PLANTS OF
THE PACIFIC
NORTHWEST
COAST
*Washington, Oregon,
British Columbia & Alaska*

PLANTS OF *THE* PACIFIC NORTHWEST COAST

Washington, Oregon, British Columbia & Alaska

Compiled and edited by

Jim Pojar and Andy MacKinnon

B.C. Forest Service, Research Program

Written by

Paul Alaback
Joe Antos
Trevor Goward
Ken Lertzman
Andy MacKinnon

Jim Pojar
Rosamund Pojar
Andrew Reed
Nancy Turner
Dale Vitt

Copyright © 1994 by the B.C. Ministry of Forests and Lone Pine Publishing
First printed in 1994   10 9 8 7 6 5 4 3
Printed in Canada

The Publisher

Lone Pine Publishing
#180, 16149 Redmond Way
Redmond, Washington 98052
USA

Lone Pine Publishing
202A – 1110 Seymour Street
Vancouver, British Columbia
Canada V6B 3N3

Lone Pine Publishing
206, 10426 – 81 Ave.
Edmonton, Alberta
Canada T6E 1X5

Canadian Cataloguing in Publication Data
Main entry under title:
Plants of the Pacific Northwest Coast

Published also as: Plants of coastal British Columbia.
Includes bibliographical references and index.
ISBN 1-55105-040-4

1. Botany—Pacific Coast (B.C.)—Handbooks, manuals, etc.
2. Botany—Pacific Coast (U.S.)—Handbooks, manuals, etc. I.
Pojar, Jim, 1948– II. MacKinnon, A. (Andrew), 1956– III.
Alaback, Paul B. IV. Title: Plants of coastal British
Columbia.
QK203.B7P62 1994   581.9711'1   C94-910289-X

Editor-in-Chief: Glenn Rollans
Botany Editor: Linda Kershaw
Design: Bruce Timothy Keith
Maps and Scans: Volker Bodegom
Layout and Production: Bruce Timothy Keith, Carol S. McKellar
Text Preparation: Jennifer Keane
Cover Design: Beata Kurpinski
Separations and Film: Elite Lithographers Co. Ltd., Edmonton, Alberta, Canada
Printing: Jasper Printing Group Ltd., Edmonton, Alberta, Canada
Front and Back Cover Photo: Alex Inselberg
Back Cover Inset Photos: Frank Boas (2), Bob Norton

Funding for this publication was provided by the British Columbia Ministry of Forests
and the Canada–British Columbia Partnership Agreement on Forest Resource Development:
FRDA II—a four-year (1991–1995), $200 million program cost-shared equally by the federal
and provincial governments.

Canadä

CANADA-BRITISH COLUMBIA
PARTNERSHIP AGREEMENT ON
FOREST RESOURCE DEVELOPMENT:
FRDA II

BC

The publisher gratefully acknowledges the assistance of Alberta Community Development,
the Department of Canadian Heritage, and the financial support provided by the Alberta Foundation
for the Arts.

Table of Contents

List of Keys

Acknowledgements

We'd first like to thank the authors who originally wrote or co-wrote the various sections of the book: Paul Alaback, Ken Lertzman and Nancy Turner (Introduction); Jim Pojar and Andy MacKinnon (vascular plants and their range maps); Dale Vitt (bryophytes and their range maps); Trevor Goward (lichens and their range maps); Andrew Reed and Nancy Turner (ethnobotanical notes); Rosamund Pojar (etymological notes); and Joe Antos and Paul Alaback (notes from Washington/Oregon and Alaska, respectively). Their work has been edited (in some cases extensively) so responsibility for technical accuracy must rest with the editors. Portions of the text were technically reviewed by George Douglas and Chris Marchant.

We are deeply grateful to the many knowledgeable Aboriginal botanists from the First Nations of the Northwest Coast and neighbouring areas who have contributed information to this publication, directly or indirectly through other literature sources. These people are mentioned by name in several of the referenced publications, particularly in Kuhnlein and Turner (1991). Some of these people are acknowledged for specific information in the ethnobotanical notations. Others who provided information used here are Randy Bouchard and Dorothy Kennedy, British Columbia Indian Language Project; Brian Compton, Department of Botany, University of British Columbia; Dana Lepofsky; and Robin Marles, Department of Botany, Brandon University, Manitoba. Most of the text about western redcedar and yellow-cedar on p. 41 is from Arlene Otke (Royal British Columbia Museum). Randy Stoltmann, Bill Beese, Steve Foster and Robert van Pelt provided information about big old trees and Leon Pavlick (Royal British Columbia Museum) supplied unpublished information about nodding semaphore grass.

Many individuals took the photographs used in this guide: Gerry Allen, Joe Antos, Frank Boas, Robin Bovey, Elizabeth Campbell, Adolf Ceska, Edward S. Curtis, (British Columbia Archives and Records Service), John DeLapp, Mathis Duerst, Blake Dickens, Robert Frisch, Jim Gillespie, Stephan Himmer, Alex Inselberg, Thomas Kaye, Linda Kershaw, Vladimir Krajina, Ron Long, Robin Love, Del Meidinger, Bill Merilees, M. Naga, Bob Norton, George Otto, Jim Pojar, L.T. Rhead, Anna Roberts, Hans Roemer, Martin Ross, Arthur Stiffe, Robert and Nancy Turner, Ted Underhill, Dale Vitt, Pat Warrington, Dave Williams, J.M. Woollett.

Original line drawings have been prepared by Trevor Goward (lichens), John Maywood (bryophytes), and Shirley Salkeld (grasses, sedges and rushes). Photo and line drawing credits are listed on pp. 7–9. Line drawings have been used with kind permission from Hitchcock *et al.* (1955-1969), Hulten (1968), Hosie (1969), and several handbooks and guides from the Royal B.C. Museum: Brayshaw (1976, 1985, 1989), Douglas (1982), Szczawinski (1962), Taylor (1966, 1973a, 1973b, 1974a, 1974b), and some unpublished works. Tara Steigenberger at the Royal B.C. Museum helped locate some drawings.

Assistance in word processing was provided by Suzanne de Grandpré, Rachele Barbuto, Trish Simoes, and Christina Stewart.

Many thanks are due to staff at Lone Pine Publishing for their assistance in putting this guide together: Glenn Rollans, Linda Kershaw, Bruce Keith, Carol McKellar, Beata Kurpinski, Volker Bodegom and Shane Kennedy.

Financial assistance in production of this guide has been provided by the B.C. Forest Service, Research and Silviculture programs and by the B.C. Forest Service and Canadian Forestry Service under the Forest Renewal Development Agreement.

Jim Pojar and Andy MacKinnon

ACKNOWLEDGEMENTS

Photo Credits (all photos used with permission; numbers refer to page and species entry)

Antos, Joe and Gerry Allen: 20a, 20b, 20c, 38, 43, 44, 45, 49, 49, 49, 50a, 50b, 61b, 63b, 64b, 72b, 81a, 88a, 91a, 105a, 105b, 107a, 109b, 111a, 111b, 112a, 112b, 119b, 125b, 128a, 128b, 134a, 134a, 136b, 138b, 155a, 156b, 157a, 160b, 161b, 164b, 165b, 173b, 176a, 179a, 181a, 183a, 187a, 197b, 203b, 206a, 209a, 219b, 221a, 230b, 232b, 234a, 240a, 259a, 263a, 263b, 265b, 267b, 270b, 271b, 275a, 286b, 287a, 288b, 293a, 299b, 304b, 305b, 312b, 313a, 315a, 319a, 319b, 323a, 332a, 333a, 342a, 352a, 425b, 427b

B.C. Forest Service: 30, 30, 32, 37, 46, 49, 72a, 74b, 86a, 90a, 155a, 179a, 308a

Boas, Frank: 51, 56a, 56a, 56b, 56b, 57a, 57a, 58a, 58b, 59a, 59b, 59b, 61a, 66, 66, 67b, 68a, 69a, 69b, 70b, 71b, 74a, 76, 77a, 78b, 80b, 85a, 86b, 89b, 94a, 95a, 95b, 96a, 100b, 101a, 101b, 102a, 102a, 102b, 103b, 103b, 104a, 104b, 109a, 109a, 111a, 115b, 118a, 119a, 121b, 121b, 122a, 123b, 132a, 133a, 138a, 139b, 141a, 147b, 149b, 155b, 163a, 165a, 165a, 167a, 168a, 168b, 174a, 175a, 175b, 177a, 177a, 177b, 179b, 180a, 180a, 180b, 182b, 185a, 185a, 186, 191b, 191b, 194a, 201a, 202a, 203a, 203a, 203b, 207b, 210b, 215a, 216b, 217a, 217a, 222a, 222b, 224a, 224b, 226b, 229a, 234b, 237a, 246a, 247b, 254b, 256a, 256b, 257a, 258a, 259b, 264a, 265a, 266b, 294a, 302a, 303a, 309b, 316b, 317a, 317b, 322a, 322b, 322b, 324a, 330a, 330b, 331b, 372b, 372b, 374a, 376a, 382a, 385a, 395a, 395a, 400b, 400b, 405a, 405b, 407b, 421, 421, 422a, 422a, 423a, 423a, 424b, 424b, 425b, 431b, 438b, 439a, 439a, 439b, 440a, 440b, 441a, 442a, 442b, 444a, 445a, 445b, 446b, 448b, 450b, 453a, 454a, 455a, 455b, 456b, 457a, 457a, 457b, 458b, 459a, 459b, 460a, 460b, 461b, 462b, 463b, 465a, 465a, 465b, 466a, 466b, 467a, 467b, 469a, 469b, 469b, 473a, 473b, 473b, 475a, 475a, 480a, 480b, 483b, 489b, 490a, 495b, 498b, 498b, 499b, 501a, 502b, 503b

Bovey, Robin: 486a, 486b, 487a, 488a, 491b, 492a, 492b, 493b, 494a, 496a, 497a, 497b, 500a, 501b, 502a, 504a

Ceska, Adolf: 48b, 89a, 106b, 166b, 169b, 245a, 293b, 313b, 324a, 325a, 332b, 343b, 347a, 354a, 383a, 391a, 396a, 403b, 413b, 432b

Curtis, Edward S., (British Columbia Archives and Records Service): 25 (Catalogue No. 74508, Neg.No. D8314); 41 (Catalogue N. 74524, Neg.No. D8330), 52b (Catalogue No. 74509, Neg.No. D8315), 404 (Catalogue No. 74456, Neg.No. D8262)

Kershaw, Linda: 47, 64a, 94a, 160b, 181b, 184b, 208b, 274a, 278b, 332a, 334b, 339a, 339b, 344a, 346b, 347a, 347b, 347b, 362a, 365a, 379a, 394a, 399b, 406b, 411a, 427a, 432b, 434b, 436a

Long, Ron: 53b, 71a, 100a, 100a, 100b, 115a, 147a, 207a, 225a, 250a, 262a, 264b, 273b, 297a, 302b, 308a, 321a, 325a, 352b, 353b

Merilees, Bill: 31, 33, 34, 34, 35, 36, 36, 36, 38, 39, 39, 39, 40, 43, 43, 47, 48a, 48a, 50a, 50a, 50b, 51, 57b, 61b, 62a, 67a, 67a, 72b, 73a, 76, 77b, 78a, 78a, 79a, 79b, 81a, 81b, 82, 84b, 85b, 90b, 90b, 92a, 93a, 93a, 95b, 96a, 96b, 103a, 103a, 106a, 112b, 115b, 118a, 120a, 129b, 131b, 132b, 133a, 133b, 134b, 138a, 141a, 142a, 143a, 143b, 145a, 146b, 148a, 151b, 157b, 163b, 166a, 166b, 167b, 167b, 168a, 169a, 175a, 179b, 182b, 185b, 192b, 193a, 193b, 194b, 196b, 198b, 199b, 205b, 206b, 206b, 214b, 216a, 218a, 231b, 232a, 232b, 234b, 235a, 239a, 243b, 251a, 251a, 258b, 260b, 261a, 261a, 261b, 270b, 272b, 275a, 276a, 276b, 277b, 278a, 278a, 279a, 279b, 280a, 280b, 281a, 282a, 284a, 287b, 290b, 290b, 291a, 292a, 292b, 293a, 297b, 298b, 304a, 304a, 306, 309a, 310b, 311a, 314a, 314b, 315b, 316a, 316b, 318b, 326a, 326b, 327a, 337a, 337b, 341b, 346a, 348a, 348a, 348b, 349, 351a, 351b, 353a, 353a, 355b, 433a

Norton, Bob: 51, 60a, 106b, 122b, 143a, 157a, 161a, 164a, 167a, 172b, 202b, 202b, 213b, 225b, 237a, 258a, 261b, 262b, 266b, 294b, 303a, 334b, 339a, 339b, 363a, 368a, 368b, 369a, 380b, 380b, 384b, 394b, 396b, 397b, 401a, 402b, 403b

Pojar, Jim: 17a, 18b, 18c, 19b, 19c, 20d, 21, 31, 31, 33, 35, 37, 37, 38, 40, 42, 44, 44, 45, 45, 46, 48b, 53a, 58a, 58b, 59a, 60a, 60b, 63a, 65b, 67b, 68b, 68b, 70a, 71b, 72a, 73b, 80a, 80b, 82, 83a, 83b, 84b, 85a, 86a, 87a, 87b, 90a, 91b, 94b, 96b, 101a, 104a, 104b, 105b, 107b, 108, 110a, 113, 114b, 116a, 116b, 118b, 119a, 121a, 123a, 123b, 125a, 126b, 127a, 129a, 130a, 130a, 130b, 131b, 132a, 136a, 137a, 137b, 137b, 138b, 139a, 140a, 140b, 141b, 145a, 148b, 149a, 152a, 152b, 153a, 153a, 153b, 153b, 156a, 156a, 160a, 160a, 161a, 162a, 162b, 164a, 169b, 172a, 172b, 173a, 173b, 174b, 175b, 176a, 176b, 177b, 178a, 178b, 181b, 183b, 184a, 184b, 185b, 187a, 187b, 187b, 188a, 192a, 192b, 194b, 195a, 195b, 196a, 199a, 199b, 201b, 204, 205b, 206a, 208a, 208b, 213a, 215a, 215b, 216a, 217b, 218b, 222a, 228a, 228b, 229b, 230b, 231a, 235a, 236a, 236b, 237b, 239b, 241a, 241a, 241b, 243b, 244a, 246b, 247a, 250a, 250b, 250b, 251a, 254a, 254b, 255a, 255b, 257a, 257b, 257b, 258b, 260a, 263a, 264a, 265a, 266a, 267a, 267a, 271a, 272a, 272a, 273a, 274b, 277a, 278b, 281b, 284b, 285a, 285b, 286a, 287b, 288a, 289a, 289b, 290a, 291b, 297b, 298a, 300a, 301a, 301b, 303b, 306, 309a, 309b, 310b, 311a, 311b, 312a, 315a, 315a, 317a, 318a, 318b, 320a, 320b, 320b, 321b, 322a, 323b, 324b, 325b, 325b, 327a, 327b, 328a, 328b, 329a, 329a, 329b, 329b, 333a, 333b, 333b, 334a, 338a, 338b, 342a, 344a, 344b, 345a, 345b, 349, 351a, 351b, 354b, 355a, 362a, 364a, 364a, 364b, 365b, 366a, 367a, 369b, 370a, 370b, 376a, 377a, 377b, 378b, 381a, 381b, 382b, 383b, 383b, 384a, 385b, 391b, 391b, 392a, 393a, 393a, 393b, 394a, 396a, 398b, 400a, 400a, 401a, 402a, 402b, 406a, 407a, 407b, 408a, 408a, 410a, 410b, 410b, 411b, 412b, 413a, 414a, 415b, 416a, 420a, 420b, 421, 422b, 423b, 424a, 424b, 425a, 426a, 426b, 430a, 430b, 431a, 432a, 433b, 434a, 435b, 438b, 443a, 475b, 481a, 494a

Roberts, Anna: 88b, 88b, 362b, 363b, 365a, 366b, 368a, 368b, 369a, 371a, 374a, 375b, 378a, 378b, 379b, 380a, 382b, 384b, 394b, 396b, 397a, 397b, 398a, 403b, 404, 404, 406a, 406b, 407a, 412a, 413a, 415a, 415b

Vitt, Dale: 440a, 440b, 441b, 442a, 442b, 443b, 444b, 445b, 446a, 446b, 448a, 449a, 449b, 450a, 450a, 451b, 452a, 452b, 453a, 453b, 454b, 455a, 456a, 456a, 457b, 458a, 459a, 459b, 460a, 461a, 461b, 462a, 463a, 463b, 464a, 464b, 464b, 465b, 466b, 467a, 468a, 468b, 468b, 469a, 470a, 470b, 471a, 471b, 472a, 472a, 472b, 474a, 474a, 474b, 474b, 475b, 475b, 476a, 476b, 477a, 477b, 478a, 478a, 478b, 478b, 479a, 479b, 480b, 481b, 482a, 482a, 482b, 483a, 483b

Williams, Dave: 485a, 485b, 487b, 488a, 488b, 488b, 489a, 490b, 491a, 494b, 496b, 498a, 498a, 499a, 501a, 501a, 503a, 504b

Woollett, J.M.: 76, 78b, 92b, 92b, 110a, 110b, 191a, 214a

Others: Campbell, Elizabeth: 40; **DeLapp, John:** 341b; **Duerst, Mathis:** 35, 46; **Dickens, Blake:** 226a; **Frisch, Robert:** 188b, 255b; **Gillespie, Jim:** 451b; **Himmer, Stephan:** 19a; **Inselberg, Alex:** cover, 17b; **Kaye, Thomas:** 344b; **Krajina, Vladimir:** 18a, 108; **Lipkin-Atka, R.:** 299a; **Love, Robin:** 77b, 100a; **Lyons, Chess:** 275b; **Meidinger, Del:** 430a; **Naga, M.:** 47; **Otto, George:** 495a, 500b; **Pierce, D.C.:** 305a; **Rhead, L.T.:** 320a; **Roemer, Hans:** 32, 42, 62b, 79b; **Ross, Martin:** 65a, 122a; **Stiffe, Arthur:** 220b, 245b, 276a; **Turner, Robert and Nancy:** 53a, 74a, 120a, 371b; **U.B.C. Botanical Gardens:** 70a; **Underhill, Ted:** 33, 93b, 183a; **Warrington, Pat:** 69a, 342b, 346b, 399a, 399b, 408b

ACKNOWLEDGEMENTS

Line Drawing Credits (all drawings used with permission; numbers refer to page and species entry)

Brayshaw, T.C. 1976. Catkin Bearing Plants (Amentiferae) of British Columbia, No.18, Occasional Paper Series, Royal B.C. Museum, Victoria, B.C.: 44, 46, 47, 50a, 81b, 81b, 83a, 87a, 87b, 88a, 88b, 89a, 89b, 92a, 108

Brayshaw, T.C. 1985. Pondweeds and Bur-reed, and Their Relatives: Aquatic Families of Monocotyledons in British Columbia. Occasional Paper No.26. Royal B.C. Museum, Victoria, B.C.: 102, 334a, 336, 337a, 337b, 342b, 343a, 343b, 344a, 345a, 345b

Brayshaw, T.C. 1989. Buttercups, Waterlilies, and Their Relatives in British Columbia. Memoir No.1, Royal B.C. Museum, Victoria: 173b, 174b, 174a, 175a, 175b, 176a, 176b, 177a, 177b, 178b, 181a, 181b, 312a, 348a, 348b, 349a, 349b

Douglas, G.W. 1982. The Sunflower Family (Asteraceae) of British Columbia. Volume 1 - Senecioneae. Occasional Paper No.23, Royal B.C. Museum, Victoria, B.C.: 109, 292b, 293b, 294a, 294b, 297a, 297b, 298a, 298b, 299a, 299b, 300a, 300b, 301a, 301b

Hitchcock, C.L., A. Cronquist, M. Ownbey and J.W. Thompson. 1955. *Vascular Plants of the Pacific Northwest.* Part 5: Compositae. University of Washington Press, Seattle, Washington: 113, 270b, 271a, 271b, 272a, 272b, 273a, 273b, 274a, 274b, 275a, 275b, 276a, 277a, 277b, 278a, 278b, 286a, 286b, 290a, 290b, 291a, 292a, 305a, 305b, 306

Hitchcock, C.L., A. Cronquist, M. Ownbey and J.W. Thompson. 1959. *Vascular Plants of the Pacific Northwest.* Part 4: Ericaceae Through Campanulaceae. University of Washington Press, Seattle, Washington: 50b, 70b, 99, 100, 227, 228a, 229a, 229b, 230a, 230b, 231a, 231b, 232a, 232b, 233, 234a, 234b, 235a, 235b, 236a, 236b, 237a, 237b, 238, 239a, 239b, 240a, 240b, 243a, 243b, 244a, 244b, 245a, 245b, 246a, 246b, 249, 251b, 252, 253, 256b, 257a, 259a, 260a, 260b, 261b, 263b, 264b, 267a, 267b, 320b, 321a, 321b, 322a, 322b, 323a, 324a, 324b, 325a, 325b, 326a, 326b, 327a, 327b, 328a, 328b, 329a, 329b, 330a, 331b, 332a, 332b, 333a, 333b, 336, 339b, 341b, 347b, 351b, 354a, 354b, 355b

Hitchcock, C.L., A. Cronquist, M. Ownbey and J.W. Thompson. 1961. *Vascular Plants of the Pacific Northwest.* Part 3: Saxifragaceae to Ericaceae. University of Washington Press, Seattle, Washington: 45, 64a, 73b, 74b, 75, 77a, 78a, 78b, 79b, 83b, 84b, 85a, 85b, 86b, 90b, 91a, 91b, 93a, 93b, 95a, 96a, 96b, 97, 98, 157b, 158, 159, 160a, 160b, 161a, 161b, 162a, 162b, 163a, 163b, 164a, 164b, 165a, 166a, 166b, 168a, 168b, 169a, 169b, 189, 198a, 202a, 202b, 203a, 203b, 204, 205b, 206b, 207a, 207b, 208b, 209a, 209b, 210a, 210b, 211, 212, 213a, 213b, 214a, 215a, 215b, 216a, 216b, 217b, 218a, 218b, 219b, 220a, 220b, 221a, 221b, 222b, 314a, 315a, 318a, 318b, 319a, 319b, 346a, 346b, 347a

Hitchcock, C.L., A. Cronquist, M. Ownbey and J.W. Thompson. 1964. *Vascular Plants of the Pacific Northwest.* Part 2: Salicaceae to Saxifragaceae. University of Washington Press, Seattle, Washington: 97, 98, 105, 125a, 125b, 126a, 126b, 127a, 127b, 128a, 128b, 129a, 129b, 130a, 130b, 131b, 132a, 132b, 133a, 133b, 134a, 134b, 136a, 136b, 137a, 137b, 138a, 138b, 139a, 140a, 140b, 141a, 141b, 142a, 142b, 143a, 143b, 145a, 145b, 146a, 146b, 147a, 147b, 148a, 148b, 149a, 149b, 150a, 150b, 151b, 152a, 152b, 153a, 153b, 154, 155a, 155b, 156a, 156b, 157a, 171, 172a, 308a, 308b, 309a, 309b, 310a, 310b, 311a, 311b, 312b, 313a, 313b, 314b, 317b, 341a, 342a

Hitchcock, C.L., A. Cronquist, M. Ownbey and J.W. Thompson. 1969. *Vascular Plants of the Pacific Northwest.* Part 1: Vascular Cryptograms, Gymnosperms and Monocotyledons. University of Washington Press, Seattle, Washington: 30, 34, 35, 37, 38, 39, 42, 43, 97, 98, 101a, 102b, 103b, 104a, 106a, 106b, 107a, 107b, 108, 109a, 109b, 110b, 111a, 111b, 112a, 112b, 114a, 114b, 115a, 116b, 118b, 119a, 119b, 122a, 122b, 123a, 123b, 344b, 345b, 364a, 364b, 365b, 367b, 369a, 370a, 370b, 371b, 372b, 373b, 374a, 374b, 381a, 381b, 383a, 384a, 385a, 385b, 386b, 387b, 388, 390, 396a, 409, 417, 418, 419, 424b, 425b, 426b, 432a, 433b, 435a, 435b, 436a, 436b

Hosie, R.C. 1969. *Native Trees of Canada.* Canadian Forest Service, Queen's Printer of Canada, Ottawa: 29, 31, 38, 40, 44, 48a, 48b, 49, 50a, 50b, 51

Hultén, Eric. 1968. *Flora of Alaska and Neighboring Territories.* Stanford University Press, Stanford, California.: 116a, 120b, 151a, 171, 173a, 183b, 208a, 219a, 227, 228b, 241b, 313, 316a, 323b, 355a

John Maywood (original line drawings): 438b, 439a, 439b, 440a, 440b, 441a, 441b, 442a, 442b, 443a, 443b, 444a, 444b, 445a, 445b, 446a, 446b, 448a, 448b, 449a, 449b, 450a, 450b, 451b, 452a, 452b, 453a, 453b, 454a, 454b, 455a, 455b, 456a, 456b, 457a, 457b, 458a, 458b, 459a, 459b, 460a, 460b, 461a, 461b, 462a, 462b, 463a, 463b, 464a, 464b, 465a, 465b, 466a, 466b, 467a, 467b, 468a, 468b, 469a, 469b, 470a, 470b, 471a, 471b, 472a, 472b, 473a, 473b, 474a, 474b, 475a, 475b, 476a, 476b, 477a, 477b, 478a, 478b, 479a, 479b, 480a, 480b, 481a, 481b, 482a, 482b, 483a, 483b

Royal B.C. Museum (original line drawings): 279a, 279b, 280a, 280b, 281a, 281b, 282a, 282b, 284a, 284b, 285a, 285b, 287a, 287b, 288a, 288b, 289a, 289b, 291b, 302a, 302b, 303a, 303b, 304a, 304b

Shirley Salkeld (original line drawings): 362a, 362b, 363a, 363b, 364a, 364b, 365a, 365b, 366a, 366b, 367a, 367b, 368a, 368b, 369a, 369b, 370a, 370b, 371a, 371b, 372a, 372b, 373a, 373b, 374a, 374b, 375a, 375b, 376a, 376b, 377a, 377b, 378a, 378b, 379a, 379b, 380a, 380b, 381b, 382a, 382b, 383a, 383b, 384a, 384b, 385a, 385b, 386a, 386b, 387a, 387b, 388, 389, 390, 391a, 391b, 392a, 392b, 393a, 393b, 394a, 394b, 395a, 395b, 396a, 396b, 397a, 397b, 398a, 398b, 399a, 399b, 400a, 400b, 401a, 401b, 402a, 402b, 403a, 403b, 404, 405a, 405b, 406a, 406b, 407a, 407b, 408a, 408b, 410a, 410b, 411a, 411b, 412a, 412b, 413a, 413b, 414a, 414b, 415a, 415b, 416a, 416b

Szczawinski, A.F. 1975. *The Heather Family (Ericaceae) of British Columbia.* Handbook No.19, Royal B.C. Museum, Victoria, B.C.: 49, 53a, 53b, 57b, 60a, 60b, 62a, 62b, 63a, 66, 99, 108, 223, 224a, 224b, 225a, 225b, 226a, 226b, 352a, 352b, 353b

Taylor, T.M.C. 1973. *The Ferns and Fern Allies of British Columbia.* Handbook No. 12. Royal B.C. Museum, Victoria, B.C.: 417, 418, 419, 421, 422b, 423b, 424a, 425a, 426a, 427a, 427b, 430a, 430b, 431a, 431b, 432b, 433a, 434a

Taylor, T.M.C. 1973. *The Rose Family (Rosaceae) of British Columbia.* Handbook No. 30. Royal B.C. Museum, Victoria, B.C.: 48a, 48b, 71a, 73a, 76, 78a, 79a, 80a, 81a, 121, 123, 182b, 183a, 184a, 184b, 185a, 185b, 186, 187b, 188a, 339a

Taylor, T.M.C. 1974. *The Pea Family (Leguminosae) of British Columbia.* Handbook No.32. Royal B.C. Museum, Victoria, B.C.: 99, 114, 189, 191a, 191b, 192a, 192b, 193a, 193b, 194a, 194b, 195a, 195b, 196a, 196b, 197a, 197b, 198b, 199a, 199b, 200, 336

Taylor , T.M.C. 1974. *The Figwort Family (Scrophulariaceae) of British Columbia.* Handbook No.33. Royal B.C. Museum, Victoria, B.C.: 126, 248, 250a, 250b, 251a, 252, 253, 254a, 254b, 255a, 255b, 256a, 257b, 258a, 258b, 259b, 261a, 261b, 262a, 262b, 263a, 264a, 265a, 265b, 266a, 266b

Trevor Goward (original line drawings): 485a, 485b, 486b, 488a, 488b, 489a, 489b, 490a, 490b, 491a, 491b, 492a, 492b, 493b, 494a, 494b, 495a, 495b, 496a, 496b, 497a, 497b, 498a, 499a, 499b, 500a, 500b, 501a, 501b, 502a, 503b, 504a, 504b

All other line drawings, original artwork from the B.C. Forest Service, Research Branch.

Additional Reading

Abrams, L. 1923, 1944, 1951. *An Illustrated Flora of the Pacific States,Washington, Oregon, and California Vol. I–IV.* Stanford University Press, Stanford, California.

Argus, G.W. 1973. *The genus Salix in Alaska and the Yukon.* National Museum of Natural Sciences Publications in Botany No. 2. National Museums of Canada, Ottawa, Ontario.

Arno, S.F., and R.P. Hammerly. 1977. *Northwest Trees.* The Mountaineers, Seattle, Washington.

Baker, M. 1969. *Discovering the Folklore of Plants.* Shire Publications Ltd., Aylesbury, England.

Coffey, T. 1993. *The History and Folklore of North American Wildflowers.* Facts on File, New York, New York.

Conard, H.S., and P.L. Redfern. 1979. *How to Know the Mosses and Liverworts.* Wm. C. Brown, Dubuque, Iowa.

Coupé, R., C.A. Ray, A. Comeau, M.V. Ketcheson and R.M. Annas (compilers). 1982. *A Guide to Some Common Plants of the Skeena Area, British Columbia.* Land Management Handbook No. 4, British Columbia Ministry of Forests, Victoria, British Columbia.

Coward, G. 1977. *Tree Book: Learning to Recognize Trees of British Columbia.* British Columbia Forest Services, Victoria, British Columbia.

Douglas, S. 1991. *Trees and Shrubs of the Queen Charlotte Islands.* Islands Ecological Research, Queen Charlotte City, British Columbia.

Fries, M.A. 1970. *Wildflowers of Mount Rainier and the Cascades.* The Mount Rainier Natural History Association and The Mountaineers, Seattle, Washington.

Garman, E.H. 1973. *Guide to the Trees and Shrubs of British Columbia.* British Columbia. Handbook No. 31, Royal British Columbia Museum, Victoria, British Columbia.

Gledhill, D. 1989. *The Names of Plants.* Second edition, Cambridge University Press, Cambridge.

Hale, M.E. 1979. *How to Know the Lichens,* Second Edition. Wm.C. Brown, Dubuque, Iowa.

Hardy, G.A., and W.V. Hardy. 1964. *Wild Flowers in the Pacific Northwest.* H.R. Larson Publishing Company, Saskatoon, Saskatchewan.

Haskin, L.L. 1934. *Wild Flowers of the Pacific Coast.* Binford and Mort, Portland, Oregon. (republished 1977, Dover Publications, New York).

Jolley, R. 1988. *Wildflowers of the Columbia Gorge.* Oregon Historical Society, Portland, Oregon.

Klinka, K., V.J. Krajina, A. Ceska, and A.M. Scagel. 1989. *Indicator Plants of Coastal British Columbia.* University of British Columbia Press, Vancouver, British Columbia.

Kozloff, E.N. 1976. *Plants and Animals of the Pacific Northwest.* J.J. Douglas Ltd., Vancouver, British Columbia.

Kruckeberg, A.R. 1991. *The Natural History of Puget Sound.* University of Washington Press, Seattle, Washington.

Larrison, E.J., G.W. Patrick, W.H. Baker, and J.A. Yaich. 1974. *Washington Wildflowers.* Seattle Audubon Society, Seattle, Washington.

MacKinnon, A., J. Pojar, and R. Coupé. 1992. *Plants of Northern British Columbia.* Lone Pine Publishing, Edmonton, Alberta.

Munz, P.A. 1964. *Shore Wildflowers of California, Oregon and Washington.* University of California Press, Berkeley and Los Angeles, California.

Pratt, V.E. 1989. *Alaskan Wildflowers.* Alaskakrafts Publishing, Anchorage, Alaska.

Richardson, D. 1975. *The Vanishing Lichens: Their History, Biology and Importance.* David & Charles, Vancouver, British Columbia.

Robuck, O.W. 1985. *The Common Plants of the Muskegs of Southeast Alaska.* Misc. Publication, U.S.D.A. Forest Service, Pacific Northwest Forest and Range Experiment Station, Portland, Oregon.

Robuck, O.W. 1989. *Common Alpine Plants of Southeast Alaska.* Misc. Publ., USDA Forest Service, Pacific Northwest Research Station, Portland, Oregon.

Ross, R.A., and H.L. Chambers. 1988. *Wildflowers of the Western Cascades.* Timber Press, Portland, Oregon.

Schofield, J.J. 1989. *Discovering Wild Plants: Alaska, Western Canada, the Northwest.* Alaska Northwest Books, Anchorage, Alaska.

Schofield, W.B. 1992. (2d edition). *Some Mosses of British Columbia.* Handbook No. 28, Royal British Columbia Museum, Victoria, British Columbia.

Stevens, J.E. 1973. *Discovering Wild Plant Names.* Shire Publications Ltd., Aylesbury, England.

Stoltmann, R. 1993. *Guide to the Record Trees of British Columbia.* Western Canada Wilderness Committee, Vancouver, British Columbia.

Szczawinski, A.F., and G.A. Hardy. 1975. *Guide to Common Edible Plants of British Columbia.* Handbook No. 20, Royal British Columbia Museum, Victoria, British Columbia.

Szczawinski, A.F., and N.J. Turner. 1978. *Edible Garden Weeds of Canada.* Edible Wild Plants of Canada. Series No. 1, National Museum of Canada, Ottawa, Ontario.

Taylor, R.J. 1990. Northwest Weeds: *The Ugly and Beautiful Villains of Fields, Gardens and Roadsides.* Mountain Press Publishing Co., Missoula, Montana.

Taylor, R.J., and G.W. Douglas. 1975. *Mountain Wild Flowers of the Pacific Northwest.* Binford and Mort, Portland, Oregon.

Turner, N.J. 1979. *Plants in British Columbia Indian Technology.* Handbook No. 38, Royal British Columbia Museum, Victoria, British Columbia.

Underhill, J.E. 1974. *Wild Berries of the Pacific Northwest.* Hancock House Publishers, Saanichton, British Columbia.

Viereck, L.A., and E.L. Little. 1972. *Alaska Trees and Shrubs.* U.S.D.A. Forest Service, Agriculture Handbook No. 410.

INTRODUCTION

ABOUT THIS GUIDE

The north Pacific coast of North America contains some of the most fascinating and distinctive ecosystems on earth—from majestic ancient forests to lush alpine meadows, sodden muskegs, open woodlands, dry rocky slopes and grasslands. The **northern Pacific coastal region** includes all of the land west of the crest of the coastal mountains, from Prince William Sound in south-central Alaska south to the Oregon Coast Range and Cascades. Some of the oldest and largest trees and the most massive, highly productive ecosystems on earth can be found here. The region spans 17° of latitude, but it is unified by mountains, rain, the forest and the sea. It includes individual species and types of ecosystems unique to the region, and others that occur elsewhere but reach their greatest development here. The plants of these ecosystems are the subject of this book.

This guide is designed for anyone interested in the plants of the north Pacific coast of North America. The guide presents a simple yet thorough account of all major land-plant groups, and some aquatics, occurring in this diverse but relatively little-known region, which we refer to as 'our region.' While most other guides attempt to cover plants occurring within particular states or provinces (and thus include many species of drier interior areas), we have tried to present information on the entire north coastal bioregion. Our region is defined on ecological rather than political and administrative grounds.

We wrote this guide with several types of users in mind: residents who want to know more about their natural surroundings; students, scientists and resource specialists who require an up-to-date reference on the plants of this region; and travellers who need a relatively simple and easy-to-use guide. When technical terms are unavoidable, they are defined in the glossary or explained in the introductions to plant groups.

This guide includes descriptions of the most common vascular plants, mosses, liverworts and lichens native to or naturalized in our region. Most primary entries include at least one colour photograph accompanied by line drawings to illustrate habit (that is, what the whole plant looks like) or details, where required. Keys are included to assist in separating some of the larger or more difficult groups.

Our region is large and so is its flora. We have tried to balance the representation of southern and northern elements, but the guide necessarily includes more southern than northern species. We sometimes feature a northern species rather than a southern if the northern occupies more of our range, even if it is not nearly as common in the more-populated southern third of our region.

Although this guide is fairly comprehensive, definitive identification of some groups of species will require consulting more-technical references. For example, more than 50 species of sedge occur in our region, and sometimes a dissecting microscope is required to distinguish their key features. The information provided in this guide is insufficient to clearly identify all of the sedges one can find in our region, but references listed in this book guide interested readers to more-comprehensive technical manuals on sedges and other difficult groups.

At the time of publication, no other guide specifically covers the plants of the northern Pacific coastal region, so working with the plants of this area has required consulting several technical manuals for surrounding areas: Hultén (1968) or Welsh (1974) for Alaska; Peck (1961) for Oregon; Hitchcock et al. (1955–1969), Hitchcock and Cronquist (1973) and Gilkey and Dennis (1967) for Oregon and Washington; Scoggan (1978, 1979), Douglas et al. (1989, 1990, 1991, 1994 in press) and Calder and Taylor (1968) for B.C. Some non-technical guides are available for various parts of our region, but few have accurate habitat and range information for the entire area. Where appropriate, we make reference to specific guides for particular areas or plant groups within our region.

This book integrates information on human uses of plants with the plants' systematic and ecological descriptions. We have compiled information on aboriginal uses of plants derived from both published and unpublished studies spanning many decades. This information appears in the notes to individual species, and it is summarized later in this introduction.

HOW TO USE THIS GUIDE

This guide is organized so that species most likely to be confused with one another appear in the same section. Trees, shrubs, wildflowers, aquatics, oddballs, grasses and grass-like plants, ferns and relatives, bryophytes and lichens comprise the major sections in the book. Within these broad sections, we have organized plants by large families and by groups of smaller families.

For most readers, the quickest way to identify an unfamiliar plant using this guide is to start by browsing through the illustrations to find those species or groups of species the plant most closely resembles. Then compare carefully the written plant descriptions to determine to which species or group the specimen belongs. Sometimes, it may not be clear which characteristics provide the most consistent distinctions between or among closely related species. To complicate matters further, the appearance of any individual plant varies with its age, the time of year, the weather, soil types, disturbances or other factors affecting growing conditions. The existence of local variants can also add to the difficulty of identifying a species.

For the most perplexing groups, especially those with closely related species, a technical key is necessary for positive identification. We have provided keys, with specialized terms kept to a minimum, for most major plant groups in this guide. These are simple, two-branched keys that rely on vegetative and floral characteristics. When flowers are necessary to distinguish among species or genera, and all that remains on the specimen is the fruit or flowers of the previous year, a bit of imagination and reconstruction may be necessary to determine the path to follow in the key. When confusion arises at a branch in the key, examine both options, then determine which looks more plausible for your specimen.

The most common and widespread species are described in the greatest detail. Less common or localized species are discussed in the 'Notes' sections under more common, closely related species. Rare species, or those whose range barely overlaps the northern Pacific coastal region, are not included. For example, we have excluded several rare boreal species that occur only near the northern limit of this book's coverage, but are common elsewhere. We have also excluded some elements of the California flora that can be found as far north as the Willamette Valley.

PLANT NAMES

Plants in this guide are listed with both common and scientific names. Scientific names are generally more widely accepted and stable than common names. For example, the scientific name *Vaccinium membranaceum* always refers to the same plant, even though different people in different places might refer to it as a blueberry, a huckleberry, or a bilberry, and as 'big,' 'big-leaved' or 'black.' However, scientific names are not always stable or universal. The bog-orchids and rein-orchids, for example, are placed in the genus *Platanthera* in this book, while other works may refer to the genus as *Habenaria*.

We used the following sources for names of plants: common names largely follow Douglas et al. (1989–1994); scientific names largely follow Douglas et al. for vascular plants, Anderson et al. (1990) for mosses, Stotler and Crandall-Stotler (1977) for liverworts and Egan (1987) for lichens. Scientific and common names are listed alphabetically in the index at the end of this guide. Where alternative scientific or common names are used in the areas covered by this guide, we have included the synonyms in the text and index.

THE REGION

The northern Pacific coastal region is defined on the west by the Pacific Ocean and on the east by the mountain massifs that surround it (see inside front and back covers). These mountains include the Chugach and St. Elias Mountains in Alaska, the Coast Mountains in British Columbia and the Cascades in Washington and Oregon. In particular, we used the alpine tundra above the subalpine mountain hemlock forest zone to define our eastern limit along these mountains. These coastally influenced alpine areas are quite distinct from the more continental alpine zones on the leeward (eastern) side of the height of land. Inland of the northern Pacific coastal region the flora changes rapidly. In the north, our region is bounded by the cold and continental boreal zone. In the south, our region is bounded by much drier intermontane forest or steppe. See maps on the inside front and back covers.

The northern limit of the range of this guide is defined by the northern extent of forest on Kodiak Island, Alaska Peninsula. Sitka spruce is still slowly expanding its range westward in this part of Alaska. Beyond the limit of forests, tundra and wetlands predominate and the plant life has more influence from the rich floras of Siberia and Japan.

For this book, we set the southern limit of our region at the Siuslaw River in the Oregon Coast Range and the MacKenzie River in the Oregon Cascades. This is an admittedly arbitrary boundary. We excluded the southern Oregon and northern California coasts because the flora of these regions contain many distinctly southern elements not shared by the north coastal flora. These differences result partly from the southern region's geological history and, in part, from its substantially warmer and drier climate.

This guide covers species of all habitats, forested and non-forested, that occur in the northern Pacific coastal region. Some of the most diverse habitats include wetlands, grasslands and alplands. One major climatic and floristic anomaly is the rainshadow belt of warm, dry habitats on southeastern Vancouver Island and the Gulf and San Juan Islands, the eastern Olympic Peninsula and in the Willamette Valley. These areas are variously called the 'saaniche' (a label used by some B.C. ecologists for the complex of vegetation—grassland, savannah, vernal meadows and seepage areas, and rock outcrop communities—that occurs on southeastern Vancouver Island and the Gulf Islands of the Strait of Georgia), 'Douglas-fir,' 'oak' or 'rainshadow' zones. One can even find prickly pear cacti (*Opuntia fragilis*) growing in the northern areas of this unique vegetation type. Many species in our region (as many as half the species of some genera) occur only in these rainshadow habitats. These are also the places where most people in the region live: Victoria, Seattle, Tacoma, Olympia and Portland all occur in or near rainshadow areas. Readers should be careful to note habitats and ranges when identifying plants—there are far fewer species to puzzle over in the more typical rainforest or alpine habitats than in the rainshadow habitats.

ABOUT THE SPECIES DISTRIBUTION MAPS

Any map is by necessity a generalization and distortion of reality. In order to cover the entire range of nearly 2,800 km on a species distribution map only 4 cm high—a scale of 1:69 million—much simplification was necessary. The challenge was to eliminate clutter while retaining the basic shape of the coast, including features such as landmark inlets. Smaller islands have been omitted or, in some cases, joined to adjacent land masses. In addition, shapes, sizes, and locations of some features have been slightly adjusted for greater clarity. These maps are based on the best information available at the time of publication. The data base grows constantly, and known ranges of species change as we learn more about our flora.

PHYSICAL ENVIRONMENT
Climate

Over a broad range of latitude, the major vegetation zones of the northern Pacific coastal region show a strong similarity in climate, ecosystem structure and dominant plant species. One key factor in this similarity is the influence of the Pacific Ocean on climate. Winters are significantly warmer, summers are significantly cooler and it is wetter year round near the Pacific Ocean than in comparable areas farther inland. Annual rainfall on the coast ranges from less than 1,000 mm to over 5,000 mm. Summer temperatures typically range from 4° to 27°C. Sea-level snow during the winter is common in the northern part of our region but relatively rare and ephemeral from Vancouver Island south. Deep accumulations of heavy, wet snow are common at high elevations throughout our region (2 to 3 m of snowpack is common in subalpine forests and much deeper accumulations can be found in higher alpine areas). This distinctly cool and wet, but moderate, climate is probably the key factor underpinning the lushness and diversity of coastal plant life.

Many plant species and plant communities occur across a broad range of latitudes in our region. As a general rule, a given species or community type will occur at lower elevations as one moves north. For example, wet ecosystems such as forests of mountain hemlock (*Tsuga mertensiana*) and blueberry (*Vaccinium* spp.) occur with many of the same species at 1,200 m on steep, north-facing, snowy subalpine environments in Oregon and on gentle, well-drained slopes at sea level in south-central Alaska. Some habitat specialists such as searocket (*Cakile edentula*) or large-headed sedge (*Carex macrocephala*), by contrast, occupy the same habitat (sandy ocean beaches) at the same elevation over the entire region.

Physiography

Two parallel belts of mountains dominate the regional landscape. In the north, the St. Elias Mountains of Alaska and the Insular Mountains of the Queen Charlotte and Vancouver Islands form a seaward band of summits. To the south, the Coast Ranges of Oregon and Washington dominate the outer coastal topography. Throughout the length of coastal British Columbia, ending at the Fraser Valley in the south, the Coast Mountains define the boundary between the coastal region and drier regions to the east. Southeast of the Fraser Valley in British Columbia, and through Washington and Oregon, the Cascade Mountains define this boundary. In the north, the trough between the St. Elias–Insular Mountains and the Coast Mountains is largely submerged beneath Hecate Strait and the Strait of Georgia. To the south, the trough between the Coast Ranges and the Cascade Mountains forms the fertile Puget Basin and Willamette Valley.

From Vancouver Island north through the Gulf of Alaska, the outer coast is made up of often mountainous barrier islands that, at times, form extensive archipelagos. Inshore of these lie complex networks of islands and steep-sided mainland fjords. South of Vancouver Island, the outer coast is mainland, not broken by extensive fjords or barrier islands. Infrequent major river systems such as the Columbia breach the long beaches and rocky headlands. South of the Olympic Peninsula, the Coast Ranges are lower and gentler than the mountains farther north.

The northern part of our region is dominated by classic glacial landforms: U-shaped valleys and cirques are frequent. Intrusive igneous rocks in sometimes spectacular exposures are also characteristic of the northern section. Thick deposits of glacial drift are restricted to valley bottoms, and impressive accumulations of glacial deposits can be found near the southern boundary of Pleistocene glaciation in the northern Puget Basin.

Remnants of volcanic activity are evident in the Pemberton-Garibaldi area of south coastal British Columbia; volcanos and soils derived from volcanic deposits increase in importance in the Cascade Range through Washington into Oregon. These mountains form the highest summits in the southern part of our region and have played an important role in large-scale disturbances to regional vegetation through recent geological time. The eruption of Mt. St. Helens provided a graphic example of the diverse impacts these volcanos have on vegetation, soils, and hydrology—and of the variety of ecosystem responses to those impacts. Refer to the map on the inside back cover for an illustration of these physiographic units.

Geology

The northern Pacific coastal region encompasses a diverse array of geological features that influence the plant cover. In the Oregon Coast Range, sandstones and mudstones dominate, except for occasional basaltic headlands. These rocks are highly weathered and extremely susceptible to landslides, but they provide a rich source of nutrients for tree growth. This is one of the most productive areas for tree growth on the west coast. Recent volcanos dominate the Cascades north to Stevens Pass. Soils derived from these deposits are deep and nutrient rich, but they are also highly susceptible to landslides and mudslides. From the North Cascades in Washington north to Alaska, a huge granitic batholith dominates the geology of the mainland coastal mountains. Steep slopes, U-shaped glacial valleys and glacial deposits dominate landscapes from the Olympics and Cascades northward. Soils from granites are more acidic and more poorly developed than soils derived from sedimentary materials, which dominate many lowland and island areas.

The geology of coastal Alaska and northern B.C. is extremely complex and forms a mosaic of many different rock types, often in close proximity. Limestone, granite, greywacke, metamorphics such as schist and even ultrabasic sedimentary rocks may occur within a few kilometres of one another. In the north, however, climate becomes the overwhelming factor limiting plant growth so that subtle distinctions among rock types become less important. Thick, acidic, organic layers can develop over all of the rock types. On the exposed outer coast from Vancouver Island north, regardless of the geological origins of the soils, stunted forests and wetland vegetation become common, primarily because of the tremendous amount of rainfall, the cool temperatures and the wind.

Areas underlain by limestone and marble are often associated with distinctive plant communities. In most coastal alpine areas, for example, ericaceous shrubs such as mountain-heathers are the dominant plants. But in alpine areas with soils derived from limestone, grasses and sedges are much more abundant. Some moss and fern species (e.g., green spleenwort, *Asplenium viride*) occur exclusively in association with limestone substrates. In the lowlands, highly productive redcedar and spruce forests often develop on limestone, especially when soils have developed over glacial till. Extensive limestone deposits occur on Vancouver Island and Prince of Wales Island.

Time

The diversity and composition of plant communities in our region have been profoundly influenced by the region's geologic history. Coastal forests of this region are among the world's most productive, not only because of an ideal climate for tree growth but also because of the rich base of genetic diversity and the long evolutionary time that has been available for adaptation to the climatic conditions. Coastal rainforest has existed for at least 2 million years, and it contains many species of great antiquity (some 70 million years or more old). Glaciations during the past 20,000 years have not significantly depleted the diversity of our region because of the abundance of refugia and migration corridors. Furthermore, forests have been in a nearly continuous state of change since the last major glacial advance. In areas such as Prince William Sound, forests are still equilibrating following the last glacial retreat that occurred, at most, 4,000 years ago. Western redcedar (*Thuja plicata*) and yellow-cedar (*Chamaecyparis nootkatensis*) have reached the northern parts of our region only recently (Hebda and Mathews 1984), after moving north from California, where they found refuge during the last glaciation.

VEGETATION
Forests

Dense, productive forests form one of the most characteristic vegetation types throughout our region. Although the greatest number of plant species are often in open patchy habitats (such as subalpine meadows, shorelines, grasslands and wetlands), forests are better known and more distinctly representative of our region. In general, forests dominate in places where there is enough annual rainfall (at our latitudes generally more than 75 cm) and a reasonably balanced nutrient supply in the soils, and where catastrophic fires and extended drought are infrequent. Under these conditions, trees can outcompete other forms of plants because trees live longer, grow taller, and can often tolerate a poor nutrient supply. Because some trees are shade-tolerant, they can persist readily under a dense forest canopy. Once established, trees can accommodate wide year-to-year fluctuations in climate better than most other kinds of plants.

One of the most striking features of the Pacific coastal forest region is the overwhelming dominance of coniferous trees and the restriction of deciduous trees (such as maple, alder, cottonwood and ash) to younger forests or frequently disturbed areas. Worldwide, most other coastal forest regions at similar latitudes have evenly mixed or largely deciduous forests. Deciduous hardwoods are poorly adapted to the summer-dry climate of the southern part of our region and the short wet summers of the northern areas. While evergreen conifers can gather sunlight and grow almost year-round, deciduous hardwoods can only grow when their leaves are out—often only a few months each year. Conifers are also more efficient at growing at low temperatures, which is why they are so common worldwide at high elevations.

Dynamics

All plant communities develop through a process called 'succession,' which involves change in community composition and structure over time. All plant communities are subject to natural disturbances of different kinds that can kill existing members of the community and 'reset' successional processes to varying degrees. Landslides, avalanches, fires, floods, volcanic eruptions and windstorms all affect plant communities and vary in their importance through our region. Most Pacific coastal forests owe their current composition and structure to a long and often idiosyncratic history of disturbances and succession.

From the central Oregon coast through central Vancouver Island, drier forests have disturbance histories in which fires have been frequent and integral in their development. By contrast, in the wettest, most maritime coastal fringe, and through much of the region north of northern Vancouver Island, fire has been insignificant in the history of forest development. Here, disturbance by wind to patches varying from one tree to many hectares is a major force shaping the development of forests. Wind often kills or snaps off the tops of the dominant canopy trees but causes little disturbance in the forest understory. This kind of disturbance creates very different patterns of stand development than would a fire. The suppressed saplings present in the forest before such a disturbance quickly grow to replace those killed, leaving little opportunity for new individuals or different species to colonize the site, as often occurs after a fire. Forests perpetuated by wind tend to have a very complex structure, with many canopy layers and ages of trees, whereas fire-origin forests more frequently have fewer layers and age classes of trees.

Old-growth forests

As young forests grow into older ones, they pass through a series of characteristic developmental stages. Old growth is the final stage of forest development. Some changes that occur as a forest develops relate to the replacement of species characteristic of early successional stages by species of later stages—usually fast-growing, shade-intolerant species such as Douglas-fir are replaced with slower-growing but more shade-tolerant species such as western hemlock. Other changes that occur as forests age are more related to forest **structure** than to **species composition**.

Productive, low-elevation, old-growth temperate rainforests are among the most massive ecosystems on earth. Tremendous accumulations of biomass result from the combination of: long periods of time between stand-destroying disturbances; the great longevity of many northwestern trees; their inherent ability to grow large; and relatively slow decomposition rates. Frequently, more than half of the total mass in these forests is in the form of dead trees, either snags or logs. Indeed, it can sometimes be difficult to find a patch of forest floor that is not actually a crumbling log in the final stages of decay. The great abundance of dead, woody material in such forests has led to the development of complex communities of organisms that depend on decomposing material in various forms for habitat or sustenance.

There are many characteristics of old forests, such as large diameter logs and snags, that are not often found in younger forests, especially young forests managed for timber production. Other structural attributes characteristic of older forests are a wide range of tree sizes and ages, and a patchy, open canopy punctuated by gaps beneath which the forest understory is especially well developed.

One can certainly find various combinations of old-growth-like characteristics in some younger forests. This is especially true for young forests regenerating without human interference after natural disturbances, or after logging in the early days of the industry, when harvesting operations were less efficient at removing all of the living trees, snags and logs. Modern forest plantations that are managed intensively for timber production on short rotations retain or develop few old-forest attributes. The challenges of redesigning forestry practices to better mimic the natural patterns of forest development, and to retain or create old-forest-like characteristics in younger forests, occupy the forefront of applied research in forest ecology and management.

Giants of their genera

	TYPICAL (OF PRODUCTIVE VERY OLD FOREST)			*MAXIMUM*		
	Age (years)	Diameter (cm)	Height (m)	Age (years)	Diameter (cm)	Height (m)
Pacific silver fir (*Abies amabilis*)	>400	90-110	45-55	750	237	72
grand fir (*Abies grandis*)	>400	90-150	45-60	>500?	202	81
noble fir (*Abies procera*)	>400	100-150	45-70	>500	275	90
yellow-cedar (*Chamaecyparis nootkatensis*)	>1000	100-150	30-40	1824 (>2000?)	365	62
western redcedar (*Thuja plicata*)	>1000	150-300	40-50	1400 (>2000?)	631	71
Sitka spruce (*Picea sitchensis*)	>500	180-230	60-75	1350	525	95
Douglas-fir (*Pseudotsuga menziesii*)	>750	150-220	70-80	1300	440	100
western hemlock (*Tsuga heterophylla*)	>500	90-120	50-65	1238	275	75
mountain hemlock (*Tsuga mertensiana*)	>500	75-100	35+	>1000	221	59

Ancient forests

The combination of long intervals between catastrophic disturbances and the presence of species with great longevity produces forests that can legitimately be considered ancient. Individual trees 600 to 1,000 years old are not uncommon, and individuals of several species can be found with ages exceeding 1,000 years. The best-known examples of such forests are the Douglas-fir forests of the southern part of our region, which established after fires or windstorms mostly between 200 and 1,000 years ago. Less well understood, but more common in the northern part of our region, are ancient forests where individual trees may only be 200 to

500 years old, but the forest itself is much older. Such ancient forests commonly occur in wet coastal areas where fires virtually never occur and the forest develops over many centuries through the slow, individual-by-individual replacement of trees. These forests also frequently occur at higher elevations on good sites where wet summers combine with persistent spring snowpacks to reduce the likelihood of fire. It is likely that the oldest individual trees in the northern Pacific coastal region are yellow-cedars growing in such circumstances.

What is temperate rainforest?

The coastal temperate rainforest of North America is the most extensive and impressive example of temperate rainforest in the world. On the west coast, it occurs only in the northern Pacific coastal region covered by this guide. Temperate rainforests are primarily distinguished from other temperate forests by the rarity of fire, their evergreenness, and their complex structure. Temperate rainforest structure is complex because of many canopy layers, a wide range of tree sizes and ages within a patch of forest, the abundance of epiphytes (plants that live on the surface of other plants, here often represented by hanging lichens, mosses and ferns), and a dense, shrubby understory. Dominance by conifers distinguishes the North American temperate rainforests from other temperate rainforests of the world.

Although North American temperate rainforest is unified by climate and physiography and has a fairly consistent evergreen coniferous aspect, it varies from south to north and from low to high elevations. **Seasonal rainforest** dominates low and middle elevations from Oregon north through eastern and central Vancouver Island. Western hemlock is the dominant tree, except in drier areas, where fires have led to even-aged Douglas-fir stands. Pacific silver fir and western redcedar are often abundant at moist, middle elevations, and western redcedar forms 'cathedral' forests, mostly on wet sites and in riparian areas.

Perhumid rainforest dominates low and middle elevations from northern Vancouver Island north to Glacier Bay and Yakutat in northern southeast Alaska. Western hemlock is still the most common tree in this zone. Pacific silver fir is common and sometimes co-dominant with western hemlock, but its range does not extend much beyond 55°N. Sitka spruce is common throughout, especially along rivers and shorelines, and it even reaches timberline in some of the coolest, wettest parts of the zone. Both redcedar and yellow-cedar are extensive in B.C., but in Alaska the cedars are restricted to wet sites, where they are usually small or stunted and often with mountain hemlock. Douglas-fir persists to about 53°N in some inner coast valleys, and as scattered individuals on steep rocky south slopes.

Subpolar rainforest occurs from the northern tip of our region south to Yakutat Bay. Summers are cool and very wet. Persistent snow is common at sea level in winter, and tidewater glaciers are common. The best examples of subpolar rainforest occur in Prince William Sound. Forest there is of recent postglacial origin (less than 4,000 years old). Mountain hemlock and Sitka spruce dominate down to sea level, but forest occupies less than 15 per cent of the land area. Timberline can be as low as 100 to 200 m above sea level.

Subalpine forest

Subalpine forest is characteristic of areas with a substantial, persistent winter snowpack. These conditions prevail only at high elevations, generally above 1,000 m in the southern part of our region, and above 800 m from southern B.C. north. In the most northern parts of the region, subalpine forest is often not distinct from the subpolar rainforest found at sea level. Mountain hemlock, yellow-cedar and Pacific silver fir are the characteristic species, although subalpine fir (*Abies lasiocarpa*) can be significant in drier, colder areas. Noble fir often dominates middle- to high-elevation forests in the Washington and Oregon mountains. From the west coast of the Queen Charlotte Islands north through coastal Alaska, Sitka spruce can also be a significant element of subalpine forests. Although fire is very infrequent in much of the subalpine zone, it plays a frequent and pervasive role along the eastern margin of the B.C. Coast Mountains and in the eastern Cascades.

Rainshadow forest

Rainshadow forest is most extensive on southeastern Vancouver Island, the Gulf and San Juan islands, the east side of the Olympic Peninsula and in the Willamette Valley. Douglas-fir and Garry oak (*Quercus garryana*) typify these dry, open forests. Where fire has been suppressed or is infrequent, grand fir and redcedar also occur. The northern distribution limits of many dry- and warm-climate species such as madrone (*Arbutus menziesii*) and prickly pear cactus occur in this zone. Rainshadow forest is the most diverse forest type in our region in terms of total numbers of plant species, and it contains some our most-endangered species and habitats.

NON-FOREST VEGETATION

Forests cover most of our region, but our region encompasses more than just forests: non-forested areas such as bogs and alpine tundra are significant components of the regional vegetation. Non-forested vegetation generally occurs where it is too wet, too saline or too cold and snowy for trees to survive, or in areas prone to disturbances that periodically kill trees—disturbances such as avalanches and fires. In our region, it is almost never too dry or too steep and rocky for trees to live; fire or some other disturbance is usually the limiting or precluding factor.

Maritime habitats

The northern Pacific coastal region has a very long coastline with a variety of both protected and exposed shores. The B.C. portion of the coast alone is 27,000 km in length. The coastline south of Puget Sound has rugged, exposed headlands punctuating long beaches and dune systems, with only a few major rivers. From Puget Sound north through B.C. and southeast Alaska, the coastline is a complex network of islands, long, steep-walled fjords, inlets, rivers and estuaries, and tidal flats. Between the forest and the sea grows a fringe of maritime vegetation adapted to exposure to salt water, wind and surf. Few vascular plants can tolerate salt spray or immersion in sea water, but those that can are often restricted to such habitats. The different types of shorelines differ primarily in the kind of substrate and degree of exposure they provide. Each supports a distinct vegetation type, and these maritime plant communities can be quite diverse. All beach habitats in exposed localities back onto a maritime forest community, typically of Sitka spruce with a dense salal (*Gaultheria shallon*) understorey.

Rocky shores are the most common type of shoreline on our coast. Terrestrial plant cover is sparse, especially on exposed rocky headlands, sea stacks and cliffs. Adaptations to the relentless buffeting by wind and salt spray, and to moisture stress, include cushion or matted growth forms and thick, waxy, succulent or densely hairy leaves. Sea plantain (*Plantago maritima*), hairy cinquefoil (*Potentilla villosa*), coastal strawberry (*Fragaria chiloensis*), northern riceroot (*Fritillaria camschatcensis*) and salal are typical of the hardy vegetation of exposed rocky shores.

Shingle beaches, composed of large gravels or cobbles, are also widespread in our region. They usually support clumps of searocket, dunegrass (*Elymus mollis*), beach pea (*Lathyrus japonicus*), giant vetch (*Vicia gigantea*), coastal strawberry, springbank clover (*Trifolium wormskjoldii*) and cleavers (*Galium aparine*). Such plants are especially common on the upper beach and among the jumble of driftwood at the furthest reach of winter storm tides and waves.

Sand beaches are widespread in Oregon and Washington, but uncommon and local in most of the rest of the region. Notable exceptions are found on the northeast Queen Charlotte Islands and the west coast of Vancouver Island. Elsewhere, beaches are mainly in small pockets behind the headlands of exposed outer coastal areas. Vegetation is sporadic, but showy species of the driftwood belt include searocket, beach-carrot (*Glehnia littoralis*) and beach pea. Further up the beach or on dunes, large-headed sedge, dune grasses, paintbrushes (*Castilleja* spp.), lupines (*Lupinus* spp.) and silver burweed (*Ambrosia chamissonis*) become common.

The most productive maritime plant communities are **tidal marshes**, especially those with brackish or low-salinity water, such as the water in estuaries. Soils are usually fine textured and nutrient rich, and they support lush meadow vegetation. Grasses and sedges, especially tufted hairgrass (*Deschampsia cespitosa*) and Lyngby's sedge (*Carex lyngbyei*), dominate, but these marshes also harbour showy species such as Pacific silverweed (*Potentilla anserina*), springbank clover and Nootka lupine (*Lupinus nootkatensis*), as well as salt-tolerant oddities such as glasswort (*Salicornia virginica*) and sea arrow-grass (*Triglochin maritimum*).

Freshwater wetlands

Wetlands are common in our region. They are extensive on the outer coast, especially on the coastal lowlands from northern Vancouver Island north to Juneau. Non-forested wetland types include **bogs**, **fens** and **marshes**. Classic bogs are acid peatlands with stagnant waters that originate as rain or snow falling directly onto the bog. In this book, we consider wetlands dominated by *Sphagnum* (peat) moss to be bogs. Fens and marshes are less acid and have more nutrients available for plants. Fens and marshes dominated by sedges and grasses—and shrubby fens with hardhack (*Spirea douglasii*), sweet gale (*Myrica gale*), Pacific crab apple (*Malus fusca*) and willows (*Salix* spp.)—are infrequent and localized along flowing water, on lake margins and at river mouths in our region. Throughout our region there are numerous, usually small, topographically controlled bogs in basins, on the margins of small lakes and on level, poorly drained terrain. The flat bogs of the Queen Charlotte Lowland and the domed bogs of the Fraser Lowland are extensive examples of this wetland type.

The colloquial term '**muskeg**' is used to refer to the complex mosaic of fens, bogs, pools, streams, exposed rock and scrubby forest that becomes increasingly common as one proceeds north. Muskeg is widespread over the north coastal lowlands and foothills, which feature an unusual landscape of low rocky hills covered with scrub forest and peatlands. You can see these areas from ferries and boats travelling north to Prince Rupert and southeast Alaska as you thread your way through the archipelagos and fjords of the Inside Passage. Stunted, gnarled shore pine, western redcedar, yellow-cedar, and both species of hemlock are scattered in muskeg areas. The pine, in particular, can assume bonsai-like forms. Pit ponds and larger pools contain skunk-cabbage (*Lysichiton americanum*), yellow pond-lily (*Nuphar polysepalum*), and various pondweeds (*Potamogeton* spp.).

Rills and streams drain the ponds, snaking between thick lawns of *Sphagnum* moss and islands of stunted forest and shrubs such as Labrador tea (*Ledum groenlandicum*), bog-laurel (*Kalmia microphylla* ssp. *occidentalis*), and common juniper (*Juniperus communis*). In the cool, humid, oceanic climate, peatlands can cover both subdued terrain and slopes of considerable steepness. Such 'blanket' or 'slope' muskeg is extensive on the west coast of the Queen Charlotte Islands and some of the exposed nearshore islands in the Hecate and Alexander Depressions. Sometimes the blanket muskeg is continuous from sea level to the alpine and has a very diverse flora with low elevation wetland species mixing with such typically subalpine species as subalpine daisy (*Erigeron peregrinus*), Indian hellebore (*Veratrum viride*), alpine-azalea (*Loiseleuria procumbens*) and partridgefoot (*Luetkea pectinata*).

Grasslands

Most grasslands in the northern Pacific coastal region originated following fires. Most of these occur in the dry intermountain corridor from the Willamette Valley north through the Puget Sound–Strait of Georgia area. In Oregon, south-facing mountaintop balds are grasslands

that were created by fire, then maintained by a combination of grazing and fire. Prehistorically, much of the Willamette Valley was a grassland maintained by annual burning. One of the few well-documented examples of natural coastal prairie is on the Olympic Peninsula in the rainshadow of the Olympic Mountains. Grasslands in our region were originally dominated by native perennial grasses, but are now dominated by Eurasian annuals and weedy grasses. These grasslands also retain many native plants such as fireweed (*Epilobium angustifolium*), lilies and various shrub species.

Disturbed habitats

These include roadsides, railroad and powerline right-of-ways, trails, recently logged areas, settled areas and other sites frequently disturbed by people. These habitats are often dominated by Eurasian weeds such as blackberries (*Rubus discolor*, *R. laciniatus*), Scotch broom (*Cytisus scoparius*) and annual grasses and composites, but native species also occur.

High-elevation habitats

Non-forested plant communities occupy high elevations throughout most of the northern Pacific coastal region, although many mountain peaks are the domain of rock, ice and permanent snow. Subalpine forest thins out with increasing elevation (around 500 to 700 m in southeast Alaska, from 800-1,000 m on the northern B.C. coast, and at 1,200 m or higher in the southern part of our region), where the snowpack is very deep and slow to melt. Picturesque clumps of trees (usually mountain hemlock, yellow-cedar and, sometimes, subalpine fir) and open heath and meadows form an attractive mosaic called **subalpine parkland**.

Heaths characteristically are dominated by dwarf, shrubby, evergreen members of the heather family, with other common species such as black crowberry (*Empetrum nigrum*), partridge-foot (*Luetkea pectinata*) and bird's-beak lousewort (*Pedicularis ornithorhyncha*). The ground cover forms a springy carpet, often so dense it obscures everything underfoot, including rocks and holes.

Coastal **mountain meadows** are less extensive than heaths but are lush, intensely green and dominated by herbs. Typical species include arrow-leaved groundsel (*Senecio triangularis*), subalpine daisy, Sitka valerian (*Valeriana sitchensis*), arctic lupine (*Lupinus arcticus*), Indian hellebore, gentians, sedges, and grasses such as purple mountain hairgrass (*Vahlodea atropurpurea*). These meadows put on a spectacular floral display in late summer.

Alpine **rocklands** and steeplands include rock outcrops, cliffs, boulder fields, fellfields, talus and scree slopes, wet runnels and gullies and avalanche tracks. The plant cover is usually sparse and discontinuous, but it includes many different saxifrages as well as ferns, buttercups, grasses, sedges and many species of lichens and bryophytes. Though often quite barren, these rocky areas are good places to look for some of the most distinctive, and often the rarest, species in our region.

BIODIVERSITY

'Biodiversity,' meaning the variety of living things and how that variety is distributed, is often defined at three levels: genetic, species and ecosystem. This considers the genetic diversity within and among the populations of given species, the patterns of abundance of populations of species and how they combine to form ecological communities, and how different types of ecosystems are distributed in space. Many other types of biological diversity can be described: for example, diversity of structure is a good example that affects wildlife living in the forests of the northern Pacific coastal region.

The species and their genetic variants and the unique ecosystems that develop in a region are of tremendous inherent value whether they are numerous or few. They represent the product of millions of years of adaptation and evolution in a particular dynamic landscape; they are quite literally irreplaceable. Each local genetic variant represents a combination of genes, which, if lost, will not be seen again. The temperate rainforests reflect, in their species composition and structure, the idiosyncratic histories of the changing climate and natural disturbances that produced them. In the structure of ancient forests, ecologists can see distinct traces of a warm period 800 years ago called the 'medieval optimum,' a cooler period during the last century called the 'little ice age,' numerous minor fluctuations in weather, and episodes of fire and wind. The forests that grow today have the potential to become ancient, given time, but as ancient forest they will necessarily be different from those we have inherited from the past.

Specific geographic areas within the northern Pacific coastal region are significant for the diversity or distinctiveness of their flora. Areas that escaped glacial advances, for example, often have a richer array of plant species than surrounding areas, and they sometimes develop local endemic species or subspecies. Well-known examples of such glacial refugia are the Queen Charlotte Islands, the Olympic Peninsula and Kodiak Island. Regionally, the greatest concentration of plant species in our region occurs in dry, fire-influenced habitats like the saaniche of southeast Vancouver Island and adjacent islands and the eastern Olympic Peninsula. These 'oases' of dry habitats surrounded by rainforest form the disjunct northern distribution limit for many plant species. However, human encroachment has greatly diminished the extent of such areas.

Centres of plant diversity tend to occur where there are major migration and climatic corridors between the harsh climates of the interior and the mild climates of the coast. Good examples of such corridors include large rivers like the Columbia, Fraser, Stikine, Skeena (pictured at right), Tatsenshini/Alsek and Taku. The greatest centre for plant diversity in Alaska is at the head of Lynn Canal, near Skagway. Many boreal species from interior B.C. and the Yukon occur there, as do many species with disjunct populations. The relatively dry rainshadow climate, historical patterns of climate change, relative isolation and corridors to the interior combine to produce the rich botanical diversity of this area.

PLANTS AND PEOPLE
Aboriginal peoples

Humans have occupied the northern Pacific coastal region for thousands of years. The archaeological record of settlements indicates the presence of people around the time of the retreat of the last glaciers, 10,000 to 14,000 years ago. The people who lived along the coast at that time apparently relied heavily on marine life, but used any available resources from the lands and forests as well. Western redcedar, which is so central to the northwest coast cultures of the present, was apparently uncommon until approximately 4,000 years ago. Other trees would have been used instead, but the giant canoes, massive houses, totem and mortuary poles and bark-fibre clothing that characterize the northwest coast culture could not have been developed until western redcedar was well established. These early peoples had an intimate relationship with the plants in their environment.

Although early European explorers described the northwest coast as untouched wilderness, in fact, the aboriginal peoples did have an impact on the landscape through selective harvesting of trees and controlled burning. Coastal people burned selected woods and meadowlands to maintain open conditions and promote the growth of desired plants including berries, nuts, root vegetables and forage plants for deer and other game. The diaries and journals of early European travellers such as David Douglas and George M. Dawson contained many observations of aboriginal landscape burning (Norton 1979; Boyd 1986; Turner 1991).

The names used for the First Nations groups in this book generally follow those used by Suttles (1990) in *Handbook of North American Indians*, volume 7, *Northwest Coast*. However, in some instances, aboriginal groups prefer other names for themselves, and we have attempted to follow these wherever possible.

The table below shows the names for aboriginal groups used in this guide, together with their equivalent names used by Suttles (1990) and others. Groups whose names are widely known (e.g., Haida, Tlingit) are not included in the table.

CONTEMPORARY ABORIGINAL GROUP NAME	PREVIOUSLY USED EQUIVALENT NAMES
Dena'ina	Taniana
Nisga'a	Nishga, Niska, Nisga
Coast Tsimshian	Kitasoo
Haisla (including Kitamaat, Hanaksiala, Kemano)	Haisla (including Kitamat, Kitlope, Kemano)
Heiltsuk	Bella Bella, Northern Kwakiutl
Oweekeno	Oowekyala
Kwakwa̱ka̱'wakw	Kwakwiutl, Southern Kwakiutl, Kwagiulth (this guide uses the form Kwakwaka'wakw in most instances)
Nuu-chah-nulth (-aht)	Nootka, Westcoast (sometimes includes Ditidaht)
Ditidaht	Nitinaht
Nuxalk (-mc)	Bella Coola
Comox	includes Sliammon (Mainland Comox)
Sechelt	Seshelt
Haq'emeylem	Sto:lo, Stalo, Halkomelem
Nlaka'pamux	Thompson
Lushootseed	Puget Sound Salish, includes: Green River, Nisqually (Skokomish), Puyallup, Skagit (Upper), Snohomish, Squaxin, Snuqualmi, Suquamish, Swinomish (Lower Skagit) [Note: in citations from Gunther (1973), these names are retained]
Straits Salish	includes: Saanich, Songish, Lummi, Samish (sometimes Clallam included)
Twana	Skokomish
Taidnapam (Sahaptin)	Upper Cowlitz (Gunther's term)
Secwepemc	Shuswap
Stl'at'imx	Lillooet
Kt'unaXa	Kootenay, Kootenai, Kutenai

Former Europeans

While the daily lives of European immigrants and other non-aboriginal residents of the Northern Pacific Coastal Region have rarely depended on a personal, intimate knowledge of plants, as did the lives of aboriginal peoples, non-aboriginal societies in our region have always relied on plant resources. Logging is the most obvious example of such dependence, and throughout our region the profits from logging the accumulated natural capital of timber in old-growth forests has been a cornerstone of historical and modern development. Plant communities contribute in many other ways as well. For instance, the streams where salmon are reared and spawn depend on the forest and riparian environments for appropriate microclimate, physical structure and energy input. Forest canopies and forest soils greatly influence patterns of run-off, and of snow accumulation and melt. Forests are now recognized as critical for maintaining water supply for many communities in our region.

Since arriving on the Pacific coast, non-aboriginal people have had a profound influence on plants and the environment. Some changes are obvious, such as the loss of habitat as forests were cleared and wetlands diked and drained for settlements, hydroelectric dams or agriculture. Other changes, many induced by forestry, involve more a manipulation of plant communities and their habitats than a permanent loss. One of the major effects of forestry in our region is a shift from the predominance of older forests to a landscape dominated by younger forests.

Some changes are more subtle than the outright loss of habitat or intentional manipulation of ecosystems. The spread, accidental or purposeful, of exotic weeds or pest plants has already had significant effects on plant communities in some parts of our region, and as modern urban and agricultural development expand, introduced species will affect areas throughout the Pacific coastal region. In some types of ecosystems, the effects of exotic species can be profound. In the dry oak woodlands of the rainshadow forest zone, ecological reserves and other areas intended to remain in their natural state have been invaded by Scotch broom, an aggressive European species that can outcompete the local flora. In forested areas near cities, many non-native species are common invaders from suburban gardens—holly (*Ilex aquifolium*) and giant knotweed (*Polygonum sachalinense*) are good examples. In many disturbed areas throughout the southern part of our region, introduced European blackberries are aggressive competitors

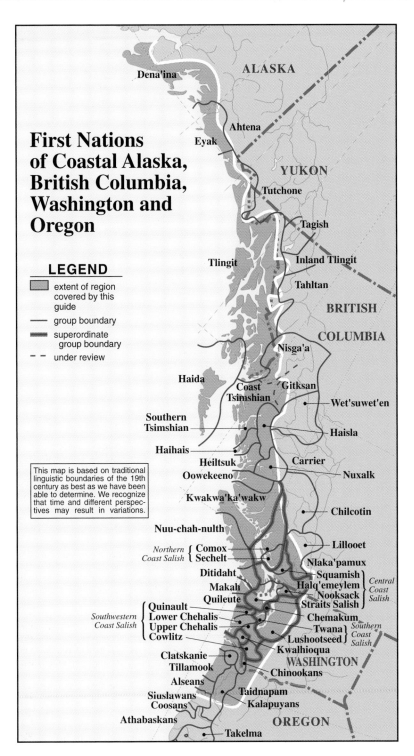

First Nations of Coastal Alaska, British Columbia, Washington and Oregon

LEGEND

- extent of region covered by this guide
- —— group boundary
- ━━ superordinate group boundary
- – – under review

This map is based on traditional linguistic boundaries of the 19th century as best as we have been able to determine. We recognize that time and different perspectives may result in variations.

ALASKA

Dena'ina

Ahtena

Eyak

YUKON

Tutchone

Tagish

Tlingit

Inland Tlingit

Tahltan

BRITISH

COLUMBIA

Nisga'a

Haida

Coast Tsimshian

Gitksan

Wet'suwet'en

Southern Tsimshian

Haisla

Haihais

Carrier

Heiltsuk

Oowekeeno

Nuxalk

Kwakwa'ka'wakw

Chilcotin

Nuu-chah-nulth

Lillooet

Northern Coast Salish { Comox — Sechelt —

Nlaka'pamux

Ditidaht

Squamish

Makah

Halq'emeylem

} *Central Coast Salish*

Quileute

Nooksack

Straits Salish

Southwestern Coast Salish { Quinault — Lower Chehalis Upper Chehalis Cowlitz —

Chemakum

Twana

} *Southern Coast Salish*

Lushootseed

Kwalhioqua

Clatskanie

Chinookans

Tillamook

WASHINGTON

Alseans

Siuslawans

Taidnapam

Coosans

Kalapuyans

Athabaskans

OREGON

Takelma

23

that effectively displace native plants. The Sitka blacktail deer introduced to the Queen Charlotte Islands earlier this century provide a sobering example of the pervasive effects that introduced herbivores can have on vegetation. The forest understorey there is now sparse and open, and tree saplings frequently develop a many-branched form after repeated browsing.

Control of wildfires throughout the rainshadow zones of the northern Pacific coastal region has fundamentally altered these ecosystems. Open meadows have gradually filled with woody vegetation to become woodlands, and woodlands have become forest. Fire intolerant species such as grand fir have filled the understorey beneath more tolerant species such as Douglas-fir and Garry oak. These changes in vegetation composition and structure have affected populations of a wide range of animal species, from moles and skunks to towhees and hawks.

Despite all these recent changes, the northern Pacific coastal region is one of the few bioregions in the world where, in many areas, there are examples of large ecosystems in which the native biodiversity remains very similar to what it was before European colonization two centuries ago. The challenge is to see that some of these ecosystems remain two centuries from now.

ETHNOBOTANY

Ethnobotany, the study of the relationships between people and plants, provides another view of the forest and its plants. Aboriginal peoples in our region have developed an intimate knowledge of plants and their uses, gained from many generations of observation and practice. In this book, some details of aboriginal relationships with particular plant species are provided, in hopes that readers will gain a greater understanding and appreciation of cultures in which wild plants have had a major role in influencing lifeways and attitudes.

Although the northwest coast peoples are often associated with a lifestyle of fishing, shellfish gathering and hunting marine mammals, plants were integral to their cultures and daily lives. Not only did plants provide aboriginal peoples with diverse foods, ranging from berries to the inner bark of trees, but many species were also sources of materials required for medicines, and for housing, fishing and hunting technologies. Plants were critical to the survival of aboriginal peoples, as they are to all of us. All aspects of people's lives, including their medicines, their religious, ceremonial and mythical traditions, their languages and their ways of looking at the world, related to plants in a variety of ways and are therefore important topics in the field of ethnobotany.

The ethnobotanical information presented in this book originated, directly or indirectly, from the knowledge and experiences of aboriginal people. In some cases, it was recorded by early ethnographers such as Franz Boas and John Swanton. Later research, focusing more directly on ethnobotanical information, was undertaken by Erna Gunther and Nancy Turner, among others. Many people today still hold profound knowledge of the plant world, and plants are still being used in traditional ways as foods, materials for implements, as medicines and in ceremonial roles. First Nations peoples are taking an increasing role in documenting and publishing their traditional knowledge.

Some parts of the northern Pacific coastal region have been more intensively studied ethnobotanically than have others. The reader will note, for example, that there are few details presented from the Oregon coast. This is not because the aboriginal peoples of the Oregon coast used plants less than other peoples in our region, but simply because little information exists relating to many of these groups, their languages and cultures (see Thompson and Kinkade 1990).

Plants as food

In the traditional diets of aboriginal peoples of the Northwest Coast, plant foods contributed both diversity and essential nutrients, supplementing the fish, seafoods, birds and game that made up the bulk of most meals. Some of the plant foods are well known to most people today; others are more obscure and little used. In all, approximately 130 different species of plants were used in some way as foods, beverages or flavourings. These include fruits (mostly fleshy berries), green vegetables (shoots and leaves), 'root' vegetables (bulbs, corms, tubers, rhizomes and true roots) and the inner bark of several tree species. Marine plants (algae or seaweeds) also contributed to the diet of northern Pacific coast peoples, but they are not covered in this book. Several plant species provided more than one type of food; for example, salmonberry (*Rubus spectabilis*) and thimbleberry (*R. parviflorus*) produced edible fruits, and their young shoots were peeled and eaten as a springtime treat.

In general, aboriginal people in our region occupied permanent villages during the winter, mostly along the shorelines and waterways of the region. Then, during the growing season, family or clan groups left the villages to travel on seasonal rounds, allowing them to harvest and process the resources they needed to sustain them through the year. Plant foods played a major role in this living pattern. Early in spring, the sweet, tender young shoots and greens of species such as cow-parsnip (*Heracleum lanatum*), fireweed, thimbleberry , salmonberry, western dock (*Rumex occidentalis*) and giant horsetail (*Equisetum telmatiea*) were harvested, often in large quantities. As these plants mature, they become tough and strong tasting and are no longer suitable as food, but in the spring they provided much-needed vitamins, especially ascorbic acid, which would have been in short supply during the winter.

In spring, when the sap starts running, the cambium and inner bark of western hemlock, Sitka spruce, black cottonwood (*Populus balsamifera* ssp. *trichocarpa*) and red alder (*Alnus rubra*) can be obtained by peeling off the outer bark and scraping the edible part from the outside of the wood or the inside of the sheets of bark. By late May and early June in the southern part of the Northwest Coast, a wide spectrum of fruits begins to ripen in succession: salmonberries and wild strawberries, followed by red elderberries (*Sambucus racemosa*), huckleberries, blueberries, blackberries, soapberries (*Shepherdia canadensis*) and thimbleberries, then gooseberries and currants (*Ribes* spp.) and salal, and finally, in late summer and fall, Pacific crab apples, highbush-cranberries (*Viburnum edule*), bog and mountain cranberries (*Oxycoccus oxycoccos*, and *Vaccinium vitis-idaea*), and evergreen huckleberries (*Vaccinium ovatum*).

Hesquiat Nuu-chah-nulth woman digging roots. E.S. Curtis (ca. 1915)

Root vegetables were important staples for many aboriginal groups. These vegetables include the edible bulbs of lily-family plants such as common camas (*Camassia quamash*), northern riceroot, chocolate lily (*Fritillaria lanceolata*), tiger lily (*Lilium columbianum*), brodiaeas (*Brodiaea* spp.) and wild onions (*Allium* spp.); tubers of arrowhead or wapato (*Sagittaria latifolia*); rootstocks of spiny woodfern (*Dryopteris expansa*); rhizomes of springbank clover and bracken fern (*Pteridium aquilinum*); and roots of Pacific silverweed, lupines, hemlock-parsley (*Conioselinum pacificum*), yampah (*Perideridia* spp.) and others. They were generally dug after the growing season, when the leaves of the plants had started to die back. For camas and the other lilies, this could be in mid-summer, while the seed stalks were still visible to aid in finding the bulbs. For others, fall through winter and early spring were considered the best gathering times.

Seaweeds were generally harvested in early to late spring. Mushrooms apparently were rarely, if at all, used as food by coastal peoples.

With the possible exception of springtime greens, most plant foods were not only eaten in season, they were also processed for use later in the year. In most cases, this meant a combination of cooking and drying. Berries, such as salal, thimbleberries, huckleberries, blueberries and currants, were often placed into a bentwood cedar box or other cooking vessel, brought to a boil with red-hot rocks and cooked to a jam-like consistency. This mixture was then poured into frames set on a base of skunk-cabbage leaves and allowed to dry into cakes. In warm weather, berries were dried individually, like raisins. Tarter fruits, such as highbush-cranberries, bog cranberries and Pacific crab apples, were often simply stored in boxes under water, sometimes mixed with oil. With time, they became softer and sweeter, and during the winter they could be taken out and eaten.

Most root vegetables were cooked in underground pits before being dried for the winter. This was an ingenious cooking technique, where large quantities of food could be processed with few utensils. There were many variations, but in general, a pit was dug and a hot fire lit in the bottom. Dense, rounded, fist-sized rocks were heated in the fire until they were red-hot, spread around the bottom of the pit and covered with a layer of grass, leaves or branches. The food to be cooked was placed in the pit in layers interspersed with fern fronds or other vegetation. Finally, more leaves or branches were piled on top, water was poured in through channels created by withdrawing posts set into the pit, and the pit was covered with a large mat and sealed with sand or dirt. The food was left to cook for periods ranging from overnight to more than 24 hours, being at once steamed, baked and smoked. When the pit was opened, the food was ready to eat or to spread out on mats to dry. Dried food, if kept in a warm, well-ventilated place, would keep through the winter. It was soaked in water overnight to rehydrate it before being served. Most plant foods were eaten with oil of some type, usually from oolichan (also spelled 'eulachon' or 'ooligan'), or from marine mammals. More recently, sugar or molasses was added to many foods.

Many plant foods were, and still are, served at special feasts and potlatches. As well, many were used as gifts and as trade or exchange items among families and between neighbouring groups. Although the aboriginal peoples of the northern Pacific Coast did not domesticate plants (with the possible exception of a type of tobacco grown in northern British Columbia and southern Alaska), they certainly managed and enhanced the production of roots and berries. Selective harvesting, burning of individual bushes and patches of certain plants, and the ownership and stewardship of particularly productive patches of 'roots' (such as camas, springbank clover, and Pacific silverweed) and fruits (such as Pacific crab apple, highbush-cranberry and salal) all served to enhance food production.

Today, few people eat wild root vegetables or tree cambium tissues, but berries are still harvested and extensively used all along the coast. Although they are used less frequently than in former years, plant foods are nevertheless highly valued and appreciated, especially by the older people. Several important health promotion programs have highlighted traditional foods as low-cost, nutritious alternatives to modern, processed foods. Nutrient analyses indicate that traditional plant foods are equal or superior to their commercial or domesticated counterparts (Kuhnlein and Turner 1991).

Plants in aboriginal technology

Plants also provided a wide range of important materials for northern coastal peoples: wood for fuel, construction and manufacture; fibrous bark, stem and leaf tissues for making mats, baskets, bags, cord, and clothing; bark and other materials for dyes and stains; pitch for glue, caulking, and waterproofing; and miscellaneous plant parts for makeshift mats and containers, abrasives, cleansers and scents.

Western redcedar is one of the most all-round useful species. It provides a range of different raw materials: wood for house posts and planks, totem poles, dugout canoes, bentwood boxes, fishing weirs and many other items; sheets of bark for siding and roofing; inner bark for mats, baskets, hats, clothing, cordage, tinder and absorbent towelling; withes (flexible branches) for pack baskets, fish traps and rope; and roots for cord and coiled baskets. It is not surprising that western redcedar was regarded as sacred and central to many important ceremonies, such as the cedar bark ceremonial dance of the Kwakwa'ka'wakw people.

Most trees and shrubs have special characteristics and were used for specific purposes. Yellow-cedar inner bark was valued for clothing and blankets, and yellow-cedar wood for carving. Bows were often made of yellow-cedar wood, especially wood from the roots. Pacific yew (*Taxus brevifolia*) was known for its tough, resilient wood, which was considered ideal for harpoon shafts, root-digging sticks, bows, clubs and wedges. Pacific crab apple had similar uses. Douglas-fir bark was used as a hot-burning fuel, and its wood was used for harpoon, spear and dipnet shafts. Sitka spruce wood, which is very light, was used for certain parts of harpoons and other implements. The dense knotwood of spruce, western hemlock and some other trees was split, steamed and fashioned into curved fishing hooks for cod and halibut. The pitch of spruce and hemlock was also used as a protective coating for implements and other items.

Red alder wood was considered the best fuel for smoking fish, and it was also used for bowls and masks. Alder bark was the most widely used source of dye, producing a range of colours from bright red-orange to dark brown. Bigleaf maple (*Acer macrophyllum*) wood was used for paddles and spindle whorls, and Douglas and vine maple (*A. glabrum, A. circinatum*) were used for small containers and snowshoe frames. The long, straight sucker shoots of oceanspray (*Holodiscus discolor*; also commonly known as 'ironwood') and mock-orange (*Philadelphus lewisii*) were used for mat-sewing needles, arrows and root-digging sticks. Bitter cherry (*Prunus emarginata*) bark was prized for its strength and toughness; it was used for wrapping the joints of implements and for a decorative overlay on some baskets. Oregon-grape (*Mahonia* spp.) bark was used to make a bright-yellow dye. Even species not generally known for their utility had some use. Cascara (*Rhamnus purshiana*) wood, for example, was apparently used for D-adze handles, and devil's-club (*Oplopanax horridus*) wood was used to make special types of fishing lures.

Many herbaceous plants were also used as materials. Cattail (*Typha latifolia*) leaves and the pithy stems of tule (bulrush; *Scirpus lacustris*) were both woven, or more often sewn, into lightweight mats that were used as walls and roofing of temporary houses, and as room dividers, wall insulation, mattresses and surfaces for drying berries and preparing food. The tough stem fibres of stinging nettle (*Urtica dioica*) and, to a lesser extent, fireweed, were spun into cord to be made into fishing nets and lines or used for sewing, binding and tying. The large, waxy-coated skunk-cabbage leaves (which are NOT edible!) and thimbleberry leaves were used as surfaces for drying berries. Fern fronds were used as makeshift placemats and interspersed between layers of food in cooking pits. Horsetail stems were used as abrasives, and mosses provided padding, towelling and diapers.

Plants as medicine

Medicinal plants comprise a large and diverse group of species, and are perhaps the least known in terms of their composition and potential application. The potent anti-cancer drug taxol, found in Pacific yew, is just one example of a promising medicine derived from a species that, though highly valued by aboriginal people, was virtually ignored by society in general. Even plants such as devil's club, whose widespread use in traditional aboriginal medicine has been described in the literature (Turner 1982), are not well documented in terms of their chemical and pharmacological properties.

It is beyond the scope of this book to describe medicinal plant uses in detail. However, it should be noted that probably several hundred plants have medicinal applications in traditional aboriginal cultures in our region. When the numbers of separate types of applications and treatments for specific ailments are included in the equation, there are literally thousands of traditional medicines derived from plants in our region.

Traditional medicinal uses range from applying tree pitch, macerated leaves, or solutions from various plant parts to wounds, burns, warts and skin infections, to chewing roots or leaves for sore throats and coughs, to drinking 'teas' made from various plants or mixtures of plants for many different purposes. Tuberculosis and other respiratory ailments, fevers, muscular aches and pains, internal haemorrhaging, stomach and digestive tract ailments, gynaecological complaints, kidney and bladder ailments and headaches were all generally treated by administering medicinal teas, in place of water or other beverages, over a period of days or weeks. Tonics, for restoring strength and maintaining health, were also administered as teas. Sore eyes and other eye problems were common, apparently because of frequent exposure to smoke from cooking and heating fires, and they were generally treated with washes or solutions applied directly to the eyes. Arthritis and rheumatism were sometimes treated by having the patient take a steambath, lying covered by a blanket for a period of time on steam-heated herbs.

Many medicinal plants are potentially toxic if taken in the wrong dosage or without proper preparation. Traditional healers, with the knowledge and experience of many generations behind them, were well aware of the potential hazards of the medicines they used. Today, some people caution, certain traditional medicines should not be used at all, because people are not following the required or prescribed lifestyles that would allow their bodies to use the medicines safely. One example of a highly toxic medicinal plant that was formerly very commonly used, but with great care, is Indian hellebore.

Traditional medicine is closely and inextricably linked with spiritual beliefs. Certain plant medicines, such as devil's club, Rocky Mountain juniper (*Juniperus scopulorum*), yellow pond-lily, and Indian consumption plant (bare-stem desert-parsley, *Lomatium nudicaule*) were valued for their special protective properties, or for their special connections with the spiritual realm. All medicines, and all plant foods and materials as well, were regarded with reverence and appreciation, and often their collection and use involved special prayers, ceremonies, and rituals.

The efficacy of many of these traditional medicines is undeniable. Time and again, accounts of cures or alleviation of symptoms have been given by aboriginal people who have undergone treatments, or who have witnessed treatments of members of their family or community. Recent research on a large selection of traditional medicinal plants from British Columbia confirms that many have antibiotic properties; some of them, such as red alder, are effective against a wide range of bacterial pathogens (McCutcheon et al. 1992).

NOTE: Although this guide records medicinal uses of plants, it is not a 'how-to' reference for using traditional plant-derived medicines, nor does it advocate the use of such medicines. We do not recommend experimentation by readers, and we caution that many plants in our region, including some with traditional medical uses, are poisonous or harmful.

Trees

Trees are single-stemmed, woody plants greater than 10 m in height when mature. Our region is predominantly forested (i.e., covered with trees), and the forests are usually dominated by evergreen conifers. A distinctive feature of our region is that, because our wet maritime climate makes large fires uncommon, some trees get very old and very big (see 'Giants of their genera' [p.16] in the Introduction to this guide).

Trees have formed the basis for human culture in our region, from the earliest peoples to the present day. The aboriginal peoples in our region used trees for food, clothing, shelter, transport, cooking and storing, and medicine. Western redcedar and yellow-cedar were of particular importance (see p. 41), and the geographical extent of the Northwest Coast peoples cultural area is approximately the same as the range of western redcedar. For non-aboriginals (from the first settlers to today), forestry has formed the basis of local and regional economies. As populations burgeon, our forests become increasingly important for other values as well: as recreational areas, sources of spiritual retreat and refreshment, and habitat for myriad other organisms, many still unknown.

Key to trees

1a. Leaves needle-like or scale-like, evergreen; seeds usually in cones,
not enclosed in a fruit (conifers) 2
  2a. Leaves scale-like, concealing the twigs 3
    3a. Leaf-covered twigs flattened; seed cones ellipsoid .... *Thuja plicata*
    3b. Leaf-covered twigs round or squarish in cross-section;
    seed cones spherical, berry-like .... *Chamaecyparis nootkatensis*
  2b. Leaves needle-like, not concealing the twigs 4
    4a. Needles in clusters 5
      5a. Needles in clusters of 5 .... *Pinus monticola*
      5a. Needles in clusters of 2 .... *Pinus contorta*
    4b. Needles not in clusters 6
      6a. Needles stalkless 7
        7a. Branches without spray-like foliage, appearing half-rounded by
        upswept needles; needles with lines of stomata on both surfaces 8
          8a. Rows of stomata on upper needle surface in a broad
          central band; seed cones without prominent bracts .... *Abies lasiocarpa*
          8a. Rows of stomata on upper needle surface in 2
          separate bands; seed cones with sharp-pointed bracts
          sticking out prominently past the scales .... *Abies procera*
        7b. Branches with spray-like foliage; needles with
        lines of stomata on lower surface only 9
          9a. Needles spread in definite 2-ranked arrangement,
          3–4 cm long; seed cones light green .... *Abies grandis*
          9b. Upper needles on twig point forward, no definite
          2-ranked arrangement; needles 1–3 cm long;
          seed cones purple .... *Abies amabilis*
      6b. Needles stalked 10
        10a. Stalks fall with needles; seed cones with
        prominent, 3-pronged bracts .... *Pseudotsuga menziesii*
        10b. Stalks or part of them remain after needles fall;
        seed cones not as above 11
          11a. Needles 4 sided, stiff, sharp-pointed .... *Picea sitchensis*
          11b. Needles 2 sided, not stiff 12
            12a. Needles of equal lengths, apparently
            alternate, sharp-pointed .... *Taxus brevifolia*
            12b. Needles of different lengths, opposite or spirally
            arranged, blunt 13
              13a. Needles flat, in 2 rows, green above, with
              two whitish bands of stomata on lower surface;
              seed cones 2–3 cm long .... *Tsuga heterophylla*
              13b. Needles half-round, keeled beneath, crowded
              on all sides of twigs, with whitish bands of stomata
              on both surfaces; seed cones 3–8 cm long .... *Tsuga mertensiana*

1b. Leaves broad and (except for *Arbutus*) annually deciduous; seed enclosed in a fruit 14

14a. Bark peeling 15

15a. Leaves evergreen, leathery, egg-shaped; bark red .... *Arbutus menziesii*

15b. Leaves annually deciduous, rarely leathery;
bark white to copper-brown .... *Betula papyrifera*

14b. Bark not peeling 16

16a. Fruits pomes (like apples); trees with thorns
(though these may be uncommon) 17

17a. Thorns abundant, smooth; flowers to 1 cm across,
unpleasantly smelly; fruits ('haws') about 1 cm long,
blackish-purple; shrubs to 7 m tall .... *Crataegus* (see 'Shrubs' section)

17b. Thorns rare, rough; flowers to 2 cm across, pleasantly fragrant; fruits
(crab apples) about 1.6 cm long, yellow to red; trees to 12 m tall .... *Malus fusca*

16b. Fruits various, but not like apples; trees without thorns 18

18a. Leaves compound (divided into leaflets); in the southern part of our region
(Washington, Oregon and a few trees on Vancouver Island) .... *Fraxinus latifolia*

18b. Leaves simple (not divided into leaflets) 19

19a. Leaves lobed 20

20a. Leaves opposite, maple-like;
fruits 2-winged samaras .... *Acer macrophyllum*

20b. Leaves alternate, oak-like; fruits acorns .... *Quercus garryana*

19b. Leaves not lobed 21

21a. Leaves opposite, smooth-margined .... *Cornus nuttallii*

21b. Leaves alternate, distinctly toothed 22

22a. Fruit a persistent, cone-like catkin; leaves
with double-toothed margins .... *Alnus rubra*

22b. Fruit not as above; leaves with single-toothed margins 23

23a. Flowers inconspicuous in catkins, without odour;
fruits dry capsules with hairy, tufted seeds; bark deeply
furrowed, without lenticels .... *Populus balsamifera* ssp. *trichocarpa*

23b. Flowers showy, fragrant; fruits fleshy cherries; bark
smooth to lightly roughened, with lenticels .... *Prunus emarginata*

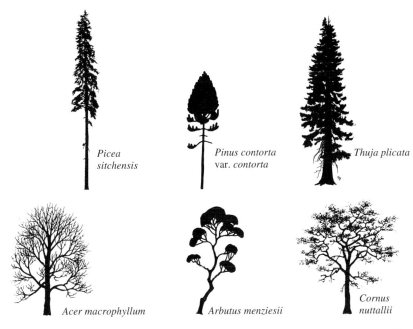

Picea sitchensis

Pinus contorta var. *contorta*

Thuja plicata

Acer macrophyllum

Arbutus menziesii

Cornus nuttallii

WESTERN HEMLOCK • *Tsuga heterophylla*

GENERAL: To 60 m tall with a narrow crown, a conspicuously drooping leader, gracefully down-sweeping branches and delicate, feathery foliage; bark rough, reddish-brown, scaly, thick and furrowed in old trees; twigs slender, roughened by the peg-like bases whose needles have fallen.

LEAVES: Needles short, flat, blunt, widely and irregularly spaced, of unequal length (5–20 mm long), producing feathery flat sprays, yellowish-green on top, whitish with 2 fine lines of stomata below, twisted at the base to appear 2-ranked.

CONES: Pollen cones numerous, small; seed cones numerous, small (about 2 cm long), oblong, purplish-green when young to light brown when mature.

ECOLOGY: Fairly dry to wet sites; well adapted to grow on humus and decaying wood, also found on mineral soil; shade-tolerant; very common from low to middle elevations.

NOTES: Western hemlock bark has a high tannin content and was used as a tanning agent, pigment and cleansing solution. The Quileute used a hemlock-bark solution for tanning hides and soaking spruce-root baskets to make them water tight. Some Coast Salish people used a red dye made from hemlock bark to colour mountain-goat wool and basket materials, and as a facial cosmetic and hair remover. The Kwakwaka'wakw steeped the bark in urine to make a black dye, and the Nuxalk, Chehalis and others used the bark steeped in water to colour fish nets brown, making them invisible to fish. The Snohomish used the dye to colour basket materials. A yellow-orange paint was prepared by the Quinault from mashed hemlock bark mixed with salmon eggs; this was used to colour dip-nets and paddles. • Western hemlock wood is moderately heavy and durable and fairly easy to carve. It was carved into implements such as spoons, roasting spits, dip-net poles, combs, spearshafts, wedges, children's bows and elderberry picking hooks. Halibut and cod hooks were fashioned from the circular grain of the trunk which surrounds the limbs, or from the dense knots. The Haida made large feast bowls from the wood of bent hemlock trunks. The Nisga'a used hemlock twigs to form the rims of birch-bark baskets. • Hemlock branches were considered an excellent bedding material. They were also frequently used by the Coast Salish and Nuu-chah-nulth for collecting herring spawn. During the spawning season, from March to June, the boughs were tied in bundles and lowered into the ocean near river estuaries. Later the spawn was collected by scraping it off the boughs, to be eaten fresh or dried. The Mainland Comox threaded oolichan and herring on hemlock boughs for drying, and used the boughs for lining steaming pits. Kwakwaka'wakw dancers wore skirts, headdresses, and head-bands of hemlock boughs, and young women lived in hemlock-bough huts for four days after their first menstruation. • The hemlock tree was used extensively as medicine by most groups of the Northwest Coast. Hemlock pitch was applied topically for a variety of purposes, including poultices or poultice coverings, linaments rubbed on the chest for colds and when mixed with deer tallow as a salve to prevent sunburn. The Nuu-chah-nulth drank a hemlock-bark tea, sometimes mixed with bark of cascara and red alder, for internal injuries and haemorrhaging. • The inner bark of hemlock was eaten by Haida, Tsimshian, Nuxalk and other central and northern coastal peoples. Ditidaht hunters and other travellers sometimes chewed on the young branch-tips of hemlock as a hunger suppressant when they were without food. • Western hemlock is the most common forest tree in Alaska and on the north coast of B.C. It is among the most shade-tolerant trees on the Pacific coast. The highest growth rate ever recorded in the temperate zone was measured in a 17-year-old hemlock forest (36 tonnes/hectare/year). Western hemlock also has the densest canopy of any tree species in the west, so that few understorey plants can grow under it, especially in middle-aged forests (30–80 years old). Western hemlock will only grow on sites with significant organic content in the soil: it will not grow on raw floodplains or on recently deglaciated sites, for example.

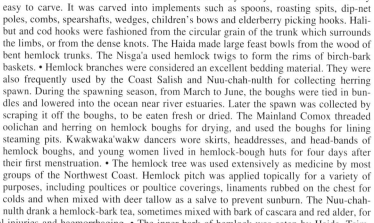

MOUNTAIN HEMLOCK • *Tsuga mertensiana*

GENERAL: Usually subalpine, to 40 m tall, often stunted at higher elevations or in muskeg; leader droops only slightly; branches droop or spread but tend to have an upward sweep at the tips; bark dark reddish-brown, deeply furrowed and ridged.

LEAVES: Similar to those of western hemlock, but needles equal in length, bluish-green, 1–3 cm long, covered equally by stomata on upper and lower surfaces, densely covering branches on all sides so sprays not flattened.

CONES: Pollen cones bluish, seed cones light to deep purple or brownish purple (or sometimes green) at flowering, becoming brown at maturity, longer (3–8 cm) than those of western hemlock.

ECOLOGY: On Vancouver Island south to Oregon, a subalpine or montane species associated with long winters and deep snowpacks; often occurs up to timberline and in subalpine parkland; north of Vancouver Island, associated with bogs and wet sites with deep organic soils, sometimes at low elevations; in Prince William Sound occurs over a broad range of sites to sea level.

NOTES: In dense forests, needles of mountain hemlock form flat sprays that are often difficult to distinguish from western hemlock. Upper branches of such trees retain typical form, and they appear darker and denser than western hemlock trees. • Because mountain hemlock is less shade-tolerant than western hemlock, it often forms the overstorey of forests with only western hemlock in the understorey. Dwarf mistletoe, a plague on pines, does not infect mountain hemlock, but Indian paint fungus (*Echinodontium tinctorium*) takes its toll on both hemlocks, as well as on the true firs. • In many areas where mountain hemlock grows, the snow does not melt until July or even August: snowpacks often reach 6 m or more deep in coastal subalpine forests. However, the soil usually does not freeze in such forests, and mountain hemlock can grow at near-freezing temperatures if its roots are not frozen. • On San Juan Ridge, northeast of Jordan River on Vancouver Island, squirrel-made caches of mountain-hemlock seed cones have been observed in the deep hoofprints of Roosevelt elk. Once covered with snow, these cones serve as a convenient winter food supply. • Unlike most conifers, mountain hemlock does not provide good shelter from the rain because some of its branches slope upwards. • *Tsuga* is from the Japanese *tsu-ga*, the elements for 'tree' and 'mother'; *mertensiana* is named for Franz Karl Mertens, a German botanist.

*mountain hemlock
(seen at left in centre photo)*

*western hemlock
(seen at right in centre photo)*

31

DOUGLAS-FIR • *Pseudotsuga menziesii* ssp. *menziesii*

GENERAL: Large, to 70 m tall (sometimes 80–90 m); crown of young trees pyramidal with a stiffly erect leader; branches spreading to drooping; buds sharply pointed; bark ultimately very thick, fluted, ridged, rough and dark brown.

LEAVES: Needles flat, yellowish-green, 2–3 cm long, with pointed tips, 1 groove on upper surface and 2 white bands of stomata on lower surface, spirally arranged, leave small, flat scar on twig upon falling; buds sharp-pointed.

CONES: Pollen cones small, reddish-brown; young seed cones hanging, oval, 5–10 cm long, green at flowering, turning reddish-brown to grey; scales papery; bracts prominently 3 forked, extend beyond scales (look for the 'mice' hiding in the cones—the bracts are their hind feet and tails).

ECOLOGY: From extremely dry, low elevation sites to moist montane sites; on the outer south coast it is replaced by western hemlock except on dry, rocky sites or in areas influenced by fire.

NOTES: Douglas-fir wood and bark was thought by most of the coastal groups to be an excellent fuel, but it had the reputation of throwing sparks and giving slivers to those handling it. The wood was also used to make items such as spear handles, harpoon shafts, spoons, dip-net poles, harpoon barbs, fire tongs, salmon weirs, caskets and halibut and cod hooks. Its pitch was used for sealing joints of implements such as harpoon heads, gaffs and fishhooks, and for caulking canoes and water vessels. The pitch, like that of many coniferous trees, was used to make a medicinal salve for wounds and skin irritations. The Nuxalk, Quinault and others made torches from the pitchy heartwood. • The Comox prepared dogfish by stuffing it with rotten, powdered Douglas-fir and burying the fish in a pit lined with the same material. • Douglas-fir is usually separated into 2 subspecies: coastal Douglas-fir (ssp. *menziesii*) and interior Douglas-fir (ssp. *glauca*). Interior Douglas-fir, which does not occur in our region, is a smaller, stockier tree with smaller cones (to 7 cm long) and bluish-green foliage. • Under natural conditions, Douglas-fir establishes primarily after fires on wetter sites, and the trees can live for over a thousand years. Thus many ancient old-growth forests contain giant Douglas-fir that represent the legacy of fires that swept the landscape many centuries ago. The trees have very thick bark, which allows them to survive moderate surface fires. • Douglas-fir is not related to the true firs (*Abies* spp.). There are only 2 species of *Pseudotsuga* in western North America. Bigcone Douglas-fir (*P. macrocarpa*) is much more restricted in range, occuring in southern California and northern Baja. Douglas-fir did not appear in our region until about 7,000 years ago. • This species was first described by naturalist-surgeon Dr. Archibald Menzies and is named after northwest explorer-botanist David Douglas. The Latin name comes from *pseudo* ('false') and *tsuga* ('hemlock').

AMABILIS FIR • *Abies amabilis*
PACIFIC SILVER FIR

GENERAL: Tall, straight, symmetrical with a **dense cylindrical or conical shape**, to 55 m tall; older bark whitish-grey with chalky white patches, smooth with resin blisters, becoming scaly with age.

LEAVES: Needles **flat**, blunt, most notched at the tip, grooved above and ridged below, to 3 cm long, **dark shiny green above, with two to many white lines of stomata underneath**; form flattened, spray-like branches, needles from the branch bottom and sides spread horizontally, **needles from the branch top lie flat against the twig and point forward**.

CONES: Pollen cones reddish; **seed cones erect, deep purple, barrel-shaped**, 8–12 cm long; fall apart while still on the tree, leaving the central 'spike' standing into winter.

ECOLOGY: On a variety of sites, but most commonly in moist forest on deep, well-drained soils above 1,000 m elevation in the southern part of its range, above 300 m in the central part and near to sea level in the north.

NOTES: In Oregon, amabilis fir is restricted to the upper montane and subalpine zones, generally occurring above 1,000 m in elevation. It is rare in the Oregon Coast Ranges. Common associates in Oregon are noble fir, Douglas-fir, and both hemlocks. In Washington and on Vancouver Island it is found at middle to high elevations (300–1,500 m) and almost to sea level on the outer coast. On the mainland coast of B.C., amabilis fir occurs in mixed stands with hemlocks, Sitka spruce and redcedar, and it grows at steadily lower elevations until the montane forest type disappears near the Alaska border. Throughout its range amabilis fir is very tolerant of shade, and small trees are often abundant in the forest understorey. • In the Cascade Mountains, *A. grandis* occurs at low elevations, but reappears on dry sites at middle elevations, where the trees are often of hybrid derivation with *A. concolor* (a species common to the south of our area). *Abies amabilis* and *A. procera* occur at middle to high elevations, with *A. amabilis* dominating tree reproduction in the forest, whereas *A. procera* establishes in areas opened by fire. *A. lasiocarpa* occurs at high elevations on relatively dry sites and extends up to timberline. • The Hesquiat and the Ditidaht called amabilis fir and grand fir by the same name and considered the two species to be very similar. The pitch of 'balsam' firs (*Abies* spp.) was chewed for enjoyment, and the Ditidaht name for both *A. amabilis* and *A. grandis* literally means 'sweet plant.' The boughs of amabilis fir have a pleasant, spicy fragrance and, along with boughs of grand fir, were used in the household as floor coverings and bedding. • The Nisga'a occasionally used amabilis fir wood for house planks, but it is soft and brittle, and therefore it was used mostly for fuel. • **True firs** (the genus *Abies*) can be distinguished from other conifers in our area by: the **circular leaf scars** left when needles are removed from their branches; their **erect cones that disintegrate in the tree** (rather than falling intact from it, as they do in our other conifers); and their **bark, which, in young trees at least, is smooth and covered with resin blisters**. When open-grown, all assume a conical form, which can be used to identify them at a distance. • Called the 'silver fir' because of the shining silvery undersides of the needles. *Amabilis* means 'lovely,' an apt name for this beautiful tree.

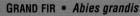

GRAND FIR • *Abies grandis*

GENERAL: Tall, straight, stately, to 80 m tall; bark greyish-brown, usually with white mottles, smooth with resin blisters when young, becoming ridged and then scaly with age.

LEAVES: Needles **flat**, tips rounded and notched (sometimes pointed on cone-bearing branches), 2–4 cm long, **dark green and grooved above, two white lines of stomata below; in two distinct horizontal rows**.

CONES: Pollen cones yellowish; seed cones **yellowish-green to green**, cylindrical, erect, 5–10 cm long, high in the crown where they fall apart through the autumn.

ECOLOGY: Dry to moist coniferous forest in rainshadow areas, usually with Douglas-fir; river flats to fairly dry slopes, from low to middle elevations.

NOTES: Grand fir is most easily distinguished from other true firs in our area by its sprays of lustrous needles in 2 distinct rows. **Needles on grand fir are usually spread so horizontally that both the upper and lower sides of the branches are clearly visible.** • Grand fir grows in drier (generally rainshadow) climates: areas with less than 150 cm of precipitation annually. It is a common understorey tree under Douglas-fir, and occasionally a co-dominant tree. Like most other true firs, it is thin-barked and therefore very sensitive to fire. Control of fires in the drier southern parts of our region has allowed widespread increase in grand fir in the last 50 years. • Kwakwaka'wakw shamans wove its branches into head-dresses and costumes and used the branches for scrubbing individuals in purification rites. The Hesquiat used its branches as incense and decorative clothing for wolf dancers. • Grand fir was occasionally used as a fuel. Some interior peoples, such as the Okanagan, also made canoes from its bark. Its pitch was applied to bows for a secure grip and rubbed on paddles and scorched for a good finish. A brown dye from its bark was used in basketry by the Straits Salish, along with a pink dye made by mixing the brown dye with red ochre. Its knots were shaped, steamed and carved into halibut hooks and other types of fish hooks by the Ditidaht, Straits Salish and other coastal groups. • Grand fir bark, sometimes mixed with stinging nettles, was boiled and the decoction used for bathing and as a general tonic by the Kwakwaka'wakw and other peoples. The Lushootseed boiled its needles to make a medicinal tea for colds. The Ditidaht sometimes brought its boughs inside as an air freshener or burned them as an incense and to make a purifying smoke to ward off sickness. Its bark was crushed with the barks of red alder and western hemlock and made into an infusion that the Ditidaht drank for internal injuries. The Hesquiat mixed pitch of young grand fir trees with oil and rubbed it on the scalp as a deodorant and to prevent balding. • A Hesquiat story tells of a woman who used grand fir boughs to stay warm after she was shunned in her village for having a child out of wedlock. • Trees at middle elevations in the Oregon Cascades **resemble white fir** (*A. concolor*) in some respects and appear to be a hybrid with this southern species. • Named 'grand' by botanist David Douglas because of the great height (to 80 m) and diameter (to 55 cm) it can attain. Sometimes called 'stinking fir,' since the crushed leaves emit a strong balsamy—some say 'catty'—odour.

SUBALPINE FIR • *Abies lasiocarpa*
ALPINE FIR

GENERAL: To 50 m tall (but usually 20–35 m tall), with **narrow, spire-shaped crown**, often stunted and hedge-like or prostrate in exposed subalpine sites; branches short, thick, not spray-like; bark thin, grey, smooth, with resin blisters.

LEAVES: Needles **thickest in the centre**, mostly blunt, sometimes notched, may be pointed on very young growth at top of tree, 2–4 cm long, **all tending to turn upward**, crowded, bluish green, with **white rows of stomata on both surfaces**.

CONES: Pollen cones small, bluish; seed cones large, cylindrical, 6–10 cm long, usually deep purple, becoming lighter-coloured with age, erect, near top of tree, as with other firs disintegrate on the tree leaving only central core.

ECOLOGY: At subalpine elevations (and as a stunted tree to treeline) but also near sea level in cold air drainages of major rivers that cut through the Coast Range in southeast Alaska and on the north coast of B.C.

NOTES: *Abies lasiocarpa* is typically a subalpine species of drier interior regions, widespread in the Rockies; in our region it is found mostly near the divide in the Cascades and the B.C. Coast Range. On the central and northern mainland, it is also common in upper valleys of inner coastal rivers, especially valleys crowned by large icefields. It often occurs in floodplain valley-bottom forests as well as at higher elevations in such cold air drainages. Isolated populations also occur in the Olympic Mountains on dry sites, more commonly in the eastern Olympics; on Vancouver Island from near Port Alberni north, but not on the Queen Charlotte Islands; and on several isolated mountain tops on the outer coast of southeast Alaska, south of Petersburg. North of the Olympics on the outer coast, it seems to be associated with glacial refugia on dry sites, especially limestone. In southeast Alaska it can be an early post-glacial colonizer. Cones are rare on

north-coastal subalpine fir, where populations are maintained mostly through layering. • The pitch and bark of subalpine fir were very important medicines in the Interior. For example, it is known as 'medicine-plant' in Secwepemc. But among northwest coast peoples, the other *Abies* species were more commonly used. • The Nlaka'pamux used the boughs of subalpine fir for bedding and covering floors. They were widely used by interior peoples as an incense. • The inner bark of subalpine fir was eaten raw by some Nlaka'pamux people. • Subalpine fir sometimes occurs on drier sites within moist subalpine landscapes where mountain hemlock and amabilis fir dominate. • Subalpine fir is often erroneously called 'balsam' or 'balsam fir,' but the true balsam fir (*Abies balsamea*) is an eastern species. Also called 'alpine fir,' which is also a misnomer, because 'alpine' suggests 'above treeline.' The name *Abies* is derived from Latin *abeo* meaning 'to rise' or 'arising' and refers to the great height that some species attain. 'Fir' is derived from the Old English *furh* or *fyrh* and the Danish *fyrr* meaning 'fire.'

NOBLE FIR • *Abies procera*

GENERAL: Tall, beautifully symmetrical, to 80 m tall, conical in shape; bark smooth with resin blisters when young, breaking up into brownish-grey plates with age.

LEAVES: Needles **roughly 4-sided** (somewhat like a spruce), or at least thicker in the middle, 2–3 cm long, bluish-green but appearing silvery due to **2 white rows of stomata below, and 1–2 rows above**, grooved on the upper surface; **twisted upward, so that the lower surface of the branch is exposed**.

CONES: Pollen cones reddish; seed cones large (10–15 cm long), erect, **scales nearly concealed by shaggy-edged, sharp-pointed bracts**.

ECOLOGY: Middle- to upper-elevation coniferous forests, often associated with amabilis fir.

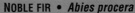

NOTES: The most 'noble' stands of *A. procera* are found in moist, middle-elevation areas with deep, rich soils. Middle-elevation forests are usually more open than low-elevation forests and occur on poorer, thinner, rockier soils in areas more frequently disturbed by wind, snow and, in some areas, fire. Magnificent stands of noble fir can occur at middle elevations in the Cascades. On one site near Mt. St. Helens, for example, an even-aged, 200-year-old forest had over 2,000 tonnes biomass/ha, or almost 10 times the living plant matter of a mature deciduous forest in eastern North America, or 2/3 that of the largest redwood forests. • Noble fir reaches a greater overall size than any other species of the genus *Abies*. The record tree (90 m tall, 2.75 m in diameter) is in the southern Washington Cascades.

• The original Latin name *Abies nobilis* had to be changed when it was discovered that another tree had already been given this name. However, the common name has persisted because of noble fir's magnificent proportions and big, heavy, shaggy cones. • Its lumber is sometimes marketed as 'Oregon Larch.' The Larch Mountains in the Cascades were so-called because they were covered with towering stands of noble fir. • The R.A.F. Mosquito planes of World War II were built with noble fir frames. • 'I...transmit one bundle of six species, exceedingly beautiful....Among these, *Abies nobilis* is by far the finest. I spent three weeks in a forest composed of this tree, and day by day could not cease to admire it....' (David Douglas, 1830, after collecting in the southern Cascades.) • '...among the many highly interesting species by which it is surrounded in its native woods, in point of elegance justly claims the pre-eminence.' (David Douglas on noble fir, 1829 notes.)

SITKA SPRUCE • *Picea sitchensis*

GENERAL: Large, commonly to 70 m tall and 2 m diameter; main branches typically long and horizontal, branchlets drooping; bark thin, reddish-brown to grey-brown, **breaking up into small scales**.

LEAVES: Needles yellowish-green or bluish-green, **stiff, very sharp**, 1–3 cm long, with 2 white lines of stomata on the upper surface, usually 2 narrower lines on the lower surface; **4-sided, somewhat flattened**.

CONES: Pollen cones red; seed cones 5–8 cm long, cylindrical, reddish-brown becoming brown, with **thin, wavy, irregularly toothed scales**.

ECOLOGY: In pure or mixed stands, often on moist, well-drained sites such as alluvial floodplains, marine terraces, headlands, recent glacial outwash, avalanche tracks; also on old logs or mounds on boggy sites; typically at low to middle elevations, but reaching timberline on the Queen Charlotte Islands and the most maritime parts of southeast Alaska.

NOTES: A quick way to identify Sitka spruce is to grab a branch in your hand: the stiff, sharp needles pointing out on all sides of the branch hurt. • Another spruce that occurs in our area, though uncommonly, is Engelmann spruce (*Picea engelmannii*). Engelmann is a species of moist subalpine coniferous forests, common east of the mountain crests but showing up sporadically from B.C. to Shasta County, California at middle and high elevations. It does not occur on Vancouver Island or the Queen Charlotte Islands. Like any spruce, Engelmann can be identified by its **4-sided needles borne on pegs** on the branches. These pegs remain on the branch after the needles have fallen. **Needles of Engelmann spruce can be rolled between your fingers**; non-spruce conifer needles are flat and will not roll. Sitka-spruce needles are somewhat flattened. • Sitka spruce freely hybridizes with the interior species white spruce (*P. glauca*), to which it is most closely related. Wherever the two species' ranges overlap, hybrids are common. These hybrids are called Lutz or Roche spruce (*P.* x *lutzii*). They are common in all major river corridors through the B.C. Coast Range, as well as in Skagway and Haines in northern southeast Alaska, and throughout the Kenai Peninsula. • Upper valleys of mainland, inner-coast rivers often have spruce that look like a hybrid between Sitka and Engelmann; these are often the same valleys that grow lots of subalpine fir. • The most ancient and majestic forests of Sitka spruce occur in low terraces of river floodplains. The Hoh River in Olympic National Park (where many of the largest trees on the Pacific coast grow) and Carmanah Pacific Park on Vancouver Island (where the tallest spruce [92 m] grows) are excellent examples.

• The sharp needles of spruce were believed to give it special powers for protection against evil thoughts. The Ditidaht and other Nuu-chah-nulth peoples used the boughs in winter dance ceremonies to protect the dancers and to 'scare' spectators. • Among the Haida, Tlingit, Tsimshian and other central and northern coastal peoples, the inner bark was eaten fresh or dried into cakes and eaten with berries. The Makah were said to eat the young shoots raw; these would have been an excellent source of vitamin C. The inner bark was eaten fresh as a laxative by the Nuxalk. The pitch was often chewed for pleasure and was also used as medicine for burns, boils, slivers and other skin irritations. Sitka spruce pitch was also used as a medicine for gonorrhoea, syphilis, colds, sore throats, internal swellings, rheumatism and toothaches. • The roots of Sitka spruce were used to make beautifully twined water-tight hats and baskets, especially among the Haida, Tlingit and other northern coastal peoples. The roots were carefully pulled out from sandy ground in the early summer, briefly 'cooked' in the fire to prevent them from turning brown, then peeled, split and bundled for later use.

TREES

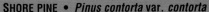

SHORE PINE • *Pinus contorta* var. *contorta*

GENERAL: Short, to 20 m tall (sometimes a straight tree to 30 m), **often with crooked trunk and irregular, pillowy crown; bark moderately thick** (greater than 2 cm thick in older trees), **scaly or deeply furrowed into plates, dark brown to blackish.**

LEAVES: Needles in pairs, often curved and twisted, **2–7 cm long**, deep green.

CONES: Pollen cones small, reddish-green in clusters on tips of branches in spring; egg-shaped seed cones, **3–5 cm long**, usually slightly curved; scales stiff and brown with **sharp prickle at tip.**

ECOLOGY: Highly adaptable, tolerant of low-nutrient conditions; found from dunes and bogs to rocky hilltops and exposed outer-coast shorelines. At low to middle elevations, occasionally subalpine on north coast.

NOTES: Another variety of *Pinus contorta* is **lodgepole pine** (*P. contorta* var. *latifolia*), which **is a taller, straighter tree** (more 'lodgepole,' less *contorta*) to 40 m tall, **with thinner, redder bark** (less than 1 cm thick), found in Lynn Canal and northern southeast Alaska, in old burned areas in large interior-influenced river valleys in the B.C. Coast Mountains and along the crest of the Cascades, especially on recent volcanic deposits in Oregon. • **Ponderosa pine** (*P. ponderosa*, also known as 'yellow pine') is an inland species over much of its range, but can be found on dry, open sites west of the Cascades in the Puget Trough and in Oregon. It is best recognized by its **long needles (10–20 cm long) in bundles of 3**, and by its splendid **cinnamon-coloured scaly bark** that smells of vanilla in the hot sun. • The Nisga'a were said to use the split and twisted roots of shore pine as rope. The Haida used peeled sheets of the bark as splints for broken limbs. The pitch was used by the Sechelt to waterproof canoes and baskets, by the Saanich to fasten arrowheads onto shafts and by the Lower Stl'atl'imx as a glue and to provide a protective coating for Indian-hemp fishing nets. • The pitch and bark were used medicinally by the Coast Salish, Nuu-chah-nulth, Kwakwaka'wakw, Nuxalk, Haida, Tsimshian, and Tlingit. The gum was applied to cuts or as a poultice for heart pain and rheumatism, or it was made into tea for tuberculosis. • Shore pine is quite tolerant of salt spray and is common along the immediate coast. It has cones that open and release the seeds upon maturity, while the cones of lodgepole pine often remain closed for years until opened by the heat of forest fires. Thus dense stands of lodgepole pine develop rapidly after fire from the abundant seed stored for years in the tree crowns. • In muskeg and subalpine habitats, shore pine assumes a **dwarf bonsai form**, 1–2 m in height and often with a twisted trunk and branches. On some peat-bogs, shore pine forms stunted forests where 100-year-old trees may be less than 5 cm in diameter. Despite this slow growth and poor regeneration it is commonly cut for Christmas trees near coastal communities.

WESTERN WHITE PINE • *Pinus monticola*

GENERAL: Medium-sized, beautifully symmetrical, **to 40 m tall (occasionally much taller)**; bark initially smooth, sometimes with resin blisters, becoming scaly, dark grey to nearly black, cinnamon-coloured underneath.

LEAVES: Needles in bundles of 5, light bluish-green, slender and flexible, **5–10 cm long.**

CONES: Pollen cones yellow, to 1 cm long; seed cones cylindrical when closed, **10–25 cm long,** yellow-green to purple when young, becoming reddish-brown and woody, scales **without prickles.**

ECOLOGY: Moist valleys to fairly open and dry slopes, from near sea level to subalpine.

NOTES: Two other **five-needle pines** occur in southern parts of our region. **Sugar pine** (*Pinus lambertiana*) **has longer cones (25–45 cm)** and pointed needles, and is found in the **southern Cascades** from Linn County, Oregon, south. Whitebark pine (*P. albicaulis*) has **shorter cones (5–8 cm long),** and is a **small, twisted tree or gnarled shrub found at high elevations** in the southern B.C. Coast Mountains and the Olympics, and in the highest parts of the Cascades from southern B.C. south. • White pine was used as a medicine by the Quinault, Lummi, Skagit, Hoh and Quileute, among other groups. A tea from the bark was drunk for stomach disorders, tuberculosis and rheumatism and to purify the blood, and it was applied externally on cuts and sores. The Kwakwaka'wakw used the pitch for stomach aches, coughs and sores. Its gum was chewed to give women fertility, and it was thought by some to cause pregnancy without intercourse. • This tree is called 'dancing tree' in Halq'emeylem. The Skagit, and various interior peoples such as the Stl'atl'imx, Okanagan, Secwepemc and Kt'unaXa, used sheets of its bark to make baskets and small canoes (the name in Secwepemc refers to this use). The Sechelt used the pitch for waterproofing and as a cleansing agent. • Western white pine would be much more widespread and abundant in our region if not for a fungus: white pine blister rust. This rust appears to have been introduced to western North America on a shipment of eastern white pine nursery stock imported into Vancouver, B.C., from France in 1910. The rust spread quickly, so that by 1922 it was established throughout most of the range of western white pine. White pine blister rust has 5 separate spore stages and requires 2 separate hosts (5-needle pines, and currants or gooseberries [*Ribes* spp.]) to complete its life cycle. Most young infected trees are quickly killed, but some white pines have a degree of natural resistance to the rust; these natural resistances are the subject of several blister-rust-resistance projects in our region that study selection and undertake breeding. • Identified on the slopes of Mt. St. Helens by David Douglas, this species gets its common name from the light colour of its wood. The Latin *monticola* means 'inhabiting mountains.'

WESTERN YEW • *Taxus brevifolia*
PACIFIC YEW

GENERAL: Evergreen **shrub to small tree, 2–15 m high**, up to 30 cm diameter; branches droop; trunk often twisted and fluted; **bark reddish, papery, scaly to shreddy.**

LEAVES: Needles **flat**, 2–3 cm long, dull green above, striped with stomata below, **ending abruptly in fine point, arranged in 2 rows in flat sprays**.

FRUITS: Male and female cones inconspicuous, **on separate trees**; although a conifer, instead of a seed cone it produces a single bony seed almost completely surrounded by a **bright red, fleshy cup** that looks like a large red huckleberry with a hole in the end; **poisonous** to humans although highly attractive to birds.

ECOLOGY: Moist mature forest at low to middle elevations in the southern part of our region, often with Douglas-fir and western hemlock in productive old-growth forests as a small understorey tree; from northern Vancouver Island north, in low-elevation, open, scrubby redcedar–western hemlock forests, as a mid-canopy or understorey tree or shrub; in Alaska and much of northern mainland B.C., only within a few km of shoreline.

NOTES: The heavy, tough, durable wood of the yew was prized by all coastal groups within its range and was often traded to the Interior. The hard wood is ideal for carving and takes on a high polish. Yew was named 'bow plant' by the Haida, Halq'emeylem and Stl'atl'imx, and 'wedge plant' in Sechelt, Squamish, and Nuu-chah-nulth. Many implements were made from yew wood, including bows, wedges, clubs, paddles, digging sticks, adze handles, harpoon shafts, spears, mat-sewing needles, awls, dip-net frames, knives, dishes, spoons, boxes, dowels and pegs, drum frames, snowshoe frames, canoe-spreaders, bark scrapers, fire tongs and combs. The Saanich used the entire trunk of a sapling to catapult spears in warfare, and they molded their yew bows to the proper curvature by first steaming them inside a bull kelp stalk. The Kwakwaka'wakw bound a bundle of yew branches to a hemlock pole for gathering sea urchins, which would get tangled in the branches. Yew is still sought today by woodcarvers. • The fleshy seed coverings were eaten by the Haida, but only in small quantities because too many were said to make women sterile. The Saanich and many Salish groups from Washington used to smoke dried yew needles, often mixed with kinnikinnick; these were very strong, and potentially harmful, smoke mixtures. • A new, potent and apparently very promising anti-cancer drug, taxol, has been identified in the bark and other parts of this tree and related yew species. It is being tested against a variety of types of cancer, including ovarian, breast and kidney cancers, and the harvesting of yew bark for this medicine has become a significant source of income for some people along the northwest coast. There are, however, concerns that the slow-growing western yew may be endangered by overharvesting. • Western yew seeds are **poisonous** and humans should avoid the fleshy 'berries,' although a wide variety of birds consume them and disperse the seeds. The foliage is poisonous to horses and cattle, especially if left to rot, but it is also a winter browse for moose. • Some dictionaries say 'yew' is from the Celtic *iw* meaning 'green,' but others say there is no such word. One explanation is that, through a series of blunders, it is derived from the Latin name ascribed to a plant by Pliny: *abiga*, which means 'abortion.' *Abiga* was misspelled and became *ajuga*, and then corrupted to *iua* or *iva*. Both 'yew' and 'ivy' appear to have the same origin. Whether or not the *abiga* of Pliny was actually the yew tree is not clear. However, if it was, it is interesting to note the possible connection between *abiga* and the Haida belief that eating too many 'berries' would make them sterile.

Cedars: Trees of Life (Adapted from an article by Arlene Otke in the Autumn 1993 issue of *Discovery*, a quarterly review of the Friends of the Royal B.C. Museum.)

> Oh, the cedar tree!
> If mankind in his infancy
> had prayed for the perfect substance
> for all materials and aesthetic needs,
> an indulgent god could have provided nothing better.
> —Bill Reid

Western redcedar and yellow-cedar (described on following pages) were extraordinarily useful trees to the aboriginal peoples of the northern Pacific coastal region, and played key roles in their cultures. From these two cedars, aboriginal people obtained the materials to provide themselves with shelter, clothing, tools and transportation. Cedars provided for these peoples from birth until death, from cradles to coffins.

A young girl learned how to collect redcedar bark each spring with her mother and grandmother. They searched for a tree about half a metre in diameter, straight and tall with few lower branches. When they found the tree they wanted, they stood under it and said a prayer.

To strip the bark from the tree, the women made a horizontal cut in the bark, a metre or more from the ground, for a third of the circumference of the tree. They used a large wedge to pry up the bark, then pulled upward and outward until it came free of the tree, leaving a long scar in the shape of an inverted V. The strip pulled from the tree might be as long as nine metres. The bark was hung up to dry, then beaten until it separated into layers ready for the making of articles such as baskets, rope or mats.

Preparation of yellow-cedar bark was more time-consuming: it had to be soaked and boiled to remove the pitch, then pounded until it was soft. The prepared bark was used especially for weaving and blankets throughout the coastal region, where it was preferred to redcedar bark because of its softness. Often it was interwoven with duck down or mountain-goat wool, or it was trimmed with these materials. Woven robes, hats and capes made from the fine, soft yellow-cedar bark repelled water and protected people from the rain. They used shredded bark as bandages, washcloths and towels.

In more open areas, women pulled up roots from the ground beyond the overhanging branches of a cedar tree, where the roots were new and pliable. They removed the outer bark from these roots and split them lengthwise in preparation for weaving baskets and cradles. These coiled cedar-root baskets, of a wide variety of shapes and sizes and often beautifully decorated with geometric patterns of reed-canary-grass stems and natural-coloured and black-dyed bark of bitter cherry, are still made by women of the Lower Stl'atl'imx, Nlaka'pamux, and various Coast Salish groups. Women also used the long, slender redcedar branches or withes to make rope, fish traps, binding material and open-weave baskets.

A redcedar bark gatherer, bundles of bark on her back, her clothing made of redcedar bark.
E.S. Curtis (ca. 1915).

WESTERN REDCEDAR • *Thuja plicata*

GENERAL: Large tree up to 60 m tall, with drooping leader; mature trees often fluted and buttressed at base; **branches tend to spread or droop slightly and then turn upward (J-shaped)**; branchlets spraylike, strongly flattened horizontally; **bark grey to reddish brown, tearing off in long fibrous strips**; wood aromatic.

LEAVES: Scale-like, opposite pairs in 4 rows, **the leaves in one pair folded, the leaves in the other not, closely pressed to stem** in overlapping shingled arrangement that looks like a flattened braid; glossy yellowish green, turning brown and shedding on branches 3–4 years old.

CONES: Pollen cones minute, numerous, reddish; **seed cones with 8–12 scales, egg-shaped**, about 1 cm long, in loose clusters, **green when immature, becoming brown, woody and turned upward**; seeds winged.

ECOLOGY: Mostly in moist to wet soils, usually in shaded forests; grows best on seepage and alluvial sites, but also occurs in drier habitats, especially on richer soils, and in bogs. Low to medium elevations.

NOTES: Incense-cedar (*Calocedrus decurrens*, sometimes called *Libocedrus decurrens*) is another tree with scale-like leaves and woody (not fleshy) seed cones. It occurs in our region only in the Oregon Cascades, usually on rather dry sites, and can be distinguished from western redcedar by its **6-scaled seed cones**. • Redcedar has been called 'the cornerstone of northwest coast Indian culture' and the large-scale use of its wood and bark delineates the cultural boundary of the northwest coast peoples within its range. The easily split, rot-resistant wood was used to make important cultural items such as dugout canoes, house planks and posts, totem and mortuary poles, bentwood boxes, baskets, clothing and hats, and a variety of tools and implements such as dishes, arrow shafts, harpoon shafts, spear poles, barbecue sticks, fish spreaders and hangers, dip-net hooks, fish clubs, masks, rattles, benches, cradles, coffins, herring rakes, canoe bailers, ceremonial drum logs, combs, fishing floats, berry-drying racks, fish weirs, spirit whistles, and paddles. It was used by the Kwakwaka'wakw and other groups to make a drill and hearth for starting friction fires. Redcedar was considered an excellent fuel, especially for drying fish, because it burns with little smoke. Few cedar trees were actually felled before European contact. Instead, fallen logs or boards split from standing trees were used. To split off cedar boards for house planks or half-logs for canoes, a series of graduated yew-wood or antler wedges were pounded into living trees along the grain. • The power of the redcedar tree was said to be so strong a person could receive strength by standing with his or her back to the tree. Redcedar was used for a variety of ailments. It is called the 'tree of life' by the Kwakwaka'wakw and is still held with highest respect by all northwest coast peoples for its healing and spiritual powers. A Coast Salish myth says the Great Spirit created redcedar in honour of a man who was always helping others: 'When he dies and where he is buried, a cedar tree will grow and be useful to the people—the roots for baskets, the bark for clothing, the wood for shelter' (Stewart 1984:27). • Western redcedar is more shade-tolerant than yellow-cedar. It is a widespread coastal species as far north as Petersburg, Alaska. It abruptly stops at Pt. Frederich Sound just as it abruptly stops at about 300 m elevation in southern southeast Alaska (it appears to be sensitive to breakage of its leader and branches by snow). It generally outcompetes yellow-cedar where their ranges overlap. In Alaska redcedar is generally not associated with riverside sites; it occurs principally on wet to boggy sites. • Western redcedar is B.C.'s provincial tree.

YELLOW-CEDAR • *Chamaecyparis nootkatensis*
YELLOW-CYPRESS, ALASKA-CEDAR

GENERAL: To 50 m tall (usually 20–40 m), with an often slightly twisted trunk (buttressed in old trees), the leader droops (like western hemlock), the **flattened branches tend to hang vertically and appear limp; bark dirty white to greyish-brown**, in vertical strips similar to that of redcedar but not tearing off in very long strips.

LEAVES: Opposite, **scale-like** in 4 rows, 3–6 mm long, leaves in all 4 rows similar, **bluish-green**, with **sharp-pointed, spreading tips**.

CONES: Pollen cones about 4 mm long; seed cones **beginning as round, bumpy, light-green 'berries'** covered with a white waxy powder, less than 1 cm long, **ripening to brownish cones with 4–6 woody, mushroom-shaped scales**; seeds winged.

ECOLOGY: In moist to wet sites; often in rocky areas, avalanche chutes, rocky ridge tops, to timberline; at middle to high elevations from southwestern B.C. south (though occasionally descending to sea level on the west coast of Vancouver Island); from northern Vancouver Island through Alaska, often associated with wet boggy sites or transitional bog-forests; reduced to a much-branched shrub in muskeg or at timberline.

NOTES: Leaves of yellow-cedar are similar to those of western redcedar, but the 4 rows of scale-leaves in this species are all the same, whereas redcedar has two opposite rows of folded leaves, and two opposite rows of non-folded leaves; also, leaves of yellow-cedar are often distinctly darker green than leaves of redcedar. Crushed leaves of yellow-cedar also have **an unpleasant, mildewy smell**, quite unlike the pleasing odour of redcedar foliage. Another way to distinguish the two species is to **stroke the branchlets away from the tip ('against the grain'): yellow-cedar is very prickly, redcedar is not**. If cones are present, they provide the easiest and most reliable way to distinguish the two species. If you do not have cones and cannot clearly see the foliage, **expose the inner bark; if it is yellowish and smells like raw potatoes, the tree is yellow-cedar**. •

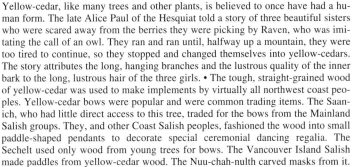

Yellow-cedar, like many trees and other plants, is believed to once have had a human form. The late Alice Paul of the Hesquiat told a story of three beautiful sisters who were scared away from the berries they were picking by Raven, who was imitating the call of an owl. They ran and ran until, halfway up a mountain, they were too tired to continue, so they stopped and changed themselves into yellow-cedars. The story attributes the long, hanging branches and the lustrous quality of the inner bark to the long, lustrous hair of the three girls. • The tough, straight-grained wood of yellow-cedar was used to make implements by virtually all northwest coast peoples. Yellow-cedar bows were popular and were common trading items. The Saanich, who had little direct access to this tree, traded for the bows from the Mainland Salish groups. They, and other Coast Salish peoples, fashioned the wood into small paddle-shaped pendants to decorate special ceremonial dancing regalia. The Sechelt used only wood from young trees for bows. The Vancouver Island Salish made paddles from yellow-cedar wood. The Nuu-chah-nulth carved masks from it. The Kwakwaka'wakw used it for paddles, chests, dishes and fishing net hoops, and they made bows from the roots. The Haida used it for digging sticks, adze handles, paddles, and dishes. • The Kwakwaka'wakw made a tea from the branch tips to treat insanity and boiled them with spruce roots to make a drink for curing kidney ailments. For a contraceptive, some Coast Salish women chewed the green cones and swallowed the juice. Yellow-cedar was used with a sweatbath as a cure for rheumatism or to 'scare away' a disease. • Yellow-cedar is also the oldest tree in our region, commonly 1,000–1,500 years in age.

RED ALDER • *Alnus rubra*

GENERAL: Deciduous, up to 25 m tall; **bark thin, grey, and smooth, often with white patches of lichens,** becoming scaly at the base with age; **wood and inner bark turn rusty-red when cut**.

LEAVES: Alternate, deciduous, broadly elliptic and sharp-pointed at the base and tip, 5–15 cm long, dull green and smooth above, rust-coloured and hairy below, the **margins wavy, slightly rolled under, with coarse, blunt teeth;** leaves remain more or less green until they drop off in late fall.

FLOWERS: Male and female flowers in hanging, cylindrical spikes (catkins), appear before the leaves; male catkins 5–12 cm long, female catkins to 2 cm long.

FRUITS: Clusters of **brownish cones to 2 cm long; remain on the tree over the winter;** contain oval, winged nutlets.

ECOLOGY: Moist woods, streambanks, floodplains, slide tracks, and recently cleared land, often in pure stands; at low elevations.

NOTES: Red alder can be easily distinguished from the always shrubby **Sitka alder** (*Alnus crispa* ssp. *sinuata*), which **has irregularly and sharply saw-toothed leaf margins that are not rolled under**. • Actinomycetes (filamentous bacteria) in the genus *Frankia* invade alders through their root hairs and stimulate cell division, forming nodules on the roots. Species of *Frankia* remove nitrogen from the air and 'fix' it in a form useful to plants. Red alder provides a home for the actinomycete, which in turn 'leaks' some of the nitrogen, making it available for the alder. In our region, nitrogen is usually the nutrient most limiting plant growth, and red alder stands can contribute up to 320 kg/ha of nitrogen per year. • Red-alder wood is considered to be the best possible fuel for smoking salmon and other types of fish. It is soft and even-grained, and is still used for making feast bowls, masks, rattles, and a variety of other items. • Its bark is used to make a red or orange dye, especially valued for colouring inner redcedar bark. The name 'red alder' may derive from this use. Variations in dye colour are obtained from different ages and quantities of the bark, and from the use of other substances such as urine to fix the colouring. Fishing nets were sometimes coloured with alder-bark dye to make them invisible to fish. • The inner bark of red alder was eaten in spring by the Straits Salish and other northwest coast peoples. Alder bark was highly valued for its medicinal qualities. A solution of the bark was used against tuberculosis and other respiratory ailments and as a tonic, and it has been credited with saving many lives. It was also used as a wash for skin infections and wounds, and is known to have strong antibiotic properties. • Red alder is an aggressive, fast-growing, but short-lived hardwood (old at 50 years) that thrives on moist, disturbed sites. Common on active river floodplains, old logging roads and in clearcuts or burns where considerable disturbance has occurred. On the north coast, it does not invade clearcuts unless mineral soil is exposed by logging disturbance. Alder improves disturbed soils by fixing atmospheric nitrogen into the soil; this is why alder forests generally have a rich understorey of grasses, sedges and ferns, but few acid-loving species such as blueberry or salal. • 'Alder' appears to be from Old English *alor* or Old High German *elo* or *elawer* meaning 'reddish-yellow,' in reference to the colour that develops when the wood is freshly exposed.

BIGLEAF MAPLE • *Acer macrophyllum*
OREGON MAPLE

GENERAL: Large, often multi-stemmed, to 35 m tall; young bark green and smooth, **older bark grey-brown, ridged, and often covered with mosses, lichens and ferns**.

LEAVES: Opposite, deciduous, **5-lobed maple leaves, 15–30 cm across**, dark green above, paler below, turning yellow in the autumn; leaf stalk exudes milky juice when cut.

FLOWERS: Greenish-yellow, about 3 mm across; numerous on short stalks in a **hanging cylindrical cluster**; appear with or before the leaves.

FRUITS: Golden-brown, **paired, winged seeds** ('samaras'), 3–6 cm long; wings spread **in a V-shape**.

ECOLOGY: Dry to moist sites, often with Douglas-fir, often on sites disturbed by fire, clearing or logging; at low to middle elevations.

NOTES: Bigleaf maple carries a greater load of mosses and other plants than any other tree species in our region. Sometimes the bark is not visible anywhere on the tree trunk and main branches. The moss layers can get so thick they form a 'soil' into which tree roots can sprout and grow. These 'canopy roots' were discovered in the canopies of mature bigleaf maples by an adventurous graduate student using modified mountain-climbing techniques. She subsequently found canopy roots on vine maple and red alder, but not on black cottonwood or any conifers. Many of the impressive moss-festooned trees of rainforests in the southern half of our region, such as on the Olympic Peninsula, are *A. macrophyllum*. • The Saanich used preparations from this maple to make an internal medicine and to treat sore throats, and the leaves were rubbed on a man's face at puberty so he would not grow thick whiskers. • This maple is called the 'paddle tree' in many First Nations languages because the wood was used to make paddles. It was also used for spindle whorls and various other implements. The big leaves are good for making temporary containers. The sprouted seeds were eaten by Nlaka'pamux. • The sap can be used to make a passable maple syrup, but this was not done originally by aboriginal peoples. It takes several times more bigleaf-maple sap than eastern-sugar-maple sap to make a given quantity of syrup. • The winged seeds descend like little helicopters, which greatly increases their dispersal. The stumps sprout vigorously after cutting (or fire) and sprouts can grow over 3 m tall in a single year. They sometimes provide strong competition to conifer seedlings and can frustrate foresters.

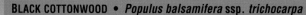

BLACK COTTONWOOD • *Populus balsamifera* ssp. *trichocarpa*

GENERAL: Large, tall, deciduous, up to 50 m tall; buds very sticky (full of resin) and fragrant; **old bark deeply furrowed, dark grey**; young shoots often angled in cross-section.

LEAVES: Alternate, deciduous, thick, oval, **5–15 cm long**, with rounded to heart-shaped base and sharp-pointed tip; margin finely round-toothed; under-surface pale and often stained with patches of brown resin beneath; **leaf stalks round**, often with a pair of glands at the junction with the blade.

FLOWERS: Male and female flowers in catkins, and on separate plants; male flowers with 40–60 stamens, female flowers with 3 stigmas; flower before leaves come up.

FRUITS: Round, green, hairy capsules that split when ripe into 3 parts; **seeds covered with white, fluffy hairs**.

ECOLOGY: On low to medium elevation, moist to wet sites; forms extensive stands on islands and floodplains along major rivers and on disturbed upland sites.

NOTES: Black cottonwood is also known as *Populus trichocarpa*. • **Trembling aspen** (*P. tremuloides*) is a smaller tree (to 25 m) with **shorter leaves (to 7 cm long)** found sporadically on southeastern Vancouver Island, around the shores of Puget Sound, and in the Cascades. It usually forms clonal stands and is best distinguished from black cottonwood by its **flat leaf-stalks**, which allow the leaves to flutter in the slightest breeze (hence the common name). • Nuxalk/Kwakwaka'wakw/Halq'emeylem/Stl'atl'imx: The sweet inner bark and cambium tissues were eaten in late spring and early summer immediately after they were harvested so they would not ferment. Hesquiat/Nuu-chah-nulth/Ditidaht: The buds were picked in the spring and boiled in deer fat to make a fragrant salve, which was molded in the bulbous float of bull kelp. Nuxalk: The gum from the buds was used in preparations for baldness, sore throats, whooping cough and tuberculosis. The buds were used as a poultice for lung pains and rheumatism, and the old, rotten leaves were boiled and used in a bath for body pains, rheumatism and stomach trouble. Stl'atl'imx/Tahltan: Cottonwood was used as a fuel for smoking fish. Coast Salish: Cottonwood was thought by the Squaxin to be an antiseptic plant; they placed the bruised leaves on cuts and made an infusion from the bark for sore throats. Quinault: This group placed the gum that exudes from the burls of cottonwood directly on cuts and wounds, and took a bark infusion for tuberculosis. • Ditidaht: The inner bark was used to reinforce other plant fibres in spinning. Vancouver Island Salish: This group occasionally made small dugout canoes from black cottonwood, a practice more common among interior tribes. The aromatic gum from the spring buds of cottonwood was used to waterproof baskets and boxes. Okanagan/Upper Halq'emeylem/Cowlitz: Friction-fire sets were made using dried cottonwood roots for the hearth and dried branches for the drill. Okanagan: Soap and a hairwash were made using ashes from cottonwood. Coast Salish/Okanagan/Stl'atl'imx: The bark was stripped off and used to make buckets for carrying and storing food. Young shoots were used to make sweatlodge frames. Nisga'a/Quinault: Temporary cabins were occasionally constructed using cottonwood bark, and the roots were twisted into rope for tying house planks and making fish traps. Okanagan/Stl'atl'imx: The aromatic gum from the spring buds was used as a glue for securing arrowheads and feathers to shafts. Cottonwood is thought to have a life of its own by the Chehalis because it shakes when there is no wind, and for this reason was never used for firewood. Okanagan/Ditidaht: The rich, yellow, aromatic gum from the buds was boiled in grease and mixed with other pigments (alder bark, larch, wolf lichen, charcoal) to make paint. • The sticky resin on black cottonwood buds and recently opened leaves has a powerful, sweet, balsamic fragrance that permeates whole river valleys in the spring and early summer. • Bees collect the resin, which is an anti-infectant, for their hives and seal intruders (such as mice) in the resin to prevent decay and protect the hive.

PAPER BIRCH • *Betula papyrifera*
WHITE BIRCH, CANOE BIRCH

GENERAL: Small to medium-sized, deciduous, to 30 m tall; **bark peeling in papery strips, white to copper-brown,** smooth and marked with brown horizontal lines of raised pores.

LEAVES: Alternate, deciduous, **oval to round, sharp-pointed,** to 10 cm long (and much longer on young growth), sometimes very shallowly lobed, dull green above, paler and hairy below; **margins doubly toothed.**

FLOWERS: Male and female flowers in separate catkins 2–4 cm long; flower at the same time or before leaves emerge; **catkins break up at maturity.**

FRUITS: Nutlets with wings broader than body.

ECOLOGY: Open to dense woods, usually moist, from lowlands to lower mountain slopes; typically on well-drained sites but also on or around bogs and other wetlands.

NOTES: In mixed second-growth forest at low elevations, be careful not to confuse bitter cherry with young, dark-barked paper birch; they can be very tricky to distinguish, unless you can see the leaves (**bitter cherry's are oblong to oval, and less pointy-tipped**). • Paper birch was used much more commonly by interior groups. The bark, which can be peeled off the tree in large, flexible, waterproof sheets, was as important to the native peoples inland from the Northwest Coast as the western redcedar was to the coastal peoples. Baskets and canoes were the most common items constructed from paper birch. The wood was also used as fuel, and the sap and inner bark as emergency food.• Paper birch thrives on burned-over and cut-over areas where it often forms pure stands, though it is later restricted to openings as the forest matures. It readily sprouts from cut stumps. • A Swedish archaeologist found what could be the world's oldest second-hand chewing gum: 9,000-year-old wads of chewed birch resin on the floor of a hut used by Stone-Age hunter-gatherers. The gum could have been medicinal: birch resin contains zylitol, a disinfectant now sold by the Finns as a natural tooth cleaner. But birch resin also contains terpenes, which could have provided a buzz; Athabaskan Indians were reported to chew birch gum much as Andean people chew coca leaves. In the Ukraine, sap from birches is used to produce a variety of beverages including wine, soft drinks and health tonics. In Alaska, parts of Canada and the northern conterminous U.S., birch is tapped and the sap is used to produce syrup, and homemade wine and beer. • The name 'birch' is derived from words in many languages, all of which mean either 'a tree whose bark is used for writing upon' or simply 'bark.' Hence, birch is the 'bark-tree.' The word 'bark' can mean either 'tree-rind' or 'vessel,' the latter reflecting its long-standing use for making canoes or water containers. *Betula* means 'pitch' because bitumen was distilled from the bark (broken clay pots were glued together with birch-bark tar in Roman Britain); *papyrifera* means 'paper-bearing.'

BITTER CHERRY • *Prunus emarginata*

GENERAL: Shrubs or small trees, 2–15 m tall; **bark reddish-brown or grey**, with horizontal rows of raised pores.

LEAVES: Alternate, deciduous, oblong to oval, 3–8 cm long, **finely toothed, rounded at the tip**, stalked, with 1 or 2 small glands at the base of the leaf blade.

FLOWERS: White or pinkish, 10–15 cm across; **5–10 in a flat-topped cluster**.

FRUITS: Bright red cherries to 1 cm diameter; bitter.

ECOLOGY: In moist forest and along streams, and as a pioneer on logged areas; at low to middle elevations.

NOTES: Another cherry more common east of our coastal mountains is **choke cherry** (*Prunus virginiana*). This shrub or small tree is most easily distinguished from bitter cherry by its **flowers and fruits, which occur in elongate clusters of more than 10 (vs. 5–10 in *P. emarginata*)**; its fruits are usually darker, to purple or even black. It grows on forest edges and in clearings, from the Strait of Georgia–Puget Sound area south to California. • Tree-sized bitter cherry can be confused with **dark-barked paper birch,** and unless it is fruiting it is most easily distinguished by its leaves. • The tough, stringy bark of bitter cherry was peeled off in horizontal or spiral strips or sheets and used for decorative overlay of coiled cedar-root baskets, and for wrapping the joints of implements such as harpoons and arrows, and the hafts of bows. Such joints were covered with pitch to make them waterproof and strong. • Cherries of this species are so bitter they are inedible.

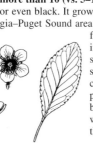

PACIFIC CRAB APPLE • *Malus fusca*

GENERAL: Shrub or small tree, **2–12 m tall, armed with sharp spur-shoots**; older bark deeply fissured.

LEAVES: Alternate, deciduous, lance- to egg-shaped, to 10 cm long, **pointed at the end, toothed, with irregular lobes**; turn red or yellow-orange in fall.

FLOWERS: White to pink, **showy, fragrant apple blossoms**, about 2 cm across; 5–12 in flat-topped clusters on spur-shoots.

FRUITS: Green becoming yellow or reddish, small (10–15 mm long) egg-shaped apples; edible but a bit tart.

ECOLOGY: Moist woods, swamps, edges of standing and flowing water, upper beaches, often fringing estuaries; low to middle elevations the length of our region.

NOTES: This species is also known as '*Pyrus fusca*.' • The small, clustered apples, though tart, are still an important food for virtually all coastal peoples. They are harvested in late summer and early fall. They are eaten fresh or stored under water, or under a mixture of water and oil, in cedarwood storage boxes. Because of their acidity, they do not require further preservation; they simply become softer and sweeter over time. • The bark was used, alone or with other plant products, for a variety of medicinal treatments for the eyes and for the stomach and digestive tract. **Like bitter-cherry bark**, crabapple bark **contains cyanide-producing compounds**, and should be used only with extreme caution.

ARBUTUS • *Arbutus menziesii*
MADRONE, PACIFIC MADRONE

GENERAL: Small to medium-sized, with heavy branches, to 30 m tall but usually much shorter; **young bark chartreuse and smooth, older bark dark brownish-red and peeling off.**

LEAVES: Alternate, **evergreen**, oval, to 15 cm long, dark shiny green above, **whitish-green below, hairless, leathery**, without teeth except sometimes on young growth.

FLOWERS: White, urn-shaped, 6–7 mm long, fragrant (like buckwheat honey); **in large drooping clusters**.

FRUITS: Orange-red berries, about 1 cm across, surface finely granular; not usually eaten by humans, but popular with birds**.**

ECOLOGY: On dry, sunny, often rocky sites, frequently with coarse-textured soils; low to middle elevations; typically associated with Douglas-fir and Garry oak.

NOTES: Another evergreen broadleaf tree (or large shrub) in our region is **chinquapin** (*Castanopsis chrysophylla*), a relative of oaks and chestnuts. It has leathery, lance-shaped leaves that are dark green above and **golden-scaly below**, white flowers **in upright catkins**, and **spiny, burr-like fruits** like small chestnuts. Chinquapin is known from a few locations at low elevations in the Puget Trough, and from low to middle elevations in Oregon. • Arbutus berries were eaten in California, but not in quantity. The Straits Salish of Vancouver Island sometimes cooked the reddish, papery bark with camas bulbs to colour them pink. Red-alder bark was also used for this purpose. The Saanich used medicinal prepa-

Castanopsis chrysophylla

rations from arbutus bark and leaves for colds, stomach problems, as a post-childbirth contraceptive, and in a ten-ingredient bark medicine for tuberculosis and spitting up blood (Turner and Hebda 1990). • A Straits Salish myth recorded by early ethnographer Diamond Jenness: Pitch used to go fishing before the sun rose, and then retire to the shade before it became strong. One day he was late and had just reached the beach when he melted. Other people rushed to share him. Douglas-fir arrived first and secured most of the pitch, which he poured over his head and body. Grand fir obtained only a little; and by the time Arbutus arrived there was none left. Therefore, Arbutus has no pitch to this day. • In a Straits Salish story, told by the late Chief Phillip Paul of the Saanich people, arbutus was the tree used by the survivors of the Great Flood (a tradition common to almost all northwest coast peoples) to anchor their canoe to the top of Mount Newton. To this day, the Saanich people do not burn arbutus in their stoves, because of the important service this tree provided long ago. • Arbutus is a magnificent evergreen tree with white flowers in the spring and red fruit in the fall, and attractive reddish bark that peels off in large strips. Its berries sometimes persist on the trees until Christmas-time. The tree looks like it belongs to warmer climates than ours. • *Arbutus* means 'strawberry tree' in Latin, in reference to the bright red fruits. It was called *madrono* (Spanish for 'strawberry tree') by Father Juan Crespi, the chronicler of the overland Portola expedition of 1769 to discover the 'lost bay' of Monterey. He named it for its resemblance to the Mediterranean strawberry tree (*A. unedo*).

GARRY OAK • *Quercus garryana*
OREGON WHITE OAK

GENERAL: Beautiful, heavy-limbed tree to 25 m tall, but often short and crooked in rocky habitats; **bark light grey, with thick furrows and ridges.**

LEAVES: Alternate, deciduous, **deeply round-lobed oak leaves** to 12 cm long, shiny dark green above, greenish-yellow and brown-hairy below; turn dull yellow-brown in fall.

FLOWERS: Male and female flowers tiny, inconspicuous; borne in separate inflorescences on the same tree, male flowers in hanging catkins, female flowers single or in small clusters; flowers as the leaves appear.

FRUITS: Acorns, 2–3 cm long, in shallow, rough-surfaced cups; sweet, tannic, edible**.**

ECOLOGY: Dry, rocky slopes or bluffs, sometimes on deep, rich, well-drained soil; low elevations.

NOTES: A similar oak with **pointy-toothed leaves tipped with bristles** is **California black oak** (*Quercus kelloggii*). Its range is from Lane County, Oregon to California. • The acorns of Garry oak were eaten by the Salish peoples of the Puget Sound region after soaking to leach out the bitter tannins. The bark was one of the ingredients in the Saanich '4 barks' medicine used against tuberculosis and other ailments (Turner and Hebda 1990).

OREGON ASH • *Fraxinus latifolia*

GENERAL: Medium-sized, to 25 m tall; bark becomes greyish-brown and fissured with age.

LEAVES: Opposite, deciduous, **pinnately compound with usually 5–7 leaflets**; leaflets to 13 cm long, oval, olive-green above, paler and woolly beneath, turning yellow in fall.

FLOWERS: Small (3 mm across), inconspicuous, yellowish (male) and greenish (female) flowers on separate trees; appear before the leaves, in bunched clusters on the twigs.

FRUITS: Paddle-shaped, 1-seeded, winged fruits (like half of a maple fruit), 3–5 cm long; in large clusters on female trees; fruit stalks very fine, almost hairlike.

ECOLOGY: On moist to wet soils at low elevations, often near streams or in other areas that are occasionally flooded.

NOTES: One use of Oregon ash seems to be for protection from snakes: traditional wisdom suggests that rattlesnakes will not crawl over an Oregon ash stick, and areas where this tree grows are free from poisonous snakes. • The origin of the word 'ash' is not clear, but most likely derives from the Latin *ascia* meaning 'axe' or *axis* meaning 'axle,' since the wood of the European ash (*Fraxinus excelsior*) is tough and was preferred for making axe-heads and axle-trees. In Anglo-Saxon the word *aesc* means 'spear.' *Aesc* can also mean 'vessel' because boats were made out of ash. The toughness of the wood makes it useful today in the manufacture of various items such as furniture and tool handles.

WESTERN FLOWERING DOGWOOD • *Cornus nuttallii*
PACIFIC DOGWOOD

GENERAL: Much-branched, irregular trees to 20 m tall; bark blackish-brown, smooth, becoming finely ridged with age.

LEAVES: Opposite, deciduous, oval, sharp-pointed at the tip and tapering towards the base, to 10 cm long, deep green above, greyish-green below, turning pinkish-red in the fall, **with characteristic 'dogwood veins' curving parallel to the leaf edge.**

FLOWERS: Greenish-white tipped with purple, small (about 5 mm across) and inconspicuous; **in tight, hemispheric clusters** surrounded by 4–6 white or pinkish-tinged, large (2–7 cm long), showy bracts, **the inflorescence appearing to be one large flower;** flower in spring, and often repeating in early fall.

FRUITS: Clusters of bright red 'berries,' each berry about 1 cm long.

ECOLOGY: At low elevations; usually on moist, well-drained sites, often along streams or gullies; in open to fairly dense, usually mixed, forest.

NOTES: Wood of western flowering dogwood was considered good for bows, arrows, implement handles and clothing hooks. The bark was boiled and used by the Nlaka'pamux to make a dark-brown dye. • Bark preparations were made for use as a blood purifier, a lung strengthener, or as a treatment for stomach troubles. It was also an ingredient used by the Saanich in their '10 barks' medicine (Turner and Hebda 1990). • The blossom of the Pacific dogwood is the floral emblem of British Columbia. • Although David

Douglas first 'discovered' this plant, he mistook it for the eastern dogwood (*Cornus florida*). Thomas Nuttall was the first scientist to recognize it as a new species when he saw it at Fort Vancouver in 1834. It was named after Nuttall by his close friend, the ornithologist and painter, John James Audubon. Audubon's painting of the band-tailed pigeon shows the Pacific dogwood in the background, because this bird was so fond of the plant's fruits. • There are several theories as to where the name 'dogwood' came from. One has it that the berries were considered unfit for even a dog to eat. Another is that it is derived from various words (French *dague*, Spanish *daga* and Sanskrit *dag*) meaning 'skewer' or 'dagger,' because the wood of the tree *C. sanguinea* was used to make skewers for butchers and other pointed instruments (daggs). • The wood is in demand for making thread spindles, piano keys, and for other purposes, but its collection is prohibited by law in B.C.

Shrubs and Small Trees

Shrubs are woody plants less than 10 m tall when mature and usually multi-stemmed.

The shrubs of our region represent a wide variety of plant families and genera; we have organized them by major plant families, and by similar species within those families.

An intriguing and very characteristic feature of the northern Pacific coastal region is the variety and abundance of shrubs in the heather family (Ericaceae). Ericaceous shrubs not only dominate the understorey of many of our forests (especially mature coniferous forests), they are also abundant and often dominant in non-forested habitats, especially at high elevations and in peatlands. One can speculate about the ecological and evolutionary reasons for the resplendence of the heather family: the development of thick, moist, acidic, organic layers in many of the region's ecosystems is a key feature.

More than 50% of our region's shrubs have fleshy fruits, which are often edible berries. This is not surprising, given the predominance of forests and the adaptive value of fruits that can be eaten and dispersed by mobile animals, rather than by some other dispersal mechanism (e.g., wind) that might not be particularly effective in the understorey of dense forest.

Fleshy, edible fruits were an important part of the diet of coastal aboriginal peoples. Berries were eaten both fresh and dried into cakes. Berries were stored for winter this way: they were mashed and either boiled in boxes or allowed to sit until thickened. The thickened jam was then poured to a 2.5 cm thickness onto skunk-cabbage leaves within rectangular cedarwood frames about 30 by 90 cm. The frames were then dried on racks over an alder-wood fire. For use the dried cakes were soaked overnight, kneaded until broken into small pieces, and mixed with oolichan grease. The mixture was often eaten with special mountain-goat spoons. The cakes were highly prized and eaten at family meals or by chiefs at feasts.

Keys are provided for currants and gooseberries (*Ribes* spp.) and for the genus *Rubus*, and a conspectus is provided for huckleberries and blueberries (*Vaccinium* spp.).

Clayoquot Nuu-chah-nulth woman picking evergreen huckleberries. E.S. Curtis (ca. 1915).

SALAL • *Gaultheria shallon*

GENERAL: Creeping to erect; spreads by layering, suckering and sprouting; height very variable (0.2–5 m tall), with hairy, branched stems.

LEAVES: Alternate, **evergreen, leathery**, thick, shiny, egg-shaped, **5-10 cm long, sharply and finely toothed**.

FLOWERS: White or pinkish, urn-shaped, 7–10 mm long; 5–15 at branch ends, flower stalks bend so that flowers are all oriented in one direction.

FRUITS: Reddish-blue to dark-purple 'berries' (actually fleshy sepals), 6–10 mm broad, edible.

ECOLOGY: Coniferous forests, rocky bluffs, to the seashore; low to medium elevations.

NOTES: Among the most common forest under-storey shrubs in our region, it forms an almost continuous shrub layer in many drier coniferous forests and is also common in some wet or boggy coniferous forests. In some areas along the coast it can form impenetrable thickets. • The dark, juicy berries were in many places on the Northwest Coast the most plentiful and important fruit for aboriginal peoples. They were eaten both fresh and dried into cakes. The Kwakwaka'wakw ate the ripe berries dipped in oolichan grease at large feasts. For trading or selling, the salal berries were mixed with currants, elderberries, or unripe salal berries. The berries were also used to sweeten other foods and the Haida used salal berries to thicken salmon eggs. In recent times, salal berries have been prepared as jam or preserves, and ripe berries from healthy bushes are hard to beat for flavour and juiciness. • The young leaves were chewed as a hunger suppressant by the Ditidaht. The leafy branches were used in pit-cooking, and cooked as a flavouring in fish soup. You can make a tiny drinking cup by shaping a salal leaf into a cone. • Salal was a favourite of David Douglas, who brought seed to Britain in 1828 for use as a garden ornamental.

WESTERN TEA-BERRY • *Gaultheria ovatifolia*
OREGON WINTERGREEN

GENERAL: Dwarf, sometimes mat-forming, to 5 cm tall; the branches to 20 cm long, brownish-hairy.

LEAVES: Alternate, **evergreen, leathery**, shiny, egg- to almost heart-shaped, **2–4 cm long, margins finely toothed**.

FLOWERS: White or pinkish, bell-shaped, to 5 mm long; **single** in leaf axils.

FRUITS: Bright red 'berries,' 6–8 mm across, edible.

ECOLOGY: Moist forest, heath and wetlands (especially bogs); middle to subalpine elevations.

NOTES: Alpine-wintergreen (*Gaultheria humifusa*) is a smaller plant (stems not usually more than 10 cm long) with smooth or only finely hairy stems, and oval leaves 1–2 cm long with margins usually without teeth. These two *Gaultheria* are best differentiated by the flowers: the sepals of western tea-berry are reddish-brown-hairy, while those of alpine-wintergreen are smooth. Range and habitat are similar for both species, though alpine-wintergreen tends to occur at higher elevations in the mountains and is only found on wet sites (e.g., moist alpine meadows, streambanks). Just to add to the confusion, hybridization between these two similar species produces plants with intermediate characteristics. • *Gaultheria* is named for Dr. Hugues Jean Gaultier (1708–1756), a French-Canadian naturalist.

Gaultheria humifusa

SPP.	HABIT	TWIGS	LEAVES
alaskaense	erect shrub 50–200 cm tall	somewhat angled, yellow-green, smooth or slightly hairy, older bark greyish	deciduous, 2.5–6 cm long, entire or with fine teeth on the lower half, lower surface glaucous, sometimes finely hairy, with scattered hairs on the midvein
ovalifolium	upright spreading shrub 40–200 cm tall	strongly angled and grooved, brown, yellow or reddish, smooth; older bark greyish	deciduous, 2–4 cm long, entire or with a few fine teeth, lower surface glaucous, without hairs on midvein
membranaceum	upright spreading shrub, 50–150 cm tall	somewhat angled, yellow-green, smooth or slightly hairy, older bark greyish, shredding	deciduous, 2–4 cm long, finely toothed along the whole leaf, lower surface paler
parvifolium	erect shrub 100–300 cm tall	strongly angled, green, usually smooth	deciduous (but with a few persistent), 1–3 cm long, smooth or slightly hairy, entire (some teeth present on young leaves)
ovatum	upright spreading shrub 50–300 cm tall	slightly hairy	evergreen, 2–5 cm long, leathery, bright glossy green above, paler below, sharply toothed the entire length, in two opposite rows
caespitosum	tufted, mat-forming shrub, 15–30 cm tall	round, yellow-green to reddish bark, usually finely hairy	deciduous, 1–3 cm long, bright green above, paler below but not glaucous, toothed from the tip to midpoint or below, prominently veined below
deliciosum[1]	low, mat-forming shrub, 15–30 cm tall (occasionally larger)	slightly angled, greenish-brown, smooth or slightly hairy	deciduous, 1.5–5 cm long, pale green above, glaucous below, toothed on the upper margins
uliginosum	erect to prostrate much-branched shrub, 10–30 cm tall	not angled, branches yellowish-green, finely hairy, old bark greyish red	deciduous, 1–3 cm long, strongly veined beneath, not toothed
vitis-idaea[2]	creeping shrub to 25 cm tall	round or slightly angled, slightly hairy	evergreen, 0.4–1.2 cm long, leathery, glossy green above, pale and with dark dots below
Oxycoccus oxycoccos	creeping shrub to 15 cm long	thin, creeping, smooth to slightly hairy	evergreen, 0.6–1 cm long, deep green above, greyish below, the margins rolled under

FLOWERS

FRUITS

HABITAT

FLOWERS	FRUITS	HABITAT
bronze to pinkish-green, about 7 mm long, wider than long, single in leaf axils; bloom after leaves develop	bluish-black to purplish-black, usually not glaucous, 7–10 mm across; stalks straight, enlarged just below berry	moist coniferous forests, low to subalpine elevations
pinkish, about 7 mm long, longer than wide, single in leaf axils; bloom before leaves develop	blue-black, usually glaucous, 6–9 mm across; stalks curved, not enlarged just below berry	bogs and moist coniferous forests and openings, low to subalpine elevations
creamy pink to yellow-pink, 5–6 mm long, a bit longer than broad, single in leaf axils	purple or reddish-black, not glaucous, 6–8 mm across	dry to moist coniferous forests, middle to alpine elevations
greenish-yellow or pinkish, a bit longer than broad, 4–5 mm long, single in leaf axils	bright red , 6–10 mm across	coniferous forests at low to middle elevations, often on rotting wood or in soils rich in rotting wood
pink, 7–8 mm long, longer than wide, in clusters of 3–10 from leaf axils	purplish-black, shiny, 4–7 mm across, occasionally glaucous, with a musky flavour	coniferous forests near the ocean
white to pink, 5–6 mm long, twice as long as wide, single in leaf axils	glaucous blue, 5–8 mm across	low-elevation bogs, sub-alpine meadows, alpine tundra
pink, 6–7 mm long, about as long as wide, single in leaf axils	glaucous blue, 6–8 mm across	subalpine meadows and open forest, alpine tundra
pink, 5–6 mm long, longer than wide, 1-4 from leaf axils	glaucous blue, 6–8 mm across	low-elevation bogs, rocky alpine tundra
pink, 4–6 mm long, 1 to several in terminal clusters	red, 6–10 mm across	coniferous forests, bogs, alpine tundra
pink, the petals distinct and strongly bent back, 1–3, terminal or lateral	pale pink to dark red, 5–8 mm across	bogs and subalpine meadows

1. see Notes for dwarf blueberry, p.58
2. see Notes for kinnikinnick, p. 67

ALASKAN BLUEBERRY • *Vaccinium alaskaense*

GENERAL: Erect to spreading, to 2 m tall; **young twigs slightly to strongly angled, yellowish-green**; old bark greyish.

LEAVES: Alternate, deciduous, oval to egg-shaped, 2–6 cm long, with or without teeth, dark green above, whitish below.

FLOWERS: Bronze to pinkish-green, round to urn-shaped, about 7 mm long, single in leaf axils; **appear with or after the leaves**.

FRUITS: Bluish-black to purplish-black berries, **without bloom**, 7–10 mm across; edible.

ECOLOGY: Moist coniferous forests, forest openings, clearings, often in soils rich in decaying wood; at low to subalpine elevations.

NOTES: Alaskan blueberry is one of the dominant shrubs in Alaskan and B.C. coastal forests, **often growing together with oval-leaved blueberry**. These two shrubs are not easy to tell apart; see the conspectus (pp. 54–55) for differentiating characteristics. One method is to turn the leaf over and bend it in two along the midvein and then examine it closely to **see if there are widely spaced 'whiskers' along the underside of the midvein**: if so, it is Alaskan blueberry and if not, it is oval-leaved blueberry (unless, of course, it is something else entirely). The berries of Alaskan blueberry are usually darker, less sweet and less prolific than those of oval-leaved blueberry. • The berries were eaten fresh or dried by virtually all coastal aboriginal groups, although the flavour was considered to be inferior to that of *V. ovalifolium*. The method for drying the berries was similar to that described for salal berries (p. 52). Recently the berries have been frozen, canned or made into jam. • Berries on some bushes are much more delicious than those on others, so you should sample widely before settling on a picking area.

OVAL-LEAVED BLUEBERRY • *Vaccinium ovalifolium*

GENERAL: Erect, slender, spreading shrub to 2 m tall; **young twigs brownish or often reddish to yellowish, angled, grooved**; old branches greyish.

LEAVES: Alternate, deciduous, oval, to 4 cm long, blunt-rounded at both ends; margins usually lacking teeth; green above, paler beneath.

FLOWERS: Pinkish, globular, urn-shaped to egg-shaped 'bells' usually longer than broad, about 7 mm long, single in axils of leaves; **appear generally before (sometimes with) the leaves**.

FRUITS: Blue-black berries with **bluish bloom**; large (6–9 mm across) and edible.

ECOLOGY: Moist coniferous forests and openings, and bogs. Middle to subalpine elevations, also at low elevations in the northern half of our region.

NOTES: Oval-leaved blueberry is Alaska's most common woodland *Vaccinium*. Along the B.C. and Alaskan coasts, it **often occurs with Alaskan blueberry**, forming a dense shrub layer in moist coniferous forests. Oval-leaved blueberry might be confused with Alaskan blueberry, but has **less astringent tasting twigs, and is generally more highly branched, with finer, often reddish, twigs**. For more assistance in separating these similar species, see the Alaskan blueberry and the conspectus (pp. 54–56). • This berry was eaten and highly regarded by all coastal aboriginal groups within the range of the species. The berries ripen in July and are distinguished from other species by their early fruiting, which occurs right after salmonberries on the coast. The berries were eaten fresh or dried into cakes, and taste like raisins when dried. They were often eaten with oil or oolichan grease, and the Gitksan sometimes preserved them in animal or fish grease.

BLACK HUCKLEBERRY • *Vaccinium membranaceum*

GENERAL: Erect to spreading, coarse, densely-branched, to 1.5 m tall; young branches yellowish-green, somewhat angled; old branches with greyish, shredding bark.

LEAVES: Alternate, deciduous, thin, lance-shaped to elliptic, **pointed at tip**, 2–4 cm long; **margins finely toothed**; glabrous, paler on lower surface; red to purple in the fall.

FLOWERS: Creamy pink to yellow-pink, urn-shaped, 5–6 mm long; single in leaf axils; appearing with or after leaves.

FRUITS: Purplish or reddish-black berries, **without bloom**; large (6–8 mm across), edible and very tasty.

ECOLOGY: Common understorey shrub in dry to moist coniferous forests, but also in open areas (e.g., burns, open subalpine slopes), from middle to high elevations.

NOTES: Black huckleberries are among the most delicious of all our *Vaccinium* species, and they are produced in great abundance on some sites, especially old burns that have only sparse tree regeneration. In parts of the Cascade Mountains the berries are picked for sale. Minore and Dubrasich (1978) estimated that black huckleberry production on their test plots in the Gifford Pinchot National Forest would have been worth almost $2,000/ha annually. They also note that 'modern fire control techniques have all but eliminated large wildfires in recent decades, and the dwindling areas now suitable for [black huckleberry]…appear insufficient to maintain the huckleberry resource.' • These juicy, flavourful berries were gathered from mid summer to fall and eaten fresh or cooked, mashed and dried into cakes. In Nuxalk taxonomy the berries are the type species of fruits and its name translates as 'berry/fruit.' The Kwakwaka'wakw cooked the berries with salmon roe, and the Sechelt smoke-dried them using the plant's own branches as fuel.

RED HUCKLEBERRY • *Vaccinium parvifolium*

GENERAL: Erect shrub to 4 m tall; **branches bright green, very strongly angled**, smooth or (when young) slightly hairy.

LEAVES: Alternate, mostly deciduous but with a few persistent; oval, to 3 cm long, **not toothed** (except occasionally on young leaves).

FLOWERS: Greenish-yellow or pinkish, bell- or urn-shaped, up to 5 mm long; single in leaf axils.

FRUITS: Bright-red, round berries, to 1 cm across; edible, a little sour for some tastes.

ECOLOGY: Coniferous forest, often at forest edges or under canopy openings, in soils rich in decaying wood, often on stumps or logs; at low to middle elevations.

NOTES: Red huckleberry is the dominant *Vaccinium* in the Oregon Coast Ranges. • These red berries were used as fish bait in streams. They were popular and were eaten fresh by all coastal aboriginal groups within the range of the plant. When gathered in quantity, they were either dried singly like raisins, mashed and dried into cakes for winter use, or stored soaked in grease or oil. The juice, though watery, was consumed as a beverage to stimulate the appetite or as a mouthwash. Berries were harvested by clubbing the branches onto the hand and letting the berries fall into a basket, or they were removed with a comb-like implement, often made of yew wood. To separate the berries from the leaves, people sometimes poured a basketful down a curvy wet plank of wood: the leaves caught in depressions, and the berries collected in a basket below. Sechelt people used to smoke-dry the berries using the branches of the bush as a part of the fuel. Sometimes the berries were mixed with other berries such as salal. The Gitksan stored the berries in grease or sometimes fresh in a cool place. • The leaves and bark were used in a decoction that was gargled for sore throats and inflamed gums. Some have said that the red huckleberry was created by Asin, the monster woman-of-the-woods, and that those who ate the berries lost their reason and were carried off to the woods.

DWARF BLUEBERRY • *Vaccinium caespitosum*
DWARF BILBERRY

GENERAL: Low-spreading, matted, **dwarf** deciduous shrub, up to 30 cm tall; twigs rounded, yellowish green to reddish, often hairy.

LEAVES: Alternate, deciduous, oblong to lance-shaped, **distinctly toothed, bright green on both sides**, less than 3 cm long, with **pronounced network of veins beneath**.

FLOWERS: Small (5–6 mm long), whitish to pink, **narrowly urn-shaped, with 5 lobes**, single in axils of leaves.

FRUITS: Blue berries **with a pale grey bloom**; edible and sweet.

ECOLOGY: Low elevation bogs, subalpine wet meadows and moist rocky ridges, and alpine tundra.

NOTES: Blue-leaved or Cascade huckleberry (*V. deliciosum*) is also found in subalpine and alpine areas, from Pemberton and southern Vancouver Island to Oregon. It is similar to dwarf blueberry, but it has **leaves with a whitish bloom beneath** (vs. bright green in dwarf blueberry) and **nearly round flowers** (vs. more elongate in dwarf blueberry). In subalpine meadows in the Cascade and Olympic Mountains, *V. deliciosum* is often abundant and produces a berry crop worthy of the species name. • Berries of dwarf blueberry are harvestable from late July until September. They were eaten fresh or dried by virtually all aboriginal peoples within its range. They were preferred to most other kinds of blueberries. They were sometimes harvested with a comb-like implement of either wood or salmon backbone. The Gitksan ate them fresh or preserved in oolichan grease. Controlled landscape burning was used to stimulate growth of blueberry species.

BOG BLUEBERRY • *Vaccinium uliginosum*

GENERAL: Low, prostrate and mat-forming to erect, freely branched, deciduous, 0.1–0.3 m tall; young twigs yellowish green, hairy, not angled; old branches greyish red.

LEAVES: Alternate, deciduous, firm, narrowly elliptic to oval, but **broadest above middle**, tip rounded but minutely pointed, **no teeth**, 1–3 cm long, **green above, pale beneath; network of veins strongly pronounced on lower surface**.

FLOWERS: Pink, urn-shaped, **usually with 4 lobes**, 5–6 mm long; 1–4 per leaf axil.

FRUITS: Blue berries, 5–10 mm across, **covered in fine waxy powder**; edible and sweet.

ECOLOGY: Low-elevation bogs, subalpine heath, and dry to moist rocky alpine tundra; uncommon south of about 52°N.

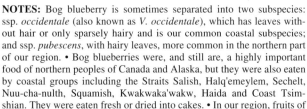

NOTES: Bog blueberry is sometimes separated into two subspecies: ssp. *occidentale* (also known as *V. occidentale*), which has leaves without hair or only sparsely hairy and is our common coastal subspecies; and ssp. *pubescens*, with hairy leaves, more common in the northern part of our region. • Bog blueberries were, and still are, a highly important food of northern peoples of Canada and Alaska, but they were also eaten by coastal groups including the Straits Salish, Halq'emeylem, Sechelt, Nuu-cha-nulth, Squamish, Kwakwaka'wakw, Haida and Coast Tsimshian. They were eaten fresh or dried into cakes. • In our region, fruits of *Vaccinium* species tend to be called blueberries if they are blue, and huckleberries if they are any other colour. • 'Blueberry' comes from the Scottish *blaeberry*, from the 15th century (probably Scandinavian) word *blae* meaning 'blue-black.'

EVERGREEN HUCKLEBERRY • *Vaccinium ovatum*

GENERAL: Erect, bushy, to 4 m tall; young stems somewhat hairy.

LEAVES: Alternate, **evergreen**, egg-shaped, **leathery, sharp-toothed, dark shiny green on top, paler below**, 2–5 cm long; distinctly 2-ranked and horizontally disposed.

FLOWERS: Pink, bell-shaped, to 8 mm long; in clusters of 3–10, in axils of leaves.

FRUITS: Deep **purplish-black** berries, shiny, small (4–7 mm broad); edible, sweet, somewhat musky in taste.

ECOLOGY: Coniferous forests (especially edges and openings) at low elevations, often on the beach fringe in the salt spray zone, usually close to tidewater.

NOTES: From north to south in our region, the common *Vaccinium* species at low elevations change: in Alaska, *V. ovalifolium* is the most common species, in B.C. it is *V. alaskaense*, and in Washington and Oregon, it is *V. parvifolium* (with *V. membranaceum* most common higher in the mountains). • These berries were used by the Nuu-chah-nulth, Sechelt, Comox, Halq'emeylem, Straits Salish, Quinault and other groups within the range of the species. They were well-liked, and people were known to travel far to collect them. They were eaten fresh, often with oil, or they were dried into cakes. They begin to ripen in early autumn, but they remain on the bushes until December, and are still treasured today as winter berries, said to taste better after the first frost.

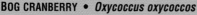

BOG CRANBERRY • *Oxycoccus oxycoccos*

GENERAL: Low-creeping, **vinelike**, dwarf shrub; stems very slender, sometimes rising 10–40 cm tall, finely hairy to smooth; bark brown to black.

LEAVES: Alternate, **evergreen**, widely spaced, **leathery**, small, 3–10 mm, sharp pointed, **with edges rolled under; grey-waxy beneath, dark green above**.

FLOWERS: Deep pink, nodding, with petals sharply bent backwards and stamens protruding (**like miniature shootingstars**); often solitary or 2–3, each on slender, long stem.

FRUITS: Pale-pink to dark red, juicy berries; small (5–10 mm broad), but appear oversized on the plant.

ECOLOGY: Half buried in *Sphagnum* hummocks of bogs at low to middle elevations, and wet subalpine meadows.

NOTES: Bog cranberry is also known as *Vaccinium oxycoccos, V. microcarpum, Oxycoccus microcarpus* and *O. quadripetalus*. • Another cranberry in our region **with evergreen leaves about 1 cm long, with black dots on the undersides, is lingonberry** or mountain-cranberry (*Vaccinium vitis-idaea*). It can be found along the coasts of B.C. and Alaska in a variety of habitats, including bogs. Lingonberry is a highly important food for the Dena'ina, Tlingit, Kaigani Haida, Haida, Nisga'a, Gitksan and other northern peoples and was used where available farther south. • The coastal peoples of the Northwest Coast usually cooked the berries of bog cranberry and served them in oolichan grease or oil. They were also eaten fresh as a snack or thirst quencher. They were stored fresh in moss or by drying into cakes. The Fraser River valley was a prime area for native harvest of cranberries, and the Halq'emeylem used to trade them to Vancouver Island and elsewhere. The berries were associated with high rank by Sechelt peoples.

FALSE AZALEA • *Menziesia ferruginea*
FOOL'S HUCKLEBERRY

GENERAL: Erect to straggly spreading shrub, to 3 m tall; young twigs covered with fine hairs, somewhat glandular and rusty coloured, sticky to the touch; bark scaly-shredding on older branches.

LEAVES: Alternate, **deciduous**, in clusters along branches; dull, thin, oblong to elliptic, blades 3–5 cm long; margins wavy, toothed; **light green to blue-green, hairy-glandular, aromatic (skunky) when crushed; end of midvein protruding at tip of leaf**.

FLOWERS: Pinkish to yellowish-white to almost salmon, urn-shaped, 6–8 mm long; several in drooping terminal clusters on previous year's growth; 4 sepals, 4 petals, 8 stamens.

FRUITS: Oval, dry, 4-valved capsules 5–7 mm long.

ECOLOGY: Shady to open coniferous woods with acid humus, moist slopes, streambanks; from sea level to subalpine in the northern half of our region; in montane to subalpine forests from Vancouver Island south.

NOTES: Some forms of false azalea have strikingly bluish-green foliage. This plant is very attractive in the fall when the leaves turn a brilliant crimson-orange. • Children of the Nisga'a used to suck the nectar from the flowers. A fungus (*Exobasidium* sp. affin. *vaccinii*) growing on the leaves of this shrub was eaten by some of the peoples of the central and north coast of B.C. (Brian Compton, personal communication 1993). The twigs and leaves were used by lower Stl'atl'imx to make a beverage tea, but it should be noted that false azalea contains some of the same **poisonous** compounds as bog-laurel (p. 65). • This plant is called 'false azalea' and 'false huckleberry' because it resembles both those plants. It is also called 'fool's huckleberry,' because the flower looks much like that of a huckleberry but the fruit is a dry, inedible capsule.

COPPERBUSH • *Cladothamnus pyroliflorus*

GENERAL: Medium-sized, to 2 m tall, leafy, with loose, shredding copper-coloured bark.

LEAVES: Alternate (usually appearing whorled), **deciduous, pale green, covered in a fine, waxy powder**, lance-shaped, broadest near tip, 2–5 cm long.

FLOWERS: Salmon or coppery, 10–15 mm long; single (sometimes 2) and terminal; style long, curved.

FRUITS: Round, many-seeded capsules 4–7 mm wide.

ECOLOGY: Moist forests (commonly mountain hemlock), stream banks, and bog edges, often in subalpine thickets with white-flowered rhododendron and false azalea.

NOTES: White-flowered rhododendron, false azalea and copperbush are all medium to tall, subalpine, heath-family shrubs that could be confused. **White-flowered rhododendron has shiny leaves with rusty hairs on the top, false azalea has glandular-hairy leaves that are often bluish-green and copperbush has hairless leaves covered with a waxy powder.** • *Cladothamnus* is one of very few genera endemic to western North America; most of our species belong to genera that include species found in other parts of the world. Though copperbush occurs as far south as Saddle Mountain in northwest Oregon, it is uncommon south of B.C. • *Cladothamnus* is from the Greek *klados* meaning 'sprout or branch' and *thamnos* meaning 'bush.' It has the name *pyroliflorus* because the flowers with their protruding styles resemble those of *Pyrola* (wintergreen). The unusual, pale-copper-coloured flowers give it its common name.

WHITE-FLOWERED RHODODENDRON
WHITE RHODODENDRON • *Rhododendron albiflorum*

GENERAL: Erect, slender, branched, with rhizomes, 1–2.5 m tall; young twigs covered with coarse reddish hairs; bark peeling.

LEAVES: Alternate, **deciduous**, in clusters along branch, especially at tip of branch; oblong to lance-shaped, elliptic, 4–9 cm long; **upper surface with fine rusty hairs; yellowish green**, turning beautiful shades of bronze, crimson and orange in the fall; **end of midvein not protruding at tip of leaf.**

FLOWERS: White to creamy, large, showy, cup-shaped, 1–2 cm across; in clusters of 2–4 on previous year's growth; petals fused at base.

FRUITS: Dry, oval capsules 6–8 mm long.

ECOLOGY: Moist coniferous forest, tree clumps in parkland, wet glades and along streams, but also on relatively dry, well-drained sites. Common at mostly subalpine elevations.

NOTES: Kamchatka rhododendron (*R. camtschaticum*) is a **low (to 30 cm)**, deciduous, sprawling to erect shrub with **pink to red (occasionally white) flowers**, found from around treeline up into alpine habitat, **from Petersburg north, and common in Prince William Sound.** • White-flowered rhododendron, rusty false azalea and copperbush are all heath-family shrubs of similar stature found in similar subalpine habitat, and they are often found together. They are easily distinguished when in flower or fruit, but when these clues are unavailable, **check the leaves. Those of rhododendron have fine rusty hairs on the upper surface, with white hairs only on the midvein underneath; leaves of false azalea are hairy on both sides; and those of copperbush are not hairy at all. Also, leaves of false azalea are sticky, and they have a midvein that protrudes beyond the end of the leaf.** • The leaves of white-flowered rhododendron were used for tea by the Okanagan. The Skokomish used the buds boiled in water as a cold and sore-throat medicine. They also chewed and swallowed the buds for stomach ulcers, or chewed and poulticed them on cuts, which they wrapped with shredded cedar bark. Many *Rhododendron* species contain some of the same **poisonous** compounds as does bog-laurel (p. 65).

PACIFIC RHODODENDRON • *R. macrophyllum*
CALIFORNIA RHODODENDRON

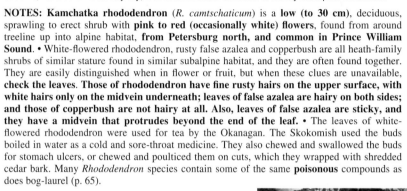

GENERAL: Erect to spreading, stout, branched, to 8 m tall.

LEAVES: Alternate, **evergreen, leathery, thick, not hairy**, oblong-elliptic, 8–20 cm long.

FLOWERS: Pink to rose-purple, bell-shaped, 5-lobed (the lobes have wavy edges), 2–4 cm long; few to many in showy terminal clusters.

FRUITS: Capsules woody, to 2 cm long.

ECOLOGY: Moist to fairly dry coniferous or mixed forests; southern B.C. (the Cascades and two locations on southeastern Vancouver Island) to northern California, from the coast to middle elevations in the mountains.

NOTES: Pacific rhododendron is the state flower of Washington. • This species forms an extensive shrub layer in forests ranging from shoreline pine groves to stands of Douglas-fir and western hemlock well up in the mountains. In the Oregon Coast Ranges it forms dense ridge-top thickets on an unusual rock type: nephaline syenite. The bushes can produce a spectacular floral display in late spring, which often matches that of cultivated *Rhododendron* species and lends a delightful colour to coniferous forests. Blooms are most profuse on plants in openings or on forest margins, although some flowers occur on bushes in very dark forest. This species sprouts well after fire or cutting and brings an encouraging touch of colour to cleared areas.

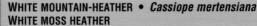

WHITE MOUNTAIN-HEATHER • *Cassiope mertensiana*
WHITE MOSS HEATHER

GENERAL: Tufted, forms extensive mats; stems up to 30 cm tall, nearly completely hidden by leaves, smooth or finely hairy, **4-angled**.

LEAVES: Opposite, evergreen, small, **scale-like**, egg- to lance-shaped, **arranged in 4 rows**, pressed flat against stem, no stalk; lower side rounded and grooved only at extreme base.

FLOWERS: White, with reddish sepals, **bell-shaped**, 5–8 mm long, more or less nodding; **several**, near branch tips.

FRUITS: Erect, 5-chambered capsules.

ECOLOGY: Alpine heath and subalpine parkland.

NOTES: A smaller version of white mountain-heather, **club-moss mountain-heather** (*C. lycopodioides*), has a **stem diameter of about 2 mm** (as opposed to 4 mm in *C. mertensiana*). It is found in habitats similar to those of white mountain-heather, from Petersburg to north coastal B.C. and the Queen Charlotte Islands. Club-moss mountain-heather is the most common *Cassiope* on the Queen Charlotte Islands. • *Cassiope* branches can be used to produce a golden-brown dye. • Individual plants of mountain-heather may be 20 years old or more; they are very slow growing. So admire them where they grow, and leave them there. • In Greek mythology, Cassiope was the mother of Andromeda (see *Andromeda polifolia*); *mertensiana* refers to F.C. Mertens (1764–1831), a German botanist. • This is another popular plant for rock gardens. It propagates from seeds, layers and cuttings.

ALASKAN MOUNTAIN-HEATHER
ALASKAN MOSS HEATHER • *Cassiope stelleriana*

GENERAL: Low-spreading, matted; stems up to 15 cm tall, minutely hairy.

LEAVES: Alternate, evergreen, **spreading, needle-like**, not pressed close to stem, linear to lance-shaped, flat on top, **rounded below, not grooved**.

FLOWERS: White or tinged pink, with reddish sepals, **broadly bell-shaped**, about 5 mm long, more or less nodding; mostly **single** at branch tips on short stalks.

FRUITS: Erect, round, 5-chambered capsules.

ECOLOGY: Alpine heaths and seepage areas, rocky slopes and gravelly creek-beds, open subalpine to above timberline.

NOTES: Alaskan mountain-heather is similar in appearance to crowberry and pink and yellow mountain-heathers, except that **those species have leaves that are grooved underneath**. • Named after Georg Wilhelm Steller, who was the first naturalist to collect, study and describe the plants and animals of Alaska when he visited with Bering's expedition in 1741.

PINK MOUNTAIN-HEATHER • *Phyllodoce empetriformis*

GENERAL: Low, much-branched, matted; stems erect, 10–40 cm tall; young stems glandular-hairy, becoming glabrous with age.

LEAVES: Alternate, evergreen, **needle-like**, linear, to 1 cm long, smooth except for tiny glands along margins; **groove on lower surface.**

FLOWERS: Showy, **pink to deep rose, bell-shaped**, about 8 mm long, erect to nodding; **one to many**, in a terminal cluster.

FRUITS: Round capsules about 4 mm across.

ECOLOGY: Subalpine and alpine heath, sometimes down into cold coniferous forest on rocky sites or seepage areas.

NOTES: This is our most common *Phyllodoce* except on the Queen Charlotte Islands and in Alaska, where yellow mountain-heather predominates. • Here is what Lewis Clark (1976) has to say about this species: 'These cheerful bells ring an invitation to high places above the timber line, to those serene and lofty slopes where peace and quiet enter our souls.' • It is called 'mountain-heather' because, superficially, it resembles the true heather (*Calluna vulgaris*) of Europe. **It also resembles crowberry, but has longer leaves and larger, more showy flowers.** • *Phyllodoce* was a sea-nymph in Greek mythology; *empetriformis* refers to the resemblance of this plant to *Empetrum nigrum* (crowberry). • Pink mountain-heather is popular as a garden ornamental, and it is easy to propagate by cuttings or by layering in sand.

YELLOW MOUNTAIN-HEATHER • *Phyllodoce glanduliflora*

GENERAL: Low, much branched, matted; stems erect, 10-40 cm tall; young stems glandular-hairy.

LEAVES: Alternate, evergreen, **needle-like**, linear, to 1 cm long, smooth except for tiny glands along margins; **groove present on lower surface.**

FLOWERS: Showy, **yellowish-green, urn-shaped**, about 8 mm long, **the flowers and their stalks sticky-glandular**, erect to nodding; **few to many**, in a terminal cluster.

FRUITS: Round capsules about 4 mm across.

ECOLOGY: Subalpine and alpine heath, sometimes down into snowy coniferous forest on rocky sites, seepage areas or middle-elevation bogs. At middle to (usually) high elevations, but down to sea level in Prince William Sound, on fresh till and outwash.

NOTES: Yellow mountain-heather is also called *P. aleutica* ssp. *glanduliflora*. • Yellow mountain-heather is very similar to pink mountain-heather, but it has **yellowish-green, urn-shaped flowers** (vs. bell-shaped in pink mountain-heather) and very **sticky-glandular flowers and flower stalks**. The two mountain-heathers often grow together and hybridize; the hybrids are described by some as *P. intermedia*, and they are most easily recognized by their pale-pink flowers.

CROWBERRY • *Empetrum nigrum*

GENERAL: Low-creeping, matted, freely branching, resembling a miniature fir tree; stems up to 20 cm tall, with long woolly hairs.

LEAVES: Evergreen, linear, **needle-like, 3–7 mm long**, minutely glandular-hairy, spreading, **in whorls of 4 or alternate** on branch; margins somewhat rolled under; **leaves grooved beneath.**

FLOWERS: Purplish crimson, **incon-spicuous**; 2–3 **in leaf axils**, appearing in very early spring; male and female flowers sometimes on different plants.

FRUITS: Juicy, **black, berrylike drupes,** with large white seeds, in small clusters.

ECOLOGY: Low, exposed coastal heathlands and bogs; rocky mountain slopes, subalpine parkland, and alpine tundra; dry to wet sites, sea level to alpine.

NOTES: See Alaskan and pink mountain-heathers (pp. 62–63), which look like crowberry when not in flower or fruit. • These berries were eaten fresh in small quantities by the Tsimshian and the Haida, but apparently not by other coastal groups. The Haida believed the berries would cause haemorrhaging if eaten in excess. The berries are juicy, but the flavour is unpleasant to some people. These berries were eaten fresh by many aboriginal groups in the Arctic, especially the Inuit. • Crowberry is a favourite food of bears. • The name 'crowberry' is thought to come from the black colour of the fruit, the fact that crows feed on it, or from the notion that it is only good for crows, not humans. Also called 'curlew berry' and 'crakeberry' (*crake* is an Old Norse word for crow). *Empetrum* is from the Greek *en petros*, or 'on rock'; *nigrum* means 'black.'

ALPINE-AZALEA • *Loiseleuria procumbens*

GENERAL: Matted, much-branched dwarf shrub, stems to 30 cm long, 2–10 cm high.

LEAVES: Opposite, evergreen, **leathery,** blades to 8 mm long, **lance-shaped to oblong,** with the edges rolled under, not toothed, green above, **whitish beneath** with dense, short hairs.

FLOWERS: Pink, bell-shaped, to 5 mm long; 1 to several in clusters at ends of twigs.

FRUITS: Oval, dark-red capsules 3–5 mm long.

ECOLOGY: Above treeline (growing with the mountain-heathers) and at low elevations in bogs, but not in between.

NOTES: The clusters of **upright, bell-shaped pink flowers** and much-branched stems with **tiny, opposite, elliptic, leathery leaves** are unmistakeable (but see *Saxifraga oppositifolia* and *S. tolmiei*, pp. 160–161). • Alpine-azalea makes an excellent rock-garden plant and is easily propagated. • Named after J.L.A. Loiseleur-Deslongchamps (1774–1849), a French botanist, this plant was originally named *Azalea procumbens* by Linnaeus because it grew in dry habitats in Lapland: *Azalea* is the Latin for 'of-dry-habitats.' The species name *procumbens* ('trailing') refers to the low, creeping growth form of the plant.

WESTERN BOG-LAUREL • *Kalmia microphylla*
SWAMP-LAUREL   ssp. *occidentalis*

GENERAL: Small, slender-branched evergreen, up to 0.5 m tall; spreads by layering and short rhizomes.

LEAVES: Opposite, narrowly lance-shaped, to 4 cm long; margins rolled under; dark-green, leathery above, **conspicuously whitish and fine-hairy beneath**.

FLOWERS: Rose-pink, saucer-shaped, about 2 cm across; 10 stamens, the tip of each tucked into a small pouch in a petal, and held under tension like a bow; at the slightest touch by an insect probing for nectar, the stamens pop out and dust the insect with pollen; several, in loose terminal clusters .

FRUITS: Five-valved capsules.

ECOLOGY: Bogs, wet mountain meadows and, in Alaska, low-productivity forests; on peaty soils; northern southeast Alaska to California.

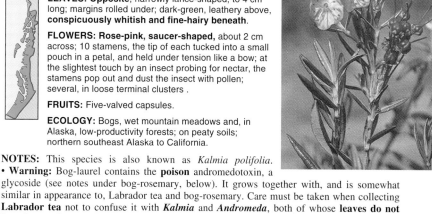

NOTES: This species is also known as *Kalmia polifolia*. • **Warning:** Bog-laurel contains the **poison** andromedotoxin, a glycoside (see notes under bog-rosemary, below). It grows together with, and is somewhat similar in appearance to, Labrador tea and bog-rosemary. Care must be taken when collecting **Labrador tea** not to confuse it with *Kalmia* and *Andromeda*, both of whose **leaves do not have brown fuzz on the underside** and do not tend to hang downwards. When in flower, all three species are easy to tell apart. • The Tlingit washed in an infusion of bog-laurel to treat skin ailments. This plant is boiled by the Haida with Labrador tea or 'little trees' (probably crowberry) to make a medicinal drink. The Kwakwaka'wakw boiled the leaves to make an extract drunk to treat spitting of blood or used to wash open sores which would not heal. • Presumably it is called 'bog-laurel' because the leaves of *Kalmia* are similar in shape to, and are aromatic like, true laurel or bay leaves. *Kalmia* is named for Peter Kalm, an 18th century student of Linnaeus; *microphylla* means 'small-leaved,' and *occidentalis* means 'western.'

BOG-ROSEMARY • *Andromeda polifolia*

GENERAL: Low-spreading evergreen; stems erect, to 80 cm tall, from creeping rhizomes.

LEAVES: Alternate, leathery, 2–3 cm long, narrowly lance-shaped to oblong, sharp-pointed; margins rolled under; **lower surface white with a fine, waxy powder, hairless**; upper surface dull-green, with sunken veins.

FLOWERS: Pinkish, small, **urn-shaped**, 2–6 in terminal stalked clusters; flower stems somewhat curved downward at tip.

FRUITS: Roundish, erect, 5-valved capsules; seeds tiny, numerous.

ECOLOGY: Bogs, fens, swamps and, in Alaska and the Queen Charlotte Islands, boggy subalpine meadows, at low to subalpine elevations.

NOTES: Highly regarded as a garden ornamental, for which horticultural varieties have been selected. • Andromeda was the daughter of Cassiopeia and Cepheus in Greek mythology. Legend has it that this beauty was chained to a rock in the midst of the ocean, just as bog-rosemary grows on little moss hummocks surrounded by swamp. The species name *polifolia* means 'many leaves.' • **Andromedotoxin** in this plant, when ingested, lowers blood pressure and causes breathing problems, dizziness, cramps, vomiting and diarrhea.

LABRADOR TEA • *Ledum groenlandicum*

GENERAL: Evergreen, much-branched, 0.5–1.5 m tall; twigs with dense, rusty hairs; with spicy fragrance.

LEAVES: Alternate, narrow, oblong to lance-shaped, **to 6 cm long**, often drooping; margins rolled under; leathery, deep-green above, with **dense, rusty hairs beneath** (hairs on young leaves may not be rusty).

FLOWERS: White, with protruding stamens, small; numerous, in short umbrella-like clusters.

FRUITS: Drooping cluster of 5-part, dry, hairy capsules.

ECOLOGY: Peatlands, bog forest; an indicator of wet, usually very acid and nutrient-poor organic soils. At low to middle elevations.

NOTES: Trapper's tea (*L. glandulosum*) is similar in most respects to *L. groenlandicum*, but is easily differentiated by its **whitish-hairy** (vs. rusty-hairy in *L. groenlandicum*) **leaf undersides**. Both species occupy similar habitats; Labrador tea is the common species in Alaska, B.C. and western Washington, and trapper's tea is the common species in the Washington Cascades and Oregon, where it occurs from the coast to high in the mountains. Trapper's tea is known to be **toxic** in concentrated doses, but interior peoples use this species as a beverage tea, apparently without ill effect. • Northern Labrador tea (*Ledum palustre* ssp. *decumbens*, also known as *L. decumbens*) is a smaller, sprawling to erect shrub with reddish hairs on stems, leaf undersides and flowers. **Leaves of northern Labrador tea are shorter** (usually less than 2 cm long) and **narrower** than those of *L. groenlandicum* or *L. glandulosum*. Northern Labrador tea is common in bogs and muskeg, and on rocky slopes, at low to high elevations in northern southeast Alaska and Prince William Sound. • Leaves, used fresh or dried, can be boiled to make a tea with an aromatic fragrance, which should be consumed in **moderation**. Excessive doses act as a strong diuretic or a cathartic, or cause intestinal disturbances. Do not confuse Labrador tea with trapper's tea, bog-laurel or bog-rosemary; all three lack brown fuzz on the underside of mature leaves, and bog-laurel and bog-rosemary have pink flowers. All three contain **toxic alkaloids** known to be poisonous to livestock, especially sheep. • Labrador-tea leaves were and still are used by many coastal peoples, and by many other aboriginal groups across Canada. European settlers and traders also valued the plant as a tea. In some areas of the Northwest Coast, it is believed the use of the tea as a beverage, rather than solely as a medicine, was introduced during the early contact period, possibly by the Hudson's Bay Company. Various methods for preparation of the leaves existed, ranging from fresh or dried leaves to elaborate pit-steaming with licorice fern rhizomes. Tea made from the leaves was ingested for colds and sore throats, especially by the Haida. It is said to be relaxing and, for some people, to cause drowsiness, possibly due to the potentially toxic glycosides present in the leaves. Others feel no such effects from it or find it prevents drowsiness.

HAIRY MANZANITA • *Arctostaphylos columbiana*

GENERAL: Erect or spreading, bushy, evergreen, to 3 m tall; young twigs and leaves very hairy, old branches with rich, reddish-brown bark that flakes and peels.

LEAVES: Alternate, egg- to lance-shaped, 2–5 cm long, **hairy all over** but more so beneath, with a **greyish-green** colour.

FLOWERS: White to pinkish, urn-shaped, 6–7 mm long; in hairy clusters borne at the ends of branches.

FRUITS: Blackish-red (coffee-coloured) berries, 6–8 mm across, mealy, edible.

ECOLOGY: Dry, sunny spots, such as rock outcrops and rocky slopes on slightly acid soil; at low elevations.

NOTES: Kinnikinnick and hairy manzanita hybridize where their ranges overlap. The resulting low shrub, sometimes described as ***Arctostaphylos* x *media*,** is intermediate in most characteristics having, for example, slightly hairy undersurfaces on its leaves (vs. mostly smooth in kinnikinnick and hairy in hairy manzanita). • While admiring hairy manzanita, watch out for **poison oak** (*Rhus diversiloba*, also known as *Toxicodendron diversilobum*), with leaves with **3–5 irregularly lobed leaflets** (somewhat like an oak leaf) that turn bright scarlet in autumn. • *Manzanita* is Spanish for 'little apples,' alluding to the appearance of the small, brown fruits. The berries were reputedly eaten by some native people, although they are said to cause severe constipation. • *Arctostaphylos* is from the Greek *arktos* ('bear') and *staphylos* ('a bunch of grapes').

KINNIKINNICK • *Arctostaphylos uva-ursi*
COMMON BEARBERRY

GENERAL: Trailing, evergreen, the ascending tips usually not over 20 cm tall, often forming mats with long, flexible rooting branches; bark brownish-red.

LEAVES: Alternate, leathery, oval- to spoon-shaped, entire, to 3 cm long; **dark-green** and somewhat shiny above, paler beneath.

FLOWERS: Pinkish-white, small (about 5 mm long), urn-shaped, drooping; several in a few-flowered terminal cluster.

FRUITS: Bright-red berries like miniature apples, 7–10 mm wide; edible but with mealy and rather tasteless pulp, and large, very hard seeds. Fruits ripen late and stay on plants into the winter.

ECOLOGY: Sandy and well-drained exposed sites, dry rocky slopes, dry forest and clearings; common and widespread, from low elevations to alpine tundra.

NOTES: Pinemat manzanita (*A. nevadensis*) is very similar to kinnikinnick but has **pointed leaves and brownish-red berries**. It is a common shrub in the Cascades of Oregon and southern Washington, where it seems to replace *A. uva-ursi*. • The leaves were used by the Haida as a diuretic in kidney diseases and infections of the urinary passage. • *Kinnikinnick* is said to be an Algonquian term meaning 'smoking mixture.' The dried leaves were smoked by a number of coastal groups within the last two centuries, including the Coast Salish and Nuu-chah-nulth of Vancouver Island, as well as the Haida and the Nuxalk, Tsimshian, Kwakwaka'wakw and other coastal mainland peoples. The Nuxalk made special smoking pipes from gooseberry stems. There is little indication of these groups smoking in pre-contact times, although the Haida, Tlingit and Tsimshian did grow and chew the leaves of a species of tobacco, now apparently extinct, in pre-contact times. Commercial tobacco, once it was available on the Northwest Coast, was preferred, although some people extended their tobacco supply by mixing it with kinnikinnick leaves.

TWINFLOWER • *Linnaea borealis*

GENERAL: Trailing, slender, semi-woody, evergreen; short (less than 10 cm tall), erect, leafy stems from long runners, more or less hairy.

LEAVES: Opposite, firm, to 1 cm long, broadly elliptic, dark green above, paler below, with a **few shallow teeth along the upper half**.

FLOWERS: Pink, trumpet-like, **nodding,** 2–5 mm long, fragrant; **in pairs,** borne on a thin Y-shaped stalk.

FRUITS: Dry nutlets with sticky, glandular hairs that readily catch onto the fur of mammals, or feathers of birds.

ECOLOGY: Open or dense forest, shrub thickets, muskeg and rocky shorelines; at various elevations up to timberline.

NOTES: The beautiful twin flowers of *Linnaea* produce one of the most fragrant perfumes of our coastal woods. • In Alaska, it occurs north to Ketchikan in bogs and open, unproductive forest, and it is very scattered to northern southeast Alaska, where it is confined to dry sites like sandy beaches and rocky bluffs near the coast. • This species was supposedly the favourite flower of Linnaeus (the Swedish 'father of taxonomy') and so was named after him by his benefactor Gronovius; *borealis* means 'northern.'

HIGHBUSH-CRANBERRY • *Viburnum edule*
SQUASHBERRY, MOOSEBERRY

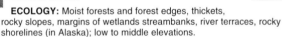

GENERAL: Straggling to erect, rhizomatous, 0.5–3.5 m tall with smooth, reddish to grey bark.

LEAVES: Opposite, shallowly **3-lobed, sharply toothed,** hairy beneath, often with a pair of teeth near the junction of the blade and stem; turning crimson in fall; leafy stalks can be sparsely glandular but not hairy.

FLOWERS: White; small clusters, **1–3 cm wide,** borne on short stems with a pair of leaves.

FRUITS: Clusters of 2–5 **red or orange,** 1-seeded, 1–1.5 cm long, **berry-like** drupes with large, flattened stones; edible, juicy, acid and tart; the over-ripe berries and decaying leaves impart a musty-sour odour to the woods in the fall.

ECOLOGY: Moist forests and forest edges, thickets, rocky slopes, margins of wetlands streambanks, river terraces, rocky shorelines (in Alaska); low to middle elevations.

NOTES: Oval-leaved viburnum (*V. ellipticum*) has **hairy-stalked,** more coarsely toothed leaves that are **not 3-lobed** and larger inflorescences (**2–5 cm wide**). It can usually be found on drier sites than highbush-cranberry, in thickets and open woods in the Cascade foothills from southern Washington to northern California. • The tart, clustered berries were an important food, especially for peoples of the central and northern coast region. The Haida were particularly fond of them, and they are the most frequently mentioned fruit in Haida myths (even though the species is not particularly common on the Queen Charlotte Islands). They were harvested in late summer and early fall, often while still hard and greenish, but they could also be obtained after the first frost of fall, since they remain on the bushes well into winter. They were stored, like wild crabapples, in boxes with water and oil, and they became softer and sweeter over time. Boxes of highbush-cranberries were considered a prestigious gift, and the berries were often served at important feasts. • The Nuxalk chewed the bark and swallowed the juice for lung colds. The Haida made a decoction from the bark which was used as an eye medicine. • The fruits are an important food source for over-wintering bird species, since they are one of the few berries available all winter. When mixed half-and-half with commercial cranberries, they make an excellent Thanksgiving cranberry sauce.

BLACK TWINBERRY • *Lonicera involucrata*
BEARBERRY HONEYSUCKLE

GENERAL: Erect to straggly, 0.5–3 m tall; **young twigs 4-angled in cross-section**, greenish.

LEAVES: Opposite, short-stalked, somewhat **elliptical to broadly lance-shaped**, pointed, often hairy beneath.

FLOWERS: Yellow, tubular with 5 lobes, 1–2 cm long; **in pairs in leaf axils**, cupped by large, green to purplish bracts.

FRUITS: Shiny, **black** 'twin' berries cupped by **2 pairs of deep-purplish-maroon bracts**; not considered palatable.

ECOLOGY: Moist forest, clearings, streamside habitats, swamps and thickets; at low to subalpine elevations.

NOTES: Utah honeysuckle (*Lonicera utahensis*) is a similar shrub with **more rounded** leaves, and **lacking big bracts** under its axillary pairs of creamy-yellow flowers and **red** fruits. It can be found at middle to high elevations in the Olympics and throughout the Cascades (B.C. to California). • The shiny, black, bitter, twinned berries are not considered edible by most people. They were given names like 'raven's food,' 'crow berry,' and 'monster's food' by northwest coast peoples. There were various taboos against eating them. For example, the Kwakwaka'wakw believed that eating the berries would cause one to become unable to speak. The bark and twigs were used in a variety of medicinal preparations, ranging from treatments for digestive tract problems to contraceptives. The Quileute and Kwakwaka'wakw peoples used the berries as a black pigment. The Haida rubbed the berries on the scalp to prevent hair from turning grey. • In coastal Alaska, black twinberry is only found near the edge of the forest on the shoreline, and in coastal meadows and bogs in the southeast Lynn Canal area, and on Kayak Island near Prince William Sound. • The honeysuckle genus *Lonicera* is named for Adam Lonitzer (1528–1586), a German naturalist; *involucrata* just means 'with an involucre,' the twin bracts surrounding the flowers and fruit.

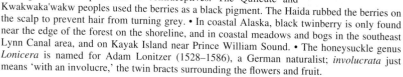

WESTERN TRUMPET HONEYSUCKLE
ORANGE HONEYSUCKLE • *Lonicera ciliosa*

GENERAL: Climbing, widely branching **vine**, sometimes reaching a height of 6 m; **twigs hollow**.

LEAVES: Opposite, deciduous, **oval**, 4–10 cm long, the **end-pair on each twig joined to form a disk**; with a whitish bloom underneath and hairs along the margins.

FLOWERS: Orange-yellow, occasionally becoming purplish on drying, 2–4 cm long, narrowly **trumpet-shaped**, flaring to 5 lobes; **in whorls above the disk-leaf** at branch ends.

FRUITS: Bunches of small (to 1 cm), **orange-red**, translucent, several-seeded berries.

ECOLOGY: Woods and thickets, from sea level to middle elevations.

NOTES: Hairy honeysuckle (*L. hispidula*) is a similar plant, although it has crawling rather than climbing, **hairy** branches, and it has **pinkish-purple** flowers **1–2 cm long**. It is found in dry, open forests, thickets and rocky ridges from southeastern Vancouver Island and the Gulf Islands to California. • The stems of *L. ciliosa* were used by interior peoples of British Columbia for weaving, binding and lashing. Saanich children liked to suck the sugar-filled nectaries at the bases of its flowers, but the berries were not eaten. Hummingbirds feed on the flowers as well. The red-to-orange berries are considered inedible, and **may be poisonous**. The plant is known as 'ghost's swing' or 'owl's swing' in several of the Coast Salish languages.

RED ELDERBERRY • *Sambucus racemosa*
RED ELDER   ssp. *pubens*

GENERAL: Shrub to small tree, to 6 m tall, with **soft, pithy twigs**; bark dark reddish-brown, warty; foliage with strong, characteristic odour.

LEAVES: Opposite, deciduous, large, **divided into 5–7 leaflets**; the leaflets lance-shaped, 5–15 cm long, pointed, sharply toothed, often somewhat hairy beneath.

FLOWERS: White to creamy, small, with a strong, unpleasant odour; numerous, in a **rounded or pyramidal parasol-like cluster**.

FRUITS: Bright-red berry-like drupes, each with 3–5 smooth seeds; not palatable when raw.

ECOLOGY: Stream banks, swampy thickets, moist clearings and open forests; sea level to middle elevations.

NOTES: Red elderberry, our common coastal variety, is *S. racemosa* ssp. *pubens* var. *arborescens*. **Black elderberry** (*S. racemosa* ssp. *pubens* var. *melanocarpa*) is a similar **interior** variety with **black or purplish-black** fruits, which occasionally shows up west of the coastal mountains. • **Blue elderberry** (*S. caerulea*) has 5 to (usually) 9 leaflets, **flat-topped** clusters of flowers, and **blue** fruits with a whitish bloom. It grows on dry to moist, fairly open, low-elevation sites from southern Vancouver Island and the adjacent mainland south to California. • Red elderberries, though small and seedy, were a highly important food for the peoples of the central and northern coast, although few people still use them today. They should always be cooked, since the raw berries may cause nausea. They were sometimes boiled to make a sauce or cooked with the stems intact. The stems and seeds were discarded later. The berries make an excellent, tangy jelly, and some people make wine from them, but they should always be cooked for this purpose. Caches of red elderberries have been found in archaeological sites dating back hundreds of years. • The stems, bark, leaves and roots, especially in fresh plants, are **toxic** due to the presence of cyanide-producing glycosides.

COMMON SNOWBERRY • *Symphoricarpos albus*
WAXBERRY

GENERAL: **Erect**, opposite-branching, rhizomatous, **0.5–2 m** tall; young stems **hairless**; twigs very fine.

LEAVES: Opposite, deciduous, elliptic to oval, 2–5 cm long, may be lobed on young stems; **margins smooth to wavy-toothed**.

FLOWERS: **Pink to white**, bell-shaped, 5–7 mm long; in short, dense clusters of few flowers, mostly terminal.

FRUITS: Clusters of **white**, **berry-like** drupes, 6–15 mm across with 2 seeds; persistent through winter.

ECOLOGY: Dry to moist, open forests, thickets, rocky slopes, river terraces, ravines, along beaches (Queen Charlotte Islands and Alaska); low to middle elevations.

NOTES: **Trailing snowberry** (*Symphoricarpos mollis*) is small (30–60 cm tall) and spreads by above-ground **trailing** stems that often root at the nodes. It has a **solid**, brownish pith in the usually **hairy** twigs (vs. hollow and glabrous in *S. albus*), and **smaller** leaves (1–3 cm long), flowers (3–5 mm long), and fruits (4–6 mm across) than common snowberry. It occurs in dry woods and openings, generally at low elevations, from southern B.C. to California. • The white, waxy-looking berries are considered **poisonous** by aboriginal peoples. They are given names like 'corpse berry' or 'snake's berry' in several languages. One Stl'atl'imx story identifies the berries as 'the saskatoon berries of the people in the Land of the Dead.' However, one or two berries were eaten by the Stl'atl'imx to settle the stomach after too much fatty food.

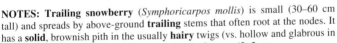

OCEANSPRAY • *Holodiscus discolor*
CREAMBUSH

GENERAL: Erect, usually with several main stems, to 4 m tall; young stems ridged, older ones with brownish, peeling bark; stems usually arch.

LEAVES: Alternate, deciduous, dull green, hairy, broadly egg-shaped to triangular, 3–6 cm long, **lobed or coarsely toothed**, in outline similar to leaves of black hawthorn (p. 73); reddish-tinged in autumn.

FLOWERS: White to cream, small (to 5 mm across); in dense terminal pyramidal, **lilac-like clusters** 10–17 cm long; flower clusters turn brown and remain on plants over winter.

FRUITS: Tiny (about 2 mm long), light-brown, **hairy achenes**.

ECOLOGY: Dry to moist, open sites (open woods, thickets, clearings, logged areas, ravine edges, coastal bluffs); mostly at low to middle elevations.

NOTES: This shrub is commonly called 'ironwood,' a name reflecting the hardness and strength of its wood. The wood was made even harder by heating it over a fire; it was then usually polished with horsetail stems. It was used to make digging sticks, spear and harpoon shafts, bows and arrow shafts by virtually all coastal groups from southern British Columbia southwards, including the Straits Salish, Halq'emeylem, Squamish, Sechelt and Kwak-waka'wakw. The Saanich and Cowichan used 'ironwood' for salmon-barbecuing sticks, inner bark scrapers, halibut hooks, cattail mat needles and, recently, knitting needles. • The Saanich, Stl'atl'imx and other groups steeped the brownish fruiting clusters of oceanspray in boiling water to make an infusion that was drunk for diarrhea, especially in children. This solution was also drunk for measles and chickenpox, and as a blood tonic. • Before the use of nails, oceanspray pegs were used in construction.

SITKA MOUNTAIN-ASH • *Sorbus sitchensis*

GENERAL: Erect, with several stems, 1–4 m tall; winter buds and young growth **with rusty hairs, not sticky**.

LEAVES: Alternate, deciduous, divided into **7–11 bluish-green leaflets, rounded at the tips**; margins **toothed mostly above middle**.

FLOWERS: White, small; not more than 80, in round-topped terminal clusters.

FRUITS: Berry-like, red, with whitish bloom; edible but extremely tart and bitter; much favoured by some birds, such as waxwings and grosbeaks.

ECOLOGY: Open, usually coniferous forest, parkland, streambanks, and clearings such as meadow edges and rockslides; occasionally in north-coast bogs at low elevations, but otherwise middle to alpine elevations.

NOTES: Western mountain-ash (*S. scopulina*) is a similar, largely interior species found less commonly in our region from Lynn Canal, Alaska, south. Western mountain-ash has **yellowish-green, sharp-pointed** leaflets, more sharply **toothed along almost their entire length**. It also has **sticky, white-hairy** young growth and winter buds, and **glossy orange to scarlet** fruits. Where ranges overlap, these two species will hybridize with each other and with the introduced rowan tree (*S. aucuparia*), which is found mostly near settlements. • The berries of both species of mountain-ash were generally not eaten by the northwest coast peoples; however, the Haida sometimes ate the berries raw. The berries are now used occasionally to make a tart jelly, which is served with game. The Nuxalk rubbed the berries on the scalp to combat lice and dandruff.

SASKATOON • *Amelanchier alnifolia*

GENERAL: Shrub to small tree, 1–5 m tall (or occasionally more); stem smooth, bark dark-grey to reddish; often spreads by rhizomes or rooting branch ends and forms dense colonies.

LEAVES: Alternate, deciduous, thin, round to oval, **regularly toothed mostly on top half** of leaf.

FLOWERS: White, large (1–2.5 cm across), 5 petals, 15–20 stamens, **showy**; in short, drooping to erect, leafy clusters of 3–20.

FRUITS: Dull-red at first, becoming **purple to nearly black**, berry-like pomes (**like miniature apples**), with a white bloom; edible, sweet.

ECOLOGY: Rocky shorelines, bluffs, talus slopes, meadows, thickets and forest edges; dry to moist open forest; roadsides; in well-drained soils. Scattered at low to middle elevations.

NOTES: On the Pacific coast, saskatoon is referred to in some works as *Amelanchier florida,* and one variety has been delightfully designated as *A. florida* var. *humptulipensis.* • Saskatoon berries were highly regarded by all groups, especially in the Interior, and they were dried into cakes for storage. The Haida called them 'sweet berries.' The Stl'atl'imx practised burning to encourage stands of saskatoon. • Saskatoon reaches supremacy as a fruit on the northern Great Plains, and horticulturists have developed several varieties for commercial and garden use. • In the Interior, saskatoon wood was commonly used for arrows, digging sticks, and drying racks. • Saskatoon provides important winter browse for ungulates (such as moose, deer and elk), and many wild bird species feast on the berries in August.

INDIAN-PLUM • *Oemleria cerasiformis*

GENERAL: Shrub or small tree 1.5–5 m tall, one of the first plants to flower in the spring; bark bitter, purplish-brown.

LEAVES: Alternate, deciduous, pale-green, broadly lance-shaped, 5–12 cm long, **not toothed**; strong **cucumber-like smell** when crushed.

FLOWERS: Greenish-white, about 1 cm across, male and female flowers on separate plants, 5 petals, 15 stamens in 3 distinct series somewhat bell-shaped, appearing **very early** in the year (usually before the leaves), unusual fragrance (something between watermelon rind and cat urine); in 5–10-cm-long clusters hanging from leaf axils.

FRUITS: Peach-coloured, ripening to **bluish-black** with a whitish bloom, **like small plums** (hence the common name), about 1 cm long; edible but bitter, with a large pit.

ECOLOGY: Dry to moist, open woods, streambanks, open areas (especially roadsides); low elevations.

NOTES: Indian-plum is also known as *Osmaronia cerasiformis*, and as 'osoberry.' • The berries were eaten in small quantities fresh, cooked or dried by the Straits Salish, Halq'emeylem, Squamish, and several Washington Salish groups. Some First Nations people call them 'choke-cherries' (but see *Prunus virginiana*, p. 48), because they are bitter and astringent, but they are quite palatable when fully ripe. The Kwakwaka'wakw ate a type of fruit, 'Indian-plum' by description, which they obtained from a small area at the upper reaches of Knight Inlet, although *O. cerasiformis* has not been recorded there. They ate these fresh, with plenty of oolichan grease, at family meals and feasts. People feasting on Indian-plum were not allowed to drink water. • Indian-plum twigs were chewed and applied to sore places. The twigs were sometimes burned and mixed with fish oil before application. The Saanich made a bark tea as a purgative and tonic.

BLACK HAWTHORN • *Crataegus douglasii*

GENERAL: Large shrubs or small trees to 10 m tall, with **thorns to 3 cm** long; bark grey, rough and **scaly**.

LEAVES: Alternate, deciduous, quite **thick, leathery**, dark-green above, paler below, oval (but broadest towards the tip), 3–6 cm long, the **top end with 5–9 lobes; margins saw-toothed**.

FLOWERS: White, stinky, about 1 cm across, 5 petals, 10–20 stamens; in clusters borne terminally or in leaf axils.

FRUITS: Blackish-purple little 'apples' about 1 cm long; edible, but with large seeds.

ECOLOGY: Moist, open places; forest edges, thickets, shorelines, streamside areas, roadsides, coastal bluffs; at low to middle elevations.

NOTES: Common hawthorn (*C. monogyna*) is a **cultivated** European species that often **naturalizes**. The leaves of *C. monogyna* are **deeply lobed (somewhat like an oak leaf)**, with showy, creamy-white flowers and clumps of **scarlet** fruits that stay on the trees over winter. It ranges from southern Vancouver Island south, at low elevations. • The thorns of black hawthorn had many practical uses, including prongs

on rakes used for catching herring, lances for probing skin blisters and boils, or for piercing ears, fish hooks and playing pieces for games. Black-hawthorn wood is very hard and was fashioned into tool handles and weapons. A winter-dance face paint was made from grease and hawthorn charcoal. The dry, seedy fruits were eaten by many coastal groups both fresh and dried, often with oil or grease. They were not highly regarded, however. The bark of black hawthorn was used to treat venereal disease, thin the blood, strengthen the heart, or reduce swellings, and it was used in steam baths. • The genus name comes from the Greek *kratos*, 'strength,' because the wood is noted for its great strength and fine grain.

PACIFIC NINEBARK • *Physocarpus capitatus*

GENERAL: Erect to spreading, to 4 m tall; arching, angled branches eventually with brown, **shredding** bark.

LEAVES: Alternate, deciduous, 3–6 cm long, **3–5 lobed, the lobes toothed**, deeply veined, shiny dark-green above, lighter and with abundant star-shaped hairs below (use hand lens).

FLOWERS: White, small (about 4 mm long), 5 petals, about 30 pink stamens; several to many in terminal, rounded clusters.

FRUITS: Reddish bunches of **dried inflated follicles** to 1 cm long, with yellowish, shiny seeds inside.

ECOLOGY: Wet, somewhat open places (streamside thickets, edges of moist woods, coastal marshes, meadows, margins of lakes and streams), occasionally on drier, shrubby sites; at low to middle elevations.

NOTES: The Nuu-chah-nulth made children's bows and other small items from the wood, and the Cowichan recently have made knitting needles from it. The Nuxalk considered this shrub highly poisonous and, along with the Coast Salish and Kwakwaka'wakw, used a tea made from a stick with the outer bark peeled off as an emetic or purgative. These three groups also used a medicine from ninebark as a laxative. The Nuxalk used medicinal preparations from ninebark for gonorrhea and scrofulous sores on the neck. • This species is called ninebark because it was believed there are nine layers of shreddy bark on the stems. Greek *physa* ('bellows' or 'bladder') and *carpos* ('fruit') form the genus name, because of the inflated follicles.

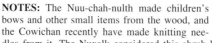

BALDHIP ROSE • *Rosa gymnocarpa*
DWARF ROSE

GENERAL: Spindly, to 1.5 m tall, **usually with numerous soft, straight prickles**, sometimes unarmed especially on younger stems, which are usually covered with stalked glands (use hand lens).

LEAVES: Alternate, deciduous, compound with an odd number (**5–9**) of **toothed leaflets**; leaflets 1–4 cm long.

FLOWERS: Pale-pink to rose, small (1–2 cm across), 5 petals, numerous stamens; usually borne **singly** at the end of branches.

FRUITS: Orange to scarlet, pear-shaped 'hips,' 6–10 mm across, **without attached sepal lobes**; 'seeds' are bony, hairy achenes.

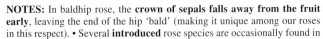

ECOLOGY: In a variety of habitats, from open to wooded, dry to moist; at low to middle elevations.

NOTES: In baldhip rose, the **crown of sepals falls away from the fruit early**, leaving the end of the hip 'bald' (making it unique among our roses in this respect). • Several **introduced** rose species are occasionally found in disturbed sites from southern B.C. south; they can usually be distinguished from our native species by the presence of **curved prickles**. • The spines of this rose were considered poisonous and thought to cause swelling and irritation if touched. A pleasant tea can be made from the young leaves and twigs and was drunk as a tonic. A decoction was also used as an eyewash for sore eyes. The leaves and bark were dried and toasted, and the resulting powder was smoked. Baldhip rose was used for protection for dance initiates, young people at puberty or relatives of the deceased. • Baldhip rose hybridizes occasionally with *Rosa acicularis* and perhaps with *R. nutkana*. • Hips of several rose species were eaten sparingly when ripe by many northwest coast groups, including the Cowichan, Saanich, Ditidaht, Nuu-chah-nulth and Makah. The outer rind of the fruit only was eaten, because the seeds contain hairs that are irritating to the digestive tract, and are said to give one 'an itchy bottom.' The hips were often considered a famine food.

NOOTKA ROSE • *Rosa nutkana*

GENERAL: Spindly, to 3 m tall, with a pair of large prickles at the base of each leaf, other prickles usually absent except on some new growth.

LEAVES: Alternate, deciduous, compound with an odd number (**5–7**) of **toothed leaflets**; leaflets elliptic, 1–7 cm long, with more or less rounded tips.

FLOWERS: Pink, large (4–8 cm across); typically borne singly at the branch tips.

FRUITS: Purplish-red, round 'hips,' 1–2 cm across, with numerous bony, hairy achenes.

ECOLOGY: In a variety of generally open habitats (shorelines, meadows, thickets, streamside areas, roadsides, clearings), at low to middle elevations.

NOTES: Another coastal rose that has paired prickles immediately below where leaves attach to the stems is **clustered wild rose** (*Rosa pisocarpa*). This species, found in wet places from Vancouver Island and the lower Fraser Valley south to California, has **several clustered flowers** (vs. solitary flowers in *R. nutkana*), smaller flowers (usually **less than 4 cm** across), and **sharp-pointed** leaflets. • Branches of all species of wild rose—along with skunk cabbage leaves, fern fronds, pine needles, or salal—were sometimes put in steaming pits, cooking baskets and root-storage pits. Cedar-root cooking baskets used for boiling foods often had rose leaves placed under and over food to flavour it and protect it from burning. • In the spring, the tender young shoots were sometimes eaten. The branches or strips of bark were boiled to make a tea used as an eyewash for cataracts or to enhance eyesight. The Makah mashed the leaves as a poultice for sore eyes and any type of abscess. The chewed leaves were applied to bee stings, and the ripe hips were steeped, mashed and fed to babies with diarrhea.

Key to *Rubus* (The Raspberry Clan)

1a. Plants unarmed
    2a. Stems erect, woody, rarely less than 50 cm tall
        3a. Petals red; leaves compound with 3 leaflets .... *R. spectabilis*
        3b. Petals white; leaves with palmate lobes like maple leaves .... *R. parviflorus*
    2b. Stems mostly trailing, seldom if ever as much as 50 cm tall
        4a. Plant either male or female, not both; leaves broadly heart-
        to kidney-shaped, shallowly lobed; flowers solitary on erect,
        leafy branches .... *R. chamaemorus* (see *R. pedatus*)
        4b. Flowers bisexual; leaves compound (except in *R. lasiococcus* and some *R.*
        arcticus)
            5a. Petals more or less reddish, 10–16 mm long; plants
            without runners .... *R. arcticus* (see *R. pedatus*)
            5b. Petals white, most less than 8 mm long; plants usually
            with runners
                6a. 5 leaflets, sometimes only 3, but lower pair divided
                nearly to base .... *R. pedatus*
                6b. Leaves not divided into leaflets, merely
                deeply lobed .... *R. lasiococcus*
1b. Plants armed with bristle-like or broad-based, often hooked prickles
    7a. Leaves (at least in part) simple and heart-shaped, evergreen;
    stipules narrowly egg-shaped, slenderly pointed; stems trailing;
    petals pink or purple .... *R. nivalis* (see *R. lasiococcus*)
    7b. Leaves nearly always compound, mostly deciduous; stipules
    various but usually slender or joined to the leaf stalks; petals mostly white
        8a. Base of the fruit fleshy, forming part of the (blackberry-like)
        ripe fruit; stems mainly trailing or clambering; plants strongly
        prickled, at least some of the prickles flattened or hooked; petals
        white or pale pink
            9a. Plants mostly with separate male and female flowers,
            female flowers with distinct rudimentary stamens, the
            male with small, non-functional ovaries; stems slender,
            trailing, armed with slender, scarcely flattened prickles;
            leaves usually with 3 leaflets, sometimes simple,
            deciduous .... *R. ursinus*
            9b. Plants with bisexual flowers; stems thick, clambering to
            erect, armed with large often flattened prickles; leaves various
                 10a. Leaves evergreen; the 5 leaflets deeply
                incised .... *R. laciniatus (see R. discolor)*
                10b. Leaves deciduous or more or less evergreen;
                the 3–5 leaflets merely toothed .... *R. discolor*
        8b. Base of the fruit dry or only slightly fleshy, usually not
        forming part of the ripened (raspberry-like) fruit; or, if fruit
        base partly succulent the petals deep pink; stems mainly
        erect or arching, rarely trailing; the prickles (except in
        R. leucodermis) neither flattened nor hooked
            11a. Petals pink to red, usually well over 1.5 cm long;
            fruit salmon-coloured to red; stems erect, not vine-like,
            often armed only (or chiefly) near the base;
            leaves not prickly .... *R. spectabilis*
            11b. Petals white, usually less than 1.5 cm long; fruit often
            red or black; leaves frequently prickly on the back
                 12a. Fruit dark reddish-blue to black; main
                prickles flattened and hooked .... *R. leucodermis*
                12b. Fruit red, occasionally yellowish; main prickles
                neither flattened nor hooked .... *R. idaeus* (see *R. leucodermis*)

SALMONBERRY • *Rubus spectabilis*

GENERAL: Erect, **largely unarmed**, branching, to 4 m tall, from branching rhizomes, often forming dense thickets; twigs **zigzag**, hairless, with **scattered prickles**; bark **golden-brown, shredding.**

LEAVES: Alternate, deciduous, usually with **3 leaflets**, dark-green, **sharply toothed.**

FLOWERS: Pink to red to reddish-purple (an unusual colour, perhaps closest to magenta), large (**about 4 cm across**); 1–2 or occasionally up to 4, on short branches.

FRUITS: Yellow or reddish, mushy raspberries; edible, but reviews range from 'insipid' to 'one of the best.'

ECOLOGY: Moist to wet places (forests, disturbed sites), often abundant along stream edges, avalanche tracks and in wet logged areas; at low to subalpine elevations.

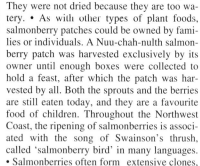

NOTES: Both sprouts and berries were eaten by all northwest coast peoples. The young stem sprouts were gathered in early spring through early summer as a green vegetable by many groups. The sprouts were peeled and eaten raw, having a sweet and juicy flavour. They were also sometimes steamed. Some groups mixed the berries in oolichan grease or dried salmon spawn, and the berries were often eaten with salmon. Salmonberries are one of the earliest berries to ripen (May–June) in our region. They were not dried because they are too watery. • As with other types of plant foods, salmonberry patches could be owned by families or individuals. A Nuu-chah-nulth salmonberry patch was harvested exclusively by its owner until enough boxes were collected to hold a feast, after which the patch was harvested by all. Both the sprouts and the berries are still eaten today, and they are a favourite food of children. Throughout the Northwest Coast, the ripening of salmonberries is associated with the song of Swainson's thrush, called 'salmonberry bird' in many languages. • Salmonberries often form extensive clones, some of which have tastier berries than others, so on berry-picking expeditions tell your group to fan out. And do not be put off by the fact that most guides list it as 'insipid'; some people really like it. It does tend to be mushy, however, and it is definitely mushier after heavy rains. (NB: do not pile salmonberries more than 5 cm deep in a pail or you will end up with mush.)

BLACK RASPBERRY • *Rubus leucodermis*
BLACKCAP

GENERAL: Erect, arching (some branches arch back to the ground), to 2 m tall; stems covered with a whitish bloom, armed with **curved, flattened prickles**.

LEAVES: Alternate, deciduous, crinkly, **3 (occasionally 5) egg-shaped, sharp-toothed leaflets** with shiny white undersides.

FLOWERS: White to pink, small (2–3 cm across); in clusters of 3–7, terminal or in leaf axils.

FRUITS: Hairy raspberries, about 1 cm across, **initially red but becoming purple to black**; edible and good.

ECOLOGY: Disturbed sites (especially burned clearcuts), thickets and open forests; common and often locally abundant, at low to middle elevations.

NOTES: **Red raspberry** (*Rubus idaeus*) is a very similar species with **red** fruits, which occurs occasionally within our range; it is the common species **east** of the Coast and Cascade Mountains. Its berries were eaten by the Nuxalk, Tsimshian and possibly the Northern Kwakwaka'wakw, as well as by indigenous interior peoples of Washington, Alaska and B.C. They were eaten fresh, or boiled and dried into cakes. • Black raspberries, along with the fruits of salal, black twinberry and wild raspberry, were mashed and used as a purple stain by the Coast Salish. In spring, the young shoots were sometimes peeled and eaten raw or cooked, but they were rarely stored. The berries were eaten fresh and dried into cakes by the Straits Salish, Halq'emeylem, Squamish, Sechelt, Comox, Kwakwaka'wakw and Nuxalk. They were eaten with dried meat or fish, or they were boiled and eaten as a dessert, often mixed with other berries. An infusion made from the roots was ingested for influenza. • In the 16th century, raspberries were called *rasps*, *raspis* or *raspises*. The name may come from the 15th-century word *raspis* (a fruit from which a drink could be made).

THIMBLEBERRY • *Rubus parviflorus*

GENERAL: Erect, **unarmed**, 0.5–3 m tall; young growth glandular-hairy; bark shredding; usually forming dense thickets through an extensive network of rhizomes.

LEAVES: Alternate, deciduous, large (**to 25 cm** across), soft, **maple-leaf shaped, 3–7 lobed**, toothed, with long glandular stalks, **finely fuzzy on both sides**.

FLOWERS: White, large (to 4 cm across), petals crinkled like tissue paper; several (3–11) in long-stemmed terminal cluster.

FRUITS: Shallowly domed, **raspberry-like** clusters of **red**, hairy drupelets; juicy, insipid to sweet depending on growing site and personal taste.

ECOLOGY: Open sites (e.g., clearings, road edges, shorelines, avalanche tracks) or open (especially red alder) forest; low elevations in the north, low to subalpine elevations in the south.

NOTES: Thimbleberries were eaten by all Northwest Coast people. The Nuu-chah-nulth were known to collect shoots in bulk. Young shoots were eaten raw (see *R. spectabilis*, p.76) • The berries are coarse and seedy, lending themselves to drying. The Nuu-chah-nulth dried the berries with smoked clams. The Kwakwaka'wakw collected thimbleberries when they were hard and pink and stored them until ripe in cedar-bark bags. They were then de-stemmed and eaten fresh, or dried the same way as salal berries. The Nuxalk considered thimbleberries to be inferior to raspberries and blackcaps, and usually mixed these three berries together when dried in cakes. The broad, maple-like leaves can be fashioned easily into makeshift berry containers.

HIMALAYAN BLACKBERRY • *Rubus discolor*

GENERAL: Erect to sprawling; stout stems **erect, then arching, then trailing** along the ground (to 10 m long) and rooting at the ends, often distinctly four-angled, armed with **stout, recurved prickles**; often forming dense, impenetrable thickets.

LEAVES: Alternate, **more or less evergreen** (some deciduous), **trifoliate** (on floral shoots) **to 5-foliate** (on vegetative shoots), 12–25 cm wide; leaflets toothed, oval, smooth-green above, covered with **white hairs below**.

FLOWERS: White to pinkish, 2–3 cm across, 5 petals; many stamens; in clusters of 5–20.

FRUITS: Blackberries 1–1.5 cm thick; edible.

ECOLOGY: An Asian species **introduced** from India via England and **widely naturalized**, in disturbed sites and streamside areas, at low elevations.

NOTES: Himalayan blackberry is also known as *R. procerus*. • Another introduced (in this case European) blackberry commonly found in disturbed sites is **evergreen blackberry** (*Rubus laciniatus*). It differs from the Himalayan blackberry primarily in leaf characteristics: the **usual 5 leaflets** of evergreen blackberry are **deeply incised and jaggedly toothed** (see silhouettes, p. 75), hairy but still **greenish on the undersurface**, and, of course, evergreen. Its range is similar to that of the Himalayan blackberry. • Himalayan blackberry is the most common introduced blackberry in our area, a favourite with berry-pickers and a staple of local blackberry festivals throughout the Pacific Northwest. • Regardless of colour, look at the way the fruits come off the plant: if they are 'hollow,' they are raspberries, and if they are solid (i.e., with a 'central core'), they are blackberries. Either way, they are likely delicious.

TRAILING BLACKBERRY • *Rubus ursinus*
DEWBERRY

GENERAL: Prostrate, **trailing**, to 5 m or more long, armed with slender, **curved, unflattened prickles**; floral canes (produced in the second year) erect, to 50 cm tall.

LEAVES: Alternate, **deciduous**, with **3 leaflets** 3–7 cm long, the terminal leaflet 3-lobed, dark-green, toothed.

FLOWERS: White or pink, large (to 4 cm across); in flat-topped purplish-hued clusters from the leaf axils; male and female flowers on separate plants.

FRUITS: Black blackberries to 1 cm long; edible and delicious.

ECOLOGY: Common and often abundant on disturbed sites, thickets and dry, open forest at low to middle elevations; behaves as a weed in some suburban and rural areas.

NOTES: The Stl'atl'imx and some Coast Salish have an origin myth for trailing blackberry. A woman was chased up a tree by a jealous husband. The blood of the woman fell from the tree and became blackberry. • A purification rite of the Coast Salish was to scrub the stems across a person's body before spirit dancing. • A tea was made with the dried leaves, which were thought to be best collected in the fall when they turn red. The leaves and roots were used to treat diarrhea, dysentery, cholera, excessive menstruation, fevers, haemorrhoids and sores in the mouth. The leaves were added to bitter medicines to sweeten the flavour. • The berries were widely used by northwest coast peoples as food. The fresh berries were harvested in July and eaten immediately or dried for winter storage. • Because the male and female plants are separate and individuals tend to spread so widely, it is not uncommon to find large patches of male bushes without any fruit. • Trailing blackberry is a commonly (and often unpleasantly) encountered blackberry. Its 'clinging' tendencies are more than compensated for by its excellent late summer fruit. Trailing blackberry is our only native blackberry.

DWARF BRAMBLE • *Rubus lasiococcus*

GENERAL: Low, to 10 cm tall, **without prickles**, the **trailing** (to 2 m long) stems rooting at the nodes.

LEAVES: Alternate, 1–3 in clusters at the nodes, **deciduous** (some persisting over winter), **3-lobed but not divided into leaflets**, toothed, 2–6 cm wide.

FLOWERS: White, small (to 1.5 cm across); 1 or 2 on long stalks.

FRUITS: Red, small (less than 1 cm across), very hairy **raspberries**.

ECOLOGY: Forests and open places (thickets, clearings, logged areas) at middle to high elevations.

NOTES: While in the mountains, also look for **snow bramble or dewberry** (*R. nivalis*), a trailing, low shrub with unlobed or 3-lobed leaves. Snow bramble has **small prickles** on its stems and **evergreen** leaves, **pink to purple** flowers, and a **red blackberry**. Its range is similar to that of *R. lasiococcus*, though it can be found on southern Vancouver Island, and reaches its southern range limit in Oregon. It is much less common, though, and tends to occur at lower elevations, and on moister sites, than *R. lasiococcus*. • Dwarf bramble is a very common understorey species in high elevation forests of the Cascade Mountains. Five-leaved bramble plays a similar role in forests farther north and occurs with dwarf bramble on wetter sites in the Cascades. Dwarf bramble has deeper roots than five-leaved bramble, which probably accounts for its ability to grow on drier sites. • 'At their best, these berries miniaturize the essence of raspberry flavour as perfectly as wild strawberries do the essence of strawberry' (Mathews 1988).

FIVE-LEAVED BRAMBLE • *Rubus pedatus*
CREEPING RASPBERRY

GENERAL: Unarmed perennial with **creeping stems (runners)**; roots at the nodes and produces short (2 cm or less), erect stems bearing 1–3 leaves.

LEAVES: Alternate, **deciduous** (some persisting through the winter), usually **divided into 5 leaflets** or oval lobes, coarsely toothed.

FLOWERS: White, small (1–2 cm across), the petals spread or bend backwards; solitary on very slender stalks.

FRUITS: Small clusters (raspberries) of bright **red** drupelets, sometimes with just one drupelet per fruit; juicy and flavourful.

ECOLOGY: Moist, mossy forest, glades, streambanks, bog forest; low to subalpine elevations.

NOTES: The Haida mixed five-leaved bramble with bog cranberries to be dried, but the raspberries required much cooking. Most coastal groups did not collect these berries because they were small, soft, and difficult to gather in large quantities. • Five-leaved bramble is commonly associated with old-growth forests. • The name 'bramble' is from the Old English *braembel*, from *brom* meaning 'wiry or thorny shrub.' The name originally referred to the blackberry *R. fruticosus*. *R. pedatus* is a strange 'bramble,' since brambles are almost always prickly. The species name *pedatus* means 'foot' and suggests, perhaps, that the 5 leaflets look like 5-toed prints in the moss.

DWARF NAGOONBERRY • *Rubus arcticus*

GENERAL: Unarmed perennial, from extensively creeping rhizomes; flowering stems erect, several, up to 10 cm tall, finely hairy.

LEAVES: Round to heart-shaped in outline, compound **with 3 leaflets** (ssp. *acaulis*, as pictured here) **or 3-lobed to nearly entire** (ssp. *stellatus*); leaflets rounded and coarsely toothed, more or less hairy.

FLOWERS: Pink to reddish-pink, showy, 2–3 cm across; usually solitary, terminal.

FRUITS: Clusters of several **red** fleshy drupelets; small raspberries about 1 cm across.

ECOLOGY: Low-elevation bogs, and wet meadows and thickets at subalpine and alpine elevations.

NOTES: This species is also known as *Rubus acaulis* or *R. stellatus*, in part. • The berries were eaten fresh by indigenous peoples of Alaska and central B.C. In Alaska, they were often mixed with cloudberries. The berries have an excellent flavour and can be eaten raw or made into jams or jellies or used for flavouring liquor. • *Rubus* means 'red' and refers to the colour of the fruits of many species. The origin of the common name 'nagoonberry' remains a mystery.

CLOUDBERRY • *Rubus chamaemorus*

GENERAL: Unarmed perennial with extensively creeping rhizomes; flowering stems erect, unbranched, up to 20 cm tall.

LEAVES: Not divided into leaflets, 1–3 per stem, round to kidney-shaped, **more or less 5-lobed**, somewhat leathery, coarsely saw-toothed.

FLOWERS: White, with spreading petals, 1–2.5 cm across; solitary, terminal, male and female flowers on separate plants.

FRUITS: Raspberry-like collections of drupelets, **at first reddish, then amber to yellow** when mature; edible, with baked-apple taste.

ECOLOGY: Low-elevation bogs.

NOTES: The berries were a staple food for peoples of the northern Northwest Coast, including the Dena'ina, Tlingit, Haida, and Coast Tsimshian. The Haida and Tsimshian picked the berries in mid-summer, when they were still hard, and stored them under water and grease in bentwood cedar boxes. Sometimes they were scalded briefly before storage. Haida people say the fruiting plants have become scarce on Haida Gwaii (the Queen Charlotte Islands) since deer were introduced. The berries are also used for food in Siberia and Scandinavia, and by the Inuit and other indigenous peoples of northern Canada and Alaska. • Cloudberry plants are either male or female, but not both. Female plants have flowers with dwarf male parts; male plants have flowers with dwarf female parts. • 'Cloudberry' comes from the Old English *clud* meaning 'rocky hill.' In the 16th century it was called 'knottberry' from the English *knot* ('rocky hill') or the Norse *knott*. According to folk tales it grew on the top of two of the highest mountains in all England, where the clouds are lower than the mountain tops all winter long.

HARDHACK • *Spiraea douglasii* ssp. *douglasii*
STEEPLEBUSH

GENERAL: Erect, leggy, much-branched, to 2 m tall; young growth reddish-brown, woolly; often forming thickets.

LEAVES: Alternate, deciduous, oblong to oval, 4–10 cm long, **toothed above the middle**, dark green above, **paler and often grey-woolly beneath**.

FLOWERS: Pink to deep rose, tiny (about 5 mm across); numerous, in a long, narrow, compact terminal cluster **several times longer than wide**.

FRUITS: Cluster of several small, smooth, **pod-like follicles**; remain on the shrub after the leaves have fallen.

ECOLOGY: Streambanks, swamps, fens, lake margins and damp meadows. Low to middle elevations.

NOTES: Hardhack was formerly known as *S. menziesii*. • **Subalpine spirea** (*S. densiflora*: inset photo) is a smaller shrub (to 70 cm tall) with **flat-topped** clusters of **pink** flowers. It grows in moist thickets, meadows, and on streambanks and open rocky slopes, at middle to subalpine elevations from southwestern B.C. south. • **Steven's spirea** (*S. stevenii*, also known as *S. beauverdiana*) has **white** flowers and **teeth almost to the base** of its leaves. It occurs on organic soils, from lowlands to alpine from Lynn Canal to Prince William Sound. • The wiry, branching twigs were used by the Nuu-chah-nulth to make broom-like implements for collecting tubular marine dentalia shells. Dentalia shells were traded as far as the Great Plains and were a form of currency among the northwest coast peoples.

SWEET GALE • *Myrica gale*

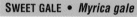

GENERAL: Aromatic wetland shrubs **to 1.5 m tall**, spread by suckers; stems slender, dark reddish, loosely branched.

LEAVES: Alternate, **deciduous**, lance-shaped but not sharply pointed, **coarsely few-toothed on the upper third**, 2–6 cm long, **dotted above and below** with **bright-yellow wax-glands**, whitish underneath.

FLOWERS: Male and female flowers borne on separate plants, in greenish-yellow, waxy **catkins** (male catkins to 2 cm long, female to 1 cm); appear before the leaves.

FRUITS: Tiny, greenish, winged nutlets about 3 mm long, in **brown, cone-like spikes**; wax glands may be evident; cones stay on through winter.

ECOLOGY: Wetlands (bogs, fens, swamps, upper fringes of salt marshes, lake margins); mostly at low elevations.

NOTES: **California wax-myrtle** (*Myrica californica*) is a larger shrub or small tree, **2–6 m** tall. Its **evergreen** leaves (5–8 cm long) have **black dots** on them (vs. yellow dots on the deciduous leaves of *M. gale*). *M. californica* can be found near the coast from Gray's Harbour, Washington, to southern California, with an isolated population between Tofino and Ucluelet on the west coast of Vancouver Island. • Sweet gale is an important nitrogen-fixing species. It is often found in the same wetlands as hardhack and, as Lyons (1952) notes, 'often loses its identity with the showier shrub.' • This plant is apparently called 'monkey bush' in Stl'atl'imx, probably because it was used for some purpose by sasquatches.

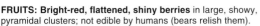

DEVIL'S CLUB • *Oplopanax horridus*

GENERAL: Erect to sprawling, 1–3 m tall; stems thick, crooked, almost unbranched but often entangled, armed with numerous, large, **yellowish spines** up to 1 cm long; wood has a sweetish odour.

LEAVES: Alternate, deciduous, large (to 35 cm across), **maple-leaf shaped**, with 7–9 sharply pointed and heavily toothed lobes; numerous **spines on underside**.

FLOWERS: Small, whitish; numerous in compact heads arranged in **pyramidal** terminal clusters.

FRUITS: Bright-red, flattened, shiny berries in large, showy, pyramidal clusters; not edible by humans (bears relish them).

ECOLOGY: Moist woods, especially in wet but well-drained seepage sites and along streams, also in avalanche tracks; low to middle elevations (sometimes in subalpine forest, and to timberline in the north).

NOTES: This spiny shrub, related to ginseng, is still highly important as a medicine and protective agent for aboriginal peoples throughout its range. At least on the B.C. coast, it is one of the most important of all medicinal plants. The roots, and especially the greenish inner bark, were the major parts used for medicine. Numerous ailments, including arthritis, ulcers and digestive tract ailments and diabetes, were treated with devil's club. • Possibly because of its diabolical spines, it is considered a highly powerful plant that can protect one against evil influences of many kinds. Devil's club sticks are used as protective charms, and charcoal from burned devil's club is used to make a protective face paint for dancers and others who are ritually vulnerable to evil influences. • The light-coloured, lightweight wood was used for making fishing lures. The Washington Klallam and Vancouver Island Nuu-chah-nulth made fish lures by peeling devil's-club sticks and cutting them into small pieces. The Manhousat Nootka carved small fish out of devil's-club sticks which would be tied near fishhooks and reeled in to snag the fish. The Ditidaht made two types of lures using devil's-club wood: one for attracting codfish to the surface where they could be speared, and another with a hook which was attached to a line and used mainly for black bass. Devil's-club stems were used by the Haida to hook octopus and black cod. • The Hesquiat scraped the spines off the bark and boiled it in water with different berries (*Vaccinium* and *Lonicera* spp.) to make a paint and basket dye. Straits Salish and the Ditidaht combined devil's-club charcoal with bear grease for ceremonial face-painting and for inserting under the skin for a blue tattoo. A black dye was made by the Dena'ina by burning devil's club and mixing the ashes with water. • The root and stem were used by the Nuxalk as a cleansing emetic and purgative, and in steam baths for rheumatism and stomach trouble. A medicine for arthritis or rheumatism used by the Ditidaht, Coast Salish and the Cowlitz was made from several pieces of stem (after scraping off the spines) infused in water and drunk exclusively for several days. Cowlitz dried the bark and pulverized it for a perfume or baby talc, and made an infusion drunk for colds and applied topically for rheumatism. The Cowichan, Sechelt and Squamish used devil's club in hot baths and as a poultice for rheumatism and pain. Lushootseed steeped the stems and drank the tea for colds, and pulverized the bark for use as a deodorant. The Skagit steeped the root and bark of devil's club with prince's pine and cascara and drank the tea for tuberculosis and to re-establish regular menstruation after childbirth. The Lummi applied the dethorned bark to a woman's breast to stop the flow of milk. Devil's-club berries were rubbed in the scalp to combat lice and dandruff and to make hair shiny. The inner bark was used to cure rheumatism and tuberculosis of the bone. The Dena'ina boiled the stems and branches and drank the tea to reduce fever. Inner bark of the root was used by the Dena'ina as a medicine for tuberculosis, stomach trouble, coughs, colds and fevers. For swollen glands, boils and other infections the Dena'ina baked and shredded the inner root bark until soft and applied it as a poultice. The Halq'emeylem used devil's club as a medicine for arthritis, and as protection from spirits in the form of a face paint made out of the ashes mixed with grease. The root and stem were used medicinally by southern Vancouver Island Salish for rheumatism and other aches and pains. The Cowichan used bark tea in the treatment of measles and the entire plant along with thistles and black hawthorn to drive away sickness. Tea made from the inner bark is taken by many people today for diabetes.

SCOTCH BROOM • *Cytisus scoparius*

GENERAL: Introduced, **unarmed**, spindly, deciduous, to 3 m tall, the branches green and strongly 5-angled.

LEAVES: Alternate, deciduous, small, with 3 leaflets when near the base of the branches, becoming simple above; pressed close to the branches.

FLOWERS: Bright-yellow, sometimes tinged with purple, typical 'pea'-flower, about 2 cm long; usually single in leaf axils.

FRUITS: Black, flattened pods, **about 4 cm** long; as the pod matures and dries, the two halves tend to warp in different directions, eventually snapping apart audibly and catapulting seeds.

ECOLOGY: Open sites, especially common on disturbed sites (e.g., along roads), but also invading natural meadows, thickets and open forest; at low elevations.

NOTES: Broom is a very widespread and invasive shrub for such a recent immigrant. It was introduced to Vancouver Island in 1850 by Captain Walter Colquhoun Grant (1822-1861), himself a recent immigrant from Scotland, from some seeds he had picked up in the Sandwich Islands (Hawaii) from the British consul, Mr. Wylie. Of the seeds he planted in Sooke, three germinated, and descendants of these three plants have subsequently colonized most of southern Vancouver Island. Broom has been so successful over much of its range that it has endangered much of our region's distinctive rainshadow flora. • Broom seeds have been used as a coffee substitute, and broom flowers have been pickled and used to make wine. However, **extreme caution** is advised: broom contains several **toxic alkaloids** that can depress the heart and nervous system. Children may be poisoned from eating the pods and seeds, which resemble small peas. • 'Broom' is derived from the Anglo-Saxon *brom* meaning 'foliage.' The word was applied to shrubs that were used for making 'besoms,' which are bunches of twigs used as brooms.

GORSE • *Ulex europaeus*

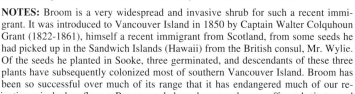

GENERAL: Introduced, **spiny**, deciduous, to 3 m tall; the branches green, strongly angled, **black-hairy**.

LEAVES: Alternate, small with 3 leaflets on young plants, **reduced to spines and scales on older plants**; the spines stiff, branched, furrowed.

FLOWERS: Yellow, typical 'pea'-flower, to 2 cm long, **smelling of coconut (or bruised peaches)**; usually single in leaf axils and concentrated near branch tips.

FRUITS: Black, hairy, flattened pods, about **2 cm long**.

ECOLOGY: Open, often disturbed sites (e.g., along roads, agricultural lands); at low elevations, usually near the ocean.

NOTES: This weedy species is viciously spiny, and it can form impenetrable thickets. It is a European species still expanding its range within our region. Gorse is fairly flammable, creating a potential fire hazard in the drier areas where it is most abundant. • 'Gorse' probably comes from the Anglo-Saxon *gorst* meaning 'a waste,' because of this plant's penchant for rough places. It is also sometimes called 'furze,' which is derived from the Anglo-Saxon *fyrs* ('fire') because it was commonly used for firewood. *Ulex*, the name used by Pliny, is of unknown origin, and *europaeus* means it comes from Europe, to where some wish it would return. • Pea-family plants such as gorse often thrive on nutrient-poor sites because they can fix nitrogen (remove it from the air). This tendency is recognized in a short verse about this Scottish plant:

Bagpipe planty,
Plenty on scanty.

Key to *Ribes* (Gooseberries and Currants)

1a. Stems with spines or prickles (gooseberries)
    2a. Stems covered with small spines, with a few larger spines at nodes; 7–15 flowers in drooping clusters; widespread .... *Ribes lacustre*
    2b. Stems with 1–3 large spines only at nodes (where leaves attach); flowers 4 or fewer per cluster; only in the southern half of the region
        3a. Leaves sticky; flowers bright-red, pendent, look like miniature fuchsias; berries reddish-brown, sticky-hairy .... *R. lobbii* (see *R. lacustre*)
        3b. Leaves not sticky; flowers green or purple; berries purplish-black, smooth .... *R. divaricatum* (see *R. lacustre*)

1b. Stems without spines or prickles (currants)
    4a. Stems, leaves, flowers and fruits covered with sticky hairs .... *R. viscosissimum*
    4b. Plants smooth or hairy, but not sticky except sometimes on the berries
        5a. Stems, leaves, flowers and fruits with yellow crystalline glands ('resin dots'); flowers greenish-white; skunky odour .... *R. bracteosum*
        5b. Plants not sprinkled with yellowish glands; flowers reddish; odours variable, but generally not unpleasant
            6a. Tall (usually taller than 1 m), erect shrubs; flowers pale to deep reddish-pink .... *R. sanguineum*
            6b. Shorter, sprawling to ascending shrubs
                7a. Leaves deeply 5-lobed, lobes sharp-pointed; flowers greenish-white, red or purple; berries purplish-black, bristly with stalked glands .... *R. laxiflorum*
                7b. Leaves 3–5 lobed, lobes rounded
                    8a. Leaves 3-lobed, flowers greenish-white to reddish-purple; berries red, smooth .... *R. triste* (see *R. laxiflorum*)
                    8b. Leaves 3–5 lobed; flowers pinkish; berries blue-black, sparsely glandular-hairy .... *R. howellii* (see *R. laxiflorum*)

RED-FLOWERING CURRANT • *Ribes sanguineum*

GENERAL: Erect, **unarmed, 1–3 m** tall, stems crooked, bark reddish-brown; young growth finely hairy.

LEAVES: Alternate, deciduous, regularly or irregularly **5-lobed**, 2–6 cm broad, lower surface paler and hairier.

FLOWERS: White to (more commonly) a distinctive **rose** colour (varies from **pale-pink to deep-red**), 7–10 mm long; in erect to drooping clusters of 10–20 or more flowers.

FRUITS: **Blue-black** round berries with glandular hairs and a white waxy bloom, 7–9 mm long; unpalatable.

ECOLOGY: Dry open woods, rocky slopes, disturbed sites (e.g., roadsides, clearings); at low to middle elevations.

NOTES: The berries are edible but insipid. They were eaten by various Coast Salish groups such as the Saanich, Cowichan, Squamish, and Sechelt, but they were not highly regarded. They were eaten fresh but not usually collected for drying. • This shrub was introduced to European horticulture by plant-hunter David Douglas. • The name *sanguineum* means 'blood-red' or 'bloody'—rather violent epithets to apply to the beautiful reddish-pink flowers, which are harbingers of spring and hummingbirds.

BLACK GOOSEBERRY • *Ribes lacustre*
BLACK SWAMP GOOSEBERRY

GENERAL: Erect to spreading, 0.5–2 m tall, covered with **numerous, small, golden prickles**, with **larger thick spines at leaf nodes**; bark on older stems cinnamon coloured.

LEAVES: Alternate, deciduous, somewhat maple-leaf shaped, 2–5 cm wide, most with **5 deeply indented lobes** and a heart-shaped base; margins toothed; upper side dark, glossy green, not glandular or hairy.

FLOWERS: Reddish to maroon, small, saucer-shaped, ovary glandular-hairy; in **drooping** clusters of 7–15.

FRUITS: Dark purple berries 6–8 mm long, **bristly** with stalked glands; palatable and with an agreeable but insipid flavour.

ECOLOGY: Moist woods and streambanks to drier forested slopes and subalpine ridges, to the shoreline in the northern half of our region; often on rotting wood.

NOTES: Wild gooseberry (*R. divaricatum*) and gummy goose-berry (*R. lobbii*) differ from black gooseberry in having 4 or fewer flowers in an inflorescence. **Wild gooseberry** has **green or purple** flowers, **1–3 spines only where leaves are attached**, and **smooth** berries. **Gummy gooseberry** is similar, with usually 3 spines per node, but it has **reddish, fuchsia-like** flowers (hummingbird favourites) and **sticky, hairy** berries. Gummy gooseberry is probably best distinguished from black gooseberry by its **sticky ('gummy') leaves** (but if your gummy 'gooseberry' lacks spines, see *R. viscosissimum*). Both *R. divaricatum* and *R. lobbii* range from southern Vancouver Island to northern California, the wild gooseberry at low elevations, the gummy gooseberry at low to middle elevations. • As with the spines of devil's club, the prickles of black gooseberry cause allergenic reactions in some individuals. Like devil's club, the prickly qualities of this shrub were thought to have special protective powers for warding off evil influences, such as those from malevolent snakes, by some groups. • Black gooseberries were eaten by most peoples of the Northwest Coast; the Sechelt, however, considered them to be poisonous. The berries were eaten fresh when ripe, but they were not collected in quantity for storage because of their small size.

STICKY CURRANT • *Ribes viscosissimum*

GENERAL: Erect to spreading, straggly, **unarmed**, 1–2 m tall, **covered with soft, sticky hairs**; bark reddish-brown and shredding with age.

LEAVES: Alternate, deciduous, **3- to 5-lobed**, toothed, 2–6 cm wide, covered with **soft, sticky hairs on both surfaces**.

FLOWERS: Greenish-white to pinkish, 6–7 mm long, bell-shaped; in erect to **drooping** clusters of 6–12.

FRUITS: Blue-black, round, **very sticky** berries; not edible.

ECOLOGY: On a variety of open and forested, moist to dry sites at middle to subalpine elevations.

NOTES: Sticky currant grows in the Cascades from southern B.C. to northern California, but not in the Olympics. • This is certainly the stickiest of our currants. The Latin *viscosus* means 'sticky' or 'viscid' and refers here to the glandular hairs that secrete a sticky gum and grow all over the plant, including the fruits. This species gives off a strong 'chemical' odour on hot, sunny days. • White pine blister rust (*Cronartium ribicola*), the fungus that kills western white pine and other 5-needle pines (such as whitebark pine), needs *Ribes* for part of its lifecycle, as the so-called 'alternate host.' • The word 'currant' refers to Corinth, home of *Uva corinthiaca*, a small grape from which we get baking currants.

STINK CURRANT • *Ribes bracteosum*

GENERAL: More or less erect, **unarmed**, to 3 m tall, all parts with round, **yellow glands**; smelling sweet-skunky or catty.

LEAVES: Alternate, deciduous, large (5–20 cm broad), maple-leaf-shaped, d**eeply 5- to 7-lobed, with yellow glands**, stinky when crushed.

FLOWERS: White to greenish-white; many (20–40) in **long erect clusters 15–30 cm** long.

FRUITS: Blue-black berries with a **whitish bloom**, in long (15–30 cm) clusters; edible, taste variable, from unpleasant to delicious.

ECOLOGY: Moist to wet places (e.g., woods, stream-banks, floodplains, shorelines, thickets, avalanche tracks) at low to subalpine elevations.

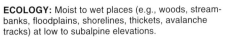

NOTES: The long clusters of flowers and fruit are distinctive; most currants and gooseberries sport just a few flowers or berries in a small clump. Note that while the crushed leaves of stink currant smell 'skunky,' all crushed leaves of *Ribes* spp. have strong smells—usually like currants. • A smaller, greenish-white-flowered, black-fruited currant is the **sticky currant** (p. 85), easily distinguished from stink currant by its **sticky leaves, branches and fruit**. • These berries have a bland flavour, but they are not unpleasant. They were widely used by northwest coast peoples. They were highly valued and collected in large quantity by some groups such as the Haida (who call them 'greyberry') and Nuxalk. They were harvested in August and September. When eaten fresh, they were consumed with grease or oil; some groups said this addition was to avoid constipation or stomach cramps.

TRAILING BLACK CURRANT • *Ribes laxiflorum*

GENERAL: Unarmed, trailing or spreading with branches running along the ground, usually less than 1 m tall, but **sometimes (in Oregon and Washington) vine-like and climbing** 5–7 m.

LEAVES: Alternate, deciduous, maple-leaf shaped, usually with **5 sharp, pointed lobes** and a heart-shaped base, 4–10 cm wide; margins toothed; smooth on top, hairy and glandular beneath; strong odour when bruised.

FLOWERS: Greenish-white to reddish-purple, saucer-shaped; glandular-hairy ovaries, flower stalks jointed and glandular-hairy, sepals 2.5–4 mm long, hairy on back, petals as wide as long; several (6–20) in **ascending to erect** clusters.

FRUITS: Purplish-black berries, with a waxy bloom and stalked **glandular hairs**, to 1 cm across; disagreeable odour and flavour.

ECOLOGY: Moist forest, avalanche tracks, clearings, roadsides; low to middle elevations.

NOTES: Two other small, red-flowered currants found on the coast are **red swamp currant** (*R. triste*), a wet forest and thicket species with **red berries and 3-lobed leaves**; and **maple-leaved currant** (*R. howellii*, also known as *R. acerifolium*), with **blue-black berries and leaves with 3–5 lobes**, most common in moist openings at high elevations. *R. howellii* occurs from the southern B.C. mainland south in the Cascades and Olympics to Oregon; *R. triste* occurs from Juneau north to Lynn Canal and scattered to Prince William Sound in Alaska, and also in the Cascades to northern Oregon. The berries of trailing black currant were used by several aboriginal groups from Alaska to Washington.

ARCTIC WILLOW • *Salix arctica*

GENERAL: Dwarf to somewhat erect, **usually prostrate or trailing** but sometimes up to 50 cm tall; branches stout, brown; twigs smooth or slightly hairy.

LEAVES: Alternate, deciduous, greyish-green, **with a whitish bloom and sparsely hairy beneath; broadly oval, 2–8 cm long**; tip blunt or pointed; **margins not toothed**; stalks 4–12 mm long; stipules, if present, tiny.

FLOWERS: Ovaries hairy; styles red in life; floral bracts dark to blackish; catkins appearing with the leaves, on leafy shoots, males to 5 cm long, females to 9 cm long.

FRUITS: Sparsely hairy capsules; styles 0.6–2.2 mm long; stalks 0.6 mm long or less; seeds very small, fluffy.

female   male

ECOLOGY: Alpine tundra to open subalpine ridges on various substrates and moisture regimes.

NOTES: Three other 'dwarf willows' commonly occur in our coastal mountains. **Cascade willow** (*S. cascadensis*) has smaller (**to 2.5 cm long**) **lance-shaped** leaves; it occurs from Pemberton south in the Cascades to Mount Rainier. **Netted willow** (*S. reticulata*) has **strongly veined**, dark green leaves that are **nearly round**, sometimes with long silky hairs beneath, and occurs from northern southeast Alaska to Yakutat and from B.C. south to California; plants south of the Queen Charlotte Islands are usually referred to as **'snow willow'** (*S. reticulata* ssp. *nivalis* or *S. nivalis*), recognized by their **fewer-flowered catkins** (2–22 flowers/catkin vs. 20–50 in ssp. *reticulata*) and by their lack of long, silky hairs on the leaf undersurfaces. **Creeping willow** (*S. stolonifera*) is perhaps most similar to arctic willow, but it has **hairless capsules** and smaller leaves (**to 2.5 cm long**) that are dark green above; it is found in Alaska and adjacent B.C. All four dwarf willows probably interbreed where their ranges overlap. • Dwarf willows, especially *S. reticulata*, are planted as ground cover in rock gardens.

VARIABLE WILLOW • *Salix commutata*
UNDERGREEN WILLOW

GENERAL: Spreading, much branched, 0.2–2 m tall; branches dark brown, sometimes remaining hairy; **twigs densely woolly.**

LEAVES: Alternate, deciduous, rounded at base, broadly oval but pointed at the tip, 4–8 cm long, margins **smooth to finely toothed**; young leaves densely hairy, **older leaves remaining somewhat hairy on both sides**; stalks 2–7 mm long; stipules leafy, to 1 cm long.

FLOWERS: Ovaries hairless, **reddish**; in catkins, appear with the leaves or after they have expanded, on leafy shoots, males to 3 cm long, females to 6 cm long.

FRUITS: Hairless capsules, brownish; styles 0.5–1 mm long; stalks 0.3–1.5 mm long.

female male

ECOLOGY: Riverside, wetland and high-elevation thickets, lakeshores, gravelly benches, fresh alluvial and morainal materials, open forests; scattered at low (in Alaska) to alpine elevations.

NOTES: Variable willow is a late-flowering species with **non-glaucous** leaves (clothed with **distinctive straggly hairs**), short leaf stalks and reddish ovaries. • **Barclay's willow** (*S. barclayi*) is a similar shrub, most easily distinguished by its twigs, which are **yellowish-green** under their hairy coats, and by its **saw-toothed leaves**, which usually develop a **whitish bloom** underneath with age. It can be found from northern southeast Alaska west to Prince William Sound and south to Mt. Adams, Washington, in the same sort of habitats as variable willow. • Twigs of Barclay's willow often end in rounded galls ('willow roses'), composed of deformed leaves and caused by insects. • If you are unsure about whether your specimen is variable willow or Barclay's willow, it may be because it is a hybrid with some characteristics of both. • In Alaska, variable willow often grows on recently exposed glacial till behind receding glaciers.

HOOKER'S WILLOW • *Salix hookeriana*

GENERAL: Large shrub or small tree to 6 m tall; **twigs stout, grey-hairy**.

LEAVES: Alternate, deciduous, **oval to egg-shaped**, pointed or rounded at the tip, 4–12 cm long, 2–6 cm wide, usually without teeth, **very hairy** when young, the top sometimes becoming nearly smooth; stalks 0.5–2 cm long; stipules small and deciduous early in the season.

FLOWERS: Bracts to 5 mm long, **dark brown to black**, very hairy; catkins **stout and very hairy, appearing before the leaves**, stalkless on short leafy branches, males to 4 cm long, females to 12 cm long.

FRUITS: Capsules to 8 mm long, **smooth to somewhat hairy**; stalks to 3 mm long but usually much shorter; styles 1–2 mm long.

ECOLOGY: Wet places, often on the edge of standing water, sometimes on sandy beaches or dunes; low elevations.

female

NOTES: The **hairy, egg-shaped leaves** help to identify this species. • The Straits Salish and the Halq'emeylem peeled the bark of this and other willow species in May or June, removed the outer part, split the inner tissue into thin strands, and twisted these into long ropes. This rope was used to make fishing lines and various types of nets, including gill-nets, reef-nets, purse-nets, bag-nets, and duck-nets. The bark was used to 'shingle' baskets. The Snohomish and Quinault made tumplines, slings and harpoon lines from the bark of this willow. The Quileute used the branches of young trees as poles for fish weirs because they were said to take root wherever they were 'planted' in the river.

PACIFIC WILLOW • *Salix lucida* ssp. *lasiandra*

GENERAL: Tall, slender shrub or tree, to 12 m tall; branches brown, glabrous; **twigs glossy, with yellow, duckbill-shaped buds**, usually hairless, **brittle at base**; bark fissured, yellowish-brown on older trees.

LEAVES: Alternate, deciduous, **lance-shaped, tapering to a long tip**, 5–15 cm long, **margins finely toothed**, young leaves reddish and densely hairy with white and rust-coloured hairs, older leaves **not hairy, with a whitish bloom beneath**; stalk 3–15 mm long, **with glands** where attached to the leaf; **stipules prominent**, kidney-shaped, also **glandular**.

FLOWERS: Bracts **pale yellow**, hairy, deciduous after flowering; catkins **appear with the leaves**, on long, leafy shoots, the males to 7 cm long, the females to 12 cm long.

FRUITS: Smooth capsules 4–8 mm long; stalks tiny (to 1 mm long); styles to 1 mm long.

ECOLOGY: River banks, floodplains, lakeshores, and wet meadows; often standing in quiet, shallow river backwaters; sea level to middle elevations.

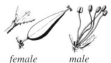

female   *male*

NOTES: Pacific willow (also known as *S. lasiandra*) is one of our largest native willows. • Two smaller, medium-to-tall willows with moderately long, narrow leaves also occur in our region. **Soft-leaved sandbar willow** (*Salix sessilifolia*) has **smaller leaves (to 8 cm long)** that are **soft, thick and quite fleshy** for a willow, with the midvein raised on both surfaces. **Geyer's willow** (*S. geyeriana*) also **has smaller leaves (to 8 cm long), minute stipules and black bracts** in the catkins (vs. yellowish in Pacific and soft-leaved willows). Both of these smaller willows range from southwestern B.C. south.

SCOULER'S WILLOW • *Salix scouleriana*

GENERAL: Tall, spindly shrub or multi-stemmed small tree 2–12 m tall; branches dark brown to yellowish-brown; **twigs densely velvety**.

LEAVES: Alternate, deciduous, broad, widest above the middle, tapering to a narrow base, pointed to rounded at tip, 3–8 cm long, **young leaves densely velvety, older leaves dark green above, hairy with some rust-coloured hairs below, or almost hairless below**; margins usually smooth but sometimes with a few rounded teeth near the tips; stalk 5–10 mm long; stipules small, pointed, fall early in the season.

FLOWERS: Ovaries densely silky; floral bracts brown to black, 4–5 mm long, hairy; catkins **appear well before the leaves**, **stalkless** on previous year's branches, males 2–4 cm long, females 2–6 cm long.

FRUITS: Silky capsules 5–8 mm long; stalks to 2 mm long; styles to 0.5 mm long.

ECOLOGY: Upland thickets, streamside areas, clearings, edges of forests and wetlands, open forests (deciduous and coniferous). At low to middle elevations.

female   male

NOTES: A more northern willow that can also form fair-sized small trees (to 8 m tall) is **Alaska or felt-leaved willow** (*S. alaxensis*). Its leaves are similar in shape to those of Scouler's willow, though narrower, but they are **densely white-woolly** underneath: its twigs are also usually **white-felty**. It occurs from sea level to alpine elevations, in fairly open, rocky situations from southeast Alaska north.

SITKA WILLOW • *Salix sitchensis*

GENERAL: Shrub or small tree 1–8 m tall; branches dark brown to grey, sparsely hairy; **twigs densely velvety, brittle at base**.

LEAVES: Alternate, deciduous, broad, tapering from above the middle to the base, 4–9 cm long, upper side bright green and sparsely silky, the **lower side satiny with short hairs pressed flat, not glaucous**; margins smooth or with tiny glandular teeth; stalks yellowish, velvety, 5–15 mm long; stipules half-oval, either fall early in the season (on slow-growing twigs) or are retained through the season (on more vigorous twigs).

FLOWERS: Bracts brown, hairy, to 2.4 mm long; catkins **appear before or with the leaves, on short leafy shoots,** males to 5 cm long, females to 8 cm long.

FRUITS: Silky capsules 3–5 mm long; stalks to 1.4 mm long; styles to 1.2 mm long.

ECOLOGY: Streamside thickets, lakeshores and wetland margins, forest edges and wet openings, clearings, avalanche tracks; low to middle elevations.

female   male

NOTES: Sitka willow is very common and abundant along rivers and streams throughout our range. It can be distinguished from Scouler's willow by its **brittle twigs and non-glaucous leaves with a satiny lustre on the underside**. • The supple, flexible nature of willow branches and bark made them extremely useful for making ropes for nets, binding and tying. The Haida used the spring catkins or pussy willows of certain species of willow as a decoration. The Straits Salish used the bark to make a grey dye for mountain goat wool. They also made reef nets from willow. Willow was used by interior groups for a variety of similar purposes, including making rope, weaving clothing and providing shredded bark for diapers. • Willows are the source of the natural precursor to aspirin, salicylic acid, found in leaves and bark.

RED-OSIER DOGWOOD • *Cornus stolonifera*

GENERAL: Freely spreading shrub with many stems, 1–6 m tall; branches opposite, lower branches often lying on ground and rooting freely; young stems smooth and round in cross-section, **often bright red**, especially after a frost.

LEAVES: Opposite, deciduous, **oval**, 5–10 cm long, mostly sharp-pointed with **5–7 prominent parallel veins** that converge at leaf tips; filmy white threads running through veins can be seen if a leaf is split crosswise and gently pulled apart; reddish in autumn.

FLOWERS: White to greenish, small (2–4 mm long); 4 petals and stamens; numerous **in dense flat-topped terminal clusters**.

FRUITS: White (occasionally blue-tinged), small (7–9 mm long) berry-like drupes, each with a somewhat flattened stone; bitter and inedible.

ECOLOGY: Moist soil, typically in swamps and streamside forest and scrub, but also in open upland forest and thickets and (in Alaska) rocky shorelines, bog-forest edges and disturbed sites; valley bottoms to middle elevations.

NOTES: This species is also known as *C. sericea*. The variety west of the Coast and Cascade Mountains is sometimes distinguished as *C. stolonifera* var. *occidentalis*, or as *C. occidentalis*. • Few people recognize this attractive, red-barked shrub as a relative of flowering dogwood. Its small, white flowers grow in more open clusters, rather than being crowded together in a 'button' surrounded by large, leafy white bracts, as are the flowers of flowering dogwood and bunchberry. • Although red-osier-dogwood berries are very bitter and contain a large central seed, they were eaten by interior aboriginal peoples, but not by coastal peoples. The bark was dried and used in smoking mixtures by aboriginal peoples to the East, but not on the Northwest Coast. The branches were sometimes used for salmon spreaders and basket rims. On the coast, the bark and twigs were used in a variety of medicinal preparations. For example, the Quileute and Straits Salish brewed a tonic tea from the bark. • It is extremely important winter browse for moose, deer and elk.

CASCARA • *Rhamnus purshiana*

GENERAL: Erect, tall shrub or small tree to 10 m tall, with thin, smooth, **silver-grey**, numbingly **bitter bark.**

LEAVES: Alternate (may seem almost opposite on new growth), deciduous (but young plants may retain their foliage over mild winters), **egg-shaped to oblong**, dark glossy green, 6–12 cm long, finely toothed, **strongly pinnately veined in furrows, the surface washboardy**.

FLOWERS: Greenish-yellow, small (3–4 mm long); 5 sepals, petals, and stamens; 8–50 in stalked, **umbrella-shaped clusters in the axils** of leaves.

FRUITS: Blue-black to purplish-black berries, 5–8 mm across; edible but not incredible.

ECOLOGY: Fairly dry to wet, often shady sites, most commonly in mixed woods, favour southern aspects with conifers or swampy bottomlands with red alder and vine maple; at low to middle elevations.

NOTES: The bark was boiled and the tea (or syrup) was drunk as a strong laxative by the Nuxalk, Coast Salish, Quileute, Nuu-chah-nulth, Kwakwaka'wakw and other groups. Cascara has been scientifically substantiated as an effective laxative. The hydroxymethyl-anthraquinones it contains cause peristalsis of the large intestine, with little or no effect on the small intestine at low dosages. The bark was often allowed to age before use because the fresh bark is said to be nauseating. The Coast Salish collected and dried the bark in strips in spring or summer. The following summer it was pounded and steeped in cold water, then boiled. Usually a handful of bark per quart of water was used. This plant was also used as a medicine for washing sores and swellings, and treating heart strain, internal strains and biliousness.

REDSTEM CEANOTHUS • *Ceanothus sanguineus*

GENERAL: Erect, 1–3 m tall; bark smooth, **reddish or purplish**; new twigs with spicy flavour.

LEAVES: Alternate, deciduous, oval, 3–10 cm long, **thin**, with **3 main veins** branching from the base of the leaf; finely toothed.

FLOWERS: White, fluffy, heavily scented clusters of small (3–5 mm across) flowers on reddish stalks **at the ends of lateral branches**.

FRUITS: Hardened, explosive, 3-chambered capsules about 4 mm long, each chamber contains a shiny brown seed.

ECOLOGY: Dry, fairly open sites: road margins, talus, dry forest openings and edges; common following fire; low to middle elevations.

NOTES: Snowbrush grows in similar habitats, but is usually shorter, **evergreen, and has thick, shiny leaves that are often sticky on top** and velvety beneath. As well, snowbrush lacks the red stems that characterize redstem ceanothus. • *Ceanothus* is the Greek name for a spiny shrub, and *sanguineus* ('bloody red') refers to the reddened flower stalks. It is sometimes called 'buckbrush' because it is a favourite food of deer. • The plant contains the **toxin** saponin • It used to be called 'soapbloom' by early settlers because the flowering twigs, when beaten in water, produce a soapy foam.

SNOWBRUSH • *Ceanothus velutinus*

GENERAL: Sprawling, spicy-scented, to 3 m tall; bark green; often forms thickets.

LEAVES: Alternate, evergreen, broadly oval, 3–6 cm long, **shiny and often sticky on top**, velvety beneath, with **3 main veins** branching from the base of the leaf (more prominently 3-veined than leaves of *C. sanguineus*), finely toothed, often tightly curling.

FLOWERS: White, small; in large pyramidal clusters (5–12 cm long) **along the lengths of side branches**.

FRUITS: 3-lobed and 3-chambered, explosive capsules 4–5 mm long.

ECOLOGY: Dry to moist, open habitats, in sunny locations, often following fire; low to middle elevations.

NOTES: Another shrub (3–7 m tall) with oval (but **opposite and wavy-margined**) evergreen leaves is **silk-tassel** (*Garrya elliptica*), common along the coast near the southern limits of our region. Female plants produce **long-persistent, hanging clusters of silky flowers** (in winter) that finally are replaced by silky-woolly fruits. • Both species of *Ceanothus* are adapted to colonize areas after fire, because they produce abundant, heat-resistant seed. The seed appears able to remain dormant in the soil for at least 200 years. It is stimulated to germinate by fire, which also creates open areas where the plants grow vigorously and can dominate early successional vegetation. These species are also able to 'fix' nitrogen in the soil. As nitrogen is almost inevitably the nutrient in shortest supply in coastal forests, this gives these shrubs a real advantage over their competition. The bushes are eventually shaded out by young trees, but the seeds remain to start a new shrub community following the next forest fire. • Leaves of snowbrush emit a sweet, spicy odour when crushed or on warm days. Other common names are tobacco-brush, cinnamon-brush, sticky laurel and mountain-balm. • In the dry Interior, the lower surfaces of the leaves are covered with dense silky or velvety hairs to prevent excessive water loss; hence the species name *velutinus*. This hairiness is not so conspicuous on the coast. • The name 'snowbrush' presumably refers to the dense covering of flowers. • The Kootenay made the leaves into a tea which was said to be good for tuberculosis.

SITKA ALDER • *Alnus crispa* ssp. *sinuata*

GENERAL: Coarse shrub or small tree, 1–5 m tall; lateral buds **pointed and lacking stalks**; bark yellowish-brown, scaly, often partially covered by lichens.

LEAVES: Alternate, thin, smooth, broadly oval with somewhat rounded base and pointed tip, 4–10 cm long, shiny and slightly sticky beneath; **margins wavy-lobed** (sinuate), **doubly saw-toothed**; turn **brownish in fall**.

FLOWERS: In male and female catkins, **opening at same time as leaves**.

FRUITS: Small **nutlets with broad wings**; female cones 1.5–2 cm long, egg-shaped, on stalks longer than cones in clusters of 3–6.

ECOLOGY: Moist sites such as edges of wet meadows, avalanche tracks, along streams, and in recently deglaciated areas; medium to subalpine elevations (to the shoreline in Alaska and parts of the Queen Charlotte Islands and northern mainland B.C.).

NOTES: This species is also known as *A. sinuata*, or *A. viridis* ssp. *sinuata*, or *A. sitchensis*. • **Mountain alder** (*A. tenuifolia*, also known as *A. incana* ssp. *tenuifolia*) is an interior species found (in our range) from northern southeast Alaska west to Prince William Sound, at low to middle elevations in wet places (e.g., edges of standing or flowing water) or on fresh till behind receding glaciers. It has very coarsely doubly-toothed leaves, **short-stalked buds**, nutlets **without wings** and **catkins appearing before the leaves**. • Sitka alder dominates shore-lines and recently deglaciated terrain in Alaska. It can also form dense shrub thickets and dominate wet avalanche tracks; apparently the snow slides over the sprawling branches without breaking them.

BEAKED HAZELNUT • *Corylus cornuta* var. *californica*
CALIFORNIA HAZELNUT

GENERAL: 1–4 m tall, with many stems; twigs, leaves and **bud scales covered in long white hairs** at least when young, hairless after first season; densely clumped or spreading widely by suckers.

LEAVES: Alternate, elliptic to oval, commonly with heart-shaped base and sharp-pointed tip, doubly saw-toothed, paler below than above, **turn yellow in fall**.

FLOWERS: Male flowers in catkins, flower **before the appearance of leaves** in the spring; female catkins very small, with protruding red stigmas.

FRUITS: Spherical, edible nuts, enclosed in tubular husks; husks light-green, covered with stiff prickly hairs and projecting beyond the nut into a beak; in clusters of 2 or 3 at ends of branches.

ECOLOGY: Moist but well-drained sites at low to middle elevations; in open forest, shady openings, thickets, clearings, rocky slopes and well-drained streamside habitats.

NOTES: Beaked hazelnut is also known as *Corylus californica*. • Hazelnuts were a favourite food of aboriginal peoples. Since beaked hazelnut has a sporadic distribution, people often had to travel to obtain them, and the nuts were an occasional trade item. The prickly husks were sometimes removed by burying the harvested nuts in the damp ground for a few weeks, allowing the husks to rot away. The nuts are a favourite food of squirrels, and some people gathered them from the winter caches of these small animals. Hazelnuts are one of the few types of seeds eaten traditionally by northwest coast peoples. They are picked in early autumn, stored until fully ripe and then eaten raw, or roasted. In some areas, the productivity of the bushes was enhanced by burning them to the ground periodically. • The long, flexible shoots were twisted into rope. • Note the unusual distribution with a northern population centred around (not surprisingly) Hazelton.

VINE MAPLE • *Acer circinatum*

GENERAL: Shrub or scraggly small tree to 7 m tall, the sprawling branches often rooting and forming new 'colonies'; stems pale green, becoming dull brown with age.

LEAVES: Maple leaves, **opposite**, deciduous, round, 5–12 cm across, **7- to 9-lobed**, toothed, hairy on the lower surface, hairy on the upper surface, at least along the veins; becoming either golden (in the shade) or bright red (in full sun) in the autumn.

FLOWERS: White, 6–9 mm broad; in clusters at the end of shoots.

FRUITS: Winged fruits 2–4 cm long; green becoming reddish or brown; in **widely spreading (almost in a straight line) pairs**.

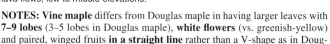

ECOLOGY: Moist to wet places, generally under other trees where some light reaches the forest floor (canopy openings, forest edges) but sometimes in open areas like shrubfields, clearcuts or lava flows; low to middle elevations.

NOTES: Vine maple differs from Douglas maple in having larger leaves with **7–9 lobes** (3–5 lobes in Douglas maple), **white flowers** (vs. greenish-yellow) and paired, winged fruits **in a straight line** rather than a V-shape as in Douglas maple. • The wood, though limited in size, is very dense and hard, and it is flexible when fresh. It was used for snowshoe frames, drum hoops, and a variety of small implements, spoons and dishes. It is often confused with Douglas maple, which many aboriginal people call 'vine maple.' • Vine maple is an eye-catching, fire-engine red in fall on open sites.

DOUGLAS MAPLE • *Acer glabrum*
ROCKY MOUNTAIN MAPLE

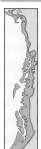

GENERAL: Shrub or small tree to 10 m tall; branches opposite; young twigs reddish, older bark greyish.

LEAVES: Opposite, deciduous, 2–8 cm across, divided into **3–5 lobes**, typical maple-leaf shape, coarsely toothed; turning bright yellowish-orange to crimson in fall.

FLOWERS: Greenish-yellow, small; male and female flowers on separate or same plant; some flowers may have both sexes; in terminal or axillary clusters of about 10, appearing with the leaves; .

FRUITS: Tan, each with a large wing, about 2–3 cm long; pairs attached **in a V-shape**.

ECOLOGY: Dry ridges to moist but well-drained seepage sites; in the northern half of our region on the inner coast along the shoreline, rocky areas, forest edges and floodplains, sometimes abundant on the lower edges of avalanche tracks; usually on drier, more open sites than vine maple; low to middle elevations.

NOTES: The wood, like that of vine maple, was used for snowshoe frames. The Salish carved miniature paddles to line ceremonial costumes and rattle with movement. The Saanich peoples of southern Vancouver Island used the bark to make an antidote for poisoning. The bright-red infestations of eriophyid mites on the leaves of this maple are called 'hummingbird's menstrual pad' in Nuxalk.

SOOPOLALLIE • *Shepherdia canadensis*
SOAPBERRY, CANADIAN BUFFALO-BERRY

GENERAL: Unarmed, spreading, 1–2 m tall; branches **brownish, covered with small, bran-like scabs**; young branches with rusty spots.

LEAVES: Opposite, deciduous, oval, 2–6 cm long; dark-greenish on upper surface, **whitish silvery felt of hairs and rusty brown spots (scales) on the undersurface.**

FLOWERS: Yellowish-brown, inconspicuous (1–2 mm long); male and female flowers on separate shrubs; 1–several in clusters on stem before leaves open out.

FRUITS: Bright red, translucent, oval, juicy berries, extremely **bitter,** soapy to touch.

ECOLOGY: Dry to moist open woods and thickets; from lowlands to middle elevation forests.

NOTES: This is more typically an 'eastside' plant, where it is widespread and often abundant. In Glacier Bay/Lynn Canal, Alaska, it occurs on burned areas with lodgepole pine and on rocky and recently deglaciated sites. It is fairly common on gravelly river terraces, often with lodgepole pine, in inner coastal valleys such as the Bella Coola and the middle Skeena-Nass. • This fruit is still widely used by aboriginal peoples in British Columbia. The berries are used to make 'Indian ice-cream,' which has a bitter taste but was often sweetened with salal berries, camas bulbs or hemlock cambium. The berries are harvested in mid-summer by shaking the bushes over a mat. The berries were put in a container with an equal amount of water and whipped until frothy with a bundle of inner cedar bark, a salal branch, thimbleberry leaves or the fingers.

COMMON JUNIPER • *Juniperus communis*
GROUND JUNIPER

GENERAL: Evergreen, **prostrate,** trailing, branched, usually less than 1 m high, forming mats or clumps to 3 m in diameter; bark very thin, reddish-brown, shredding, scaly.

LEAVES: Needle-like to narrowly lance-shaped, jointed to the branchlet, usually stiff, **very prickly,** whitish below, dark-green above, mostly in 3s.

FRUITS: Female cones **berry-like,** pale green at first, **bluish-black when mature,** very fleshy, covered in white-grey bloom, maturing in the second season; male and female cones on separate plants.

ECOLOGY: Dry, open woods, gravelly ridges, outcrops, muskeg and open rocky slopes; from lowland bogs to subalpine ridges and alpine tundra.

NOTES: Rocky Mountain juniper (*Juniperus scopulorum*) is an uncommon **shrubby tree,** found in dry, rocky habitats in the Strait of Georgia–Puget Sound area. Its young leaves are similar to those of the common juniper, but **most of its leaves are scale-like,** like those of western redcedar. • Common juniper was considered an important medicine for interior peoples, but it was not widely used on the Northwest Coast. The Haida and other coastal peoples sometimes referred to it as 'swamp boughs,' because it often grows in peat bogs. It was used medicinally for childbirth and to treat urinary infections, but it must be used with caution because it can cause uterine contractions, and hence miscarriages in pregnant women. • Juniper berries are commonly used in European cooking as a flavouring for soups, stews, cordials and gin. • The species name *communis* means 'common,' which this species is over much of the globe. Common juniper is the only circumpolar conifer of the northern hemisphere.

FALSEBOX • *Pachistima myrsinites*
MOUNTAIN BOXWOOD, OREGON BOXWOOD

GENERAL: Low, dense, **evergreen**, erect or prostrate, 20–80 cm tall; branches reddish-brown, 4-ridged, otherwise smooth.

LEAVES: Opposite or nearly so, oval to elliptic, 1–3 cm long, thick, leathery, shiny; **margins toothed** and slightly rolled under.

FLOWERS: Maroon, very small (3–4 mm wide), fragrant; 4 petals and stamens; numerous in small axillary clusters all along the branches.

FRUITS: Small, oval, 1- to 2-seeded capsules; seeds mostly covered by a white, fleshy outgrowth called the aril.

ECOLOGY: Coniferous forest, rocky openings, dry mountain slopes; low to middle elevations.

NOTES: The genus name is spelled various ways, commonly as *Paxistima*. • Another deciduous, opposite-leaved shrub in this family (Celastraceae, the staff-tree family) is the **western wahoo** (*Euonymus occidentalis*). It has **greenish/purplish-mottled to purplish-red flowers** and seeds covered by a reddish-orange aril, similar in construction to a cashew. Western wahoo is found near Courtenay, Vancouver Island, and uncommonly through Washington and Oregon in forests and thickets at low to middle elevations. • This low, upright shrub with leathery, evergreen leaves **looks somewhat like kinnikinnick, but falsebox has no berries and its leaf margins are toothed**, not smooth. • It provides good winter browse for deer. • The branches provide decorative greenery in floral arrangements, often to the detriment of populations near urban centres.

DULL OREGON-GRAPE • *Mahonia nervosa*

GENERAL: Erect, rhizomatous, **evergreen**, stiff-branched shrub, to 60 cm tall; **leaves like holly; bark and wood yellowish**.

LEAVES: Clustered, long, alternate, turning reddish or purplish in winter, with **9–19 leathery leaflets**, somewhat shiny on both surfaces; leaflets oblong to egg-shaped, with several prominent spiny teeth (resembling English holly).

FLOWERS: Bright **yellow**, flower parts in 6s; many-flowered erect clusters to 20 cm long.

FRUITS: Blue berries about 1 cm across with few large seeds and a whitish bloom, in elongated clusters, edible.

ECOLOGY: Dry to fairly moist, open to closed forests at low to middle elevations.

NOTES: The Oregon-grapes are also known as *Berberis* spp. (e.g., *Berberis nervosa*). • **Tall Oregon-grape** (*Mahonia aquifolium*) is similar, but with **5–9 leaflets** per leaf, glossy above and less so beneath, each leaflet with **1 central vein** (vs. 3 in *M. nervosa*). It is commonly found in drier, more open, (often rocky) sites than is dull Oregon-grape, from southern B.C. to central Oregon. • Dull Oregon-grape is particularly common in second-growth, closed-canopy Douglas-fir forests (e.g., 50–100 years old). • The tart, purple berries of both Oregon-grapes were eaten, but generally not in quantity. Often they were mixed with salal or some other sweeter fruit. Today they are used for jelly, and some people make wine from them. An excellent jelly can be made using two cups Oregon-grape juice, two cups salal juice, five cups sugar and one box pectin crystals. • The bark is bright yellow inside, due to an alkaloid, berberine. The shredded bark of the stems and roots was used to make a bright-yellow dye for basket materials. The bark and berries were also used medicinally for liver, gall-bladder and eye problems. One Saanich woman noted that eating the berries in quantity was the only antidote known for shellfish poisoning. Great **caution** was used, because this drug is very potent.

MOCK-ORANGE • *Philadelphus lewisii*

GENERAL: Erect, loosely branched, to 3 m tall; bark brown, checking and eventually flaking off.

LEAVES: Opposite, deciduous, **short-stalked**, **oval to egg-shaped**, 3–5 cm long, light green, margins essentially smooth (some teeth on young leaves), with **3 major veins** from the leaf base.

FLOWERS: White, 2–3 cm broad, fragrant, usually with 4 petals, numerous stamens; 3–15 in clusters at the end of lateral branches.

FRUITS: Oval, **woody**, 4-chambered **capsules** about 1 cm long.

ECOLOGY: A variety of different habitats, from open forests and forest edges on moist rich sites to open brushy areas on dry, rocky soils; low to middle elevations.

NOTES: Our coastal plants are sometimes described as *P. lewisii* var. *gordonianus*, or *P. gordonianus*. • This species is extremely variable in both vegetative and floral characters and appears to be particularly responsive to local ecological conditions. • The wood is strong and hard; it never cracks or warps when properly prepared. It is most widely used for making implements among the Interior Salish. On the coast, the Saanich used the wood for bows and arrows, and the Lummi of Washington made combs, netting shuttles and, recently, knitting needles. The Cowlitz also used the wood for combs, and the Skagit made arrow shafts. • The leaves and flowers foam into a lather when bruised and rubbed with the hands. This lather was used for cleansing the skin by the Snohomish and Cowlitz, as well by various interior groups. • This shrub has showy and aromatic flowers, and it has horticultural potential in native plant gardens. The commonly grown garden plant in the Pacific Northwest is the European *P. coronarius*. • Aristotle gave the name *Philadelphus* to a tree, now unknown, to commemorate Pharoah Ptolemy II Philadelphus (308–246 B.C.). Somehow the name, which means 'brotherly love,' was applied to this shrub. It has nothing to do with the city of Philadelphia, where a whole block once burned after the police bombed a house to keep the peace.

WHIPPLEVINE • *Whipplea modesta*

GENERAL: Main stems woody, slender, **trailing** and freely rooting, up to 1 m long, with numerous short, erect, herbaceous, flowering shoots, coarse-hairy throughout.

LEAVES: Opposite, nearly stalkless, withering but remaining on the branches, **oval to egg-shaped**, 1–2.5 cm long, vaguely toothed, with **3 main veins**.

FLOWERS: White, small, 3–4 mm long, 5–6 petals, 8–12 stamens; borne in terminal clusters of 5–10.

FRUITS: Roundish **capsules**, separating into 4–5 **leathery**, 1-seeded segments.

ECOLOGY: Dry, rocky, open areas or open forest, clearings, cutbanks; at low to middle elevations.

NOTES: Whipplevine occurs **only at the southern end** of our region; its affinities are more with the Californian than the northern Pacific flora. • Named for Lt. A.W. Whipple, 1818–1863, who commanded the U.S. Railroad Expedition of 1853–1854. Whether *modesta* means that the plant or Lt. Whipple is modest is not clear. *Whipplea modesta* is also called *yerba de selva*: Spanish for 'forest herb.'

Wildflowers

This section includes all non-woody flowering plants except the aquatics, the 'oddballs' and the grasses, sedges and rushes. It is divided into 24 parts. Twenty-three of these represent the major plant families, and the 24th includes flowers from other, smaller, families.

Plants representing the 23 major plant families are illustrated below and on the following page. If the leaves, flowers and fruit of your 'unknown plant' resemble one of those shown, then you are probably in the right family. If not, your plant may belong to a smaller family, and it might be found in 'Other Families,' 'Aquatics,' or 'Oddballs' (a collection of some flowering plant oddities—including parasites and carnivores) sections.

We have organized this and other sections of the book by families, so that similar species can be compared easily. The identification of the family to which a plant belongs is often the first step in its complete identification, especially for less-common species that are not illustrated and cannot be picture-keyed. The order of the families more or less follows that set out in some of the major technical references for the region, such as Hultén (1968) and Hitchcock and Cronquist (1973); it is presumed to reflect increasing evolutionary complexity and specialization—particularly in flower structure. Within families and within the constraints of this guide's format, we have ordered entries to allow easy comparison of similar genera and species.

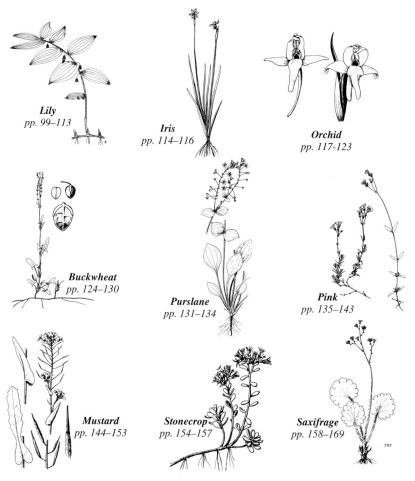

Lily
pp. 99–113

Iris
pp. 114–116

Orchid
pp. 117-123

Buckwheat
pp. 124–130

Purslane
pp. 131–134

Pink
pp. 135–143

Mustard
pp. 144–153

Stonecrop
pp. 154–157

Saxifrage
pp. 158–169

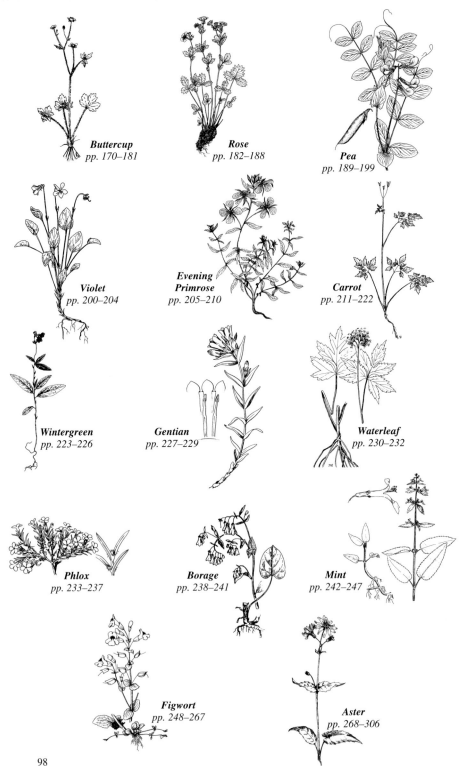

Buttercup
pp. 170–181

Rose
pp. 182–188

Pea
pp. 189–199

Violet
pp. 200–204

Evening Primrose
pp. 205–210

Carrot
pp. 211–222

Wintergreen
pp. 223–226

Gentian
pp. 227–229

Waterleaf
pp. 230–232

Phlox
pp. 233–237

Borage
pp. 238–241

Mint
pp. 242–247

Figwort
pp. 248–267

Aster
pp. 268–306

Liliaceae (Lily Family)

The Liliaceae is a large and varied family, mostly of perennial herbs from rhizomes, bulbs or fleshy roots. The parallel-veined leaves are either all basal, or alternate or whorled along the stem. The radially symmetric flowers, which are often large and showy, have flower parts in 3s (except for *Maianthemum*, which is in 4s), and a single superior ovary. The fruit is a 3-chambered capsule or a berry.

Onions, garlic, leeks and asparagus are edible members of this family, but some members, such as death-camas (*Zygadenus*) are very poisonous. Beautiful garden ornamentals in the lily family include tulips, lilies, day lilies (*Hemerocallis*), hyacinths, scillas and hostas.

Key to Genera of the Lily Family

1a. Petals and sepals totalling 4; leaves usually 2, heart-shaped .... *Maianthemum*
1b. Petals and sepals totalling 6; leaves various 2
    2a. Leaves in a single whorl of 3 atop stem; sepals green, petals white or purplish .... *Trillium*
    2b. Leaves not in a single whorl of 3 3
        3a. Sepals and petals very dissimilar in size 4
            4a. Plants with rhizomes; leaves mottled, oval; stamens 3 .... *Scoliopus* (see *Clintonia*)
            4b. Plants from a bulb; leaves linear, grass-like, not mottled; stamens 6 .... *Calochortus*
        3b. Sepals and petals similar in size 5
            5a. Flowers in umbels or heads; bulbs or corms present; leaves linear & basal 6
                6a. Plants with onion odour; flowers to 1.5 or so cm long .... *Allium*
                6b. Plants lacking onion odour; flowerss 1.5-4 cm long .... *Brodiaea*
            5b. Flowers solitary or in racemes or panicles (branching clusters); not in umbels 7
                7a. Leaves linear, stiff, tough, evergreen in large basal tuft .... *Xerophyllum*
                7b. Leaves soft, not persisting for more than 1 year 8
                    8a. Leaves mostly on the flowering stems, not strongly reduced in size upwards 9
                        9a. Plants from scaly bulbs; leaves often whorled 10
                            10a. Sepals/petals (tepals) 4–10 cm long, orange .... *Lilium*
                            10b. Tepals 1–3.5 cm long, dark green to brown or black .... *Fritillaria*
                        9b. Plants from rhizomes; leaves alternate, not whorled 11
                            11a. Flowers numerous (more than 10) in terminal clusters 12
                                12a. Styles 3; tepals 6–17 mm long; leaves prominently ribbed .... *Veratrum*
                                12b. Styles 1; tepals 2–7 mm long; leaves not prominently ribbed .... *Smilacina*
                            11b. Flowers 1 to few, borne singly along stems or in small clusters at tips 13
                                13a. Flowers scattered along lower side of stems, often concealed by leaves .... *Streptopus*
                                13b. Flowers 1 to 3 at tips of branches of stem .... *Disporum*
                    8b. Leaves mostly basal; flowering stems bare or with leaves greatly reduced upwards 14
                      14a. Styles 3, distinct to ovary 15
                          15a. Plants with rhizomes; leaves 2-ranked and iris-like .... *Tofieldia*
                          15b. Plants with neither 2-ranked nor iris-like 16
                              16a. Stems slender and weak; flowers in racemes, nodding on slender stalks, tubular bell-shaped; tepals greenish-yellow to purplish-green .... *Stenanthium*
                              16b. Stems stout; flowers stiffly erect, not nodding, saucer-shaped; tepals creamy white. .... *Zygadenus*
                    14b. Styles 1, or 3 but fused more than half their length 17
                        17a. Leaves several, linear to narrowly lance-shaped 18
                          18a. Flowers 1–2, white; plants to 15 cm tall, subalpine to alpine .... *Lloydia*
                          18b. Flowers 10 or more, blue; plants > 20 cm tall, of the lowlands .... *Camassia*
                      17b. Leaves usually 2, lance–shaped to oblong elliptic 19
                        19a. Plants with rhizomes; flowers white; fruits blue berries .... *Clintonia*
                      19b. Plants from corms; flowers white, yellow, or pink; tepals strongly turned backward; fruits dry capsules .... *Erythronium*

FALSE SOLOMON'S-SEAL • *Smilacina racemosa*

GENERAL: Perennial from **stout**, fleshy rhizomes; stems erect or (usually) stiffly arched, **0.3–1.0 m tall**, unbranched, finely hairy above, often growing in clumps.

LEAVES: Broad, **elliptical**, 7–20 cm long, alternating along the stem in 2 rows, with strong parallel veins and somewhat clasping bases; margins without hairs.

FLOWERS: Creamy white, small, **numerous, stalks very short; in branched, egg- or pyramid-shaped terminal cluster**, strongly perfumed and showy *en masse*.

FRUITS: Red (sometimes dotted with purple), fleshy, round berries, showy, 5–7 mm across.

ECOLOGY: Moist forests, streambanks, meadows and clearings; widespread at low to subalpine elevations.

NOTES: The berries of false Solomon's-seal are edible, but not especially palatable. Kwakwaka'wakw hunters and berry-pickers ate the raw berries on occasion. The Gitksan boiled the roots and drank the tea as a strong medicine for rheumatism, sore back and kidney trouble, and as a purgative. The roots were also mashed and bound on cuts. The Coast Salish also used the root as a poultice. • The name 'Solomon's-seal' (originally given to *Polygonatum multiflorum*) is traditionally thought to refer to the rhizomes of this species. They bear surface scars, or show markings when freshly cut, which resemble the seal of Solomon: a 6-pointed star. However, Grigson (1974) claims the original medieval Latin refers to one of the flowers hanging like a seal on a document. *S. racemosa* resembles *P. multiflorum*—hence 'false' Solomon's-seal. • False Solomon's-seal makes a good ornamental foliage plant in shaded gardens, and it is easy to transplant.

STAR-FLOWERED FALSE SOLOMON'S-SEAL • *Smilacina stellata*

GENERAL: Perennial from **slender**, pale, wide-ranging rhizomes; stems erect, arching, unbranched, **20–60 cm tall**, finely hairy.

LEAVES: Alternate in 2 rows, **lance-shaped**, 5–15 cm long, flat, sometimes folded down centre (usually when plant is growing in the open), with prominent veins and somewhat clasping bases; margins without hairs.

FLOWERS: Creamy white, star-like; **few (5–10) in short, unbranched, terminal cluster**.

FRUITS: Round, **greenish-yellow** berries with 3 or 6 blue-purple stripes, changing to **dark blue or reddish-black** at maturity, 7–10 mm across.

ECOLOGY: Moist (less commonly dry) forest, often abundant in alluvial or deciduous forest, also in clearings and meadows and among low shrubs; common from valley bottoms to (occasionally) timberline.

NOTES: The leaves of this species are set more at right angles to the stem than are those of *S. racemosa*. • The berries are edible, but not especially palatable. They were usually classed with false-lily-of-the-valley berries in quality and appearance. The Nuxalk occasionally chewed the raw berries, swallowing the juice and spitting out the seeds and skin.

CLASPING TWISTEDSTALK • *Streptopus amplexifolius*

GENERAL: Perennial from thick, short rhizomes covered with fibrous roots; stems **0.4–1.0 m or more tall**, smooth, **branched**, sometimes bent at nodes (zig-zag).

LEAVES: Oval to oval-lance-shaped, pointed, 5–14 cm long, clasping the stem at base, **glaucous beneath**; margins may have inconspicuous, irregularly spaced teeth.

FLOWERS: Greenish-white, bell-shaped with flaring tips, hanging, **on thin, kinked stalks**; 1-2 from each leaf axil along stem.

FRUITS: Yellow to red, oval-oblong berries (sometimes turning dark purple), about 1 cm long.

ECOLOGY: Moist, rich forest, streambanks, avalanche tracks, subalpine thickets, clearings; widespread at low to subalpine elevations.

NOTES: The **branched stem** separates this species from **other twistedstalks**; the **axillary flower attachment** separates it from the terminal-flowered **fairybells** (*Disporum* spp., which also have branched stems). • Young shoots of clasping twistedstalk were eaten by some of the Alaska peoples, but apparently this was learned from the Europeans. Most aboriginal people regard the plants and berries as poisonous. Stems of this plant were used by the Haida for a poultice on cuts. The Haida called the berries 'owl-berries' or 'witch-berries' in Skidegate and 'black-bear berries' in Masset, and the Kwakwaka'wakw called them 'frog-berries.' Makah women chewed and ingested the root to induce labour in case of protracted delay. • The name twistedstalk refers either to the zig-zag stem, or to the strongly bent flower stalks. *Streptopus* is from the Greek *streptos* (twisted) and *podus* (foot), and *amplexifolius* is from the Latin *amplexor* (to surround) and *folius* (leaf).

ROSY TWISTEDSTALK • *Streptopus roseus*

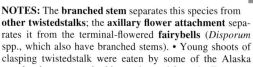

GENERAL: Perennial from slender rhizomes; stems **usually unbranched**, not conspicuously bent or zig-zag, **15–30 cm tall**, with a sparse fringe of hairs at the nodes (where leaves arise).

LEAVES: Mostly oval to elliptic, 5–9 cm long, **not clasping** at base, **shiny beneath**; margin with irregularly spaced hairs.

FLOWERS: Usually **rose-coloured with white tips**, (sometimes greenish-yellow streaked with reddish-purple), bell-shaped, **on curved (not kinked) stalks**; single from leaf axils.

FRUITS: Red, round to oblong berries.

ECOLOGY: Moist forest, forest openings, streambanks, clearings and meadows; at low to subalpine elevations.

NOTES: Rosy twistedstalk is distinguished from **clasping twistedstalk** by the unbranched stem, rose-coloured flowers on non-kinked stalks, non-clasping leaves, fringe of hairs at each node and shiny underside of the leaves. • **Small twistedstalk** (*Streptopus streptopoides*) is a **small (to 20 cm tall)** species with a few purplish-green **saucer-shaped flowers**, which is found in dense coniferous forest at middle to subalpine elevations from Alaska to Washington.

HOOKER'S FAIRYBELLS • *Disporum hookeri*

GENERAL: Perennial from slender rhizomes; stems with **few branches**, to 1 m tall, with irregularly curled hairs.

LEAVES: Alternate, oval to lance-shaped with pointed tips, stalkless and somewhat clasping at base, **slightly hairy** on upper surface and margins, prominently veined, 5–13 cm long.

FLOWERS: Creamy **white**, narrow, bell-shaped, style usually hairy; 1–3 (usually 2) hanging **from tip of branch**.

FRUITS: Lemon-yellow to orange-red (ultimately), egg-shaped berries, **often hairy**; 4–6 seeds.

ECOLOGY: Moist coniferous or mixed forest at low elevations.

NOTES: Also in our region is **Smith's fairybells** (*Disporum smithii*), which has a **smooth stem and leaves** (vs. a hairy stem and hairy-margined leaves in Hooker's fairybells), a **smooth** (not hairy) berry, and **longer tepals** (longer than 1.5 cm, vs. usually shorter than 1.5 cm in *D. hookeri*). Its range is from southern Vancouver Island to California, in habitats similar to those of Hooker's fairybells. • Some interior groups of British Columbia ate the berries of this plant, but most northwest coast peoples considered them poisonous, and associated them with snakes or ghosts. • The pointed leaf tips of Hooker's fairybells, sometimes called 'drip tips,' provide a way for the leaves to shed the ample rain that falls where this species often grows.

WESTERN TRILLIUM • *Trillium ovatum*

GENERAL: Showy, hairless perennial to 45 cm tall from short, stout, fleshy rhizomes.

LEAVES: In **whorls of usually** 3 (up to 5), triangular-oval with a 'drip-tip,' to 18 cm long, unstalked.

FLOWERS: White (turning pink to purple with age), 3 white petals (to 5 cm long) with 3 green sepals beneath; single, terminal **on a stalk**.

FRUITS: Oval, green, berry-like capsules with wing-like ridges; seeds numerous, egg-shaped, in a sticky mass when first shed.

ECOLOGY: Moist to wet woods, streambanks, shaded open areas; at low to middle elevations.

NOTES: A dwarf (to 10 cm tall) form with **pale-pink flowers** occurs in a few places on western Vancouver Island and has been called *T. hibbersonii*, or *T. ovatum* forma *hibbersonii*. • **Sessile trillium** (*T. chloropetalum*) has **mottled leaves** and **non-stalked, greenish-white, yellow or purple flowers** (vs. stalked white flowers in *T. ovatum*). Its range extends from about Olympia south through the Willamette valley, in moist, open forests. • Each seed has a little, oil-rich appendage that is attractive to ants. The ants lug the seeds back to their nests, where they eat the appendages or feed them to the larvae and then discard the remaining seeds on their rubbish piles. This is a reasonably effective mechanism for seed dispersal, especially for plants of the dim, becalmed forest floor. Ants disperse up to 30% of the spring-flowering, herbaceous species in the deciduous forests of eastern North America. Our forest flora is less dependent, but we do have several spring-flowering 'ant plants,' including bleeding heart, inside-out flower and wild ginger, as well as trilliums. • Genus and common names come from the Latin *trillium* meaning 'in 3s,' referring to the leaves, petals, sepals and stigmas. The flower blooms early in the spring (March to May), just as the robins appear or 'wake up,' giving rise to the alternative common name 'wake-robin.'

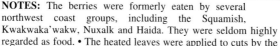

FALSE LILY-OF-THE-VALLEY • *Maianthemum dilatatum*

GENERAL: Perennial from slender, branched, creeping rhizomes; stems erect, 10–40 cm tall.

LEAVES: Alternate, 1–3 **(usually 2)**, **broadly heart-shaped**, smooth on top, to 10 cm long, **with long stalks**.

FLOWERS: Small, **white**, with **flower parts in 4s** (unlike usual 3s of most species in the lily family), delicately perfumed; several to many in **terminal cylindric cluster**.

FRUITS: Small, round berries, light green and mottled brown at first, becoming red, to 6 mm diameter.

ECOLOGY: Moist to wet, usually shady woods, riverside areas, at low to middle elevations; sometimes forms the dominant groundcover in Sitka-spruce forests near the sea.

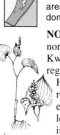

NOTES: The berries were formerly eaten by several northwest coast groups, including the Squamish, Kwakwaka'wakw, Nuxalk and Haida. They were seldom highly regarded as food. • The heated leaves were applied to cuts by the Haida, and the young leaves were eaten as a 'spring purge.' The roots were poulticed on sore eyes. The Quinault rubbed sore eyes with the pounded roots, and the Squamish rubbed the leaves on sore eyes. The Cowichan drank a root tea for healing internal injuries. The Makah chewed the long roots and swallowed the juice to reverse sterility. A medicine from the root was applied to the eye to remove a 'white growth' (possibly cataracts). The Ohiet used the leaves as a poultice on small cuts. Some Nuu-chah-nulth people believed that the berries could only be eaten ripe, with oil, or they would cause stomach pains. • In one Haida myth, a feast for supernatural beings included highbush-cranberries, wild crabapples, salal-berry cakes, lupine-root cakes and false-lily-of-the-valley berries with grease.

STICKY FALSE ASPHODEL • *Tofieldia glutinosa*

GENERAL: Perennial from fairly stout, vertical rhizomes covered with fibrous remains of old leaf bases; stems to 40 cm tall, smooth below, very **glandular-hairy and sticky** on upper part of stem.

LEAVES: Basal (2–4), sheathing, **iris-like**, half the length of stem; often 1 or 2 much smaller ones on stem.

FLOWERS: Small, **white or greenish-white**, anthers often purplish and conspicuous; several in **dense, terminal clusters**.

FRUITS: Large, erect, **reddish-purple capsules**; seeds numerous, enclosed within a spongy coat.

ECOLOGY: In the open in bogs, fens, wet meadows, streambanks; sometimes locally abundant, from valley bottoms to alpine elevations.

NOTES: The origin of the name 'asphodel' is obscure, but ancient. It is the flower of the Elysian Fields: Homer's meadows of asphodel inhabited by the souls of the dead. This would fit with one possible origin: from the Greek *a* meaning 'not' and *spodos* meaning 'ashes.' Another source says it is from the Greek *a* ('not') and *sphallo* ('I surpass'), meaning 'a stately plant of great beauty.' In medieval England the name was somehow corrupted to the now widely used 'daffodil' (*Narcissus* spp.). • *Tofieldia* is named for English botanist Thomas Tofield (1730–1779).

> And rest at last, where souls unbodied dwell
> In ever-flow'ring meads of asphodel.
> —Homer: *The Odyssey* (xxiv.1.19 of Pope's translation)

QUEEN'S CUP • *Clintonia uniflora*

GENERAL: Perennial from slender, creeping **rhizomes**; stems mostly underground, short, to 15 cm tall.

LEAVES: 2–3 in basal rosette, 7–15 (sometimes 25) cm long, oblong or elliptic with sheathing base, slightly fleshy and shiny; noticeably hairy margin.

FLOWERS: Large, white, cup-shaped, erect; solitary (rarely 2) on a long stalk.

FRUITS: Single, bright **metallic blue berries**.

ECOLOGY: Moist forest, forest openings, clearings; widely distributed and often abundant at low to subalpine elevations.

NOTES: Another lily with large, fleshy, paired basal leaves is *Scoliopus hallii*, found in damp woods from Tilamook County, Oregon, south. This species, called (in polite circles) **'slink lily'** or **'fetid adder's tongue,'** has **purple-mottled leaves** and a **greyish-yellow flower** with the delicate **scent of rotting flesh** (useful for attracting pollinating flies). • The beautiful, pure-white, cup-shaped flower with a crown of golden stamens deserves the name 'queen's cup.' Another common name, 'blue-bead lily,' refers to the single blue berry. The berries, however, are considered unpalatable, although grouse reportedly eat them. • The Bella Coola call the fruit 'wolf's berry,' and they regard it as inedible for humans. • *Clintonia* is named in memory of New York State Governor and botanist DeWitt Clinton (1769–1828).

WHITE FAWN LILY • *Erythronium oregonum*

GENERAL: Perennial herb to 30 cm tall from a segmented **corm**.

LEAVES: Basal, paired, lance-shaped to oblong, to 20 cm long, **mottled** with pale green and dark brown.

FLOWERS: White (often marked with orange-yellow at the base), the tepals **'bent back'**; usually single, terminal, **nodding**.

FRUITS: Erect, broadly club-shaped **capsules** 3–4 cm long, notched near the tip.

ECOLOGY: Well-drained, open, often grassy areas, open to fairly dense, rocky woodlands; at low elevations.

NOTES: Distinction of *Erythronium* species is quite easy: *E. grandiflorum* and *E. montanum* (inset photo) both have plain, **pale-green leaves**; the former has **yellow flowers** and the latter has **white flowers**. Plants with **mottled leaves** are either the **white-flowered *E. oregonum*** or the **pink-flowered *E. revolutum*** (confined to Vancouver Island and areas south). • *Erythronium* species have unusual below-ground structures, consisting of a bulb with only one scale, and a segmented corm made of round annual segments, just like a string of beads. The bulbs of flowering specimens are usually at least 10 cm deep. • John Burroughs is said to have named this species 'fawn lily' because he thought the two leaves looked like the pricked ears of a fawn. More likely, 'fawn' alludes to the mottled leaf colouring. *Erythronium* comes from the Greek *erythros* for 'red,' in reference to some pinkish-flowered species that was used in ancient times to make a dye.

PINK FAWN LILY • *Erythronium revolutum*

GENERAL: Perennial herb from a thick, segmented, scaly **corm**; to 35 cm tall.

LEAVES: Basal, paired, broadly lance-shaped, to 20 cm long, **green mottled with white**.

FLOWERS: Rose-pink, the tepals **bent back**; single, terminal, **nodding**.

FRUITS: Erect, narrowly club-shaped **capsules** 3–4 cm long, abruptly narrowed at the base.

ECOLOGY: Open to moderately dense moist woodlands, riverside areas, meadows and other open areas; at low elevations.

NOTES: The Kwakwaka'wakw and possibly the Nuu-chah-nulth ate the bulbs of pink fawn lily. The Kwakwaka'wakw dug them with special yew-wood spades when the leaves first sprouted in the spring. The bulbs were stored in ventilated baskets in a cool place. Some Kwakwaka'wakw people liked to eat them on hot days because they were cool and moist inside. They had a slightly bitter, milky taste. For a feast they were steamed in tall cedar boxes and served with large quantities of oolichan grease. Water was always taken after eating these corms; otherwise, it was said, one would get sick.

YELLOW GLACIER LILY • *Erythronium grandiflorum*

GENERAL: Perennial herb to 30 cm tall from an elongate, segmented **corm**.

LEAVES: Basal, paired, bright yellow-green, **not mottled**, oblong to oval, to 20 cm long, clasping the flowering stem base.

FLOWERS: Golden-yellow, nodding, the tepals **strongly recurved**; usually single, atop a leafless, unbranched stem.

FRUITS: Erect, club-shaped **capsules** about 3 cm long; seeds brown, papery.

ECOLOGY: Moist open areas (meadows, avalanche tracks, subalpine parkland); middle to alpine elevations.

NOTES: A similar lily with **non-mottled leaves** but with **white flowers** with yellow centres is **avalanche lily** (*E. montanum*). Avalanche lily is a subalpine species ranging from Vancouver Island and the Mt. Waddington area south in the Olympics and Cascades to northern Oregon. Mathews (1988) notes that avalanche lilies are more common in the Olympics and glacier lilies are more common in the Cascades, but this depends on where you are in the Cascades: avalanche lily is abundant from Mt. Rainier to Mt. Hood but it is almost absent elsewhere, while glacier lily is widespread but less abundant. • Glacier lily corms were an important food of indigenous peoples of the Interior Plateau. They were not generally used by northwest coast peoples, however the Nuxalk sometimes obtained them through trade. • The common names 'avalanche lily' and 'glacier lily' are used interchangeably in some books, which can be confusing. Perhaps it is best to simply preface common names with 'white' or 'yellow' to avoid confusion. • The common names 'avalanche' and 'glacier' lily refer to the fact that these species bloom at the edge of melting snow banks. However, where they carpet alpine meadows, one could easily fancy an avalanche of fine snow or pollen had covered the ground.

HOOKER'S ONION • *Allium acuminatum*

GENERAL: Perennial herb to 30 cm tall, from a small, deeply-buried, grey-brown, egg-shaped **bulb with a fibrous network on the surface**; entire plant with characteristic **onion odour and taste**.

LEAVES: 1–2, basal, long and narrow, grass-like, **withering** before the flowers appear.

FLOWERS: Rose, occasionally white, **stiff and parchment-like, tepals turn back at the tips**; in **upright** umbels with 7–25 flowers with 2 bracts under the umbel.

FRUITS: Capsules with 3 obscure ridges; seeds black.

ECOLOGY: Usually in open, rocky sites, occasionally in dry to moist open forest; at low elevations.

NOTES: Several other onions occur in our region, generally from southern Vancouver Island south. They can be difficult to distinguish; keys and descriptions are provided in Hitchcock and Cronquist (1973) and Taylor (1966). • **Slimleaf onion** (*A. amplectens*) is very similar to Hooker's onion but has **white to pink flowers** with tepals that **do not turn up at the tips**. It occurs in the same sorts of dry open habitats, scattered from the Strait of Georgia–Puget Sound area south to California. • **Olympic onion** (*A. crenulatum*) usually has **2 thick, flat leaves** curved to 1 side, a **flattened winged** stem, and upright umbels of **pink** flowers. It is scattered on dry rocky outcrops, rock slides and gravelly balds, usually at alpine elevations but occasionally in the lowlands, from southern Vancouver Island and the Gulf Islands to southwestern Oregon. • The small, strong-tasting bulbs of Hooker's onion were occasionally eaten by some northwest coast groups. Note that this is a relatively restricted species, however, and should not be harvested from the wild.

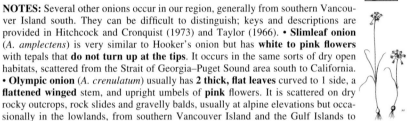

NODDING ONION • *Allium cernuum*

GENERAL: Perennial, from oval, long-tapering, faintly pink-coated, usually **clustered bulbs, smelling strongly of onion**; stems slender, leafless, somewhat angled, up to 50 cm tall.

LEAVES: Several per bulb, basal, linear, grass-like, flat or channelled, **remaining green** during flowering.

FLOWERS: Pink to rose-purple, bell-shaped; numerous in **nodding**, umbrella-shaped clusters; bracts below umbel soon deciduous.

FRUITS: 3-lobed capsules.

ECOLOGY: Dry open woods and exposed grassy places, rocky crevices and sandy soils, often with Douglas-fir; scattered but locally common; at low elevations.

NOTES: Nodding onion was eaten sparingly by a few groups of the Northwest Coast, including the Cowichan, Sechelt, Squamish, Comox, Nuxalk, Tsimshian, Makah and Kwakwaka'wakw, who marked the growing plants in spring (May or June) and came back in August to dig the bulbs. They were steamed in pits lined with pine boughs and covered with lichens and alder boughs. The Mainland Comox cooked them with seals and ducks, to take away the 'fishy' flavour. Once properly cooked, the onions lose their strong odour and flavour and become very sweet and blackish in colour. The cooked onions were a delicacy. They were eaten immediately after cooking or dried in strings or on mats or they were pressed into thin cakes. This plant contains the sugar inulin, which is converted to the more digestible fructose after cooking (see camas). • **CAUTION:** Wild onion bulbs often grow in the same habitat as, and can be confused with, those of **death-camas**, but the latter do **not** have an onion odour. If confused, do *not* try a taste test. • Lewis and Clark noted that wild onions were a remedy for flatulence induced by eating camas bulbs. • *Allium* is the genus that contains not only onions but also garlic, leeks and chives.

HARVEST BRODIAEA • *Brodiaea coronaria*

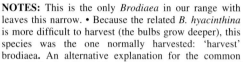

GENERAL: Perennial herb to 30 cm tall, from a deeply buried **round, scaly corm** about 2 cm across.

LEAVES: Basal, 1–3, **grass-like, 2–3 mm wide, drying out** before the flowers appear.

FLOWERS: Violet-purple, vase-shaped, 2–4 cm long, unequally stalked; in **loose umbels** of 2–10 (usually 3–5) flowers.

FRUITS: Non-stalked, egg-shaped capsules.

ECOLOGY: Open, often gravelly sites (grassy meadows and slopes, rocky areas); at low elevations.

NOTES: This is the only *Brodiaea* in our range with leaves this narrow. • Because the related *B. hyacinthina* is more difficult to harvest (the bulbs grow deeper), this species was the one normally harvested: 'harvest' brodiaea. An alternative explanation for the common name is that brodiaeas bloom later in summer than most lilies. • This genus is named after Scottish botanist James Brodie (1744–1824). • 'On the Point near the Ship [Restoration Point, Puget Sound] where…a few families of Indians live in very Mean Huts or Sheds formed of slender Rafters & covered with Mats. Several of the women were digging on the Point which excited my curiosity to know what they were digging for & found it to be a little bulbous root of a liliaceous plant which on searching about for the flower of it I discovered to be a new *Genus* of the Triandia monogina [i.e. *Brodiaea*]. This root with the young shoots of Raspberrie & a species of Barnacle formed at this time the chief part of their wretched subsistence' (Archibald Menzies, on the *Discovery* under Capt. George Vancouver, May 28, 1792). • Harvest brodiaea is suitable as a rock garden plant; it is introduced and cultivated in the United Kingdom.

FOOL'S ONION • *Brodiaea hyacinthina*

GENERAL: Perennial herb to 70 cm tall, from a **round, scaly corm** about 2 cm across.

LEAVES: 1–2, basal, **grass-like, to 1 cm wide**, 40 cm long, **usually not withered** by the time the flowers are out.

FLOWERS: Mostly **white (to light blue)** with a bluish-green midvein, bell-shaped, 1–1.5 cm long; numerous in an **upright cluster** atop 3–5 bracts.

FRUITS: Stalked capsules.

ECOLOGY: Open, grassy areas at low elevations, to mountain meadows.

NOTES: Fool's onion is also known as *Triteleia hyacinthina*. • Two other *Brodiaea* species in our area are Howell's brodiaea (*B. howellii*, also known as *Triteleia howellii*) and compact harvest lily (*B. congesta*). *B. howellii* has **1–2 leaves** and typically **pale blue**, more-tubular flowers than *B. hyacinthina*. *B. howellii* can be found from southeastern Vancouver Island and the Gulf Islands south. *B. congesta* has **2–3 leaves** and individual **pinkish or bluish-purple flowers** with very short (less than 1 cm long) stalks (hence the flowering head is dense, or 'congested'). Its range is from northern Washington to the southern limit of our region, primarily in drier climates; it is very common in the Willamette valley but only scattered northwards. • *B. hyacinthina* is also known as the 'hyacinth brodiaea,' because the flowers somewhat resemble hyacinths (*Hyacinthus* spp.), which are typically purplish-blue. Hyacinth was either Homer's name for a flower that sprang from the blood of Hyakinthos, or from an earlier (Thraco-pelagian) word for the blue colour of water. • As the name implies, the plant somewhat resembles an onion, but it has no onion flavour or smell.

COMMON CAMAS • *Camassia quamash*

GENERAL: Perennial herb to 70 cm tall, from a deep, egg-shaped, 2-cm-long **bulb**.

LEAVES: Numerous, basal, grass-like, to 2 cm wide and 50 cm long.

FLOWERS: Pale to deep blue, occasionally white, to 3.5 cm long; 5 to many in a **terminal spike**.

FRUITS: Egg-shaped capsules to 2.5 cm long; stalk curved in towards stem.

ECOLOGY: Grassy slopes and meadows, low to middle elevations; southeast Vancouver Island (also in a bog on the Brooks Peninsula) south to California; one record from Haines, Alaska.

NOTES: Camas is one of several beautiful lily-family plants restricted, in our region, to rainshadow climates. An entry from the journal of Meriwether Lewis of June 12, 1806, hints at how abundant camas meadows must have been prior to their depletion due to agriculture and urban sprawl: 'The quawmash is now in blume and from the colour of its bloom at a short distance it resembles lakes of fine clear water, so complete in this deseption that on first sight I could have sworn it was water.' • The great camas (*C. leichtlinii*) is less common than common camas, but it can be expected in similar habitats and over a similar range. The two camas species are distinguishable mainly by flower characteristics: the **tepals of the great camas eventually twist together** to cover and protect the fruit, and those of the common camas do not; the common camas has 5 tepals curved upward and the 6th curved downward; and the great camas will have **no more than 1–3 flowers fully open at one time**, while the common camas may have many more. • Camas was an important staple food, and the bulbs were eaten wherever available. The bulbs were harvested during or soon after flowering, so as not to confuse them with death-camas. Among the Vancouver Island Coast Salish, camas is semi-cultivated. The camas beds could be owned and inherited, and each season they were cleared of stones, and weeds and brush, often through controlled burning in summer. Harvesting the bulbs was a seasonal event often involving setting up temporary living shelters. It could last for several weeks, with entire families participating. The bulbs were dug with pointed digging sticks; only the larger ones were taken, and the smaller ones were left to grow. Usually steamed in large pits for 24 hours or more, the bulbs were sweet when cooked and they were often used to sweeten other foods. Because most of the bulb's carbohydrate is in the form of a long-chain sugar, inulin, which is neither very digestible nor very palatable, prolonged cooking was necessary to break down the inulin into its component fructose molecules. The properly cooked bulbs are markedly sweet and much more digestible. The steaming pits could be quite large: as much as 50 kg of bulbs could be cooked at a time. The cooked bulbs could be served right away, often at large feasts and potlatches, or sun-dried for trade or storage. • **WARNING: Death-camas often grows in the same habitat as the edible blue camas species. Although death-camas flowers are cream-coloured, the bulbs are very similar to blue camas bulbs, but they are highly toxic and potentially fatal.** • 'A hole is scraped in the ground, in which are placed a number of flat stones on which the fire is placed and kept burning until sufficiently warm, when it is taken away. The cakes, which are formed by cutting or bruising the roots and then compressing into small bricks, are placed on the stones and covered with leaves, moss, or dry grass, with a layer of earth on the outside, and left until baked or roasted, which generally takes a night. They are moist when newly taken off the stones, and are hung up to dry. Then they are placed on shelves or boxes for winter use. When warm they taste much like a baked pear. It is not improbable that a very palatable beverage might be made from them. Lewis observes that when eaten in a large quantity they occasion bowel complaints. Assuredly they produce flatulence: when in the Indian hut I was almost blown out by strength of wind.' (journal of David Douglas) • The common camas is also known as 'early camas,' because it flowers several weeks before great camas.

MEADOW DEATH-CAMAS • *Zygadenus venenosus*

GENERAL: Perennial from oval **bulbs** covered with blackish scales; stems to 60 cm tall.

LEAVES: Mainly basal, grasslike, channelled, to 30 cm long, becoming smaller up the stem.

FLOWERS: Creamy-white, bell- or saucer-shaped, with green glands at the base of the petals, foul-smelling; many in **fairly compact, terminal cluster.**

FRUITS: Cylindrical capsules to 1.5 cm long, with brown, spindle-shaped seeds.

ECOLOGY: Open forests and forest edges, damp (at least in spring) meadows, and rocky or grassy slopes, at low to middle elevations.

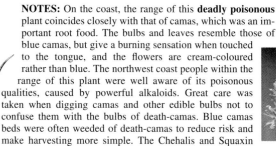

NOTES: On the coast, the range of this **deadly poisonous** plant coincides closely with that of camas, which was an important root food. The bulbs and leaves resemble those of blue camas, but give a burning sensation when touched to the tongue, and the flowers are cream-coloured rather than blue. The northwest coast people within the range of this plant were well aware of its poisonous qualities, caused by powerful alkaloids. Great care was taken when digging camas and other edible bulbs not to confuse them with the bulbs of death-camas. Blue camas beds were often weeded of death-camas to reduce risk and make harvesting more simple. The Chehalis and Squaxin used this plant as a violent emetic. It was also applied as a poultice to sprains, bruises, boils, rheumatism and pain in general. • **WARNING:** The bulb and leaves are **poisonous** to humans and grazing animals. Symptoms include vomiting, lowered body temperature, difficult breathing and finally coma. • The genus name means 'joined glands,' referring to pairs of glands inside the flowers of another species in the genus.

ALP LILY • *Lloydia serotina*

GENERAL: Small (4–15 cm tall) **alpine** perennial from oblong, scaly **bulbs** sometimes connected by thin rhizomes.

LEAVES: Narrow, grass-like, basal, somewhat fleshy, to 15 cm long, but with 2–3, smaller, alternate leaves on the stem.

FLOWERS: Yellowish-white with purple or green veins, to 2 cm across, erect or drooping in poor weather; **solitary to few atop the stems**.

FRUITS: Oval capsules to 8 mm long; seeds numerous, flattened and crescent-shaped.

ECOLOGY: Rocky ridges and ledges, meadows, subalpine parkland and alpine tundra.

NOTES: This small lily is much more common (even abundant) in alpine areas of the north and only scattered in the south. Its main area of distribution is in Europe and Asia. • Plants on the Queen Charlotte Islands are larger, with greenish veins on the flowers. • Alp lily is named for Welsh naturalist Edward Llwyd (1660–1709). This is one of the earlier flowers to appear in the alpine, so the species name *serotina* ('late-flowering') is a misnomer. However, it may be that the word is derived from the verb *sero* ('to weave together') in reference to the fine web like network of rhizomes. • Alp lily is probably the only relatively showy, lily-and-related-family species of the northern hemisphere that has a circumpolar, arctic-alpine distribution.

NORTHERN RICE ROOT • *Fritillaria camschatcensis*
BLACK LILY

GENERAL: Sturdy, glabrous, perennial herb to 60 cm tall, from a scaly **bulb with numerous rice-like bulblets**.

LEAVES: In **3 main whorls of 5–10**, sometimes alternate above, lance-shaped, to 8 cm long.

FLOWERS: Bronze to purple-brown, bell-shaped with flaring mouths, to 3 cm long, nodding, foul-smelling; usually **several from axils** of small upper leaves.

FRUITS: Upright, **6-angled capsules, without wings**; seeds numerous, flat.

ECOLOGY: Moist open places; meadows, stream-banks, often at edges of salt marshes or along shorelines; sea level to subalpine.

NOTES: The bulbs, resembling tight clusters of white rice, were eaten by virtually all northwest coast peoples, including the Nuu-chah-nulth, Comox, Kwakwaka'wakw, Heiltsuk, Haisla, Nuxalk, Haida, Coast Tsimshian, Kaigani Haida, Tlingit, Dena'ina, Kodiak and Aleuts. The bulbs grow relatively close to the surface and are easily extracted. They were dug, usually in spring before flowering or in summer or fall after flowering, using a digging stick, a wooden spade or bare hands. They were cooked immediately, or they could be partially dried then stored in a cool place. They were cooked by steaming for about 30 minutes in a cedarwood box, by boiling for a short time then mashing to a paste or occasionally by baking in ashes. They were usually eaten with oil such as oolichan grease, and more recently they were eaten with molasses or sugar. They were also cooked in stews and soups with fish or meat, or eaten raw with fish eggs. The Gitksan sometimes toasted the kernels and served them with the inner bark of western hemlock. The Kaigani Haida sometimes boiled them with the chopped leaves of western dock. Even when cooked they are slightly bitter, and some people used to soak them overnight to reduce the bitter flavour. A few people still use them, but in many areas their edibility has been forgotten. • The plants are pollinated by flies attracted to the flowers by their colour and the smell of rotting meat or faeces. • This plant is also known as chocolate lily, Indian rice and Eskimo potato.

CHOCOLATE LILY • *Fritillaria lanceolata*

GENERAL: Perennial, glabrous herb to 80 cm tall, from a scaly **bulb with numerous rice-like bulblets**.

LEAVES: In **1–2 whorls of 3–5**, sometimes alternate, lance-shaped, 5–15 cm long.

FLOWERS: Dark purple mottled with greenish-yellow, bell-shaped, to 4 cm long, nodding; **single or in clusters of 2–5**, terminal.

FRUITS: Upright, **6-angled capsules, with wings** on the angles; seeds many, flat.

ECOLOGY: Open places (grassy meadows, bluffs) and open woods, from sea level to nearly subalpine; along the coast and inland along the major drainages.

NOTES: Northern rice root has **several, brighter-green whorls of 5–10 leaves**, compared to 1 or 2 whorls of 3 leaves in chocolate lily. The greenish, usually single flowers of chocolate lily are distinct from the **dark bronze-purple flowers** of northern rice root. • Bulbs of chocolate lily were eaten by the Coast Salish, including the Squamish, Sechelt, Halq'emeylem and Straits Salish. They were steamed in pits or, more recently, boiled in metal pots. The bulblets are said to be tender and delicate, resembling rice, except for having a slightly bitter taste. Note that these flowers, also known as 'checker lily' and 'mission bells,' are quite rare in many places and should be left undisturbed.

TIGER LILY • *Lilium columbianum*

GENERAL: Hairless perennial, from deep-seated, oval, white **bulb** (3–5 cm diameter) with **thick scales**; stems slender, **to 1.2 m tall.**

LEAVES: Narrowly lance-shaped, 4–10 cm long, usually arranged **in several whorls** of 6–9 on stem; upper stem leaves may be scattered.

FLOWERS: Bright-orange with deep-red or purple spots near centre; large, **showy, nodding; tepals curved backwards**; few to many flowers at top of stem.

FRUITS: Barrel-shaped **capsules, with low ridges**; seeds numerous, flat.

ECOLOGY: Meadows, thickets, open forest and clearings; at low to subalpine elevations.

NOTES: The bulbs were steamed and eaten by the Coast Salish, Nuu-chah-nulth peoples and most northwest coast peoples in western Washington. They are bitter or peppery tasting, and they therefore tended to be used more as a flavouring or condiment than as food by themselves. The bulbs were dug at various times: in spring before flowering, during flowering in early summer, immediately after flowering or in the fall after the leaves had died down. For the fall harvest, stakes were sometimes set out in the summer to mark the bulbs. Some people say the bulbs taste better after flowering. The bulbs were generally steamed or boiled, but were also pit-cooked. After cooking, they were usually dried for winter storage. The fresh or dried bulbs were cooked in soups with meat or fish. • The name 'tiger' probably comes from the colours of the flowers. Also called 'Columbia lily' and 'Oregon lily.' The spots on the petals give rise to the superstition that smelling the tiger lily will give you freckles.

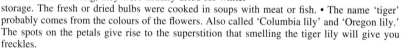

MOUNTAINBELLS • *Stenanthium occidentale*

GENERAL: Perennial, to 50 cm tall from an oval **bulb** 2–4 cm long.

LEAVES: Basal, 2–3, sheathing the stem base, to 30 cm long, narrow and grass-like.

FLOWERS: Greenish- or brownish-purple, broadly **bell-shaped**, nodding, with a tangy perfume; tepals with **tips recurved**, to 1.5 cm long; in an elongate **terminal spike**.

FRUITS: Erect, oblong **capsules** to 2 cm long; seeds flat and winged.

ECOLOGY: Wet open forest, rock faces, thickets, and meadows, usually at high elevations, but occasionally to sea level.

NOTES: Mountainbells are known to some people as 'poison onions,' and are said to be **poisonous** (Turner *et al.* 1990), but they are not widely recognized by aboriginal people. • *S. occidentale* is also called 'bronze-bells,' because the pretty bell-shaped flowers turn a deep purplish-green. They have a lovely perfume. • The Latin name is derived from the Greek *stenos* ('narrow') and *anthos* ('flower'), in reference to the flower's narrow tepals.

SUBALPINE MARIPOSA LILY • *Calochortus subalpinus*
MOUNTAIN CAT'S-EAR

GENERAL: Perennial herb to 30 cm tall, from a deep **bulb**.

LEAVES: Single, flattened, basal, to 30 cm long and 1.5 cm wide, about as long as the flowering stem, grass-like.

FLOWERS: Yellowish-white, sometimes tinged with lavender, often with a **purple crescent** on each petal and a **purple dot** on each sepal, 3–4 cm across; **1–5 in a terminal cluster** on an **unbranched** flowering stem.

FRUITS: Elliptic, sharp-pointed, **3-winged nodding capsules**.

ECOLOGY: Open forests and dry meadows at middle to subalpine elevations; Cascade Mountains from southern Washington south to the Three Sisters in central Oregon.

NOTES: Tolmie's mariposa lily (*C. tolmiei*) has **branched** stems and **white to cream-coloured flowers**, often tinged with purple or rose but unspotted; its range is from Forest Grove, Oregon, southwards in the Willamette valley, on dry rocky slopes. • The Spanish settlers named this lovely flower the 'mariposa' lily after the butterfly (or *mariposa*). Another common name is 'sego lily,' *seego* being a Shoshonean word for an 'edible bulb' (equivalent to 'camas'). *Pah-see-go* was 'water sego' or 'camas' to distinguish it from the dryland sego, *Calochortus*. • The heroine in Zane Grey's book *The Rainbow Trail* was called 'Sego Lily,' and she was a beautiful child reared amidst desolate surroundings. • *Calochortus* is from the Greek *kalo* (beautiful) and *chortos* (grass). • The name 'tulip' (a word that means 'turban') was applied to members of this genus (e.g., 'Mormon tulip'), as the flower was supposed to resemble an inverted cap. Also called 'cat's-ear' because of the hairy throats of the flowers.

BEAR-GRASS • *Xerophyllum tenax*

GENERAL: Large (to 1.5 m tall) perennial herb, from short, stout rhizomes.

LEAVES: Basal leaves grass-like, tough, wiry, evergreen, numerous **in large clumps**, long (to 90 cm), with finely toothed margins; stem leaves similar but shorter, and becoming still shorter the farther up the stem you go.

FLOWERS: White, tiny, saucer-shaped, long-stalked, fragrant; in a dense, **showy, pyramidal terminal cluster** that is at first bulbous and nippled; populations may flower irregularly every few years.

FRUITS: Oval **3-lobed capsules** to 6 mm long, each with a few small seeds.

ECOLOGY: Open areas (clearings, meadows) and open to fairly dense forest from near sea level (on the Olympic Peninsula) to the subalpine (very commonly into the krummholz).

NOTES: The flowering stems (and all their leaves) die after fruiting. • This species is abundant in some drier subalpine meadows, and it dominates the forest understorey in many subalpine forests in the Cascade Mountains. • Bears eat the fleshy leaf bases in the spring, hence the common name 'bear-grass.' Aboriginal peoples made hats, baskets and capes from the tough (*tenax*) dry (*xero*) leaves (*phyllum*). • Bear-grass has been introduced into cultivation at the University of British Columbia Botanical Garden, but it is a very difficult plant to cultivate and should not be removed from the wild.

INDIAN HELLEBORE • *Veratrum viride*
GREEN FALSE HELLEBORE, CORN LILY

GENERAL: Perennial from short, stout, erect rhizomes; stems **unbranched, often clustered**, robust, **0.7–2.0 m tall**, leafy and hairy throughout.

LEAVES: Large (10–35 cm long), broad, oblong to elliptic, pointed at tip, clasping at base, **prominently ribbed** (accordion-pleated), hairy beneath, getting narrower above.

FLOWERS: Star-shaped, **pale-green** with dark-green centres, with a musky odour; **numerous in thin, branched, terminal clusters with drooping tassels**.

FRUITS: Oblong or oval **capsules**, straw-coloured to dark-brown, containing flattish, broadly winged, brown, papery seeds.

ECOLOGY: Wet thickets, meadows, bogs and swamps, moist to wet, usually open forests, lowland (especially on the north coast) to alpine meadows; most abundant at subalpine elevations, in cold wet meadows and at late snowmelt patches in the forest.

NOTES: In similar habitats in Washington and Oregon you may encounter **California false hellebore** (*V. californicum*), which has **larger, whitish flowers** (tepals more than 1 cm long, vs. less than 1 cm long in *V. viride*), and an inflorescence with branches that **do not droop** as they do in Indian hellebore. • **WARNING:** Indian hellebore is one of the most **violently poisonous** plants on the Northwest Coast, a fact recognized by all indigenous groups. This plant was, and still is, highly respected, for even to eat a small portion of it would result in loss of consciousness, followed by death. It is sometimes known as 'skookum' root, the Chinook jargon for 'strong, powerful.' This plant was an important and respected medicine, used by most northwest coast groups. The Tlingit used an Indian-hellebore medicine for colds. The Nisga'a used small quantities of the root for toothache. There is one report of a Haisla who was cured of tuberculosis by placing a lozenge of dried Indian-hellebore root under his tongue for a day. It is said that his face went numb, but he recovered. The Haida made a poultice for sprains, bruises, and rashes, and a medicine for colds. It was believed almost any disease could be cured with Indian hellebore. The Haida also treated kidney and bladder troubles and acute fevers with this plant. The Nuxalk made preparations for chronic coughs, gonorrhea, constipation, stomach pains, chest pains, heart trouble and for toothache or rotting teeth. The Kwakwaka'wakw made medicinal preparations for constipation, internal back and chest pains, colds and to abort pregnancy. The Nuu-chah-nulth rubbed the mashed root on sores or rheumatic areas to stop pain, and as a general liniment. Among the Coast Salish this plant was utilized by the Quinault, Squamish, Sechelt, Mainland Comox, Southern Vancouver Island Salish and other groups for similar cures. • Some species of this genus are powdered to form the garden insecticide 'hellebore.' People who drink water in which hellebore is growing have reported stomach cramps. Other symptoms of hellebore poisoning include frothing at the mouth, blurred vision, 'lockjaw,' vomiting and diarrhea. • *Veratrum* presumably refers to the dark flowers or blackish rhizome (*vera* means 'true'; *atrum* means 'black'). The origin of the name 'hellebore' is obscure; true hellebores are species of *Helleborus* and do not bear much resemblance to *Veratrum* species. *Helleborus* was a supposed remedy for madness.

Iridaceae (Iris Family)

The iris family is medium-sized and occurs over much of the earth, except in the coldest regions. Its centre of distribution is in Africa. Members of the family are mostly perennial herbs from rhizomes, bulbs or corms, with one to several stems, or stemless. The leaves are mostly basal and numerous, overlapping in 2 ranks, linear and grasslike to sword-shaped, and with parallel veins. Flowers usually occur in clusters atop the stem, subtended individually or in clusters by 2 leaf-like bracts. The usually showy flowers have radial or bilateral symmetry and 6 petal-like segments in 2 series, all generally fused basally. The flowers have 3 stamens and 1 inferior ovary, 1 style and 3 stigmas. The fruit is a 3-chambered capsule that splits lengthwise into 3 segments and has several to many seeds.

The family has several economically important ornamentals, including iris, gladiolus, crocus, freesia and others. The stigmas of *Crocus sativa* are used in preparation of saffron, and the rhizomes of several irises are commercial sources of orris root, used as an aromatic flavouring in dentifrices.

Sisyrinchium   *Iris*

BLUE-EYED-GRASS • *Sisyrinchium idahoense* var. *macounii*
IDAHO BLUE-EYED-GRASS

GENERAL: Showy tufted perennial **to 40 cm tall**; stems usually flattened and **wing-margined**.

LEAVES: Mostly basal, long (to 20 cm long) and very narrow (usually less than 2 mm broad).

FLOWERS: Blue to bluish-purple, often with a yellow 'eye,' small (about 2 cm across); terminal cluster of 1–5 flowers, above a pair of sheathing, leaf-like bracts.

FRUITS: Egg-shaped capsules to 6 mm long, with black seeds.

ECOLOGY: Moist to wet grassy meadows, vernal seepage areas, marshes, roadside ditches; at low to middle elevations.

NOTES: This species used to be included in '*S. angustifolium*,' which was previously used to lump all of our blue-flowered *Sisyrinchium*s. It is also known as *S. segetum*, *S. macounii* and *S. bellum*. • A **shorter** coastal blue-flowered species with **wider leaves** (**2.5–5.5 mm** wide) and **wider stems** (averaging **2.4 mm** wide vs. less than 2.4 mm for Idaho blue-eyed-grass) is **shore blue-eyed-grass** (*S. littorale*). It is a common but scattered species of coastal meadows, marshes, beaches and cliff faces from southeast Alaska to Washington. • The name 'blue-eyed-grass' is very apt for flowers that appear like beautiful blue 'eyes' from the side of a grass-like stem. *Sisyrinchium* was Theophrastus' name for an iris. • Shore blue-eyed-grass grows mostly along ocean shores, giving rise to both its common and species name (*littorale*).

GOLDEN-EYED-GRASS • *Sisyrinchium californicum*

GENERAL: Showy, tufted perennial to 40 cm tall; stems flattened and **winged**.

LEAVES: Mostly basal, long (to 30 cm long) and narrow (5 mm wide), clumped.

FLOWERS: Yellow with purplish-brown veins, short-stalked; 6 tepals each to 1.2 cm long; 2–7 flowers, in a terminal cluster above 2 sheathing, leaf-like bracts.

FRUITS: Egg-shaped capsules to 12 mm long, with black, pitted seeds.

ECOLOGY: Moist to wet edges of wetlands (ponds, seepage areas, bogs); scattered at low elevations.

NOTES: The flower segments of *Sisyrinchium* species are not differentiated into petals and sepals, and so they are usually referred to as 'tepals.' The flowers are well-protected, with 2 larger leaf-like bracts below the inflorescence, and bracts at the base of individual flowers. The flowers of golden-eyed-grass usually open in the morning, and are closed up by mid-day. • A characteristic feature of golden-eyed-grass is that it **turns purplish-black when dried** in a plant press. • The common name 'golden-eyed-grass' refers to the yellow 'eyes' (flowers) peering out among grass-like leaves.

SATIN-FLOWER • *Sisyrinchium douglasii*
DOUGLAS' BLUE-EYED-GRASS

GENERAL: Showy tufted perennial to 30 cm tall; stems flattened but **not winged**.

LEAVES: Of two types: basal leaves bract-like, to 2 cm long; stem leaves to 15 cm long, 3 mm wide.

FLOWERS: Reddish-purple, 'satiny' in appearance, large (to 4 cm across); usually 2, terminal, above 2 sheathing, leaf-like bracts (one longer than the flowers, one shorter).

FRUITS: Capsules to 1 cm long, with brown, finely pitted seeds.

ECOLOGY: Dry rocky bluffs and meadows, open oak woodlands; at low to middle elevations.

NOTES: Satin-flower is also known as *Olsynium douglasii*, *Sisyrinchium grandiflorum*, grass-widows, and purple-eyed-grass. • Clark (1973) waxes eloquent in describing satin-flower as 'the reigning queen of the genus. Indeed, a slope covered with these sprightly bells, sensitive to every whisper of wind, is one of the floral delights of early spring.' • The pink-purple flowers have a satiny sheen that sparkles in the spring sunshine, giving rise to the common name 'satin-flower.' Satin-flower is yet another species named after early explorer and botanist David Douglas (1798–1834). • Satin-flower is one of our earliest spring flowers, often blooming as early as February with spring-gold and blue-eyed Mary.

WILD-FLAG • *Iris setosa*

GENERAL: Showy perennial herb **to 70 cm tall**, densely tufted, from a short, thick rhizome; stems often branched.

LEAVES: Long and (for an *Iris*) fairly wide (**often more than 1 cm wide**), **sword-shaped**.

FLOWERS: Blue with dark veins; sepals 5–6 cm long, 3, showy, spreading; **petals small (to 2 cm long), 3, sharp-pointed**; usually 1 or 2 flowers, terminal.

FRUITS: Egg-shaped, angled capsules, 3–4 cm long.

ECOLOGY: Wet meadows, wetland edges, marshes, lakeshores; at low to middle elevations.

NOTES: Western blue iris (*I. missouriensis*) is another blue-flowered iris, but it has **narrower leaves (less than 1 cm wide) and larger (3–6 cm), blunt-tipped petals**. It's an uncommon species, occasional on the B.C. coast and as far south as Puget Sound (where it is rare). Many of these locales represent introductions. • **WARNING:** Wild-flag is **poisonous**, especially the rhizome. • *Iris* is from the Latin meaning 'rainbow,' alluding to the different colours of the flowers. *Iris* species are also called 'flags' because the sepals hang out like banners. • The species name *setosa* means 'bristly,' perhaps referring to the sharp petal tips.

OREGON IRIS • *Iris tenax*

GENERAL: Showy, clumped perennial herb **to 40 cm tall**, from slender rhizomes.

LEAVES: Chiefly basal, long (to 40 cm long) and narrow (**5 mm wide**), tough; 1–4 stem leaves.

FLOWERS: Blue to purple, often lavender, occasionally white to pinkish or even yellow, **sepals and petals to 6 cm long**; 1–2 flowers on flowering stems to 35 cm tall.

FRUITS: Angled capsules to 3.5 cm long.

ECOLOGY: Open areas (grassy meadows, fields, pastures, roadsides, logged areas) and open woodland (deciduous or coniferous); at low to middle elevations.

NOTES: An **introduced yellow-flowered** iris occasionally found in wetlands in southern B.C. and Washington is **yellow-flag** (*I. pseudoacorus*). This is a European species perhaps adopted by Louis VII as a floral symbol for the Second Crusade, hence 'fleur de Louis' and eventually 'fleur-de-lis.' Others suggest, however, that the *fleur-de-lis* may represent a halberd-head, or even a toad. • Early explorer/botanist David Douglas found aboriginal peoples braiding iris leaves into snares for animals as large as elk: 'It will hold the strongest bullock and is not thicker than the little finger' (cited in Mathews 1988). The specific name *tenax* ('tenacious') recognizes the toughness of Oregon-iris leaves. • There is a French legend that a shield charged with irises was brought to Clovis (a 5th-century king of the Franks) from heaven while he was battling the Saracens. Another legend has Clovis trapped on a bend of the Rhine by a superior force of Goths. He was saved by noticing that yellow-flag grew far out in the river, revealing shallows across which the Franks retreated.

Orchidaceae (Orchid Family)

The orchids are a very large family (ca. 23,000 species), vying with the Asteraceae for top spot, distributed primarily in the tropics. Our region has a fair number of orchids, but except for *Calypso* and *Cypripedium*, they are not particularly showy. Still, they are beautiful in their own modest way: their flowers are intricate, complex and often wonderfully scented. The orchid flower is distinctive: strikingly bilaterally symmetrical, with 3 sepals (one usually modified) and 3 petals (the lower one usually modified into a lip, sometimes inflated into a pouch or with a hollow appendage [a spur] extending from it). The inferior ovary and its stalk are twisted through a semicircle (180°). The fruit is usually a 1-chambered capsule with very numerous, very small seeds.

Economically the orchids are important primarily for the numerous ornamentals they supply to the florist and horticultural trade. Natural vanilla extract comes from capsules of the tropical genus *Vanilla*.

It is important to remember that many of our orchids have established an intimate relationship between their roots and the fungi growing in the soil. This makes them very difficult to transplant, and they are best left in the wild to be enjoyed.

Key to Genera of the Orchid Family

1a. Plants saprophytes, without green stems and leaves; stems
reddish-brown to yellow; roots coral-like .... *Corallorhiza*
1b. Plants not saprophytes, with green stems and leaves
(leaves may be withered by flowering time) 2
  2a. Lip of flower inflated, pouch-like 3
    3a. Leaf solitary, basal; flower rose-purple, 2–3 cm long .... *Calypso*
    3b. Leaves several, extending up stem; flowers white
    or yellow, 3–5 cm long .... *Cypripedium*
  2b. Lip of flower not inflated and pouch-like 4
    4a. Lip of flower spurred at the base 5
      5a. Lip 3 lobed at tip; bracts greatly exceeding
      flowers .... *Coeloglossum* (see *Platanthera stricta*)
      5b. Lip not lobed or notched at tip; bracts not usually
      exceeding flowers .... *Platanthera*
    4b. Lip of flower not spurred 6
      6a. Leaves all basal 7
        7a. Leaves evergreen and fleshy, mottled or veined
        with white, more than 2 .... *Goodyera*
        7b. Leaves not evergreen and mottled 8
          8a. Leaves 1 (rarely 2), 3–6 cm long, prominently
          several veined .... *Malaxis* (see *Hammarbya*)
          8b. Leaves 2 or 3, less than 3 cm long,
          indistinctly few veined .... *Hammarbya*
      6b. Leaves (or at least some of them) on stems 9
        9a. Leaves 2, opposite and stalkless .... *Listera*
        9b. Leaves several, alternate, strongly reduced upward .... *Spiranthes*

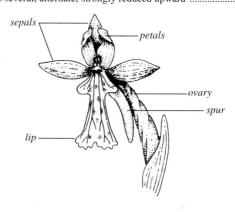

FAIRYSLIPPER • *Calypso bulbosa*

GENERAL: Perennial from a round or oval, **bulb-like corm**; stems delicate, yellow-purple to brown-purple, covered in membranous sheathing bracts, **10–25 cm long**.

LEAVES: Single, dark-green, produced at top of corm in fall and persistent through winter, withering in summer, **broadly egg-shaped**, mostly 3–6 cm long.

FLOWERS: Rose-purple, large, showy, solitary, with a sweet fragrance, 3 sepals and 2 petals (narrow, pointed, and twisted) sit erect above the lip; lower lip large, **slipper-like**, yellow to whitish, streaked and spotted with purple, with a cluster of golden hairs above and a spotted, double spur below the lip.

FRUITS: Erect capsules about 1 cm long.

ECOLOGY: Mostly in forests, often in soil rich with leaf mould; lowlands to middle elevations; rare in southeast Alaska, where usually near beaches in dense forest.

NOTES: This beautiful (and deliciously perfumed) little orchid, although widespread, is rapidly being exterminated in populated areas due to trampling and especially picking. The corms are attached by means of delicate roots that are easily broken even by the lightest tug on the stem. Hence, when the flower is picked, the plant usually dies. • The Haida called the corms 'black cod grease' because of their rich, butter-like flavour. They ate them in small quantities, but their use today is not recommended because the plants are relatively rare in many places. Haida girls ate the corms raw to enhance their bustlines. • Calypso, the goddess daughter of Atlas, was Homer's beautiful nymph hidden in the woods and found by Ulysses when he was wrecked on the island of Ogygia. *Calypso* means 'concealment.' Other common names include Cytherea, Venus slipper, hider-of-the-north, pink slipper-orchid, and false ladyslipper. Cytherea is another name for Aphrodite: the goddess of love, beauty and marriage.

MOUNTAIN LADYSLIPPER • *Cypripedium montanum*

GENERAL: Perennial, somewhat **rhizomatous herb**; stems **20–70 (sometimes to 100) cm tall**, glandular to somewhat hairy, simple or branched.

LEAVES: Elliptic to egg-shaped, alternate, to 12 cm long, 5 cm wide, **all along the stem**, with the bases of the lower ones wrapped around (sheathing) the stem.

FLOWERS: White with purple veins, fragrant, the lip inflated into a **showy pouch**, other petals and sepals copper-coloured, long and twisted; usually 2 flowers per stem.

FRUITS: Ascending oblong capsules, 2–3 cm long.

ECOLOGY: Dry to moist, usually fairly open woods, often deciduous or with a deciduous component, commonly on rich humus; also on disturbed sites such as roadsides; scattered but locally abundant, at low to middle (and sometimes subalpine) elevations.

NOTES: The flowers of the mountain ladyslipper resemble the fairyslipper in that their lip has been expanded into a pouch. The flowers differ from *Calypso*'s in colour and size (*Cypripedium* has larger flowers, sometimes called 'moccasin flowers'). In addition, mountain ladyslipper has numerous leaves, and it is much taller than the fairyslipper. • Mountain ladyslipper is threatened by over-collecting; would-be growers should be aware that this orchid reportedly takes 15 years to flower. • 'Ladyslipper' and 'moccasin flower' both refer to the shape of the lower lip of the flower. *Cypripedium* means 'Aphrodite's foot,' as *Kypris* was an old name for Aphrodite (Venus).

WESTERN CORALROOT • *Corallorhiza maculata* ssp. *mertensiana*

GENERAL: Perennial **saprophyte** from branched, coral-like rhizomes; stems to 50 cm tall, **purplish to reddish-brown**, or often light yellow to tan.

LEAVES: Reduced to thin, semi-transparent sheaths.

FLOWERS: Pink to reddish-purple, the **lip not spotted**; flowers few to 30 in a loose, terminal cluster.

FRUITS: Nodding, oval capsules about 2 cm long.

ECOLOGY: Rich humus in moist to fairly dry coniferous or mixed forest, often in heavy shade; widespread at low to middle elevations.

NOTES: The **spotted coralroot** (*C. maculata* ssp. *maculata*) is similar, but its **lip is white with magenta spots** (inset photo and line drawing); it can be found in the same habitats

as western coralroot, from Prince of Wales Island and Bella Coola south to California (but not on the Queen Charlotte Islands). • Members of the genus *Corallorhiza* are saprophytic orchids— that is, they derive their nutrients from decaying organic matter, while most plants make their own food. Because of this, the coralroots lack the green colour that is characteristic of most plants. • *Corallorhiza* literally means 'coral-like root' and *maculata* means 'spotted.'

STRIPED CORALROOT • *Corallorhiza striata*

GENERAL: Perennial **saprophyte** from branched, coral-like rhizomes; **stems purplish tinged**, 15–50 cm tall.

LEAVES: Thin, semi-transparent, sheathing scales.

FLOWERS: Pink to yellowish-pink with 3 purplish stripes on each sepal; lip tongue-shaped, not lobed, stripes on lip merging to solid brown-purple; 7–25 flowers drooping in fairly loose terminal clusters.

FRUITS: Nodding, elliptic capsules about 1 cm long.

ECOLOGY: Moist humus in shady coniferous and deciduous forests; streambanks, ravines; common at low to middle elevations.

NOTES: As in other species of coralroot, an occasional 'albino' specimen is pale yellow throughout. • *Corallorhiza striata* is called 'striped coralroot' because of the stripes on

its sepals. It is also called 'madder-stripes' in reference to the flower colour, sometimes described as madder-purple. The coralroots are also sometimes called 'chicken toes.' • All 3 coralroots mentioned here typically flower in late spring, often with starflowers, fairybells, vanilla-leaf, false lily-of-the-valley, wild roses, orange honeysuckle, red huckleberry, thimbleberry, and salal. What a time to be in the woods!

RATTLESNAKE-PLANTAIN • *Goodyera oblongifolia*

GENERAL: Evergreen perennial from short creeping rhizomes, with fibrous roots; stems 20–45 cm tall, stout and stiff, glandular-hairy; spreads very rapidly by vegetative multiplication.

LEAVES: In **basal rosette**, thick, **dark green, mottled or striped** with white, especially along midrib, oval or oblong to narrowly elliptic, 3–10 cm long.

FLOWERS: Dull-white to greenish, petals and 1 of the sepals form a hood over the lip; numerous in long, dense, downy, terminal spike with most of the flowers oriented to one side.

FRUITS: Erect capsules to 1 cm long.

ECOLOGY: On humus among mosses in dry to moist, shady, coniferous forests; common from lowlands to middle elevations.

NOTES: According to the 'Doctrine of Signs,' early settlers believed that because the markings on the leaves of the rattlesnake-plantain resembled snakeskin markings, this plant could be used in treatment of rattlesnake bites. Presumably, it was also thought to resemble a plantain (*Plantago major*) because of the similarity of the flattened basal leaf rosettes of the 2 species. • Some northwest coast peoples, such as the Saanich, used the plants as a good luck charm. Stl'atl'imx children used to make 'balloons' from the leaves, by rubbing them until the top and bottom layers separated and then blowing through the stem to inflate them. This plant was known to some interior plateau peoples as a medicine for childbirth, and as a poultice for cuts and sores for which the leaves were split open, and the moist inner part placed over the wound. • *Goodyera* is named for John Goodyer, a 17th-century English botanist.

BOG ADDER'S-MOUTH ORCHID • *Hammarbya paludosa*

GENERAL: Perennial **to 20 cm tall**, spreading by **stolons from corms** buried in humus and moss.

LEAVES: Pale-green, small (to 3 cm long), **2–3 in a basal cluster**, their bases sheathing the stem.

FLOWERS: Yellow-green, tiny; lip ovate, **not lobed**; numerous flowers in a slender terminal spike.

FRUITS: Egg-shaped capsules to 4 mm long.

ECOLOGY: Bogs and muskeg at low to middle elevations; uncommon (though abundant where it appears).

NOTES: This species is also known as *Malaxis paludosa*. • **One-leaved malaxis** (*M. monophyllos*, also known as white adder's-tongue) is a very similar species with a **3-lobed, pointed lip** and (usually) a **single basal leaf**. It can be found in wet sites (often in moist forests or along streams and beaches) from Alaska to southeastern Vancouver Island. One variety of this species (**var. *diphyllos***), known in our region only from the Queen Charlotte Islands, has **2 basal leaves**, but the lip is still lobed and pointed. The small bog-orchid (*Platanthera chorisiana*) grows in similar habitats to those of bog adder's-mouth orchid, scattered from Vancouver Island north. It could be confused with either *H. paludosa* or *M. monophyllos*, because it is only 5–12 cm tall and has 2 broad leaves at the middle of the stem and a short spike of very small, greenish flowers. However, it has tuber-like roots and flowers with spurred lips.

NORTHWESTERN TWAYBLADE • *Listera caurina*

GENERAL: Perennial from slender creeping **rhizomes**; stems **to 30 cm tall, very hairy above leaves.**

LEAVES: A single pair near mid-length of stem, **broad, egg-shaped** and pointed, to 6 cm long, opposite, clasping at base.

FLOWERS: Pale-green to yellowish; lip rounded and with a pair of horn-like teeth at base; 5–25 flowers in a terminal elongated cluster.

FRUITS: Egg-shaped capsules to 6 mm long.

ECOLOGY: Moist to wet, mossy coniferous forests, wet meadows, stream-banks; from low to subalpine elevations.

NOTES: Broad-leaved twayblade (*L. convallarioides*) is similar, but has a **lip that is more notched** and has shorter, broader, more **triangular teeth at its base**. It can be found in the same habitats, over the same range (but very rare in southeastern Alaska) as northwestern

twayblade. • *Listera* species earned the name 'twayblade' because of the two small blades found on the flowering stem. For the same reason, they are sometimes called 'big-ears.' • The species name *caurina* means 'of the northwest wind.'

HEART-LEAVED TWAYBLADE • *Listera cordata*

GENERAL: Perennial from slender creeping **rhizomes**; stems **to 20 cm tall, smooth to glandular-hairy above leaves.**

LEAVES: A single pair near mid-length of stem, **broad, heart-shaped**, to 4 cm long, opposite, clasping at base.

FLOWERS: Pale-green to purplish-brown; lip divided into 2 linear or lance-shaped lobes and with a pair of horn-like teeth at base; 5–16 flowers in terminal elongated cluster.

FRUITS: Egg-shaped capsules.

ECOLOGY: Moist to wet, mossy coniferous forests, along streams or in bogs; usually at middle elevations.

NOTES: The intricate pollination mechanisms of *Listera* species fascinated Charles Darwin, who studied them intensively. The pollen is blown out explosively within a drop of viscous fluid that glues the pollen masses to unsuspecting insects (or to your finger if you touch the top of the column). Heart-leaved twayblade flowers have an unpleasant odour that attracts flies and fungus gnats. • The genus *Listera* is named for English naturalist M. Lister (1638–1712); *cordata* means 'heart-shaped' and refers to the leaves, as does the common name. Also called 'mannikin twayblade'; 'mannikin' means 'a dwarf' or 'little man.'

WHITE BOG-ORCHID • *Platanthera dilatata*
WHITE REIN-ORCHID

GENERAL: Perennial from fleshy tuber-like roots; stems erect, to 70 cm tall, smooth, **leafy** throughout.

LEAVES: Gradually getting smaller up the stem, sheathing, oblong to broadly lance-shaped.

FLOWERS: White to greenish-tinged, waxy, small but **very fragrant; spur slender, cylindrical, curved, longer than lip**; 5–30 flowers in loose to densely packed terminal spikes.

FRUITS: Elliptic capsules.

ECOLOGY: Swamps, bogs, fens, marshes, wet meadows, moist seepage slopes, along streams and lake edges, also in subalpine meadows, swampy coniferous forests and clearings; at middle to high elevations.

NOTES: **Slender bog-orchid** (*P. stricta*) occurs in similar habitats throughout our region and resembles white bog-orchid, but it has **green flowers with scrotiform spurs** and fewer leaves that are more rounded at the tip. • This genus of orchids is referred to in some guides as *Habenaria*. Do not confuse *Habenaria* with *habañera*, a sultry Spanish dance made famous by Bizet's *Carmen*. Carmen was intrigued by José's initial indifference to her charms; the flowers of rein-orchid may initially appear indifferent, but they are curiously contrived and intriguing. • This is a very fragrant species, often smelled before being sighted. Another common name for this species is 'scent-candle.' Szczawinski (1959) describes the perfume as a mix of cloves, vanilla, and mock-orange. • Some interior aboriginal groups believed the plant to be poisonous to humans and animals. The Shuswap used extracts as poison to sprinkle on baits for coyote and grizzlies. Other sources report that the tuber-like roots are edible. Care should be taken until the exact poisonous nature of this plant is clarified. • The name 'rein'-orchid comes from the Latin *habenas* meaning a 'strap' or 'rein' and refers to the thong-like shape of the lip and spur.

SLENDER BOG-ORCHID • *Platanthera stricta*
SLENDER REIN-ORCHID

GENERAL: Perennial from fleshy, spindle-shaped tuber-like roots; stems erect, stout, to 1 m tall, smooth, **leafy**.

LEAVES: Gradually getting smaller up the stem, sheathing, lance-shaped, to 15 cm long.

FLOWERS: Green, sometimes brownish-tinged, waxy, **not fragrant; spur inflated and sac-like**, sometimes purplish, **shorter than lip**; 5–30 flowers in slender terminal clusters.

FRUITS: Elliptic capsules to 1.5 cm long.

ECOLOGY: Wet meadows, coniferous forests, along streams and lake edges, swamps and bogs, also in subalpine meadows; at low to middle elevations.

NOTES: This species is also known as *P. saccata*. • Two other green-flowered, non-scented rein-orchids are the green-flowered bog-orchid (*P. hyperborea*) and the frog-orchid (*Coeloglossum viride*, also known as *P. viridis*). The **green-flowered bog-orchid** is most similar to the slender bog-orchid, but it has a **cylindrical spur** on its flower; it is found in wet, open places through most of our region. The **frog-orchid has an inflated spur** and a **lip with 2–3 lobes** (lips of the other rein-orchids are entire). It is found (less commonly) from southeast Alaska to southern B.C., in wetlands, dry to moist forest, thickets and meadows, and on grassy shores. • The species name *stricta* means the same thing as the common name: 'slender.'

ALASKA REIN-ORCHID • *Platanthera unalascensis*

GENERAL: Perennial from fibrous roots with 1–3 tubers; stems erect, to 90 cm tall, **leafless**.

LEAVES: Basal, 2–4, lance-shaped but broadest near the tip, to 20 cm long, soon withering.

FLOWERS: Green or greenish-white, not fragrant; spur cylindrical, about the same length as the lip; flowers numerous in narrow clusters.

FRUITS: Elliptic capsules to 1 cm long.

ECOLOGY: Dry to moist coniferous forests, meadows, riverside areas; at low to middle elevations, uncommon north of 55°N.

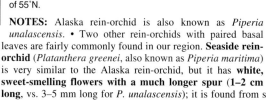

NOTES: Alaska rein-orchid is also known as *Piperia unalascensis*. • Two other rein-orchids with paired basal leaves are fairly commonly found in our region. **Seaside rein-orchid** (*Platanthera greenei*, also known as *Piperia maritima*) is very similar to the Alaska rein-orchid, but it has **white, sweet-smelling flowers with a much longer spur (1–2 cm long**, vs. 3–5 mm long for *P. unalascensis*); it is found from southeast Vancouver Island and the Gulf and San Juan Islands south (one collection from the Queen Charlotte Islands) in grassy meadows and on rocky slopes, at mostly low elevations. **Round-leaved rein-orchid** (*P. orbiculata*) has **round basal leaves that lie flat** on the ground; it occurs in similar habitats, and over a similar range, as the Alaska rein-orchid, but it is much less common, and it is absent from the Queen Charlotte Islands. • The common name 'rein-orchid' derives from the Latin *habenos* meaning 'strap, rein or thong,' and refers to the strap-shaped lip and spur. The species name recognizes that the plant was described from Unalaska.

LADIES' TRESSES • *Spiranthes romanzoffiana*

GENERAL: Perennial to 50 cm tall from fleshy, tuberous roots.

LEAVES: Basal, 2–5, long and narrow (to 20 cm long, 5–10 mm broad), reduced to sheathing bracts above base.

FLOWERS: White or creamy to greenish-white, petals converge and form a hood; in a dense spike, with flowers in 1–4 rows **arranged in spiral fashion** around the spike .

FRUITS: Dry, many-seeded capsules.

ECOLOGY: Dry to moist woodland, meadows, streamside areas, lakeshores, bogs and marshes; at low to middle elevations, less common north of 55°N.

NOTES: The flowers are supposed to resemble braided ladies hair, although the name is more appropriate for its original owner *Neottia spiralis*, a Eurasian orchid. This species was named after Nikolei Rumliantzev, Count Romanzoff (1754–1826), a Russian patron of science, and the person who sent Kotzebue to explore Alaska.

Polygonaceae (Buckwheat Family)

The Polygonaceae are annual or perennial, sometimes twining, herbs, with stems often with swollen nodes. The alternate leaves usually have sheathing stipules at the base of the leaf stalks (*Eriogonum* is an exception). The small, sometimes unisexual flowers typically are numerous in terminal or axillary clusters. The flowers are radially symmetric with 6 (sometimes only 3, 4 or 5) undifferentiated, distinct, scale-like sepals/petals typically in 2 whorls of 3 each. The inner series of scales is sometimes enlarged or modified with hooks, spines, wings or bumps, and sometimes the scales are persistent, enlarged and membranous in fruit. Stamens are mostly 6–9; the ovary is single, superior, 1-chambered. The fruit is a flat, angled or winged, nut-like achene with 1 seed.

The buckwheats are a medium-sized family mostly of northern temperate regions, although *Polygonum* occurs on all continents. The family is of little economic importance, although buckwheat (*Fagopyrum*) and rhubarb (*Rheum*) are significant foods. Ornamentals include mountain-rose vine (*Antigonon*), silver-lace vine (*Polygonum aubertii*), sachaline (*Polygonum sachalinense*) and related coarse perennials, and sea-grape (*Coccoloba uvifera*). Some species are rascally little weeds.

Key to Genera of the Buckwheat Family

1a. Leaves without sheathing stipules; flowers clustered in umbels or heads;stamens 9 .... *Eriogonum*
1b. Leaves with collar-like sheathing stipules surrounding bases of leaf stalks; stamens 4–6 2
  2a. Leaves all basal, kidney-shaped; sepals 4 .... *Oxyria*
  2b. Stems with alternate leaves; leaves not kidney-shaped; sepals 3, 5 or 6 3
    3a. Sepals 6; stamens 6; fruits usually winged .... *Rumex*
    3b. Sepals 5; stamens 5; fruits angled, but not usually winged .... *Polygonum*

Key to Knotweeds (*Polygonum*)

1a. Annuals, usually with small taproots; more of less clear & colourless 2
  2a. Flower stalks curved sharply downwards; flowers in axils of bracts,
  not bunched .... *P. douglasii*
  2b. Flower stalks erect or spreading; flowers often crowded in short clusters 3
    3a. Leaves elliptic to roundish, 5–15 mm long;
    achenes blackish, shining .... *P. minimum* (see *P. douglasii*)
    3b. Achenes yellowish to brown 4
      4a. Mature achenes smooth, yellowish-brown; plants of
      sea beaches and salt marshes .... *P. fowleri* (see *P. douglasii*)
      4b. Achenes wrinkled and bumpy, dark brown; weedy species of
      disturbed habitats .... *P. aviculare* (see *P. douglasii*)
1b. Perennials (sometimes annual), usually with rhizomes; stipules usually
red or brown, cylindric or funnel-like 5
  5a. Flowers in a single spike-like cluster atop few-leaved or leafless stem 6
    6a. Spike-like flower clusters white to pinkish, at least 1.5 cm thick .... *P. bistortoides*
    6b. Spike-like flower clusters white, < 1.5 cm thick; lower flowers
    replaced by bulblets .... *P. viviparum* (see *P. bistortoides*)
  5b. Flowers in clusters in leaf axils as well as terminal; stems leafy 7
    7a. Plants erect, strongly rhizomatous introduced, escaped from cultivation 8
      8a. Leaves heart-shaped; fruits keeled; stems to 4 m tall .... *P. sachalinense*
      8b. Leaves squared-off at base; stems mostly to 1 m tall 9
        9a. Fruits strongly winged .... *P. cuspidatum* (see *P. sachalinense*)
        9b. Fruits not winged .... *P. polystachyum* (see *P. sachalinense*)
    7b. Plants generally reclining or spreading, if erect less than 1 m tall, native 10
      10a. Stems perennial, woody-based, covered with clear, torn stipules;
      along coastline, usually on sand dunes .... *P. paronychia*
      10b. Stems annual, herbaceous to the base 11
        11a. Plants subalpine to alpine, with enlarged fleshy root crowns 12
          12a. Flowers in small clusters in leaf axils; leaves oval to oblong;
          stems ascending to erect, < 50 cm tall .... *P. newberryi*
          12b. Flowers in loose showy leafy terminal clusters; leaves lance-shaped;
          stems erect, 80–200 cm tall .... *P. phytolaccaefolium* (see *P. newberryi*)
        11b. Plants not alpine 13
          13a. Flowers rose-coloured, in 1 or 2 head-like clusters; plants
          aquatic or amphibious .... *P. amphibium* (see *P. lapathifolium*)
          13b. Flowers white or green to pinkish, in several small spike-like
          clusters; plants in wet places, but not aquatic .... *P. lapathifolium*

AMERICAN BISTORT • *Polygonum bistortoides*

GENERAL: Perennial from a short, thick, erect or ascending rhizome; flowering stems 1 to several, unbranched, **20–70 cm tall**.

LEAVES: Mostly basal, long-stalked, the blade oblong to elliptic or lance-shaped, to 15–20 cm long, with brownish sheathing stipules at the base; stem leaves few, smaller, becoming sessile upwards.

FLOWERS: White to pinkish, with 5 small (4–5 mm long) petal-like lobes and 8 stamens **sticking out** from flowers; **numerous in terminal, spike-like clusters** 2–5 cm long and **about 2 cm thick**.

FRUITS: Achenes, smooth, lustrous yellowish brown, 3-angled.

ECOLOGY: Common in moist to wet meadows and streambanks at subalpine and alpine elevations.

NOTES: American bistort is also known as *Bistorta bistortoides*. • *Polygonum viviparum* (**alpine bistort**, also known as *Bistorta vivipara*) is a smaller (usually) plant with **spike-like clusters less than 1.5 cm thick**, and lower flowers usually replaced by **bulblets**. It is normally an alpine species, but it descends to near sea level in periglacial habitats. It is fairly common in the Alaska portion of our region, rare on Queen Charlotte Islands, and it is occasional south in the mainland mountains to the North Cascades. • *Polygonum* is Greek for 'many' (*poly*) 'knees' (*gonu*), and *bistortoides* comes from the Latin *bis* (twice) and *torta* (twisted): 'many knees, twice twisted,' in reference to the jointed stems and twisted rhizomes.

BLACK KNOTWEED • *Polygonum paronychia*
BEACH KNOTWEED

GENERAL: Semi-shrubby, branched perennial; **branches prostrate and spreading, or ascending**, freely rooting, clothed with remains of membranous torn stipules.

LEAVES: Narrowly oblong but with **rolled-under margins** and thus **linear in outline**, numerous, 1–3 cm long, with prominent fringed midrib beneath; sheathing stipules **with frilly tips**.

FLOWERS: White to pink, short-stalked, 5 petal-like flower segments, 5–6 mm long, 8 stamens; **clustered in upper leaf axils**.

FRUITS: Achenes, smooth, shining, black, 3-angled.

ECOLOGY: Coastal dunes and sandy beaches; strictly low elevations. Scattered in suitable habitats.

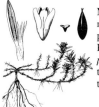

NOTES: The common name 'knotweed' refers to the many-jointed stems. • A poultice of black knotweed was used in Europe to treat 'whitlows' or inflammations 'beside the nail' (Latin *paronychia*). • *P. aviculare* (see Douglas' knotweed, p. 127) was known as the 'hindering knotweed' or 'knotgrass' from the belief that it would hinder the growth of children.

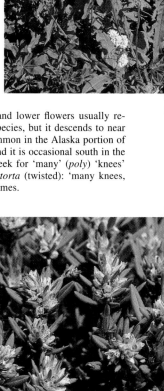

GIANT KNOTWEED • *Polygonum sachalinense*
SACHALINE

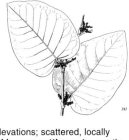

GENERAL: Huge, strongly rhizomatous, hairless perennial; **stems erect, leafy, hollow, reed- or cane-like**, reddish, **to 4 m tall** but still herbaceous.

LEAVES: Heart-shaped, big (15–30 cm long, at least 2/3 as wide), with tubular, sheathing stipules at the base.

FLOWERS: Greenish-white, with 5 flower segments, 2–3 mm long; **numerous in small panicles in upper leaf axils.**

FRUITS: Achenes, smooth, shining, black, 3-angled.

ECOLOGY: Moist ravines, ditches, waste places; low elevations; scattered, locally common, **in disturbed areas especially in and around human settlements**, mostly in the southern half of the region but to be expected in north coastal towns as well.

NOTES: Japanese knotweed (*P. cuspidatum*) and Himalayan knotweed (*P. polystachyum*) both resemble the giant knotweed, but **Japanese knotweed** has **egg-shaped, abruptly pointed leaves** more or less **squared off at the base** and flowers about 2 mm long, whereas **Himalayan knotweed has oblong lance- to egg-shaped leaves often heart-shaped or with 2 small lobes at the base** and flowers 3–4 mm long. Neither species is quite as huge as giant knotweed; both are introductions from Asia and have become established in several places in the region. Himalayan knotweed is known from the Queen Charlotte Islands. • **Introduced and cultivated** for gardens, giant knotweed is an aggressive native of Japan and Sakhalin Island that has frequently escaped and become well established. • The young shoots of giant knotweed are edible and have a tart, tangy flavour reminiscent of rhubarb. They can be cooked as a potherb, but should not be eaten excessively because they contain oxalic acid (see sheep sorrel, p. 129). • The species name means 'from Sakhalin Island.'

NEWBERRY'S KNOTWEED • *Polygonum newberryi*
FLEECEFLOWER

GENERAL: Perennial from a **thick, fleshy** root and branched crown; stems several, leafy, ascending to erect, simple to branched, hairless to finely hairy, 15–35 cm tall; shoots come up deep red in spring.

LEAVES: Numerous, **broadly lance-shaped to oblong-oval**, mostly blunt-tipped, short-stalked, **2–5 cm long**, hairless to downy on both surfaces, with brownish, long-sheathing stipules at the base.

FLOWERS: Greenish-white to pinkish, 3–4 mm long; in **small clusters wedged in axils of upper leaves**.

FRUITS: Achenes, yellowish-brown, smooth, shining, 3-angled.

ECOLOGY: Rocky, open slopes and ridges, often on talus, scree or semibarren pumice; at **subalpine and alpine** elevations.

NOTES: Alpine knotweed (*P. phytolaccaefolium*) also inhabits subalpine to alpine ridges, talus slopes and meadows, commonly in the Washington-Oregon Cascades. It also has a thick root and branched crown, but it is a **tall (0.5–2 m)** plant with leaves that are **lance-shaped and often longer than 8 cm**. It has numerous flowers in **open, loose panicles**. • *P. newberryi* is called 'fleeceflower' because of the fine fuzz over most of the plant. • John Newberry was surgeon-naturalist (specializing in geology and herpetology) on an 1858 U.S. Army expedition searching for a railway route along the east side of the Cascades from California to the Dalles of the Columbia River.

DOUGLAS' KNOTWEED • *Polygonum douglasii*

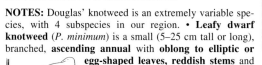

GENERAL: Taprooted annual; stems simple to freely branched, **erect to ascending**, 10–50 cm tall, **greenish**.

LEAVES: Linear to narrowly oblong or lance-shaped, numerous but not strongly overlapping, 1–6 cm long, sessile or nearly so, jointed at the base; stipules short, sheathing, raggedly torn at tip.

FLOWERS: Greenish with white or reddish margins, small, with 5 flower segments 2–4 mm long; several to many in **long loose** (somewhat short) **racemes** with 1–4 flowers per node, on short downcurved or spreading stalks.

FRUITS: Achenes, black, smooth, shining, 3-angled.

ECOLOGY: Dry to moist, often gravelly or disturbed, open sites; common at low to middle elevations.

NOTES: Douglas' knotweed is an extremely variable species, with 4 subspecies in our region. • **Leafy dwarf knotweed** (*P. minimum*) is a small (5–25 cm tall or long), branched, **ascending annual** with **oblong to elliptic or egg-shaped leaves, reddish stems** and greenish-black achenes. It is scattered in dry open sites, usually at high elevations, from southern B.C. (south of 53°N) to California; also reported from Haines, Alaska. **Fowler's knotweed** (*P. fowleri*) is a **prostrate maritime annual,** with somewhat **fleshy, oblong to egg-shaped leaves**, and yellowish-brown achenes. It grows in tidal marshes and on sandy or gravelly sea beaches, scattered from central B.C. north through south coastal Alaska. **Common knotweed** (*P. aviculare*) is a widespread **weedy annual** with **bluish-green, oblong to elliptic or lance-shaped leaves**. Also known as doorweed, knotgrass or matgrass, it grows in a variety of disturbed, open, often dry or compacted sites, throughout the region but more commonly in the southern half. • *P. aviculare* was known as the 'hindering knotweed' or 'knotgrass' from the belief that it would hinder the growth of children.

WILLOW WEED • *Polygonum lapathifolium*
DOCKLEAF SMARTWEED

GENERAL: Annual with an erect, usually branched, leafy stem **20–80 cm tall**.

LEAVES: Lance-shaped to oblong or elliptic, 4–20 cm long, hairless to hairy; sheathing stipules brownish, 5–20 mm long, upper margin with slender, soft bristles but not raggedly torn.

FLOWERS: Greenish, white or pink, with 4 or 5 flower segments, the outer 2 larger and strongly 3-veined; several to many borne in **spike-like** racemes (which are **often aggregated in open panicles**) on glandular stalks (or stalkless).

FRUITS: Achenes, brown, smooth, shining, lens-shaped.

ECOLOGY: Moist meadows, wet shorelines, ditches, roadsides, gardens, fields, swamps; low to middle elevations. Common in the southern half of the region, from southwestern B.C. south; uncommon, widely scattered on the north coast.

NOTES: All of the smartweeds in our region are weedy in moist to wet sites, scattered mostly in the southern half of the region, rare northwards. They include marshpepper smartweed (*P. hydropiper*), water-pepper (*P. hydropiperoides*), lady's-thumb (*P. persicaria*, also called common smartweed) and dotted smartweed (*P. punctatum*). They are difficult to distinguish, even with technical manuals. However, *P. amphibium* (**water smartweed**) is an unmistakable **aquatic** (see 'Aquatics' section, p.342) **or creeping species** with long-stalked, narrowly elliptic to oblong, often floating leaves and 1–2 rose-coloured, terminal, compact, thick spikes (see p. 342). • Several species of *Polygonum* were called 'smartweed,' or 'arsmart' in the old days, because of the irritating effect of the leaves 'when used in these parts' (Gerarde's Herbal). There is no explanation as to why anyone would want to use the plant on these parts in the first place.

SULFUR BUCKWHEAT • *Eriogonum umbellatum*

GENERAL: Perennial from a **strong taproot and branched crown**; branches **usually prostrate and forming mats** to 60 cm wide, but sometimes ascending and the **upright flowering stems** 5–40 cm tall, **usually white-woolly**.

LEAVES: All basal, elliptic, oval, spoon- or egg-shaped, narrowed to a slender stalk, **usually grey-woolly below and greenish above**, the blades 1–4 cm long; without sheathing stipules at the base.

FLOWERS: Light to deep yellow, sometimes pink-tinged, small, with 6 flower lobes and 9 stamens; numerous, in **compact headlike clusters (umbels)** on stalks arising from a whorl of several narrow, leaf-like bracts.

FRUITS: Achenes, smooth, 3-angled.

ECOLOGY: Dry gravelly ridges, talus slopes, rock ledges and crevices, common from middle to high elevations.

NOTES: Barestem buckwheat (*E. nudum*) has **white to pink** flowers in several, small, tight umbels; the flowers are interspersed with feathery, hairy bracts. It grows in dry to moist meadows, on rock outcrops, along trails and roadsides; scattered from low to subalpine elevations in the Washington and Oregon Cascades. **Northern buckwheat** (*E. compositum*) has bluish-green, long-stalked, **narrowly egg-shaped to deltoid leaves** that are **squared off or heart-shaped at the base**, and it has **creamy-white to lemon-yellow** flowers in broad, compound umbels. It is locally common on dry ridges and rock outcrops in the Oregon Cascades, ranging mostly east of our region. • The true 'buckwheat' (*Fagopyrum*) was widely cultivated in Europe for fodder, and its triangular seeds were ground to make flour. *E. umbellatum*'s inverted umbrella-shaped clusters of sulphur-coloured flowers and its similarity to buckwheat give rise to the common name. *Eriogonum* means 'woolly' (*erio*) 'knees' (*gonu*).

ALPINE BUCKWHEAT • *Eriogonum pyrolifolium*
DIRTY SOCKS

GENERAL: Tufted perennial from a strong taproot and woody, simple to branched crown; flower stems several, unbranched, leafless, **usually long-hairy,** 4–15 cm tall, **often red**; numerous dried old leaves at the base of the plant.

LEAVES: All basal, numerous, stalked, **elliptic to oval,** greenish-yellow and usually **hairless above,** commonly **greyish-hairy (sometimes hairless and green) below,** the blades 1–5 cm long.

FLOWERS: White or greenish-white to pinkish, glandular-hairy and reddish-fuzzy, **foul-smelling;** anthers purplish; in small, tight umbels with only 2 bracts below inflorescence.

FRUITS: Achenes, 3-angled.

ECOLOGY: Dry scree, talus and rocky ridges; most common on pumice; at high elevations.

NOTES: Oval-leaved or cushion buckwheat (*E. ovalifolium* var. *nivale*) is locally common on dry alpine ridges and talus slopes in the Cascades and Olympic Mountains. It is a **tiny** (**1–6 cm tall** flowering stems), **densely matted** plant with **silvery-white, elliptic to oval** leaves, and **creamy-white to rose-tinged flowers** in single headlike clusters. • You will not forget the common name 'dirty socks' once you have smelled the flowers of *E. pyrolifolium*.

MOUNTAIN SORREL • *Oxyria digyna*

GENERAL: Hairless, often **reddish-tinged** perennial from long fleshy taproot and branching crown; stems usually several, 5–60 cm tall; juice acrid, vinegary.

LEAVES: Mostly basal, kidney- to heart-shaped, long-stalked, with sheathing stipules at the base; flowering stems leafless or often with a single leaf below the inflorescence.

FLOWERS: Greenish to reddish, small, short-stalked, **flower scales 4**, about 2 mm long; usually numerous and crowded in panicle 2–20 cm long.

FRUITS: Achenes, **flattened, lens-shaped**, 3–6 mm wide, **prominently winged**.

ECOLOGY: Moist, often gravelly or rocky, open sites (talus and scree slopes, ledges, gullies, streambanks, snowbeds) from middle to high elevations; common through most of our region, uncommon on the Queen Charlotte Islands.

NOTES: The leaves of mountain sorrel can be eaten as a salad green (but check the next note before you do). • 'Sorrel' is from the French *surelle*, the diminutive of the Lower German *suur* meaning 'sour,' from the acidity of the leaves. The genus name *Oxyria* also means 'acid-tasting.'

SHEEP SORREL • *Rumex acetosella*
SOUR WEED

GENERAL: Hairless perennial with slender, widely spreading **rhizomes**; stems thin, 1 to several, unbranched below the inflorescence, **15–50 cm tall**.

LEAVES: Numerous, variable, narrowly **arrowhead-shaped** with spreading basal lobes, 1–8 cm long; basal leaves long stalked; stem leaves short stalked to sessile; above each leaf base a membranous sheath (modified stipule) surrounds the stem.

FLOWERS: Reddish or yellowish, small; 3 sepals and 3 petals, scale-like; male and female flowers on **separate plants**; male plants have long stamens hanging like red chandeliers from the flowers; numerous in **loose**, narrow, **leafless** panicles.

FRUITS: Achenes, nut-like, lustrous yellowish-brown, 3-angled, enveloped in scales 1–2 mm long that **lack a basal grain-like swelling**; stalks jointed immediately under the fruit.

ECOLOGY: Disturbed sites at low to middle elevations: roadsides, abandoned fields, pastures, gardens, lawns, beaches, pathways, waste places; also sometimes established in undisturbed open forest; common in much of our region, especially in and around human settlements.

NOTES: Sheep sorrel was introduced from Europe, but many aboriginal peoples, especially children, learned to enjoy eating the tart leaves, which are rich in vitamin C and taste something like rhubarb. The sour taste is due to the presence of oxalic acid, so these leaves should not be eaten in large quantities, since oxalic acid can produce oxalate salts that interfere with the body's calcium metabolism. • This troublesome weed spreads by seeds and fragile rhizomes that easily break into pieces that can each resprout. • The common name 'sour weed' and species name both arise because of the sour-tasting leaves. *Rumex* is Pliny's name for 'sorrel,' which again means 'sour' (see note under mountain sorrel).

CURLED DOCK • *Rumex crispus*

GENERAL: Robust perennial from **stout taproot** that is yellowish when cut; stems unbranched below flower clusters, **50–100 cm or more tall**.

LEAVES: Oblong to lance-shaped, rounded at base, to 40 cm long by **5 cm wide**, with crisp curly edges; basal leaves long-stalked; stem leaves short-stalked to stalkless, reduced in size upwards, with sheathing stipules at the base.

FLOWERS: Greenish to dull rusty-brown, small, inconspicuous; numerous, **whorled in dense, leafy-bracted** clusters (to 40 cm in length) along upper part of stem and its branches.

FRUITS: Achenes, lustrous reddish-brown, 3-angled, enveloped in the inner 3 flower scales which are enlarged to 4–5 mm long when in fruit, **net-veined, and usually each with a grain-like swelling** centred towards the base; fruiting clusters dense, brownish; stalks with a swollen joint below midlength.

ECOLOGY: Waste places, roadsides, meadows, cultivated fields and pastures; also in undisturbed sites such as upper parts of tidal marshes and the driftwood zone of beaches; common at low elevations throughout southern part of our region (south of 54°), scattered northwards, uncommon in coastal Alaska.

NOTES: Bitter or broadleaved dock (*R. obtusifolius*) resembles *R. crispus* but has much **broader (to 15 cm)** leaves that are **heart-shaped** at the base and inner flower scales with **toothed margins**. It is also an introduced weed of moist roadsides and fields, occurring fairly frequently the length of our region but rarely on the Queen Charlotte Islands or in southern southeast Alaska. **Clustered dock** (*R. conglomeratus*) has **open** panicles with **well-separated whorls** of flowers. It is another introduced perennial weed, scattered but locally common from Strait of Georgia–Puget Sound area south to California.

WESTERN DOCK • *Rumex occidentalis*

GENERAL: Perennial from a stout **taproot**, hairless or sometimes sparsely hairy; stems erect, usually single and **unbranched** below inflorescence, usually reddish-tinged, **0.5–2 m tall**.

LEAVES: Basal leaves several, oblong egg-shaped to oblong lance-shaped, 6–40 cm long, **3–15 cm wide**, long-stalked, **heart-shaped to squared off** at the base, usually with somewhat wavy or crisped margins; stem leaves few, smaller; sheathing stipules at leaf bases.

FLOWERS: Greenish, small, inconspicuous; numerous in large, dense, rather narrow panicle that has a **few leafy bracts** in the lower part.

FRUITS: Achenes, lustrous brown, 3-angled, enveloped in the inner 3 flower scales which are greatly enlarged (4-10 cm) in fruit, net veined, but **without grain-like swellings**; stalks obscurely jointed near midlength.

ECOLOGY: Moist to wet meadows, shorelines, stream-banks, tideflats, beaches; low to middle elevations; scattered but locally common throughout our region, rare in southeast Alaska.

NOTES: This species includes *Rumex fenestratus*. • **Willow or narrow-leaved dock** (*R. salicifolius*, sometimes called *R. mexicanus* or *R. transitorius*) is a perennial with **stems that branch** from the lower nodes, narrowly lance-shaped to oblong leaves (**0.3–3 cm broad**) and fruiting inner scales 2–4 mm long, usually **with grain-like swellings**. It occurs sporadically at low to middle elevations, from coastal dunes, beaches (driftwood zone) and tidal marshes to streambanks, shores, fields, roadsides, and moist mountain meadows. **Golden dock** (*R. maritimus*) is a **branching annual** with long narrow leaves and **leafy whorled** flower clusters. Its enlarged inner flower scales have **long, slender teeth plus grain-like swellings**; the entire plant is **yellowish** when in fruit. It grows in marshes and along shorelines and streambanks, mostly in the southern half of the region, and it is absent from the Queen Charlotte Islands and coastal Alaska.

Portulacaceae (Purslane Family)

The Portulacaceae is a small family with centres of distribution in western North America and southern South America. In our region they are annual or perennial herbs with usually fleshy, alternate or opposite, undivided leaves. The radially symmetric flowers usually have 2 greenish sepals (several in *Lewisia*), 4–6 distinct or basally fused petals, 4–6 or more stamens, and a single superior ovary. The fruit is a 1-chambered capsule with several to many, or sometimes solitary, seeds.

The family includes several notable ornamentals, especially moss-rose (*Portulaca grandiflora*) and many species of *Lewisia*, *Talinum* and *Calandrinia*. Purslane (*Portulaca oleracea*) is used to a limited extent as a potherb and salad green.

Key to the genera of the Purslane Family

1a. Flowers red to crimson-purple, in leaf axils or tightly clustered atop stem .... *Calandrinia*
1b. Flowers white to pinkish, solitary or usually clustered loosely atop stem 2
    2a. Stem with several usually alternate leaves; without a basal
    rosette of leaves .... *Montia*
    2b. Stem with one pair of opposite leaves, or leaves whorled, or
    two opposite leaves fused into one with the stem coming through;
    with a basal rosette of leaves 3
        3a. Leaves thick, fleshy; petals 7–9 .... *Lewisia*
        3b. Leaves not markedly thick and fleshy; petals 5 .... *Claytonia*

RED MAIDS • *Calandrinia ciliata*
DESERT ROCK PURSLANE

GENERAL: Annual, low and spreading to upright; stems several, **leafy**, simple to branched from the base, 5–35 cm long.

LEAVES: Alternate, somewhat fleshy, linear to lance-shaped, narrowed to slender stalks, sparsely hairy, 1–7 cm long.

FLOWERS: Red to crimson-purple, fairly small (3–8 mm long); 2 sepals; usually 5 petals, quickly withering; few to several on stalks in the axils of upper leaves and in small groups at stem tips.

FRUITS: Capsules, somewhat papery, opening from the top into 3 segments; seeds numerous, lens-shaped, black, shiny.

ECOLOGY: Vernally moist, gravelly or compacted soil; open, low elevation, grassy meadows, clearings; scattered, locally common.

NOTES: The name red maids is very apt for these charming, diminutive red flowers nestled close to the ground. The genus is named for Calandrini, an eighteenth-century Swiss botanist. Purslane ('herb of the womb') is apparently ultimately derived from the Latin *porcella*, 'little sow,' a vulgar term for 'vagina'—definitely less polite than this beautiful plant deserves. • 'Its modest charms are best appreciated from a kneeling position, appropriate in the presence of the divine handiwork represented in these small jewels' (Clark, 1973).

SMALL-LEAVED MONTIA • *Montia parvifolia*
STREAMBANK SPRING-BEAUTY

GENERAL: Somewhat succulent, hairless, **often reddish perennial**, from long slender **rhizomes and stolons**, sometimes forming large patches; flowering stems single from the nodes of the rhizomes, erect to ascending, 10–30 cm tall, sometimes with **bulb-like buds** in the leaf axils.

LEAVES: Basal leaves **oval to egg- or lance-shaped**, 1–6 cm long, stalked; stem leaves several, **alternate**, smaller and narrower than basal leaves.

FLOWERS: Pink or white with pink veins; 2 sepals; 5 petals, 7–15 mm long; mostly 3–8 in a small cluster atop stem.

FRUITS: Capsules, egg-shaped, opening into 3 segments; usually 2 seeds, black, lustrous.

ECOLOGY: Moist, mossy rocky outcrops, streambanks, rocky gullies, rocky beaches; common from sea level to middle elevations.

NOTES: Small-leaved montia is also called *Claytonia parvifolia*. • **Toad-lily or Chamisso's montia** (*Montia chamissoi*, sometimes called *Claytonia chamissoi*) is also a perennial with rhizomes and stolons, but it has several pairs of **opposite, broadly egg-shaped** stem leaves. It occurs in wet habitats (bogs, marshes, seeps, springs, streambanks) at low to middle elevations perhaps throughout our region, but uncommonly. **Blinks or water chickweed** (*M. fontana*) is a little **annual**, often sprawling and branched, with several **pairs of lance-shaped** stem leaves, and small **white** flowers. It grows in wet meadows, springs and shallow water, also at low to middle elevations the length of our region, and it too is uncommon. • *Montia* is named after the Italian botanist Giuseppe Monti (1682–1760).

NARROW-LEAVED MONTIA • *Montia linearis*

GENERAL: Low **annual**, sometimes freely branched from base; stems 1 to several, leafy, ascending to upright, **5–20 cm tall**.

LEAVES: Alternate, linear, 1.5–5 cm long.

FLOWERS: White, small (**3–4 mm** long); 2 sepals; 5 petals; 5–12 in loose, one-sided clusters.

FRUITS: Capsules, opening into 3 segments; seeds black, shining, lens-shaped.

ECOLOGY: Moist to dry, sandy or rocky sites; low to middle elevations; common from southwestern B.C. south, scattered northwards to about 55°.

NOTES: In the southern part of the region we have several small annual species that are difficult to distinguish. **Dwarf montia** (*M. dichotoma*) is like *M. linearis* but **smaller (2–8 cm tall)**, with **very narrow** leaves, and flowers about **2 mm** long. **Branching montia** (*M. diffusa*) has distinctly stalked, **lance-shaped to nearly circular** leaves. **Howell's montia** (*M. howellii*) is spreading and has **narrow** leaves 5–20 mm long, but its tiny flowers (about **1 mm** long) occur in clusters along the stem at leaf axils. All 3 of these species occur sporadically in moist, lowland habitats from the Strait of Georgia–Puget Sound area south to California.

SIBERIAN MINER'S-LETTUCE • *Claytonia sibirica*
CANDY FLOWER

GENERAL: Somewhat succulent **annual (or short-lived perennial)** from slender **taproot or short rhizome**; stems usually several, spreading to erect, leafy, 10–40 cm tall.

LEAVES: Basal leaves several to many, **long stalked**, 3–30 cm long, the blades **lance- or egg-shaped to elliptic**, 1–6 cm long; **stem leaves 2, opposite, stalkless**, egg- to lance-shaped, to 7 cm long.

FLOWERS: White to pink, stalked; 2 sepals; 5 petals, 6–12 mm long; in 1–3, many-flowered clusters.

FRUITS: Capsules, opening into 3 segments; seeds 1–3, black, lustrous.

ECOLOGY: Common on moist, often shady sites (forests, thickets, upper beaches, streambanks, meadows, clearings); low to middle elevations.

NOTES: This species is also called *Montia sibirica*. • **Heart-leaved spring-beauty** (*Montia cordifolia*) could be confused with *C. sibirica*, but it has **strictly white** petals, wide basal leaves **somewhat heart-shaped** at the base, and inflorescences **without bracts**. It grows in wet sites near streams and ponds at middle elevations, scattered from southern Vancouver Island south. • Leaves of Siberian miner's-lettuce are edible, but they were not used as food by aboriginal people. • The Tlingit mixed the leaves with pitch and mountain-hemlock bark to externally treat syphilis sores. The Nuu-chah-nulth pounded the plant and, with no water added, applied it to the abdomen as a remedy for constipation. The women chewed and swallowed the whole plant to hasten or induce labour. The Songish soaked the leaves and applied them to the head as a remedy for a headache. Quinault women chewed the whole plant during pregnancy so the baby would be soft when born.

MINER'S-LETTUCE • *Claytonia perfoliata*

GENERAL: Somewhat succulent **annual** from slender **taproot**; flowering stems several, ascending to upright, **5–30 cm tall**.

LEAVES: Basal leaves numerous, narrowly **spoon-shaped to lance- or egg-shaped, long stalked**, 2–10 cm long; stem leaves 2, opposite and usually fused, forming a disk around the stem above midlength.

FLOWERS: White or pinkish, stalked, nodding; 2 sepals; 5 petals, 3–7 mm long; several to many in clusters 1–8 cm long above the leaf disk.

FRUITS: Capsules, opening into 3 segments; seeds usually 3, black, shining.

ECOLOGY: Moist (at least in spring), open to shady, often sandy, forests, thickets, meadows; common at low to medium elevations.

NOTES: This species (also known as *Montia perfoliata*) is extremely variable in size, colour and shape of leaves, and size of flowers. **Pale spring-beauty** (*Claytonia spathulata*, also called *Montia spathulata*) is similar but smaller (**1–8 cm** tall) with **linear** basal leaves and a **pair of lance-shaped, partially fused** stem leaves. The whole plant has a **glaucous, pale-green or bluish** cast. It occurs from the Strait of Georgia–Puget Sound area south to California on dry to moist open sites, from low to middle elevations. • *Claytonia* is named for John Clayton (1685–1773), an American botanist who made early collections in the eastern U.S. that contributed to Gronovius's *Flora Virginica*. The unusual upper leaves are fused around the stem, which appears to perforate them (hence *perfoliata*). Called miner's-lettuce because early miners and settlers used it as a salad vegetable.

WESTERN SPRING-BEAUTY • *Claytonia lanceolata*

GENERAL: Hairless, somewhat fleshy **perennial** from a deep, **bulb-like, marble-sized corm**; flowering stems 1 to several, 5–20 cm tall.

LEAVES: Basal leaves usually 1 or 2, **commonly withering or lacking** in flowering plants, lance-shaped, 7–15 cm long; **stem leaves 2, opposite**, stalkless, **egg- to lance-shaped**, attached near or above midlength of stem.

FLOWERS: White or pale pink (sometimes yellow), often with deep-pink veins, stalked; 2 sepals; 5 petals, 5–15 mm long; few to several in loose, often 1-sided clusters atop the stems.

FRUITS: Capsules, egg-shaped, opening into 3 segments; seeds usually 3–6, black, shining.

ECOLOGY: Moist meadows, snowbeds, open slopes; middle to high elevations; common from mainland southwestern B.C. (rare on Vancouver Island) south to California.

NOTES: This plant has been used most extensively by aboriginal people in the southern and central Interior of British Columbia. In fact, in the Chilcotin territory, the Potato Mountains are named after this plant. The corms were collected with digging sticks during late May or June and eaten either raw or cooked. The corms can be stored raw in underground caches or cooked and dried for winter. Western spring-beauty was also eaten by the Carrier, Nlaka'pamux, Stl'atl'imx, Secwepemc, Okanagan, and Kt'unaXa peoples, but apparently it was not used on the Northwest Coast. • Of the flowers that bloom in the alpine spring, this is one of the prettiest.

COLUMBIA LEWISIA • *Lewisia columbiana*

GENERAL: Succulent perennial from a **large, branched, fleshy root**; flowering stems usually several, 5–30 cm tall, **leafless** but with several bracts.

LEAVES: Basal, numerous, narrowly **spoon- to lance-shaped**, 2–10 cm long.

FLOWERS: White with pink veins to rose, 5–13 mm long, stalked; sepals 2, glandular toothed; usually **7–9 petals**; several to many in an open, branched cluster with **glandular, toothed bracts**.

FRUITS: Capsules, egg-shaped, 1-chambered, **opening near the base and splitting upward**; seeds usually 3, brownish-red to black, lustrous.

ECOLOGY: Exposed gravelly or rocky ridges, slopes, outcrops; middle to high elevations; scattered, locally common.

NOTES: Three-leaved lewisia (*L. triphylla*) has roundish **bulb-like corms**, usually **lacks basal leaves**, but has **2–3 semiwhorled stem leaves**. It occurs from middle to high elevations on moist, sandy snowbed or spring-seepage sites, scattered from southern Vancouver Island south in the Cascades to California, mostly east of our region. • As a much-favoured rock garden subject, Columbia lewisia and other lewisias have suffered from the depredations of unscrupulous alpine gardeners. • *Lewisia columbiana* is named after Capt. Meriwether Lewis of the Lewis and Clark expeditions, who explored, among other areas, the Columbia River valley.

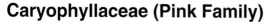

Caryophyllaceae (Pink Family)

The Caryophyllaceae is a family of annual or perennial herbs that characteristically have: stems with swollen nodes; opposite, mostly narrow leaves; radially symmetric flowers with 4–5 sepals (sometimes fused into a tube), 4–5 distinct petals, 5–10 stamens, and a single superior ovary; fruits that are 1-chambered capsules opening at the top by valves, teeth or lids, or sometimes are bladder-like utricles; and numerous seeds (sometimes solitary).

This is a medium-sized family primarily of northern temperate regions, with a centre of distribution in the Mediterranean basin. The family includes a large number of commercially important ornamentals, notably carnation (*Dianthus caryophyllus*) and many other species of *Dianthus*, baby's-breath (*Gypsophila*), catchfly (*Silene*), maltese cross (*Lychnis*), sandwort (*Arenaria*) and *Cerastium*, which includes mouse-ear chickweeds and dusty miller. Several species are widespread weeds, including chickweeds (*Cerastium* and *Stellaria*), spurry (*Spergula*) and pearlwort (*Sagina*).

Key to Genera of the Pink Family

1a. Leaves whorled .... *Spergula*
1b. Leaves opposite 2
  2a. Nodes each with a pair of papery, membranous stipules .... *Spergularia*
  2b. Stipules absent 3
    3a. Sepals united for at least half their length 4
      4a. Styles generally 3 (sometimes 4 or 5); fused sepals usually glandular, often inflated .... *Silene*
      4b. Styles generally 5 (sometimes 4); fused sepals not glandular, not inflated .... *Lychnis*
    3b. Sepals distinct or nearly so 5
      5a. Plant fleshy, succulent, maritime; seeds 3–4 mm long .... *Honkenya*
      5b. Plants not markedly succulent; seeds rarely over 1.5 mm long 6
        6a. Styles 4 or 5 7
          7a. Styles mostly 5; capsules cylindric, bent near tip; petals 2 lobed .... *Cerastium*
          7b. Styles 4 or 5; capsules oval; petals not 2 lobed (sometimes lacking); plants low and matted .... *Sagina*
        6b. Styles usually 3 8
          8a. Petals deeply notched or 2 cleft .... *Stellaria*
          8b. Petals entire to shallowly lobed 9
            9a. Leaves elliptic to oblong, 1–4 cm long, usually wider than 3 mm .... *Moehringia*
            9b. Leaves linear or awl-shaped, if elliptic less than 1 cm long and 3 mm wide 10
              10a. Capsules opening by 6 teeth .... *Arenaria*
              10b. Capsules opening by 3 teeth .... *Minuartia*

Moss campion, *silene acaulis*

135

CANADIAN SAND-SPURRY • *Spergularia canadensis*

GENERAL: Hairless to glandular-hairy **annual from taproot**; stems leafy, usually several, clumped, erect or ascending to prostrate, 4–30 cm long, about 1 mm thick.

LEAVES: Opposite, **somewhat fleshy**, linear, 1–4.5 cm long, **blunt or pointed at tip**, usually lacking axillary clusters of secondary leaves.

FLOWERS: White to pinkish, small; petals 1–3 mm long; sepals as long or longer than petals; stamens 2–5; few to many in leaf axils, erect to spreading or reflexed.

FRUITS: Capsules, longer than sepals, opening by 3 valves; seeds several, about 1 mm long, light brown, usually with a distinctive **membranous wing**.

ECOLOGY: Common on sea beaches, tidal marshes, mudflats, saline or brackish soil.

NOTES: **Canadian sand-spurry** is a common, **annual, native** species of tidelands. • **Salt marsh sandspurry** (*S. marina*) is an **introduced annual** species of coastal mudflats and tidelands, fairly common from southwestern B.C. south. It has **abruptly pointy-tipped leaves** and **wingless seeds**. • *Spergularia* means 'resembling the genus *Spergula*.' One source says *Spergula* is a contraction of *asparagula* or 'asparagus' because of the similarity of the plants. Another says that *Spergula* is from the Latin *spargo* meaning 'to scatter,' in reference to the dehiscent discharge of the seeds from the fruit capsule. Whichever is the case, 'spurry' is derived from *Spergula* and was originally given to *S. arvensis*, which was cultivated as a forage crop. An old name for *S. arvensis* is 'franke,' which means 'a stall or sty,' since the plant was used to fatten cattle.

BEACH SAND-SPURRY • *Spergularia macrotheca*

GENERAL: Glandular-hairy **perennial from a woody root and a branched stem-base**; stems several, leafy, reclining to ascending, to 40 cm long, 1–2 mm thick.

LEAVES: Two to several per node, linear, 1.5–5 cm long, **abruptly pointy-tipped**.

FLOWERS: Pink, small; sepals 5–9 mm long; petals shorter than sepals; stamens 10; several to many in leaf axils, erect to ascending.

FRUITS: Capsules, slightly longer than sepals, opening by 3 valves; seeds several, dark reddish-brown, 0.7–0.9 mm long, **wingless or with a narrow rim**.

ECOLOGY: Salt marshes and sandy, coastal beaches; uncommon in Strait of Georgia area, common south to California.

NOTES: **Beach sand-spurry** is a common **native perennial** species in the southern part of our region. • **Red sand-spurry** (*S. rubra*) is an **introduced weedy annual** of gardens, disturbed sites and waste places, common from southwestern B.C. south, but uncommon northwards. It has **clusters of dark-green**, somewhat fleshy, narrowly linear leaves. It also has lustrous **silvery stipules, pinkish** flowers, and dark-brown, **wingless**, finely pebbled seeds. **Spurry, corn-spurry, or stickwort** (*S. arvensis*) is a widespread, **introduced annual weed** of fields, roadsides and waste places that forms diffuse clumps with **whorled, hairlike, yellowish-green leaves**, small **white** flowers, and black, plump, narrowly winged seeds often covered with white bumps or pegs. • The species name *macrotheca* means 'large box,' in reference to the seed capsule.

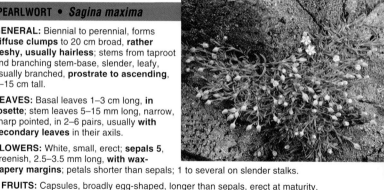

COASTAL PEARLWORT • *Sagina maxima*

GENERAL: Biennial to perennial, forms **diffuse clumps** to 20 cm broad, **rather fleshy, usually hairless**; stems from taproot and branching stem-base, slender, leafy, usually branched, **prostrate to ascending**, 2–15 cm tall.

LEAVES: Basal leaves 1–3 cm long, **in rosette**; stem leaves 5–15 mm long, narrow, sharp pointed, in 2–6 pairs, usually **with secondary leaves** in their axils.

FLOWERS: White, small, erect; **sepals 5**, greenish, 2.5–3.5 mm long, **with wax-papery margins**; petals shorter than sepals; 1 to several on slender stalks.

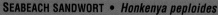

FRUITS: Capsules, broadly egg-shaped, longer than sepals, erect at maturity, opening into 5 segments; seeds several, 0.3–0.5 mm long, lustrous.

ECOLOGY: Common on moist, sandy or gravelly beaches, sea bluffs, bird rocks, salt marshes; **strictly maritime**.

NOTES: This species is also known as *S. crassicaulis*. **Bird's-eye pearlwort** (*S. procumbens*) is also a hairless biennial to perennial, but it is an **introduced weed** of moist lawns, roadsides, gardens, sea cliffs and pond margins, common at low elevations from southwestern B.C. to California, and less frequent northward to the Queen Charlotte Islands. It has tiny flowers, usually with **4 sepals and petals**, and dull seeds 0.3 mm long. **Western pearlwort** (*S. decumbens*, also called *S. occidentalis*) is a loosely branched **annual lacking a basal rosette**, with **hairlike** stems and leaves, but **without axillary clusters** of secondary leaves. It grows at low elevations in moist grassy areas, edges of spring pools, and forest openings, scattered in the southern half of the region, and it is also reported from southeast Alaska. In northern southeast Alaska and Prince of Wales Sound, **snow pearlwort** (*S. nivalis*, also called *S. intermedia*), occurs from sea beaches and bluffs to snow beds high in the mountains. It forms **dark-green tufts** or clumps and usually has **4 sepals with purple margins**. **Arctic pearlwort** (*S. saginoides*) forms **yellowish-green mats** and usually has **5 sepals with white or clear margins**. It grows in moist, often muddy areas from low to high elevations, fairly commonly in the Cascades and also in northern southeast Alaska. • One source says *Sagina* spp. are called pearlworts because they were used to treat an eye infection called 'pearl.' Another says it refers to either the small, unopened flower bud or the fruit. *Sagina* means 'fodder' and derives from the fact that this was once used as animal feed.

SEABEACH SANDWORT • *Honkenya peploides*

GENERAL: **Fleshy**, hairless perennial from **taproot and branching, buried stem-base**, forming **mats** 10–80 cm broad or more; stems numerous, leafy, **trailing**, branched, with upturned flowering ends 5–30 cm tall.

LEAVES: In 3–10 pairs, **elliptic-oblong to egg-shaped**, 1–5 cm long, **fleshy, yellowish-green**.

FLOWERS: White or greenish-white, small; petals often shorter than sepals; usually 10 stamens; 3 styles; scattered singly on short stalks in leaf axils.

FRUITS: Spherical capsules, longer than sepals, opening by 3–5 valves; seeds 5–10, brown, smooth, shining, about **3 mm long**.

ECOLOGY: Common on sandy, gravelly or rocky **ocean beaches**, often among driftwood.

NOTES: Seabeach sandwort is also known as *Arenaria peploides*. • Sandwort ('sand-plant') is a name for beach species of *Arenaria*, a genus to which this plant formerly belonged. *Honkenya* is named for G. A. Honckeny (1724–1805), a German botanist.

BIG-LEAVED SANDWORT • *Moehringia macrophylla*

GENERAL: Perennial from slender **rhizomes**, often forming **loose mats**; stems leafy, declining to erect, rounded to 4-angled, usually branching, finely hairy, 5–20 cm tall.

LEAVES: Opposite, narrowly **elliptic to lance-shaped, 2–6 cm long, pointy-tipped**, hairless to finely hairy.

FLOWERS: White, on slender stalks; sepals 3–6 mm long, **sharp-pointed; petals shorter to longer than sepals**; 2–5 in small open clusters.

FRUITS: Capsules, spherical to egg-shaped, shorter than sepals, opening by 6 valves; seeds few, smooth, with a fleshy appendage.

ECOLOGY: Moist to dry forests, thickets and open, rocky slopes; low to middle elevations; common in the southern half of our region, rare northwards.

NOTES: Big-leaved sandwort is also known as *Arenaria macrophylla*. • **Blunt-leaved sandwort** (*M. lateriflora*, also called *Arenaria lateriflora*) is similar but has **smaller (1–4 cm long) leaves blunt or rounded** at the tip, and oblong, **rounded, white-margined sepals**. It also occurs in moist to dry forests, thickets, and meadows and along forest edges, from low to middle elevations. It is scattered the length of our region, more commonly along its eastern edge, and rarely on the Queen Charlotte Islands and Vancouver Island. • The common name and the species name of big-leaved sandwort (*macrophylla*, meaning 'big-leaved') reflect that its leaves are larger than those of most sandworts. The genus is named for P.H.G. Moehring (1710–1792), a German naturalist.

THREAD-LEAVED SANDWORT • *Arenaria capillaris*
ssp. *americana*

GENERAL: Tufted perennial from a **branched crown**, forming **loose mats** to 20 cm wide; stems numerous, leafy, glandular-hairy on their upper part, 5–30 cm tall, covered with **withered leaves at base**.

LEAVES: Basal leaves numerous, **narrowly linear**, light green (often glaucous), erect or curved, 2–5 cm long; stem leaves in 2–5 pairs, about half as long as basal leaves.

FLOWERS: White, **fairly showy**; sepals egg-shaped, wing-margined and often purplish tinged; **petals about twice as long as sepals**; 3 styles; usually few in small, **flat-topped clusters**.

FRUITS: Capsules, egg-shaped, about twice as long as the sepals, opening by 6 valves; seeds about 2 mm long, kidney-shaped, flattened.

ECOLOGY: Dry rocky slopes and mountain meadows, from middle to high elevations; common in the Cascades and Olympic Mountains, rare on Vancouver Island.

NOTES: Thread-leaved sandwort also occurs in Alaska and the Yukon (inland of our region) as ssp. *capillaris*. • The species name *capillaris* refers to the very slender, hair-like leaves.

BOREAL SANDWORT • *Minuartia rubella*
REDDISH SANDWORT

GENERAL: Dwarf, **tufted perennial or biennial**, from a **taproot and branched crown**, forming **cushions or mats** 5–20 cm wide; basal shoots **clothed with persistent leaves**; flowering stem very thin, leafy, simple or 2-branched, 2–15 cm tall, **densely glandular-hairy**.

LEAVES: Basal leaves **lance-shaped to linear**, 3-ribbed, 3–12 mm long; stem leaves 2–6 pairs, similar to the basal ones but reduced in size upwards.

FLOWERS: White, small; on glandular-hairy stalks; sepals 3–4 mm long, pointy tipped, **reddish-purple; petals slightly shorter to slightly longer than sepals**; 3 styles; solitary or more commonly 2–5 in an open cluster.

FRUITS: Capsules, narrowly egg-shaped, somewhat longer than sepals, opening by **3–4 valves**; seeds about 0.5 mm long, reddish-brown.

ECOLOGY: Common on gravelly or sandy soils, rock outcrops, talus slopes, usually at **high elevations**; absent from outer coast.

NOTES: Slender sandwort (*M. tenella*, also called *Arenaria stricta* var. *puberulenta*) is also glandular-hairy, but it is a slender, **branching annual, not at all matted**, 10–25 cm tall, with open, diffuse flower clusters. It occurs in relatively dry grassy openings and on rocky slopes and coastal bluffs, at **low to middle elevations**. It is common from southwestern B.C. to northern Oregon and rare on the Queen Charlotte Islands. • Boreal sandwort is one of a group of **dwarf, tufted, alpine perennials** in the pink family (Caryophyllaceae). Most have small narrow leaves and all have fairly small, white flowers, but *Minuartia* and *Arenaria* (sandworts) and *Sagina* (pearlworts) have **entire or shallowly notched petals**, whereas *Stellaria* and *Cerastium* have **deeply notched or 2-cleft petals**. All are plants of rocky slopes, scree, ledges and tundra. • The genus *Minuartia* is named after Juan Minuart, a Spanish botanist (1693–1768). The sepals are often reddish-purple, hence the common name 'reddish sandwort' and the species name *rubella*.

CRISP SANDWORT • *Stellaria crispa*

GENERAL: Low, **spreading, often clumped or matted perennial** from slender rhizomes, **hairless**; stems weak, prostrate to ascending, mostly unbranched, 5–50 cm long.

LEAVES: In numerous pairs, **lance- to egg-shaped, stalkless** or lower ones short-stalked, sharply pointed at tip; thin **margin translucent and minutely crisped (wavy) like potato chips**.

FLOWERS: White, very small; 5 sepals; **petals usually lacking, or shorter than sepals**; 3 styles; **single** in leaf axils and at stem tips.

FRUITS: Straw-coloured or brownish capsules nearly twice as long as the sepals, opening by **6 teeth**; seeds about 1 mm long, brown, slightly roughened.

ECOLOGY: Moist sites such as shady alder forests and thickets, streambanks, seepage areas, clearings, old grown-over logging roads; common at low to middle elevations.

NOTES: Chickweed (*S. media*) is a widespread **introduced weed** of gardens, lawns, cultivated fields and pastures. It is an **annual** with trailing, branching stems and numerous egg-shaped to elliptic leaves. Chickweed has **stalked leaves** and **longitudinal lines of hairs** along the stems. • Occasional specimens of crisp starwort resemble northern starwort (*S. calycantha*). • The name *wort* is frequently encountered in compound plant names. It derives from the old English *wyrt* which generally means 'plant' or 'vegetable' and was often applied to plants having some medicinal value. • Crisp starwort acquired its common and Latin names from the star-shaped flower (Latin *stella*) and the 'crisped' (wavy) margins of the leaves.

NORTHERN STARWORT • *Stellaria calycantha*

GENERAL: Low, often **sprawling or matted perennial** from long rhizomes; stems slender, prostrate to ascending or erect, 5–50 cm or more long, **hairless to sparsely hairy.**

LEAVES: Opposite, stalkless, **elliptic to narrowly lance-shaped,** 0.5–5 cm long, thin, hairless except for a few long basal hairs; **margins minutely saw-toothed.**

FLOWERS: White or greenish, small; **petals from nearly as long as sepals to absent**; solitary and in leaf axils or **more commonly in open terminal groups.**

FRUITS: Straw-coloured to purplish capsules, much longer than flowers, opening by 6 teeth; seeds 0.5–1 mm long, reddish-brown.

ECOLOGY: Scattered, locally common in wet meadows, thickets, streambanks, glades, open moist forests, clearings and roadsides; low to moderately high elevations.

NOTES: • Northern starwort is very variable in size of leaves and flowers, degree of branching of the inflorescence and hairiness of the stem. It includes *S. sitchana.* • **Long-leaved starwort** (*S. longifolia*) is similar to *S. calycantha* but has very narrow, more or less **linear leaves and a long-branched, more-open inflorescence.** It occupies habitats similar to those of *S. calycantha* and is said to occur from Yakutat to southwestern B.C., but it seems uncommon at best. **Simcoe starwort** (*S. simcoei*, also called *S. calycantha* ssp. *interior* and var. *simcoei*) has **wider leaves (egg-shaped)** and **very hairy** upper stems. It occurs from southwestern B.C. and the Olympics south through the Cascades, mostly in middle- to high-elevation meadows and along streambanks. **Long-stalked starwort** (*S. longipes*; includes *S. monantha*, *S. laeta*, *S. alaskana*, *S. edwardsii*) is a small, often dwarfed perennial with **stiff, shiny, sharply pointed, very narrow leaves** and **petals as long as or longer than the sepals.** It grows from low-elevation, gravelly lakeshores and streambanks to alpine tundra and is scattered the length of our region, but mostly along its inland margin and typically at high elevations in the south. • The species name *calycantha* is from *calyc*, the Latin for 'calyx,' and *antho*, meaning 'flower,' because the petals are much reduced, leaving the calyx to form the flower.

SALT MARSH STARWORT • *Stellaria humifusa*

GENERAL: Hairless, **yellow-green perennial** from slender rhizomes, **often mat-forming**; stems 5–40 cm long.

LEAVES: Opposite, stalkless, **thick and fleshy,** lance-shaped to elliptic, 4–15 mm long.

FLOWERS: White, small; sepals 3.5–5 mm long; **petals usually slightly longer than sepals; usually solitary** in leaf axils, on fairly stout stalks.

FRUITS: Straw-coloured capsules, egg-shaped, about as long as sepals, opening by 6 teeth; seeds brown, about 1 mm long.

ECOLOGY: Salt marshes, mudflats, gravelly and sandy shores; common **beach species.**

NOTES: Shining starwort (*S. nitens*) occupies open, grassy habitats at low to middle elevations in the Strait of Georgia–Puget Sound area south to California. It is a **delicate annual** with erect, **very thin stems,** and its leaves grow mostly on the lower part of the stems. • Salt marsh starwort varies greatly according to habitat. Plants in competition with lush grass and sedge vegetation are elongate and twining, while plants colonizing mudflats and exposed gravel beaches are matted and much branched, and they have smaller leaves. • The species name *humifusa* means 'sprawling or spreading over the ground.'

FIELD CHICKWEED • *Cerastium arvense*

GENERAL: Tufted or clumped, greyish-green perennial; stems trailing to ascending or erect, 5–50 cm long or tall; **glandular-hairy on upper part** of stems and among the flowers.

LEAVES: Opposite, **linear to narrowly lance-shaped or oblong**, 1–3 cm long, fine hairy, pointed at tip; **most stem leaves have secondary leafy tufts in their axils.**

FLOWERS: White, **fairly showy**, on glandular-hairy stalks; petals 5, **deeply notched at tip, 8–12 mm long, 2–3 times as long as sepals**; 5 styles; few to several in an open, **flat-topped cluster.**

FRUITS: Cylindric, many-seeded capsules opening by **10 teeth**.

ECOLOGY: Dry ground on rocky slopes, outcrops, grassy bluffs, meadows, screes, gravelly openings and clearings; scattered, locally common, from low to high elevations but usually below timberline.

NOTES: Bering chickweed (*C. beeringianum*) is a **matted to sprawling, arctic-alpine** species that resembles field chickweed but has **broader leaves, generally rounded** at the tip, that **lack sterile axillary shoots**, and it has fewer flowers. It occurs on high mountains the length of our region, but mostly along its inland margin except in northern southeast Alaska and Prince William Sound, where it is more widespread. **Fisher's chickweed** (*C. fischerianum*) occurs at low elevations on gravelly shores and open hillsides, sporadically from northern Vancouver Island and the Queen Charlotte Islands north. It is similar to Bering chickweed but is **larger, with coarser stems (1–1.5 mm diameter) and conspicuous yellowish hairs**.

DOUGLAS' CAMPION • *Silene douglasii*
DOUGLAS' CATCHFLY

GENERAL: Loosely tufted perennial from a **stout taproot and branching crown**; stems numerous, bent at base, unbranched, 10–50 cm tall, **finely and densely hairy all over**.

LEAVES: Opposite; basal leaves smaller than main stem leaves and often withered by flowering time; stem leaves 2–8 pairs, lance-shaped, 2–8 cm long, hairy.

FLOWERS: White to greenish or pinkish; sepals **12–15 mm long, fused into a chalice, usually hairy**; petals 12–16 mm long, 2-lobed at tip, with **2 appendages 1–2 mm long** at juncture of blade (horizontal or spreading part of petal) and claw (the vertical basal part); usually 3 styles; solitary, or more commonly 2 to several in terminal clusters.

FRUITS: Capsules, **1-chambered, 8–12 mm long, stalked, borne within the calyx (united sepals), which becomes inflated and papery in fruit**; seeds reddish-brown, roughened.

ECOLOGY: Common on dry, open slopes and grassy areas; low to middle elevations.

NOTES: Menzies' campion or catchfly (*S. menziesii*) has white flowers and capsules, both **less than 10 mm long**, and is **generally glandular-hairy**, at least on the leaves and the upper part of the stems. It occurs occasionally in northern southeast Alaska and Prince William Sound, and commonly from southwestern B.C. south in the Cascades to California (not on the Olympic Peninsula), in moist meadows and open forest at low to middle elevations. **Parry's campion or catchfly** (*S. parryi*) has **mostly basal** leaves, is **glandular-hairy**, and has **white (or greenish- to purplish-tinged) petals that appear 4-lobed** at the tip. It occurs on dry to moist meadows and in open forests, from middle to alpine elevations and is common from the southwestern B.C. mainland south to the Olympics and Washington Cascades.

BLADDER CAMPION • *Silene vulgaris*

GENERAL: Perennial from strong taproot; stems leafy, branched and bent or sometimes rhizome-like at base, **mostly hairless**.

LEAVES: Opposite, egg- to lance-shaped, 3–8 cm long, stalkless, the lower pairs joined at the base.

FLOWERS: White; sepals about 1 cm long, **fused into a chalice, hairless, veined, becoming membranous with age**; petals about 15 mm long, **deeply 2-lobed at tip, without appendages (or with 2 mere bumps)** at juncture of blade and claw; usually 3 styles; several to many in **open, loosely flat-topped clusters**.

FRUITS: Capsules, **3-chambered**, stalked; seeds brown, warty-roughened.

ECOLOGY: Common on roadsides, fields, waste places; mostly at low elevations.

NOTES: Bladder campion is a weedy introduced species, also known as *S. cucubalus*. • **Scouler's campion or catchfly** (*S. scouleri*) is a **native, densely hairy perennial** with numerous **lance-shaped leaves** and numerous, **greenish-white to purplish flowers in a long, narrow, several-tiered inflorescence**. Its **petals appear 4-lobed** at their tips. It occurs at low elevations near the sea in dry meadows and on gravelly bluffs, scattered from the Strait of Georgia–Puget Sound area south to California. **White cockle or campion** (*S. alba*, also called *Lychnis alba*) is similar but has **male and female flowers on separate plants** with **2-lobed petals** and 5 styles. It is an **introduced perennial** scattered in the southern half of our region, in fields and waste places and on roadsides from low to middle elevations. • The name 'campion' (or 'champion') comes from Europe, where flowers of red campion (*Silene dioica*) were used to adorn chaplets (wreaths) placed on heads of champions at public games. • 'Bladder' campion comes from the fact that the calyx is strongly inflated, or bladder-like. The species name *vulgaris* does not refer to the bladder, but means 'the usual, common, or vulgar' species.

SLEEPY CATCHFLY • *Silene antirrhina*

GENERAL: Annual; stems leafy, erect, simple to branched, hairy below, hairless above, usually **glandular in bands below the nodes**, 20–80 cm tall.

LEAVES: Opposite, hairless to hairy; basal leaves lance- to spoon-shaped, 3–6 cm long; stem leaves narrowly lance-shaped.

FLOWERS: White to pink; sepals 4–10 mm long, **united into a hairless, veined tube**; blades of **petals 2–4 mm long**; 3 styles; few to many in a **flat-topped cluster**.

FRUITS: Capsules, 3 chambered, short stalked; seeds blackish, with rows of small bumps.

ECOLOGY: Roadsides, fields, clearings and open forests; common at low to middle elevations.

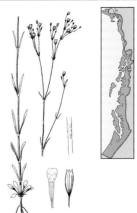

NOTES: Sleepy catchfly is weedy but apparently native. • We also have two **introduced weedy, hairy annuals** that have **hairy sepals** and are common in the southern half of our region. They are **night-flowering catchfly** (*S. noctiflora*, also called *Melandrium noctiflorum*, or **sticky cockle**), which has **2 or more flowers per node**, and **small-flowered catchfly** (*S. gallica*), which has **1 flower per node**. • *Silene* comes from the Latin *sialon* for 'saliva,' in reference to the glandular hairs on the stem. These sticky (glutinous) hairs act like flypaper, giving rise to the common name catchfly for many members of this genus. An alternative derivation for *Silene* is that it is from Seilenos, a woodland satyr and frequent companion of Bacchus.

MOSS CAMPION • *Silene acaulis*

GENERAL: Hairless, tufted perennial from woody roots and branched, thickened stem-base, forming **compact, hemispherical or flat cushions** to 50 cm broad; stems 3–6 cm tall, with **densely crowded branches.**

LEAVES: Mostly basal, withering and **persistent** for many years, **linear to narrowly lance-shaped, stiff, sharply pointed**, hairless or with stiff hairs on margins, stalkless.

FLOWERS: Showy, pink, lilac or pale purple (rarely white); stalkless or short-stalked; petals 8–12 mm long; **single.**

FRUITS: 3-chambered capsules; seeds light brown.

ECOLOGY: Moist but well-drained sites in **high mountains**, such as in rock crevices or on cliffs and ledges, also on gravelly, exposed ridges and turfy tundra barrens; common alpine species in suitable habitats in most of our region, rare in southern southeast Alaska and on the Queen Charlotte Islands.

NOTES: One of our most beautiful alpine cushion plants, and an excellent plant for rock gardens. • Craighead et al. (1963) describe, with stirring patriotism, the occurrence of moss campion with alpine forget-me-not and white phlox: 'Growing thus together, they appear to be a single cushion of varicoloured flowers—the red, white and blue symbolizing the complete freedom that comes to all outdoor lovers in the vastness of the mountains.'

ROSE CAMPION • *Lychnis coronaria*

GENERAL: Grey-woolly perennial from a usually branched stem-base; stems 1 to several, stout, unbranched, leafy, **40–100 cm tall.**

LEAVES: Basal leaves numerous, lance-shaped, 5–10 cm long; stem leaves opposite, 5–10 pairs from **swollen nodes**, gradually reduced in size and becoming stalkless up the stem.

FLOWERS: Showy, deep-red; sepals about 15 mm long, hairy, veined; blade of petals 10–15 mm long, **heart-shaped**; 5 styles; **several in a loosely branched, flat-topped cluster.**

FRUITS: Capsules, 1-chambered, **opening by 5 teeth**; seeds purplish-brown, warty in concentric rings.

ECOLOGY: Roadsides, railroad right-of-ways, clearings, waste places; common at low elevations.

NOTES: Introduced from Europe as a garden ornamental, rose campion frequently escapes and persists. • *Lychnis* is Latin for 'lamp.' One source says that this is because the leaves were used as wicks for oil lamps, but another says it is in reference to the brightly coloured flowers found in this genus. • This species gets its common name from the colour of its flowers. The species name *coronaria* means 'garlanding, forming a crown' and possibly refers to the crown of five teeth atop the fruit capsule.

Brassicaceae (Mustard Family)

The mustards are a large family distributed primarily in the cooler regions of the northern hemisphere. *Draba, Cardamine* and *Arabis* are large genera in our region. The family has considerable economic importance because of its food crops, weeds and ornamentals. Important food crops include cabbage, cauliflower, broccoli, rutabaga, kohlrabi, Brussels sprouts (all from *Brassica oleracea*), turnips (*Brassica rapa*), rapeseed (*Brassica napus*), radish (*Raphanus*), and watercress (*Nasturtium*). The family produces two condiments, mustard (*Brassica*) and horseradish (*Armoracia*). Troublesome weeds like shepherd's purse (*Capsella bursa-pastoris*), mustards (*Brassica, Barbarea*), flixweeds (*Descurainia*) and peppergrass (*Lepidium*) are widespread. Ornamentals include wallflower (*Cheiranthus, Erysimum*), honesty (*Lunaria*), stocks (*Matthiola*), rocket (*Hesperis*), candytuft (*Iberis*), sweet alyssum (*Lobularia*) and rock cress (*Arabis*).

The family consists mainly of annual, biennial or perennial herbs with watery sap, and often with forked or stellate hairs; leaves are alternate and simple. Flowers are radially symmetrical, typically in racemes, and have 4 sepals, 4 petals, 6 stamens and 1 superior 2-chambered ovary. Fruits are usually pod-like with 2 chambers separated by a membranous partition and opening by two valves; if long they are called 'siliques,' if short 'silicles.'

Key to Genera of the Mustard Family

1a. Pods composed of 2 segments, flowers white to purplish; plants maritime .... *Cakile*
1b. Pods not divided into 2 segments 2
  2a. Pods silicles, oval, elliptic, oblong or heart-shaped (scarcely longer than wide) 3
    3a. Silicles flattened in same plane as partition, not roundish or
    circular in cross-section .... *Draba*
    3b. Silicles not strongly flattened, but swollen and roundish in cross-section,
    or flattened at right angles to the partition between chambers of the pod 4
      4a. Plants aquatic; leaves all basal, linear, ... *Subularia (see* 'Aquatics'*)*
      4b. Plants not truly aquatic, not with all basal, needle-like leaves 5
        5a. Plants with fleshy leaves and seashore habitat; basal leaves
        with kidney-shaped to oval blades on long, slender stalks .... *Cochlearia*
        5b. Plants not usually maritime; basal leaves various 6
          6a. Silicles inflated or swollen, petals yellow or sometimes white .... *Rorippa*
          6b. Silicles somewhat compressed at right angles to the partition;
          flowers mostly white 7
            7a. Silicles heart-shaped to triangular .... *Capsella*
            7b. Silicles not heart-shaped or triangular 8
              8a. Seeds 1 per chamber; silicles usually < 5 mm long .... *Lepidium*
              8b. Seeds 2 to several per chamber; stem leaves with
              ear-like clasping basal lobes; silicles > 5 mm long .... *Thlaspi*
  2b. Pods siliques, long and narrow, at least 3 times as long as wide 9
    9a. Leaves (at least the basal and lower stem-leaves) pinnately lobed or divided 10
      10a. Flowers white to pink or purple .... *Cardamine*
      10b. Flowers yellow 11
        11a. Stem leaves with basal, clasping, ear-like lobes .... *Barbarea*
        11b. Stem leaves not clasping 12
          12a. Siliques long, linear and narrow; seeds in 1 series;
          valves 3 nerved .... *Sisymbrium*
          12b. Siliques oval to linear; seeds in 2 series; valves nerveless .... *Rorippa*
    9b. Leaves not pinnately lobed or divided, sometimes toothed, lobed or lyre-shaped 13
      13a. Flowers yellow or orange 14
        14a. Siliques linear (at least 8 times as long as broad); seeds in
        1 series; appressed, 2-pronged hairs on stems and leaves .... *Erysimum*
        14b. Siliques at most narrowly cylindric; seeds in 2 series;
        star-shaped or branched hairs .... *Draba*
      13b. Flowers white to pink or purple 15
        15a. Plants with forked, star-like, branched or tree-like hairs 16
          16a. Siliques relatively short, less than 8 times long as broad .... *Draba*
          16b. Siliques much longer, usually at least 8 times long as broad .... *Arabis*
        15b. Plants hairless or with unbranched hairs only 17
          17a. Leaves all basal, or stem leaves not with ear-like clasping
          basal lobes, often pinnately lobed or compound .... *Cardamine*
          17b. Stem leaves with ear-like clasping lobes at base, leaves at
          most lyre-shaped, often merely toothed or entire .... *Arabis*

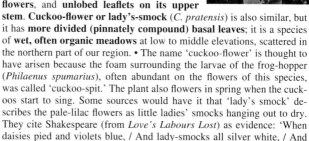

ANGLED BITTER-CRESS • *Cardamine angulata*

GENERAL: Perennial herb to 70 cm tall, from extensive, **slender rhizomes**; stems unbranched.

LEAVES: Mostly on the stem but some basal, **compound with usually 3 leaflets**, the leaflets to 7 cm long, lobed.

FLOWERS: White to pink; 4 petals each **to 1.2 cm long**; several in a terminal cluster.

FRUITS: Erect siliques to 4 cm long.

ECOLOGY: Moist forests and stream-banks at low elevations.

NOTES: **Beautiful bitter-cress** (*C. pulcherrima*, also known as **slender toothwort**) is a similar species of **moist to wet forests** at low elevations, from the Strait of Georgia–Puget Sound area south. *C. pulcherrima* is a charming smaller plant (to 30 cm tall) with **pink to red flowers**, and **unlobed leaflets on its upper stem**. **Cuckoo-flower or lady's-smock** (*C. pratensis*) is also similar, but it has **more divided (pinnately compound) basal leaves**; it is a species of **wet, often organic meadows** at low to middle elevations, scattered in the northern part of our region. • The name 'cuckoo-flower' is thought to have arisen because the foam surrounding the larvae of the frog-hopper (*Philaenus spumarius*), often abundant on the flowers of this species, was called 'cuckoo-spit.' The plant also flowers in spring when the cuckoos start to sing. Some sources would have it that 'lady's smock' describes the pale-lilac flowers as little ladies' smocks hanging out to dry. They cite Shakespeare (from *Love's Labours Lost*) as evidence: 'When daisies pied and violets blue, / And lady-smocks all silver white, / And cuckoo-buds of yellow hue, / Do paint the meadows with delight. / When shepherds pipe on oaten straws, / And maidens bleach their summer smocks...'. • Angled bitter-cress was originally placed in the genus *Dentaria* ('tooth') and, according to the medieval Doctrine of Signs (or Signatures), the resemblance of the white, rounded rhizomes to teeth indicated that this plant would alleviate dental problems.

ALPINE BITTER-CRESS • *Cardamine bellidifolia*

GENERAL: Smooth, **tufted, dwarf perennial alpine** herb to 10 cm tall, from a **taproot**.

LEAVES: Forming a **basal rosette**, blades to 3 cm long, **oval with vaguely toothed margins**; leaf stalks 2–4 times as long as the blades.

FLOWERS: White, 4 petals each **to 5 mm long**; in few-flowered clusters atop the stem.

FRUITS: Erect siliques to 3.5 cm long.

ECOLOGY: Moist gravelly and rocky sites in the **subalpine and alpine** zones.

NOTES: *Cardamine* is an ancient name for 'cress,' a plant used for salads. 'Cress' appears to be derived from an Old English word of Indo-European origin meaning 'to nibble or eat.' The leaves of *Cardamine* species can be somewhat bitter, giving rise to 'bitter-cress' *Cardamine* is from the Greek 'kardamon,' because the taste is similar to kardamon or water-cress. Kardamon comes from *kardia* ('heart') and *damao* ('sedative'), because this plant was formerly used as a heart sedative; *bellidifolia* means the leaves of alpine bitter-cress look like those of English daisy (*Bellis perennis*, see p. 282).

WESTERN BITTER-CRESS • *Cardamine occidentalis*

GENERAL: Perennial herb from short, slender rhizomes, the **rhizomes forming tubers** at the bases of the stems; flowering stems to 40 cm long, erect (at least at the tip) to reclining and rooting at the nodes; often partially submerged.

LEAVES: Basal leaves lyrate (deeply divided with opposite paired lobes and a larger lobe at the end), in a loose rosette; stem leaves alternate, similar to basal leaves but becoming simpler as you go up the stem.

FLOWERS: White, 4 petals each **3–5 mm long**; several in elongate to rounded terminal clusters.

FRUITS: Erect siliques to 3.5 cm long.

ECOLOGY: Along the **edges of flowing and standing water**, at low elevations.

NOTES: Another bitter-cress of wet sites is **Brewer's bitter-cress** (*C. breweri*), similar to western bitter-cress but with some **simple basal leaves** and **without the enlarged, tuberous rhizomes**. It is also found in and around water, often partially submerged, at low to middle elevations from southern B.C. (not on the Queen Charlotte Islands) to California. • The species name *occidentalis* means 'western.'

FEW-SEEDED BITTER-CRESS • *Cardamine oligosperma*
LITTLE WESTERN BITTER-CRESS

GENERAL: Annual or biennial herb from a taproot; stems usually branched, 10–45 cm tall.

LEAVES: Basal and stem leaves lyrate (see western bitter-cress, above), basal leaves in a rosette, stem leaves alternate.

FLOWERS: White, 4 petals each **2–4 mm long**; several in elongate terminal clusters.

FRUITS: Erect siliques to 2.5 cm long.

ECOLOGY: A variety of wet, fairly open sites, from disturbed areas to open forest, at low to middle elevations.

NOTES: Two similar bitter-cresses are Pennsylvanian bitter-cress (*C. pensylvanica*) and Siberian bitter-cress (*C. umbellata*, also known as *C. oligosperma* var. *kamtschatica*). **Siberian bitter-cress** is an extremely variable rhizomatous perennial, with **flowers crowded near the top of the stem** (so as to **resemble an 'umbel,'** the characteristic inflorescence of the carrot family); it is an uncommon species of low to middle-elevation streambanks throughout our region. **Pennsylvanian bitter-cress** is like few-seeded bitter-cress in most respects, but its **leaf stalks are smooth** (vs. those of *C. oligosperma*, which have hairs) and its **mature fruits (siliques) are less than 1 mm thick** (those of *C. oligosperma* are greater than 1 mm thick). Pennsylvanian bitter-cress has similar habitats and distribution to *C. oligosperma*. • The species name *oligosperma* means 'few seeded.'

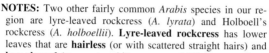

HAIRY ROCKCRESS • *Arabis hirsuta*

GENERAL: Biennial or short-lived perennial herb from a taproot; stems unbranched, to 1 m tall, hairy at base.

LEAVES: Basal leaves to 8 cm long, **hairy, lance-shaped, often purplish underneath**; stem leaves alternate, 5–15, somewhat lance-shaped, to 12 cm long.

FLOWERS: White to somewhat pinkish, to 9 mm long; in many-flowered, simple or branched terminal clusters.

FRUITS: Smooth siliques to 8 cm long, **erect to spreading**.

ECOLOGY: Beaches, bluffs, rocky slopes, gravel bars and disturbed sites at low to middle elevations.

NOTES: Two other fairly common *Arabis* species in our region are lyre-leaved rockcress (*A. lyrata*) and Holboell's rockcress (*A. holboellii*). **Lyre-leaved rockcress** has lower leaves that are **hairless** (or with scattered straight hairs) and **lyre-shaped** (see western bitter-cress, p. 146); it ranges from low to subalpine elevations (subalpine only in Washington and Oregon) in moist to wet habitats (forests, streamsides, lakeshores), throughout our region. **Holboell's rockcress** is similar to hairy rockcress, but has basal leaves with **star-shaped hairs** (use a hand lens), **pink to purple flowers** and **siliques bent downward**; it can be found from southeastern Vancouver Island and the Gulf Islands south to California, at low to (most commonly) subalpine elevations in a variety of open habitats. • You sometimes find individuals of rockcress infected by a rust fungus; instead of forming simple rosettes of basal leaves, these plants develop long stems crowned by flower-like clusters of bright-yellow, diseased leaves. These fungal pseudoflowers resemble buttercups, and they deceive flies who, attracted by the colour, shape and a sticky, sweet-smelling secretion, land on what appears to be a yellow flower surface, which is coated with fungal 'sperm' and 'eggs.' As the flies shuttle among the counterfeit flowers, they improve the rust's reproductive success by a sort of cross-fertilization.

FIELD PENNYCRESS • *Thlaspi arvense*

GENERAL: Introduced, hairless, yellow-green annual weed, to 50 cm tall.

LEAVES: Basal leaves few, to 6 cm long, **wavy to divided**, usually falling off by the time flowers are out; stem leaves similar to basal leaves at bottom, **arrowhead-shaped above** (with the basal lobes directed back).

FLOWERS: White, 4 petals to 4 mm long; in **long terminal clusters**.

FRUITS: Silicles to 1.7 cm long, **broadly heart-shaped, flattened, winged all around**.

ECOLOGY: Disturbed sites, fields; at low to middle elevations, throughout our region (but rare on the Queen Charlotte Islands and B.C.'s mid-coast).

NOTES: The round, flat fruits (silicles) look like shiny, silver pennies and give rise to the common name 'pennycress.' This species is also called 'stinkweed,' since the **foliage emits a rank odour when crushed**. Dairy products and meat may be tainted if cattle graze on it; excessive grazing by livestock may also result in poisoning. • Pennycress is also called 'Jim Hill mustard' after James J. Hill (1838–1916), famous railroad builder because the plant spread along the transcontinental railroads he helped build. • *Thlaspi* was the name used by Dioscorides for the 'cress of corruption and ruination,' and it was a medieval name for a poisonous buttercup. The word appears to be from the Greek *thlao* which means 'I compress,' presumably describing the flattened fruits. • In the old times it was also called 'mithridate mustard' because it was part of a mixture, known as 'Mithridaticum,' which was hailed as 'the antidote to all poisons.' This mixture was named after its inventor, Mithridates (a King of Pontus), and it later became known as 'Venice treacle' as its composition changed (see wormseed mustard, p. 152).

FIELD MUSTARD • *Brassica campestris*
RAPE

GENERAL: Weedy, introduced annual herb, to 1 m tall, from a thin taproot, **generally not hairy, but covered with a whitish bloom**.

LEAVES: Basal leaves lyrate (see western bitter-cress, p. 146), with 2–4 lateral lobes; stem leaves alternate, with basal lobes, **eventually clasping** the stem as you move up.

FLOWERS: Pale-yellow, 4 petals each to 1 cm long; **in small clusters** terminally and from leaf axils.

FRUITS: Siliques to 7 cm long, **with slender 'beak'** at tip.

ECOLOGY: Disturbed sites at low to middle elevations.

NOTES: This species is also known as *Brassica rapa*. • Several species of mustard (*Brassica* spp.) can be found in weedy places in our region; all are introduced species, and *B. campestris* is the most common. • The young leaves of field mustard were eaten as a potherb by some aboriginal peoples, such as the Stl'atl'imx. • Rapeseed farmers will be pleased to note that there is no sexual connotation in the origin of the name 'rape.' Rather, it derives from the Latin *rapa* or *rapum* for 'turnip,' since this species was formerly considered a subspecies of *B. rapa*, the cultivated turnip. • The word 'mustard' appears to be from the Latin *mustum* for 'new wine' (the first pressings of the grapes). The new wine used to be mixed with the powdered seeds of the mustard plant (*B. alba*) to form 'mustard sauce.'

PRAIRIE PEPPER-GRASS • *Lepidium densiflorum*

GENERAL: Introduced, finely hairy annual herb; **freely branched** stems to 50 cm tall

LEAVES: Basal leaves in a rosette, to 10 cm long, **shallowly or deeply toothed**; stem leaves alternate, smaller and simpler as you go up.

FLOWERS: White and about 1 mm long, but petals usually absent; numerous in branched terminal cluster.

FRUITS: Oblong, flattened silicles to 4 mm long.

ECOLOGY: Relatively dry openings and disturbed sites at low to middle elevations.

NOTES: Tall pepper-grass (*L. virginicum*) has **disc-shaped silicles and white petals to 3 mm long**; it can be found in disturbed sites or along beaches from southern Vancouver Island, the Gulf Islands and the adjacent mainland south through the Puget Sound area. • 'Pepper-grass' appears to have derived from pepper-wort, the name given to *L. latifolium* because of its acrid taste.

AMERICAN WINTER CRESS • *Barbarea orthoceras*

GENERAL: Biennial herb from a woody base and taproot; stems erect, **angled, usually hairless**, to 80 cm tall.

LEAVES: Basal leaves lyrate (see western bitter-cress, p. 146), to 12 cm long; leaves becoming smaller and simpler as you go up the stem.

FLOWERS: Yellow, small (**to 5 mm** long), with 4 petals; in small terminal clusters.

FRUITS: Siliques to 5 cm long, **somewhat 4-angled, without a distinct beak** at the tip.

ECOLOGY: Moist to wet forest and openings (meadows, streambanks, beaches) at low to middle elevations.

NOTES: Bitter winter cress (*B. vulgaris*) is a very similar weedy species, found in wet, disturbed places in the Strait of Georgia–Puget Sound area. The upper stem leaves of bitter winter cress are **not nearly so deeply divided** as are those of American winter cress. • Species of *Barbarea* were formerly called 'Saint Barbara's cress' after a saint of the 4th century. They were so-called because they were traditionally eaten in winter around St. Barbara's Day: December 4th. A German interpretation is that winter cresses are eaten by 'barbel,' a type of fresh-water carp.

SHEPHERD'S PURSE • *Capsella bursa-pastoris*

GENERAL: Finely hairy annual; stems to 50 cm tall, simple to (usually) branched.

LEAVES: Basal leaves in a rosette, to 6 cm long including the stalks, broadly lance-shaped, **usually toothed to pinnately divided**; stem leaves alternate, stalkless and **clasping** (with pairs of ear-like lobes at the leaf bases), lance-shaped to oblong, irregularly toothed.

FLOWERS: White, small; 4 petals each **to 3 mm** long; usually numerous, at first clustered densely along the stem, later spreading out as they mature and the fruits develop.

FRUITS: Strongly flattened, triangular to heart-shaped silicles; seeds numerous, sticky when wet; typically buds, flowers and fruits are present at the same time on a single plant.

ECOLOGY: Waste places, roadsides, fields, paths, gardens, barnyards; from low to subalpine elevations; common in most places where there is human-caused disturbance.

NOTES: Originally from Europe, shepherd's purse has become a **very widespread weed** throughout our region and most of North America. It can be troublesome in cultivated fields and gardens. Shepherd's purse often harbours fungi that can be transmitted to cabbage, turnips and other members of the mustard family. • This weedy plant has been used in Europe for centuries as a source of edible greens and spicy seeds. Some Nlaka'pamux people used to eat the young, peppery leaves of this introduced weed. • The distinctive fruits are responsible for both the scientific and common names. *Capsella* is Latin for 'little box,' *bursa* for 'purse,' *pastor* for 'shepherd.'

149

MARSH YELLOW CRESS • *Rorippa palustris*

GENERAL: Annual or biennial herb, **erect**, simple to branched stems **to 1 m tall**.

LEAVES: Alternate, **large (to 17 cm long)**; lower stem leaves more finely divided, leaves up the stem becoming simply toothed, some with basal lobes.

FLOWERS: Light yellow, 4 petals **to 2 mm** long; in clusters terminally and in leaf axils.

FRUITS: Sausage-shaped, straight siliques to 1 cm long.

ECOLOGY: Wet, open areas (meadows, lakeshores, swamps, roadside ditches) at low to middle elevations.

NOTES: This species is also known as *R. islandica*. • **Western yellow cress** (*R. curvisiliqua*) is a smaller, **more creeping** plant (**to 40 cm** tall) with **curved siliques on short stalks (2–4 mm** long, vs. 4–12 mm long in *R. palustris*). Its habitat is similar to that of marsh yellow cress (though it can also be found in open woods); its range is from the south coast of B.C. to California. • **Water cress** (*R. nasturtium-aquaticum* or *Nasturtium officinale*) is an edible European **aquatic** that has been widely **introduced** to ditches, springs and quiet waterways in settled areas.

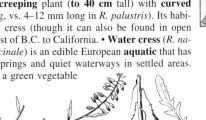

Aboriginal peoples adopted its use as a green vegetable long ago. The Saanich used to pick the leaves of this plant at Shady Creek, near Brentwood on Vancouver Island, and eat them raw. • *Rorippa* is from the Old Saxon name for this plant: *rorippen*. The species name *palustris* describes its habitat: marshy places.

HEDGE MUSTARD • *Sisymbrium officinale*

GENERAL: Introduced hairy annual herb to 80 cm tall, often extensively branched and **ungainly**, with a distinctive **sweetish smell**.

LEAVES: Basal leaves lyrate (see western bittercress, p. 146), to 20 cm long; stem leaves reduced, lobed.

FLOWERS: Pale yellow, 4 petals **to 4 mm** long; in terminal clusters.

FRUITS: Erect, dagger-like siliques, **tightly pressed** to the stem, **to 1.5 cm long**.

ECOLOGY: Disturbed sites, throughout our region near human habitation, most common from Vancouver Island south.

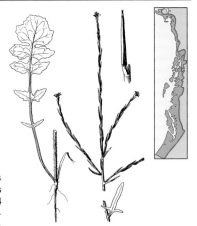

NOTES: Tall tumble-mustard (*S. altissimum*) is another **introduced annual**, with **larger petals (5–8 mm long)** and **larger siliques (more than 4 cm long) not tightly pressed** to the stem. Habitats and range are similar to those of hedge mustard. Some Stl'atl'imx people have adopted the use of the young leaves of tall tumble-mustard as a potherb; they know it by the name 'Italian weed.' The habit of the mature plant breaking off and being blown around by the wind gives rise to the name 'tumble-mustard.' • An old name for hedge mustard is 'crambling rocket': a *crambe* was a cabbage or mustard and 'rocket' derives from the Italian *ruchetta* and French *roquette*. These are the names for a Mediterranean species, *Eruca sativa*, a very hot-tasting salad plant.

NORTH PACIFIC DRABA • *Draba hyperborea*

GENERAL: Perennial, **loosely tufted** herbs of coastal sea-bluffs, from **thick taproots**; stems erect, to 25 cm tall.

LEAVES: Mostly basal, **yellowish-green**, lance- to wedge-shaped, **large (to 30 cm long), succulent, coarsely toothed in the upper half**, with long, broad leaf stalks; stem leaves 3–10, smaller, not toothed.

FLOWERS: Pale-yellow, 4 petals each **to 6 mm** long; in elongate, many-flowered, terminal clusters.

FRUITS: Large (to 2.2 cm long), dark-brown siliques.

ECOLOGY: Rocky cliffs and bluffs **along the sea coast**, often on exposed offshore islets.

NOTES: Calder and Taylor (1968) note that, in the Queen Charlotte Islands at least, north Pacific draba is often found in the nitrogen-rich environments of sea-bird nesting sites. They speculate that this species may be distributed by glaucous-winged gulls. • *Draba* is from the Greek *drabe*, ascribed to *Lepidium draba* (Arabian mustard) and meaning 'bitter or acrid.'

COMMON DRABA • *Draba verna*
WHITLOW-GRASS

GENERAL: **Introduced annual** herb from a taproot; flowering **stems leafless**, 5–25 cm tall.

LEAVES: In a basal rosette, **spoon-shaped, slightly toothed**, to 2.5 cm long, hairy.

FLOWERS: White; 4 petals **about 2.5 mm** long, **2-lobed** (like Mickey Mouse ears); in terminal clusters that elongate with age.

FRUITS: Elliptic silicles, **to 1 cm** long.

ECOLOGY: Dry, open, often disturbed sites at **low to middle elevations**.

NOTES: Another annual (or biennial) *Draba*, **Alaska draba** (*D. stenoloba*), occupies moist to drier meadows in the **subalpine and alpine** throughout our region (but is absent from the Queen Charlotte Islands); it has **creamy-yellow flowers and leafy stems**. • *Draba* is a taxonomically difficult genus of 12 or so

species in our region. These species are annual, biennial or perennial; generally from taproots; often with simple or variously branched hairs; with a basal rosette of leaves or sometimes with stem leaves; with small, yellow or white flowers; and with relatively short, oval to lance-shaped, flattened fruits. Some species grow in lowland habitats (usually disturbed or open grassy areas), but most are small, tufted or cushion-forming alpine species. Positive identification often requires material with both flowers and fruits, and reference to technical floras and keys. Regardless of their technical difficulty, drabas are charming plants, especially in the alpine tundra, where they produce little explosions of colour under extremely trying circumstances. • Drabas were formerly used for treating 'whitlows' (inflammations of the finger-tip, especially next to the nail). This plant was placed in the 16th century in the genus *Paronychia*, which is the Latin for 'beside the nail.'

LANCE-FRUITED DRABA • *Draba lonchocarpa*

GENERAL: Tufted, hairy perennial from taproot and branched stem base; flowering stems to 15 cm tall, **leafless or with 1–3 leaves.**

LEAVES: Mostly in a basal rosette, lance- to egg-shaped, to 1.5 cm long, **usually densely covered with star-shaped hairs; midribs of old leaves firm and persistent** on the basal tuft; stem leaves small, toothed.

FLOWERS: White; 4 petals **to 5 mm** long; few to several in terminal clusters.

FRUITS: Lance-shaped to oblong silicles, to 12 mm long, hairless or hairy, **often twisted.**

ECOLOGY: Rocky ridges, scree slopes, cliffs, dry meadows and tundra, **subalpine and alpine** elevations.

NOTES: Snow draba (*Draba nivalis*) is another **dwarf, tufted, alpine** draba that has **white** flowers and appears **ash-coloured** because of hairiness. It occupies high-elevation habitats similar to those of lance-fruited draba. If you really, really want to distinguish them (and some of the other alpine drabas), pull out your compound microscope: the **star-shaped hairs** on the leaves are **greater than 0.2 mm** in diameter in *D. lonchocarpa*, and **less than 0.2 mm** in diameter in *D. nivalis*. Tiny hairs are often the key to the recondite world of *Draba* taxonomy.

WORMSEED MUSTARD • *Erysimum cheiranthoides*

GENERAL: Slightly hairy, introduced annual herb **to 1 m tall**, from a **taproot (line drawing below; photo is *E. arenicola*).**

LEAVES: Alternate, **narrowly lance-shaped**, to 8 cm long, **with or without teeth.**

FLOWERS: Pale-yellow, 4 petals each **to 5 mm** long; in terminal clusters that elongate with age.

FRUITS: Nearly erect siliques to 3 cm long, **round to square** in cross-section.

ECOLOGY: Moist disturbed sites at low elevations.

NOTES: When in **alpine** regions of Vancouver Island, the Olympics and Cascades, look for the **perennial sand-dwelling wallflower** (*E. arenicola, photo*), with **longer (greater than 1.5 cm long) lemon-yellow petals** and **flattened** siliques. If your Cascade foothills *Erysimum* is **greyish-hairy** with **yellow to orange flowers** and **3-D** siliques, it is likely **prairie rocket** (*E. asperum*), which finds its northern range limit in southern B.C. (in the Cascades). • Wormseed mustard was one of the 72 ingredients of the 'Venice treacle,' which was fashionable in the Middle Ages as an antidote for all animal poisons. This mixture was formerly known as 'Mythridaticum' (see *Thlaspi arvense*, p. 147). It became a 'treacle' (from the Dutch *triakel* and Latin *theriaca* for 'a small animal') after Andromachus, physician to the Emperor Nero, added vipers to the mixture. This mixture was also a famous vermifuge, which may explain where the name 'wormseed' came from. • The Latin *Erysimum* is from *erysio* meaning 'to draw,' as in 'drawing out pain' or causing blisters, because *Erysimum* species were often used as poultices.

SCURVY GRASS • *Cochlearia officinalis*

GENERAL: Fleshy, hairless, biennial or perennial, seashore herb; **stems horizontal becoming vertical at tips**, to 30 cm long.

LEAVES: Basal leaves in a rosette; blades **round to kidney-shaped, to 2 cm long, stalks several times longer**; stem leaves longer and narrower, with short (or no) stalks.

FLOWERS: White, 4 petals **to 5 mm** long; few to several in cluster atop stem.

FRUITS: Silicles **spherical to oval**, 4–10 mm long; in elongate terminal clusters.

ECOLOGY: Sandy **shorelines, mudflats, marshes**; at low elevations north from Gray's Harbour, Washington.

NOTES: Because it is rich in vitamin C, scurvy grass helped some of the early explorers of the Arctic survive their long winter exiles in places like Novaya Zemlya and Spitsbergen. Parties who gathered scurvy grass and stored it ('freeze-dried') for winter use tended to survive; those who didn't tended to die of malnutrition compounded by scurvy. • The Latin *Cochlearia* (from *cochlear*, meaning 'spoon') and another common name, 'spoonwort,' both refer to the spoon-shaped basal leaves.

AMERICAN SEAROCKET • *Cakile edentula*

GENERAL: Fleshy, branched, **annual seashore** herb from taproot; stems **somewhat sprawling**, to 50 cm tall or long.

LEAVES: Alternate, **to 7 cm long, oblong, lobed, somewhat fleshy**, with broad stalks.

FLOWERS: White to purplish-tinged, 4 petals **to 8 mm** long; several in short clusters at the ends of branches or from leaf axils.

FRUITS: Siliques to 2.5 cm long; **thick, 2-jointed, the upper segment tapering to a flattened beak**.

ECOLOGY: Sandy **beaches** along the ocean.

NOTES: European searocket (*C. maritima*) is an uncommon introduced species with **more finely divided leaves and larger flowers**. It is found on Graham Island (in the Queen Charlotte Islands), and sporadically along the west coast of Vancouver Island and points south, on sandy beaches. • American searocket has a strange distribution: the Atlantic and Great Lakes regions, and our coast. It has been suggested that it has been introduced on the Pacific coast. • Studies have shown this species responds to burial in sand with enhanced growth and production of more seeds per plant. • The name 'rocket' derives from the Italian *ruchetta* and French *roquette*. These are the names for a Mediterranean species, *Eruca sativa*, a very hot-tasting salad plant. The fruits are 'toothless' (*edentula*), unlike those of European searocket.

Crassulaceae (Stonecrop Family)

Crassulaceae is a medium-sized, widely distributed family, that for the most part inhabits the drier parts of the earth, but which is almost absent from Australia and Oceania. It includes annual or perennial succulent herbs, with fleshy, opposite, whorled or alternate, mostly persistent, usually simple and unlobed leaves that lack stipules. The flowers are radially symmetrical and have 4–30 distinct sepals; petals in the same numbers as sepals, distinct; stamens typically in 2 whorls and as many or twice as many as petals; and ovaries usually as many as petals, distinct, superior, and each subtended by a scale-like, nectar-producing gland. Their fruits are 1-chambered follicles, usually with many seeds.

Members of the Crassulaceae are important primarily as ornamentals, and many are grown as novelties by fans of succulent plants.

Brittle prickly pear cactus is also a succulent plant and has been included in this section, but it belongs to the Cactus Family (Cactaceae).

Key to *Sedum* (Stonecrops)

1a. Flowers usually purple; leaves mostly on the flowering stems, strongly flattened .... *S. integrifolium*
1b. Flowers yellow; leaves mostly basal 2
  2a. Leaves of flowering stems mainly opposite .... *S. divergens*
  2b. Leaves of flowering stems alternate 3
    3a. Leaves usually broadest above mid-length and tapered to the base, flattened 4
      4a. Petals 8–13 mm long, long-pointed; follicles erect .... *S. oreganum*
      4b. Petals 6–10 mm long, not with long pointy tips; follicles spreading .... *S. spathulifolium*
    3b. Leaves usually broadest below mid-length, tapering to tip or to both ends, either strongly keeled or rounded in cross-section 5
      5a. Leaves strongly keeled, with long, pointy tips; follicles widely divergent .... *S. stenopetalum*
      5b. Leaves not strongly keeled, sometimes falling off by flowering time, round in cross-section, not with long, pointy tips; follicles erect .... *S. lanceolatum*

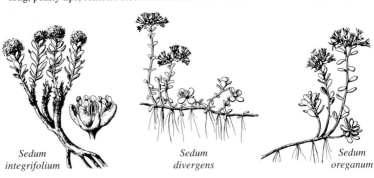

Sedum
integrifolium

Sedum
divergens

Sedum
oreganum

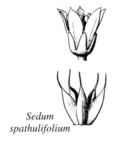

Sedum
spathulifolium

Sedum
lanceolatum

BROAD-LEAVED STONECROP • *Sedum spathulifolium*

GENERAL: Perennial, succulent herb to 20 cm tall, from stout rhizomes.

LEAVES: Alternate, crowded, **oblong to wedge- or spoon-shaped,** fleshy, **flattened,** to 2 cm long, 1 cm wide, crowded, **sage-green, reddish in full sun;** leaf surface **glaucous** (covered with a white-waxy powder), sometimes wrinkled.

FLOWERS: Bright yellow; petals **to 1 cm** long, in 5s, lance-shaped, **pointed;** in flat-topped clusters atop leafy, flowering stems.

FRUITS: Erect follicles, the 5 segments joined at the base and **spreading at the tips;** seeds numerous.

ECOLOGY: Rocky outcrops, cliffs, coastal bluffs, forest openings on coarse soils; at low to middle elevations.

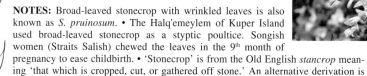

NOTES: Broad-leaved stonecrop with wrinkled leaves is also known as *S. pruinosum.* • The Halq'emeylem of Kuper Island used broad-leaved stonecrop as a styptic poultice. Songish women (Straits Salish) chewed the leaves in the 9th month of pregnancy to ease childbirth. • 'Stonecrop' is from the Old English *stancrop* meaning 'that which is cropped, cut, or gathered off stone.' An alternative derivation is that 'crop' also means 'a top, or bunch of flowers.' • The charming name 'livelong' is also used for *Sedum*, because these plants remain green long after they have been picked, and were used to test a lover's fidelity. On Midsummer's Eve, young girls would pick two pieces, one representing themselves and the other their lover. These were set up on a slate or trencher, and the length of time his piece lived and whether or not it turned towards hers indicated the strength of his fidelity. Stonecrop was also called 'lovelong' and 'midsummer men' for the same reason. • Stonecrop growing on the roof was believed to protect a house from fire and lightning. • *Sedum*, from the Latin *sedeo* ('to sit'), aptly describes the habit of many species; *spathulifolium* means 'spoon-shaped leaves.'

ROSEROOT • *Sedum integrifolium*

GENERAL: Hairless, succulent perennial with branched rhizomes that produce clustered annual stems, 5–20 cm tall and clothed with many persistent leaves; rhizomes thick, fleshy, scaly and **fragrant** when cut.

LEAVES: Oval to oblong, flattened, irregularly toothed to smooth-edged, much smaller and scale- like below, larger (0.5–4 cm long) further up the stem; **green to pinkish.**

FLOWERS: Usually dark purple, sometimes yellow or pink; parts often in 4s; petals oblong, somewhat fleshy, **2–4 mm** long; in dense, head- like clusters at tips of leafy stems.

FRUITS: Red or purplish follicles, more or less erect with divergent tips.

ECOLOGY: Moist rocky sites (headlands, cliffs, talus and scree slopes) and tundra meadows, at all elevations in the north and primarily high elevations in the south.

NOTES: Roseroot is also known as *S. rosea.* • Native people in Alaska ate the suc- culent leaves and young shoots raw or boiled them as greens. The Inuit would eat the boiled rootstocks with walrus blubber or other fats. The plants are best collected before flowering since they tend to become bitter and fibrous in late summer. • Decoctions of roseroot were also used by Alaskan Athapaskan groups for sore throats and colds, and as an eye-wash. • The common name roseroot derives from the fact that the rhizome, when cut or bruised, emits the fragrance of roses. Another common name, 'king's crown,' may refer to the flowers, which are arranged in a dense, crown-like cluster at the top of the stem.

OREGON STONECROP • *Sedum oreganum*

GENERAL: Perennial, sprawling, succulent herb from rhizomes, with ascending branches, to 15 cm tall.

LEAVES: Alternate, crowded, **egg- to spoon-shaped**, to 2.5 cm long, **somewhat flattened** but fleshy; **green becoming bronze**, **somewhat glaucous** (whitish from a fine, waxy powder).

FLOWERS: Yellow, becoming pinkish with age; petals in 5s, lance-shaped and **long-pointed**, **to 12 mm** long, **united basally for 1–3 mm**; numerous, crowded atop flowering stems.

FRUITS: Upright, 5-segmented follicles, **not spreading** much.

ECOLOGY: Rock ledges, rocky ridges and talus slopes, often at the edges of forest; at low to middle elevations.

NOTES: Creamy stonecrop (*S. oregonense*) is a similar species but it has **opposite leaves** on the sterile shoots and **pointed but not long-tipped** petals **joined for about 3 mm** at their bases. It is a mid-elevation Cascade species from Mt. Hood south, in habitats similar to those of *S. oreganum*. • The Nuxalk ate the leaves of Oregon stonecrop, like those of spreading stonecrop. Makah women ingested the leaves to promote menstruation. • The fleshy leaves of stonecrops are an adaptation for enduring drought in their usually dry habitats. • Another common name for stonecrops is 'orpine,' the name given originally to yellow-flowered species of this genus, but ironically now mainly used for the pink-flowered *Sedum telephium* of Europe. It is from the French *orpin* or Latin *auropigmentum* meaning 'gold-pigment,' and applies well to many of our species.

SPREADING STONECROP • *Sedum divergens*

GENERAL: Creeping, mat-forming, succulent perennial from rhizomes; stems upright, to 15 cm tall.

LEAVES: Opposite or nearly so, to 8 mm long, fleshy, finely bumpy, **oval on horizontal stems, oblong to spoon-shaped on flowering stems, green to bright red**.

FLOWERS: Bright yellow; petals 5, lance-shaped, to 9 mm long; 5–15 in clusters atop erect flowering stems.

FRUITS: Star-shaped cluster of buff-coloured follicles, the 5 segments joined at the base but spreading above.

ECOLOGY: Rocky cliffs and headlands, ledges, lava fields and talus slopes at low to high elevations; often forms semicircles on scree or rock outcrops.

NOTES: The Haida, Nisga'a, Nuxalk and Lower Stl'atl'imx formerly relished the crisp leaves of spreading stonecrop as food. The Haida collected it from small offshore islands and rocky headlands and ate the leaves, which they called 'berries,' raw. The Nisga'a collected it in quantity from the lava beds of the Nass Valley; they still use it in the springtime. • The Haida used the leaves in a female tonic. The Nuxalk heated the leaves and applied them externally to the breast to start the flow of milk following childbirth. They drank a tea brewed from the stalks to ease childbirth.

STONECROP

LANCE-LEAVED STONECROP • *Sedum lanceolatum*

GENERAL: Hairless, succulent perennial from a slender rhizome; stems 5–25 cm high, tufted.

LEAVES: Alternate, narrowly lance-shaped to elliptic, but **rounded in cross-section** and fleshy; mostly near the base (the **stem leaves tend to drop off** before the plant flowers) and crowded on sterile shoots; sometimes covered with a white-waxy powder; often turning bronze in autumn.

FLOWERS: Yellow; parts in 5s; petals narrowly lance-shaped, 6–9 mm long; in dense flat-topped clusters.

FRUITS: Erect follicles.

ECOLOGY: Dry to moist, rocky, open sites at low to subalpine elevations.

NOTES: The leaves of all stonecrops are edible, but should be eaten only in moderation since some have emetic and cathartic properties and can cause headaches. • The reddish colour of the leaves in some of our stonecrops is enhanced by sunlight and occurs most often in plants on warm, exposed sites. • Some species of stonecrop were used in a vermifuge or treacle and were known as 'trip-madam,' 'prick-madam' or 'pricket'—all corruptions of 'triacle-madame,' from the French *triacque* and *triaquette* for a worming medicine.

BRITTLE PRICKLY-PEAR CACTUS • *Opuntia fragilis*

GENERAL: Low, mat-forming, **succulent perennial,** to 15 cm tall; **stems flattened, broad and fleshy, in 2–5 segments,** the upper segments easily broken off; with large spines and smaller bristles.

LEAVES: Reduced to **large spines** (to 3 cm long) and **smaller yellowish bristles** from axillary white-woolly 'cushions' (areolae).

FLOWERS: Yellow, showy, large (to 5 cm across), borne on the areolae, with numerous thin (like tissue paper) petals; stamens numerous, with reddish stalks.

FRUITS: Dry, pear-shaped, slightly spiny berries to 2 cm long.

ECOLOGY: Dry, open sites on sandy or gravelly soils; at low elevations.

NOTES: The succulent stems of the prickly-pear were roasted and eaten as a green vegetable by interior peoples, but they were apparently little used on the coast. • Archibald Menzies reported this species from the Gulf Islands in May 1792: 'was not a little surprizd to meet with the Cactus Opuntia thus far to the Northward, it grew plentifully but in a very dwarf state on the Eastern point of the Island which is low flat & dry sandy soil' (cited in Clark, 1976). • The name 'cactus,' from Greek *kaktos* (any kind of prickly plant), was originally ascribed to the prickly 'cardoon' or thistle, *Cynaria cardunculus*. The great Swedish taxonomist Linnaeus is reputed to have borrowed the name to describe the unfamiliar plants from the Americas, now known as the Cactaceae. The stem segments are pear-shaped and, as many a bare-footed child in summer will attest to, covered in horribly sharp spines.

Saxifragaceae (Saxifrage Family)

Saxifragaceae is a widespread, medium-sized family that (understood here not to include *Ribes*, the gooseberries and currants) includes mostly perennial herbs with alternate or basal, simple leaves that lack stipules; flower clusters terminal; flowers mostly radially symmetrical, with 4–5 sometimes fused sepals, 4–5 separate petals (sometimes smaller than sepals or absent), stamens of same number as and alternate with petals or twice as many (except only 3 stamens in *Tolmiea*); superior to inferior ovaries that are single or 2–5 and separate; fruit a 1–5 chambered capsule; and seeds several to many.

The family is particularly diverse in western North America, with several endemic species and genera. *Saxifraga* is the largest genus. The family is economically important for ornamentals such as saxifrages, coral-bells (*Heuchera*), astilbe, bergenia and piggyback plant (*Tolmiea*).

The Saxifragaceae is similar to the Rosaceae, but it has leaves with stipules and usually fewer ovaries and stamens, and it is allied to the Crassulaceae, which have different numbers of floral parts and ovaries subtended by scale-like glands.

Key to Genera of the Saxifrage Family (Saxifragaceae)

1a. Flowering stems leafless or with a few small leaves of bracts, leaves in a basal rosette 2

  2a. Fertile stamens 5 3

    3a. Flowers single atop stem; fertile stamens alternating with clusters of gland-tipped sterile stamens .... *Parnassia*

    3b. Flowers more than 1 in a cluster; sterile stamens lacking 4

      4a. Petals divided and feather-like, or 3 lobed .... *Mitella*

      4b. Petals entire, not divided .... *Heuchera*

  2b. Fertile stamens 10 5

    5a. Leaves leathery; ovaries separate almost to base; inflorescence tightly bunched atop stem .... *Leptarrhena*

    5b. Leaves not leathery; ovaries united considerably above the base; inflorescence usually open and loose, not tightly bunched atop stem .... *Saxifraga*

1b. Flowering stems distinctly leafy 6

    6a. Petals lacking; flowers greenish, inconspicuous; sepals 4; stamens 4 or 8 .... *Chrysosplenium*

    6b. Petals present or sepals 5 and stamens (3) 5 or 10; flowers often showy 7

      7a. Stamens 3; flowers greenish to purplish-brown; petals thread-like, entire .... *Tolmiea*

      7b. Stamens 5 or 10 8

        8a. Stamens 5 9

          9a. Petals deeply divided and feather-like, or lobed 10

            10a. Petals with 3–7 short, blunt lobes .... *Elmera* (see *Tellima*)

            10b. Petals deeply divided, with narrow, hair-like segments .... *Mitella*

          9b. Petals entire, not divided into narrow segments or blunt lobes 11

            11a. Ovary and capsule 1-chambered; inflorescence often spike-like .... *Heuchera*

            11b. Ovary and capsule 2-chambered; inflorescence open .... *Boykinia*

        8b. Stamens 10 12

          12a. Ovary and capsule 2 chambered .... *Saxifraga*

          12b. Ovary and capsule 1 chambered 13

            13a. Petals entire, linear; capsule opening by 2 unequal segments .... *Tiarella*

            13b. Petals divided, lobed, or fringed 14

               14a. Petals frilly, pinnately divided into 5–10 linear lobes; leaves shallowly lobed .... *Tellima*

               14b. Petals palmately divided into narrowly oblong lobes; leaves deeply palmately cleft or lobed .... *Lithophragma*

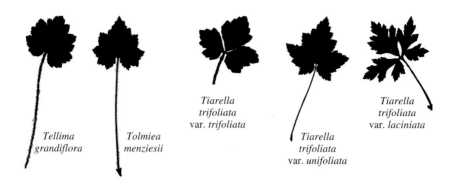

*Tellima
grandiflora*

*Tolmiea
menziesii*

*Tiarella
trifoliata*
var. *trifoliata*

*Tiarella
trifoliata*
var. *unifoliata*

*Tiarella
trifoliata*
var. *laciniata*

*Heuchera
micrantha*

*Heuchera
glabra*

*Boykinia
elata*

*Mitella
pentandra*

*Mitella
breweri*

159

PURPLE MOUNTAIN SAXIFRAGE • *Saxifraga oppositifolia*

GENERAL: Densely or loosely matted, **cushion-forming** perennial with **condensed, crowded, or trailing branches.**

LEAVES: Very small (1–4 mm long), oblong to oval, **leathery, bristly-hairy,** overlapping and **scale-like, opposite, arranged in 4 rows.**

FLOWERS: Showy, **lilac or purple** (rarely white); to 1 cm long; single at branch tips; one of the earliest flowering species of the alpine zone.

FRUITS: Capsules, 6–9 mm long, with slender spreading tips.

ECOLOGY: Moist but well-drained, alpine cliffs, ledges, gravelly ridges and scree and exposed tundra; most abundant on calcium-rich substrates; in Alaska can also occur near sea level on glacier forelands or in areas of cold-air drainage; common in northern southeast Alaska (north of Juneau), where often associated with recently deglaciated terrain; scattered on high mountains south to the Olympic and Cascade mountains of Washington; rare on the Queen Charlotte Islands and Vancouver Island.

NOTES: Saxifrage comes from the Latin *saxum* (rock) and *frangere* (to break), since these plants were thought to break the rocks upon which they grew. Because of this, plants were ground up and fed to patients with gallstones as a supposed cure; saxifrages may also be called 'breakstone.' Other old beliefs are that the fresh roots of saxifrages can remove freckles and relieve toothaches. • The species name *oppositifolia* means 'opposite-leaved.'

SPOTTED SAXIFRAGE • *Saxifraga bronchialis*
PRICKLY SAXIFRAGE

GENERAL: Matted, **cushion-like** perennial, with a branched stem-base from a taproot; **branches closely covered with withered, persistent leaves**; flowering stems glandular-hairy, with several small, **alternate** leaves, 5–15 cm tall.

LEAVES: Leathery, evergreen, rigid, closely crowded and overlapping, lance-shaped to oblong to spoon-shaped, entire, coarsely **bristly-hairy along the margins, spine-tipped.**

FLOWERS: White to yellowish, usually spotted with yellow or red; 1-2 cm across; few to several in a somewhat flat-topped cluster.

FRUITS: Oblong, often purplish, 2-beaked capsules.

ECOLOGY: Cliffs, rock crevices, talus slopes, scree slopes, gravelly flats; usually non-forested habitats; from middle to (more typically) high elevations, through most of our region.

NOTES: Some taxonomists split 2 other species or subspecies off from *S. bronchialis*: Funston's saxifrage (*S. funstonii*) of the northernmost part of our region (Juneau and Glacier Bay north), and *S. vespertina* of Washington and Oregon. • The related **three-toothed saxifrage** (*S. tricuspidata*) has leathery **3-toothed leaves without marginal bristles**. It occurs occasionally in the northern part of our region, but it is typically an interior species. **Taylor's saxifrage** (*S. taylori*) has leathery **3-toothed leaves that also have marginal bristles**; this species is confined to the mountains of the Queen Charlotte Islands and northern Vancouver Island.

TOLMIE'S SAXIFRAGE • *Saxifraga tolmiei*

GENERAL: Low, **mat-forming** perennial with numerous sterile, leafy shoots; flowering stems 2–8 cm tall, with stalked glands.

LEAVES: Entire, hairless or the bases sparsely long-hairy, **fleshy** and slightly rolled over on the edges, 2–10 mm long, alternate, **club-shaped to spoon-shaped**.

FLOWERS: White, saucer-shaped, with 5 well-separated, spreading petals; 1–3.

FRUITS: 2-lobed, oval capsules, 7–12 mm long, purplish mottled.

ECOLOGY: In moist talus, scree or rock crevices, typically watered by melting snow, or near streams or in snowbeds in alpine tundra; common at high elevations.

NOTES: The sausage-like, fleshy leaves give *S. tolmiei* the look of a *Sedum* or stonecrop. This saxifrage is able to survive with a very short growing season. The plants are often found—and can be the most common species—in areas with very deep, long-lasting snowbanks that do not melt until August. • William Fraser Tolmie (1812–86) was the Hudson's Bay Company physician at Fort Vancouver in 1832 and a botanical collector in northwestern North America.

TUFTED SAXIFRAGE • *Saxifraga cespitosa*

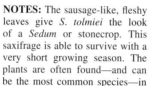

GENERAL: Loosely to densely **tufted** or **matted** perennial, from a taproot; stem bases branched, clothed in old, withered leaves; flowering stems glandular-hairy, with 1 to several small leaves, 3–15 cm tall.

LEAVES: Wedge-shaped, 0.5–2 cm long, with **3–5 narrow lobes at the tip**, often glandular-hairy, gradually narrow to broad stalks.

FLOWERS: White to yellowish, sepals often purplish; 1 to several in a loose cluster.

FRUITS: Capsules, 5–10 mm long.

ECOLOGY: Rocky slopes, cliffs, ledges, gravelly ridges; common from sea level outcrops to alpine tundra in much of our region, but less common in the southern part.

NOTES: Tufted saxifrage is a wide-ranging and highly variable circumboreal species. • Two tiny, few-flowered alpine species with toothed leaves also occur at high elevations in the coastal mountains. **Brook saxifrage** (*Saxifraga rivularis*) has **3–5 toothed**, roughly **heart-shaped** leaves with distinct stalks. **Wedge-leaved saxifrage** (*S. adscendens*) has leaves shaped more like those of tufted saxifrage, but with **3 shallow lobes at the tip**, and the plants are **not densely matted**.

WOOD SAXIFRAGE • *Saxifraga mertensiana*
MERTENS' SAXIFRAGE

GENERAL: Perennial from short, thick, scaly rhizomes that sometimes have bulblets at the tip; flowering stems 15–40 cm tall, with spreading glandular hairs and 1–3 basal leaves.

LEAVES: Circular to kidney-shaped, heart-shaped at base, coarsely lobed (lobes themselves sharp-toothed), with distinct hairy stalks several times as long as leaf blades, sparsely hairy, thick, somewhat succulent and brittle, often with bulblets in their axils.

FLOWERS: White, at least some flowers replaced by pinkish bulblets; few to several in an open cluster.

FRUITS: Capsules, broadly egg-shaped, about 5 mm long.

ECOLOGY: Rocky or gravelly stream-banks, wet ledges and rocks, spray zone near waterfalls, from sea level to subalpine; common but rarely abundant.

NOTES: **Heart-leaved saxifrage** (*Saxifraga nelsoniana,* also called *S. punctata*) also has **circular to kidney-shaped**, long-stalked leaves that are **heart-shaped at the base**, but they have **only one set of teeth**, and the plants **never have bulblets**. *S. nelsoniana* is common in moist rocky habitats from middle to alpine elevations throughout all but the southernmost part of the region. • Mertens' saxifrage is named after Carl Heinrich Mertens (1796–1830), the first collector at Sitka, Alaska.

RED-STEMMED SAXIFRAGE • *Saxifraga lyallii*
LYALL'S SAXIFRAGE

GENERAL: Perennial from basal rosette and rhizomes; flowering stems leafless, hairless to hairy, reddish to purplish.

LEAVES: Fan- or wedge- to spoon-shaped, coarsely toothed but not at the base, abruptly narrowing to stalks about as long as the leaf blades, hairless to hairy.

FLOWERS: White; few to several in open groups.

FRUITS: 2-, 3- or 4-beaked capsules, 6–11 mm long, often bright red when mature.

ECOLOGY: Stream-banks, seepage areas, snowbeds and other wet places in the mountains; mostly in the alpine zone, but also along creeks in ravines in subalpine forest; widespread throughout much of our region.

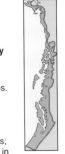

NOTES: Stream saxifrage (*Saxifraga odontoloma,* also called *S. arguta*) has **kidney-shaped** leaves that are **coarsely toothed all around the margin** and have **stalks several times as long as the leaf blades**. It is also a species of stream-banks and moist, shady rocks at middle to high elevations, and it is frequent from southwestern B.C. to California. It sometimes hybridizes with *S. lyallii*.

ALASKA SAXIFRAGE • *Saxifraga ferruginea*

GENERAL: Perennial from a short, erect, unbranched stem-base; flowering stems 1 to several, glandular-hairy, leafless, **10–35 cm tall.**

LEAVES: Narrowly **wedge- to spoon-shaped, all basal, with 5–15 teeth, taper gradually to broad, winged stalks.**

FLOWERS: White to purplish, sometimes replaced by **bulblets; petals distinctly stalked, the upper 3 usually larger and with 2 yellow spots;** several to many in open clusters.

FRUITS: Capsules, 3–6 mm long.

ECOLOGY: Moist, mossy outcrops, stream-banks, wet rocks; frequent throughout our region in open habitats, from sea level to alpine.

NOTES: Alaska saxifrage is a widespread and very variable species; it can form large, showy colonies on exposed, rocky headlands and sea-bird islands, where it tends to be a robust plant with thick, fleshy, densely hairy leaves. • **Alpine saxifrage** (*Saxifraga nivalis*) is a **smaller (5–20 cm tall)**, strictly alpine species that has **elliptic to oval, several-toothed leaves** and densely clustered flowers. It occurs occasionally in coastal mountains in the northern part of our region. • Another common name, 'rusty saxifrage,' and the species name *ferruginea* both refer to the rusty sepals of Alaska saxifrage.

WESTERN SAXIFRAGE • *Saxifraga occidentalis*

GENERAL: Perennial, from **basal rosettes** with short rhizomes, usually forming small clumps; flowering stems 10–25 cm tall, leafless, reddish glandular-hairy.

LEAVES: Elliptic to egg-shaped, 3–8 cm long and 1–3 cm wide, with **15–30 coarse teeth.**

FLOWERS: White to pinkish, several to many in an open to compact cluster.

FRUITS: Capsules, 3–6 mm long, greenish to reddish-purple.

ECOLOGY: Moist to dry, grassy or mossy openings, rocky slopes, rock outcrops, meadows; frequent from low to high elevations in the southern part of the region, scattered on the mainland north of Vancouver Island.

NOTES: The closely related **rusty-haired saxifrage** (*Saxifraga rufidula,* line drawing on left) has **flat-topped** inflorescence and leaves with very **regular teeth (resembling the cogs on a gear wheel)** and often with **dense rusty hairs** on the undersides. Rusty-haired saxifrage is common on rock outcrops from low to high elevations in the southern part of our region, and is locally abundant on southern Vancouver Island, the Olympic Peninsula and the Columbia River gorge. **Grassland saxifrage** (*S. integrifolia*) has **entire or wavy-margined leaves** and a compact **conical** inflorescence. **Oregon saxifrage** (*S. oregana*) has **entire to wavy-toothed leaves** and a **long, narrow to open** inflorescence. **Grassland saxifrage** occupies dry, grassy slopes to moist banks and meadows, at low to middle elevations from southwestern B.C. to California. Oregon saxifrage prefers bogs, stream-banks and wet meadows from low to middle elevations in Washington and Oregon.

LEATHERLEAF SAXIFRAGE • *Leptarrhena pyrolifolia*

GENERAL: Perennial with robust, widely spreading rhizomes; flowering stems unbranched, glandular-hairy, 20–40 cm tall, with 1–3 smaller leaves, purplish-red in fall.

LEAVES: Mostly basal, oval to oblong, hairless, **leathery, glossy-green, rough and deeply veined above**, pale-green below; margins round-toothed.

FLOWERS: White, small; in a tight cluster at the stem tip.

FRUITS: Consist of 2 follicles that are **bright purplish-red**, as is the fruiting stem; seeds with a long, loose, tailed coat.

ECOLOGY: Stream-banks, flushes, mossy seepage areas, subalpine and alpine thickets and meadows; widespread in suitable habitats at high elevations south to Mt. Jefferson.

NOTES: Hitchcock et al. (1971) note that leatherleaf saxifrage 'takes well to cultivation and, because of its deep green leathery leaves and usually reddish follicles, is well worth a place in the native garden or in a moist spot in the rockery.' The brightly coloured fruiting cluster is very showy. • The species name means '*Pyrola*-like leaves'—that is, leathery and bright green. *Leptarrhena* is from the Greek *leptos* for 'slender' and *arrhen* or 'male,' and it refers to the slender filaments of the stamens.

SMALL-FLOWERED WOODLAND STAR • *Lithophragma parviflorum*

GENERAL: Perennial from slender rhizomes with numerous **rice-grain-sized bulblets**; flowering stems 10–40 cm tall, glandular-hairy, usually purplish towards the top, with 1–3 leaves.

LEAVES: Mostly basal, long-stalked, **circular to kidney-shaped** in outline but **deeply divided into 5 main divisions that are themselves 3-cleft, hairy**; upper stem leaves nearly stalkless.

FLOWERS: White to pink or somewhat purplish; petals 5–10 mm long, usually **deeply 3-lobed** at tip; **5 to 11 flowers in** compact to elongated (up to 15 cm long) clusters.

FRUITS: Capsules, 3-chambered and 3-beaked at tip; seeds wrinkled and ridged.

ECOLOGY: Dry, open, grassy slopes, gravelly or rocky openings in dry forest such as Garry oak woodland, coastal bluffs; common from low to middle elevations in the southern part of our region, especially in the Strait of Georgia–Puget Sound area, the Columbia Gorge and the Willamette Valley.

NOTES: Smooth woodland star (*Lithophragma glabrum,* which includes *L. bulbifera*) has minutely spiny seeds, virtually **hairless** basal leaves, and **2–5** flowers; often **bulblets** in the axils of the stem leaves replace some of the flowers. It occurs in much the same habitats and over a similar range as small-flowered woodland star, but it is less common. • These species are presumably called 'woodland stars' because of the star-like white flowers. The genus name, from the Greek *lithos* ('stone') and *phragma* ('wall or hedge'), implies that some species of *Lithophragma* (not this one) grow near walls or hedges.

FIVE-STAMENED MITREWORT • *Mitella pentandra*

GENERAL: Perennial from rhizomes, occasionally with creeping above-ground shoots; flowering stems **20–40 cm tall**, generally leafless, glandular-hairy to hairless.

LEAVES: Few, **basal**, oval to heart-shaped, **4–8 cm long**, shallowly 5–9 lobed, round-toothed, with stiffly erect **hairs on both surfaces**.

FLOWERS: Greenish, small, saucer-shaped, blossoming upwards; petals dissected into 2–5 pairs of threadlike segments (look like a television antenna); **stamens 5, located opposite the petals**; in a long narrow cluster of 6–25.

FRUITS: Capsules, which shed their top half to expose the shiny, black seeds nestled in a shallow cup.

ECOLOGY: Moist woods, especially along streams, wet meadows, forest glades, clearings and avalanche tracks; middle elevation forests to subalpine parkland, but probably most common at subalpine elevations.

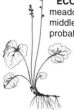

NOTES: **Common or bare-stemmed mitrewort** (*Mitella nuda*) is a smaller species (**3–20 cm tall**) with heart- to kidney-shaped leaves **1–3 cm long** and flowers with **10 stamens**. *M. nuda* is primarily an interior species of bogs, swamps, stream-banks and wet forest, but does occur in the B.C. Coast and northern Cascade Mountains along the eastern boundary of our region. • Without flowers, five-stamened mitrewort can be very difficult to distinguish from several genera and species of the Saxifragaceae with similar foliage (e.g., *Boykinia, Elmera, Mitella, Heuchera, Tellima, Tiarella, Tolmiea*). Refer to the key and silhouette diagrams (pp. 158–159) for help. • Seed dispersal is (at least partly) by a 'splash-cup' mechanism; this is also true for other species of *Mitella* and for *Chrysosplenium* (see notes under ground ivy-leaved water-carpet, p. 169). • The common and Latin names come from the diminutive of *mitra*, which means 'cap' or 'mitre.' Presumably the seed capsule was thought to resemble a bishop's mitre, though one reference suggests that it looks more like 'a tattered French-Canadian toque.'

BREWER'S MITREWORT • *Mitella breweri*

GENERAL: Perennial from rhizomes; flowering stems 15–40 cm tall, leafless, hairless to glandular-hairy.

LEAVES: Basal, heart- to kidney-shaped, shallowly 7–11 lobed, round-toothed, **hairless to sparsely hairy**.

FLOWERS: Greenish-yellow, small, saucer-shaped; petals dissected into 2–5 pairs of threadlike segments; **stamens 5, alternate with petals**; in a long narrow cluster of 20–60.

FRUITS: Capsules, much like those of five-stamened mitrewort.

ECOLOGY: Moist forest and glades, stream-banks, and gullies, from middle to subalpine elevations; fairly frequent but scattered, locally abundant in some mountain-hemlock forests in the southern half of our region.

NOTES: **Oval-leaved mitrewort** (*Mitella ovalis*), a lowland species of stream-banks, gullies, and shady forest from southern Vancouver Island south to California, is similar, but has smaller, very **hairy, oblong to oval** leaves. **Three-toothed mitrewort** (*M. trifida*) has leaves similar to those of oval-leaved mitrewort but has **white, 3-lobed petals** and inhabits moist mid-elevation forest from southern Vancouver Island to California. **Leafy mitrewort** (*M. caulescens*) is our only species of *Mitella* that has **stem leaves (1–3)** and that **blossoms from the top downward**. It occurs at low to middle elevations in moist, shaded forest, wet meadows and swamps, from southern Vancouver Island and the Chilliwack River south to California.

SMOOTH ALUMROOT • *Heuchera glabra*

GENERAL: Perennial from short, stout rhizomes; flowering stems 1 to several, clothed at base with persistent brown leaf bases and stipules, hairless to sparsely hairy below but becoming glandular-hairy in the inflorescence, 15–60 cm tall.

LEAVES: Mainly basal, long-stalked, heart-shaped, broader than long, 5-lobed, coarsely sharp-toothed, **hairless to sparsely glandular-hairy** on lower surface; stem leaves 1 or 2, much smaller.

FLOWERS: White, small; numerous, on thin stalks in **large open groups**.

FRUITS: Many-seeded, beaked capsules; seeds small, brown, somewhat banana-shaped, covered in rows of tiny spines.

ECOLOGY: Rocky meadows, mossy talus slopes, wet cliffs, crevices, moist slabs and boulders (as in the spray zone around waterfalls), at middle to high elevations virtually the length of the region (to Mt. Hood, Oregon); on the north coast can occur near sea level in rocky places.

NOTES: The pounded, dried roots of several *Heuchera* species are reputed to have been used by North American native people and herbalists as a poultice applied to cuts and sores to stop bleeding and promote healing. The Tlingit used this plant to cure inflammation of the testicles. • Johann Heinrich von Heucher (1677–1747) was a Professor of Medicine in Wittenburg, Germany.

SMALL-FLOWERED ALUMROOT • *Heuchera micrantha*

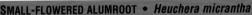

GENERAL: Perennial from rhizomes; flowering stems 1 to several, clothed at base with persistent brown leaf bases and stipules, long-hairy below to glandular-hairy in inflorescence, **15–60 cm tall**.

LEAVES: Mainly basal, long-stalked, kidney- or heart-shaped to oblong, 5–7 lobed, sharp- to round-toothed, usually **hairy on the leaf stalk and lower surface;** often lacking stem leaves.

FLOWERS: White, small; numerous in **open clusters**.

FRUITS: Many-seeded, beaked capsules; seeds small, black, egg-shaped, covered in rows of tiny spines.

ECOLOGY: Stream-banks, rock crevices, mossy talus slopes, from low to subalpine elevations; common in the southern half of our region, rare in the Coast Mountains of northern B.C. mainland.

NOTES: Small-flowered alumroot has leaf blades mostly **longer than broad,** and **long-hairy leaf stalks,** in contrast to smooth alumroot, which occupies similar habitats. • **Meadow alumroot** (*Heuchera chlorantha*) has a **long, narrow** inflorescence and **greenish-white** flowers. It is a **larger (40–100 cm tall)** species of moist, grassy bluffs, rocky slopes and forest edges from low to middle elevations. It is frequent on the eastern Queen Charlotte Islands and southern Vancouver Island and the adjacent mainland, south to Oregon. • The leaves of meadow alumroot were used by the Haida with skunk-cabbage leaves to make a sweat bath for people suffering from rheumatism, fever and other ailments. The Skagit pounded small-flowered alumroot and rubbed it on the hair of little girls to make it grow thick. They also used a poultice of small-flowered alumroot on cuts. • Our native alumroots are closely related to the cultivated Mexican 'coral bells' (*H. sanguinea*).

COAST BOYKINIA • *Boykinia elata*

GENERAL: Perennial, with rhizomes; stems **leafy, 15–60 cm tall**, with brownish to reddish, often glandular hairs.

LEAVES: Lower leaves long stalked, heart- to kidney-shaped, 2–8 cm wide, 5–7 cleft and with multiple, sharp-pointed teeth; leaves becoming stalkless further up stem; stipules consist of a **bit of a wing and several long, brownish bristles**.

FLOWERS: White; numerous in an open, compound grouping, branches of inflorescence densely glandular and reddish.

FRUITS: Capsules, beaked, with numerous, minutely spiny, black seeds.

ECOLOGY: Stream-banks, moist mossy rocks, moist forest, from sea level to middle elevations; common in the southern half of our region.

NOTES: Large boykinia (*Boykinia major*) has stout stems **30–100 cm tall**, unequally 3–7 lobed leaves up to 20 cm wide and **conspicuous, leafy stipules**. It occurs in wet meadows and along streams in Washington and Oregon. Its leaves are suggestive of false bugbane (p. 179), but they have brownish membranous stipules, whereas the leaves of false bugbane lack stipules. • This genus is named after Dr. Samuel Boykin (1786–1848), a naturalist in Georgia, U.S.A.

FRINGECUP • *Tellima grandiflora*

GENERAL: Perennial, with short rhizomes; flowering stems curved at base, 40–80 cm tall, very hairy on lower part, becoming glandular higher up towards flowers.

LEAVES: Basal leaves with long, very hairy stalks, more or less **heart-shaped** in outline, **5–8 cm wide**, shallowly 5–7 lobed and coarsely toothed, sparsely hairy; stem leaves 1–3, smaller.

FLOWERS: Greenish-white to sometimes reddish (darker with age), very fragrant; petals frilly, divided into **5–10 lobes**; **10 stamens**; 10–35 in loose clusters.

FRUITS: Capsules, about 10 mm long, with numerous, brown, wrinkled-warty seeds.

ECOLOGY: Moist forest, glades, stream-banks, avalanche tracks, thickets, clearings; common from low to middle elevations.

NOTES: Elmera (*Elmera racemosa*, inset photo) is somewhat similar to *Tellima*, but has **kidney-shaped leaves 3–5 cm wide**, flowering stems 10–25 cm tall, **white flowers with 3–7 lobed petals** and **5 stamens**. Elmera grows in rocky crevices and on ledges and talus slopes, scattered at mostly high elevations in the Cascade Mountains south of the Fraser River to Oregon, and also in the Olympic Mountains. *Elmera* has only 1 species, which in the past was placed either in *Heuchera* or *Tellima*. It seems most closely related to *Tellima*, from which it differs in number of stamens and degree of dissection of the petals. • The Skagit pounded fringecup, boiled it and drank the tea for any kind of sickness, especially lack of appetite. It was also known as a 'special' medicine to some Ditidaht people. • Fringecup was said to be eaten by woodland elves to improve night vision. • The highly divided petals form a fringe around the edge of the floral disc, giving rise to the common name. • *Tellima* is an anagram of *Mitella*.

PIGGY-BACK PLANT • *Tolmiea menziesii*
YOUTH-ON-AGE

GENERAL: Perennial with well-developed rhizomes; flowering stems 40–80 cm tall, hairy and somewhat glandular in the inflorescence.

LEAVES: Principal leaves basal, hairy, with long hairy stalks, heart-shaped, palmately 5–7 lobed and coarsely toothed, up to 10 cm long and about as wide, **sometimes with buds at the base** of the leaf blade; stem leaves few, smaller.

FLOWERS: Brownish-purple, 6–10 mm long; **petals 4, ribbon-like**; sepals 5, 3 large and 2 small, greenish-purple; **3 stamens**; several to many in long clusters.

FRUITS: Capsules, slender, 9–14 mm long, equally 2-valved; seeds numerous, brown, finely spiny.

ECOLOGY: Moist forest, glades, stream-banks, old logging roads with red alder; frequent at low to middle elevations.

NOTES: Piggy-back plant is commonly sold as a house plant. Despite its habitat, this is one of the few of our native species that can handle the low humidity of modern homes. • Small buds at the base of the leaf blades develop into **'daughter' plants**, giving rise to both the common names. • The genus is named after William Fraser Tolmie (1812–86), the Hudson's Bay Company physician at Fort Vancouver in 1832 and a botanical collector in northwestern North America; the species is named after Archibald Menzies, the first European botanist to explore the Pacific North American coast.

FOAMFLOWER • *Tiarella trifoliata*

GENERAL: Perennial with slender, short rhizomes; stems erect or ascending, glandular-hairy, 15–60 cm tall.

LEAVES: Main leaves basal, with long stalks and **3 leaflets** that are **irregularly lobed and coarsely toothed**, sparsely hairy; **stem leaves (1 to few) reduced in size** and with shorter stalks.

FLOWERS: Tiny, delicate, white, at the end of short wire-like stalks; several to many in elongate clusters.

FRUITS: Few-seeded capsules borne horizontally, open by splitting between the small upper valve and the larger lower valve to form structures that **resemble sugar scoops**; seeds smooth, black, shining.

ECOLOGY: Moist, shady coniferous forests, seepage areas, stream-banks, also in clearings; widespread at low to middle and sometimes subalpine elevations.

NOTES: Foamflower includes three varieties, each of which has been considered a separate species by some taxonomists. Variety *trifoliata* is as described above. *T. trifoliata* **var.** *unifoliata* (top drawing) has **simple** rather than compound leaves, merely **shallowly 3–5 lobed (maple-leaf-like)**. These 2 varieties occur throughout our region, but var. *unifoliata* tends to grow at higher elevations (above 300–650 m, depending on latitude) from mid-coastal B.C. south; it is less common and occurs to sea level north to northern southeast Alaska. *T. trifoliata* **var.** *laciniata* (lower drawing) has **3 leaflets deeply cleft** nearly their full length. It ranges from Vancouver Island and the adjacent islands and mainland south to Washington. • *Tiarella* species are called 'foamflowers' because the flowers appear like specks of foam. They are sometimes called 'sugar-scoops,' in reference to the unusual shape of the opened capsules. *Tiarella* is the diminutive of the Latin for a 'tiara,' which was a turban-like head-dress of ancient Persians, not the glittering diamond affair worn by Princess Diana.

GROUND IVY-LEAVED WATER-CARPET • *Chrysosplenium glechomaefolium*

GENERAL: Weak, hairless, mat-forming perennial **with stolons** (runners); stems somewhat succulent, usually branched in 2s, prostrate, ascending at tips, up to 20 cm long.

LEAVES: Opposite (except for the uppermost), on stalks up to 1 cm long, **oval to egg-shaped**, up to 2 cm long, **shallowly 15–20 toothed**.

FLOWERS: Greenish, small, inconspicuous, short-stalked; petals lacking; **4 sepals; 8 stamens**; single in the axils of upper leaves.

FRUITS: Capsules, 3–4 mm long, when ripe and open form **shallow cups** filled with several smooth, plump, purplish-black seeds.

ECOLOGY: Moist to wet seepage areas, springs, swamps; scattered at low to middle elevations.

NOTES: **Northern water-carpet** (*Chrysosplenium tetrandrum*) has **alternate** leaves with **merely 3–7 broad teeth**, and flowers with **4 stamens**. It occurs occasionally in the northern part of our region (north of 55°) along streams, in seepage areas, swamps and wet clearings. • The shallow cups of the ripe capsules are well-suited for splash-cup dispersal, whereby raindrops scoring direct hits eject the small, smooth seeds. • The common names come from the carpet-like, golden-coloured growth form of the plant and its preference for wet habitats. *Chrysosplenium* is from the Greek *chrysos* ('gold') and *splen* ('spleen'), from an old belief that it had some medicinal value. 'Golden-saxifrage' is another common name for the genus.

FRINGED GRASS-OF-PARNASSUS • *Parnassia fimbriata*

GENERAL: Hairless perennial from short rhizomes; flowering stems 1 to several, 15–30 cm tall, with a **clasping leaf about halfway or further up on the stem**.

LEAVES: Mostly basal, **broadly kidney-shaped**, glossy-green.

FLOWERS: White, with greenish or yellowish veins, showy; petals 5, nearly twice as long as the sepals, lower margins **fringed with hairs** in a comb-like arrangement; fertile stamens (the 5 with anthers) alternating with broad, gland-tipped sterile stamens that are divided into 5–9 segments or finger-like lobes; **solitary** on stem.

FRUITS: Capsules, with numerous, angled, loosely wrapped seeds.

ECOLOGY: In wet meadows, bogs, fens, along streams and in open and forested seepage areas; common throughout our region, generally at middle to alpine elevations, but in Alaska to sea level, especially in bogs.

NOTES: **Northern grass-of-Parnassus** (*Parnassia palustris*) is similar but its stem leaf is usually attached **below mid-stem**, the basal leaves usually are not deeply lobed at their base, and the petals **do not have a marginal fringe**. Northern grass-of-Parnassus occurs in wet, spongy habitats only in the northern-most part of our region (north of Juneau and west to Prince William Sound). • Dioscorides described a grass-like plant growing on the side of Mt. Parnassus. This 'grass' was taken to be *P. palustris*. Obviously, this was a mistake, because *Parnassia* species are not even remotely grass-like, but the name stuck.

Ranunculaceae (Buttercup Family)

The Ranunculaceae is a fairly large family, chiefly of cooler temperate regions and especially of the northern hemisphere. Members are mostly annual or perennial herbs, occasionally shrubs or vines (*Clematis*), with mostly alternate leaves (opposite in some *Ranunculus*), often compound or deeply divided (exception *Caltha*) and lacking stipules (see Rosaceae, p. 182). Flowers are radially symmetric, except in *Aconitum* and *Delphinium*, and solitary to numerous. Flowers have both sepals and petals or undifferentiated, usually showy segments; the segments are distinct and free and variable in number; stamens are usually many, spirally arranged; ovaries are several to many, distinct, spirally arranged and superior. Fruits are typically 1-chambered follicles (dry fruits opening on the front suture and each the product of a single ovary), achenes (*Ranunculus*), or berries (*Actaea*). Flowers produce several to many seeds.

The family has many important ornamentals, with several species each from the genera *Anemone, Delphinium, Aconitum, Aquilegia, Helleborus, Thalictrum* (meadowrue), *Paeonia, Ranunculus* and *Trollius* (globeflower). *Aconitum* is a source of anti-fever compounds important in internal medicine. Several species are strongly poisonous, most notably some in *Delphinium* and *Aconitum*.

Brayshaw (1989) is a well-illustrated treatment that includes most of the buttercup-family species that occur in our region.

Key to the Genera of the Buttercup Family

1a. Flowers bilaterally symmetric 2
  2a. Upper sepal hooded but not spurred; petals 2, covered by hood .... *Aconitum*
  2b. Upper sepal spurred but not hooded; petals 4, not concealed by sepals .... *Delphinium*
1b. Flowers radially symmetric 3
  3a. Petals prominently spurred; flowers red and yellow (our region) .... *Aquilegia*
  3b. Petals not prominently spurred; flowers mostly white or yellow 4
    4a. Ovaries 1; fruits red or white berries .... *Actaea*
    4b. Ovaries usually 2 or more; fruits achenes or follicles 5
      5a. Fruits 1-seeded achenes, not splitting when mature 6
        6a. Flowers with both sepals and petals; petals
        showier than sepals .... *Ranunculus*
        6b. Flowers with sepals only, or with sepals and less showy petals.................. 7
          7a. Sepals relatively small and inconspicuous, usually greenish
          or white, less showy than stamens; stem leaves (if any) alternate 8
            8a. Leaves simple, palmately lobed; flowers
            with both sexes .... *Trautvetteria*
            8b. Leaves 2 or 3 times compound; flowers
            sometimes unisexual .... *Thalictrum*
          7b. Sepals conspicuous, showier than stamens;
          stem leaves usually whorled .... *Anemone*
      5b. Fruits 2- to many-seeded follicles, splitting when mature 9
        9a. Leaves divided 1–3 times into 3s 10
          10a. Leaves leathery and evergreen; rhizomes bright yellow .... *Coptis*
          10b. Leaves herbaceous; rhizomes not yellow 11
            11a. Plants 1–2 m tall; follicles 1–3 .... *Cimicifuga* (see *Trautvetteria*)
            11b. Plants 10–80 cm tall; follicles 4 .... *Isopyrum*
        9b. Leaves simple or palmately compound, not divided into 3s 12
          12a. Leaves simple; margins merely toothed, not lobed .... *Caltha*
          12b. Leaves deeply 5-lobed to palmately compound .... *Trollius*

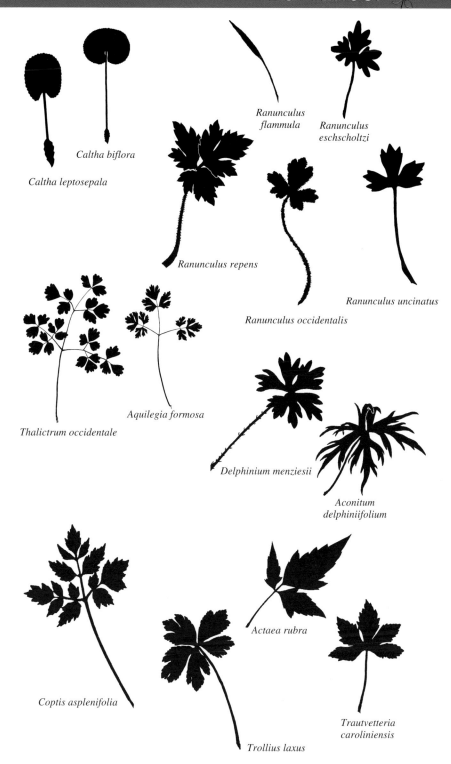

Caltha biflora

Caltha leptosepala

Ranunculus
flammula

Ranunculus
eschscholtzi

Ranunculus repens

Ranunculus occidentalis

Ranunculus uncinatus

Thalictrum occidentale

Aquilegia formosa

Delphinium menziesii

Aconitum
delphiniifolium

Coptis asplenifolia

Actaea rubra

Trautvetteria
caroliniensis

Trollius laxus

THREE-LEAVED ANEMONE • *Anemone deltoidea*

GENERAL: Perennial from slender, creeping rhizomes; stems 10–30 cm tall, hairless or with scattered hairs.

LEAVES: Basal leaves mostly solitary, with 3 egg-shaped, **deeply and coarsely toothed**, usually hairless leaflets; stem leaves in a whorl of 3 below the flower, to 8 cm long, similar to leaflets of the basal leaves.

FLOWERS: Showy, **white, 4–6 cm wide**; usually 5 petal-like sepals; solitary on long stalks.

FRUITS: Plump egg-shaped achenes, hairless above, **hairy on the lower portion**.

ECOLOGY: Common in moist forest and glades at low to middle elevations; apparently one collection from the Olympic Mountains.

NOTES: Northern anemone (*A. parviflora*) is similar, a 5–30 cm tall perennial with wedge-shaped, **toothed and deeply lobed** basal leaflets and stem leaves, solitary, **frosty-white flowers (2.5–5 cm wide**, 5 or 6 sepals) that are often **tinged with blue on the outside**, and densely woolly achenes. It is primarily an alpine species of moist tundra, heath, seepage areas, snowbeds and scree. It is fairly common along the mainland mountains from Alaska to the Cascades of northern Washington, and it is scattered on the Queen Charlotte Islands and Vancouver Island. **Lyall's anemone** (*A. lyallii*) has **compound stem leaves** of 3 thin, coarsely toothed and lobed leaflets, **small (12–20 mm wide) white to pale bluish or pinkish** flowers, and finely hairy achenes. **Oregon anemone** (*A. oregana*) also has **compound stem leaves** of 3 coarsely toothed and lobed leaflets, but it has **larger (20–40 mm wide), bluish or reddish-purple to pale-pink** flowers, and finely hairy achenes. Lyall's anemone grows in moist meadows, thickets and forest from low to subalpine elevations. It is common from Vancouver Island and the adjacent mainland south to California, and it is found sporadically north to 55°N. Oregon anemone occurs in moist forests, thickets, marshes and wet openings, commonly in the Washington/Oregon Cascades and also in the Oregon Coast Ranges and Olympic Mountains.

CUT-LEAF ANEMONE • *Anemone multifida*

GENERAL: Hairy, tufted perennial with 1 to many stems from a thickened, commonly branched stem base, **15–60 cm tall**.

LEAVES: Basal leaves long stalked, numerous, **divided into 3 leaflets that themselves are divided 2 or 3 times**; leaves that cradle the flower stems are short stalked but dissected similarly to basal leaves.

FLOWERS: Fairly showy, **creamy-white, yellowish or pinkish** and tinged with red, blue or purple, particularly on outer surface, sometimes bright red-pink; flowers single or less commonly in long-stalked clusters of up to 4.

FRUITS: Silky-woolly achenes, borne in egg-shaped or spherical clusters about 1 cm wide; styles short.

ECOLOGY: From dry, rocky, exposed slopes and open forest in the foothills and valleys to timberline; dry open woods, scrub and rocky meadows through most of our region; less common on the outer coast.

NOTES: Alpine or Drummond's anemone (*A. drummondii*) has leaves divided much like those of cut-leaf anemone, but it is **smaller (10–20 cm tall), sparsely hairy to nearly hairless**, and it has **white or bluish** flowers. It grows on subalpine and alpine ledges and rocky slopes, scattered from southwestern B.C. south to the Olympic Mountains and along the Cascades to California. It reappears rarely along the inland margin of the region north of 55°N. **Yellow anemone** (*A. richardsonii*) is a **small (5–15 cm tall)**, delicate herb with **simple, palmately-lobed** basal leaves and solitary, **bright-yellow** flowers. It is a plant of thickets, creekbanks, seepage areas and tundra, generally where wet, at middle to alpine elevations in the northwestern part of our region, north of about 53°N; absent from the outer coast.

NARCISSUS ANEMONE • *Anemone narcissiflora*

GENERAL: Perennial from woody base; stems erect, 5–60 cm tall, **hairless to spreading-hairy**.

LEAVES: Mainly basal, divided into 3 broad lobes that are themselves **deeply divided into narrow, pointed segments**; stem leaves clustered just below flowers.

FLOWERS: Creamy-white with bluish tinge on back, showy, **2–5 cm wide**, roughly twice as large as those of cut-leaf anemone and about the same size as those of northern anemone, 1 per stem, or in terminal clusters of 2–5.

FRUITS: Hairless achenes; **short** styles.

ECOLOGY: Meadows, heath, grassy or rocky slopes, grassy glades in subalpine thickets and sometimes in forest openings; common in **northern half of our region**, typically at higher elevations but descending northwards.

NOTES: Alaskan and Siberian native people ate the early spring growth on the upper end of the root. It has a waxy, mealy texture and taste. The leaves were eaten like cress and 'Eskimo ice cream' was made from greens and oil beaten to a creamy consistency. • Anemone roots were considered to have powerful healing properties and were used for treating wounds. • Common and species names recognize the vague resemblance of the showy flowers to those of the narcissus.

WESTERN ANEMONE • *Anemone occidentalis*
WESTERN PASQUE FLOWER, TOW-HEADED BABY, MOPTOP

GENERAL: Stout, **very hairy** perennial from a thick, short, branched stem-base surmounting a taproot; stems 10–30 cm tall at flowering, elongating to 30–60 cm in fruit.

LEAVES: Basal leaves tufted, long stalked, 2–3 times **divided into narrow segments**; stem leaves more or less stalkless.

FLOWERS: Large (4–7 cm wide), white, often tinged with blue outside; solitary; flowering starts before the leaves expand.

FRUITS: Hairy achenes with **very long**, drooping, wavy, **feathery-hairy styles**; numerous on a cylindrical receptacle, forming a large, long-stalked, **showy head**.

ECOLOGY: Subalpine and alpine meadows and rocky slopes; common in the **southern part of our region**.

NOTES: Western anemone flowers as soon as the snow leaves the ground. It is showy in flower, but particularly conspicuous and attractive in fruit. • The genus name is derived from the Greek *anemos* ('wind'), giving rise to 'windflower,' a name often given to members of this genus. One myth is that anemones sprang from the tears that Venus shed over the body of Adonis. The fact that the tears were then blown away suggests her grief was short-lived. Pliny claimed anemones are called 'windflowers' because the flowers never open when the wind is blowing. • 'Tow-headed babies' and 'mop-tops' aptly describe the heads of soft whitish-hairy seeds. • The true 'pasque flower' is *A. patens*, so-called because it flowers at Easter. • The Upper Cowlitz made tea from some anemone species, which they drank to treat tuberculosis. The dose had to be small so as not to burn the stomach. • **WARNING:** This plant, and most others in the buttercup family, are poisonous when fresh (see creeping buttercup, p. 176).

ALPINE WHITE MARSH-MARIGOLD • *Caltha leptosepala*

GENERAL: Fleshy, hairless perennial, 5–30 cm tall, from short, erect, buried stem-bases or short rhizomes.

LEAVES: All basal or with 1 on the stem, **oblong to oval, longer than broad** with a somewhat heart- or arrowhead-shaped base, to 6 cm long, **nearly smooth-edged to blunt-toothed**, waxy green.

FLOWERS: Showy, **white or greenish, often tinged with blue** on the outside and with a greenish-yellow centre, 2–4 cm wide; 1 or sometimes 2 per stem.

FRUITS: Cluster of **almost stalkless** follicles.

ECOLOGY: Wet meadows, seepage areas, stream-banks and snow-beds at subalpine and alpine elevations; common in most of our region.

NOTES: The taxonomy of alpine white marsh-marigold and broad-leaved marsh-marigold (see below) is somewhat confusing. Douglas et al. (1991) lump them as varieties of one species. Hitchcock and Cronquist (1973) seem to think that alpine white marsh-marigold does not even occur in the Cascades, but most other sources indicate it does. Wide-leaved plants are much more common in the Cascades in our experience, but narrower leaves also occur. • The leaves and flower buds were eaten raw or cooked by Alaskan native people, who also boiled the long, white roots, which look like sauerkraut when cooked. Soaked in saltwater and vinegar, the flower buds apparently make an acceptable substitute for capers. The related yellow marsh-marigold (see below) was also eaten, but it contains the poison helleborin which must be destroyed by cooking. • The common name 'marigold' appears to come from the Anglo-Saxon *meargealla*, which means 'horse-gall,' because the unopened buds presumably resembled galls.

BROAD-LEAVED MARSH-MARIGOLD • *Caltha biflora*
TWO-FLOWERED MARSH-MARIGOLD

GENERAL: Somewhat fleshy, hairless perennial, 10–40 cm tall, from short, erect, buried stem-bases or short rhizomes.

LEAVES: Mostly basal, 4–10 cm long and **as wide or wider, circular to kidney-shaped** with a heart-shaped base; **margins regularly blunt toothed**.

FLOWERS: Showy, **white above and usually below**, 1.5–4 cm wide; usually 2 on a stem with one leaf.

FRUITS: Cluster of **distinctly stalked** follicles.

ECOLOGY: Bogs, fens, seepage areas, wet forest; common from low to subalpine elevations (in the north) or mostly subalpine and alpine elevations (in the south).

NOTES: Yellow marsh-marigold (*Caltha palustris* ssp. *asarifolia*) has leaves somewhat similar to those of broad-leaved marsh-marigold, but it has **arching to creeping stems with several leaves** and **yellow flowers**. It is a species of low-elevation swamps, bogs and shallow pools, occurring almost the length of the region, fairly commonly in Alaska but rarely south through B.C. to Oregon. **Deer-cabbage** (*Fauria crista-galli*, p. 325) is an unrelated species with leaves very similar to those of broad-leaved marsh-marigold. When these 2 species occur together (as they commonly do, especially in the northern half of our region) and are not in flower, remember that the **lobes at the base of the leaves of broad-leaved marsh-marigold touch or overlap, while those of deer-cabbage do not**—they usually do not even come close. • The species name means 'two-flowered.' Marsh-marigolds were sometimes called 'mare-blobs' from the Anglo-Saxon *mere* or *myre* meaning 'marsh' and *blob* meaning 'bladder,' referring to the round, bud-shaped flowers growing in marshes.

GLOBEFLOWER • *Trollius laxus*

GENERAL: Hairless perennial with short stem-base and strong fibrous roots; stems erect, 1 to several, 10–50 cm tall.

LEAVES: Basal leaves with broad, membranous sheaths at the base of long stalks, the blade **palmately divided into 5 oval-shaped main segments, which are further divided and toothed;** stem-leaves short stalked to stalkless as you go upwards.

FLOWERS: Showy, 2–4 cm wide, **greenish-white to creamy-white** sometimes with pinkish tinge; stalks long, elongate with age; single.

FRUITS: Fruiting heads cone-shaped, composed of several-veined, many-seeded follicles.

ECOLOGY: Wet meadows, seepage areas, stream-banks, and snowbeds at high elevations, down into the subalpine zone along streams and in seepage areas, usually blossoming just as the snow recedes; common along the eastern part of the southern half of our region.

NOTES: Globeflower should not be confused with *Caltha* **or white anemones**, which **usually have a bluish tinge** on the outside of the flowers. • The common name 'globeflower' is derived from the globular shape of the flower, at least of the European species *T. europaeus*. *Trollius* is thought to derive from the Swiss-German *Trollblume* given to *Trollius europaeus*, named after the Swedish *Troll* (a malignant supernatural being) because the plant contains acrid, poisonous substances. It was also called *locken gowan* after a similar mythical creature in Scotland known as a *gowan*. Another name, 'cabbage-daisy,' acknowledges the shape of the flower.

SUBALPINE BUTTERCUP • *Ranunculus eschscholtzii*
MOUNTAIN BUTTERCUP, SNOWPATCH BUTTERCUP

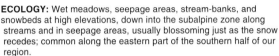

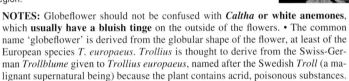

GENERAL: Perennial with fibrous roots; stems 1 to several, erect, **hairless**, 5–25 cm tall.

LEAVES: Basal leaves on slender stalks, kidney-shaped to oval in outline, **usually 3-lobed and then divided again**; stem leaves lacking or stalkless; all leaves hairless.

FLOWERS: Yellow, 15–30 mm wide; petals 5; sepals 5, **hairless or with yellowish or brownish hairs**, dropping off soon after flower opens; 1–3, terminal.

FRUITS: Smooth achenes, essentially hairless, with short, slender, **straight to somewhat curved beaks**, 20–50 or more in an elongate cluster.

ECOLOGY: Mountain meadows, avalanche tracks, talus slopes, into subalpine forest along stream-banks, often blooming at edges of melting snowbanks or along streams; a subalpine-alpine species, common except in the southernmost part of our region; uncommon in the Oregon and southern Washington Cascades (maybe the volcanic substrates are a problem), in the North Cascades much more common on the east side.

NOTES: 2 species in our region somewhat resemble subalpine buttercup. **Snow buttercup** (*R. nivalis*) can be distinguished by its **densely brown-hairy sepals**; the hairs are much darker than those on the sepals of subalpine buttercup. Snow buttercup grows in wet alpine tundra, along creeks and in moist meadows, seepage areas and snowbanks, occasionally in our region **north of 58°N**. **Cooley's buttercup** (*R. cooleyae,* inset photo) has hairless basal leaves that are circular in outline, no stem leaves and a **single flower with 8–15 narrow petals**. It is a species of snowbeds, rocky gullies and moist scree at high elevations in the northern 2/3 of our region, south to the Olympic Mountains and North Cascades.

WESTERN BUTTERCUP • *Ranunculus occidentalis*

GENERAL: Perennial with fibrous roots, **usually hairy**; stems 1 to several, erect to somewhat spreading, branched, hollow, 15–60 cm tall.

LEAVES: Basal leaves long stalked, variously lobed but normally with **3 wedge-shaped, coarsely lobed and toothed divisions**; stem leaves alternate, short stalked, deeply divided, smaller and narrower as you go upwards.

FLOWERS: Yellow, 10–25 mm wide; sepals and petals normally 5 (to 8); sepals hairy, bent downwards and falling off early; several at the ends of long stalks.

FRUITS: Smooth, usually hairless achenes, with **minutely hooked beaks**; 5–20 in a spherical head.

ECOLOGY: Moist meadows, grassy slopes, coastal bluffs, sea-bird islands, open or shaded forest, clearings; common from sea level to subalpine elevations.

NOTES: Straight-beaked buttercup (*R. orthorhynchus*) has hairy, **pinnate, basal leaves with 3–7 leaflets**, and it has larger achenes with **long, straight beaks**. It occupies moist meadows, stream-banks and shores, including sea beaches and upper tidal marshes, from low to middle elevations, and it is fairly common south of about 58°N. **Pacific buttercup** (*R. pacificus*) has **basal leaves with 3 stalked leaflets**, and achenes with **short, hooked beaks**. It grows in moist meadows and along stream-banks, very commonly in (but apparently restricted to) southeast Alaska. It may be most closely related to Macoun's buttercup (see p. 177), but it has larger (15–25 mm wide vs. 5–15 mm wide) flowers.

CREEPING BUTTERCUP • *Ranunculus repens*

GENERAL: **Hairy** perennial from fibrous roots, **with stolons (to 100 cm long) rooting at the nodes**, giving rise to several erect flowering stems.

LEAVES: Dark-green, often with pale spots; long-stalked, triangular in outline, with **3 leaflets that are themselves lobed and toothed**; stem leaves alternate, smaller and shorter stalked.

FLOWERS: Deep yellow, **large (10–35 mm wide)**; sepals hairy, spreading; terminal on erect stems or their branches.

FRUITS: Hairless smooth achenes with short, stout, **strongly curved to nearly straight beaks.**

ECOLOGY: Moist disturbed sites; fields, pastures, gardens, lawns, ditches, clearings; common at low elevations, especially in settled areas.

NOTES: Meadow buttercup (*R. acris*) is another hairy, large-flowered, introduced and weedy perennial, but it has **tall, erect stems and no stolons**. Meadow buttercup resembles creeping buttercup, but it has **smaller achenes with shorter (about 0.5 mm** vs. 1–2 mm long) beaks, and spreading rather than reflexed sepals. Meadow buttercup grows in moist meadows, hay pastures, roadsides and clearings. It is common at low elevations throughout the region, but more so in the southern half. • **WARNING:** Many members of the Ranunculaceae, including these species, contain chemicals that can cause severe irritation and blistering of skin, or inflammation of tissues of mouth, throat and digestive tract when swallowed. However, meadow buttercup is considered to be harmless in hay because the poisonous material is volatile and evaporates when the hay is cured. • The irritant compound protoanemonin causes redness and blistering when the leaves are applied to the skin.

LITTLE BUTTERCUP • *Ranunculus uncinatus*
SMALL-FLOWERED BUTTERCUP

GENERAL: Annual or perennial; stems single, erect, **hairy to hairless**, usually unbranched, hollow, 20–90 cm tall.

LEAVES: Mostly basal with long stalks; blades simple, heart- to kidney-shaped in outline, **deeply divided into 3 lobes which are again divided into toothed lobes**, hairy below; somewhat similar to those of western and creeping buttercup; stem leaves 1–2, alternate, with lobes more lance-shaped and transitional between basal leaves and the bracts at top of stem.

FLOWERS: Yellow, very **small (3–8 mm wide)**, 5 petals; single at ends of several stalks clustered together above large, lance-shaped leafy bracts.

FRUITS: Achenes small, with a **small hooked beak**, in rounded clusters of 5–30; receptacle (axis to which achenes attach) **hairless**.

ECOLOGY: Native species common at low to middle elevations; often in shady, moist soil in woodlands, thickets, meadows, glades, beaches and along streams; also in disturbed, trampled areas.

NOTES: Includes *R. bongardii*. • **Macoun's buttercup** (*R. macounii*) and **Pennsylvania or bristly buttercup** (*R. pensylvanicus*) are also small-flowered, native perennials, similar to little buttercup but with **compound basal leaves of stalked leaflets** and with **straight-beaked achenes** on **hairy** receptacles. **Macoun's buttercup** has somewhat **sprawling stems**, often rooting at the nodes, spherical fruiting **receptacles to 5 mm long**, and it is fairly common, mostly in the B.C. and Alaska portions of our region. **Pennsylvania buttercup** has **erect stems** and fruiting **receptacles to 12 mm** long, and it is scattered from Alaska to Washington.

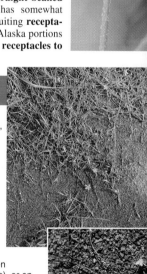

LESSER SPEARWORT • *Ranunculus flammula*
CREEPING SPEARWORT

GENERAL: Amphibious, mostly hairless perennial; vegetative stems are **strawberry-like stolons**, often arched, creeping in mud and rooting at the nodes; flowering stems 5–10 cm tall.

LEAVES: Appearing basal, **linear to lance-shaped or elliptic**, long stalked to nearly stalkless; margins **mostly smooth**.

FLOWERS: Yellow, **5–20 mm wide**; sepals and petals mostly 5; solitary, terminal on erect stalks 2–10 cm long.

FRUITS: Achenes, plump, egg-shaped, hairless, with **short curved beaks**, several to many (5–50) in a somewhat spherical cluster.

ECOLOGY: In shallow water of lake margins or ditches (often becoming terrestrial later as water level recedes), or on wet, muddy shorelines and in wet meadows and marshes; common and widespread at low to middle elevations.

NOTES: Includes *R. reptans*. • Lesser spearwort is a very variable species, especially in leaf shape and size, as is often the case in amphibious plants. • **Water-plantain buttercup** (*R. alismaefolius*) has **erect stems** not rooting at the nodes, 10–60 cm tall, and **lance- to egg-shaped, often toothed**, stout-stalked leaves. It grows in shallow water, on shorelines and in moist swales and meadows, from low to high elevations, from southern Vancouver Island south to California. **Shore buttercup** (*R. cymbalaria*) has undivided, basal, **egg-, heart- or kidney-shaped** leaves with **scalloped, blunt-toothed** margins. It has **strawberry-like runners** that root at the nodes and 50–200 longitudinally ribbed achenes in a columnar head. It grows on moist saline or brackish shorelines, tidal flats and marshes, wet ditches and muddy clearings, scattered the length of our region.

FERN-LEAVED GOLDTHREAD • *Coptis asplenifolia*

GENERAL: Evergreen perennial, mostly hairless, 10–30 cm tall, with widespread, **golden-yellow rhizomes**.

LEAVES: All basal, **fern-like**, divided into 5 or more lobed and toothed, dark, shiny leaflets that are 2–6 cm long.

FLOWERS: Pale greenish-white; sepals 5–6, tapering, linear, 6–15 mm long, flared back; petals 5–6, 4–7 mm long, narrowly strap-shaped above a broadened glandular base; **2 or 3**, nodding on a leafless flowering stalk that is **taller than the leaves** at flowering time.

FRUITS: Follicles, 7–9 mm long, on stalks about as long, up to 12, upright and spreading in a head when ripe, each contains 5–10 seeds that are exposed as the follicle splits open on its upper side; the whole adapted for splash-cup dispersal.

ECOLOGY: Moist forest, bogs, at low to middle elevations; common and widespread in the northern 2/3 of our region.

NOTES: Cut-leaved goldthread (*Coptis laciniata*) is common in moist forests in the southern part of our region, from west-central Washington south to California. Cut-leaved goldthread closely resembles fern-leaved goldthread, but it has divided leaves with **3 deeply lobed leaflets**, and flowering stalks that are **shorter than the leaves**. **Three-leaved goldthread** (*C. trifolia*) has leaves with **3 leaflets toothed but scarcely lobed** 1–2 cm long, and **solitary white** flowers. It grows in bogs, wet forest and seepage areas from low to middle elevations over much the same range in our region as fern-leaved goldthread, but less commonly. • All goldthreads have a touch of yellow at the base of the leaf stalks. • The evergreen leaves of fern-leaved goldthread are important deer forage on the north coast. • The bright-yellow thread-like rhizomes give rise to the name 'goldthread.' *Coptis*, from the Greek *kopto*, 'to cut' and *asplenifolia*, meaning 'leaves like *Asplenium*,' both refer to the finely divided (fern-like) leaves.

QUEEN CHARLOTTE ISOPYRUM • *Isopyrum savilei*

GENERAL: Delicate, hairless perennial from rhizomes; stems leafy, **10–35 cm tall**.

LEAVES: Both basal and stem leaves, but not always with both kinds; basal leaves **compound, divided in 3s**, on long, slender stalks; stem leaves usually 2, similarly divided, the leaflets round lobed, blue-green below.

FLOWERS: White, 15–30 mm wide; 5 petal-like sepals; **solitary** at top of stem.

FRUITS: Follicles, several in a stalkless, divergent cluster, each containing 2 to several pear-shaped seeds.

ECOLOGY: Moist, shady cliffs, talus slopes, rocky gullies and runnels, usually at high elevations but sometimes descending to near sea level; scattered, locally common on the Queen Charlotte Islands, northwestern Vancouver Island (Brooks Peninsula) and Porcher Island, south of Prince Rupert.

NOTES: Hall's isopyrum (*Isopyrum hallii*) occurs occasionally in southwestern Washington south to the Columbia River gorge and the Willamette Valley, in moist forest and along stream-banks. It has **fleshy roots** and **3–10 white to pink** flowers in several flat or rounded clusters atop **40–80 cm** tall stems. • *Isopyrum savilei* was named for D.B.O. Savile, a Canadian research botanist in Ottawa and collector of plants on the Queen Charlotte Islands. *Isopyrum* is from the Greek *isos* ('equal') and *pyros* ('wheat'), in reference to the grain-like fruits.

BANEBERRY • *Actaea rubra*

GENERAL: Rhizomatous, hairless to sparsely hairy perennial with 1 to several, erect, sparingly branched, leafy stems, **0.4–1.0 m tall.**

LEAVES: Few; 1 near-basal leaf large and long stalked, and 1 or 2 smaller, alternate stem leaves, large, crinkly, **2–3 times divided in 3s, the segments coarsely toothed and lobed.**

FLOWERS: Small, white, and numerous; sepals 3–5, 2–4 mm long, soon deciduous; petals 5–10, white, spoon-shaped, shorter than sepals; in **rounded clusters**, on long stalks.

FRUITS: Smooth, glossy, red or white **berries**; the red form is more common.

ECOLOGY: Moist, shady forest, stream-banks, and clearings; common at low to subalpine elevations.

NOTES: WARNING: The berries, foliage, and roots are all highly poisonous. As few as 6 berries can induce vomiting, bloody diarrhea and finally paralysis of respiration. The rootstock is a violent purgative and emetic. The common name 'baneberry' obviously refers to the plant's severely poisonous nature and comes from the Anglo-Saxon word *bana* meaning 'murderous.' • The Stl'atl'imx name means 'it makes you sick.' The Quileute chewed the leaves and spat them on a boil to bring it to a head. The Quinault also chewed the leaves and spat them on wounds. • Baneberry's leaf shape is similar to that of *Osmorhiza* species (p. 217); compare their silhouettes.

FALSE BUGBANE • *Trautvetteria caroliniensis*

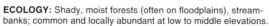

GENERAL: Widely rhizomatous perennial; stems scattered on rhizomes, producing colonies, hairless below but thinly curly-hairy (at least in the inflorescence), erect, **0.5–1 m tall.**

LEAVES: Mainly basal, 10–30 cm wide, **palmately cleft** into 5–11 coarsely toothed lobes, with **impressed veins** and long stalks; stem leaves smaller and less divided.

FLOWERS: White, about 2 cm wide; sepals 3–5, falling off as flowers open; petals lacking; stamens 50–70, white, 5–10 mm long, dilated upwards; **flower showiness largely due to the tufted white stamens; in flat-topped**, stalked clusters.

FRUITS: Achenes, papery, **longitudinally ribbed**, 3–4 mm long, with **hooked beaks**.

ECOLOGY: Shady, moist forests (often on floodplains), stream-banks; common and locally abundant at low to middle elevations.

NOTES: Tall bugbane (*Cimicifuga elata*) is a somewhat similar species with **tall (1–2 m)** branched stems, **large compound leaves (somewhat like those of *Actaea* see above)**, numerous, small, **white-stamened** flowers in a **narrow**, terminal, branched inflorescence, and several-seeded **follicles**. It occurs in moist forest at low to middle elevations, from the Lower Fraser Valley and the Olympic Peninsula south to northwestern Oregon. • False bugbane, like other plants in the buttercup family, contains an irritant compound, protoanemonin, which causes redness and blistering when the leaves are applied to the skin. The Nuxalk pounded the roots in water and prepared a poultice to treat boils, but it caused intensive burning and blistering and so was not used on children. • This plant is called 'false bugbane' because of its similarity to the true bugbane, *Cimicifuga elata*, which has an unpleasant odour and was sometimes used as a bedbug repellant. The genus is named for Ernest Rudolph von Trautvetter (1809–89), director of the Botanical Garden in St. Petersburg.

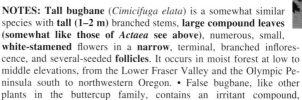

WESTERN MEADOWRUE • *Thalictrum occidentale*

GENERAL: Rhizomatous perennial; stems leafy, hairless to finely glandular-hairy, 40–100 cm tall; young stems purplish.

LEAVES: Mostly from the stem, hairless, **bluish-green, delicately divided 3–4 times in 3s**; each leaflet 3 lobed, on thin stalk.

FLOWERS: Small, male and female flowers on **separate plants; female** flowers with inconspicuous **greenish-white** sepals (no petals); **male** flowers with prominent **hanging stamens and dangling purple anthers**; in loose clusters at top of plant.

FRUITS: Short-stalked, hairless achenes with **3 prominent veins** on each side.

ECOLOGY: Open forest (usually mixed or deciduous), thickets, meadows, slide tracks, and grassy openings, from the lowlands to subalpine parkland.

NOTES: Alpine meadowrue (*T. alpinum*) is a **dwarf, high-elevation species** with **glossy, mostly basal** leaves. It occurs occasionally on the Queen Charlotte Islands and in northern southeast Alaska.
• **Few-flowered meadowrue** (*T. sparsiflorum*) is similar to western meadowrue but has male and female flowers on the **same plant**, and has **long-stalked achenes**. It grows in moist meadows, thickets and forests in the northernmost part of our region (northern southeast Alaska to Prince William Sound). • 'Rue' is derived from the Latin *ruta*, as in *Ruta graveolens*, and means 'bitter-leaved.'

RED COLUMBINE • *Aquilegia formosa*

GENERAL: Perennial herb from **taproot**; stems simple, erect, to 1 m tall, hairless below, sparsely hairy and somewhat glandular in the inflorescence.

LEAVES: Mainly basal, **twice divided in 3s**; blades hairless to hairy, green above, paler and glaucous beneath.

FLOWERS: Red and yellow with 5 long, straight, **reddish spurs** with bulbous, glandular tips; central tuft of stamens and styles **protruding**; usually 2–5 flowers, sometimes more numerous in vigourous plants, drooping.

FRUITS: Usually 5 erect follicles with hairy, spreading tips and numerous black, wrinkled seeds.

ECOLOGY: Variety of moist, open to partly shaded sites; meadows, rocky slopes and beaches, forest glades, clearings, roadsides; common from the lowlands to timberline.

NOTES: Leaves of columbine and meadowrue are similar in general appearance; compare their silhouettes. • The flowers are very attractive to hummingbirds and butterflies. • This plant is called 'red rain-flowers' in Haida. Haida children were warned not to pick the flowers or it would rain. The Nuxalk called it 'grizzly-bear's den' (for some reason). • The Quileute scraped columbine roots with a sharp rock and smeared the milky pulp on sores to help form a scar. The leaves were also chewed and spat on sores. Aboriginals in other parts of North America used various parts in medicinal preparations for diarrhea, dizziness, aching joints and possibly venereal disease. • The common name is derived from the Latin *columbina* meaning 'dove-like.' The arched petals and spurs of the flowers resemble a quintet of doves arranged in a ring around a dish (a favourite device of ancient artists). Another old name for this species is 'culverwort,' from the Anglo-Saxon *culfre* ('pigeon') and *wort* ('plant').

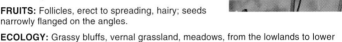

MENZIES' LARKSPUR • *Delphinium menziesii*

GENERAL: Short **(to 50 cm tall)** perennial from **tuberous** roots; stems single, slender, weakly attached to the tubers, simple or branched, hairless or hairy.

LEAVES: Mostly on the stem and stalked, the few basal leaves long stalked, upper stem leaves smaller and stalkless; main leaf blades **palmately 2 or 3 times divided** into narrowly oblong to wedge-shaped segments.

FLOWERS: Deep-blue to purplish with some white or pale-blue, and a prominent, straight, 13–18 mm long, nectar-containing **spur**; 3–20 in fairly open, loose, simple to branched, terminal clusters.

FRUITS: Follicles, erect to spreading, hairy; seeds narrowly flanged on the angles.

ECOLOGY: Grassy bluffs, vernal grassland, meadows, from the lowlands to lower mountain slopes; common in the southern half of our region.

NOTES: Tall larkspur (*Delphinium glaucum*) is a stout perennial with several hairless, hollow stems **0.5–2 m tall**, from tough **fibrous** roots. It has flowers **6–12 mm long** in a long, loose, hairless or sparsely hairy inflorescence. It occurs in high-elevation meadows and seepage areas from the Olympic and Cascade mountains of Washington south to California. It also ranges north to Alaska but mostly inland of our region. **Trollius-leaved larkspur** (*D. trolliifolium*) is also a stout perennial with several hollow stems **0.6–1.5 m tall, from short, thick rhizomes or somewhat woody roots**. It has flowers **15–25 mm long** in a long loose inflorescence with fine, yellowish hairs. Trollius-leaved larkspur grows in moist shady forest and along stream-banks from southwestern Washington to California. • Some larkspurs (containing delphinine) are poisonous to cattle and highly toxic to humans; symptoms of poisoning include abdominal pain, nausea, depressed respiration and eventually asphyxiation.

MOUNTAIN MONKSHOOD • *Aconitum delphiniifolium*

GENERAL: Perennial herb from **tuberous taproots**, 0.1 to 1.2 m tall; stems single, slender, hollow, unbranched, hairy above.

LEAVES: Mostly from the stem, alternate, **deeply palmately 5 lobed**; lobes themselves incised and toothed; hairless.

FLOWERS: Large, showy, **usually dark blue-purple**, but sometimes tinged with green, yellow, or white; upper part of each flower **hood-like**, hood **wider than high** in side view; single or several in terminal clusters.

FRUITS: 3–5, hairless to sparsely hairy follicles; seeds with membranous ridges like screws.

ECOLOGY: Moist open forest, thickets, glades, meadows, stream-banks and tundra; from lowlands to alplands.

NOTES: This species varies widely in size. Alpine plants are often dwarfed (less than 10 cm tall) and have but a single flower, in contrast to robust, valley-bottom individuals that exceed 1 m in height and have 10 or more flowers. • **Columbian monkshood** (*A. columbianum*) has leaves that are **palmately divided, but not to the base**, and hoods that are **higher than wide** in side view. It occurs in moist forest and meadows and along stream-banks, at middle to subalpine elevations, fairly commonly in the Washington and Oregon Cascades. • General leaf shape for mountain monkshood is similar to that of *Delphinium*, some species of *Ranunculus*, and *Geranium*—compare their leaf silhouettes. Mountain monkshood typically has narrower leaf lobes. • All parts of the plant are highly poisonous, especially to livestock. The tubers contain aconitin, an ester alkaloid that paralyses the nerves and lowers body temperature and blood pressure.

Rosaceae (Rose Family)

Members of the rose family are trees, shrubs or herbs, and they are often thorny. They have alternate, simple or pinnately compound leaves, usually with stipules (appendages at the base of the leaf stalk). Flowers are radially symmetric, typically with 5 sepals united at the base, 5 petals arising from a cup or saucer-like structure atop the flower stalk, numerous stamens in several whorls and 1 compound or several simple ovaries. Fruits are achenes, follicles, apple-like pomes, cherry-like drupes or raspberry-like aggregations of drupelets. The family is characterized by the presence of stipules, the general 5-part plan of the flower, and the presence of cup-like hypanthia.

Rosaceae is a large family of considerable economic importance in temperate regions. Fruit-producers include apple (*Malus*), pear (*Pyrus*), quince (*Cydonia*), cherry, plum, prune, peach, nectarine, apricot, almond (all species of *Prunus*), blackberry, raspberry, loganberry (species of *Rubus*) and strawberry (*Fragaria*). Notable ornamental trees and shrubs occur within the family, for example spiraea (*Spirea*), ninebark (*Physocarpus*), cotoneaster (*Cotoneaster*), hawthorn (*Crataegus*), flowering quince (*Chaenomeles*), mountain-ash (*Sorbus*), Japanese cherry (*Prunus*), rose (*Rosa*) and shrubby cinquefoil (*Potentilla fruticosa*).

This section treats mostly herbaceous members of the rose family. Several woody species of the family are described in 'Shrubs,' pp. 71–81.

GOAT'SBEARD • *Aruncus dioicus*

GENERAL: Robust perennial, from stout short-creeping rhizomes; stems several, hairless, **1–2 m tall**.

LEAVES: Lower leaves large, usually **3 times compound, the leaflets sharply toothed and pointed**, the upper leaves smaller and less compounded; green and usually hairless above, hairy and paler below.

FLOWERS: **White, tiny** (petals about 1 mm long), male and female flowers on **separate plants; densely packed** in elongated, terminal, much divided clusters; the **branchlets spike-like**.

FRUITS: Straw-coloured follicles about 3 mm long.

ECOLOGY: In 'edge' habitats (edges of roadsides, forests and streams) at low to middle elevations; common to the north B.C. coast, rare north of there.

NOTES: Goat'sbeard is also known as *A. sylvester* and 'spaghetti flower.' • The Tlingit made a preparation from the root for curing diseases of the blood. The roots were made into tea by the Nuxalk for stomach pain, gonorrhea, and as a diuretic. The roots were also boiled in mountain-goat grease for treating smallpox. The Kwakwaka'wakw prepared a cough medicine from the dried root which was soaked, scraped and held in the mouth. The Lummi chewed the leaves to help cure smallpox. The Skagit burned the twigs (and possibly the roots) and mixed the ashes with bear grease to make a salve used on swellings, especially of the throat. The Klallam also made such a salve and applied it to sores which would not heal. The Skagit made a root infusion which was drunk as a cure for colds and sore throats. The Mainland Comox steeped the roots and drank the solution for any swelling, and they also used the solution to bathe the swollen area. The whole plant was burned and the charcoal was rubbed over swellings or powdered in water and drunk to prevent internal bleeding. An infusion of the roots was given to Squamish women just before giving birth, in order to 'help heal the insides.' The Makah ground the root with a little water and ingested the mixture for treatment of kidney pain. The leaves were chewed as a remedy for spitting blood and showing signs of tuberculosis. The Makah also made a medicine for gonorrhea from the roots. • The name 'goat'sbeard' refers to the large, fluffy, white flower clusters; *Aruncus* is from the Greek *aryngos* ('goat'sbeard').

COASTAL STRAWBERRY • *Fragaria chiloensis*

GENERAL: Perennial maritime herb to 25 cm tall; short, thick rootstocks connected by **short, hairy runners**.

LEAVES: Basal, on long stalks (to 20 cm long); leaflets 3, **thick, leathery**, strongly veined, coarsely toothed, the terminal tooth shorter than its neighbours.

FLOWERS: White, to 3.5 cm across, with 5–7 petals; 5–9 flowers on a leafless flowering stalk to 30 cm tall.

FRUITS: A small, hairy **strawberry** to 1.5 cm across.

ECOLOGY: Common on **sand dunes and sea bluffs**; never far from the sea.

NOTES: Our other 2 common strawberries have thinner, non-leathery leaves and are found in a variety of habitats (not restricted to areas near the ocean). Woodland strawberry (*F. vesca,* inset photo) and wild strawberry (*F. virginiana*) are very similar. The best way to tell them apart is that the **terminal tooth** on leaflets of **woodland strawberry** is **longer** than the adjoining teeth, while the **terminal tooth** of **wild strawberry** is **narrower and shorter** than its neighbours. Another good character is that the leaves of **wild strawberry** are often **bluish-green** on top. Woodland strawberry is a species of openings and open forests, at low to subalpine elevations south of about 55°N; wild strawberry is more typically an interior species, but it can be found in similar habitats from southern Vancouver Island south. • Coastal strawberries can be made into jam or other preserves, but probably the most satisfying way to eat them is to pop them into the mouth as soon as they are picked. Haida people say that the coastal strawberries used to be much more plentiful before deer were introduced to the Queen Charlotte Islands; now, one can hardly find any berries. Strawberries were only eaten fresh, being too juicy to dry like other berries. The Saanich and Mainland Comox steeped the fresh leaves to make a clear, sweet tea. The Mainland Comox often added fresh thimbleberry and trailing wild blackberry leaves to this tea. • The Quileute chewed the leaves and applied them as a poultice on burns. The Skokomish made tea from the entire plant for diarrhea. The Haida used coastal strawberry leaves as an ingredient in a female tonic. Strawberry leaves are well known for their use in anti-diarrhea medicines, especially for children.

YELLOW MOUNTAIN-AVENS • *Dryas drummondii*

GENERAL: Low, **prostrate, evergreen shrub**, with freely rooting, trailing woody stems.

LEAVES: Alternate, withering but not immediately dropping, **oblong to oval**, to 2 cm long, broadest above the middle, leathery, wrinkly, **dark-green above, densely covered in white hairs below; margins scalloped**.

FLOWERS: Pale yellow, 2–3 cm across, single on leafless stems (15–25 cm tall), nodding.

FRUITS: Numerous **achenes**, each with a silky, golden-yellow, **feathery plume** which becomes twisted around others and later opens up to a fluffy mass; each seed is eventually carried off by its own 'parachute' in the wind.

ECOLOGY: A common pioneer on gravelly river bars, rocky slopes, roadsides, and (in Alaska) periglacial habitats; from the lowlands up into the alpine tundra.

NOTES: In similar habitats in the Lynn Canal/Glacier Bay area, look for **entire-leaved mountain-avens** (*D. integrifolia*), which has **white flowers** and more-**lance-shaped leaves**. • The name *Dryas* is Latin and Greek for 'wood nymph.' • Yellow mountain-avens is much cultivated as a dwarf rock-garden plant.

183

PARTRIDGEFOOT • *Luetkea pectinata*

GENERAL: Prostrate, **mat-forming, evergreen semi-shrub**; flowering stem up to 15 cm tall, leafy.

LEAVES: Numerous, mostly crowded in **thick basal tufts, fan-shaped**, 2- to 3-times 3-**dissected**, withering and persistent for many years; stem leaves alternate.

FLOWERS: Small (petals about 3 mm long), **white**; in a **dense terminal cluster** on an upright leafy, flowering stem.

FRUITS: Several-seeded **follicles** to 4 mm long.

ECOLOGY: Common in meadows, heath and on scree slopes; from middle to alpine elevations.

NOTES: Partridgefoot is an extremely common plant in most alpine areas in our region. • The common name 'partridgefoot' refers to the finely divided leaves that somewhat resemble the footprint of a partridge or ptarmigan. It is also called 'creeping spirea' or 'mountain spirea,' and it was formerly know as *Spiraea pectinata*. *Luetkea* commemorates Count F. P. Lütke, a 19th-century Russian sea captain and explorer; *pectinata* means 'pectinate' (like the teeth of a comb) and here refers to the leaves.

SIBBALDIA • *Sibbaldia procumbens*

GENERAL: Low, tufted, hairy, **mat-forming** perennial **herb from crawling woody stems**.

LEAVES: Basal, **3-foliate**; leaflets **wedge-shaped**, 3- to 5-toothed, often purplish beneath.

FLOWERS: Yellow; petals small (to 4 mm long), surrounded by larger, hairy sepals and bracts; in dense axillary and terminal clusters.

FRUITS: Brown, pear-shaped **achenes**.

ECOLOGY: Open gravelly areas (rocky outcrops and slopes, meadows) at middle to alpine elevations.

NOTES: Is it sibbaldia or is it one of those alpine cinquefoils? Check the flower: **sibbaldia has 5 or 10 stamens** and **tiny (less than 5 mm long) petals; cinquefoils** have **more than 10 stamens** and **conspicuous flowers (petals more than 5 mm long)**. • It is unfortunate this delightful plant does not have a more interesting common name—no offence to Sir Robert Sibbald (1614–1722), professor of medicine, Edinburgh, after whom it is named.

LARGE-LEAVED AVENS • *Geum macrophyllum*

GENERAL: Hairy perennial with short rhizomes, stems **to 1 m tall**.

LEAVES: Basal leaves long stalked, with heart- to kidney-shaped **terminal segment many times larger than the several smaller leaflets below**; stem leaves few, stalkless or nearly so, deeply 3 lobed or 3 parted.

FLOWERS: Bright-yellow, saucer-shaped; **petals to 6 mm long**; at the tips of the branches, single or in a few-flowered cluster.

FRUITS: Clusters of **short-hairy achenes** that have elongate styles with a distinctive **S-shaped bend** near the tip; cling to any rough surface, have a 'stick-tight' mode of dispersal by animals, including humans wearing wool socks.

ECOLOGY: Open areas and open forests; common at low to middle elevations.

NOTES: Large-leaved avens produces small, brown, hooked fruits that catch easily on cloth-ing and pets' hair. The Nuxalk name for them is 'lice.' • The Nuxalk made tea from the roots for stomach pains, and the leaves were poulticed on boils by the Nuxalk, Quileute, Snohomish and Quinault. The Quileute and the Klallam chewed the leaves during labour, because these plants ap-peared at the time seals gave birth to their pups. The Southern Vancouver Island Salish ate the leaves before visiting a dying person to protect the visitor from harmful germs. Chehalis women made tea from the leaves to avoid conception; this only worked after a women had previously given birth. Cowichan men chewed the leaves and fed them to their wives when they were pregnant to 'straighten out her womb' and aid delivery. The Squamish used the leaves to make a diuretic tea. An eyewash was also prepared from the leaves. The Haida boiled the roots to make a steambath to treat rheumatism. • The species name *macrophyllum* means the same thing as the common name: 'big-leaved.'

CALTHA-LEAVED AVENS • *Geum calthifolium*

GENERAL: Hairy perennial herb **to 25 cm tall** from a stout, creeping, branching rhizome.

LEAVES: Basal leaves long stalked; blades circular, coarsely and irregularly toothed, **larger terminal leaflets with 1–3 tiny leaflets below**; stem leaves without stalks, coarsely toothed and lobed.

FLOWERS: Yellow, large; 5 **petals about 1 cm long**; 1–2 on largely leafless stems.

FRUITS: Bristly-hairy achenes to 1.5 cm long, with **straight styles**.

ECOLOGY: Bogs at low elevations, wet subalpine slopes and alpine meadows; uncommon, but can be locally abundant.

NOTES: If on the Queen Charlotte Islands your avens has **5–7 leaflets** per leaf, it may be **Queen Charlotte avens** (*G. schofieldii*), one of the species originally known only from these misty isles, but since found on the Brooks Penninsula, northwestern Vancouver Island. This species, found in wet rock crevices, is named for legendary B.C. bryologist Wilf Schofield. • The name 'avens' appears to come from the old French *avence* or medieval Latin *avancia,* derived from the Greek word for 'antidote,' because spe-cies of avens were supposed to ward off 'the devil and evil spirits, venomous ser-pents and wild beasts.' • *G. calthifolium* is called 'caltha-leaved' (*calthifolium*) be-cause its leaves are similar to those of some species of *Caltha*, p. 174.

SILVERWEED • *Potentilla anserina* ssp. *pacifica*

GENERAL: Perennial hairy herb from **long runners**.

LEAVES: Basal, to 40 cm long, erect, **compound, pinnate** with a mix of large and small leaflets that are **woolly beneath**.

FLOWERS: Yellow; petals oval, to 1.3 cm long; **single on leafless stalks** to 2 cm tall.

FRUITS: Flattened oval achenes to 2 mm long.

ECOLOGY: Wet spots (marsh edges, stream sides), sandy spots (beaches and dunes), usually near the sea, but not restricted to maritime habitats; common at low to middle elevations, less common further north.

NOTES: Silverweed is not easily confused with other coastal cinquefoils; it is the only one with runners and leafless flowering stalks bearing single flowers. It is also known as *P. pacifica* and *P. egedii*. • Two perennial cinquefoils that are fairly common near the southern end of our region are sticky cinquefoil (*P. glandulosa*) and graceful cinquefoil (*P. gracilis*). **Sticky cinquefoil** is a species of open forests and meadows at middle elevations from about 50°N south; it is covered with glands and is **noticeably sticky**. **Graceful cinquefoil** has **palmately compound leaves** (the leaflets spread out from a single point), and it occurs in meadows and clearings at low to middle elevations mostly in the southern half of our region. • The roots of silverweed were used as food by almost all coastal groups (Turner and Kuhnlein 1982). They were frequently associated with springbank clover roots, since they grow in the same habitat and were prepared the same way. As with springbank clover, silverweed patches were often owned by certain chiefs, especially among the Nuu-chah-nulth, Kwakwaka'wakw and Haida. Like the clover roots, silverweed roots are of two types: short, curly roots near the surface and long, fleshy taproots. They were dug by women in late fall or early spring and had to be steam-cooked to remove the bitter flavour when raw. Once cooked, they taste similar to sweet potatoes, but still retain some bitter flavour. Among the Nuu-chah-nulth, silverweed roots were second only to bracken rhizomes in importance as a root vegetable. The Kwakwaka'wakw preferred silverweed roots dug in Knight and Kingcome Inlets; those from the Nimpkish River were too gnarled from the gravelly soil. They put short roots in baskets and coiled up the long ones, tying them in bundles. The roots were dried or stored fresh in a cool place. According to Kwakwaka'wakw tradition, the men cooked silverweed roots at a feast. They packed alternating layers of curly and long roots over red-hot rocks and dried fern leaves in a tall, cedar steaming box. They poured hot water over the roots, covered them with a mat and waited until the mat sank down, indicating that the roots had softened. The chiefs and high-ranking persons ate the long roots and the commoners ate the curly roots. Leftovers from a silverweed feast were taken home to the wives. Water could be drunk afterwards. • The roots were also collected and boiled by the Haida, who drank the tea a purgative. The roots mixed with other herbs were used for medicinal preparations. The Kwakwaka'wakw boiled the roots, mixed them with fish oil and applied them as a poultice. They also pressed the roots and applied the juice to inflamed eyes. • The common name 'silverweed' describes the silky-grey, hairy appearance of the plant.

VILLOUS CINQUEFOIL • *Potentilla villosa*

GENERAL: Hairy perennial herb to 30 cm tall from **short, thick, scaly, woody rhizomes**.

LEAVES: Basal leaves **compound in 3s** with long, hairy stalks; leaflets thick, leathery, broadly triangular, **white-woolly below** (becoming hairless above), coarsely toothed on upper half, 1–2 cm long; stem leaves similar but reduced, becoming stalkless and in 2s.

FLOWERS: Yellow; petals to 8 mm long; **1–2 at the top of leafy flowering stalks**.

FRUITS: Smooth achenes to 1.5 mm long.

ECOLOGY: Common in open areas (beaches, sea bluffs, rocky slopes, meadows) at all elevations.

NOTES: Villous cinquefoil is much smaller (not much more than 10 cm tall) at high elevations. • One-flowered cinquefoil (*P. uniflora,* also called *P. ledebouriana*) can be mistaken for puny versions of villous cinquefoil, but **one-flowered cinquefoil** has generally **smaller flowers** (petals 4–5 mm long) than villous cinquefoil, and **villous cinquefoil is hairier overall**. One-flowered cinquefoil occurs from the southern B.C. coast north, but not on Vancouver Island or the Queen Charlotte Islands. • The most distinctive cinquefoil in this large and difficult genus is marsh cinquefoil (*P. palustris*), with its dark red to purple flowers and wetland habitat (vs. white or yellow flowers and generally drier habitats for the rest). In this book, it is described in the 'Aquatics' section (p. 339). • The species name *villosa* simply means 'villous' ('hairy').

FAN-LEAVED CINQUEFOIL • *Potentilla flabellifolia*

GENERAL: Perennial herb to 30 cm tall from a dense, **branched, creeping, woody base**.

LEAVES: Basal and stem, **compound with 3 leaflets**; leaflets egg- to fan-shaped, deeply toothed, to 2.5 cm long, mostly hairless.

FLOWERS: Yellow; petals to 1 cm long, somewhat heart-shaped; **several terminally on leafy stems**.

FRUITS: Smooth, dark achenes, 1–2 mm long.

ECOLOGY: Moist meadows and scree slopes at subalpine to alpine elevations south of 51°N; scattered but sometimes locally abundant.

NOTES: 2 other high-elevation cinquefoils with compound leave are **diverse-leaved cinquefoil** (*P. diversifolia*), in which the **leaflets all arise from one point**

(like the fingers on a hand), and **Drummond's cinquefoil** (*P. drummondii*), in which the **5–9 leaflets arise in opposite pairs**. Diverse-leaved cinquefoil occurs throughout our region; Drummond's can be found south of about 55°N. • The species name *flabellifolia* means, appropriately enough, 'fan-leaved.'

SITKA BURNET • *Sanguisorba canadensis*
CANADA BURNET   ssp. *latifolia*

GENERAL: Perennial, hairless, freely rhizomatous; flowering stems 25–100 cm tall.

LEAVES: Mostly basal, with attached membranous stipules; blades 10–30 cm long, **divided into 9–17** egg-shaped to oblong, coarsely toothed leaflets; leaves of flowering stems 1–3, reduced upwards, with leaflet-like stipules.

FLOWERS: Greenish-white or yellowish-white, numerous and small; petals absent; sepals to 2.5 mm long; arranged in **dense cylindrical heads** (sometimes tapering at the top).

FRUITS: Achenes enclosed in plant tissue under the sepals, slightly winged.

ECOLOGY: Wet places (bogs, swamps, stream-banks); common at middle to subalpine elevations.

NOTES: Sitka burnet is known as *S. sitchensis* or *S. stipulata* by some taxonomists. • Herbalists recommend that the leaves be made into an herbal tea, and that root decoctions may be used for internal and external bleeding, dysentery, or genital discharges. • The name 'burnet' comes from the old French word *brunette* meaning 'brown.' It is applied to European species of *Sanguisorba* because their flowers are a rich, red-brown colour. • *Sanguisorba* and another common name, 'burnet blood-wort,' refer to the plant's supposed power to stop bleeding.

GREAT BURNET • *Sanguisorba officinalis*
ssp. *microcephala*

GENERAL: Perennial herb 20–80 cm tall, from a stout rhizome.

LEAVES: Basal leaves **compound with 9–11 leaflets;** leaflets coarsely toothed, green above, paler beneath; stem leaves few, similar to basal leaves but smaller and with fewer leaflets.

FLOWERS: No petals; **sepals purplish to maroon,** in 4s, about 2.5 mm long; in dense **egg-shaped to round clusters** atop stems.

FRUITS: Achenes enclosed in plant tissue under the sepals, slightly winged.

ECOLOGY: Wetlands (bogs, muskegs, swamps) at low to middle (sometime subalpine) elevations.

NOTES: This species is also known as *S. microcephala.* • One way to differentiate great burnet from Sitka burnet is to check the stamens ('male bits'). *S. sitchensis* has **stamens** that are **2–3 times as long** as the surrounding sepals and consequently **stick out** of the flower; the **stamens** of *S. officinalis* are **about as long as** the sepals (or slightly longer). • Another *Sanguisorba* with **purple sepals** and egg-shaped to round inflorescences is **Menzies' burnet** (*S. menziesii*), but it also has **long stamens** (like Sitka burnet). It occurs where the ranges of the other two species overlap, and is likely a hybrid. • The species name *officinalis* indicates that this is a plant with medicinal value. • Menzies' burnet is yet another species named after Archibald Menzies, the first botanist to explore the Pacific North American coast.

Fabaceae (Pea Family)

The peas are a large family of (in our region) herbs and shrubs that have mostly alternate, compound (mostly pinnately so, sometimes palmately) leaves that usually have stipules. The flowers are (in our species) bilaterally symmetric, of 5 fused sepals, 5 distinct petals, 5 or 10 stamens and 1 superior ovary. The fruit is a 1-chambered pod ('legume') with several to many seeds in 2 alternating rows. The family is also known as Leguminosae. • Flowers of our species are butterfly-like, with 5 unequal petals; an upright 'standard,' a lateral pair of 'wings,' and 2 inner, joined petals forming a 'keel,' which envelops the stamens and pistil.

Lupinus (lupines) and *Trifolium* (clovers) are the largest genera in our region. The pea family is probably the 3rd largest in the world, after the Asteraceae and Orchidaceae, and it is also one of the most economically important families. Its species provide food, fodder, dyes, gums, resins, oils, medicines and timber. Members of over 150 genera are grown as ornamentals. Food products include garden peas (*Pisum*), lentils (*Lens*), peanut (*Arachis*), beans (*Phaseolus*) and soybean (*Glycine*); fodder and forage plants include clover, alfalfa (*Medicago*), lupine, vetch (*Vicia*), birds-foot trefoil (*Lotus*) and sweet clover (*Melilotus*). Outstanding ornamentals are wisteria, sweet pea (*Lathyrus*), lupines, redbud (*Cercis*), acacia and mimosa.

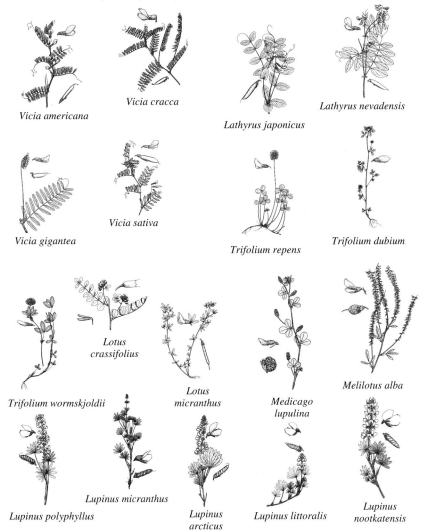

Vicia americana

Vicia cracca

Lathyrus japonicus

Lathyrus nevadensis

Vicia gigantea

Vicia sativa

Trifolium repens

Trifolium dubium

Trifolium wormskjoldii

Lotus crassifolius

Lotus micranthus

Medicago lupulina

Melilotus alba

Lupinus polyphyllus

Lupinus micranthus

Lupinus arcticus

Lupinus littoralis

Lupinus nootkatensis

Key to Pea Family (Fabaceae)

1a. Leaves with an even number of opposite leaflets, the terminal leaflet represented by a tendril 2

  2a. Hairs on the style all around the tip, like a bottlebrush (*Vicia* spp., the vetches) 3

    3a. Leaflets 8–18 4

      4a. Perennial; tendrils simple or branched; flowers 4–10 in clusters; pods to 3 cm long; native herbs of fields, thickets, and open deciduous and mixed forests .... *Vicia americana*

      4b. Annual; tendrils branched; flowers 1–3 in leaf axils; pods to 7 cm long; introduced weeds of waste places and pastures .... *Vicia sativa*

    3b. Leaflets 16–24 5

      5a. Stems solid; flowers blue-purple, less than 15 mm long, in clusters of 20–50; introduced weeds .... *Vicia cracca*

      5b. Stems hollow; flowers yellowish-white to orange (often tinged with purple), more than 15 mm long, in clusters of 7–20; native, often in maritime habitats .... *Vicia gigantea*

  2b. Hairs at the tip of the style arranged on 1 side, like a toothbrush (*Lathyrus* spp., the peavines) 6

    6a. Tendrils branched; pods hairy; plants of maritime habitats, ocean beaches and dunes .... *Lathyrus japonicus*

    6b. Tendrils unbranched; pods smooth; plants in a variety of habitats. .... *Lathyrus nevadensis*

1b. Leaves with an odd number of opposite leaflets (including a terminal leaflet), or palmate (the leaflets radiating from a common point like the fingers on a hand) 7

  7a. Leaves with an odd number of leaflets 8

    8a. Leaves with 7–15 leaflets .... *Lotus crassifolius*

    8b. Leaves with 3 leaflets 9

      9a. Leaflets entire (not toothed) .... *Lotus micranthus*

      9b. Leaflets toothed 10

        10a. Flowers in narrow, elongate clusters; tall, erect plant to 2 m tall .... *Melilotus alba*

        10b. Flowers in short, dense clusters; crawling to somewhat erect plants to 50 cm tall 11

          11a. Flowers remaining on the plant after blooming; pods straight (*Trifolium* spp., the clovers) 12

            12a. Flowers yellow, about 3 mm long; heads 6–7 mm diameter; annual .... *Trifolium dubium*

            12b. Flowers white to pink, or purple, to 1 cm long; heads 2–3 cm diameter; perennial 13

              13a. Flowers white to pink .... *Trifolium repens*

              13b. Flowers purple .... *Trifolium wormskjoldii*

          11b. Flowers falling from the plant after blooming; pods spiral .... *Medicago lupulina*

  7b. Leaves palmate (*Lupinus* spp., the lupines) 14

    14a. Leaflets 10–17 .... *Lupinus polyphyllus*

    14b. Leaflets 5–8 15

      15a. Plants annual .... *Lupinus polycarpus*

      15b. Plants perennial 16

        16a. Leaflets sparsely hairy on their upper surface; stems with rust-coloured hairs on stems and leaf stalks; plants of sandy sea-beaches and dunes .... *Lupinus littoralis*

        16b. Leaflets smooth (not hairy) above; stems and leaf stalks not with rust-coloured hairs; plants of varied habitats 17

          17a. Flowers numerous in dense clusters; erect herbs of low to middle (sometimes high) elevations; stalks of basal leaves about as long as diameter of leaf .... *Lupinus nootkatensis*

          17b. Flowers several in elongate clusters; bushy herbs most common and abundant at high elevations; stalks of basal leaves 2 or more times as long as diameter of leaf .... *Lupinus arcticus*

BEACH PEA • *Lathyrus japonicus*

GENERAL: Perennial herb from slender rhizomes; angled stems to 1.5 m long, trailing or climbing on or over other plants.

LEAVES: Compound with an even number **(6–12)** of leaflets and tipped with **curling tendrils**; leaflets opposite, to 7 cm long.

FLOWERS: Reddish-purple to blue, pea-like, to 3 cm long; in loose clusters of 2–8.

FRUITS: Hairy pods to 7 cm long.

ECOLOGY: Sandy beaches and dunes, upper gravel beaches amongst driftwood, along the **immediate coast**.

NOTES: This species is also known as *L. maritimus*. • Two similar red- to purple-flowered peavines of coastal dunes and tidal flats are **grey beach peavine** (*L. littoralis*), which is **grey-hairy all over and lacks tendrils**, and the less common **marsh peavine** (*L. palustris*), which has **'winged' stems** (two of the 'angles' stretched out), **tendrils and (usually) 6 leaflets**. *L. littoralis* and *L. japonicus* are usually found on sand, *L. palustris* in marshes and on mudflats. *L. japonicus* and *L. palustris* are found throughout our region, while *L. littoralis* is found only from southern Vancouver Island south and on the northern Queen Charlotte Islands. • The Dena'ina ate beach pea seeds raw or boiled and preserved in seal oil. This plant, along with giant vetch, was called 'Raven's canoe' by the Haida, because of the shape of its seed pods, which are black when ripe. • *Lathyrus* is from the Greek word *thouros* meaning 'something exciting,' from the belief that the seeds had some medicinal value.

PURPLE PEAVINE • *Lathyrus nevadensis*

GENERAL: Perennial herb with creeping rhizomes and erect to clambering, angled stems, to 1 m tall.

LEAVES: Compound with **4–10 leaflets**, tipped with **straight, unbranched tendrils**; leaflets opposite, to 12 cm long.

FLOWERS: Bluish-purple to mauve-red, pea-like, to 2.5 cm long; in terminal clusters of 2–7 flowers.

FRUITS: Hairless pods to 7 cm long.

ECOLOGY: Moist to dry open woods and clearings; at low to middle elevations.

NOTES: The tendrils of purple peavine are sometimes called 'bristles' because they are unbranched (and rarely used for climbing); this and the habitat should help distinguish it from beach pea and similar maritime species. • **Leafy peavine** (*L. polyphyllus*) is a fairly common, westside Cascades species of drier forests and meadows, with **bluish-purple flowers and 10–16 leaflets**; its northern range limit is in the Puget Trough. Several **introduced, weedy peavines with 2 leaflets** (e.g. broad-leaved peavine, *L. latifolius*; meadow peavine, *L. pratensis*; grass peavine, *L. sphaericus*) can be found in waste places from southern Vancouver Island south; these are described in Taylor (1974b) and Hitchcock and Cronquist (1973). • Purple peavine is often confused with American vetch (p. 192). Where the two grow together, **purple peavine generally appears more robust and has fewer and larger leaflets** than American vetch. Another way of telling them apart is by looking at the style. The hairs at the tip of the style of *Lathyrus* are arranged on one side so that they resemble a **toothbrush**. The hairs on the style of *Vicia*, however, bristle all around the tip, like a **bottle-brush**.

AMERICAN VETCH • *Vicia americana*

GENERAL: Perennial, trailing or climbing herb, **often in tangled masses**; stems to 1 m long.

LEAVES: Compound with **8–18 leaflets**, tipped with **simple or branched tendrils**; leaflets opposite, to 3.5 cm long.

FLOWERS: Bluish-purple to reddish-purple, pea-like, **to 2 cm long**; in **loose terminal clusters of 3–9**.

FRUITS: Hairless pods to 3 cm long.

ECOLOGY: Fields, thickets, and open deciduous or mixed forest, at low to middle elevations.

NOTES: Hairy vetch (*V. hirsuta*) has **small (about 4 mm long), white to pale-blue flowers**. It is an introduced, **annual,** European species found on disturbed sites south of 50°N latitude (and rare on the Queen Charlotte Islands). • **WARNING:** several species of vetch have been reported to be toxic to livestock and children. The seeds in the pods may attract a child's curiousity, so be careful. • The name vetch is from *vicia*, which is thought to be derived from the Latin *vincio* ('to bind'), in reference to the climbing habit and twining tendrils of these plants.

TUFTED VETCH • *Vicia cracca*
BIRD VETCH

GENERAL: Introduced perennial herb with climbing or trailing, angled stems to 2 m long.

LEAVES: Compound, with terminal, **branched tendrils; leaflets 16–24**, to 3 cm long, with pointed tips.

FLOWERS: Blue to reddish-purple, pea-like, to 1.2 cm long; in **dense, 1-sided clusters of 20–50 flowers**.

FRUITS: Hairless pods to 3 cm long.

ECOLOGY: Openings, thickets, open forest; at low to middle elevations.

NOTES: Woolly vetch (*V. villosa*) is a similar introduced, **annual or biennial** species, **very hairy** overall, with flowers that can be **2-toned in colour** (e.g., purple and white, red and white). It is a species of disturbed sites found from Vancouver Island and the adjacent mainland south, and on the Queen Charlotte Islands (near human habitation). • An old common name for vetches was 'strangletare'; a 'tare' was a weed of wheat fields.

GIANT VETCH • *Vicia gigantea*

GENERAL: Succulent perennial herb, **stout hollow** stems upright or climbing, to 2 m long.

LEAVES: Compound, somewhat hairy, with a terminal, branched tendril; **18–26** leaflets to 3.5 cm long, with pointy tips.

FLOWERS: Yellowish-white to orange, often tinged with purple, pea-like, to 1.8 cm long; in **1-sided, long-stalked clusters of 7–20** flowers.

FRUITS: Hairless pods to 4 cm long.

ECOLOGY: Disturbed sites, openings, and edges of forests and streams; at low elevations.

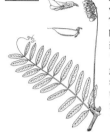

NOTES: The Makah used the leaves and vines to cover sprouts when steaming. The seeds were eaten in small quantities by the Nuu-chah-nulth and Kaigani Haida. The Saanich, who called this plant 'canoe plant,' prepared a hair tonic from giant vetch by crushing and boiling the stems and roots. A similar solution was used by canoe racers, who bathed with it for strength. In Haida this species, like beach pea, is known as 'Raven's canoe.'

COMMON VETCH • *Vicia sativa*

GENERAL: Perennial, slightly hairy herb with **slender, angled**, solid stems upright or climbing, to 1 m long.

LEAVES: Compound, with a branched tendril at the end; **8–16** leaflets to 3.5 cm long, pointy-tipped.

FLOWERS: Purple (occasionally white), pea-like, to 3 cm long; **in pairs on very short stalks in leaf axils**.

FRUITS: Pods to 7 cm long.

ECOLOGY: Waste places, pastures; at low elevations south from about 50°N, and rare on the Queen Charlotte Islands.

NOTES: This species (introduced from Eurasia) is also known as *V. angustifolia*. • Common vetch was once cultivated widely in Europe for fodder—hence *sativa* ('sown').

ARCTIC LUPINE • *Lupinus arcticus*

GENERAL: Perennial bushy herb with several **erect** stems from a branched rhizome; stems to 60 cm tall, slender, hollow, long-hairy.

LEAVES: Mostly arising from near the base, with **long stalks**, palmately compound; 6–8 leaflets, to 5 cm long, most with sharp, pointed tips.

FLOWERS: Bluish, pea-like, to 2 cm long; several in an elongated cluster.

FRUITS: Hairy pods to 4 cm long.

ECOLOGY: Open areas at all elevations, but most commonly and abundantly at middle to subalpine elevations.

NOTES: This species is also known as *L. latifolius.* • 2 **yellow-flowered** lupines have been introduced from California to the southern part of our region. **Dense-flowered lupine** (*L. densiflorus*, also called *L. microcarpus*) is (unlike arctic lupine) an **annual**, and is found in our region only around Victoria and coastal Puget Sound; and **tree lupine** (*L. arboreus*) is a **perennial shrub**, introduced here and there from Victoria southwards, perhaps to stabilize dunes (Hitchcock & Cronquist 1973). • While in subalpine and alpine areas, look for **dwarf mountain lupine** (*L. lyallii*, also known as *L. lepidus* var. *lobbii*), a **small (leaflets to 1.5 cm long)**, clumped, **silky-hairy** species of alpine meadows and scree slopes, which can be found from the southern B.C. mainland (south of 53°N) south to California.

SEASHORE LUPINE • *Lupinus littoralis*

GENERAL: Perennial herb from bright-yellow roots; slender, hairy, **trailing** stems to 60 cm long; **often in mats**.

LEAVES: Palmately compound; 6–8 leaflets to 2.5 cm long.

FLOWERS: Pea-like, to 1.2 cm long; banner pale blue to white; wings bright blue; in loose, many-flowered clusters to 15 cm in length.

FRUITS: Hairy pods to 3.5 cm long.

ECOLOGY: Sandy beaches and dunes along the **immediate coast**.

NOTES: The roots were roasted or pit-cooked and eaten by the Haida, Tlingit, Lower Chinook and probably other northwest coast groups. They were peeled before eating and were often dipped in oolichan grease. The Haida dried the roots into cakes for winter use. They were called 'black bear's tail.' Note that several lupines are known to **contain toxic alkaloids, and should be considered poisonous** until demonstrated otherwise. • This species is also known as 'Chinook licorice,' perhaps because of the appearance or taste of the dried roots.

NOOTKA LUPINE • *Lupinus nootkatensis*

GENERAL: Perennial herb, dies back annually to a thick rhizome; hairy, hollow, erect stems **to 1 m tall**.

LEAVES: Palmately compound, **from the stem; 5–8 leaflets**, to 6 cm long, **shaggy-hairy beneath**.

FLOWERS: Blue (sometimes tinged pink or white), pea-like, to 2 cm long; in dense clusters as much as 30 cm long.

FRUITS: Hairy or silky pods to 6 cm long.

ECOLOGY: A variety of open habitats (gravel bars, meadows, tidal marshes, open slopes) at low to middle (sometimes subalpine) elevations.

NOTES: While on sandy or gravelly soils at low to alpine elevations, look for **prairie lupine** (*L. lepidus*), **a short (to 40 cm tall), silky-hairy**, variable species (or complex of species) ranging from extreme southern Vancouver Island to California. • The roots of Nootka lupine, like those of beach lupine, were roasted or pit-cooked by the Nuxalk and Kwakwaka'wakw. Note that some lupines

contain toxic alkaloids and should not be used without special knowledge of preparation techniques. • Grizzly bears relish the roots of Nootka lupine and make large feeding excavations on north coastal estuarine marshes where both lupines and bears thrive.

LARGE-LEAVED LUPINE • *Lupinus polyphyllus*

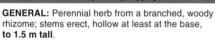

GENERAL: Perennial herb from a branched, woody rhizome; stems erect, hollow at least at the base, **to 1.5 m tall**.

LEAVES: Palmately compound; **10–17 leaflets**, to 12 cm long; **longest leaf stalks basal**, 10–60 cm long.

FLOWERS: Blue to violet, pea-like, to 1.5 cm long; in dense clusters to 40 cm long.

FRUITS: Hairy pods to 5 cm long.

ECOLOGY: Moist to wet, open habitats (seashore, streamside, wet meadows) and disturbed sites; at low to middle elevations.

NOTES: There seems to be some confusion as to exactly what the origin of 'lupine' is. One source says it is derived from the Latin *lupus*, for 'wolf,' because it was a pea 'only fit for wolves.' • Another reports that it is 'wolfish' because it depletes the soil of its nutrients, which is a serious misinterpretation because lupines fix nitrogen and actually fertilize poor soils (see notes under small hop-clover, p. 197). However there is a possibility that *Lupinus* comes from the Greek *lopos*, 'a husk,' or *lepo*, a 'hull' or 'peel,' in reference to the fruit. • Large-leaved lupine is widely cultivated as a garden ornamental; many colours and shades of this hardy perennial have been developed. • A good reference work for lupines in our region is Dunn and Gillett (1966).

SMALL-FLOWERED LUPINE • *Lupinus polycarpus*

GENERAL: Annual, brown-hairy herb 10–45 cm tall, erect or nearly so.

LEAVES: Palmately compound; 5–8 leaflets, to 4 cm long, hairy below.

FLOWERS: Blue, pea-like, small (to 7 mm long); in short clusters.

FRUITS: Slightly hairy pods to 3 cm long.

ECOLOGY: Open, gravelly and sandy sites; at low elevations.

NOTES: This species is also known as *L. micranthus.* • Another annual lupine found in similar sites over a similar range is two-coloured lupine (*L. bicolor,* also known as *L. micranthus* in part). The simplest way to distinguish them is to examine the leaflets; those of **small-flowered lupine** are generally **smooth above**, those of **two-coloured lupine** are **hairy above.**

WHITE CLOVER • *Trifolium repens*

GENERAL: Introduced **perennial** herb with **creeping** stems to 60 cm long, rooting at the nodes.

LEAVES: With **3 leaflets** (rarely and luckily 4); leaflets to 2 cm long, finely toothed; leaf stalks to 14 cm long.

FLOWERS: White or pinkish, pea-like, about 1 cm long; in dense, round, **long-stalked heads** up to 2 cm in diameter.

FRUITS: Pods about 5 mm long.

ECOLOGY: Disturbed sites (fields, roadsides), occasionally in other open, grassy sites; low to subalpine elevations.

NOTES: 2 other introduced, perennial clovers found in our range are red clover (*T. pratense*) and alsike clover (*T. hybridum*). **Red clover** has **red** flowering heads with leaves **immediately below** them. **Alsike clover** is the most similar to white clover, but it has **more upright stems and pinker flowers**; it is a hybrid between red and white clover. Both red and alsike clover are, like white clover, introduced European species, and can be found in similar habitats throughout our region. • 'Clover' is from the Latin *clava* meaning 'club,' as in playing cards, describing the shape of the leaves.

SMALL HOP-CLOVER • *Trifolium dubium*

GENERAL: Somewhat hairy, introduced **annual** clover; stems **clambering to curving upward**, to 50 cm tall.

LEAVES: Compound, 3-foliate; leaflets to 2 cm long, with small teeth on the upper half.

FLOWERS: Yellow becoming brown, pea-like, small (about 3 mm long); in round clusters of 5–25 flowers, **about 6–7 mm in diameter.**

FRUITS: Pods about 3 mm long.

ECOLOGY: Disturbed sites and grassy fields and lawns; at low elevations.

NOTES: A similar yellow-flowered introduced annual clover is **low hop-clover** (*Trifolium campestre*, also called *T. procumbens*), found in the same sorts of habitats from Vancouver Island and the lower Fraser Valley south to California. Its flowering heads are **larger, over 8 mm** across with more than 30 flowers. • Plants in the pea family commonly harbour nitrogen-fixing bacteria (*Rhizoctonia* spp.) in their roots. These bacteria pull nitrogen out of the air and 'leak' it into the soil in a form plants can use. Nitrogen is the nutrient in most limited supply over most of our region. For this reason, species such as clovers, alfalfa, sweet-clovers and lupines increase soil fertility where they grow. • Small hop-clover is an introduced Eurasian weed.

SPRINGBANK CLOVER • *Trifolium wormskjoldii*

GENERAL: Perennial herb with creeping rhizome; stems branched, prostrate, to 30 cm long, tips turning up.

LEAVES: Compound, 3-foliate; leaflets to 3 cm long, pointed at tip, finely toothed.

FLOWERS: Red to purple, often tipped with white, pea-like, to 1.2 cm long; in dense heads of 2–60 flowers, to 3 cm across.

FRUITS: Pods with 1–4 seeds.

ECOLOGY: Moist to wet, open places from low to middle elevations.

NOTES: Springbank clover differs from other perennial clovers described in this guide in having an **'involucre'**: a cluster of bracts under the flowering head. Two other native, small-headed clovers with involucres in our region are thimble clover (*T. microdon*) and small-headed clover (*T. microcephalum*). **Thimble clover** has **white to pinky-rose** flowers in **heads to 8 mm in diameter**, and it is found in dry to moist, open, usually grassy spots at low elevations south from about 50°N. **Small-headed clover** has **lilac to pinkish** flowers in **heads to 1 cm across**, with habitat and range similar to thimble clover. Several other clovers occur in our range, particularly from southern Vancouver Island south; more information is available in Hitchcock and Cronquist (1973). • The long, fleshy, white rhizomes of springbank clover were an important food source to northwest coast peoples, including the Haida, Kwakwaka'wakw, Nuu-chah-nulth (including the Ditidaht), Nuxalk, Comox, Sechelt, Straits Salish and Makah. The rhizomes were commonly harvested and prepared together with the roots of silverweed (p. 186). Both were usually dug in the fall, after the leaves had died down for the winter. They both grow in dense patches along estuaries. Among the Kwakwaka'wakw and other groups, these patches were divided into beds which were owned by families or individuals and passed on from generation to generation. Stones, sticks and intruding vegetation were removed from these beds, and the constant annual cultivation of the soil during the harvesting process undoubtedly enhanced the habitat of these beds. At some point within the historical period, the Nuxalk transplanted these species and tended them like garden vegetables. They pried out the rhizomes with a digging stick and wrapped them in fist-sized bundles using one of the roots as a tie. Occasionally they were eaten raw, but typically they were steamed in a box or an underground cooking pit. Usually the rhizomes were eaten dipped in fat or oolichan oil. The rhizomes were also dried for winter use. The Nuxalk stored them raw in underground boxes. Their flavour is sweet, similar to that of young green peas.

PEA

BIG DEERVETCH • *Lotus crassifolius*

GENERAL: Perennial herb to 1 m tall, **erect to spreading**, from rhizomes.

LEAVES: Compound, **stalked; leaflets 7–15**, opposite, to 4 cm long, green above, pale green to grey below.

FLOWERS: Yellowish or white, tinged with purple, pea-like, to **1.3 cm long**; in terminal round-topped **clusters of up to 20 flowers.**

FRUITS: Broad pods to 4.5 cm long.

ECOLOGY: Moist forests, riparian areas; from low to middle elevations.

NOTES: A similar perennial *Lotus* species with yellow flowers and **5 leaflets** is **birds-foot trefoil** (*L. corniculatus*), which has leaves **without stalks**. It is an introduced European species of moist to wet, open, grassy places from southern Vancouver Island south. • Other pea family plants in our region with an odd number of leaflets (i.e., with a terminal leaflet) probably are members of the genera *Oxytropis* or *Onobrychis*. **Field locoweed** (*Oxytropis campestris*) has **8–12 yellowish-white flowers on leafless stems** and can be found in drier, open areas at middle to alpine elevations from Alaska to Oregon. (NB: Taxonomists have recently split *Oxytropis campestris* into several different species; for more information, consult Douglas *et al.* 1990). **Saintfoin** (*Onobrychis viciifolia*), which bears its **pink to red** flowers in **dense, clover-like inflorescences**, is an introduced Eurasian weed found in waste places from southeast Vancouver Island to northern Washington (Whidbey Island, Yakima County). For more information on these genera, consult Taylor (1974b) or one of the regional floras. • The large, fleshy leaves (hence *crassifolius*) are presumably appealing to deer.

SMALL-FLOWERED LOTUS • *Lotus micranthus*

GENERAL: Annual, slender-stemmed herb with **crawling to erect** stems to 30 cm long.

LEAVES: Compound, essentially **stalkless; leaflets 3–5**, opposite, to 1.2 cm long, often covered with a whitish bloom.

FLOWERS: Yellow, often reddish-tinged, pea-like, **small (to 5 mm long); single, on long stalks** from leaf axils.

FRUITS: Pods **to 3 cm long, constricted** between seeds.

ECOLOGY: Open sites, from the seashore to middle elevations.

NOTES: Two other annual species of *Lotus* are found in our region. **Spanish-clover** (*L. purshianus*) is very similar to *L. micranthus* but has usually **3 leaflets** and pods **not evidently constricted** between seeds; it is a species of coarse-textured soils in open woods or clearings from Vancouver Island (Cowichan Lake only) to California. **Meadow birds-foot trefoil** (*L. denticulatus*) has **3–4 leaflets (usually more on one side than the other), non-stalked** flowers in leaf axils and **smaller pods (less than 1.5 cm long)** than the other 2 species. It is a species of open places from southern Vancouver Island and the adjacent mainland to California. • Several species of *Lotus* are called 'birds-foot trefoil' because they resemble the true 'birds-foot' (*Ornithopus perpusillus*), a species with curved (claw-like) legumes.

BLACK MEDIC • *Medicago lupulina*

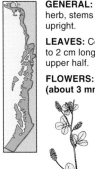

GENERAL: Annual introduced weedy herb, stems to 50 cm long, crawling or upright.

LEAVES: Compound, **3-foliate**; leaflets to 2 cm long, finely toothed on the upper half.

FLOWERS: Yellow, pea-like, **tiny (about 3 mm long)**; in compact clusters to 8 mm long.

FRUITS: Black, kidney-shaped, **veined, spiral** pods with 1 seed.

ECOLOGY: Disturbed sites at low elevations.

NOTES: **Small hop-clover** (p. 197) is similar to black medic but has **straight**, not coiled, pods. • **Alfalfa** or **lucerne** (*Medicago sativa*) is another introduced Eurasian weed; it is found on disturbed sites and in or near cultivated fields throughout our region. It is a **perennial** species with **larger (6–10 mm) purple** flowers, but it is otherwise similar. • *Medicago* is from *medike*, a name given by Dioscorides to a plant from Medea, ancient Persia, where alfalfa (*M. sativa*) was first grown. Alfalfa was imported into Greece at the time of the Persian wars under Darius. 'Black' refers to the colour of the seed pods of black medic.

WHITE SWEET-CLOVER • *Melilotus alba*

GENERAL: Tall, sweet-smelling annual (occasional biennial) from a taproot, **to 2 m tall**; stems erect, much-branched.

LEAVES: Compound, 3-foliate; leaflets to 2 cm long, **lance-shaped to oblong**, toothed.

FLOWERS: White, small (4–5 mm long), pea-like; numerous and crowded in long, slender, tapering, **spike-like clusters**.

FRUITS: Hairless pods about 4–5 mm long; **surface veined, black** when ripe.

ECOLOGY: Waste places, roadsides, cultivated fields; scattered at low to middle elevations, wherever roads and settlement occur.

NOTES: **Yellow sweet-clover** (*Melilotus officinalis*) is similar but has **yellow** flowers, **wider oblong-elliptic** leaflets and pods that are **yellowish-brown and not strongly net-veined** when ripe; it is much less common in our region than *M. alba*. Both species are weedy and were introduced as forage crops: white sweet-clover from Eurasia and yellow sweet-clover from the Mediterranean. • The sweet fragrance of the sweet-clovers comes from coumarin, which also imparts a very sweet smell to sweetgrass (*Hierochloe* spp.) and fresh cut hay. If allowed to degrade (e.g., through rotting of hay), the coumarin can break down into compounds that prevent blood from clotting, leading to death of hay-fed animals from even minor injuries. • In some areas, sweet-clovers are important nectar plants for honeybees.

Violaceae (Violet Family)

The violets are a widely distributed (occurring on all continents) medium-sized family of shrubs or herbs, in our region all herbs. They have alternate, simple (sometimes lobed or divided) leaves with minute or leafy stipules. The (in our region) bilaterally symmetric flowers are usually single and showy, with 5 distinct sepals and 5 distinct petals, the lowermost of which is spurred and larger than the others. They have 5 stamens and 1 superior ovary. The 1-chambered capsule (which sometimes opens explosively) has numerous seeds. In *Viola*, the stamens possess a finger-like, curved, nectar-secreting horn. In midsummer, after the normal flowering season is past, small, closed flowers without petals are produced on short stalks near the ground.

The family is economically important in the florist's trade, with over 120 species of *Viola* cultivated as ornamentals. The popular pansy is a *Viola*.

Key to Violets

1a. Plants lacking above-ground stems, the leaves and flower stalks arise from stolons (runners) and thick rhizomes; flowers white to lavender .... *Viola palustris*
1b. Plants with leafy, above-ground stems; flowers arise from leaf axils 2
  2a. Flowers partially or wholly yellow
    3a. Some parts (underside of older leaves, capsules) purple-spotted; leaves leathery, persistent .... *V. sempervirens*
    3b. Leaves and capsules not purple-spotted; leaves annually deciduous 4
      4a. Leaf bases heart-shaped; leaf blades about as long as broad (measured from the point where the stalk attaches to the blade) 5
        5a. Petals all clear yellow on both surfaces, lower three petals purple-pencilled on the inside .... *V. glabella*
        5b. Petals white with yellow bases, upper petals (especially) purple tinged on back .... *V. canadensis*
      4b. Leaf bases not heart-shaped; leaf blades elliptic to lance-shaped, 1.5 to twice as long as broad .... *V. praemorsa*
  2b. Flowers not yellow 6
    6a. Petals white to pale violet; stipules entire; above-ground stems well developed .... *V. canadensis*
    6b. Petals deep violet to purple; stipules toothed; above-ground stems shorter than flower stalks 7
      7a. Flowers large (15–25 mm long); head of style not bearded; spur thick, much less than half as long as the blade of the lowest petal .... *V. langsdorfii*
      7b. Flowers smaller (5–15 mm long); head of style bearded; spur slender, more than half as long as blade of lowest petal .... *V. adunca*

V. palustris	*V. sempervirens*	*V. glabella*	*V. canadensis*

V. praemorsa	*V. langsdorfii*	*V. adunca*

200

EARLY BLUE VIOLET • *Viola adunca*

GENERAL: Perennial with short to long, **slender** rhizomes, **usually stemless in early part of season, later develops aerial stems** to 10 cm tall, starts to flower in early part of growing season.

LEAVES: Generally oval to heart-shaped at base, hairy or hairless, with blades to 3 cm long and margins finely round-toothed; stipules **reddish-brown** or with reddish-brown flecks, narrowly lance-shaped, margins slender-toothed or somewhat ragged.

FLOWERS: To 1.5 cm long, with a **slender spur** half as long as lowest petal; petals **blue to deep violet**,

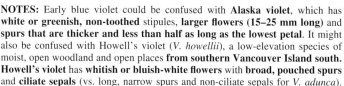

the lower 3 often white at base and purple-pencilled, the lateral pair white-bearded.

FRUITS: Small capsules opening explosively by 3 valves.

ECOLOGY: Dry to moist meadows, open woods, grasslands and open, disturbed ground; from lowlands to near timberline throughout our region.

NOTES: Early blue violet could be confused with **Alaska violet**, which has **white or greenish, non-toothed** stipules, **larger flowers (15–25 mm long)** and **spurs that are thicker and less than half as long as the lowest petal**. It might also be confused with Howell's violet (*V. howellii*), a low-elevation species of moist, open woodland and open places **from southern Vancouver Island south.** Howell's violet has **whitish or bluish-white flowers** with **broad, pouched spurs** and **ciliate sepals** (vs. long, narrow spurs and non-ciliate sepals for *V. adunca*).
• The leaves and flowers of all violet species can be eaten raw in salads, used as potherbs or made into a tea. Candied violet flowers are used for cake decorations. In the southern U.S. the leaves are often added to soups as a thickening agent. Flowers and leaves have long been used in various herbal remedies as poultices and a laxative for children and to relieve coughs and lung congestion.

ALASKA VIOLET • *Viola langsdorfii*

GENERAL: Small, perennial violet to 15 cm tall from **thick** rootstock and creeping rhizomes.

LEAVES: Round to heart- or kidney-shaped, somewhat pointed, to 5 cm long, the edges scalloped; stipules **white or greenish**, round to lance-shaped, with smooth margins.

FLOWERS: Bluish-violet, large (15–25 mm long), long-stalked; 3 lower petals dark-pencilled, lateral petals white-bearded, lowermost petal with a **short, sac-like spur**; usually single, terminal on flowering stalk.

FRUITS: Explosive capsules.

ECOLOGY: Moist meadows, grassy outcrops and talus, scree slopes, streambanks, bogs, often at the edges of snowbanks; common at low to high elevations; mostly in low-elevation, coastal bogs in Washington and Oregon.

NOTES: As noted by Clark (1973), violet flowers are elaborately designed to ensure pollination. Pencilling on lower petals serves as a 'honey guide' to lure bumblebees (short-spurred species) or butterflies (long-spurred species). The mouth of the nectary is guarded by two modified stamens. An insect arriving for a sip cannot help but bump against these stamens (acquiring pollen) at the same time as 'beards' on the lateral petals comb its body to remove pollen it may be carrying from other violet flowers. • There is a lot of folklore about violets. If violets bloom in autumn, there is going to be a death or an epidemic. It is unlucky to bring only a small number of flowers into the house; this may harm the laying capacity of hens (this also applies to primroses and snowdrops); spiteful neighbours might encourage children to take only one flower home. Violets worn as a wreath around the neck were said to prevent drunkenness.

MARSH VIOLET • *Viola palustris*

GENERAL: Perennial with **slender, spreading rhizomes and creeping stolons,** but **without aerial stems.**

LEAVES: Arise directly from rhizomes or stolons, **delicate, heart- to kidney-shaped, not hairy**; stipules lance-shaped, with smooth margins.

FLOWERS: Fairly large (10–15 mm long), with conspicuous sac-like spur; petals **white to lavender, generally tinged with violet or blue on back,** lateral pair sparsely white-bearded; flowering stems come directly from rhizomes.

FRUITS: Ellipsoid, greenish capsules.

ECOLOGY: Wetlands (swamps, fens, marshes, bog margins), wet seepage areas in forests and along streambanks; common at low to subalpine elevations.

NOTES: **Dwarf marsh violet** (*V. epipsila* ssp. *repens*) is very similar but usually produces **only 2 leaves** with the flowers (vs. 3 in *V. palustris*), and these leaves are **smaller: 1.0–2.5 cm long in flower to 3.5 cm long in fruit** (vs. 2.5–5 cm long in flower to 7 cm long in fruit in *V. palustris*). Dwarf marsh violet can be found in habitats similar to marsh violet, but often at higher elevations (subalpine to alpine), from southeast Alaska north.

CANADA VIOLET • *Viola canadensis*

GENERAL: Perennial with **short, thick rhizomes** and often with slender, **creeping stolons; stems leafy,** to 40 cm tall.

LEAVES: Heart-shaped, long-stemmed, sharply pointed at tip, usually hairy on one or both surfaces, margin saw-toothed.

FLOWERS: White with yellow base; petals **about 1.5 cm long,** lower 3 with purple lines, upper 2 purplish tinged on back, **lateral petals bearded;** flowers occur on upper portion of the stem.

FRUITS: Brown seeds in explosive capsules.

ECOLOGY: In moist to fairly dry woodland and forest (usually mixed or deciduous), often on floodplains, clearings; mostly at low to middle elevations.

NOTES: Another white-flowered violet with stolons is **small white violet** (*V. pallens*, also known as *V. macloskeyi* ssp. *pallens* or *V. palustris* ssp. *brevipes*). It is like Canada violet, but less hairy, with **smaller flowers (to 8 mm long), lateral petals not bearded** and leaves and sepals without fine hairs on the margins. Small white violet is a middle-elevation species of wet forests and bogs, from about 58°N south to California. (See notes for *V. adunca* on p. 201 for a description of Howell's violet, which can also have white flowers.) • The first, showy blossoms of violets often do not produce seed. Greenish flowers, borne later in the season either underground or right at the soil's surface, do not open and are self-fertilized, ensuring seed production. • Canada violet is easily transplanted and often invasive in a garden setting.

STREAM VIOLET • *Viola glabella*
YELLOW WOOD VIOLET

GENERAL: Perennial to 50 cm tall with spreading, **scaly, fleshy rhizome; flower stem leafless except on uppermost section**.

LEAVES: Heart-shaped, sharply pointed at tip, to 5 cm across, dark green and shiny above, toothed, without or more commonly with hairs; basal leaves stalked.

FLOWERS: Yellow, to 1.5 cm long, 3 lower petals with purple lines, lateral pair **white-bearded**, the lowest petal well separated from the rest, short-spurred; flowers occur mostly on upper portion of stem.

FRUITS: Brown seeds in explosive capsules.

ECOLOGY: Moist forests, glades, clearings, or along streams; common at all elevations.

NOTES: 2 other perennial yellow violets lacking stolons are **round-leaved yellow violet** (*V. orbiculata*), and Queen Charlotte twinflower violet (*V. biflora* ssp. *carlottae*). • **Round-leaved yellow violet** is most similar to stream violet, from which it is best distinguished by **oval to circular** leaf shape (see inset photo below); it is a species of moist woods and openings at middle to alpine elevations, from about 56°N south to Oregon, but absent from the Queen Charlotte Islands. • If the sepals have a conspicuous **purple-black stripe**, it is likely **Queen Charlotte twinflower violet**, found only on the Queen Charlotte Islands and Brooks Peninsula, Vancouver Island (with an unconfirmed report from Cray, Alaska). Its habitat is moist, open areas (meadows, rock outcrops), usually at subalpine to alpine elevations but occasionally to sea level.

TRAILING YELLOW VIOLET • *Viola sempervirens*
EVERGREEN VIOLET

GENERAL: Evergreen perennial to 8 cm tall from scaly rhizomes; plants usually fine-hairy and **some parts purple-spotted, often mat-forming**.

LEAVES: Heart- to kidney-shaped (quite variable), to 3 cm across, **thick and leathery**, coarsely toothed, older leaves often purple-spotted beneath; stipules thin, brown, lance-shaped.

FLOWERS: Pale yellow, 1.5 cm across, lower 3 petals purple-pencilled, lateral pair **yellow-bearded**, lowermost with a short, sac-like spur.

FRUITS: Purple-spotted capsules with brown seeds.

ECOLOGY: Common in moist forests at low to middle elevations.

NOTES: Round-leaved yellow violet (*V. orbiculata*, **inset photo**) closely resembles trailing yellow violet, but it lacks stolons and its leaves are **relatively thin and not purple-blotched,** and they wither over winter • Some violets (usually those with flowers held higher than the leaves) have a sort of explosive seed-dispersal mechanism, in which the drying capsule walls fold in on themselves, eventually expelling the seeds under pressure, catapulting them into the air. Some violet seeds also have outgrowths called 'oil-bodies.' Ants eat the oil-bodies after carrying the seeds off and leaving them at some distance from the parent plant.

YELLOW MONTANE VIOLET • *Viola praemorsa*
PRAIRIE VIOLET

GENERAL: Perennial from **short, erect** rhizomes; above-ground stems to 15 cm tall.

LEAVES: Egg- to broadly lance-shaped, 5–10 cm long, hairy and somewhat fleshy; stipules entire or with a few teeth.

FLOWERS: Petals **yellow**, upper pair **brownish-backed**, lower 3 purple-veined, lateral pair bearded, lowermost with a sac-like spur.

FRUITS: Brown seeds in explosive capsules.

ECOLOGY: Dry grassy slopes, meadows and Garry-oak savannah, at low elevations.

NOTES: Yellow montane violet is also known as *V. nuttallii* var. *praemorsa*. • Pansies are violets; the name 'pansy' is from the French *pensée*, meaning 'a thought' or 'remembrance' *à la* Proust (a notion similar to 'forget-me-not').

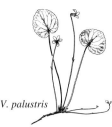

V. adunca

V. langsdorfii

V. palustris

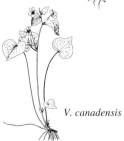

V. canadensis

V. glabella

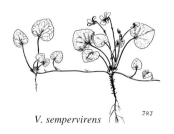

V. sempervirens

JRJ

V. praemorsa

Onagraceae (Evening-Primrose Family)

This is a relatively small family worldwide, but significant in our region, with quite a few abundant and conspicuous species. Plants in the family are mostly (all in our region) herbs with simple, alternate or opposite leaves. Flowers are solitary in the leaf axils or numerous in terminal spikes or racemes. Flowers have radial symmetry, typically 4 sepals, 4 petals, 4–8 stamens and 1 inferior ovary. Fruits are usually 4-chambered capsules with several to many hairless or hairy seeds (hairy in *Epilobium*) or bristly 1–2 seeded nutlets in *Circaea*. The family is distinguished by flowers with the numerical plan of 4, with the inferior ovary surmounted by a cup-like crown from whose rim emerge sepals, petals and stamens.

The family is important economically primarily for flower gardens; species of most genera are cultivated as ornamentals. The predominantly tropical American genus *Fuchsia* provides many species of ornamental shrubs.

Key to the Willowherbs (*Epilobium*)

1a. Plants annual from taproot; leaves mostly opposite; skin over lower portion
of stem shedding .... *E. minutum*
1b. Plants perennial, with fibrous roots or rhizomes; skin on lower portion of stem shedding 2
   2a. Flowers large, more than 3 cm across 3
      3a. Flowers yellow; petals notched at tip; leaves opposite .... *E.luteum*
      3b. Flowers purplish or pink; petals rounded at tip; leaves alternate 4
         4a. Flowers usually at least 15 per cluster; plants widely rhizomatous;
         veins visible on undersurface of leaves .... *E. angustifolium*
         4b. Flowers usually less than 12 per cluster; plants clumped;
         veins not visible on lower leaf surfaces .... *E.latifolium*
   2b. Flowers small, less than 2 cm across 5
      5a. Plants not clumped, forming leafy rosettes or bulb-like offsets;
      stem-bases erect .... *E. ciliatum*
      5b. Plants clumped, with short leafy stolons; stem-bases bent and spreading 6
         6a. Stems 5–20 cm tall; stem leaves not toothed; capsules
         less than 4 cm long .... *E. anagallidifolium*
         6b. Stems 10–50 cm tall; stem leaves usually toothed;
         capsules 4–10 cm long .... *E.hornemannii*

YELLOW WILLOWHERB • *Epilobium luteum*

GENERAL: Perennial from stout, widespread rhizomes; **bulb-like offsets** present; stem leafy, mostly unbranched, upright, 20–80 cm tall, often with **lines of hairs** running down from the leaf bases.

LEAVES: Opposite, stalkless, lance-shaped to elliptic, 2–8 cm long, mostly hairless, the margins finely toothed.

FLOWERS: Yellow, stalked; sepals 4; petals 4, 12–19 mm long, **notched** at tip and with wavy margins; stigmas 4 lobed; 2–10 in the axils of small upper leaves.

FRUITS: Pod-like capsules, 4–8 cm long, linear, glandular-hairy; seeds rusty- or dingy-hairy.

ECOLOGY: Steambanks, seepage areas in forest, around springs and lakes; scattered, locally common, at middle to subalpine elevations the length of our region; absent from the outer coast from southern southeast Alaska south.

NOTES: Yellow-flowered willowherb is a distinctive, **late-flowering** (July to September) species. • Species of *Epilobium* are called 'willowherbs' because of the resemblance of their leaves to those of the weeping willow (*Salix babylonica*). *Epilobium* comes from the Greek *epi* ('upon') and *lobos* ('pod'), in reference to the sepals and petals being located on top of the long 'pod' (ovary or fruit). • Both the common name and the species name *luteum* refer to this willowherb's most evident feature, its yellow flowers.

FIREWEED • *Epilobium angustifolium*
ROSEBAY WILLOWHERB

GENERAL: Perennial from **rhizome-like roots**; stem leafy, usually unbranched, 0.8–3 m tall, often purplish and short-hairy in the upper part.

LEAVES: Alternate, lance-shaped, stalkless, 5–20 cm long, green and often short-hairy above, paler, hairless and **distinctly veined below**, smooth-margined.

FLOWERS: Rose to purple, large (2–4 cm across), stalked; sepals 4; petals 4; stigma 4 lobed; several to many **(more than 15)** in long cluster atop stem.

FRUITS: Pod-like capsules, 4–9 cm long, narrow, green to red, 4 chambered, splitting open to disgorge hundreds of fluffy, white seeds.

ECOLOGY: Moist to fairly dry disturbed areas, including clearings, roadsides and especially recently burned sites; also in meadows, thickets, on avalanche tracks, and along riverbars; common throughout our region, but only locally abundant on the outer coast.

NOTES: The Haida used the outer stem fibres of fireweed to make cord. They peeled off the outer layer of the stem, dried it, and later soaked it in water and twisted or spun it into twine, used especially for making fishing nets. The Coast Salish used the seed fluff in weaving and padding. The Saanich and other Vancouver Island groups along with the Squamish and Puget Sound groups added the seed fluff to dog hair or mountain-goat wool and wove the mixture into blankets and clothing. The Saanich used fireweed seed fluff mixed with duck feathers to stuff mattresses. The Quinault and Skokomish mixed fireweed fluff with duck feathers to make blankets. • The Haida, Nisga'a, Gitksan and some other peoples ate the central pith of fireweed stems in the early spring. This plant was sometimes called *asperge* by the French Canadian voyageurs, and it was used by them as a green potherb. The leaves are rich in vitamin C and can also be used to make a tea. • Fireweed is especially evident along roads and railways and on old burns, hence the common name. The flowers produce ample nectar, which makes an excellent honey.

BROAD-LEAVED WILLOWHERB • *Epilobium latifolium*
RIVER BEAUTY

GENERAL: Low-growing, **matted** perennial from a stout woody stem-base, **without rhizomes**; stem leafy, reclining to erect, fine greyish-hairy above, 5–40 cm tall.

LEAVES: Opposite below, alternate above, lance-shaped to elliptic or oval, stalkless or nearly so, somewhat fleshy, often with whitish-grey bloom, 1–8 cm long; margin smooth or finely toothed; **veins not distinct on undersurface**.

FLOWERS: Pink to purple (sometimes white), stalked, large and showy (3–6 cm across), sepals, petals, and stigma lobes 4; **3–12 in loose, short** terminal cluster.

FRUITS: Pod-like capsules, 3–10 cm long, somewhat hairy, usually purplish; seeds numerous, tawny-hairy.

ECOLOGY: Sandy, gravelly soils on riverbars, streambanks, roadsides and on drier high-elevation slopes, often on talus or scree; common most of the length of our region, more common in the north; rare on the Queen Charlotte Islands and adjacent outer-mainland coast.

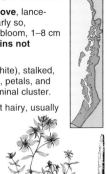

NOTES: Within the species there is considerable variation in the size and shape of leaves. An albino form is occasionally encountered. • 'River-beauty' is a great common name for this species—it often adorns gravelly streamsides, especially at more-northerly latitudes.

SMALL-FLOWERED WILLOWHERB • *Epilobium minutum*

GENERAL: Finely **hairy, taprooted annual**; stem leafy, upright, often branched, 5–45 cm tall.

LEAVES: Mostly opposite, oblong to lance-shaped, short-stalked, 1–2.5 cm long; margins smooth.

FLOWERS: White to pink, small; petals 4, **2–4 mm long**, notched at tip; stamens 8; stalked **in upper leaf axils**.

FRUITS: Pod-like capsules, narrowly club-shaped, slightly curved, 1.5–2.5 cm long, 4 chambered; seeds yellow-hairy.

ECOLOGY: Dry, often sandy or gravelly open sites, rocky bluffs and ridges; frequent in open disturbed sites, including clearcuts; low to middle elevations; common in the southern half of the region, scattered northwards.

NOTES: Tall annual willowherb (*E. brachycarpum*, also called *E. paniculatum*) is also a taprooted annual of dry, gravelly or disturbed sites at low to middle elevations, and it is common in the southern part of the region. *E. brachycarpum* is a **larger plant, 30–120 cm tall**, with stems **hairless below** the inflorescence, **mostly alternate** leaves, and **pale-pink to rose petals 3–12 mm long**. • **Dwarf groundsmoke** (*Gayophytum humile*) is another annual of dry, sandy sites, common at low to middle elevations in the Oregon Cascades. It is **low, much branched**, with **alternate linear** leaves and **white to pinkish, small (about 1 mm long)** flowers growing stalkless in **crowded spikes**. Dwarf groundsmoke is such a wispy plant that it resembles a whiff of smoke lying close to the ground. The genus name literally translates as 'Gay's plant,' and was named for G. Gay, a 19th-century French botanist and explorer who was the author of a flora of Chile.

PURPLE-LEAVED WILLOWHERB • *Epilobium ciliatum*

GENERAL: Perennial with **short or no rhizomes**; bulb-like buds (offsets) present or absent; stems leafy, **erect**, simple or branched above, hairy or glandular in the upper part, 15–150 cm tall.

LEAVES: Opposite, lance-shaped to oval or elliptic, pointed, toothed, short-stalked or stalkless, crowded or overlapping to remotely spaced.

FLOWERS: White, pink or rose-purple, small **(2–8 mm long)**; few to numerous in erect, **leafy-bracted cluster atop stem**.

FRUITS: Pod-like capsules, 3–10 cm long, hairy; seeds somewhat rough and hairy.

ECOLOGY: Moist, open habitats generally; streamsides, lakeshores, moist meadows and thickets, glades, disturbed sites such as roadsides and clearcuts; common from sea level to middle elevations.

NOTES: Purple-leaved willowherb is part of a large complex, including what some taxonomists distinguish as *E. adenocaulon*, *E. glandulosum* and *E. watsonii*. It is highly variable. *E. ciliatum* **ssp. *ciliatum*** (the widespread weedy subspecies) is usually **branched** above, has relatively **narrow** and uncrowded stem leaves and **smaller, usually paler** flowers than the typically **unbranched ssp. *glandulosum*.** Subspecies *glandulosum* has **broader** stem leaves that are often crowded around the flowers, **larger, darker-purple** flowers, and **bulb-like offsets** from rhizomes, which the tighter-flowered ssp. *watsonii* lacks. The less-common narrow-fruited willowherb (*E. leptocarpum*) and delicate willowherb (*E. delicatum*) would also key out to this complex, and they can be distinguished by their leaves, flowers and offsets—but you will have to use technical manuals to sort things out.

HORNEMANN'S WILLOWHERB • *Epilobium hornemannii*

GENERAL: Perennial, spreading by **rhizomes but lacking bulb-like offsets**; stems leafy, mostly unbranched, often with short, leafy shoots at the base, **10–50 cm tall**.

LEAVES: Opposite, elliptic to oblong or oval, short-stalked, mostly hairless; **margins bluntly toothed or nearly smooth to sharp-toothed**.

FLOWERS: Pink to rose-purple, small (4–8 mm long); petals 4, notched; few to several, stalked, nodding to erect in compact cluster atop stem.

FRUITS: Pod-like capsules **4–10 cm long**, sparsely hairy, stalked; seeds somewhat roughened, hairy.

ECOLOGY: Wet rocks, cliffs, streambanks; low to subalpine elevations.

NOTES: This species includes *E. alpinum* var. *nutans* and *E. behringianum*. • **White-flowered willowherb** (*E. lactiflorum*) is similar but has **white** flowers. It too is widespread in wet meadows, streambanks and seepage areas, at middle to high elevations throughout our region. **Smooth willowherb** (*E. glaberrimum*) is also similar and has **pink to rose-purple** flowers but, unlike the other 2 species, **lacks raised, hairy lines** running down the stem from the leaf bases. It grows in middle elevation, open moist forests and along streambanks, commonly from southwestern B.C. south to California. • This species is named for Jens Wilken Hornemann (1770–1841), a professor of botany from Copenhagen.

ALPINE WILLOWHERB • *Epilobium anagallidifolium*

GENERAL: Low, usually **matted**, mostly hairless perennial, spreading by **rhizomes and stolons**; roots **slender and loose**; stems 5–20 cm tall, leafy, curved at base, simple to branched, often reddish-purple.

LEAVES: Generally opposite, about equally spaced, small (5–20 mm long), **oblong to narrowly elliptic**, blunt, usually short-stalked, with **smooth to wavy margins**.

FLOWERS: Pink to rose-purple, small (3–6 mm long); petals notched at tip; solitary to few, often nodding.

FRUITS: Pod-like capsules, linear to narrowly club-shaped, 2–4 cm long; seeds about 1 mm long, net-veined, with smooth body and hairy tip.

ECOLOGY: Moist banks and rocks, scree slopes, alpine meadows, seepage sites, springs and streambanks, often above timberline; common throughout our region at high elevations, although the species occasionally descends to lower elevations on northern coastal floodplains.

NOTES: This species is also known as *Epilobium alpinum* in part. • **Club-fruited willowherb** (*E. clavatum*, also known as *E. alpinum* var. *clavatum*) is similar but has **wiry, tangled roots, hairy** inflorescences that are erect in bud, **egg-shaped to narrowly elliptic** leaves and seeds 1–2 mm long with a bumpy surface and hairs easily detached from the tip. It grows on moist, open, grassy or rocky slopes at middle to high elevations, and it is fairly common the length of the region. • The almost-impossible-to-pronounce species name means 'with leaves like *Anagallis*'; *anagallis*, in turn, is Latin for 'unpretentious, without boasting, without adornment,' and aptly describes this tiny, inconspicuous plant.

FAREWELL-TO-SPRING • *Clarkia amoena*

GENERAL: Taprooted annual; stems **spreading to upright**, simple to freely branched, leafy, 10–100 cm tall.

LEAVES: Alternate, linear to lance-shaped, smooth-edged, 2–7 cm long.

FLOWERS: Pink to rose-purple, showy; petals 4, **dark-spotted** in the centre, **1–4 cm long**; stamens 8; few to several in loose, leafy-bracted clusters.

FRUITS: Capsules, pod-like, long (1–4.5 cm), narrow, **straight to curved**, 8-ribbed, 4-chambered; seeds numerous, angled, not hairy.

ECOLOGY: Relatively dry, grassy open slopes and bluffs, forest edges at low elevations; scattered, locally common, more common through Washington and Oregon.

NOTES: The green sepals that encase the unopened buds have the peculiar habit of bursting along 1 side only and bending back in a single piece, as the flowers expand. • The common name acknowledges this species's habit of flowering in midsummer, as the grass dries and turns brown and when most other flowers are past. For this reason, *Clarkia amoena* is also sometimes called 'summer's darling,' or 'herald-of-summer' much-less-melancholy names. • The species name *amoena* means 'charming,' which this plant is indeed. *Clarkia* is for Capt. William Clark of the famous Lewis and Clark expeditions. (It is nice to see Capt. Clark get some recognition—many of our plants are named after Lewis.)

CONTORTED-POD EVENING-PRIMROSE • *Camissonia contorta*

GENERAL: Small, spreading, hairy, **taprooted annual**; stem simple or branched and **often sprawling**, leafy, 5–25 cm tall.

LEAVES: Alternate, linear to narrowly lance-shaped, 5–30 mm long, the margins smooth or lightly toothed.

FLOWERS: Yellow, small **(2.5–4 mm long)**; petals 4; stamens 8, in 2 unequal sets of 4; stalkless or short-stalked in open leafy clusters.

FRUITS: Capsules, pod-like, long and narrow (2–4 cm long, 1 mm thick), **arched to nearly coiled**, 4-chambered; seeds numerous, not hairy.

ECOLOGY: Open, gravelly or sandy areas (including beaches) at low elevations; scattered, locally common.

NOTES: Contorted-pod evening-primrose is also known as *Oenothera contorta*. • The eastern North American *Oenothera biennis* is called 'evening-primrose' because its pale yellow, primrose-coloured flowers open in the evening (at sunset). The meaning of *Oenothera* is not clear. It is probably from the Greek meaning 'wine-scented,' although one source says it means 'wine-catching' (the roots having been taken after a meal to induce further wine-drinking) and another says it means 'ass-catcher' (with no explanation why; perhaps it has something to do with people's behaviour after drinking all that wine?). • The pods are twisted or contorted, leading to the common and species names.

DENSE SPIKE-PRIMROSE • *Boisduvalia densiflora*

GENERAL: Hairy, sometimes glandular **annual**; stem leafy, simple to branched, **15–100 cm tall**.

LEAVES: Alternate, numerous, lance-shaped, stalkless, 1–5 cm long; margins smooth to irregularly toothed.

FLOWERS: Pale-pink to purple, small **(3–10 mm long)**; petals 4, **notched**; stamens 8; stalkless and numerous in crowded, leafy, terminal and lateral spikes.

FRUITS: Capsules, long and **straight**, pod-like, 4-ribbed, 4-chambered; seeds 3–6 per chamber, flattened, hairless.

ECOLOGY: Moist meadows, open slopes at low elevations; scattered, locally common.

NOTES: Brook spike-primrose (*Boisduvalia stricta*) also occurs in moist, open sites at low elevations. It is rare on southeast Vancouver Island and fairly common in Oregon. It is a **smaller (10–50 cm tall), densely hairy** annual, usually **branched** from the base, with pink to purple flowers **2 mm long** and **curved** capsules. • The numerous seeds of dense spike-primrose were reported to have been gathered for food by some aboriginal

JRJ

groups. They are small but oil-rich, with a taste and consistency somewhat like those of flax-seed • The spike-primroses look rather like some weedy species of *Epilobium*, but they have alternate leaves and hairless seeds. • The somewhat primrose-like flowers of *B. densiflora* grow in dense spikes, giving rise to the common name. The genus was named for French naturalist J.A. Boisduval (1801–1879).

ENCHANTER'S-NIGHTSHADE • *Circaea alpina*

GENERAL: Tender, juicy perennial, from slender rhizome with **tuberous thickenings**; stems leafy, simple to branched, hairless on the lower half, somewhat hairy above, 10–50 cm tall.

LEAVES: Opposite, heart- to egg-shaped, short-stalked, with pointed tips and remotely toothed margins, short-hairy on the lower surface, 2–6 cm long; **leaf stalks with narrow wings**.

FLOWERS: White to pale pink, small (1–1.5 mm long); **petals 2**, each deeply notched; in clusters of 8–12 atop a long stalk.

FRUITS: Indehiscent capsules, top- or pear-shaped, covered with **short, hooked bristles**, 1-chambered and 1-seeded.

ECOLOGY: Cool, damp forest and other moist, rich sites, often on floodplains or along streams, from valley bottoms to middle elevations; common.

NOTES: The name 'enchanter's-nightshade' results, in part, from some confusion. *Circaea* is named after the Greek goddess Circe—an enchantress—who supposedly used this plant 'as a tempting powder in some amorous concerns' (Hitchcock et al. 1961). The application of 'nightshade' to this plant is, however, a mystery. The name was originally applied to deadly nightshade (*Atropa bella-donna*) and European nightshade (*Solanum dulcamara*); see notes under European nightshade (p. 325) for the story of how these plants came to be called 'nightshades.' Somehow, the name has been subsequently transferred to *Circaea*. • The species name *alpina* is not great for our region—the alpine is one of the places you are least likely to find this plant.

Apiaceae (Carrot Family)

The carrots, also known as the Umbelliferae, are a medium-large family mostly of the northern hemisphere, and well represented in our region. The plants are mostly biennial or perennial, aromatic herbs, with stems usually with a large pith that shrivels at maturity leaving them hollow. They have alternate, often basal, usually pinnately or palmately compound leaves that usually have sheathing bases on the leaf stalks. The radially symmetric, individually small flowers are usually numerous in compact, simple or compound 'umbels,' or umbrella-shaped inflorescences, often subtended by an involucre of bracts. Flowers have sepals fused to the ovary with the 5 lobes distinct; 5 distinct petals; 5 stamens alternate with the petals, arising from a disc atop the single, inferior, 2-chambered ovary. The fruit is a schizocarp (a dry fruit that splits into 2 halves), the halves flattened or rounded, often ribbed, and sometimes winged or spiny; each half ('mericarp') is 1-seeded and suspended after dehiscence by a slender wiry stalk.

This economically important family produces food, condiments, and ornamentals. Foodplants include carrot (*Daucus*), parsnip (*Pastinaca*), celery (*Apium*) and parsley (*Petroselinum*). Flavouring comes from anise (*Pimpinella*), caraway (*Carum*), dill (*Anethum*), chervil (*Anthriscus*), fennel (*Foeniculum*) and lovage (*Ligustichum*). Water-hemlock (*Cicuta*) and poison-hemlock (*Conium*) possess resins or alkaloids in lethally poisonous quantities. Cultivated ornamentals include angelica (*Angelica*), goutweed (*Aegopodium*), sea holly (*Eryngium*) and blue laceflower (*Trachymene*).

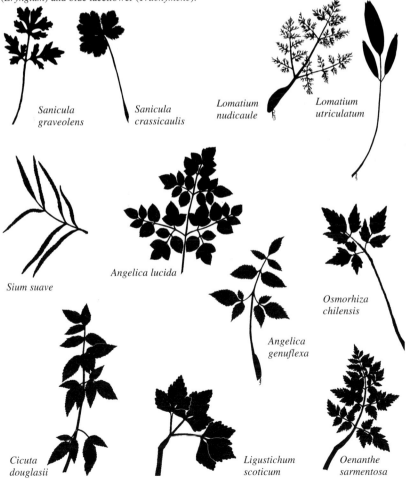

Sanicula graveolens

Sanicula crassicaulis

Lomatium nudicaule

Lomatium utriculatum

Sium suave

Angelica lucida

Osmorhiza chilensis

Angelica genuflexa

Cicuta douglasii

Ligustichum scoticum

Oenanthe sarmentosa

211

Key to the Genera of the Carrot Family (Apiaceae)

1a. Leaves simple, entire, hollow, tubular .... *Lilaeopsis*
1b. Leaves compound or deeply cleft 2
  2a. Most leaves compound with well-defined leaflets, not dissected
  into small, narrow segments 3
    3a. Leaflets 3, large, at least 10 cm across .... *Heracleum*
    3b. Leaflets more than 3, usually less than 10 cm across 4
      4a. Plants from fibrous or fleshy- thickened, clustered roots 5
        5a. Leaves palmately lobed or compound;
        fruits with hooked bristles .... *Sanicula*
        5b. Leaves pinnately compound 6
          6a. Stem-base thickened, hollow, with transverse
          partitions; some of the roots usually tuberous-thickened;
          veins in leaflets running to notches between the
          marginal teeth .... *Cicuta*
          6b. Stem-base without transverse partitions;
          roots not tuberous-thickened; veins not directed
          to marginal notches 7
            7a. Plants semi-prostrate to scrambling-ascending;
            sepal teeth well-developed; veins in leaflets
            extending to meet the marginal teeth .... *Oenanthe*
            7b. Plants erect; sepal teeth tiny or lacking;
            veins in leaflets not extending to meet the
            marginal teeth .... *Sium*
      4b. Plants from taproots or stout, vertical rhizomes 8
        8a. Plants low (to 10 cm tall); umbels with a series of
        tight, head-like clusters; flowers stalkless;
        plants of sea beaches .... *Glehnia*
        8b. Plants usually taller than 10 cm; umbels not
        with a series of tight, head-like clusters; flowers stalked 9
          9a. Fruits flattened crosswise 10
          10a. Flowers white or pinkish .... *Angelica*
          10b. Flowers yellow .... *Lomatium*
          9b. Fruits rounded in cross-section or flattened lengthwise 11
          11a. Leaves with well-defined leaflets;
          fruits 8–22 mm long, not winged .... *Osmorhiza*
          11b. Leaflets not always well-defined;
          fruits 2–6 mm long, usually winged .... *Ligusticum*
  2b. Most leaves dissected into small, narrow segments,
  without well-defined leaflets 12
    12a. Stems purple-spotted; robust biennial weeds 0.5–3 m tall .... *Conium*
    12b. Stems not purple-spotted; habit various 13
      13a. Fruits bristly or prickly 14
        14a. Bristles of the fruit in straight rows
        corresponding to the ribs .... *Daucus*
        14b. Bristles of the fruit not in straight rows .... *Sanicula*
      13b. Fruits not bristly or prickly 15
        15a. Plants of the seashore (mainly) .... *Conioselinum*
        15b. Plants mostly not maritime 16
          16a. Plants with stout, elongated taproots 17
          17a. Fruits flattened crosswise .... *Lomatium*
          17b. Fruits flattened lengthwise .... *Ligusticum*
          16b. Plants with fibrous or fleshy roots 18
          18a. Stem-base thickened, tuberous, chambered .... *Cicuta*
          18b. Stem-base not tuberous-thickened and chambered 19
            19a. Fruits flattened crosswise, or lengthwise
            and long and narrow; plants
            definitely taprooted .... *Lomatium*
            19b. Fruits nearly spherical, not long
            and narrow; plants with clustered roots .... *Perideridia*

WESTERN LILAEOPSIS • *Lilaeopsis occidentalis*

GENERAL: Small, perennial herb with rhizomes; **erect stem lacking**.

LEAVES: Narrow, hollow **tubes**, 3–15 cm long, 1–4 mm wide, with 5–11 **partitions**.

FLOWERS: White, inconspicuous; 5–12 in small umbrella-shaped clusters on slender stalks that are 0.5–4 cm long (usually much **shorter** than the leaves) and ascending to arched.

FRUITS: Egg-shaped, about 2 mm long, hairless, with pale, **prominent, corky-thickened ribs**.

ECOLOGY: Mudflats, tidal marshes, sandy or muddy beaches and shores along and near the coast, strictly at low elevations; common but scattered in mostly maritime habitats.

NOTES: *Lilaeopsis* is named for its resemblance to the genus *Lilaea* (the flowering quillwort). *Lilaea* was named after the French botanist Alire Raffeneau Delile (1778–1850). The species name *occidentalis* simply means 'western.'

COW-PARSNIP • *Heracleum lanatum*

GENERAL: Very large, hairy perennial from **stout taproot or cluster of fleshy fibrous roots**; stems single, leafy, hollow, 1–3 m tall, with strong pungent odour when mature.

LEAVES: Large, stalked, compound, **divided into 3 large (10–40 cm long and wide) segments,** each coarsely toothed and **palmately lobed**, woolly-hairy at least when young; upper leaves sometimes simple, maple-leaf-like; base of leaf stalk conspicuously **inflated and winged**.

FLOWERS: White, small; numerous, in a large, flat-topped, terminal umbrella-like cluster, with 1–4 secondary umbels from side shoots; involucral bracts 5–10, narrow, deciduous.

FRUITS: Egg- to heart-shaped, 7–12 mm long, flattened, with or without hairs, 1-seeded, **aromatic, sunflower-seed-like;** lateral ribs **broadly winged**.

ECOLOGY: Streambanks, moist slopes and clearings, upper beaches and marshes, meadows, thickets, avalanche tracks, roadsides; common from sea level to subalpine elevations.

NOTES: This species is also known as *H. sphondylium*. • **WARNING:** Besides taking care not to confuse this species with the violently poisonous water-hemlock (p. 215) and poison-hemlock (p. 220), watch out for **giant cow-parsnip** (*Heracleum mantegazzianum*, also called **giant hogweed**), **a huge (1.5–4.5 m tall)** garden escapee that can cause acute phototoxicity (severe skin rashes and persistent blisters after handling the plant and exposure to sunlight) and is known from the Strait of Georgia area. It probably occurs elsewhere in settled parts of our region. (**Note** that cow-parsnip also contains furanocoumarins, which can cause skin damage, especially to light-sensitive individuals.) • Cow-parsnip was used by virtually every group on the Northwest Coast as a green vegetable. The young stalks and leaf stems, before the flowers matured, were peeled and eaten raw or occasionally boiled. Because of the furanocoumarins, found in its outer skin, cow-parsnip was considered poisonous by some groups. The coastal peoples called this plant 'Indian Celery,' because the peeled young stems are mild and sweet, despite the strong odour of the leaves and outer skin.

PACIFIC SANICLE • *Sanicula crassicaulis*

GENERAL: **Taprooted** perennial; stem solitary, **erect**, leafy, 25–120 cm tall.

LEAVES: Alternate; basal and lower stem leaves long stalked, more or less **palmately 3–5 lobed**; lobes sharply toothed; middle and upper stem leaves smaller, becoming stalkless.

FLOWERS: Yellow or sometimes purple-tinged, small; 8–13 in small, compact, rounded clusters less than 1 cm wide on long stalks subtended by leafy bracts.

FRUITS: Ellipsoidal to spherical **burs**, 2–5 mm long, 2–4 mm wide, covered (except sometimes at the base) with **stout, hooked prickles**.

ECOLOGY: Common in moist to dry, open forest, thickets and shoreline bluffs, at low elevations; rare on the Queen Charlotte Islands.

NOTES: Footsteps of spring (*Sanicula arctopoides*, also called bear's-foot sanicle) is a **prostrate to ascending** perennial with branched stems, somewhat succulent, **yellowish, rosette-forming** leaves, and heads of **bright-yellow** flowers **nested in a ring of prominent bracts**. It grows on grassy bluffs, always along or near the sea, scattered from the southern tip of Vancouver Island south to California. **Black sanicle** or **snake-root** (*S. marilandica*) has **fibrous roots, greenish-white flowers,** and **palmately cleft** leaves that look somewhat like those of **palmate coltsfoot** (p. 294) or **false bugbane** (p. 179). It has been collected at Kitimat, B.C., and several places in the middle Skeena River valley. • Sanicles are unpopular in pastures for dairy cattle, because if eaten they can impart an unpleasant flavour to the milk. • The species name *crassicaulis* means 'thick-stemmed.'

SIERRA SANICLE • *Sanicula graveolens*

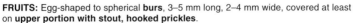

GENERAL: **Taprooted** perennial; stem solitary, erect, often branched, leafy, 5–50 cm tall.

LEAVES: Alternate; lowermost stem leaves long stalked, often attached below ground level and **seeming to arise separately from the stem, pinnately divided in 3s**; primary divisions also lobed and toothed, lowermost pair separated from the upper by a **narrow, smooth stalk**; middle and upper stem leaves few, smaller, often becoming stalkless.

FLOWERS: Yellowish, small; 10–15 in small, compact, rounded clusters on short stalks subtended by narrow bracts.

FRUITS: Egg-shaped to spherical **burs**, 3–5 mm long, 2–4 mm wide, covered at least on **upper portion with stout, hooked prickles**.

ECOLOGY: Relatively dry, open forest, glades, rocky slopes, from low to fairly high elevations; scattered, locally common, in the southern part of our region; occurs rarely also in the middle Nass and Skeena valleys.

NOTES: Purple sanicle (*Sanicula bipinnatifida*) has **purple flowers** and pinnately divided leaves, with a distinctly **sharp-toothed leaf axis**. It grows in dry open forest, meadows and on bluffs and rocky slopes at low elevations, scattered from southeastern Vancouver Island south to California. • The most likely origin of the name 'sanicle' appears to be from the Latin *sanus*, meaning 'whole' or 'sound,' or *sanare* meaning 'to heal.' The plant was understood to have curative properties, as in the proverbial axiom, 'He who keeps sanicle has no business with a doctor.' A 16th-century herbal says, 'The iyce of Sanicle dronken, doth make whole and sound all inward, and outwarde woundes and hurtes.' However, others claim that the word is derived from Saint (*San*) Nicholas based on a story of how he obtained the favour of God to restore to life 2 children who had been murdered and pickled in a pork tub. • The species name *graveolens* means 'strong-smelling.'

DOUGLAS' WATER-HEMLOCK • *Cicuta douglasii*

GENERAL: Stout perennial from a taproot or cluster of tuberous roots; stems solitary or few together from a **tuberous-thickened and chambered base**, leafy, hairless, 0.5–2 m tall.

LEAVES: Both basal and along the stem, **divided 1–3 times** producing many **lance-shaped to oblong** leaflets, sharply pointed and toothed; **lateral veins end at the base of the teeth**.

FLOWERS: White to greenish, small; numerous, in several to many small, compact clusters aggregated in several compound umbels; **involucral bracts mostly lacking**.

FRUITS: Egg-shaped to orbicular, 2–4 mm long, hairless, with **corky-thickened unequal ribs**.

ECOLOGY: Marshes, edges of streams and ponds, wet ditches and clearings; common from lowlands to middle elevations.

NOTES: WARNING: Extremely poisonous if ingested. Even small amounts can be deadly, to both humans and livestock. All parts of the plant are poisonous, but the roots and stem-base especially so. The basal parts of 1 plant can kill a cow. • An important feature that aids in identification of *C. douglasii* and serves to distinguish it from other similar plants (e.g., *Angelica, Heracleum, Sium*) is the arrangement of the leaf veins. The lateral veins of its leaflets end at the base of the marginal teeth rather than at the points. Also, the thickened stem-base, when cut lengthwise, clearly

reveals the chambers (not found in *Heracleum, Sium, Oenanthe, Osmorhiza, Conioselinum, Daucus, Ligustichum*; but see *Angelica*) and an evil-looking orange-yellow resin. • Aboriginal elders maintain that the only antidote to poisoning from this plant is drinking salmon-head soup or salmon oil. The roots were occasionally used externally as a poultice for swellings, but because of their extreme toxicity, their use is not recommended.

WATER-PARSNIP • *Sium suave*

GENERAL: Terrestrial to semiaquatic perennial from a very short, erect stem-base **(not chambered)** with **fibrous roots that sometimes are tuberous-thickened**; stem stout, leafy, hollow, strongly ridged, generally branched above, 50–120 cm tall.

LEAVES: Emergent leaves **once-divided** into 7–15 leaflets that are **lance-shaped to linear**, saw-toothed; leaf stalks with sheathing bases; submerged leaves much more finely divided; primary lateral veins of the leaflets not directed towards the base of the teeth.

FLOWERS: White, small; numerous in dense umbrella-like heads; **involucral bracts 6–10, narrow, reflexed**.

FRUITS: Oval to elliptic, 2–3 mm long, **prominently ribbed**.

ECOLOGY: Common in swamps, low marshy ground, riverbanks and lake-shores, and in shallow water; from low to middle elevations.

NOTES: The Nuxalk ate the long, fleshy roots both raw and cooked. The roots were an important food for many interior peoples and young shoots are said to be edible. Older plants and flowers should be avoided because they could be **toxic** and have been implicated in livestock poisonings. • All care should be taken to correctly identify the plant because of its **similarity to the poisonous water-hemlock**. In contrast to water-hemlock, **water-parsnip has stem-bases neither swollen nor chambered and leaves that are only once-divided**.

BEACH-CARROT • *Glehnia littoralis* ssp. *leiocarpa*

GENERAL: Perennial from **stout woody taproo**t; stemless or with short stems and strongly sheathing leaf stalks **buried in the sand.**

LEAVES: Spreading, often prostrate, **thick and firm**, hairless above, **white-woolly beneath**, once- or twice-divided in 3s; leaflets broadly **elliptic to egg-shaped**, coarsely toothed.

FLOWERS: White, small; in several compact clusters on hairy stalks that are 1.5–5 cm long.

FRUITS: Oblong egg-shaped to spherical, 6–13 mm long, somewhat flattened, hairless or hairy towards tip, with broadly **corky-winged ribs.**

ECOLOGY: Coastal dunes and sandy beaches; scattered the length of our region, but in Alaska only on Kodiak Island and in the Yakutat area.

NOTES: Beach carrot is also known as beach silver-top and as *Glehnia leiocarpa.* • This species also occurs along the north Pacific coast of Asia, an interesting distribution pattern shared by several north coastal species. • Its leaves are covered in dense white woolly hairs on the undersides that give it a silvery appearance. • Peter von Glehn, for whom the plant was named, was a Russian botanist and curator of the St. Petersburg Botanic Garden until 1876. The plant grows on beach dunes (*littoralis*).

PACIFIC WATER-PARSLEY • *Oenanthe sarmentosa*

GENERAL: Fibrous-rooted hairless perennial; stems **soft, weak, reclining to ascending, often rooting at nodes**, freely branched, to 1 m long.

LEAVES: Oblong to egg-shaped in outline, 2–3 times coarsely pinnately divided; leaflets toothed and cleft with **primary lateral veins directed to the teeth.**

FLOWERS: White, small; in 5–20 compact clusters on 1–3 cm long stalks subtended by 0-few, narrow, leafy bracts.

FRUITS: Barrel-shaped, 2.5-3.5 mm long, about 2 mm wide, with **ribs broader than the narrow intervals.**

ECOLOGY: Low wet sites, in thickets, along streams and sloughs, in marshes, wet meadows and clearings and at forest edges, often in temporary standing water; at low to middle elevations; common throughout the region except for northern southeast Alaska.

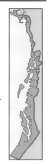

NOTES: This plant was an important purgative and emetic used by the Ditidaht. The Southern Vancouver Island Salish chewed the roots or soaked them in water and drank this for stomach disorders and headaches. It was also used as a childbirth medicine, to shorten labour. **WARNING:** It is reputed to be poisonous, with toxins related to those of water-hemlock. • Since some species of the genus were used in the past in Greece for flavouring wine, they were called *Oenanthe* from the Greek *ionois* ('wine') and *anthos* ('flower'). The leaves are somewhat parsley-like, and when the stems touch or lie on the ground they send out long runners from the nodes, which is described by the term *sarmentosa*.

MOUNTAIN SWEET-CICELY • *Osmorhiza chilensis*

GENERAL: Perennial from **taproot**; stems **solitary or sometimes 2–3**, slender, leafy, 30–100 cm tall, branched above.

LEAVES: Twice divided into 3s; **9 leaflets coarsely toothed, more or less hairy, thin**; basal leaves several, long stalked; stem leaves 1–3, short stalked.

FLOWERS: Greenish-white, inconspicuous; in several loose umbels that are short-stalked when flowering but become open and long stalked in fruit; involucral bracts absent.

FRUITS: Black, needle-like, 12–22 mm long, narrowing (constricted) below tip, broadening into a beak, bristly-hairy, often catching on clothing or fur.

ECOLOGY: Open forest (coniferous and deciduous), forest edges, thickets, glades; common from low to middle elevations.

NOTES: Mountain sweet-cicely is very similar to **blunt-fruited sweet-cicely** (*O. depauperata*). The 2 can be distinguished by close examination with a hand-lens of the mature fruits. In *O. depauperata*, the fruit is **club- or baseball-bat-shaped** with **no constriction** below the tip. *O. depauperata* occupies habitats similar to those of *O. chilensis*, but it is scattered mostly in northern southeast Alaska and the Prince William Sound area, and it is apparently lacking in the southern half of the region. **Western sweet-cicely** (*O. occidentalis*) is distinctive with its **yellow** flowers, **hairless** fruits and **clustered** stems. It grows in moist thickets and openings, from low to middle elevations, sporadically in the Cascades of Washington and Oregon and in the Olympic Mountains.

PURPLE SWEET-CICELY • *Osmorhiza purpurea*

GENERAL: Perennial from well-developed **taproot**; stem **single**, slender, 20–70 cm tall.

LEAVES: Deltoid in general outline, twice-divided into 3s; **9 sharp-pointed leaflets coarsely toothed and usually hairless**, thin, yellowish-green.

FLOWERS: Pink to purplish (sometimes greenish-white), small; several to many in 2–6 spreading heads aggregated in 1 to few compound umbels; involucral bracts absent.

FRUITS: Dark, **spindle-shaped, 8–13 mm long**, bristly-hairy, **with constriction** below the beaked tip; beak cone-shaped, broader than tall.

ECOLOGY: Common in (usually) coniferous forests or openings, stream-banks, river flats, meadows, avalanche tracks, from lowlands to subalpine meadows; probably most common overall at middle elevations.

NOTES: This plant can be easily confused with *O. chilensis* and *O. depauperata*, both of which have **hairy leaves**, however. It also differs from *O. depauperata* in that the fruit has a constriction or narrowing below the tip and the flowers tend to be pink-purplish. It can also be distinguished from *O. chilensis* by close examination of the fruit. **In *O. purpurea*, the fruit is generally smaller and the cone-shaped beak is broader than tall, whereas in *O. chilensis* the beak is as tall as it is broad**. Overall, *O. purpurea* is smaller. • 'Cicely' is from the Greek *seseli* meaning 'a carrot family plant used in medicine'; it has been confounded with the girls' name 'Cicely.' It is called 'sweet-cicely' because of the licorice-like odour of the root when crushed.

KNEELING ANGELICA • *Angelica genuflexa*

GENERAL: Stout perennial from a **taproot**; stem leafy, hairless, hollow, arising from erect, **tuberous, chambered stem-base; stem 1–1.5 m tall, often purplish and glaucous**.

LEAVES: Compound, with 3 major divisions divided in turn; **primary divisions bent back** (not directed forward as in other similar species); **leaf stalk also bent** above the first pair of primary leaflets; ultimate leaflets egg-shaped to lance-shaped, coarsely toothed; **veins tending to end at the points of the teeth**; leaf stalks with inflated bases sheathing the main stem.

FLOWERS: White or pinkish, small; in numerous small, compact heads, all arranged together in several umbrella-shaped clusters; involucral bracts lacking.

FRUITS: Rounded, 3–4 mm long, hairless, with **broadly winged lateral ribs**.

ECOLOGY: Moist thickets, forest openings and edges, swamps, streambanks, wet ditches and clearings; common at low to middle elevations through the northern 2/3 of our region, sporadic southwards through Washington and Oregon.

NOTES: Sharptooth angelica (*A. arguta*) is similar but **does not have bent leaves and leaf stalks**. It grows in moist to wet sites (streambanks, wet meadows, marshes, swamps) at low to middle elevations. It is scattered from southernmost B.C. to California, and it is more common in Oregon. • Care must be taken not to confuse kneeling angelica with the poisonous water-hemlock. Both have tuberous-thickened and chambered stem-bases, but the **kinks in the leaves of kneeling angelica** give it away. • The Bella Coola used the stems as breathing tubes when hiding under water in times of trouble. • The species name *genuflexa*, meaning 'to genuflect,' refers to the bending 'knees' in the leaf stalks.

SEA-WATCH • *Angelica lucida*

GENERAL: Stout perennial from **strong taproot**; stem single, leafy, 50–140 cm tall.

LEAVES: Hairless, 2–3 times divided in 3s; leaflets egg-shaped to deltoid, 2–7 cm long, irregularly toothed; stem leaf stalks inflated, with expanded sheathing bases.

FLOWERS: White, small; numerous in 20–45 small compact heads in 1-several compound umbels; involucral bracts lacking.

FRUITS: Oblong-elliptic, 4–9 mm long, hairless, with **corky-thickened, thin-edged ribs**.

ECOLOGY: Common on moist beaches, coastal bluffs, meadows, streambanks; mostly maritime and at low elevations from Vancouver Island south, also inland, from sea level to subalpine elevations in the north.

NOTES: Stems and leaf stalks of sea-watch were eaten by aboriginal people, who called them 'wild celery.' • In Siberia the root was carried as an amulet against polar bears, and the fumes of the roasted root were inhaled by Siberian Inuit as a seasickness remedy. • *Angelica* is Latin for 'angel' and is derived from *Archangelica* - a name applied to a plant that was reputedly revealed to Matthaeus Sylvaticus by an archangel as a remedy for cholera and plague. Therefore *Angelica* is believed to have healing powers. Another interpretation suggests that *Archangelica* was applied to these plants because they bloom around the feast of the Apparition of St. Michael (May 8th according to the old calendar) and hence were believed to be protection against bad spirits, witches and a disease of cattle called 'elfshot.' • The species name *lucida* means 'glittering' or 'shining' and may refer to the pale colour of the plant.

BEACH LOVAGE • *Ligusticum scoticum*

GENERAL: Stout, hairless perennial from **thick taproot**; stems single, leafy, 10–80 cm tall, reddish-purple at base.

LEAVES: Thick, firm, mostly twice-divided in 3s; **leaflets usually 9, egg-shaped**, 2–6 cm long, coarsely toothed; stem leaf stalks with long, often purplish, but **not greatly expanded** basal sheaths.

FLOWERS: White or pinkish, small; numerous in 5–16 small compact heads in 1-several compound umbels; involucral bracts few to several, narrow.

FRUITS: Oblong, 7–8 mm long, hairless, with **narrowly winged ribs**.

ECOLOGY: Common on beaches, coastal bluffs and headlands; **strictly maritime** at low elevations.

NOTES: *L. scoticum* occurs on both the Atlantic and Pacific coasts of North America; the plants in our region are usually treated as a separate subspecies, ssp. *hultenii*. **Beach lovage** is our only *Ligusticum* that **does not** have much-divided, fern-like or parsley-like leaves. When beach lovage and sea-watch are growing together and are not in flower or fruit, they can easily be confused. However, **sea watch** usually has **more leaflets, more-expanded sheaths** on the leaf stalks and transverse **partitions** within the root crown (partitions that beach lovage lacks). • Species name *scoticum* means 'from Scotland.'

GRAY'S LOVAGE • *Ligusticum grayi*

GENERAL: Hairless, taprooted perennial; stems 20–60 cm tall, clothed at base with **fibrous remains** of leaf sheaths.

LEAVES: Mostly basal, divided into **numerous toothed or cleft leaflets** to 3 cm long; stem leaves 1 or 2, much reduced.

FLOWERS: White, small; several to many in 7–14 small compact heads in 1–3 compound umbels; involucral bracts lacking.

FRUITS: Elliptic-oblong, 4–6 mm long, hairless, with **narrowly winged ribs**.

ECOLOGY: Moist to dry, open or forested slopes and mountain meadows; common at **middle to subalpine elevations**.

NOTES: Parsely-leaved lovage (*L. apiifolium*) is similar but has **well-developed stem leaves** and fruits with **wingless ribs**. It grows at **low elevations** in thickets, along forest edges and fencerows and on sparsely wooded slopes and grassy meadows; it is common from Washington to California. **Calder's lovage** (*L. calderi*) is also similar to Gray's lovage and shares its mainly basal leaves and fibrous root crowns, but it is **restricted** (apparently) to the B.C. coast, the Queen Charlotte Islands, adjacent nearshore islands, and northern Vancouver Island (Brooks Peninsula). It grows from the lowlands to alpine elevations in wet rocky habitats, boggy slopes and alpine heath, and it is scattered but locally common. • 'Lovage' seems to have derived from an old word *love-ache,* meaning 'love-parsley,' which appeared in a translation of Pliny the Elder. However, the hint of an amorous connection is misleading, since *love-ache* is more likely a misspelling or corruption of *levisticum* derived from *Ligusticum. Ligusticum* was a name used by Dioscorides for a plant from Liguria in Italy. • Calder's lovage is named for Jim Calder, a Canadian botanist and student of the flora of the Queen Charlotte Islands. Gray's lovage is named for either Asa Gray (1810–1888), a professor of botany at Harvard, or S.F. Gray (1766–1836), a British botanist.

PACIFIC HEMLOCK-PARSLEY • *Conioselinum pacificum*

GENERAL: Essentially hairless, sometimes glaucous perennial from a short, stout **rhizomatous stem-base with a cluster of fleshy roots or a taproot**; stem single, leafy, 20–120 cm tall.

LEAVES: All on the stem, egg-shaped to deltoid in outline, **2–3 times pinnately dissected**, with lobed or cleft leaflets; leaf stalks sheathing at base.

FLOWERS: White, small; numerous in 8–30 small compact heads in 1-several compound umbels; involucral bracts 1 to few and linear, or lacking.

FRUITS: Oblong-oval, 5–8 mm long, hairless, ribbed; the **lateral ribs have broad, thin wings**.

ECOLOGY: Common on gravelly beaches, sandy shores, upper tidal marshes, grassy bluffs and headlands, sometimes in open boggy forests; **mostly along or near the coastline**.

NOTES: This species is also known as *C. chinense*. • Pacific hemlock-parsley could be confused with Calder's lovage (notes, p. 219) where the two occur in close proximity, as they do on rocky sea bluffs on the Queen Charlotte Islands. However, **Calder's lovage** can be readily distinguished by its **fibrous root crown**. • Pacific hemlock-parsley has been identified by ethnobotanist Brian Compton as the 'Indian carrot' or 'wild carrot' of the Kwakwaka'wakw, Nuxalk, Heiltsuk, Haisla, Oowekela, Sechelt, Halq'emeylem, probably the Squamish and other northwest coast groups. The carrot-like taproots were dug in the spring, cooked and eaten by people long ago; however, few aboriginal people today recall their use. • The Latin *Conioselinum* is derived from the Greek *Conio*, 'hemlock' and 'poison,' and *selenum* signifying 'any umbelliferous or celery-like plant with lustrous petals.'

POISON-HEMLOCK • *Conium maculatum*

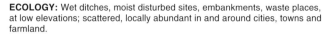

GENERAL: Robust, hairless biennial from a stout, whitish taproot, with a disagreeable odour especially when crushed; stem freely branched, leafy, **purple-blotched**, hollow, **0.5–3 m tall**.

LEAVES: Large (15–30 cm long), **pinnately dissected (fern-like)**, with small ultimate segments, giving the plant a **lacy** appearance; leaf stalks enlarged and sheathing at the base.

FLOWERS: White, small; numerous, in many terminal and axillary, compound umbels; involucral bracts small, lance-shaped.

FRUITS: Egg-shaped, somewhat flattened, about 2 mm long, hairless, with **prominent, raised, often wavy ribs**.

ECOLOGY: Wet ditches, moist disturbed sites, embankments, waste places, at low elevations; scattered, locally abundant in and around cities, towns and farmland.

NOTES: WARNING: Extremely poisonous; sickness and death can result from ingestion of leaves, roots or seeds. This plant was originally introduced from Europe, and has become a common weed of waste ground, pastures, fields, roadsides, ditches and sometimes gardens. Poison-hemlock is known to be toxic to both humans and animals, and it has often caused fatal poisonings. Some people mistake the finely dissected leaves for parsley or the seeds for anise, with fatal results. • It was a draught prepared from this plant with which Socrates killed himself in 399 BC. • The word 'hemlock' is from old english *haelm* or *haem* meaning 'straw' or 'stalk' and *leac* meaning 'plant,' applied originally to any plant in the Apiaceae with hollow stalks (like straw) left after flowering.

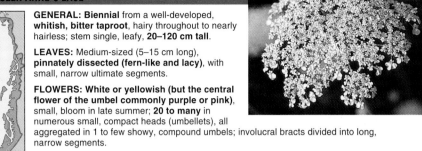

WILD CARROT • *Daucus carota*
QUEEN ANNE'S LACE

GENERAL: Biennial from a well-developed, **whitish, bitter taproot**, hairy throughout to nearly hairless; stem single, leafy, **20–120 cm tall**.

LEAVES: Medium-sized (5–15 cm long), **pinnately dissected (fern-like and lacy)**, with small, narrow ultimate segments.

FLOWERS: White or yellowish (but the central flower of the umbel commonly purple or pink), small, bloom in late summer; **20 to many** in numerous small, compact heads (umbellets), all aggregated in 1 to few showy, compound umbels; involucral bracts divided into long, narrow segments.

FRUITS: Egg-shaped, 3–4 mm long, ribbed and **armed with barbed prickles along alternate ribs**; inflorescence narrower in fruit than in flower, with the outer, longer stalks arching inwards, producing a **'bird's nest'** effect.

ECOLOGY: Common on roadsides, fields, pastures, waste places, moist clearings, at low elevations.

NOTES: Introduced from Eurasia, wild carrot is now established as a weed throughout much of North America. This is the wild ancestor of the cultivated carrot. • **American wild carrot** (*D. pusillus*) is a **native annual,** smaller **(to 70 cm tall)** and **more slender** than *D. carota*, and with **fewer flowers (5–12)** per umbellet. It is a species of dry, open, rocky or grassy sites at low elevations, scattered but locally common in the Strait of Georgia–Puget Sound area south to California. • *Daucus carota* literally translated means 'carrot carrot.' A prettier name is 'Queen Anne's lace,' which refers to the lacy, white flower heads. In Britain, however, this is also the common name for cow parsley (*Anthriscus sylvestris*), apparently named after one of three possible Queen Annes.

GAIRDNER'S YAMPAH • *Perideridia gairdneri*

GENERAL: Slender, hairless perennial from **tuberous-thickened root**; stems leafy, solitary, 40–120 cm tall.

LEAVES: Several, well distributed along stem, once or sometimes twice pinnately divided into **long, narrow segments**; leaf stalks not much inflated and sheathing basally.

FLOWERS: White or pinkish, small; several to many in small compact heads united in 1 to several compound umbels; involucral bracts lacking.

FRUITS: Nearly spherical, 2–3 mm long and wide, slightly flattened, hairless, **prominently ribbed**.

ECOLOGY: Dry to vernally moist open forest, meadows and mossy or grassy slopes; low to middle elevations; scattered but locally common.

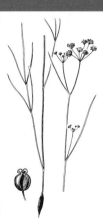

NOTES: This plant and many of its relatives were known as 'wild carrot,' and its roots were eaten by the Straits Salish and other groups within its range, as they were by the interior peoples from south-central B.C. to the Great Basin. • The root, known as 'yampah,' was pounded by native people to make a flour, and Lewis and Clark described it as having a flavour 'not unlike annis seed.' The plant is also called 'wild caroway' because it both smells and looks somewhat like the caroway plant (*Carum carvi*). • The genus was named *Perideridia* by Heinrich Reichenbach of Dresden, but we do not know what it means. It is suggested that it may have derived from the Greek *peri* meaning 'around' and *derris* meaning 'leather coat,' in reference to the tough-coated root. • *Gairdneri* acknowldges Meredith Gairdner (1809–1837), surgeon to the Hudson's Bay Company and collector of plants in the American northwest.

INDIAN CONSUMPTION PLANT • *Lomatium nudicaule*
BARE-STEM DESERT-PARSLEY

GENERAL: Hairless, strongly **blue-glaucous** perennial from a **stout taproot**; flowering stems 20–90 cm tall at maturity, solitary or several.

LEAVES: Mostly basal, large, firm, 1–3 times divided; leaflets 3–30, **oblong to egg-shaped**, veiny, often stalked, **entire or coarsely toothed**.

FLOWERS: Yellow, small; several to many in well-separated compact heads on stalks of unequal length; involucral bracts absent.

FRUITS: Oblong to elliptic, 7–15 mm long, flattened, with **broad wings and distinct ribs**.

ECOLOGY: Dry, open or sparsely treed sites; **low to middle elevations**; scattered, locally common.

NOTES: Martindale's or few-fruited lomatium (*L. martindalei*) also has relatively large, blue-green leaflets, but they are **strongly toothed or cleft**; it has **yellow to yellowish-white** flowers and a **taproot often with a deep-seated thickening**. *L. martindalei* occurs on rocky slopes, outcrops, scree, and in dry meadows, at **middle to alpine elevations**; it is scattered but locally common from southwestern B.C. and the Olympic Mountains south to southern Oregon, in both the Coast and Cascade ranges. • The young leaves of Indian consumption plant, which taste like celery, were eaten raw or cooked as a potherb by the Interior Salish peoples of British Columbia and Washington, and some indigenous peoples of Oregon. They were, and still are in some places, a popular springtime vegetable. They are rich in vitamin C. The seeds were used for flavouring stews, soups, teas and tobacco. Because of its powerful medicinal qualities, this plant is still valued by the Coast Salish, Ditidaht and Kwakwaka'wakw. The plant was widely used during the last century for the treatment of 'consumption' (tuberculosis). The Saanich, Songish and Cowichan chewed the seeds for colds, sore throats, and tuberculosis.

SPRING-GOLD • *Lomatium utriculatum*
FINE-LEAVED DESERT-PARSLEY

GENERAL: Hairless or short-hairy perennial from a long, fairly **slender taproot**; stems leafy, 10–60 cm tall.

LEAVES: Some basal, but **most from the stem**, soft, **lacy, much dissected** into small, very narrow segments; leaf stalks **abruptly inflated and sheathing** at the base.

FLOWERS: Bright-yellow, small; several to many in up to 15 compact heads aggregated in a compound umbel; no involucral bracts at the base of the compound umbel, but each umbellet has well-developed, **egg-shaped**, toothed bracts.

FRUITS: Oblong to elliptic, 5–11 mm long, somewhat granular-roughened when young, usually hairless at maturity, flattened, **broadly winged and with prominent ribs**.

ECOLOGY: Dry, open, rocky slopes, grassy bluffs and vernal meadows at low elevations; locally common.

NOTES: Fern-leaved desert-parsley (*Lomatium dissectum*) occurs in similar habitats and over a similar range in our region, although it does extend up to middle elevations in the mountains. It also has finely dissected, fern-like leaves, but its flowers are **yellow or purple**, and the bracts of its umbellets are **very narrow**. • Spring-gold taproots may have been one of the 'wild carrots' eaten by the peoples of southern Vancouver Island. Related species, often called 'biscuit-roots,' comprise a major portion of the root vegetables used by interior plateau peoples of British Columbia, Washington, Idaho and Montana. • *Lomatium* comes from the Latin *loma* meaning a `border' and refers to the winged or ribbed fruits. 'Spring gold' describes the splashes of yellow flowers that appear in the early spring.

Pyrolaceae (Wintergreen Family)

The wintergreen family consists of herbaceous or woody-based perennials with simple, alternate, opposite or whorled leaves that are either evergreen or much reduced and lacking chlorophyll. The flowers are radially or slightly bilaterally symmetric, and have 4–5 more or less distinct sepals, 4–5 more or less distinct petals (united in *Pterospora*), 8 or 10 stamens with anthers that open by pores or slits and a single superior ovary. The fruit is a 4–5 chambered capsule that produces numerous tiny, dust-like seeds.

The wintergreen family is often included as part of the larger heather family (Ericaceae), but it can be distinguished by the usually separate (not fused) petals. Taxonomy places the unusual, fleshy, chlorophyll-lacking, white to brownish or reddish species such as Indian-pipe (*Monotropa uniflora*) and candystick (*Allotropa virgata*) in the Pyrolaceae, but we have described these and related species in a gallery of unusual plants (see 'Oddballs,' pp. 350–355).

Key to Pyrolaceae

1a. Stems leafy; leaves elliptic to lance-shaped 2
    2a. Flowers 1–3; stem reddish, to 15 cm tall; leaves alternate,
    bluish-green, toothed along their length .... *Chimaphila menziesii*
    2a. Flowers 3–15; stem greenish, to 35 mm tall; leaves whorled,
    bright green, toothed above the middle .... *Chimaphila umbellata*
1b. Stems largely leafless (leaves in a basal whorl); leaves oval to round 3
    3a. Flowers single, waxy-white .... *Moneses uniflora*
    3b. Flowers numerous in clusters, colour variable 4
        4a. Flowers all on 1 side of the flowering stem .... *Orthilia secunda*
        4b. Flowers arranged around the flowering stem 5
            5a. Leaves mottled on the upper surface; flowers yellowish
            or greenish-white; southern B.C. south .... *Pyrola picta*
            5b. Leaves uniformly green on the upper surface; flowers
            pinkish to purplish-red; throughout the region .... *Pyrola asarifolia*

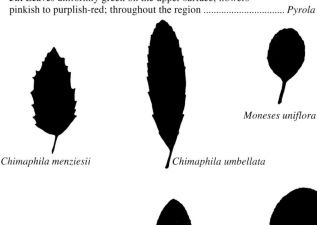

Chimaphila menziesii

Chimaphila umbellata

Moneses uniflora

Orthilia secunda

Pyrola picta

Pyrola asarifolia

SINGLE DELIGHT • *Moneses uniflora*
WAX-FLOWER

GENERAL: Delicate evergreen perennial, from very slender creeping rhizome; flowering stem 3–17 cm tall.

LEAVES: Mainly basal, but sometimes opposite or in whorls of 3, **oval-elliptic,** thin, veiny, **toothed,** 1–3 cm long.

FLOWERS: White, waxy, fragrant, 1.5–2.5 cm across; petals 5, spreading; 10 stamens; large prominent style and stigma; **solitary, nodding** atop a long leafless stalk with 1 or 2 bracts about midlength.

FRUITS: Spherical, erect capsules that split lengthwise into 5 parts when dry; seeds tiny, numerous.

ECOLOGY: Open to dense, usually moist coniferous forests with moss ground cover, in humus or on rotting wood; common at low to middle elevations.

NOTES: This species is also known as one-flowered wintergreen and as *Pyrola uniflora.* • When lacking flowers, single delight could be confused with one-sided wintergreen (p. 225), whose leaves are less veined and usually larger. • The Kwakwaka'wakw use this plant as a poultice on swellings and pains, causing blisters on the skin. These were opened with broken mussel shells and smeared with fish oil. When the loose skin peeled off, the sore was washed with an extract of gooseberry roots and covered with plantain leaves until it healed. • The Haida gathered and dried these plants in July. The flowering or fruiting stems were removed, and the vegetative parts of the plant were brewed as a tea drunk for many different ailments, including colds and flu, smallpox and cancer, and for 'power' and good luck. The tea was sometimes taken with oolichan grease. For coughs, the lichen *Lobaria oregana* and licorice-fern (p. 489) rhizomes were mixed with the tea. Single delight was also boiled with Labrador tea (p. 66). The Makah made a tea from the entire plant for coughs. • The delicate, waxy-white, fragrant, solitary flowers justly deserve the name 'single delight.' *Moneses* derives from the Greek *monos* ('one') and *hesia* ('delight').

PINK WINTERGREEN • *Pyrola asarifolia*

GENERAL: Evergreen perennial with long, branched rhizome; flowering stem **to 40 cm tall,** with a few papery bracts.

LEAVES: Numerous in **basal rosette, circular to elliptic or heart-shaped, leathery, shiny, smooth-margined to slightly toothed,** dark green on top, purplish beneath; leaf stalks as long as blades, **2–8 cm.**

FLOWERS: Pinkish to purplish-red, bell- or cup-shaped; style long, **curved and bent downwards;** 8–25 in a long, loose cluster.

FRUITS: Spherical capsules, 5 chambered.

ECOLOGY: Moist, usually wooded, sites, in both coniferous and deciduous stands, including cottonwood-spruce floodplain forests; also in thickets, meadows, and heath; common from low elevations to near timberline through most of our region.

NOTES: This is the largest and most handsome wintergreen in our forests. • **Arctic wintergreen** (*Pyrola grandiflora*) is quite similar but has **white** flowers and, in our region, **occurs only in Prince William Sound. Green wintergreen** (*P. chlorantha*, also called *P. virens*) has similarly shaped but **yellowish to greenish-white** flowers, and smaller, oval to elliptic leaves (blades 0.7–3.5 cm long) pale green above, deeper green beneath. **Lesser wintergreen** (*P. minor*) also has small, oval to elliptic leaves, but its **pale-pink to creamy-white** flowers have short, **straight** styles. Both green and lesser wintergreen grow in mossy, usually coniferous forest, from low to middle elevations; they are common the length of our region but mostly along its eastern or inland margin, and they are absent from the Queen Charlotte Islands. • Pink wintergreen is known as 'bear's ears' or 'frog's plant' in various coastal languages; it was sometimes used as a poultice for sores and swellings.

WHITE-VEINED WINTERGREEN • *Pyrola picta*

GENERAL: Evergreen perennial from slender rhizomes; non-flowering shoots with several leaves; flowering stem usually single with a few papery bracts, reddish-brown, 10–30 cm tall.

LEAVES: Several in a **basal rosette**, plants sometimes leafless with several narrow bracts at base of stem; **egg-shaped to rounded-elliptic**, leathery, **deep-green but upper surface pale-mottled** along the main veins, 2–7 cm long; margins thickened, smooth to irregularly toothed.

FLOWERS: Yellowish or greenish-white, sometimes tinged with purple, bowl-shaped, 6–8 mm long and about 1 cm across; style longer than stamens, **strongly curved** downwards; 10–25 on short, spreading stalks in a narrow cluster.

FRUITS: Spherical capsules, 5-chambered, opening from the base upwards.

ECOLOGY: Common in dry to moist, coniferous forests; low to middle elevations.

NOTES: The **leafless, possibly saprophytic** forms of this species and other Pyrolas have often been classified as *P. aphylla* (**leafless wintergreen**), which is not a true species. **Nootka wintergreen** (*P. dentata*) is similar but has **narrower, lance-shaped, pale or bluish-green** leaves that **lack the whitened veins**. It is scattered in dry, coniferous forests at low to middle elevations from southeastern Vancouver Island and the adjacent mainland south to California. **White wintergreen** (*P. elliptica*) has **broadly elliptic, unmottled** leaves and **white or creamy** flowers. It is an uncommon species of dry to moist coniferous forests in southwestern B.C. • The leaves of **white-veined wintergreen** are **broader and tougher** than the similarly mottled leaves of rattlesnake-plantain (p. 120). • *Pyrola* comes from the Latin *pyrus* ('pear'), because *Pyrola* leaves are often pear-shaped; *picta* means 'brightly marked, painted' and refers to the white 'veins' on the leaves.

ONE-SIDED WINTERGREEN • *Orthilia secunda*

GENERAL: Evergreen perennial from slender, much-branched rhizome; stems single, leafy and often woody towards base, with several bracts above, 5–20 cm tall.

LEAVES: Mostly basal but some along lower part of stem, several to numerous, oval-elliptic, **toothed**, clear-green above, paler beneath.

FLOWERS: Pale-green to white, bell-shaped, 5–6 mm across, nodding; style **straight**, projecting beyond flower; 4–20 in elongated narrow cluster with **flowers all directed to 1 side**.

FRUITS: Spherical, erect, 5-chambered capsules.

ECOLOGY: Dry to moist, usually mossy, coniferous forests; low to subalpine elevations; common throughout our region, except rare on the Queen Charlotte Islands.

NOTES: One-sided wintergreen is also known as *Pyrola secunda*. • The leaves of wintergreens contain acids that are effective in the treatment of skin eruptions, and mashed leaves of several *Pyrola* species traditionally have been used by herbalists as skin salves or poultices for snake and insect bites. • The species name *secunda* refers to the one-sided ('second') arrangement of flowers and fruit in this species. • The common name 'wintergreen' appears originally to have been applied to ivy, because it stayed green through the winter. The name has subsequently been applied to *Pyrola*s because they are evergreen. 'Oil of wintergreen' is obtained not from *Pyrola*s but from an eastern North American plant, *Gaultheria procumbens* (false wintergreen), which is related to salal and alpine-wintergreen (p. 53).

PRINCE'S-PINE • *Chimaphila umbellata*
PIPSISSEWA

GENERAL: Stout, slightly woody, dwarf evergreen shrub, with creeping rhizome; stems up **to 35 cm tall**, simple or branched, greenish, without hairs.

LEAVES: Whorled, evergreen, 3–7 cm long, **bright-green and shiny** above; **narrowly oblong, sharply toothed mostly above the middle**.

FLOWERS: Whitish-pink to rose, waxy, 5–7 mm long, saucer-shaped, faintly perfumed, nodding; **several (3–15)** in a small, loose cluster.

FRUITS: Roundish, erect capsules, 5–7 mm across.

ECOLOGY: Well-drained sites in open or dense coniferous forests, clearings; in humus and on rotting wood at low to middle elevations; not on the outer coast.

NOTES: In Alaska and north-coastal B.C., this is a rare coastal species that is more common in the interior; it is sometimes found in the understorey along major mainland rivers with linkages to the interior. • The leaves of prince's-pine were put in a bath by the Saanich as a linament for sore muscles, especially by canoe-pullers and sprinters. They are also used to brew a tea for colds and influenza by the Stl'atl'imx and other peoples. • Prince's-pine has shown hypoglycemic (blood-sugar-lowering) and anti-diuretic (urine-reducing) properties in experiments. • *Chimaphila* comes from Greek *cheima* ('winter') and *philos* ('loving') and refers to this plant's evergreen habit. 'Prince's-pine' may refer to its appearance—a miniature pine tree fit for a prince?

MENZIES' PIPSISSEWA • *Chimaphila menziesii*

GENERAL: Slender, slightly woody, dwarf evergreen shrub, with creeping rhizome; stems up **to 15 cm tall**, simple or branched, reddish, without hairs.

LEAVES: Alternate, evergreen, 2–5 cm long, **dull bluish-green; lance-shaped to oval, usually sharply toothed along their length**.

FLOWERS: Creamy-white, sometimes pink, waxy, 5–7 mm long, fragrant, saucer-shaped, nodding; ovary plump, green, surrounded by ten reddish stamens; **few (1–3)** in a small, loose cluster; flowering stems with fine hairs.

FRUITS: Roundish, erect capsules, 5 mm broad.

ECOLOGY: Well-drained sites in open or dense coniferous forests, clearings; in humus and on rotting wood at low to middle elevations; not on the outer coast.

NOTES: This species is like a smaller version of *C. umbellata*, and it is best differentiated by its leaves or (if present) its inflorescence. • The common name 'pipsissewa' is an adaptation of the Cree name *pipisisikweu*, meaning 'it-breaks-into-small-pieces,' because the leaves contain a substance that was supposed to dissolve kidney stones. • Menzies' pipsissewa is named after naturalist Dr. Archibald Menzies.

Gentianaceae (Gentian Family)

The Gentianaceae is a small to medium-sized family of worldwide distribution. It consists primarily of herbs with opposite, simple leaves. Its flowers are radially symmetric, usually showy, wheel- or bell-shaped and borne in flat-topped or rounded clusters; they have 4 or 5 fused sepals, 4 or 5 fused and tubular petals, stamens of the same number as the petals and alternate with them, and 1 superior, 1-chambered ovary. The fruit is a 1-chambered capsule, usually with numerous seeds. The family is of little economic importance except for the numerous cultivated ornamentals, most notably gentians (*Gentiana*), centaury (*Centaurium*) and *Exacum*.

Key to Gentian Family (Gentianaceae)

1a. Flowers yellowish to salmon-red;
plants annual .... *Centaurium erythraea* (see *Swertia perennis*)
1b. Flowers white to blue or purple 2
    2a. Stem leaves narrow, lance-shaped; flowers flat or saucer-shaped;
    wetland plants of Alaska, Queen Charlotte Islands and B.C.'s north coast 3
        3a. Leaves to 3 cm long;
        plants annual or biennial .... *Lomatogonium rotatum* (see *Swertia perennis*)
        3b. Leaves 4–15 cm long; plants perennial .... *Swertia perennis*
    2b. Stem leaves broader, egg-shaped; flowers tubular,
    funnel-like or nearly bell-shaped; habitats and ranges various 4
        4a. Flower tubes without pleats between the petals;
        plants annual .... *Gentianella amarella* (see *Gentiana douglasiana*)
        4b. Flower tubes with accordion-like pleats between the petals;
        plants annual or perennial (*Gentiana*) 5
            5a. Plants annual; flowers small (3–10 mm long),
            white with purple markings .... *Gentiana douglasiana*
            5b. Plants perennial; flowers usually larger, some shade of blue 6
                6a. Plants 25–100 cm tall; stem leaves usually >10 pairs;
                plants of wetland habitats at low elevations .... *Gentiana sceptrum*
                6b. Plants to 40 cm tall; stem leaves usually <10 pairs;
                plants of various habitats, usually subalpine to alpine 7
                    7a. Flowers smaller (1–2 cm long), deep glaucous blue,
                    greenish inky blue, or occasionally yellowish to white;
                    northern part of our region .... *Gentiana glauca* (see *G. platypetala*)
                    7b. Flowers larger (2.5–4 cm long), bright to deep blue,
                      streaked or spotted with green 8
                        8a. Sepals divided into 2 parts, the lobes apparent
                        only as teeth on the edge; flowers bright blue;
                        northern half of our region .... *Gentiana platypetala*
                        8b. Sepals forming a tube, with well-developed
                        lobes; flowers deep blue; Cascade
                      and Olympic mountains .... *Gentiana calycosa* (see *G. sceptrum*)

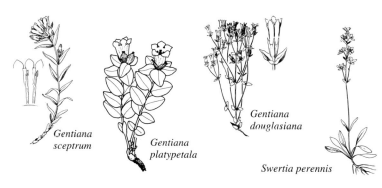

*Gentiana
sceptrum*

*Gentiana
platypetala*

*Gentiana
douglasiana*

Swertia perennis

KING GENTIAN • *Gentiana sceptrum*

GENERAL: Clustered perennial from thick fleshy roots; stems 1 to many, leafy, hairless, 25–100 cm tall.

LEAVES: Opposite, 10–15 pairs; lowest few pairs reduced to short bracts; upper leaves largest, 3–6 cm long, **oblong-lance-shaped, ascending**.

FLOWERS: Blue, often streaked or spotted with green, 3–4.5 cm long, tubular with 5 flaring, oval lobes, folded or pleated (accordion-like) between the lobes, the pleats squared off or rounded at the top; **sepals fused into a short tube with 5 well-developed lobes, usually several** in a cluster atop the stem, with a few others **on short stalks** in upper leaf axils.

FRUITS: Capsules, 1-chambered; seeds numerous, small, spindle-shaped.

ECOLOGY: Bogs, fens, wet meadows, lake margins; low elevations; common in the **southern half** of our region, especially near tidewater; scattered, locally abundant, north to the Skeena River.

NOTES: Mountain bog gentian (*G. calycosa*) grows in wet meadows, swamps and along streambanks, at high elevations in the Cascades and Olympic mountains. It has **solitary, stalkless**, deep-blue flowers, and the pleats between the petal lobes are (unlike those of *G. sceptrum*) **frilly** at the top. • The European *G. lutea* was supposedly named after an Illyrian king called Gentius who discovered its medicinal properties. The root was a source of 'medicinal bitters' (tonic) and a flavouring for liqueurs. The rich, blue flowers atop the stem supposedly look like a sceptre (*sceptrum*)—hence it is the 'king gentian.'

BROAD-PETALLED GENTIAN • *Gentiana platypetala*

GENERAL: Hairless, clustered perennial from a thick rhizome; stems 1 to several, leafy, 10–40 cm tall.

LEAVES: Opposite, lowest few pairs reduced to bracts; upper leaves largest, 1.5–3 cm long, **egg-shaped to elliptic, usually spreading and strongly divergent.**

FLOWERS: Bright-blue, spotted with green inside, **2.5–4 cm long**, funnel-shaped with 5 flaring lobes; **sepals growing together, forming 2 lips, the 5 individual lobes merely teeth** at the margin; **solitary and stalkless** atop stems.

FRUITS: Capsules, 1-chambered, elliptic-oblong; seeds small, numerous.

ECOLOGY: Meadows, grassy slopes, lake-shores, bogs, talus slopes and weathered rock outcrops; usually subalpine to alpine, sometimes descending to low elevations on exposed outer coast; common on the **north coast** (Queen Charlotte Islands north through the Alaskan portion of our region), rare on northern Vancouver Island and B.C. mainland.

NOTES: Inky or glaucous gentian (*G. glauca*) is an alpine species fairly common in the northern part of our region, from northern southeast Alaska to Prince William Sound. This perennial is 4–15 cm tall and has hairless, **yellowish-green** stems, somewhat fleshy **basal leaves in a rosette**, 1–4 pairs of elliptic to oval stem leaves and a **terminal cluster** of erect, tubular, **8–16 mm long**, deep glaucous-blue, greenish inky-blue or rarely yellowish to white flowers. • The species name *platypetala* is Latin for 'broad-petalled.'

SWAMP GENTIAN • *Gentiana douglasiana*

GENERAL: Hairless, **taprooted annual**; stems **often branched**, angled, 5–25 cm tall.

LEAVES: Basal leaves forming a small rosette; stem leaves opposite, few, egg-shaped to elliptic, 3–10 mm long.

FLOWERS: White with purplish spots or streaks, tubular or funnel-shaped, 9–14 mm long; tube yellowish-green, flaring into 5 lobes that have folds between and are white on top, bluish on the bottom; flowers solitary or several in a more or less flat-topped cluster atop stem, plus some in leaf axils.

FRUITS: Capsules, oblong, flattened, wing-margined; seeds small, numerous, dark brown, spindle-shaped.

ECOLOGY: Bogs, fens, wet meadows; low to subalpine elevations; common from Prince William Sound, Alaska, south to Vancouver Island, known also from Lake Ozette and Snoqualmie Pass, Washington.

NOTES: Northern gentian (*G. amarella,* also known as *Gentianella amarella*) is also an annual, but has 5–8 pairs of lance-oblong to narrowly egg-shaped leaves and blue, tubular flowers. The flowers do not have folds between the petal lobes, but the lobes are frilly within at the base. Northern gentian is scattered in moist meadows, and clearings the length of the region. • Swamp gentian is yet another west-coast species named after intrepid explorer and botanist David Douglas.

ALPINE BOG SWERTIA • *Swertia perennis*

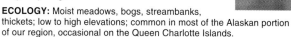

GENERAL: Hairless **perennial from rhizomes**; stems leafy, upright, unbranched, 10–60 cm tall.

LEAVES: Basal leaves egg-shaped to oblong-elliptic, long stalked, 4–25 cm long; stem leaves in a few pairs, reduced in size upwards, short stalked to stalkless.

FLOWERS: Dark bluish-purple to whitish, often flecked with green or white, 10–16 mm long, **circular and flat**, with 5 pointed petals; solitary to several on stalks in leaf axils and in clusters atop stem.

FRUITS: Capsules, 1-chambered, narrowly egg-shaped, flattened; seeds dark, flattened or angular, irregularly winged.

ECOLOGY: Moist meadows, bogs, streambanks, thickets; low to high elevations; common in most of the Alaskan portion of our region, occasional on the Queen Charlotte Islands.

NOTES: Marsh felwort (*Lomatogonium rotatum*) is an **annual** 5–50 cm tall, with **basal leaves soon withering**, several pairs of narrow stem leaves, and 1 to several, **blue to whitish, often spotted or striped** flowers similar in size and shape to those of *Swertia*. Marsh felwort also grows in wet meadows, marshes, and bogs and on shores at middle to high elevations, mostly in northern southeast Alaska, but also at Prince William Sound and at one locality near Ketchikan. • In the southern part of our region (the Strait of Georgia area south), in moist meadows, grassland and clearings at low elevations, watch for another **small annual, common or European centaury** (*Centaurium erythraea,* also known as *C. umbellatum*). It is an introduced species, with several basal leaves, several pairs of egg- to lance-shaped stem leaves, and **yellowish to salmon-red, phlox-like** flowers that are numerous and crowded in terminal clusters. • *Swertia* is named for Emanuel Sweert, a Dutch gardener and author who lived in the 16th century.

Hydrophyllaceae (Waterleaf Family)

The Hydrophyllaceae is a family of annual or perennial herbs, often rough-hairy, bristly or glandular. The leaves are alternate or opposite, often in basal rosettes, and entire or pinnately divided. The inflorescence is typically coiled. The radially symmetric flowers have 5 partially fused sepals, 5 petals fused into funnel-, bell-, or bowl-shapes with overlapping lobes, 5 stamens alternate with the petals and a single superior ovary. The fruit is a 1-chambered capsule with several to many seeds, which sometimes are pitted, spiny or sculptured. The family is related to the Polemoniaceae, but it is distinguished by the coiled inflorescences and overlapping petals.

The Hydrophyllaceae is a small but widely distributed family, occurring on all continents except Australia, and it is particularly abundant in western North America. *Phacelia* is the largest genus.

The family has little economic importance but some species of *Phacelia* and *Nemophila* (baby blue-eyes) are grown as garden ornamentals.

*Hydrophyllum
fendleri*

*Phacelia
hastata*

SITKA MISTMAIDEN • *Romanzoffia sitchensis*
SITKA ROMANZOFFIA

GENERAL: Short (5–30 cm tall), **tufted** perennial herb of wet, rocky places, from **short, woody rhizomes**; stems slender, lax.

LEAVES: Mostly basal; blades **round to kidney-shaped**, to 4 cm across, **shallowly lobed**; stalks to 15 cm long, their bases swollen and overlapping.

FLOWERS: White with a golden 'eye,' bell-shaped, **to 1 cm across**; several in long, loose terminal clusters.

FRUITS: Oblong 2-chambered capsules; seeds numerous.

ECOLOGY: Moist to wet cliffs, talus slopes, gravel bars; at middle to high elevations over most of its range but descending to sea level in the north and to low elevations in the Columbia gorge.

NOTES: Tracy's mistmaiden (*R. tracyi*, also known as *R. unalaschensis*, **inset photo**) grows on **ocean bluffs** (often in sea-spray) from southern Vancouver Island and the adjacent mainland south. It is smaller (to 10 cm tall) than Sitka mistmaiden, and it grows from conspicuous, **brownish-woolly tubers**. • **Small-flowered nemophila** (*Nemophila parviflora*) is a hairy **annual** member of the waterleaf family with **alternate, 5-lobed leaves** and small (**1–3 mm wide**) **solitary, lavender** flowers **from the leaf axils**. It is a species of shady (usually forested) sites at low to middle elevations, from southern B.C. south. It is also called 'grove-lover'; *Nemophila* is from the greek *nemos* ('grove') and *philos* ('lover'). • *Romanzoffia* species **look much like saxifrages**, but the 5 petals of *Romanzoffia* are **fused at the base into a tube** and the fruit is a **capsule**; *Saxifraga* species have distinct petals and a fruit of 2 follicles. • 'Mistmaiden' is an appropriate name for both *R. sitchensis* and *R. tracyi*, but especially for Tracy's mistmaiden, since the pretty, white, pristine flowers are often shrouded in mist from the ocean spray. • The genus is named after Nikolai Rumiantzev, Count Romanzoff (1754–1826), a Russian patron of botany and sponsor of Kotzebue's expedition to the Pacific northwest coast. • Samuel Mills Tracy (1847–1920), who lends his name to *R. tracyi*, was with the United States Department of Agriculture.

FENDLER'S WATERLEAF • *Hydrophyllum fendleri*

GENERAL: Perennial herb from a short, thick rhizome and fleshy, fibrous roots; stems solitary, leafy, hairy, 20–80 cm tall.

LEAVES: Alternate, large; blade to 25 cm long and 15 cm wide, deeply divided into an odd number (**7–15**) of sharp-pointed, sharply toothed segments.

FLOWERS: White to purplish, bell-shaped, to 8 mm across, the 5 stamens sticking out; sepals **long-hairy**; numerous, terminal in compact clusters on stalks from upper leaf axils.

FRUITS: Capsules, 1-chambered, opening by 2 valves; 1–3 seeds.

ECOLOGY: Generally moist, open areas and thickets, at **middle to subalpine** elevations.

NOTES: Fendler's waterleaf has **leaf blades that are longer than wide, with 7–15 segments; Pacific waterleaf** (below) has **leaf blades about as long as wide, with usually 5 segments.** • 'Waterleaf' is a translation of the genus name *Hydrophyllum*, from the Latin *hydro* ('water') and *phyllos* ('leaf'). It is not clear why this name was given to the genus, although some species have leaves splotched as if with water-marks, some have very juicy, watery leaves and some prefer wet habitats.

PACIFIC WATERLEAF • *Hydrophyllum tenuipes*

GENERAL: Perennial herb from a rhizome and fleshy, fibrous roots; stems solitary, leafy, usually hairy, to 80 cm tall.

LEAVES: Alternate, large (to 15 cm long and wide), hairy, divided into **usually 5** (up to 9), pointed and coarsely toothed segments.

FLOWERS: Greenish-white to lavender (occasionally blue or purple), bell-shaped, 5–7 mm long, the stamens and pistil sticking out; sepals **bristly on margins**; numerous, terminal in compact clusters on stalks from upper leaf axils.

FRUITS: Capsules, 1-chambered, opening by 2 valves; 1–3 seeds.

ECOLOGY: Moist, open forests at **low to middle** elevations.

NOTES: Pacific waterleaf is a true shade-lover that is at its best on moist, rich bottomlands. The whole plant has a soft, fuzzy appearance. The roots of Pacific waterleaf were eaten by the Cowlitz of western Washington, according to Erna Gunther (1973). The roots of a related species, ballhead waterleaf (*H. capitatum*), were eaten by the plateau peoples of the Interior. • Hitchcock et al. (1959) report that plants at the 'mouth of the Columbia; Port Angeles; [and] Hoh River' have blue or purple flowers.

SILVERLEAF PHACELIA • *Phacelia hastata*

GENERAL: Perennial herb **to 50 cm tall or more**, from a taproot and branched, woody stem-base; stems several, ascending to upright.

LEAVES: Alternate, **broadly lance-shaped** (some with a small pair of basal lobes); blades to 12 cm long, **strongly veined, usually silvery-hairy.**

FLOWERS: White to purple, bell-shaped, to 7 mm across; stamens sticking out and giving the terminal flowering cluster a 'fuzzy' appearance.

FRUITS: Capsules, 2-chambered; 2 to several seeds per chamber.

ECOLOGY: Dry, open, often sandy places (meadows, rocky slopes, forest openings) at low to subalpine elevations.

NOTES: Narrow-sepalled phacelia (*P. leptosepala*, sometimes called *P. hastata* var. *leptosepala*) is similar in most respects, but it tends to be a lower (less than 50 cm tall), **often creeping plant**, and **often lacks the distinctive silvery leaves** of silverleaf phacelia. *P. leptosepala* occupies the same habitats as *P. hastata*, but at **higher** (usually middle to subalpine) elevations. The common name 'narrow-sepalled phacelia' is derived from the scientific name (*leptosepala* means 'narrow-sepalled'). • *P. hastata* is called 'silverleaf' because of the fine silvery hairs on the leaves. The species name *hastata* suggests the leaves are shaped like arrow-heads (which they can be, if equipped with basal lobes).

SILKY PHACELIA • *Phacelia sericea*
SKY-PILOT

GENERAL: Perennial, **silky-hairy** herb to **30 cm tall**, from a taproot and branched, woody stem-base; stems several, ascending to erect.

LEAVES: Alternate, **divided like a feather** with the divisions sometimes divided again, becoming simpler (less divided, shorter leaf stalks) higher up the stem.

FLOWERS: Dark-blue to purple, bell-shaped, to 6 mm long, hairy; numerous, terminal in a bottle-brush-like cluster to 15 cm long, the long **yellow or orange stamens** stick out making it appear 'fuzzy.'

FRUITS: Pointed, 2-chambered capsules with 8–18 pitted seeds.

ECOLOGY: Dry, often rocky, open places (and forest openings) at middle to alpine elevations.

NOTES: The dense, silky hairs on the leaves provide a wonderful contrast for the deep-purple flowers with their bright-yellow to orange, protruding stamens.

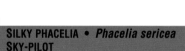

Polemoniaceae (Phlox Family)

The Polemoniaceae is a mostly North American, small family of annual to perennial plants (mostly herbs), with usually alternate, entire leaves, or palmately or pinnately divided leaves. The flowers of plants in this family are often showy, phlox-like or wheel-shaped and radially symmetric, with sepals fused into a 5-lobed tube, petals fused into usually a well-developed tube spreading into 5 lobes, 5 stamens arising from the corolla tube at various and unequal heights, and a superior ovary. The fruit is a 3-chambered capsule with few to many seeds that sometimes have a mucilaginous coat (*Collomia, Gilia, Linanthus, Microsteris, Polemonium*). The family seems to be most closely related to the Convolvulaceae (morning glory family). The economic importance of Polemoniaceae centres on a few garden ornamentals: species of *Phlox*, Jacob's-ladder (*Polemonium*), cup-and-saucer-vine (*Cobaea*) and *Linanthus*.

Showy flowers of this family are good places to observe pollinators, such as bees, butterflies, hoverflies and hummingbirds.

Key to Phlox Family (Polemoniaceae)

1a. Leaves opposite, sometimes alternate at the top 2

    2a. Leaves palmately lobed (the lobes spreading from a common
    point like the fingers on a hand); annuals .... *Linanthus bicolor*

    2b. Leaves not lobed 3

        3a. Leaves alternate at the top; annuals .... *Microsteris gracilis*

        3b. Leaves opposite throughout; perennials .... *Phlox diffusa*

1b. Leaves alternate, sometimes opposite at the bottom 4

    4a. Perennial, glandular-hairy plants; ill-smelling when bruised;
    leaves compound (divided into leaflets) 5

        5a. Leaves with numerous, crowded, deeply lobed leaflets;
        flowers 15–30 mm long .... *Polemonium viscosum*

        5b. Leaves with 11–25 opposite leaflets;
        flowers 7–13 mm long .... *Polemonium pulcherrimum*

    4b. Annual plants; may or may not be ill-smelling when bruised;
    leaves simple (not divided into leaflets), but often deeply lobed 6

        6a. Leaves spiny; plant skunky-smelling .... *Navarretia squarrosa*

        6b. Leaves not spiny; plants not skunky-smelling 7

            7a. Plants slimy-hairy, at least on upper portions;
            flowers pink or lavender, 1–2 cm long .... *Collomia heterophylla*

            7b. Plants not slimy-hairy; flowers light blue, to 1 cm long .... *Gilia capitata*

Phlox diffusa

BICOLORED FLAXFLOWER • *Linanthus bicolor*

GENERAL: Slender, **taprooted annual**; stems leafy, sometimes branched at the base, finely hairy, to 15 cm tall.

LEAVES: Opposite, stalkless, firm, **palmately cleft** into several narrow, **whiskery segments**, so that the pair of divided leaves **looks like a whorl** of 6–14 linear leaves; leaves of inflorescence longer and more whiskery than those below.

FLOWERS: Pink to purplish or white, with a long (to 3 cm), slender tube abruptly flaring in a **yellow throat** from which the 5 pinkish, 2–4 mm long flower lobes spread; flowers **stalkless** in a **leafy cluster** atop the stem.

FRUITS: Capsules, 3-chambered; **several** seeds per chamber.

ECOLOGY: Scattered in open, dry to vernally moist sites at low elevations.

NOTES: Harkness' flaxflower (*L. harknessii*) has stems branched above, and **stalked, white (not bicoloured)** flowers in an open, branching cluster. It grows on dry slopes, outcrops and meadows, and in forest openings, from low to middle elevations, and it is common in the Cascades from Kittitas County, Washington, south to California. • In order to really appreciate this plant's yellow, tube-like flowers tipped with pink, it is necessary to lie flat on your belly and use a hand lens. • Seeds of some *Linanthus* species become mucilaginous when moistened. • *Linanthus* means 'flaxflower,' so-called because of the similarity of these flowers to the flowers of flax (*Linum*).

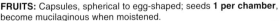

PINK MICROSTERIS • *Microsteris gracilis*

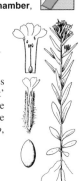

GENERAL: Taprooted annuals; stems erect, leafy, simple or branched, 3–30 cm tall.

LEAVES: Alternate above, opposite below, linear to lance-elliptic, 1–5 cm long, hairy to glandular (at least the upper leaves).

FLOWERS: Pink to violet lobes spreading from a 5–15 mm long, **whitish tube**; sepals united in a glandular-hairy tube consisting of 5 slender **green segments separated by wax-papery areas, ruptured** by the maturing capsule; flowers mostly in pairs near ends of stem and branches, or sometimes single.

FRUITS: Capsules, spherical to egg-shaped; seeds **1 per chamber**, become mucilaginous when moistened.

ECOLOGY: Dry to moist slopes, clearings, rock outcrops, gravelly roadsides, meadows at low to middle elevations; common in the southern half of our region, infrequent further north.

NOTES: Pink microsteris is a native species that behaves like a weed on disturbed soils. • This is another 'belly plant' whose beauty is often overlooked because of its diminutive size. Take the time to 'stoop and smell the flowers.' • The genus name is from the Latin *mikros*, 'small' and *sterizo*, 'to support.'

VARI-LEAVED COLLOMIA • *Collomia heterophylla*

GENERAL: Taprooted annual, slimy-hairy at least on upper portions; stems simple or more commonly branched (often several stems from the base), leafy, 5–40 cm tall.

LEAVES: Alternate, mostly **deeply pinnately lobed and coarsely toothed**; blades to 3.5 cm long, with long, spreading hairs; upper leaves smaller, less cleft.

FLOWERS: Pink or lavender, with 5 short **(3–4 mm) lobes** spreading from a tube 8–17 mm long; 5 sepals united in a short tube of **uniform, papery texture, not ruptured** by developing capsule; flowers several in dense clusters atop stem, cradled by entire or merely toothed upper leaves.

FRUITS: Capsules, ellipsoidal, 3-chambered; seeds **2–3 per chamber,** become mucilaginous when moistened.

ECOLOGY: Common in dry to moist forest openings, meadows, streambanks, gravelly roadsides and cutbanks, at low elevations.

NOTES: Narrow-leaved collomia (*C. linearis*, **inset photo**) has numerous, **narrow, entire** leaves and **pink or bluish to white** flowers 8–15 mm long, with **lobes 1.5–3 mm long**. It is common from low to middle elevations from southwestern B.C. south, and sporadic northwards, on dry to moist, open, sometimes disturbed sites. **Large-flowered collomia** (*C. grandiflora*) is similar to *C. linearis* but tends to be a **larger** plant with broader leaves, and it has **salmon or yellowish** flowers **20–30 mm long**. It grows in dry, open or lightly forested areas at low to middle elevations, from southwestern B.C. south. **Alpine collomia** (*C. debilis*) is a **dwarf, sprawling perennial** with **blue, lavender or pink to white** flowers. It grows at **high elevations** on rocky slopes and talus, in the Washington-Oregon Cascades and the Olympic Mountains. • Vari-leaved collomia is a native species, but it is somewhat weedy in disturbed soils. • *Collomia* is from the Greek *kolla* for 'glue,' since the seeds have a coat that turns very sticky when wet.

SKUNKWEED • *Navarretia squarrosa*

GENERAL: Taprooted, prickly, glandular-hairy, skunky-smelling annual; stems erect, leafy, simple or branched, to 40 cm tall.

LEAVES: Alternate, firm and **spiny, pinnately lobed,** to 6 cm long.

FLOWERS: Pale to deep-blue; sepals half-united in a short tube with **wax-papery intervals** between the 5 sharp-pointed lobes 8–14 mm long; petals 5, fused into a 9–12 mm long tube spreading into 2–3 mm long lobes; **stamens included within** the floral tube; numerous in dense, relatively large (to 3 cm wide) heads with leafy bracts.

FRUITS: Capsules, oblong-elliptic, 3-chambered; seeds **6–9 per chamber,** become mucilaginous when moistened.

ECOLOGY: Scattered, locally common in dry to moist meadows and grassy open sites at low elevations.

NOTES: Needle-leaved navarretia (*N. intertexta*) has **lightly hairy (not glandular)** stems, **white to pale-blue** flowers, **stamens that stick out** from the floral tube and 2-chambered capsules. It is scattered in our region over much the same range as skunkweed, in moist meadows and on open slopes and the edges of vernal pools, from low to middle elevations. • *Navarettia* is named for Father Ferdinand Navarette, a Spanish physician. One wonders if he would have appreciated his name associated with a plant that smells so skunky.

GLOBE GILIA • *Gilia capitata*
BLUEFIELD GILIA

GENERAL: Taprooted annual; stems upright, leafy, slender, simple or branching from the upper nodes, hairless to glandular-hairy, 15–100 cm tall (line drawing below; **photograph is *G. aggregata***).

LEAVES: Basal and alternate on the stem, reduced in size upwards, 2–10 cm long, once or twice pinnately lobed with very narrow segments.

FLOWERS: Light-blue, small (6–10 mm long); stalkless and numerous in dense, bractless, **ball-shaped heads** at tips of stems and branches.

FRUITS: Capsules, more or less spherical, 3-chambered; seeds 1–3 per chamber, become mucilaginous when wet.

ECOLOGY: Fairly common in dry to moist open meadows, rock outcrops, rocky slopes, clearings, and roadsides, at low to middle elevations; escaped from cultivation and established in a few places in southeast Alaska.

NOTES: Scarlet gilia or skyrocket (*Ipomopsis aggregata*, also known as *G. aggregata*, **photo above**) is a biennial or short-lived perennial with a long, showy cluster of **bright-red (to orange or yellowish)** flowers. It occurs occasionally in our region in dry, rocky, open sites at fairly high elevations from southern Washington south. It is very common east of the Cascades. The scarlet, trumpet-shaped flowers are very attractive to hummingbirds and humans. • *Gilia* is named for the 16th-century Spanish botanist, Felipe Luis Gil. The common names come from the globe-shaped clusters of pale-blue flowers.

SPREADING PHLOX • *Phlox diffusa*

GENERAL: Taprooted, mat-forming perennial, 5–10 cm tall; when in flower, foliage often nearly hidden by lavish blooms.

LEAVES: Opposite, linear, entire, fused at the base in pairs, green and hairless except for hairy lower edges, 5–20 mm long.

FLOWERS: Showy, **pink to lavender or whitish**; 5 sepals fused into whitened, long-hairy tube with sharp lobes; petals fused into tube 9–17 mm long, spreading flat into 5–9 mm long lobes; **solitary and stalkless** at ends of stems and branches.

FRUITS: Capsules, 3-chambered; seeds usually 1 per chamber, **not mucilaginous** when moistened.

ECOLOGY: Open, rocky slopes, scree, talus, rock outcrops, and open forest; middle to high elevations; common from southwestern B.C. south to California.

NOTES: *Phlox* is the Greek word for 'flame' and was given to this group of plants for their bright flowers. The species name *diffusa* means 'spreading.'

SHOWY JACOB'S-LADDER • *Polemonium pulcherrimum*

GENERAL: Taprooted perennial, with **several** erect to ascending or sprawling stems from branched, thickened stem-bases, 5–35 cm tall, glandular or glandular-hairy (at least in the inflorescence), ill smelling when bruised.

LEAVES: Mostly basal, often tufted, **pinnately compound (ladder-like); leaflets 11–25**, opposite or offset, egg-shaped to circular, **often glandular-hairy**, at least when young.

FLOWERS: Blue (occasionally white) with yellow centres, showy, **bell-shaped, 7–13 mm long** and as wide; petals rounded at tip; in crowded clusters.

FRUITS: Capsules, 3-chambered; seeds several per chamber, become mucilaginous when moistened.

ECOLOGY: Fairly dry, rocky or sandy, open sites; also in open forest; lowlands to high elevations, at progressively higher altitudes further south; common the length of our region, but mostly absent from the outer coast and rare on the Queen Charlotte Islands.

NOTES: Northern Jacob's-ladder (*P. boreale*) has **larger (15–20 mm long)** flowers, and occurs in alpine tundra and scree in the **northern-most part** of our region (Prince William Sound to northern southeast Alaska). **Tall Jacob's-ladder** (*P. caeruleum*, also called *P. acutiflorum*) is 30–100 cm tall, with **solitary** stems, **19–27 hairless leaflets** per leaf, and **pale-blue to purplish**, usually pointy-tipped petals. It is also a northern species (Prince William Sound to northern southeast Alaska) of moist meadows, streambanks, thickets and tundra, from middle to high elevations. • If you look closely at the beautiful flowers of showy Jacob's-ladder, you can see a bright-orange ring at their base.

SKUNKY JACOB'S-LADDER • *Polemonium viscosum*

GENERAL: Low, often dwarfed perennial from stout taproot and branched crown, 10–40 cm tall, **densely glandular-hairy and very skunky smelling.**

LEAVES: Mostly basal, to 20 cm long, with **numerous, crowded leaflets that are divided into 2–5 deep lobes** and so **appear whorled.**

FLOWERS: Blue, funnel-shaped, 15–30 mm long, longer than wide; several to many in **dense, head-like clusters.**

FRUITS: Capsules, 3-chambered; seeds several per chamber, become mucilaginous when moistened.

ECOLOGY: Dry, rocky, open sites at **high elevations**; scattered in the Coast Mountains of southern B.C.

NOTES: Elegant Jacob's-ladder (*P. elegans*) has **undivided leaflets in 13–27 crowded pairs** and flowers **12–15 mm long**; in other respects it is very similar to skunky Jacob's-ladder, including its sticky hairs and skunky smell. It occurs on alpine cliffs, scree and rocky ridges in the Cascades from southernmost B.C. south, seemingly replacing skunky Jacob's-ladder in the Washington Cascades. **Great Jacob's-ladder** (*P. carneum*) grows in **wetter habitats** (streambanks, moist thickets, forest edges and meadows) from **low to middle elevations** in the Washington-Oregon Cascades and in western Washington. It has large flowers borne **singly or in small clusters** on stems 30–100 cm tall. Flower colour is variable: **light tan, salmon, yellow, lavender or bluish white**. • Jacob's-ladders have sweet-smelling flowers, but in several species the fragrance can be overwhelmed by the skunky smell of the rest of the plant. Researchers have suggested that the foul smell serves to repel nectar-feeding ants, which can rob the nectaries without pollinating the flowers.

Boraginaceae (Borage Family)

The borages are a fairly large, widely distributed family, all representatives of which are herbs in our region. Typically they are rough or stiff-hairy (sometimes hairless) with simple, usually alternate, usually smooth-margined leaves and stems that are round, not square, in cross section. The flowers are usually in tight, one-sided, fiddlehead-like clusters that uncoil as the flowers open. Flowers usually have radial symmetry; 5 distinct or basally fused sepals; petals fused into a tube that flares into 5 lobes; 5 stamens, alternate with the petal lobes; and a superior ovary, deeply cut with the style attached at the base. The fruit is usually made up of 4 sculptured or hairy nutlets (sometimes smooth and shiny). The flower tube is sometimes closed in by appendages or scales on the insides of the petals.

The family has a little economic importance, mostly in cultivated ornamentals such as blue-bells (*Mertensia*), forget-me-nots (*Myosotis*), heliotrope (*Heliotropium*), borage (*Borago*), hound's-tongue (*Cynoglossum*), lungwort (*Pulmonaria*), and viper's bugloss (*Echium*). Some species, such as comfrey (*Symphytum*), have medicinal value.

Key to Borage Family (Boraginaceae)

1a. Flowers blue to pink, in open to dense clusters; plants perennial 2
  2a. Stems ascending to upright; flowers 9–19 mm long,
  sepals hairy; fairly widespread in meadows, thickets,
  stream-banks and open forest .... *Mertensia paniculata*
  2b. Stems sprawling; flowers 4–12 mm long, sepals smooth; sandy/gravelly
  beaches and river-banks in northern parts of our region .... *Mertensia maritima*
1b. Flowers white, yellow or blue, in coiled clusters; plants annual 3
  3a. Flowers blue; nutlets round, smooth, and shiny .... *Myosotis laxa*
  3b. Flowers white or yellow; nutlets egg-shaped and warty,
  bumpy or bristly (occasionally smooth) 4
    4a. Lower leaves opposite, upper leaves alternate;
    flowers white; plants to 20 cm tall or long .... *Plagiobothrys scouleri*
    4b. All leaves alternate; flowers yellow or white
    with a yellow centre; plants to 50 cm tall or more 5
      5a. Flowers yellow; nutlets wrinkled and warty .... *Amsinckia menziesii*
      5b. Flowers white with a yellow centre;
      nutlets minutely bumpy or smooth .... *Cryptantha intermedia* var. *grandiflora*

Cryptantha intermedia
var. *grandiflora*

Plagiobothrys
Scouleri

Amsinckia menziesii

Myosotis laxa

Mertensia
paniculata

Mertensia
maritima

LARGE-FLOWERED CRYPTANTHA • *Cryptantha intermedia var. grandiflora*

GENERAL: Taprooted, stiffly hairy annual; stems leafy, simple or branched, 5–50 cm tall.

LEAVES: Alternate, narrowly oblong to linear-lance-shaped.

FLOWERS: White with a yellow eye in the centre; sepals 5, spreading-hairy; petals fused basally into a short tube that spreads into 5 lobes each 2–4 mm long; numerous in coiled spikes that straighten and lengthen with maturity.

FRUITS: Nutlets, 1–4 clustered together, egg-shaped, minutely bumpy or smooth.

ECOLOGY: Dry, open slopes at low elevations; fairly common in the Washington-Oregon portion of our region; rare in southwestern B.C.

NOTES: Common cryptantha (*Cryptantha affinis*) has small flowers 1–2 mm wide and compressed nutlets, and it is scattered in dry to moist, mostly open sites from southwestern B.C. south, at low to middle elevations. **Torrey's cryptantha** (*C. torreyana*) ranges from southeastern Vancouver Island south to California, with an isolated occurrence near Haines, Alaska. It also occurs in dry to moist, open sites at low to middle elevations. It has very small flowers (about 1 mm wide) and nutlets that are not compressed. Both of these annual species are somewhat weedy, and they are much more common east of our region. • Several species of this genus have flowers that never open and appear hidden, which is the meaning of *Cryptantha*. The flowers in large-flowered cryptantha look like miniature, white forget-me-nots. • John Torrey (1796–1873) was an American botanist and the author of 5 major floras.

SCOULER'S POPCORNFLOWER • *Plagiobothrys scouleri*

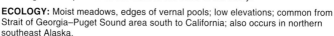

GENERAL: Stiffly hairy annual with taproot or fibrous roots; stems leafy, single and upright to several and sprawling, to 20 cm tall or long.

LEAVES: Lower 1–4 pairs opposite, the upper alternate, linear, to 6 cm long.

FLOWERS: White, small (1–4 mm wide); 5 sepals; petals fused basally into a short tube that spreads into 5 lobes; several in long, coiled, loosely flowered spikes.

FRUITS: Nutlets, usually 4, clustered together, egg-shaped, bumpy and sometimes also bristly, with a lateral scar or groove at point of attachment to the base of the ovary.

ECOLOGY: Moist meadows, edges of vernal pools; low elevations; common from Strait of Georgia–Puget Sound area south to California; also occurs in northern southeast Alaska.

NOTES: Fragrant popcornflower (*Plagiobothrys figuratus*) is somewhat similar but has **large (5–10 mm wide), fragrant** flowers that are **white with a yellow eye**. It occurs sporadically from southeastern Vancouver Island and the Gulf Islands south to southwestern Oregon (especially in the Puget Trough and Willamette valley), in low-elevation meadows and moist clearings and fields. **Slender popcornflower** (*P. tenellus*) has a **basal rosette** of leaves, and stem leaves that are **all alternate**. It occurs infrequently in dry, open sites at low elevations, from the Strait of Georgia area south to California, mostly east of the Cascades. • *Plagiobothrys* comes from the Greek *plagios* for 'placed sideways' and *bothros* for 'pit,' and it refers to the groove on the nutlet (fruit). John Scouler was a Scottish botanist (1804–71) who collected extensively in western North America.

SMALL-FLOWERED FIDDLENECK • *Amsinckia menziesii*

GENERAL: Taprooted, bristly-hairy annual; stems leafy, simple to branched, 15–80 cm tall.

LEAVES: Alternate, linear to oblong or lance-shaped, 2–12 cm long.

FLOWERS: Yellow, small (**1–3 mm wide**); sepals 5, stiff-hairy; petals fused basally into tube 4–7 mm long that spreads into 5 lobes; several to many in coiled spikes.

FRUITS: Nutlets, 4 clustered together, egg-shaped, **wrinkled and warty.**

ECOLOGY: Dry to moist fields, clearings and disturbed sites; low to middle elevations; common in the Washington-Oregon portion of our region, also occurs in northern southeast Alaska.

NOTES: Seaside fiddleneck (*Amsinckia spectabilis*) occurs near or along the seashore and is scattered from the Queen Charlotte Islands south to California. It has **finely toothed leaves** and flowers that are **2.5–5 mm wide**. **Bugloss fiddleneck** (*A. lycopsoides*) has **orange-yellow flowers with hairy throats**. It is a weedy species of dry, disturbed sites from southeast Alaska to California and is scattered mostly along the eastern boundary of our region. • The flowers of *A. menziesii* are arranged like the scroll-neck of a fiddle and unfurl (just as a 'fiddlehead' fern does) with the youngest flowers at the very tip. • The genus was named for Wilhelm Amsinck, a patron of Hamburg Botanical Garden in the 19th century, and the species was named for Archibald Menzies, a northwestern explorer.

SMALL-FLOWERED FORGET-ME-NOT • *Myosotis laxa*

GENERAL: Fibrous-rooted, lightly hairy, short-lived perennial or annual; stems leafy, slender and weak, often curved or bent at the base, 10–40 cm tall.

LEAVES: Alternate, lance-shaped to oblong, 2–8 cm long.

FLOWERS: Blue, small (**2–5 mm wide**), stalked; sepals 5, tightly hairy; petals fused basally into short tube spreading to 5 lobes; several to many in loose, coiled racemes.

FRUITS: Nutlets, 4 clustered together, brown to blackish, **smooth and shining.**

ECOLOGY: Common in moist, open areas, sometimes in shallow water, swamps, wet ditches, margins of pools; at low elevations.

NOTES: We have several other forget-me-not species in our region, all of which were introduced from Europe. **Marsh forget-me-not** (*Myosotis scorpioides*, also called *M. palustris*) is similar to small-flowered forget-me-not, but has **creeping stem-bases and stolons**, and **bigger flowers (5–10 mm wide)**. It occurs in moist to wet sites, from low to middle elevations, and it is common from southwestern B.C. south; it is sporadic northwards (including the Queen Charlotte Islands and northern southeast Alaska). **Wood forget-me-not** (*M. sylvatica* var. *sylvatica*) also has flowers 4–10 mm wide (usually blue but occasionally white or pink), **lax but not creeping** stems and **sepals with spreading hairs, some of which are hooked**. It is the **cultivated ornamental** plant, which has escaped and is found frequently at low elevations from southwestern B.C. south. **Common forget-me-not** (*M. discolor*) has **small (1–2 mm wide)** flowers that are **at first yellow**, and that **change to blue** with age. It grows in moist meadows and along roadsides at low elevations and is scattered from the Strait of Georgia–Puget Sound area south. • One source says the name 'forget-me-not' dates back to 1561, recognizing that a blue flower traditionally was worn to retain a lover's affection. Another source says the name was originally applied to ground pine (*Ajuga chamaepitys*) because of the nauseating taste it left in one's mouth. • A 'forget-me-not' was said to be a good plant to give travellers who started their journey on February 29th. Steel tempered with the juice of forget-me-not was said to be hard enough to cut stone. Forget-me-not was used to treat dog or snake bites.

TALL BLUEBELLS • *Mertensia paniculata*

GENERAL: Perennial from a branched stem-base or stout rhizomes; stems **few to several, leafy**, ascending or upright, 20–150 cm tall.

LEAVES: Basal leaves **long stalked and egg-to heart-shaped, distinctly veined**; stem leaves alternate, numerous, short stalked to stalkless, lance- to egg-shaped, hairy above and beneath or hairless on lower surface, 3–15 cm long.

FLOWERS: Blue (sometimes pink), bell-shaped, 9–19 mm long; sepals 5, **hairy**; petals fused at base into a tube flaring into 5 lobes; few to many in compact to open clusters atop stems.

FRUITS: Nutlets, 4 clustered together, **wrinkled**.

ECOLOGY: Fairly common in moist to wet meadows, thickets, streambanks, open forest; **at all elevations**.

NOTES: Broad-leaved bluebells (*M. platyphylla*) is very similar to tall bluebells but has **mostly single** stems and **longer (3.5–5 mm vs. 2–3.5 mm) anthers**. It occurs on stream-banks and in moist thickets and forest at lower elevations, from the western base of the Cascades to the coast, from the southern Puget Sound area south through the Willamette valley. **Bluebuttons or hound's-tongue** (*Cynoglossum grande*) has similar leaves, but they are **confined to the lower half or third** of the stem; its blue or violet flowers are more like forget-me-nots than bell-shaped, and its nutlets are **prickly at the top**. It grows in open forests at lower elevations from the Puget Trough through the Columbia gorge and Willamette valley. • 'Hound's-tongue' is from the Old English *hundes tunge*. *Cynoglossum* is from the Greek *cynos* for 'dog' and *glossa* for 'tongue.' The name was given originally to *Cynoglossum officinale* because the shape and rough texture of the leaves are like those of a dog's tongue. In the old days, it was used to treat skin diseases and dog-bite. A piece placed in the shoe was believed to protect you from being barked at by strange dogs.

OYSTERLEAF • *Mertensia maritima*
SEA BLUEBELLS

GENERAL: Fleshy, hairless and glaucous perennial from a branched, often underground, stem-base and taproot; stems leafy, several to many, sprawling, 10–100 cm long.

LEAVES: Alternate, fleshy, **broadly lance-to egg-shaped or elliptic**, 1–12 cm long, hairless or upper surface dotted with blister-like growths.

FLOWERS: Blue or rarely white, or pink in bud, bell-shaped, 4–12 mm long; sepals 5, **hairless**; petals united in a short, basal tube flaring into 5 lobes; several to many in compact to open, somewhat rounded clusters.

FRUITS: Nutlets, 4 clustered together, somewhat flattened, smooth or slightly wrinkled.

ECOLOGY: Sandy and gravelly beaches, spits, bars and, less commonly, riverbanks; scattered **along the coastline**.

NOTES: This is a handsome, widespread, seashore species with a circumpolar range, most common on Arctic shores. • The genus *Mertensia* is named for F.C. Mertens (1764–1831), a German botanist.

Lamiaceae (Mint Family)

Lamiaceae is a large, cosmopolitan family mostly of annual or perennial herbs. Mints characteristically have square stems in cross-section, opposite leaves and aromatic oils. The inflorescence usually appears to be whorled and often spike-like or head-like at the top of the stem, although *Scutellaria* has solitary flowers in leaf axils. The flowers are normally strongly bilaterally symmetric (except in *Mentha*) with 5 fused sepals and 5 petals that are usually fused into a 5-lobed, 2-lipped tube. Stamens are 2 or 4; the ovary is superior and 4-lobed and the single style arises from the navel of the lobed ovary. The fruit typically consists of 4 nutlets.

The mint family shares its distinctive 4-lobed ovary and 'gynobasic' style with the borage family, but borages have round stems, generally alternate leaves and usually radially symmetric flowers.

This family is also known as the Labiatae. The mint family is an important source of volatile, aromatic oils and garden ornamentals. Aromatic oil producers include sage (*Salvia*), lavender (*Lavendula*), rosemary (*Rosmarinus*) and mint (*Mentha* spp.). Other important culinary herbs prized for flavour or aroma include pot marjoram (*Origanum*), hyssop (*Hyssopus*), basil (*Ocimum*), thyme (*Thymus*) and savory (*Satureja*). Hoarhound (*Marrubium*) is used in medicine and confectionery. The principal garden ornamentals in this genus include: salvia (*Salvia*), bugloss (*Ajuga*), dragonhead (*Dracocephalum*), bee-balm (*Monarda*) and skullcap (*Scutellaria*), as well as species of *Coleus, Nepeta, Stachys, Teucrium, Thymus* and *Lavendula*.

Key to Genera of the Mint Family (Lamiaceae)

1a. Sepals fused into 2 small lips, the upper lip with a raised, hood-like appendage .... *Scutellaria*
1b. Sepals arranged in various ways, but without an appendage on top 2
  2a. Petals fused into a 4-lobed tube; flowers less than 1 cm long 3
    3a. 4 flower lobes arranged regularly (equally) around flower; flowers pink to light purple (sometimes white), 4–7 mm long; plants pleasantly scented .... *Mentha*
    3b. 4 flower lobes arranged in two lips, the upper lip undivided, the lower lip with 3 lobes; flowers white, 2–4 mm long; plants without an obvious scent .... *Lycopus*
  2b. Petals fused into a 2-lipped tube; flowers usually more than 1 cm long 4
    4a. Flower clusters terminal (atop the stem) 5
      5a. Sepals fused into 2 quite different lips; flowers usually dark purplish; leaf margins smooth or vaguely toothed .... *Prunella*
      5b. Sepals fused into a regular tube with 5 sharp lobes; flowers white to pinkish, or deep red-purple; leaf margins regularly toothed .... *Stachys*
    4b. Flower clusters in leaf axils 6
      6a. Middle lobe of lower lip of petals constricted at base; leaves heart-shaped, 1–2.5 cm long; flowers pink-purple, 12–18 mm long ... *Lamium*
      6b. Middle lobe of lower lip of petals not constricted at base 7
        7a. Taprooted annuals, standing upright; leaves egg- or lance-shaped, 3–10 cm long; flowers pink-purple, 15–23 mm long .... *Galeopsis*
        7b. Creeping perennials from stolons or rhizomes, rooting at the nodes 8
          8a. Flowers white or purple-tinged, 7–10 mm long; native, aromatic plants usually in open, dry forests .... *Satureja*
          8b. Flowers bluish-purple, 12–24 mm long; introduced, non-scented plants often on moist or disturbed sites ..... *Glecoma*

Lamium amplexicaule

Stachys cooleyae

NORTHERN WATER HOREHOUND • *Lycopus uniflorus*
BUGLEWEED

GENERAL: Perennial from **tubers** with long, slender rhizomes and stolons; stems erect, single, quadrangular, leafy, usually unbranched, finely hairy, 10–50 cm tall.

LEAVES: Opposite, lance-shaped to elliptic, short-stalked, 2–8 cm long, not much reduced in size up the stem; margins coarsely and irregularly toothed.

FLOWERS: White or pinkish, small (2–4 mm long), stalkless, 2-lipped; lower lip 3 lobed and hairy within; stamens 2; ovary 4 lobed; several to many in whorled clusters in leaf axils.

FRUITS: 4 hard, **ridged,** 1-seeded nutlets.

ECOLOGY: Marshes, streambanks, lakeshores, wet thickets, bogs; common at low to middle elevations in the southern half of our region, less common northwards.

NOTES: This species is widely distributed in North America and also occurs in Siberia and Japan. • The fleshy, white, tuberous roots of bugleweed were formerly eaten by some interior plateau peoples, but apparently not by peoples on the Northwest Coast. • The common name 'bugleweed' comes from another plant, bugloss (*L. arvensis*), whose name in turn is derived from the Greek *bous* ('ox') and *glossa* ('tongue'), since its leaves are rough and shaped like ox tongues. *L. uniflorus* is called 'water horehound' for its likeness to the true horehound (*Marrubium vulgare*), another mint. The word 'horehound' may come from the Latin *urinaria*, since the plant was used to treat urinary diseases.

MARSH SKULLCAP • *Scutellaria galericulata*

GENERAL: Perennial with slender rhizomes; stems erect, quadrangular, single or a few together, leafy, simple or branched, hairy (especially along the angles) to less often hairless or glandular, 20–90 cm tall.

LEAVES: Opposite, lance-shaped to oblong-egg-shaped, very short-stalked, hairless above, short-hairy below, 2–5 cm long; margins blunt-toothed.

FLOWERS: Blue or pink-purple, streaked with white, **medium-sized (1.5–2 cm long); sepals fused into 2 small lips,** the upper lip with a raised appendage; petals fused into a 2-lipped tube, the upper lip hooded; stamens 4; 4-lobed ovary; flowers stalkless and **solitary in the axils** of slightly reduced upper leaves.

FRUITS: 4 yellowish, **warty** nutlets.

ECOLOGY: Wet meadows, marshes, streambanks, lakeshores, wet roadside ditches; common at low to middle elevations.

NOTES: Blue skullcap (*S. lateriflora,* **inset photo**) has **several to many** flowers in **elongate clusters** from the leaf axils and at the top of the stem. It occurs in moist bottomlands, meadows and grassy clearings from southwestern B.C. south, at low to middle elevations. Marsh skullcap has a broad circumboreal distribution, over much of North America, Europe and Siberia. • The shape of the fused sepals resembles a helmet (*galericulata* means 'helmet-shaped') or 'skullcap.' The genus name is from *scutella* ('tray'), and refers to the appendage on the upper side of the calyx.

FIELD MINT • *Mentha arvensis*

GENERAL: Aromatic **perennial from creeping rhizomes**; stems leafy, ascending to upright, simple or branched, quadrangular, hairy, 15–80 cm tall.

LEAVES: Opposite, **lance-shaped to oval**, 1–8 cm long, short-stalked, usually gland-dotted; margins **saw-toothed**.

FLOWERS: White to pale-purple or pink, 4–7 mm long; sepals fused into a glandular-hairy, 5-lobed tube; petals fused into a short 4-lobed tube; stamens 4, sticking out from flowers; 4-lobed ovary; numerous in **whorled clusters in leaf axils**.

FRUITS: 4 nutlets.

ECOLOGY: Streambanks, wet meadows and clearings, springs, seepage areas, lakeshores, beaver wetlands; common at low to middle elevations.

NOTES: Field mint is an extremely variable, widely distributed, circumboreal species. • This aromatic plant is widely used as a tea and flavouring. To make mint tea, simply place a small handful of the dried leaves in a teapot, pour on boiling water and allow to steep for a few minutes. This tea is said to be especially good for digestion. • The Nuxalk boiled this plant and drank the tea for stomach pains. The Quileute used it as a 'smelling and rubbing' medicine. The Chehalis and the Upper Cowlitz used the leaves to brew a tea as a cold remedy. • 'Mint' comes from the Latin *mentha* (or *menta*) and the Greek *minthe*. Minthe was a nymph who was turned into a mint plant by Proserpina in a fit of jealousy.

COMMON DEAD-NETTLE • *Lamium amplexicaule*
HENBIT DEAD-NETTLE

GENERAL: Taprooted annual, generally branched from the base; stems several, leafy, quadrangular, weak, ascending from **bent bases**, 10–40 cm tall.

LEAVES: Opposite, **heart-shaped, coarsely blunt-toothed**, 1–2.5 cm long, lightly hairy; lower leaves stalked, **upper leaves stalkless** and clasping at the base.

FLOWERS: Lavender-purple, 12–18 mm long, stalkless; sepals united in a hairy, 5-lobed tube; petals fused into a long tube with 2 lips, the upper lip hooded and hairy outside, the lower lip 2 lobed; 4 stamens; 4-lobed ovary; flowers several in a few, **well-spaced clusters in leaf axils**.

FRUITS: 4 nutlets, 3-angled, squared off at tip.

ECOLOGY: Fields, grassy clearings, waste areas; common at low to middle elevations in the southern half of our region, rare northward.

NOTES: Purple dead-nettle (*Lamium purpureum*) has **heart-shaped to deltoid** leaves that **all have stalks** and are **shallowly toothed**. The upper leaves are **reddish-purple** and partially conceal the flowers, which are smaller and paler than those of common dead-nettle. These 2 annual dead-nettles have similar ranges and habitat preferences; both are weedy introductions from Eurasia. • Words similar to 'nettle' appear in many languages and all derive from the Indo-European verb *ne* meaning 'to spin or sew,' reflecting the widespread use of the nettle (*Urtica*) as a source of thread. These nettle-like plants are 'dead' in the sense that they don't sting when touched. The name 'henbit' comes from the fact that hens like to nibble at its leaves. *Lamium* is from the Greek *laimos* ('throat'), because of the constricted throat of the petal tube.

YERBA BUENA • *Satureja douglasii*

GENERAL: Aromatic, inconspicuously hairy **perennial** herb from a woody rhizome; **stems prostrate** and often rooting, to 1 m long, often with short, ascending branches.

LEAVES: Opposite, bright-green, **egg-shaped to nearly round**, rounded at tip, short-stalked, 1–3.5 cm long; margins irregularly blunt-toothed.

FLOWERS: White or purple-tinged, 7–10 mm long; sepals fused into a hairy, ribbed, 5-lobed tube; petals united into a hairy tube surmounted by 2 short lips, the lower lip 3 lobed; 4 stamens; 4-lobed ovary; flowers **solitary** on slender stalks from the leaf **axils**.

FRUITS: 4 nutlets.

ECOLOGY: Open, well-drained, coniferous forest, rocky thickets, often associated with Garry oak and arbutus, at low to middle elevations; common in the southern half of the region, and a rare introduction in southeast Alaska.

NOTES: Yerba buena emits a strong but pleasing fragrance when crushed between the fingers. • This plant has a history linked with the Pacific coast. In the early contact period the Spanish priests of California recognized its virtues and gave the plant its name, meaning 'good plant' in Spanish. The Hudson Bay voyageurs and trappers learned from indigenous peoples of its use for making a delightful beverage. San Francisco was called Yerba Buena until 1847, when it received its present name. • Leaves of yerba buena were used in medicinal (and non-medicinal) teas by many northwest coast groups. The Halq'emeylem of Kuper Island mixed the leaves of this plant with *Lomatium nudicaule* to make a tea for colds. The Saanich made a tea from the leaves which was thought to be good for the blood. When hunting for deer, yerba-buena leaves were crushed and rubbed on the body to disguise the human odour. • *Satureja* means 'culinary herb,' reflecting its wide use in cooking.

GROUND-IVY • *Glecoma hederacea*
CREEPING CHARLIE

GENERAL: Perennial from stolons; stems trailing and rooting at the nodes, branches upright, leafy, square in cross-section, hairy at least at the nodes, 10–40 cm long.

LEAVES: Opposite, **heart- to kidney-shaped**, hairy or hairless, stalked, coarsely blunt-toothed, 1–3 cm long.

FLOWERS: Bluish-purple, sometimes with darker blotches, 12–24 mm long; sepals fused into a hairy tube with 5 spine-tipped lobes; petals united in a trumpet-shaped tube flaring into 2 lips, the upper lip 2 lobed, the lower 3 lobed; 4 stamens; 4-lobed ovary; flowers **few** on short stalks in loose clusters from upper leaf **axils**.

FRUITS: 4 nutlets, brown, finely pebbled.

ECOLOGY: Moist, shady clearings, waste places, thickets, open forest, also often in lawns, at low elevations; common in the southern half of our region, rare northwards.

NOTES: Ground-ivy is a native of Eurasia which was introduced as a garden ornamental, but has escaped and become widely established in North America. Other common names for this species are gill-over-the-ground and field balm. • The name 'ivy' has, by a series of mistakes, the same origin as 'yew' (see *Taxus brevifolia*, p. 40) and came from the Latin *abija*, corrupted to *ajuga* and then to *iua* or *iva*. The identity of the 'Charlie' in 'creeping Charlie' is a mystery; 'creeping' and 'ground-ivy' both refer to the running stolons that spread along the ground.

SELF-HEAL • *Prunella vulgaris*
HEAL-ALL

GENERAL: Fibrous-rooted **perennial** from a short rhizome or stem-base; stems solitary or clustered, erect to spreading or even reclining, leafy, square in cross-section, usually unbranched, 10–50 cm long or tall.

LEAVES: Opposite, relatively few, lance-egg-shaped to oblong or elliptic, minutely hairy to hairless, stalked; margins **smooth or obscurely toothed**.

FLOWERS: Purplish to pink (occasionally white), 1–2 cm long, **short-stalked**; sepals united in a 2-lipped, spine-tipped tube; petals fused into a 2-lipped tube, upper lip hooded and bonnet-like, lower lip 3 lobed **(the middle lobe fringed)**; 4 stamens; 4-lobed ovary; numerous in dense, **spike-like cluster atop** the stem.

FRUITS: 4 nutlets.

ECOLOGY: Moist roadsides, clearings, fields, lawns, forest edges; common at low to middle elevations.

NOTES: Self-heal apparently consists of native plants (ssp. *lanceolata*) and introduced plants from Eurasia (ssp. *vulgaris*). The species now occurs on all continents. • The Nuxalk boiled the entire plant and drank a weak tea for the heart. The Quinault and Quileute put the juice on boils. The leaves were placed on cuts, bruises and skin inflammations, and the plants were also crushed and mixed with grease as an ointment. • The widespread traditional use of this plant for healing purposes gave rise to the common names used today. It is featured in the old French proverb, 'no one wants a surgeon who keeps Prunelle.' *Prunella* is from the German *die Braune* or 'quinsy,' for which this plant was used as a cure. • Older common names such as 'hook-heal' and 'carpenter's herb' refer to the fact that the plant was used to heal wounds inflicted by sharp-edged tools. Also called 'sickle-wort,' because the flowers in profile resemble sickles.

HEMP-NETTLE • *Galeopsis tetrahit*

GENERAL: Taprooted annual; stems simple or branched above, leafy, erect, square in cross-section, stiff-hairy (especially below the joints), often swollen below the joints, 20–80 cm tall.

LEAVES: Opposite, egg- or lance-shaped to elliptic, stalked, **coarsely blunt-toothed**, more or less coarse-hairy, 3–10 cm long.

FLOWERS: Pale-purple, pink or whitish, hairy, 15–23 mm long, **stalkless**; sepals fused into a ribbed tube with 5 spine-tipped lobes; petals fused into a 2-lipped tube, the lower lip 3 lobed and **with a pair of protuberances or nipples** on the upper side near the base; 4 stamens; 4-lobed ovary; numerous in 2–6 **dense clusters in leaf axils**.

FRUITS: 4 egg-shaped, grey-brown nutlets, surface sprinkled with **whitish warts**.

ECOLOGY: Weedy species of fields, waste places, clearings, roadsides and gardens; common at low to middle elevations.

NOTES: Hemp-nettle (which includes *G. bifida*) has been introduced from Eurasia. It appears to have originated as a hybrid between 2 other European species of *Galeopsis*. • The bristly hairs along the stems are strong enough to penetrate the skin when the plant is handled, as are the spiny flower clusters. • The common name was originally 'hemp dead-nettle' because of the resemblance of the flowers to those of dead-nettle (see *Lamium amplexicaule*, p. 244) and the leaves to those of hemp (*Cannabis sativa*). It was apparently known to 16th-century botanists as *Cannabis sylvestris*. *Galeopsis* means 'weasel-like,' but we are not sure why the plant deserves this characterization.

MEXICAN HEDGE-NETTLE • *Stachys mexicana*

GENERAL: Perennial from rhizomes; stems erect, leafy, simple or branched, square in cross-section, spreading-hairy on the angles, 30–100 cm tall.

LEAVES: Opposite, **lance-egg-shaped**, sparsely hairy on both sides, **stalked**, coarsely toothed, 2–12 cm long.

FLOWERS: Pale-pink to pink-purple, hairy, **12–18 mm long**, stalkless; sepals united in a tube with 5 spine-tipped lobes; petals fused into a 2-lipped tube, the lower lip 3-lobed; 4 stamens; 4-lobed ovary; several to many in open **terminal** clusters, **often with additional clusters in leaf axils.**

FRUITS: 4 nutlets.

ECOLOGY: Moist clearings, logged-over areas, thickets, forest edges; scattered, locally common at low elevations, mostly near the coast.

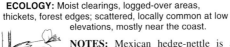

NOTES: Mexican hedge-nettle is also called *S. emersonii* and *S. ciliata*. • **Swamp hedge-nettle** (*S. palustris*) has **mostly stalkless** leaves and **purplish, white-spotted** flowers. It grows in wet meadows and roadside ditches, and on streambanks and lakeshores, and it is scattered at low elevations from southern southeast Alaska to Oregon, mostly in the eastern part of our region. • The odour given off by hedge-nettles when bruised is pungent, fishy and rather unpleasant, not mint-like.

COOLEY'S HEDGE-NETTLE • *Stachys cooleyae*

GENERAL: Perennial from rhizomes; stems erect, leafy, mostly unbranched, square in cross-section, bristly-hairy on the angles, 70–150 cm tall.

LEAVES: Opposite, **deltoid or heart-egg-shaped**, long-hairy on both sides, stalked, coarsely blunt-toothed, 6–15 cm long.

FLOWERS: Deep red-purple, hairy, **23–40 mm long**, stalkless; sepals united in a tube with 5 spine-tipped lobes; petals fused into a 2-lipped tube, the lower lip 3 lobed; 4 stamens; 4-lobed ovary; several to many in open **terminal** clusters.

FRUITS: 4 nutlets.

ECOLOGY: Moist roadsides, clearings, thickets and open woods; common at low elevations.

NOTES: Taxonomists are not unanimous about the distinction between Cooley's and Mexican hedge-nettle. In fact, Calder and Taylor (1968) maintain that they are all *Stachys cooleyae* in our region. • The reddish-purple, deep-throated flowers are attractive to hummingbirds. • The Saanich made a spring tonic by steeping the crushed rhizomes in hot water. The Green River and Puyallup people used this plant for healing boils. The Quileute made a steam bath to cure rheumatism by putting the leaves in an alder tub with hot rocks, sitting on the tub, and covering themselves with an elkskin or bearskin. • The Haida of the Queen Charlotte Islands apparently used to chew the young stems of this plant, sucking out the juice and discarding the fibre. The Quinault sucked the nectar from the purple flowers. Other northwest coast groups did not consider it edible. • This 'nettle,' which often grows along hedgerows, was first described from Nanaimo on July 18, 1891, by Grace Cooley, a professor from New Jersey. *Stachys* means 'a spike' (as in an ear of grain) and refers to the inflorescence.

Scrophulariaceae (Figwort Family)

The figworts are a large family both globally and in our region. *Pedicularis, Penstemon* and *Castilleja* are particularly large genera here. In our region, the family is represented by herbs with alternate or opposite leaves that are simple, entire or lobed.

Some plants in this family are chlorophyll-containing parasites or partial parasites (*Melampyrum, Pedicularis, Castilleja*).

The flowers typically are strongly bilaterally symmetric, with a tube of fused petals, often conspicuous (*Penstemon* or *Digitalis*), 2 lipped (*Collinsia, Linaria*), and 4–5 lobed; *Veronica* and *Verbascum* are weakly bilaterally symmetric, short-tubed exceptions to this rule. Brightly coloured bracts occur in *Castilleja* and *Orthocarpus*. Stamens are commonly 4 (a 5th stamen is represented by a sterile filament in *Penstemon*, or reduced to a scale in *Scrophularia*); *Veronica* has only 2 stamens and *Verbascum* has 5. The ovary is single and superior. The fruit is typically a 2-chambered capsule; seeds are numerous, smooth or variously surfaced and angled or winged.

The family includes the drug plant *Digitalis*, but otherwise is principally economically valued for its garden ornamentals. Notable ornamentals are the snapdragons (*Antirrhinum*), speedwells (*Veronica*), beardtongues (*Penstemon*), monkey-flowers (*Mimulus*), foxgloves (*Digitalis*) and slipperflowers (*Calceolaria*).

Key to Genera of the Figwort Family (Scrophulariaceae)

1a. Stem leaves mainly alternate 2
  2a. Leaves chiefly basal; flowers usually blue,
  bell- or wheel-shaped, not 2 lipped, with 5 distinct sepals .... *Synthyris*
  2b. Leaves not all basal, some stem leaves well developed;
  flowers not as above 3
    3a. Flowers spurred at the base .... *Linaria*
    3b. Flowers without spurs 4
      4a. Stamens 5; flowers yellow, saucer-shaped;
      plants densely hairy all over .... *Verbascum*
      4b. Stamens 4; flowers tubular to bell-shaped 5
        5a. Flowers barely 2 lipped .... *Digitalis*
        5b. Flowers distinctly 2 lipped 6
          6a. Leaves toothed (more than 5 teeth) or strongly dissected,
          often basal as well as on the stem; calyx lobes mostly 5,
          sometimes only 4 or 2 .... *Pedicularis*
          6b. Leaves all on the stem, entire or few toothed or few lobed,
          not strongly dissected; calyx lobes 2–4 7
            7a. Plants perennial; upper flower lip or beak
            much longer than lower lip .... *Castilleja*
            7b. Plants annual; upper flower lip
            about same size as lower lip .... *Orthocarpus*
1b. Stem leaves mainly opposite or whorled 8
  8a. Calyx with 4 lobes 9
    9a. Stamens 2; flowers barely 2 lipped, blue to pink or white .... *Veronica*
    9b. Stamens 4; flowers distinctly 2 lipped, yellow to whitish 10
      10a. Leaves entire; seeds 2–4 .... *Melampyrum*
      10b. Leaves toothed; seeds numerous 11
        11a. Calyx inflated in fruit, flattened; plants not glandular-hairy .... *Rhinanthus*
        11b. Calyx not inflated in fruit, not markedly flattened;
        plants glandular-hairy .... *Parentucellia*
  8b. Calyx with 5 lobes 12
    12a. Filaments (stamen stalks) 5, one of these sterile (not bearing an anther) 13
      13a. Sterile filament a knob or scale; leaves all on stem .... *Scrophularia*
      13b. Sterile filament long; leaves basal and on stem 14
        14a. Seeds winged; filaments not nectar-producing .... *Nothochelone*
        14b. Seeds not winged; filaments of upper stamens
        nectar-producing towards base .... *Penstemon*
    12b. Filaments (stamen stalks) 2 or 4 15
      15a. Flowers yellow or pink-purple .... *Mimulus*
      15b. Flowers blue or blue and white .... *Collinsia*

*Synthyris
reniformis*

*Linaria
vulgaris*

*Verbascum
thapsus*

*Digitalis
purpurea*

*Pedicularis
oederi*

*Castilleja
parviflora*

*Orthocarpus
imbricatus*

*Veronica
beccabunga
ssp. americana*

*Melampyrum
lineare*

*Rhinanthus
minor*

*Parentucellia
viscosa*

*Nothochelone
nemorosa*

*Penstemon
davidsonii*

*Scrophularia
californica*

*Mimulus
alsinoides*

*Collinsia
parviflora*

249

BUTTER-AND-EGGS • *Linaria vulgaris*
COMMON TOADFLAX

GENERAL: Perennial herb from creeping **rhizomes**, erect, often branched above, **ill-smelling**, hairless throughout and somewhat glaucous, **20–80 cm tall**.

LEAVES: Alternate, stalkless, smooth-margined, numerous, **linear to narrowly lance-shaped**, 2–10 cm long.

FLOWERS: Yellow with a central, bearded, **orange patch**; **snapdragon-like** with a **long, straight spur at the base**; in spike-like clusters at first compact, then elongating.

FRUITS: Capsules, broadly cylindric, 2-celled; seeds numerous, flattened, with tiny bumps, winged.

ECOLOGY: Fields, roadsides, gardens, waste places; common at low to middle elevations in settled parts of southern half of our region, scattered further north near towns.

NOTES: Dalmatian toadflax (*L. genistifolia* ssp. *dalmatica*, also called *L. dalmatica*, **inset photo**) also has **yellow** flowers but is a **larger (up to 1 m tall)** plant with **egg-shaped** leaves. It is scattered and locally abundant on roadsides and disturbed sites mostly in drier parts of the southern half of our region. **Blue toadflax** (*L. canadensis*) is a **native annual or biennial** species with **blue** flowers, a **sticky inflorescence** and a basal rosette of short prostrate stems. It is occasional on moist, sandy, open sites from the Strait of Georgia–Puget Sound area south. **Purple toadflax** (*L. purpurea*) is an **introduced, purple-flowered perennial**, occasionally **escaped from gardens**. • Butter-and-eggs is a Eurasian weed now widely established in North America. • The pretty, yellow flowers tinged with reddish-orange are the reason this plant is called butter-and-eggs.

GREAT MULLEIN • *Verbascum thapsus*
COMMON MULLEIN

GENERAL: Coarse, **biennial** herb from **thick taproot**, in the 1st year producing a rosette of basal leaves, in the 2nd year a single erect stem **0.4–2 m tall**; virtually entire plant **thickly covered with branched hairs, woolly to the touch**.

LEAVES: Basal leaves broadly lance-shaped, tapering to a stalked base, entire or obscurely round toothed or crimped, up to 45 cm long; stem leaves alternate, numerous, progressively smaller up the stem, becoming stalkless and clasping the stem.

FLOWERS: Yellow or rarely whitish, concave and **circular in outline**, 1–3 cm wide; petals fused into a short tube with 5 spreading lobes; stamens 5, the upper 3 yellow-hairy, the lower 2 longer and hairless; flowers more or less stalkless in a dense, spike-like inflorescence.

FRUITS: Capsules, egg-shaped; seeds small, numerous.

ECOLOGY: Common on roadsides, fields, dry open waste places; mostly at low elevations.

NOTES: Taylor (1990) notes that 'sore-footed hitchhikers can take advantage of the soft padded, natural insoles (the leaves)' of mullein. • Legend has it that this plant was used by Ulysses, Mercury and Circe in their incantations and witchcraft. • The name 'mullein' is from the word *mol* from the Latin *mollis* meaning 'soft,' in reference to the lovely, softly felted leaves. It is also called 'hedge-taper' and 'torch'; the plants were apparently once dipped in suet and burned as candles or torches. These names have also been explained as referring to the tall inflorescence with its yellow flowers gradually opening from the bottom up, like a slow-burning torch or taper. • Great mullein is a Eurasian weed now widely established in much of temperate North America.

COMMON FOXGLOVE • *Digitalis purpurea*

GENERAL: Big, **usually biennial** herb; **stems leafy**, erect, unbranched, greyish-hairy becoming glandular upwards, **0.5–1.8 m tall**.

LEAVES: Alternate, **egg- to lance-shaped**, coarsely toothed, **green and soft-hairy above, grey-woolly below**, narrowed to a winged stalk, 15–40 cm long, biggest and most numerous at the base, reduced in size upwards.

FLOWERS: Pink-purple with deeper-purple spots inside; petals fused into a **long, gaping tube**, 4–6 cm long; stamens 4; flowers numerous, stalked, **somewhat drooping** in a long, **1-sided** raceme.

FRUITS: Capsules, egg-shaped; numerous, very small seeds.

ECOLOGY: Roadsides, fields, forest edges, mostly at low elevations; common in the southern part of our region, especially near settlements; occasionally also on the Queen Charlotte Islands and in southeast Alaska.

NOTES: This famous medicinal plant was introduced to the Northwest Coast from Europe. It contains cardiac glycosides and is highly poisonous, affecting muscle tissue and circulation. The heart drug digitalis, derived from this plant, is used today by hundreds of thousands of people suffering from heart disease. • A fanciful explanation for the common name is that the finger-like flowers are 'gloves for foxes,' possibly because they grow in disturbed soil favoured by foxes for denning. However, a more likely explanation is that it was originally called *foxes-gliew* or 'foxes music,' which then became *foxes-glofa*. *Gliew* was the Anglo-Saxon word for a ring of bells hung on an arched support (a tintinnabulum), which the rows of bell-like flowers of this plant do resemble. An old tale has it that bad fairies gave the flowers to the fox to wear so that he could steal silently around the chicken coop. • *Digitalis* is from the Latin for 'thimble.'

SPRING QUEEN • *Synthyris reniformis*

GENERAL: Perennial herb from a short rhizome or stem-base; flowering **stems leafless**, up to 15 cm tall.

LEAVES: All basal, on long stalks, **heart- to kidney-shaped, palmately veined**, shallowly lobed (the lobes themselves round-toothed), sparsely hairy, 2–8 cm long and wide.

FLOWERS: Blue-violet, bell-shaped, 5–7 mm long, 4-lobed; 2 stamens; flowers few in short clusters at the ends of stalks that are weak and curved (reclining in fruit).

FRUITS: Capsules, compressed, notched at summit, twice as wide as high, long-hairy on margins; seeds 2 per cell, with thick, incurved margins.

ECOLOGY: Open coniferous forest, glades, forest edges; common at low elevations; flowers very early.

NOTES: Cut-leaf synthyris (*S. pinnatifida*, with deeply lobed basal leaves) and **fringed synthyris** (*S. schizantha*, with heart- to kidney-shaped basal leaves but flower lobes deeply slashed at tips) occur in the Olympic Mountains; *S. schizantha* also occurs in the Cascades near Mount Rainier and in the northern Oregon Coast Range. Both species are quite uncommon. The variety of *S. pinnatifida* in the Olympics is a rare alpine endemic; the species is common in the Rocky Mountains, but it does not occur in the Cascades. • Spring queen is also called 'snow queen' because it sometimes flowers as early as December or January, or 'kittentails,' perhaps because of the ciliate fruits.

Key to Louseworts (*Pedicularis*) and Paintbrushes (*Castilleja*)

1a. Leaves with more than 5 teeth or strongly dissected, often basal as well as along the stem; calyx lobes mostly 5, sometimes only 2 or 4 .... ***Pedicularis***

   2a. Stem leaves whorled .... *P. verticillata* (see *P. oederi*)

   2b. Stem leaves alternate or lacking 3

      3a. Leaves merely toothed; calyx lobes 2 .... ***P. racemosa***

      3b. Leaves pinnately lobed to twice pinnately dissected 4

         4a. Stems branched; calyx 2 cleft and raggedly toothed; plants annuals or biennials ....***P. parviflora***

         4b. Stems unbranched; calyx lobes 5; plants perennials 5

            5a. Stems leafy throughout; basal leaves, if present, not much larger than the stem leaves .... ***P. bracteosa***

            5b. Stem leaves few and reduced; leaves mostly basal 6

               6a. Flower hoods with distinct beaks at least 2 mm long 7

                  7a. Beaks straight, 2–4 mm long .... ***P. ornithorhyncha***

                  7b. Beaks strongly curved, usually more than 4 mm long 8

                     8a. Beaks curved upwards; flowers resembling an elephant's head with the trunk uplifted .... ***P. groenlandica***

                     8b. Beaks curved down .... *P. contorta* (see *P. groenlandica*)

               6b. Flower hoods beakless, or with little points less than 1 mm long 9

                  9a. Flowers yellow; plants slightly hairy .... ***P. oederi***

                  9b. Flowers pink to rose-coloured; plants white-woolly all over .... *P. lanata* (see *P. oederi*)

1b. Leaves all along the stem, entire or few toothed or few lobed, not strongly dissected; calyx lobes 4 .... ***Castilleja***

  2c. Leaves usually entire (sometimes the uppermost somewhat lobed); floral bracts entire or lobed but not deeply divided 3

    3c. Bracts of the 'paintbrush' yellow or yellowish 4

      4c. Upper leaves narrowly lance-shaped, entire, long-pointed at tip; plants of the northern part of our region .... ***C. unalaschcensis***

      4d. Upper leaves oblong to egg-shaped, usually with 1–3 pairs of short lateral lobes; plants of the southern part of our region .... *C. lutescens* (see *C. unalaschcensis*)

    3d. Bracts of the 'paintbrush' usually red to purplish 5

      5c. Stems mostly 10–30 cm tall, usually unbranched; bracts crimson to purplish; flowers 20–30 mm long .... *C. rhexifolia* (see *C. miniata*)

      5d. Stems mostly taller than 30 cm, often branched; bracts reddish (scarlet) or sometimes red-orange to yellowish; flowers mostly 30–40 cm long 6

        6c. Bracts rather narrow and strongly lobed; stems mostly erect; leaves usually lance-shaped or narrower; widely distributed .... ***C. miniata***

        6d. Bracts broader and rounded; stems reclining or bent at base; leaves often egg-shaped; plants of Oregon coast .... *C. litoralis* (see *C. miniata*)

  2d. Upper leaves and bracts deeply cleft into 3–7 linear lobes 7

    7c. Plants with long, stiff hairs .... ***C. hispida***

    7d. Plants without long, stiff hairs 8

      8c. Leaves and bracts mostly 3 parted; midblade usually much wider than lateral lobes; bracts purple, crimson, rose, pink or white .... ***C. parviflora***

      8d. Leaves and bracts mostly 5 parted; midblade not much wider than lateral lobes; bracts scarlet or crimson .... *C. rupicola* (see *C. hispida*)

SICKLETOP LOUSEWORT • *Pedicularis racemosa*

GENERAL: Perennial herb from a woody stem-base; stems leafy, clustered, hairless throughout or sparsely hairy above, 15–50 cm tall.

LEAVES: Lowermost leaves small, the others all along the stem, alternate, short stalked, lance-shaped to narrowly oblong, **undivided but doubly saw-toothed**, up to 10 cm long.

FLOWERS: Mostly pink to purplish in our region, **sometimes whitish**; upper lip strongly arched, tapering into a **sickle-shaped, downwardly curved beak** that reaches the prominent lower lip; inflorescence long, leafy-bracted.

FRUITS: Capsules, hairless, flattened, curved.

ECOLOGY: Open coniferous forest, glades, dry meadows, open rocky slopes; common at middle to subalpine elevations.

NOTES: The common name 'lousewort,' applied to most species of *Pedicularis*, dates back to the 17ᵗʰ century. It was formerly thought that cattle grazing in fields where the European *P. sylvatica* grew in abundance became infested with lice. It is more likely that these pastures were poor and supported weak, unhealthy and lice-ridden stock. • *P. racemosa* is called 'sickletop' because of its sickle-shaped flowers.

BRACTED LOUSEWORT • *Pedicularis bracteosa*
WOOD BETONY

GENERAL: Erect perennials up to 1 m tall, coarsely fibrous-rooted, or some of the roots tuberous-thickened; plant hairless below the inflorescence; stems leafy, unbranched.

LEAVES: Finely divided or fern-like, doubly toothed with short or no stalk, **mostly borne on flowering stems**.

FLOWERS: Yellowish to red or purple; upper lip hooded, beakless or with short beak at tip; numerous in dense, elongate terminal cluster above several hairy, leafy bracts.

FRUITS: Hairless, flattened, curved capsules.

ECOLOGY: Moist, open forest, thickets, meadows, and clearings in the mountains; common, locally abundant at subalpine to alpine elevations (occasionally lower) from southern mainland B.C. (53°N) south to California; rare on Vancouver Island.

NOTES: Thompson women incorporated the leaf pattern in basket designs. • 'Betony' comes from an old Gallic word meaning 'medicinal plant.' Another common name for this species is 'fernleaf.'

SMALL-FLOWERED LOUSEWORT • *Pedicularis parviflora*

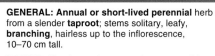

GENERAL: **Annual or short-lived perennial** herb from a slender **taproot**; stems solitary, leafy, **branching**, hairless up to the inflorescence, 10–70 cm tall.

LEAVES: Mostly on the stem, alternate, stalkless, **pinnately lobed**, the lobes with blunt teeth.

FLOWERS: Purple or bicoloured; upper lip **slightly hooded, beakless**, with or without small teeth near the tip; inflorescence fairly long, leafy-bracted, the lower flowers remote and in leaf axils or the flowers clustered at the ends of branches.

FRUITS: Hairless capsules 8–17 mm long, partially enclosed by dry, expanded and partly fused sepals.

ECOLOGY: Wet meadows, bogs, marshes, at low to middle elevations; fairly common in the northern part of our region (from the Queen Charlotte Islands north), scattered southwards.

NOTES: This species includes *Pedicularis macrodonta* and *P. pennellii* ssp. *insularis*. • The species name (*parviflora*) and the common name mean the same thing: 'small-flowered.'

OEDER'S LOUSEWORT • *Pedicularis oederi*

GENERAL: Perennial herb from short, woody stem-base with several **thick, yellowish, spindle-shaped roots**; stems thick, hairy (at least up among the flowers), 5–25 cm tall.

LEAVES: Mostly basal, thick, dark green, stalked, **pinnately lobed** and the lobes sharp-toothed; stem leaves alternate, few and reduced in size.

FLOWERS: Yellow; upper lip hooded, beakless and without teeth at the tip, which is **brownish-red with 2 red spots**; inflorescence **dense, spike-like**, with leaf-like bracts.

FRUITS: Capsules, hairless, lance-shaped to oblong.

ECOLOGY: Tundra, heath, rocky slopes and cliffs at high elevations; fairly common in northern part of our region.

NOTES: Whorled lousewort (*P. verticillata*, **inset photo**) has **whorled stem leaves** in addition to pinnately lobed, sharp-toothed basal leaves and **purplish-red to rose-pink flowers also in whorls**. It is a high-elevation species scattered in the northern part of our region, from the Queen Charlotte Islands north. **Woolly lousewort** (*P. lanata*, also called *P. kanei*) has **pink to purple** flowers in a dense, oblong, **white-woolly spike**. It occurs infrequently in dry, rocky, alpine tundra from the Queen Charlotte Islands north through Alaska. • Oeder's lousewort is named for Georg Christian von Oeder (1728–91), professor of botany, Copenhagen, the first editor of *Flora Danica*.

FIGWORT

BIRD'S-BEAK LOUSEWORT • *Pedicularis ornithorhyncha*

GENERAL: Perennial herb from **fibrous-rooted** stem-base; stems sparingly leafy, unbranched, hairless up to the hairy inflorescence, 8–30 cm tall.

LEAVES: Mostly basal, stalked, **deeply lobed** and the lobes toothed, 3–12 cm long; stem leaves few, smaller, alternate.

FLOWERS: Purple; upper lip **hooded and extended to a straight beak** 2–4 mm long; flowers several to many in a dense, terminal **cluster**.

FRUITS: Capsules, hairless, flattened, curved.

ECOLOGY: Common in subalpine and alpine meadows, heath, streambanks, rocky slopes.

NOTES: Bird's-beak lousewort is an attractive plant, commonly found in heather meadows. It often blooms soon after snowmelt. • Young stems and roots of some species of *Pedicularis* can be eaten raw or boiled until tender, but they should only be eaten in an emergency, because several species are uncommon and often locally rare. • The species name *ornithorhyncha* means 'bird's beak' and, like the common name, refers to the shape of its flowers.

ELEPHANT'S HEAD • *Pedicularis groenlandica*

GENERAL: Perennial; stems unbranched, often clustered, 20–70 cm tall, hairless, sometimes reddish-purple.

LEAVES: Basal leaves **finely divided, fern-like**, the divisions sharply toothed; stem leaves several, progressively smaller towards top of stem.

FLOWERS: Pink-purple to reddish; upper lip **strongly hooded and beaked, resembling the head and trunk of an elephant**; flowers many in a dense, terminal **spike**.

FRUITS: Hairless, flattened, curved capsules.

ECOLOGY: Fens, wet meadows, seepage areas, edges of mountain streams; common at middle to high elevations.

NOTES: **Coil-beaked lousewort** (*P. contorta*) also has a beak curved from the hooded upper lip, but the **beak curves downward in a twisted crescent**. *P. contorta* occurs in fairly dry, open forest and meadows at middle to high elevations, and it is common in the Cascades of Oregon and Washington; it is found at one locality on the south side of the Olympic Mountains. • The common names 'elephant's head' (the flowers do look remarkably like an elephant's head, with the long, curved upper lip resembling the trunk) and 'coil-beak' both describe the appearance of the flowers.

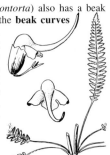

SMALL-FLOWERED PAINTBRUSH • *Castilleja parviflora*

GENERAL: Perennial from a woody base; stems clustered, erect or ascending, usually **not more than 30 cm tall**, unbranched, hairy above; whole plant becoming black when dry.

LEAVES: Alternate, oval to lance-shaped, all except few lowest ones **divided into 3–5 lobes**, somewhat hairy.

FLOWERS: Greenish, tubular, with two lips; upper lip edged with violet-purple; inconspicuous, hidden among **rose-pink to crimson or magenta (sometimes white)**, leafy, lobed and hairy bracts.

FRUITS: 2-celled capsules; seeds numerous.

ECOLOGY: Subalpine and alpine meadows, heath and stream-banks.

NOTES: Note that the 'brush' is not the flowers themselves, but the leafy bracts surrounding the greenish flowers. The showy, leafy bracts resemble a brush dipped in paint, hence the common name. • *Castilleja* species are partially parasitic on the roots of other plants; they are therefore extremely difficult to transplant. • Small-flowered paintbrush is a colourful species of high-elevation meadows, and its colour varies. In some areas (e.g., North Cascades) the brushes are **whitish**. • The genus is named for Don Domingo Castillejo, a Spanish botanist of the 18th century.

UNALASKA PAINTBRUSH • *Castilleja unalaschcensis*

GENERAL: Perennial herb from a short, stout, scaly, branched stem-base; stems several, hairless to hairy (especially upwards), **20–80 cm tall**.

LEAVES: Alternate, rough-hairy to nearly hairless, lance- to egg-shaped, **usually entire**.

FLOWERS: Greenish, tubular, 15–30 cm long, concealed by **yellow to greenish-yellow**, oval bracts that are entire or with 1–2 pairs of very short, blunt lobes; inflorescence hairy, oblong.

FRUITS: 2-celled capsules; seeds numerous.

ECOLOGY: Grassy meadows, beaches, upper parts of tidal marshes, rocky sea bluffs, open forest; common at low to middle and sometimes subalpine elevations.

NOTES: Unalaska paintbrush is also known as *C. pallida* var. *unalaschcensis*. • **Golden paintbrush** (*C. levisecta*, **inset photo**) is a rare species of grassy, low-elevation meadows of southeastern Vancouver Island and western Washington (it used to be more widespread). It has **golden-yellow, sticky-hairy** inflorescences.

COMMON RED PAINTBRUSH • *Castilleja miniata*

GENERAL: Perennial; stems few, erect or ascending from a woody base, **20–80 cm tall**, hairless to short-hairy or somewhat sticky hairy.

LEAVES: Narrow, sharp-pointed, **linear to lance-shaped, usually entire**, but sometimes upper ones with 3 shallow lobes, with or without fine hairs.

FLOWERS: Greenish, tubular, inconspicuous, mostly concealed by several, showy, **bright-red to scarlet, sharp-toothed and pointed**, hairy bracts; calyx lobes **sharp pointed**.

FRUITS: 2-celled capsules.

ECOLOGY: Open woods and meadows, thickets, grassy slopes, tidal marshes, clearings, gravel bars, roadsides; at low to high elevations.

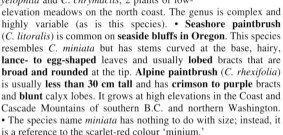

NOTES: This is the most common species of *Castilleja* in our region. *C. miniata* includes *C. hyetophila* and *C. chrymactis*, 2 plants of low-elevation meadows on the north coast. The genus is complex and highly variable (as is this species). • **Seashore paintbrush** (*C. litoralis*) is common on **seaside bluffs in Oregon**. This species resembles *C. miniata* but has stems curved at the base, hairy, **lance- to egg-shaped** leaves and usually **lobed** bracts that are **broad and rounded** at the tip. **Alpine paintbrush** (*C. rhexifolia*) is usually **less than 30 cm tall** and has **crimson to purple** bracts and **blunt** calyx lobes. It grows at high elevations in the Coast and Cascade Mountains of southern B.C. and northern Washington. • The species name *miniata* has nothing to do with size; instead, it is a reference to the scarlet-red colour 'minium.'

HARSH PAINTBRUSH • *Castilleja hispida*

GENERAL: Perennial herb from a woody stem-base; stems clustered, ascending or erect, usually unbranched and **stiffly hairy**, 20–60 cm tall.

LEAVES: Alternate, lance-shaped, hairy; lower leaves small, entire; upper leaves usually with **1–2 pairs of narrow, lateral lobes**.

FLOWERS: Greenish, 20–40 mm long, partly concealed by **scarlet (sometimes yellow)** bracts that are broad, **deeply 3–5 lobed**, and hairy; inflorescence showy, short and broad at first, elongating later.

FRUITS: 2-chambered capsules; seeds numerous.

ECOLOGY: Grassy slopes, dry meadows, forest openings and edges; at **low to middle elevations**; in the southern half of our region.

NOTES: Harsh paintbrush is similar to both **common red paintbrush**, which has mostly **entire** leaves, and **cliff paintbrush** (*C. rupicola*), which has **curled hairs**. Cliff paintbrush also has a showy scarlet inflorescence, but it tends to be **short and few-flowered**, its flowers stick out more from the bracts and its leaves have narrower, deeper lobes. Cliff paintbrush is a species of cliffs and rocky slopes at **high elevations**, and it is scattered in the Cascade Mountains from the Skagit Valley in B.C. south to central Oregon.

MOUNTAIN OWL-CLOVER • *Orthocarpus imbricatus*

GENERAL: Annual herb; stems slender, simple or branched above, 10–35 cm tall.

LEAVES: All on the stem, **alternate**, linear to narrowly lance-shaped, entire, sparsely hairy; bracts abruptly differentiated from leaves.

FLOWERS: Purplish, with a beak-like upper lip, 10–13 mm long, largely hidden by **showy petal-like** bracts, which are broad, blunt, and have **pink-purple tips**; flowering spike dense, showy.

FRUITS: Capsules, elliptic, with numerous seeds with loose, netted coat.

ECOLOGY: Relatively dry meadows, rocky slopes, and outcrops with thin soil; common at **middle to high elevations** in the Olympic Mountains and the Cascades of Washington and Oregon; known from 1 site on southern Vancouver Island.

NOTES: Several other species of *Orthocarpus*, all of them annual root parasites, occur sporadically in the southern part of our region, primarily at low to middle elevations in meadows and open grassy sites in the Strait of Georgia–Puget Sound area south interruptedly to Oregon. **Dwarf owl-clover** (*Orthocarpus pusillus*) is very small, often has **purplish** leaves, and has red-purple or sometimes yellow flowers **4–6 mm long. Rosy owl-clover** (*O. bracteosus*) has showy, **pink-purple** flowers **12–20 mm long. Narrow-leaved owl-clover** (*O. attenuatus*) has narrow, white flowers **10–25 mm long**, with purple spots. **Paintbrush owl-clover** (*O. castillejoides*) has wider **yellow flowers 14–22 mm long**, with purple markings. It grows in **salt marshes**. • *Orthocarpus* means 'straight' (*orthos*) 'fruit' (*karpos*), in reference to the capsules.

COW-WHEAT • *Melampyrum lineare*

GENERAL: Slender **annual**; stems leafy, simple or with a few branches, glandular especially in the upper part, 10–30 cm tall.

LEAVES: Opposite, with short stalks, linear or lance-shaped, 2–5 cm long.

FLOWERS: White or pinkish, tubular with yellow patch in throat, 2-lipped, 5–12 mm long, surrounded by **green, leafy** bracts.

FRUITS: Curved, asymmetrical capsules, with usually 4 relatively large (about 3 mm in diameter) seeds.

ECOLOGY: Open forest, grassy openings, dry, well-drained sites, especially on coarse outwash, terraces, rocky slopes and ridges; sporadic, locally common at low to middle elevations.

NOTES: The name 'cow-wheat' was originally applied to the European *M. arvense* which was 'freely cropped by passing cattle, to which it was fed in times of scarcity.' Linnaeus claimed cows produced the yellowest butter after eating it. Another source says it got its common name because its seeds resemble wheat, but are useless to humans. Despite all this, our *M. lineare* is much too small and scattered to be a forage plant.

YELLOW RATTLE • *Rhinanthus minor*
RATTLEBOX

GENERAL: Annual herb; stems leafy, erect, simple or few branched, **thinly hairy,** 10–80 cm tall.

LEAVES: Opposite, stalkless, lance-shaped, coarsely toothed, rough-hairy, 2–7 cm long.

FLOWERS: Yellow, 9–14 mm long, 2-lipped; upper lip hooded; lower lip 3 lobed; **sepals fused, like a flattened balloon** with 4 teeth at the mouth when plants in fruit; 4 stamens; flowers in leafy-bracted terminal spikes.

FRUITS: Capsules, flattened, circular, completely enclosed by the sepal balloon; seeds numerous, winged.

ECOLOGY: Meadows, fields, open grassy sites, beaches, roadsides, moist clearings; common (locally abundant) at low to middle elevations throughout our region, except in Washington and Oregon, where infrequent.

NOTES: Yellow rattle is also known as *R. crista-galli.* • Both common names refer to the fact that the seeds rattle around inside the capsule at maturity. *Rhinanthus* is from the Greek *rhin* ('snout') and *anthos* ('flower'), in reference to the unusual shape of the flower.

YELLOW PARENTUCELLIA • *Parentucellia viscosa*

GENERAL: Annual herb with fibrous roots; stems leafy, erect, unbranched, **coarsely hairy becoming stalked-glandular** up towards the flowers, 10–70 cm tall.

LEAVES: Opposite (mostly), stalkless, lance-shaped to narrowly egg-shaped, coarsely toothed, distinctly veined, hairy, 1–4 cm long.

FLOWERS: Yellow, about 2 cm long, 2-lipped; upper lip hooded; lower lip 3 lobed; 4 stamens; **fused sepals sticky-hairy, not inflated;** flowers in axils of leafy-bracted, spike-like raceme.

FRUITS: Capsules, lance-shaped; seeds numerous, small, smooth.

ECOLOGY: Moist grassy sites, clearings, pastures; common in settled areas.

NOTES: Eyebright (*Euphrasia*) is a genus of similar but **smaller** plants; our species are 3–30 cm tall with **3–10 mm long, whitish,** 2-lipped flowers. The upper lip is hooded with a **dark blotch** inside; the lower lip is white with **purple veins** and is said to resemble a bloodshot eye. Eastern eyebright (*E. nemorosa,* also called *E. officinalis* or *E. americana*) is a weedy European species established in fields, roadsides, and waste places, and it is scattered at low elevations in southwestern B.C. and western Washington. Arctic eyebright (*E. arctica,* which includes *E. mollis*) is a species of wet meadows, bogs and moist river gravels on the north coast (primarily southeast Alaska). • Yellow parentucellia is a weedy species introduced from the Mediterranean region. • *Parentucellia* is named for Thomas Parentucelli, founder of the Rome Botanical Garden.

CALIFORNIA FIGWORT • *Scrophularia californica*

GENERAL: Perennial herb from **thickened** roots; stems clustered, leafy, **stout, 4-angled, sticky-hairy in the upper part**.

LEAVES: Opposite, stalked, saw-toothed, triangular-egg- to lance-shaped, only gradually reduced in size upwards, finely hairy, about 10 cm long.

FLOWERS: Brownish to maroon, 9–15 mm long, **2-lipped**; upper lip pointing forward, 2 lobed; lower lip shorter, 3 lobed; 4 fertile stamens; flowers numerous in a terminal, open, branched, leafless inflorescence.

FRUITS: Capsules, **pear-shaped**; seeds numerous, angular, wrinkled.

ECOLOGY: Streambanks, moist openings and clearings, thickets, at low elevations; scattered, locally abundant.

NOTES: Lance-leaved figwort (*S. lanceolata*) is similar and has a similar range on the coast, but it has **yellowish-green** flowers. • Why are plants in the genus *Scrophularia* 'figworts'? The Romans thought that haemorrhoids looked like figs, so *ficus* meant both the disease and the fruit. *Scrophularia nodosa* had swellings on its roots, and in the Doctrine of Signatures (according to which plants were thought to aid the body part or ailment they resembled) it was one of the *ficariae*: a plant used to treat the disease *ficus* (i.e, piles). It was *ficaria major*, whereas *Ranunculus ficaria* (celandine), which has swollen tubers, was *ficaria minor*. • *Scrophularia* is Latin for a plant used in the treatment of 'scrophulus' swellings.

AMERICAN BROOKLIME • *Veronica beccabunga*
ssp. *americana*

GENERAL: Perennial from shallow, **creeping rhizomes, or rooting from trailing stems**; stems somewhat succulent, simple, erect or ascending, 10–70 cm tall, **hairless**.

LEAVES: Opposite, usually 3–5 pairs on the flowering stem, oval to lance-shaped, short-stalked, sharply pointed and toothed.

FLOWERS: Blue (violet to lilac), saucer-shaped, **not strongly lipped**, with 2 large, spreading stamens; in long, loose clusters along the stem.

FRUITS: Round capsules.

ECOLOGY: Wet ground or shallow water, marshes, seepage areas, along springs and streams, wet clearings and ditches, and skidder tracks; common at low to middle elevations.

NOTES: American brooklime is also known as *V. americana*. • **Bractless hedge-hyssop** (*Gratiola ebracteata*) is a small **annual** 5–15 cm tall with lance-shaped, opposite leaves, **whitish or yellow tubular flowers solitary in leaf axils**, and spherical capsules. It grows on muddy shores and in shallow water, wet ditches and drying pools; it is scattered at low elevations in the Strait of Georgia–Puget Sound area south to California. • The leaves of American brooklime are edible and used widely as a salad vegetable and potherb. Care should be taken to avoid plants growing in polluted water. • Brooklimes have been used for centuries to treat urinary and kidney complaints and as a blood purifier. • The name 'brooklime' comes from Europe, where *V. beccabunga* grows along streams or brooks in wet mud where birds may become trapped or 'limed' (an expression for ensnaring birds in sticky materials).

THYME-LEAVED SPEEDWELL • *Veronica serpyllifolia*

GENERAL: Perennial herb from creeping, branching rhizomes; stems 10–30 cm long, also **creeping and forming mats**, rooting at the nodes, finely hairy.

LEAVES: Opposite, elliptic to egg-shaped, **entire or weakly toothed**; the lower leaves short stalked, **hairless**, 1–2.5 cm long.

FLOWERS: Bright-blue or whitish with dark-blue lines, 4–8 mm wide, saucer-shaped, stalked; several to many in terminal racemes that become long and lax.

FRUITS: Capsules, heart-shaped, notched, finely glandular-hairy; seeds small, numerous.

ECOLOGY: Moist meadows, streambanks, clearings, often on disturbed sites; common but rarely abundant, from low to sometimes high elevations.

NOTES: Most of the plants in our region represent the native *V. serpyllifolia* var. *humifusa*, not the introduced, pale-flowered var. *serpyllifolia*. • Several other species occur in our region, often in wet meadows, ditches and clearings. **Purslane speedwell** (*V. peregrina*, also called neckweed, which is an annual with **white** flowers on **very short** stalks in a long **terminal** inflorescence) and **marsh speedwell** (*V. scutellata*, which is a **perennial** with **white or blue** flowers on **long** stalks in **axillary** clusters) are both scattered the length of our region. **Wall speedwell** (*V. arvensis*, which is an **annual** European weed with **blue-violet** flowers on **very short** stalks in a long, **lax terminal** inflorescence) and **slender speedwell** (*V. filiformis*, which is a **perennial** Asian weed with **single blue-purple** flowers on **long** stalks in leaf **axils**) are locally common in settled parts of the southern half of our region. • The common name 'veronica' is also used. It may be derived from an Arabic word meaning 'beautiful memory,' in reference to the pretty flowers. An alternative derivation is that some flowers bear markings resembling those on the handkerchief of St. Veronica after she used it to wipe the face of Jesus as he carried the cross (the *vera iconica*, meaning 'true likeness'). • The species name *serpyllifolia* means 'thyme-leaved.'

ALPINE SPEEDWELL • *Veronica wormskjoldii*

GENERAL: Perennial from shallow rhizomes; stems simple, **erect**, 7–30 cm tall, sparsely to densely **hairy, sticky or glandular among flowers**.

LEAVES: All on the stem, opposite, elliptic to oval or lance-shaped, rounded to pointed at tip, **slightly toothed, smooth to hairy**.

FLOWERS: Blue-violet with cream-coloured centre, saucer-shaped, with prominent style and 2 stamens; stalks sticky-glandular; few to several in cluster at top of stem.

FRUITS: Heart-shaped, hairy capsules.

ECOLOGY: Meadows, streambanks, seepage areas and moist, open slopes, at middle to high elevations in the mountains.

NOTES: Cusick's speedwell (*V. cusickii*) is also a rhizomatous perennial of high-elevation meadows and rocky slopes, which is fairly common and locally abundant in the Washington Cascades (to Manning Park, B.C.) and in the Olympic Mountains. It has **entire, hairless** leaves and longer styles and stamens than alpine speedwell. • The name 'speedwell' was applied originally to *V. officinalis*, which was used medicinally as a strengthening and wound-healing plant and against coughs. Alternative meanings of 'speedwell' are 'get well,' 'prosper well,' or 'go on well.' Another meaning comes from the fact that the petals fall off as soon as the flowers are picked, hence 'farewell' or 'God speed.' • This species is named for Morten Wormskjold (1783–1845), a Danish lieutenant on Kotzebue's first expedition to Alaska, who collected at Kodiak and Sitka.

SMALL-FLOWERED BLUE-EYED MARY • *Collinsia parviflora*

GENERAL: Annual herb; stems leafy, usually erect or ascending, sometimes long and sprawling, simple or branched, minutely hairy plus often glandular in upper part, 5–40 cm tall.

LEAVES: Middle and upper leaves opposite to whorled, mostly stalkless, oblong to lance-shaped, entire or somewhat toothed, usually hairless, 1–4 cm long, becoming smaller and bract-like in the inflorescence; lower leaves oblong to spoon-shaped, relatively long stalked.

FLOWERS: Blue with some white, 4–8 mm long, strongly 2-lipped; upper lip white, 2 lobed; lower lip deep blue, 3 lobed; 4 stamens; flowers on hairy stalks, single in the leaf axils below but clustered at upper nodes.

FRUITS: Capsules, football-shaped, 3–5 mm long; seeds usually 4, with thickened margins, smooth, reddish-brown.

ECOLOGY: Open, grassy, vernally moist slopes, mossy rock outcrops, gravelly flats; common at low to middle and sometimes higher elevations; absent from the wetter outer coast.

NOTES: Large-flowered blue-eyed Mary (*C. grandiflora,* **inset photo**) is stouter and more erect, and it has larger, violet-blue-and-white flowers, **8–17 mm long**. It occupies similar habitats to those of *C. parviflora* but is restricted to the southern part of our region, from the Strait of Georgia–Puget Sound area south to California. • The common name refers to the pretty, blue flowers; the 'Mary' referred to is likely the mother of Jesus. The genus was named for Zacheus Collins (1764–1831), an early American botanist. • The species names *parviflora* ('small-flowered') and *grandiflora* ('large-flowered') can be used in the field to distinguish our 2 common species.

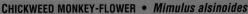

CHICKWEED MONKEY-FLOWER • *Mimulus alsinoides*

GENERAL: Annual herb; stems leafy, slender, nearly hairless to somewhat glandular-hairy, simple or freely branched, 5–30 cm tall.

LEAVES: Opposite, stalked, elliptic to triangular-egg-shaped, irregularly toothed, thin, hairless, yellowish-green, 3–5 veined.

FLOWERS: Yellow, with a reddish-brown blotch on the lower lip, **8–14 mm long**, 2-lipped; 4 stamens; flowers 1 to few on long stalks at each node.

FRUITS: Capsules, oblong-pointed; seeds numerous.

ECOLOGY: Vernally moist, often shady, mossy ledges, cliffs, rocky slopes; common at mostly low elevations.

NOTES: The name 'monkey-flower' comes from the grinning, ape-like faces of the flowers. The Latin *mimulus* means 'little actor'; it is the diminutive of *mimus* meaning a buffoon or actor in a farce or mime. The species name means 'like *alsine*' (a chickweed-like plant), and this in turn gives rise to the common name.

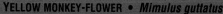

YELLOW MONKEY-FLOWER • *Mimulus guttatus*

GENERAL: Annual from fibrous roots **or perennial** from creeping stolons and rhizomes or rooting from stem nodes; stems leafy, erect or trailing, simple or branched, **10–80 cm tall**, sometimes small and dwarfed, hairless (usually) to sparsely hairy.

LEAVES: In pairs, oval, coarsely toothed, lower ones stalked, upper ones clasping the stem, smooth or covered with fine hairs.

FLOWERS: Yellow, 2-lipped, large, **20–40 mm long**, trumpet-shaped, long-stalked; lower lip with one large or several small, crimson to brownish-red spots; throat hairy; several to many in loose terminal clusters.

FRUITS: After flowers drop, the fused sepals become inflated and surround a many-seeded, 10–20 mm long, broadly oblong capsule.

ECOLOGY: Wet ledges, crevices, weeping rock faces, seepage areas, along streams, near springs, on gravel bars, in wet ditches and clearings; common from lowlands to high elevations in the mountains.

NOTES: Mountain monkey-flower (*M. tilingii*, **inset photo**) is a **dwarf (5–20 cm tall), creeping**, perennial, **alpine and subalpine** species with **leafy stems** and a **few** terminal yellow flowers that are very like (and just as large as) those of yellow monkey-flower. The flowers look almost too big for the stems. *M. tilingii* grows in mossy alpine seepage sites and along stream banks, sporadically from 54°N south to California; it is absent from the Queen Charlotte Islands. **Primrose monkey-flower** (*M. primuloides*) is a **densely matted** perennial with **basal leaves** and **single, yellow**, trumpet-shaped flowers on long stalks. It grows in wet meadows and bogs in the Washington and Oregon Cascades, and in the Olympic Mountains.

MUSK-FLOWER • *Mimulus moschatus*

GENERAL: Perennial, slimy-hairy, sometimes musk-scented, from slender, well-developed rhizomes; stems leafy, lax, often prostrate or creeping, freely branched, 10–70 cm long.

LEAVES: Opposite, more or less stalkless, egg-shaped, entire or vaguely toothed, 1–8 cm long.

FLOWERS: Yellow, about **2 cm long,** funnel-like, with dark lines or spots, **weakly 2-lipped;** 4 stamens; few per node on long slender stalks.

FRUITS: Pointed capsules.

ECOLOGY: Stream-banks, moist meadows, rocky seepage areas, thickets, roadsides, other moist shaded habitats; common from low to middle elevations.

NOTES: **Tooth-leaved monkey-flower** (*M. dentatus*) is similar but has merely hairy (**not slimy**) leaves and **strongly 2-lipped** flowers **2.5–4 cm long**. It also grows on stream-banks and in moist forest from southern Vancouver Island to California, chiefly in the western Olympic Mountains and the Washington-Oregon Coast Ranges. • Musk-flower was widely grown in England after David Douglas brought seeds back around 1828. It was highly prized for its musk-like scent, which was said to rival the perfume of mignonette (*Reseda odorata*). For some strange reason, the flowers, whether domesticated or in the wild, lost their perfume at the same time as their popularity in English gardens waned. A possible explanation for this unusual phenomenon may be found in Sheldrake's theory of 'morphic resonance,' also known as the '100th monkey' effect.

PINK MONKEY-FLOWER • *Mimulus lewisii*

GENERAL: Perennial from stout, branching rhizomes; stems thick, clustered, leafy, mostly simple, 30–100 cm tall, **sticky and softly hairy.**

LEAVES: Large, clasping the stem in pairs, oval with sharply pointed tips, conspicuously veined; **widely spaced teeth** on margin.

FLOWERS: Rose-red to pale-pink, large (30–55 mm long), showy, trumpet-shaped, strongly 2-lipped; lower lip marked with yellow and a few hairs; few to several on long stalks from upper leaf axils.

FRUITS: Capsules, oblong, 10–20 cm long; seeds numerous.

ECOLOGY: Common in and along streams (especially ice-cold ones) and in other wet clearings, also in the forest along avalanche tracks, at middle to high elevations in the mountains.

NOTES: Brewer's monkey-flower (*M. breweri*) is a delicate annual, usually less than 15 cm tall, with reddish to light-purple flowers. It grows on rocky slopes, outcrops and scree, and in meadows, at middle elevations in the Cascades from southern B.C. through Washington and Oregon. • The monkey-flowers have very sensitive, 2-lobed stigmas that will close if touched with a pin, straw, piece of grass or insect's tongue. • *M. lewisii* is named for Capt. Meriweather Lewis of the Lewis and Clark Expedition of 1806 and it is sometimes called 'Lewis' monkey-flower.'

WOODLAND PENSTEMON • *Nothochelone nemorosa*
TURTLEHEAD

GENERAL: Perennial herb from a branched, woody stem-base; stems several, leafy, erect, **hairless or finely hairy,** 40–80 cm tall.

LEAVES: Opposite, short-stalked, thin, lance- to egg-shaped, **saw-toothed,** mostly hairless, 4–11 cm long.

FLOWERS: Blue-purple or pink-purple, about 3 cm long, glandular-hairy on outside, tubular, distinctly 2-lipped; **upper lip shorter;** 4 fertile stamens, hairy at the base and long-woolly on the anthers; flowers several in loose, branched, glandular-hairy panicles.

FRUITS: Capsules, leathery, 11–17 mm long; seeds flattened, **wing-margined.**

ECOLOGY: Common in moist forest and rocky slopes from low to subalpine elevations.

NOTES: Woodland penstemon is also known as *Penstemon nemorosus.* • The genus name *Nothochelone* is from the Greek *notho* ('false') and *chelone* (the name of another genus). The name *chelone* itself means 'turtle' or 'tortoise.' It has been suggested that the front view of the flower might resemble the squat head of a turtle.

COAST PENSTEMON • *Penstemon serrulatus*

GENERAL: Perennial herb from a branching, woody base; stems several, leafy, hairless or hairy, **20–70 cm tall**.

LEAVES: Opposite, hairless, stalkless, lance-shaped to oblong egg-shaped, **saw-toothed**, 3–8 cm long; **lower leaves reduced** in size, often stalked.

FLOWERS: Deep-blue to dark-purple, 17–25 mm long, tubular, hairless inside and out, stalked; 4 fertile stamens, anthers hairless; in 1 to several compact clusters.

FRUITS: Capsules, 5–8 mm long.

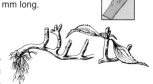

ECOLOGY: Streambanks, moist rocky slopes, gullies, from low to middle or subalpine elevations; common in the southern 2/3 of our region.

NOTES: Broad-leaved penstemon (*P. ovatus*) has **triangular-egg-shaped**, saw-toothed leaves and deep-blue-purple flowers to 20 cm long, but it has a **glandular-hairy** inflorescence. It is a species of open forest, mossy ledges and outcrops at low to middle elevations from southwestern B.C. to northern Oregon. • The common and scientific name 'penstemon' is from the Latin *pente* ('5') and *stemon* ('stamens') because the flower has 5 stamens: 4 fertile and 1 sterile.

SMALL-FLOWERED PENSTEMON • *Penstemon procerus*
SLENDER BLUE PENSTEMON

GENERAL: Perennial from a woody stem-base; stems tufted, erect, **5–40 cm tall**, smooth.

LEAVES: Opposite, oval to lance-shaped, **lacking teeth; basal leaves** with short stalks, stem leaves lacking stalks.

FLOWERS: Blue-purple, sometimes tinged pink (occasionally white), petals fused to form a tube that is not strongly 2 lipped and is relatively small **(6–12 mm long)**; 4 fertile stamens; flowers 1 to several in dense clusters arranged in whorls around the stem and at its tip.

FRUITS: Capsules, 4–5 mm long; seeds numerous.

ECOLOGY: Dry, sandy banks, gravelly ridges, open, rocky slopes, grassy hillsides, dry meadows and open woods; fairly common at middle to high elevations.

NOTES: Penstemons are sometimes also called 'beard-tongues' because of the hairy throats, and especially the hairy lower lip, of the flowers. Some species also have hairy sterile stamens or hairy anthers on the fertile stamens.

DAVIDSON'S PENSTEMON • *Penstemon davidsonii*

GENERAL: Low, **shrubby** perennial forming **dense mats** via creeping stems; flowering stems **5–10 cm tall**, short-hairy.

LEAVES: Evergreen, opposite, thick and firm, **hairless but not glaucous,** entire or short-toothed, **5–15 mm** long, blunt-tipped.

FLOWERS: Purple to blue-lavender, 25–35 mm long, tubular with a widened, hairy throat, 2-lipped, stalked; 4 fertile stamens, with **densely woolly anthers;** few in racemes.

FRUITS: Capsules, leathery, 8–10 mm long; seeds angled, narrowly winged.

ECOLOGY: Frequent on rocky ledges, slabs, talus slopes, at middle to high elevations.

NOTES: Rock penstemon (*P. rupicola*) also forms dense, shrubby mats with evergreen leaves, but it has **pink to rose-purple** flowers and **glaucous, often hairy** leaves. It grows on cliffs, ledges and rocky slopes in the Cascades of Washington and Oregon. Both species are very showy, adding brilliant patches of colour to cliffs and rocky slopes high in the mountains. • Davidson's penstemon is named for Dr. George Davidson, who first collected it in California.

CARDWELL'S PENSTEMON • *Penstemon cardwellii*

GENERAL: Low **shrub 10–30 cm tall;** stems curved and sometimes rooting at base.

LEAVES: Opposite, hairless, larger towards the base or on short, sterile shoots, elliptic, toothed to nearly entire, short-stalked or stalkless, **15–35 mm** long.

FLOWERS: Bright-purple to deep-blue-violet, 30–40 mm long, tubular, widened and white-hairy at mouth; 4 fertile stamens, stalked, with **long-woolly anthers;** flowers stalked, several in compact terminal clusters and in axils of upper leaves.

FRUITS: Capsules.

ECOLOGY: Common in open forest, forest edges, rocky slopes, and cutbanks at middle elevations.

NOTES: The plants spread vegetatively to form large mats, often on disturbed rocky sites such as road cuts. Large patches occur in some spots on Mt. St. Helens where the forest was destroyed in the 1980 eruption and volcanic rubble covers the old forest soil.

Asteraceae (Sunflower Family)

The composites, or the plants of the sunflower family (the Asteraceae, also known as Compositae) form the largest plant family in the world (or perhaps the second largest, after the orchids), with over 21,000 species.

Composites are easily recognized by their inflorescence, which is often mistaken for a single large flower but is actually made up of numerous individual flowers on the broadened top of the stem. These flowers can be of two forms: tubular and sitting on the broadened stem top (**disk flowers**) or strap-shaped and arranged around the edges of the stem top (**ray flowers**) (When you play 'loves me, loves me not' you are plucking ray flowers). A plant may have ray flowers only, disk flowers only, or both. Each individual flower has 5 united petals, 5 stamens, and an inferior, 1-chambered ovary. What originally were the sepals are interpreted to have been modified into hairs (collectively called the '**pappus**') that crown the summit of the single-seeded fruits (achenes) and which assist in wind-dispersal (as in the downy parachute of a dandelion seed), or less commonly into scales, awns or hooks. Attached to the rim of the head is an involucre consisting of scale-like or somewhat leaf-like bracts, called '**involucral bracts**.'

The family is cosmopolitan in range but especially well adapted to fairly dry, temperate and cooler climates. It has considerable economic importance through food plants such as lettuce (*Lactuca*), globe artichoke (*Cynara*), endive and chicory (species of *Cichorium*), salsify (*Tragopogon*) and sunflower (*Helianthus*). The contact insecticide pyrethrum comes from *Chrysanthemum coccineum*. Many species are noxious weeds, while others are used in medicinal preparations or herbal teas. Many genera provide ornamentals, including perennial asters, chrysanthemum, coreopsis, cosmos, dahlia, gerbera, strawflowers (*Helichrysum, Helipterum, Xeranthemum*), sunflower (*Helianthus*), cineraria (*Senecio*), edelweiss (*Leontodon*), marigolds (*Tagetes*), zinnia and globe thistle (*Echinops*).

A key to genera is provided below, as are keys to species within some of the larger genera (*Erigeron* and *Aster*, p. 283; *Arnica* and *Senecio*, pp. 295–96). Many more species occur on the Northwest Coast than are covered in this guide. The best additional reference is Douglas (1982), but this covers only part of the family (including the genera *Arnica*, *Petasites* and *Senecio*), and only for British Columbia. Additional volumes in the series are expected to be published very soon by the Royal B.C. Museum to cover the rest of the composites. Cronquist (1955, vol. 1 of Hitchcock et al. 1955–69) is still very useful but covers only the southern half of our region.

Key to Genera of the Sunflower Family

1a. Flowers all ray-like or strap-shaped; plants with milky juice .... Group I
1b. Flowers not all ray-like, some or all of them tubular; plants mostly with watery juice 2
  2a. Ray flowers present 3
    3a. Ray flowers white, pink, purple, red or blue, never yellow or orange .... Group II
    3b. Ray flowers mostly yellow or orange 4
      4a. Pappus chaffy (of bracts or scales) or of firm awns, or absent .... Group III
      4b. Pappus of hair-like or feathery bristles .... Group IV
  2b. Ray flowers lacking, all flowers tubular 5
    5a. Pappus of hair-like or feathery bristles .... Group V
    5b. Pappus of scales or awns, or a mere crown .... Group VI

Group I: Flowers all ray-like or strap-shaped; juice milky (the dandelion tribe)

1a. Achenes without a pappus .... *Lapsana*
1b. Achenes with a pappus 2
  2a. Pappus of simple bristles only (these sometimes finely barbed) 3
    3a. Plants without stem leaves, leaves all in basal rosette; heads solitary 4
      4a. Achenes roughened with tiny spines and ridges .... *Taraxacum*
      4b. Achenes smooth or nearly so 5
        5a. Achenes beaked .... *Agoseris*
        5b. Achenes beakless .... *Microseris* and some *Agoseris glauca*
    3b. Plants with at least some stem leaves; heads few to several 6
      6a. Stem leaves well-developed, broad, usually over 1 cm wide 7
        7a. Leaves simple, toothed; flowers white; achenes cylindric .... *Prenanthes*
        7b. Leaves, or at least some of them, deeply lobed;
        flowers yellow or blue; achenes flattened 8
          8a. Achenes beaked (or beakless in *Lactuca biennis*);
          leaves not clasping-lobed at base .... *Lactuca*
          8b. Achenes beakless; leaves with ear-like, clasping lobes at base .... *Sonchus*
      6b. Stem leaves narrow, usually less than 1 cm wide, reduced in size up the stem 9

9a. Perennials from a short rhizome,
not taprooted; pappus tan or brown .... *Hieracium*
    9b. Annuals, biennials or perennials from a
taproot or fibrous roots; pappus mostly white .... *Crepis*
2b. Pappus of feathery bristles, of bristles and scales, or minute scales 10
    10a. Pappus of minute scales; flowers blue .... *Cichorium*
    10b. Pappus well-developed; flowers yellow, orange or purple 11
        11a. Pappus of narrow scales, each bearing a long bristle .... *Microseris*
        11b. Pappus of feathery bristles 12
            12a. Plume branches of the pappus interwebbed;
stems leafy; leaves somewhat grass-like .... *Tragopogon*
            12b. Plume branches of the pappus not interwebbed; leaves all basal .... *Hypochaeris*

Group II: Heads with both ray and disk flowers; ray flowers white, pink, purple, red or blue

1a. Pappus none, or a mere crown, or of scales or awns; receptacle naked or chaffy-bracted 2
    2a. Leaves all basal; pappus lacking .... *Bellis*
    2b. Plants with at least some stem leaves; pappus present or absent 3
        3a. Ray flowers few (usually 3–5), short, less than 5 mm long; perennials .... *Achillea*
        3b. Ray flowers more numerous, over 5 mm long 4
            4a. Receptacle chaffy-bracted or bristly, at least towards the middle; annuals .... *Anthemis*
            4b. Receptacle naked 5
                5a. Leaves entire to toothed or broadly lobed; perennials .... *Leucanthemum*
                5b. Leaves pinnately dissected, with very narrow,
hair-like lobes; annuals or biennials .... *Matricaria*
1b. Pappus of hair-like bristles; receptacle naked 2
    6a. Basal leaves long-stalked, heart- or arrowhead-shaped,
or palmately-lobed; stem leaves greatly reduced, bract-like .... *Petasites*
    6b. Basal leaves not as above; stem leaves ample or reduced 7
        7a. Ray flowers numerous, hair-like, short (scarcely longer than disk flowers); annuals .... *Conyza*
        7b. Ray flowers few to numerous, well-developed, conspicuous,
usually obviously surpassing the disk flowers .... *Aster* and *Erigeron* (p. 283)

Group III: Heads with both ray and disk flowers; ray flowers yellow or orange; pappus chaffy or of firm bracts or absent

1a. Receptacle chaffy-bracted or bristly throughout; pappus of barbed awns .... *Bidens*
1b. Receptacle naked, or with a single row of bracts between the ray and disk flowers 2
    2a. Ray flowers well-developed, conspicuous, mostly 5–30 mm long 3
        3a. Pappus of firm, deciduous awns; involucres sticky-resinous .... *Grindelia*
        3b. Pappus of chaffy or clear scales, or a mere crown, or absent;
involucres usually not resinous (but sometimes hairy or glandular) 4
            4a. Leaves pinnately divided; ray flowers ascending, minutely notched at tip .... *Eriophyllum*
            4b. Leaves simple, toothed; ray flowers bent down, prominently 3 lobed at tip .... *Helenium*
    2b. Ray flowers short, inconspicuous, mostly 1–5 mm long, or, if longer,
(in some *Madia*) then receptacle with a row of bracts between the ray and disk flowers 5
        5a. Leaves strongly dissected, fern-like .... *Tanacetum*
        5b. Leaves entire to toothed; involucres glandular .... *Madia*

Group IV: Heads with both ray and disk flowers; ray flowers yellow or orange; pappus of mostly hair-like, sometimes feathery, bristles

1a. Stem leaves, except some of the reduced uppermost ones, opposite .... *Arnica* (pp. 295–96)
1b. Leaves alternate, or all basal 2
    2a. Involucral bracts in 1 equal series .... *Senecio* (pp. 295–96)
    2b. Involucral bracts in 2 or more series, equal or overlapping 3
        3a. Pappus double, bristles of the outer series distinctly shorter than the inner .... *Erigeron aureus*
        3b. Pappus single, bristles not divided into an inner and outer series 4
            4a. Plants shrubby .... *Haplopappus*
            4b. Plants herbaceous .... *Solidago*

Group V: Heads of disk flowers only; pappus of hair-like or feathery bristles

1a. Leaves spiny .... *Cirsium*
1b. Leaves not spiny and thistle-like 2
    2a. Flowers all bisexual and fertile; leaves simple and smooth-margined .... *Luina*
    2b. Flowers all, or at least the outer ones, female 3
        3a. Basal leaves heart- or arrowhead-shaped .... *Petasites*
        3b. Basal leaves, if any, not heart- or arrowhead-shaped 4
            4a. Plants taprooted annuals or perennials .... *Gnaphalium*
            4b. Plants fibrous-rooted perennials, often with rhizomes or stolons 5
                5a. Basal leaves usually conspicuous, tufted; stem leaves reduced
upwards, often few or lacking .... *Antennaria*
                5b. Basal leaves soon deciduous, not larger than the numerous stem leaves .... *Anaphalis*

Group VI: Heads of disk flowers only; pappus of scales, awns or a mere crown

1a. Involucral bracts with short, hooked bristles .... *Arctium*
1b. Involucral bracts not with hooked prickles 2
   2a. Receptacles chaffy or bristly all over; pappus of barbed awns .... *Bidens*
   2b. Receptacles naked, or with a single row of chaffy bracts between the ray and disk flowers 3
      3a. Lowermost leaves deltoid to somewhat kidney-shaped,
        white-woolly beneath; involucral bracts only 4–5 ....*Adenocaulon*
      3b. Lowermost leaves not deltoid to kidney-shaped; involucral bracts usually numerous 4
         4a. Involucral bracts equal-sized, in a single series, each wholly enclosing an achene ...... *Madia*
         4b. Involucral bracts in several series, each not enveloping an achene 5
            5a. Heads in an elongate cluster, relatively small, usually numerous .... *Artemisia*
            5b. Heads in an open, round- or flat-topped inflorescence, small to large,
            solitary to few, sometimes numerous; receptacles hemispherical or conical .... *Matricaria*

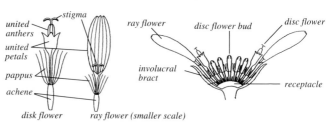

stigma, united anthers, united petals, pappus, achene — disk flower; ray flower (smaller scale); ray flower, disc flower bud, disc flower, involucral bract, receptacle

---

COMMON DANDELION • *Taraxacum officinale*

GENERAL: Perennial herb with **milky juice**, with a simple or branched stem base and a thick, often blackish **taproot**; flowering stems solitary to several, naked, 5–60 cm tall, rarely taller.

LEAVES: All basal, oblong to spoon-shaped, 5–40 cm long, **toothed or, more usually, pinnately lobed or divided,** often with an enlarged terminal segment, tapering to a more or less winged stalk.

FLOWERS: Heads **yellow, solitary**, made up of ray flowers only; involucral bracts hairless, the **inner bracts not horned**, the outer bracts **reflexed**.

FRUITS: Achenes, greyish-brown, long beaked (beak 2.5–4 times as long as body), ribbed, spiny on upper portion; pappus hairs white.

ECOLOGY: An **introduced**, weedy species of disturbed sites at low to middle elevations.

NOTES: Horned dandelion (*T. ceratophorum*, which includes *T. eriophorum* and *T. lyratum*) is a complex of **native**, often dwarf plants with **inner involucral bracts that are often horned**. It occurs at **middle to high elevations** and is common except in the southern part of our region, but mostly along the mountains of its eastern margin. **Red-seeded dandelion** (*T. laevigatum*) is an **introduced**, weedy species of roadsides, fields, pastures and lawns, which is fairly frequent at low elevations in the southern half of our region. *T. laevigatum* has leaves deeply and narrowly lobed for their entire length and **without an enlarged terminal segment**; its **inner involucral bracts are usually horned** and its outer bracts are erect to loose but usually **not reflexed**. It has red to reddish-brown achenes with beaks mostly 1–2 times as long as the body. • The young leaves of common dandelion were eaten raw or cooked in recent times by the Halq'emeylem, Nlaka'pamux and some indigenous peoples of Alaska. • This plant was imported to North America on early sailing ships. The young leaves make a good vegetable green. The cooked roots can be eaten as a vegetable or dried and ground for use as a coffee substitute. The flowers can be used to make dandelion wine and the whole plant can be brewed to make beer.

APARGIDIUM • *Microseris borealis*

GENERAL: Perennial herb with **milky juice,** essentially hairless, from a short, taprooted stem-base; flowering stem solitary, naked or with 1–2 small bracts, often curved at base, 10–50 cm tall.

LEAVES: All basal, **narrowly lance-shaped to lance-oblong, entire to remotely toothed or lobed,** long (5–25 cm), hairless, gradually tapering to pointed tip.

FLOWERS: Heads **yellow, solitary,** consisting of ray flowers only; involucral bracts 10–13 mm high, in several rows, sparsely dark hairy.

FRUITS: Achenes, columnar, ribbed, beakless, **hairless**; pappus of fine, **brownish bristles that are connected at base**.

ECOLOGY: Sphagnum bogs, wet meadows, wet rocky slopes; common most of the length of our region, especially on the outer coast from Vancouver Island north, from sea level to subalpine elevations; scattered in Washington and more common in the mountains than along the coast.

NOTES: Apargidium is also known as *Apargidium boreale*. • Coast microseris (*M. bigelovii*) and cut-leaf microseris (*M. laciniata*) occur sporadically in the southern part of our region, in moist meadows and on open slopes, from southern Vancouver Island (*M. bigelovii*) or Washington (*M. laciniata*) south to California. **Coast microseris** is an **annual** with **inconspicuous** flowers barely exceeding the involucral bracts. **Cut-leaf microseris** is a branched, several-headed perennial. Both species have **awned or bristle-tipped pappus scales.** • The common name is from the former Latin name for this species: *Apargidium boreale. Apargidium* means 'resembling *Apargia*,' which is a synonym for the genus *Leontodon* (hawkbit). *Leon* means 'lion' and *odous* means 'tooth,' and refers to the toothed leaves. *Microseris* means 'small' (*micro*) 'chicory' (*seris*), from the resemblance of some species to a smaller version of chicory.

ALPINE MICROSERIS • *Microseris alpestris*

GENERAL: Perennial herb with **milky juice,** from a stout taproot, essentially hairless; flowering stem naked or with a single bract, 3–35 cm tall.

LEAVES: All basal, **narrowly lance-shaped, generally coarsely few-toothed to deeply divided,** 5–15 cm long.

FLOWERS: Heads **yellow, solitary,** of ray flowers only; involucral bracts 12–20 mm high, tapered to a pointed tip, with tiny, **dark-purple dots**.

FRUITS: Achenes, columnar, ribbed, 5–8 mm long, beakless, the slightly narrowed top portion **finely hairy**; pappus of fine, **whitish, somewhat flattened bristles**.

ECOLOGY: High-elevation meadows and open slopes, from subalpine to above timberline.

NOTES: Dwarf hulsea (*Hulsea nana*) is a dwarf (to 10 cm tall), aromatic, **glandular-hairy,** perennial herb with a stout taproot and mostly basal, shallowly lobed leaves and large, yellow, solitary heads with **both disk and ray flowers**. It grows on high elevation cinder cones and pumice fields in the Cascades, from Mt. Rainier to Mt. Lassen. It is one of the few plants that occurs in such habitats, where it can be the most abundant species. • The species name *alpestris* means 'of the mountains.'

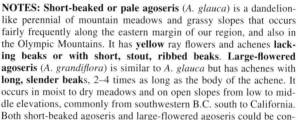

ORANGE AGOSERIS • *Agoseris aurantiaca*

GENERAL: Perennial herb with **milky juice**, from a taproot and simple or branching stem-base, mostly 10–60 cm tall.

LEAVES: All basal, **narrowly to broadly lance-shaped, entire to few-lobed**, long-stalked, hairless or somewhat hairy.

FLOWERS: Heads **burnt orange**, often becoming pink or purplish with age, solitary, large, consisting only of ray flowers.

FRUITS: Achenes, abruptly **long beaked**; pappus hairs white.

ECOLOGY: Dry to moist meadows, thickets, and forest openings from middle to high elevations.

NOTES: Short-beaked or pale agoseris (*A. glauca*) is a dandelion-like perennial of mountain meadows and grassy slopes that occurs fairly frequently along the eastern margin of our region, and also in the Olympic Mountains. It has **yellow** ray flowers and achenes **lacking beaks or with short, stout, ribbed beaks. Large-flowered agoseris** (*A. grandiflora*) is similar to *A. glauca* but has achenes with **long, slender beak**s, 2–4 times as long as the body of the achene. It occurs in moist to dry meadows and on open slopes from low to middle elevations, commonly from southwestern B.C. south to California. Both short-beaked agoseris and large-flowered agoseris could be confused with apargidium (p. 271). **Apargidium** has **beakless** achenes with pappus bristles **connected at the base**, whereas large-flowered agoseris has long-beaked achenes with distinct pappus bristles. Both apargidium and large-flowered agoseris have outer involucral bracts less than half the length of the inner ones. Short-beaked agoseris has beakless or short-beaked achenes with distinct pappus bristles, and outer involucral bracts more than half the length of the inner ones. • The leaves, and especially the latex of some *Agoseris* and *Hieracium* species were chewed for pleasure by some interior aboriginal groups.

SMOOTH HAWKSBEARD • *Crepis capillaris*

GENERAL: Annual or biennial herb with **milky juice**, from a thin taproot; stems erect, simple or branched, sparsely hairy, 20–90 cm tall.

LEAVES: Basal leaves stalked, **lance-shaped, toothed to divided**, hairless to hairy with stiff, yellow hairs; **stem leaves** reduced in size upwards, lance-shaped, stalkless and with **clasping flanges** at the base.

FLOWERS: Heads **yellow**, ray flowers only, 20–60 flowered; involucral bracts 5–8 mm high, cottony-hairy and often glandular as well, but **hairless on inner surface**; several to numerous heads in an open cluster.

FRUITS: Achenes, ribbed, **light brown**, narrowed upward but **not beaked**; pappus hairs white.

ECOLOGY: Meadows, fields, lawns, pastures, roadsides; common at low elevations in settled areas in the southern part of our region, sporadic north of Vancouver Island.

NOTES: Smooth hawksbeard is a weedy species of disturbed sites, introduced from Europe. **Annual hawksbeard** (*C. tectorum*) is another annual weedy species of disturbed areas, but it has inner involucral bracts that are **hairy on the inner surface**, and **purplish-brown** achenes. **Elegant hawksbeard** (*C. elegans*) and **dwarf hawksbeard** (*C. nana*) are **native perennial** species with **mainly basal** leaves. *C. elegans* occurs on **gravelly or sandy river bars** along the mainland rivers of northern southeast Alaska. *C. nana* is an uncommon, **dwarf, densely tufted alpine** species scattered the length of our region but mostly along its eastern margin and further inland.

WHITE-FLOWERED HAWKWEED • *Hieracium albiflorum*

GENERAL: Perennial herb with **milky juice**, from **fibrous-rooted**, commonly unbranched, short stem-base; stems solitary, **30–120 cm tall**.

LEAVES: Mostly basal, oblong to broadly lance-shaped, narrowed to a stalk or upper ones stalkless, **bristly with short, rigid hairs** on the upper surface; margins entire or wavy toothed.

FLOWERS: Heads **white**, made up of only ray flowers; involucral bracts in 1 row; several to many heads in open clusters.

FRUITS: Achenes, several-veined; pappus bristles tawny.

ECOLOGY: Relatively dry, open forests, meadows, clearings, and roadsides; common at **low to middle elevations** through most of our region except the wettest undisturbed parts of the outer coast.

NOTES: The name 'hawkweed' comes from a belief by the ancient Greeks that hawks would tear apart a plant called the hieracion (from the Greek *hierax* meaning 'hawk') and wet their eyes with the juice to clear their eyesight.

SLENDER HAWKWEED • *Hieracium gracile*

GENERAL: Perennial herb with **milky juice**, with a slender, horizontal **rhizome** and a short stem-base; stems few to several, unbranched, **8–25 cm tall**.

LEAVES: Mostly basal, broadly lance- to spoon-shaped, narrowed below to a stalk, entire or toothed, hairless or sometimes inconspicuously hairy and glandular on both surfaces; stem leaves absent or few and much reduced.

FLOWERS: Heads **yellow**, all ray flowers; involucral bracts roughly the same size, with fine **blackish and black-glandular hairs**; similar hairs on the flower stalks; few to several heads in small clusters.

FRUITS: Achenes, veined; pappus bristles dirty-white to straw-coloured.

ECOLOGY: Subalpine and alpine meadows, heath and snowbed tundra; common at **high elevations**.

NOTES: This species could be mistaken for the closely related **woolly hawkweed** (*H. triste*). Woolly hawkweed, however, has **larger** heads and **longer, greyish-black hairs** (its heads and stalks look quite **shaggy**), but **no glands**. Woolly hawkweed is common in the northern part of our region, from the Queen Charlotte Islands northwards. • The species name *gracile* means 'slender,' as in the common name.

NARROW-LEAVED HAWKWEED • *Hieracium umbellatum*

GENERAL: Perennial herb with **milky juice**, from a **short woody rhizome**; stems solitary or few, hairless or nearly so below, commonly having **star-like hairs above**, 40–120 cm tall.

LEAVES: Basal leaves few, soon deciduous; lower stem leaves small, soon deciduous; upper stem leaves strongly reduced; **middle leaves lance-shaped**, stalkless, entire or somewhat toothed, with short, stiff, **star-like hairs.**

FLOWERS: Heads **yellow**, consisting only of ray flowers; involucral bracts graduated, overlapping, hairless or nearly so, smoky green to blackish; few to many heads in a **flat-topped cluster.**

FRUITS: Ribbed achenes.

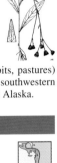

ECOLOGY: Fairly dry, open forests and meadows, clearings, and roadsides, scattered at low to middle elevations in the Strait of Georgia–Puget Sound area and uncommon south in the Cascades.

NOTES: There are **several other yellow-headed** species of hawkweed to watch out for at low to middle elevations. Some are natives and some are introduced weeds and can be expected to occur in disturbed habitats such as along roads and railway embankments. They are best identified using more-technical manuals. • Orange hawkweed (*H. aurantiacum*, also called devil's paintbrush) is another weedy introduced European species, and it is unmistakable with its **basal rosettes** of leaves, **spreading stolons and rhizomes**, and showy **red-orange** heads. It is scattered but locally abundant in disturbed sites (roadsides, gravel pits, pastures) along major transportation corridors in the southern half of our region (especially southwestern B.C.), and from a few places on the Queen Charlotte Islands to northern southeast Alaska.

HAIRY CAT'S-EAR • *Hypochaeris radicata*

GENERAL: Perennial herb with **milky juice**, from somewhat fleshy roots; stems usually several, simple or branched, 15–60 cm tall, hairless to hairy, leafless but with several scale-like bracts, enlarged below the flower heads.

LEAVES: All basal, oblong-lance-shaped, wavy-toothed or divided, somewhat glaucous on undersurface, **spreading-hairy** on both sides.

FLOWERS: Heads **yellow, open in sunny or dull weather**, of ray flowers only; involucral bracts 10–15 mm high (up to 25 mm in fruit), overlapping, hairless or stiffly hairy; **usually several heads**, at ends of branches,.

FRUITS: Achenes, cylindrical, veined, minutely roughened, orange-brown, **slender-beaked**; pappus of feathery bristles.

ECOLOGY: Roadsides, lawns, pastures, disturbed ground; common at low elevations in and around settled areas, especially in the southern half of our region, also found north to the Queen Charlotte Islands and scattered near towns in southeast Alaska.

NOTES: Smooth cat's-ear (*H. glabra*) is another weedy species introduced from Europe, but it is an essentially **hairless annual** with smaller flowering heads that **open only in full sunlight**. It is common in disturbed areas, especially in sandy soils, in the southern part of our region, from the Strait of Georgia–Puget Sound area south. **Autumn hawkbit** (*Leontodon autumnalis*) is an introduced **perennial weed** locally common in pastures and fields and on roadsides from southwestern B.C. to Oregon. **Hairy hawkbit** (*L. taraxacoides*, also called *L. nudicaulis*) is another introduced **weedy perennial** of disturbed habitats on the Queen Charlotte Islands and found north from the Strait of Georgia–Puget Sound area south along the coast to California. **Autumn hawkbit** is very similar to hairy cat's-ear, but it has **beakless achenes**. Hairy hawkbit has a **single-headed**, naked flowering stem.

YELLOW SALSIFY • *Tragopogon dubius*

GENERAL: Biennial or annual herb with **milky juice**, from **taproot; stems leafy**, often branched, 30–100 cm tall, **noticeably enlarged** beneath flowering or fruiting heads.

LEAVES: Long, narrow, **entire, somewhat grass-like**, tapering uniformly from base to tip, clasping stem at base, alternate, cottony-hairy when young.

FLOWERS: Heads **pale yellow**, of ray flowers only; involucral bracts **form a cone in bud**, in 1 equal series, 2.5–4 cm long, distinctly longer than ray flowers, to 4–7 cm long in fruit; **solitary heads** at ends of branches.

FRUITS: Achenes, slender, 25–35 mm long, gradually narrowed to a stout beak; pappus a single series of large, **feathery bristles united at the base**.

ECOLOGY: Roadsides, fields, relatively dry waste places; common at low elevations in settled parts of the southern half of our region.

NOTES: Yellow salsify is a weedy species introduced from Europe, as is common salsify (*T. porrifolius*, also called oyster plant). **Common salsify** has **purple** flowers and tends to grow in moister habitats than does yellow salsify. • The coagulated latex of yellow salsify was chewed by some Nlaka'pamux and other people of interior British Columbia. • 'Salsify' is from the French *salsifis* and Latin *solsequium*, derived in turn from *sol* meaning 'sun' and *sequium* meaning 'follower.' Although the flowers do not actually follow the sun, they do close up at midday or in cloudy weather, a habit that makes them often hard to find and earns them the name 'Jack-go-to-bed-at-noon.'

PRICKLY SOW-THISTLE • *Sonchus asper*

GENERAL: Annual or sometimes biennial herb with **milky juice**, from short **pale taproot**, 10–100 cm tall; **stems leafy**, hollow, hairless except for some gland-tipped hairs in the inflorescence.

LEAVES: Alternate, stalkless and with **large, rounded flanges clasping the stem**; middle and upper leaves **elliptic to egg-shaped**; margins usually **prickly-toothed but sometimes also lobed**.

FLOWERS: Heads **yellow**, of ray flowers only, 1.5–2.5 cm wide; involucral bracts 9–14 mm high, somewhat glandular-hairy; **several heads in flat-topped clusters**.

FRUITS: Flattened achenes with usually 6–8 ribs; pappus hairs white, often in 2 series.

ECOLOGY: Roadsides, fields, gardens, waste places; common at low to middle elevations in settled areas, mostly in the southern half of our region but also established in several places near towns on the Queen Charlotte Islands and in southeast Alaska.

NOTES: Prickly sow-thistle is a cosmopolitan weed, introduced from Europe. • **Common sow-thistle** (*S. oleraceus*) is also a taprooted, weedy annual with distribution and ecology similar to those of prickly sow-thistle. However, common sow-thistle usually has **soft, pinnately divided** leaves with **sharp-pointed, clasping flanges**, and its achenes are both 6–10 ribbed and **cross-wrinkled**. **Perennial sow-thistle** (*S. arvensis*) is a perennial with **extensive rhizomes**, 0.4–2 m tall, with **pinnately lobed**, prickly-toothed leaves and **dark-yellow** heads 3–5 cm wide. It grows in cultivated fields, pastures, roadsides, clearings, meadows and thickets; it is common at low to middle elevations in settled parts of our region, mostly in the southern half. • Sow-thistles can be separated from the true thistles (*Cirsium* spp.) by breaking their stems. **Sow-thistles have milky latex; true thistles do not.** • The young leaves of sow-thistles can be eaten raw in salads or cooked as a vegetable.

NIPPLEWORT • *Lapsana communis*

GENERAL: Annual herb with **milky juice**, from a **taproot; stems leafy**, simple or branched above, hairless to glandular hairy, 30–150 cm tall.

LEAVES: Alternate, thin, **stalked, broadly egg-shaped**, with **toothed to lobed** (the basal leaves) margins, sparsely hairy to hairless.

FLOWERS: Heads **yellow**, of ray flowers only; involucral bracts in 2 series, 5–8 mm high, hairless; usually numerous heads on slender hairless stalks.

FRUITS: Achenes, **sausage-shaped, curved**, hairless, 3–5 mm long; **no pappus**.

ECOLOGY: Fields, roadsides, disturbed areas, sometimes in open forest; common at low to middle elevations in the southern part of our region, sporadic northwards.

NOTES: Nipplewort is a weedy species introduced from Eurasia. • In our region, *Lapsana* is the only member of its tribe (that is, genera with ray flowers only and milky juice) **without a pappus**. • This plant was used to treat sore or cracked nipples or ulcerated breasts. In French it is called *herbes aux mamelles*. • The Latin *Lapsana* is from the Greek *lapazo* meaning 'purge,' implying medicinal use.

WALL LETTUCE • *Lactuca muralis*

GENERAL: Annual or biennial herb with **milky juice**, from a taproot; **stems leafy**, slender, hairless, 30–100 cm tall.

LEAVES: Alternate; basal and lower stem leaves 6–20 cm long, lance-shaped in outline, **deeply lobed with a broad, ivy-like terminal lobe, with flanges at the clasping base**, glaucous on the lower surface; middle and upper leaves few and much smaller.

FLOWERS: Heads **yellow**, narrow, 5 flowered; involucral bracts 9–11 mm high; usually numerous heads in an open cluster.

FRUITS: Achenes, **flattened**, with several veins or ribs on each face, about 4 mm long including the short beak; pappus of numerous **whitish bristles**.

ECOLOGY: Moist forest, glades and forest edges, clearings, roadsides; common and often abundant at low to middle elevations.

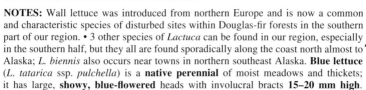

NOTES: Wall lettuce was introduced from northern Europe and is now a common and characteristic species of disturbed sites within Douglas-fir forests in the southern part of our region. • 3 other species of *Lactuca* can be found in our region, especially in the southern half, but they all are found sporadically along the coast north almost to Alaska; *L. biennis* also occurs near towns in northern southeast Alaska. **Blue lettuce** (*L. tatarica* ssp. *pulchella*) is a **native perennial** of moist meadows and thickets; it has large, **showy, blue-flowered** heads with involucral bracts **15–20 mm high**. **Tall blue lettuce** (*L. biennis*) and **prickly lettuce** (*L. serriola*) are both **annuals or biennials**. Tall blue lettuce is a big (0.5–2.5 m tall) **native** species of moist meadows, thickets and openings; it has **blue or white-flowered** heads with involucral bracts **9–14 mm long**, short-beaked achenes, and **brownish** pappus hairs. **Prickly lettuce** is an **introduced weed** of roadsides, fields and disturbed areas; it is 30–150 cm tall and has **spiny stems, yellow-flowered heads** with involucral bracts **10–15 mm high**, long-beaked achenes, and **white** pappus hairs. • This weedy plant is a relative of garden lettuce. The leaves are edible, but rather bitter. • The common name is a direct translation of the Latin *Lactuca* meaning 'lettuce' and *muralis* meaning 'wall.'

WESTERN RATTLESNAKE-ROOT • *Prenanthes alata*

GENERAL: Perennial herb from somewhat **tuberous-thickened** roots, with **milky juice**; stems leafy, single but often branched above, sparsely hairy, 20–80 cm tall.

LEAVES: Mostly on the stem, thin; middle and lower leaves with **winged stalks, arrowhead-shaped, coarsely and irregularly sharp-toothed**; upper leaves smaller and becoming stalkless.

FLOWERS: White to pinkish heads, of 10–15 ray flowers; involucral bracts 7–14 mm high, sparsely hairy; few to many heads in open, somewhat flat-topped groups.

FRUITS: Achenes, cylindrical, several veined, beakless, hairless, 4–6 mm long; pappus hairs **brownish**.

ECOLOGY: Stream-banks, wet rocks, shoreline bluffs and rocky beaches, forest edges and openings; common at low to middle elevations.

NOTES: At first glance and when not in flower, western rattlesnake-root looks 'a lotta' like arrow-leaved groundsel (p. 298), which, however, does not have milky juice or distinctly winged leaf stalks. • The origin of the common name is not clear, but the name suggests the plant was used to ward off rattlesnakes or treat their bites. *Prenanthes* is from the Greek and means 'drooping' (*prenes*) 'flower' (*anthos*). The leaf stalks are winged—hence the name *alata* which means 'winged with protruding ridges that are wider than thick.'

CHICORY • *Cichorium intybus*

GENERAL: Perennial herb with **milky juice**, from a **deep taproot**; stems branching, leafy, 30–150 cm tall, hairless or hairy.

LEAVES: Alternate; lower leaves stalked, **lance-shaped, with deeply toothed to lobed margins**; upper leaves reduced, stalkless, toothed (not lobed) to entire.

FLOWERS: Heads **blue or rarely white**, of ray flowers only, up to 4 cm wide; involucral bracts in two series, 9–15 mm high, outer bracts shorter and loose; several to many heads but usually 1–3 together on long branches from the axils of very small upper leaves.

FRUITS: Achenes, small (2–3 mm long), hairless, somewhat ribbed and 5 angled; pappus of 2–3 series of **scales**.

ECOLOGY: Roadside, fields, waste areas; common in settled parts of the southern half of our region.

NOTES: This introduced weed, native to Eurasia, is now established in many parts of the world. • Chicory is related to Belgium endive (*C. endiva*), whose leaves are eaten as a salad green. The taproots, which contain the complex carbohydrate inulin, can be roasted, ground and used as a coffee substitute (see Turner and Szczawinski, 1978). • Chicory and *Cichorium* are from the original Arabic name for wild chicory. The blanched leaves of chicory are reportedly the esteemed *barbe-de-capucin* used in France for winter salads.

SILVER BURWEED • *Ambrosia chamissonis*

GENERAL: Somewhat succulent perennial herb, forming **large clumps** 20–100 cm tall; stems branched at base, leafy, spreading hairy.

LEAVES: Mostly alternate, stalked, **toothed to deeply divided and crinkly edged**, 2–7 cm long, generally **silvery-hairy.**

FLOWERS: Heads **small, greenish**, of disk flowers only, unisexual; male heads more or less stalkless in leafless terminal spikes; female heads usually below the male ones, in the axils of leaves and bracts, with **involucral bracts that have several rows of prickles.**

FRUITS: Achenes, enclosed within the involucral bracts, the whole forming 6–11 mm long **burs** with 2–4 series of somewhat flattened prickles; **no pappus.**

ECOLOGY: Coastal dunes, sandy or gravelly beaches; common in suitable habitats.

NOTES: Silver burweed is also known as *Franseria chamissonis*. • Ambrosia was food for the Greek gods. The name was given to plants that smelled sweet, because they were thought to render a person long-lived, just as ambrosia did the immortals.

MOUNTAIN SAGEWORT • *Artemisia norvegica* ssp. *saxatilis*

GENERAL: Perennial herb, from a branching stem-base; stems **single or a few together**, 20–60 cm tall, with short runners and sterile rosettes.

LEAVES: Hairless to finely hairy; basal leaves stalked, **pinnately deeply divided, the ultimate segments linear**; stem leaves few, stalkless, progressively reduced upwards.

FLOWERS: Heads **yellowish**, often tinged with red, of disk flowers only, up to 1 cm wide, **often nodding**; involucres 3–7 mm high, of greenish, dark-margined bracts; several to many heads in a narrow, often **spike-like cluster.**

FRUITS: Hairless achenes; **no pappus hairs.**

ECOLOGY: Alpine tundra and exposed rocky ridges, subalpine and alpine meadows and heath, subalpine thickets and open forest, recent periglacial habitats in coastal Alaska; fairly common at **high elevations** in the northern part of the region, less so in the south.

NOTES: Mountain sagwort is also known as *Artemisia arctica*. • **Suksdorf's mugwort** (*A. suksdorfii*) has clustered stems with **elliptic to lance-shaped, coarsely toothed or lobed** leaves that are **green above and cottony white-hairy below.** It is a native perennial species of coastal bluffs and rocky, gravelly or sandy beaches, and it is common from Vancouver Island (especially the Strait of Georgia–Puget Sound area) south to California. **Western mugwort** (*A. ludoviciana*) is a native perennial with **mostly stem leaves that are lance-shaped, mostly entire, and white-woolly** at least on the upper surface. Although it mainly occurs east of the southern part of our region, western mugwort is fairly common in drier mountain meadows of the Cascades, and it is also found in the Olympic Mountains. **Northern wormwood** (*A. campestris* ssp. *pacifica*, also called *A. campestris* var. *scouleriana*) is occasional in relatively dry, open, sandy or rocky habitats from the Strait of Georgia–Puget Sound area south. It is a native perennial with **mostly basal, deeply divided, loosely hairy** leaves and much smaller heads than those of mountain sagwort. • Most artemisias are aromatic, but mountain sagwort does not have the typical sage smell. • The genus *Artemisia* includes several well-known, pungently aromatic species used as vermifuges (hence the common name 'wormwood').

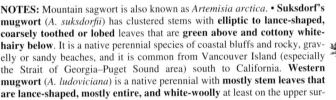

YARROW • *Achillea millefolium*

GENERAL: Perennial **aromatic** herb, usually rhizomatous, 10–100 cm tall.

LEAVES: Fern-like, stalked below and stalkless above, alternate, **pinnately dissected,** the divisions again dissected.

FLOWERS: Ray flowers usually about 5, **white to sometimes pink or reddish**; disk flowers 10–30, cream coloured; involucral bracts dry, overlapping in several series, often dark margined; heads numerous, in a short, **flat or round-topped cluster.**

FRUITS: Hairless, flattened achenes; **pappus lacking.**

ECOLOGY: On dry to moist, well-drained, open sites, meadows, rocky slopes, gravel bars, roadsides, clearings, sometimes in open forest, at low to high elevations; often weedy at lower elevations; common and widespread.

NOTES: Also known as *A. borealis*. • Taxonomically this is one of the most complex species in our flora, and it has been the subject of extensive studies. It is probably best, at least for ecological purposes on the northwest coast of North America, to recognize a single, variable species. • Yarrow was used in a wide variety of medicinal preparations: by the Haida as a poultice; by the Tsimshian as a sore throat gargle; by the Nuxalk as a bronchitis medication; by the Kwakwaka'wakw for a variety of purposes; by the Ditidaht as a childbirth medicine and by other Nuu-chah-nulth as a cold and cough medicine; by the Sechelt for colds and by the Squamish to cure measles; by the Cowichan as a blood purifier; by the Songish as a headache poultice and by the Saanich as a styptic and poultice; by the Swinomish as a bath for invalids; by the Klallam as a cold medicine with bitter-cherry bark; by the Quinault as a general tonic and eyewash; by the Squaxin as a stomach tonic; by the Skagit and Snohomish as a diarrhea medicine; and by the Makah as a childbirth medicine.

PINEAPPLE WEED • *Matricaria discoidea*

GENERAL: Annual herb, **pineapple-scented,** hairless; stems leafy, usually branched, 5–45 cm tall.

LEAVES: Basal leaves usually withered by flowering time; stem leaves alternate, **divided 1–3 times into short, narrow segments,** 1–5 cm long.

FLOWERS: Heads **greenish-yellow, conical, lacking ray flowers**; involucral bracts 2–5 mm long, with broad, pale margins; heads few to numerous.

FRUITS: Achenes, veined, beakless, hairless; **pappus a short, membranous crown.**

ECOLOGY: Roadsides, disturbed soils, waste places, often where soil has been trampled or compacted; common throughout our region in suitably disturbed habitats, from low to middle elevations.

NOTES: This weedy species is also known as *M. matricarioides*. • **Scentless mayweed** (*M. perforata*, also called false-chamomile and *M. inodora* or *M. maritima*) is **scentless** and has showy heads with **white ray flowers** and **hemispheric disks**. It is a weedy European species established on roadsides and other disturbed sites sporadically through our region. **Wild chamomile** (*M. recutita*, also called sweet false-chamomile and *M. chamomilla*) is another relatively infrequent introduction. It also has showy heads with **white ray flowers**, but it is **aromatic** and has a **conical, pointed disk**. • Pineapple weed has a definite pineapple scent when crushed, and it has been used as a fragrant stuffing for sachets and pillows by some aboriginal people in recent times. • *Matricaria* means 'mother-care' from its former use in the treatment of uterine infections. The flower heads are disk-shaped—hence *discoidea*.

DUNE TANSY • *Tanacetum bipinnatum* ssp. *huronense*

GENERAL: Perennial, aromatic (smelling of camphor) herb from rhizomes; stems stout, leafy, 20–60 cm tall, moderately hairy.

LEAVES: Basal leaves 5–30 cm long, **2 or 3 times intricately divided**, ultimate segments very narrow; stem leaves similar to basal, gradually reduced in size upwards.

FLOWERS: Ray flowers yellow, 2–7 mm long; disks yellow, button-like, 8–15 mm wide; involucral bracts 5–10 mm high, with light-coloured margins; heads few to several in **compact, somewhat flat-topped cluster**.

FRUITS: Achenes, ribbed and glandular; **pappus a tiny crown**.

ECOLOGY: Coastal sand dunes; scattered; frequently associated with other typical dune species such as large-headed sedge (p. 393) and seashore bluegrass (p. 377).

NOTES: This species is also known as *T. douglasii*, *T. huronense* and *Chrysanthemum bipinnatum*. • Common tansy (*T. vulgare*) is an introduced weed of roadsides, railway embankments and other disturbed areas that is common at low elevations in the southern half of the region and sporadic further north. Common tansy has numerous (20–200) rayless flower heads and hairless but gland-dotted leaves. Feverfew (*T. parthenium*) has white ray flowers and less-divided leaves. It, too, has been introduced, mainly from gardens, and it has become established in disturbed sites fairly commonly from southwestern B.C. south. • Dune tansy is called, in the Haida language, 'sloppy yellow beach leaves.' Common tansy has been used recently as a good luck charm by some aboriginal peoples of southern Vancouver Island. • In Britain, the bitter juice of common tansy was used to flavour Easter cakes. Sometimes a piece of the plant was placed in the shoe to relieve ague. • Common tansy was sold in 16th-century apothecaries as both 'anathasia' and 'tanacetum' for placing under the winding sheets of the dead to repel vermin.

BRASS BUTTONS • *Cotula coronopifolia*
MUD-DISK

GENERAL: Hairless, **aromatic, somewhat succulent, perennial** herb; stems leafy, often trailing and rooting at the nodes, 5–30 cm tall.

LEAVES: Alternate, stalkless, with sheathing bases, **narrowly oblong, entire or with a few coarse teeth or narrow lobes**, 1–6 cm long.

FLOWERS: Heads **yellow**, 5–11 mm wide, **of disk flowers only**; involucral bracts in 2 series, 3–5 mm high, hairless, yellowish with clear margins; **heads solitary** at ends of branches.

FRUITS: Achenes, those of the outer flowers flattened, winged, and long stalked, those of the central flowers 2-veined and short stalked; **no pappus**.

ECOLOGY: Beaches, tidal mudflats and marshes; scattered in the northern part of our region, common from Vancouver Island and the adjacent mainland south to California.

NOTES: Brass buttons is a South African species **introduced** and widely distributed along the beaches of the world. • **Fleshy jaumea** (*Jaumea carnosa*) is a **succulent native perennial** with **opposite**, narrowly oblong leaves and usually solitary yellow heads with **small, narrow ray flowers**. It occurs sporadically from southern Vancouver Island to California in habitats similar to those of brass buttons. • *Cotula* is from the Greek *kotyle*, 'a little cup,' so-called because the bright-yellow 'brass button' flowers suggest a cup turned face down. The species name means 'crowned' or 'encircled' and may refer to the involucral bracts cradling the cup.

MAYWEED • *Anthemis cotula*
STINKING CHAMOMILE

GENERAL: Annual, **ill-scented** herb from **taproot**; stems erect, leafy, simple or branched, essentially hairless, 10–60 cm tall.

LEAVES: Alternate, **2–3 times divided into narrow, sparsely hairy, gland-dotted segments**.

FLOWERS: Ray flowers white, commonly 10–20, 5–10 mm long; disk flowers yellow, numerous; involucral bracts in several rows, overlapping, firm, narrow, with long-pointed tips; receptacle with **chaffy scales only in the middle**; heads solitary at ends of uppermost branches.

FRUITS: Achenes, slightly flattened, **10-ribbed, glandular-bumpy; no pappus**.

ECOLOGY: Fields, roadsides, disturbed soils; common at low elevations in the settled part of the southern half of our region, uncommon on the north coast, where it is found mostly near towns.

NOTES: 2 other introduced weedy species occur in our region. **Corn chamomile** (*A. arvensis*) is similar to mayweed but has achenes with **smooth ribs** and a recep-

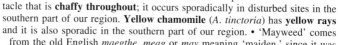

tacle that is **chaffy throughout**; it occurs sporadically in disturbed sites in the southern part of our region. **Yellow chamomile** (*A. tinctoria*) has **yellow rays** and it is also sporadic in the southern part of our region. • 'Mayweed' comes from the old English *maegthe, meag* or *may* meaning 'maiden,' since it was widely used for 'complaints of young women.' Many old names for daisy-like flowers are similarly derived from words associated with young women. The reasoning was that flowers with white rays resembled the moon. Therefore, they were thought to influence the monthly cycles of young women or complaints related to the womb. In ancient times, all such flowers were dedicated to the virgin goddess of the night (Artemis or Diana). Later, in Christian times, the dedication was transferred to Mary Magdalene and Saint Margaret; some white-rayed daisies are called 'marguerite.'

OXEYE DAISY • *Leucanthemum vulgare*

GENERAL: Perennial from a well-developed, woody rhizome, typically **smelling strongly of sage**; stems 20–80 cm tall, simple or once branched, hairless to slightly hairy.

LEAVES: Basal leaves stalked, broadly or narrowly **spoon-shaped**, with **rounded teeth and lobes** on the margin; stem leaves alternate, becoming stalkless upwards, oblong, toothed to lobed.

FLOWERS: Ray flowers white, 1–2 cm long; disks yellow, 1–2 cm across; heads solitary at ends of branches.

FRUITS: Achenes black, with **about 10 white ribs; no pappus**.

ECOLOGY: Fields, meadows, roadsides, clearings; primarily at low elevations in the settled portions of the southern half of our region, but also established on the Queen Charlotte Islands and in southeast Alaska.

NOTES: This species is also known as *Chrysanthemum leucanthemum*. • **Arctic daisy** (*L. arcticum*, also called *Chrysanthemum arcticum*) has leaves that are **wedge-shaped with 3–7 blunt, often toothed lobes**. It is a **native, perennial, maritime** species of rocky or gravelly beaches and salt marshes, and occurs sporadically from Observatory Inlet, B.C., north through southeast Alaska. • Oxeye daisy is an introduced weed of European origin that is widespread and often very abundant in disturbed places, especially roadsides. It also invades fields and meadows, where it competes aggressively, especially under grazing pressure, to form dense and extensive populations. • The young leaves of oxeye daisy are edible and very sweet. The flower heads can be used to make a wine similar to dandelion wine.

ENGLISH DAISY • *Bellis perennis*

GENERAL: Fibrous-rooted **perennial** herb, spreading-hairy; flowering stems leafless, **2–20 cm tall**.

LEAVES: All basal, with short to long stalks, **elliptic to oval or circular**, rounded at tip; margins entire or toothed.

FLOWERS: Ray flowers **white to pink or purple**, numerous; disk flowers yellow; involucral bracts 5–6 mm high, often purplish-tinged, blunt at tip, hairy; heads solitary.

FRUITS: Achenes, flattened, 2 veined, soft-hairy; **no pappus**.

ECOLOGY: Lawns, pastures, roadsides, waste places; common throughout our region in or near settlements.

NOTES: English daisy is a **cultivated ornamental** species, which was introduced from Europe and is now widely established along the coast. • Daisy, or 'day's eye,' is from the Anglo-Saxon *doeges-sege* meaning 'eye of the day' because the flowers open and close with changes in daylight, or because the yellow disk resembles the sun. *Bellis* means 'pretty' and there is a legend that the genus was named after the Belides, one of whom died in fear of Vertumnus, the god of spring, and sank to the earth in the form of a daisy.

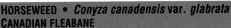

HORSEWEED • *Conyza canadensis* var. *glabrata*
CANADIAN FLEABANE

GENERAL: Annual, hairless to sparsely hairy herb; stems leafy, **20–100 cm tall**.

LEAVES: Alternate, numerous, the lower ones **lance-shaped**, stalked, up to 10 cm wide, the others narrower and more or less stalkless.

FLOWERS: Ray flowers **white, very short, narrow** and inconspicuous; disk flowers yellow, few; involucral bracts 3–4 mm high, overlapping, hairless; heads small, numerous in an open inflorescence.

FRUITS: Achenes, bristly; **white pappus hairs**.

ECOLOGY: Weedy species of roadsides and disturbed areas; frequent at low elevations.

NOTES: Horseweed is closely related to *Erigeron*, and has been named *Erigeron canadensis* by some. • **Annual fleabane** or daisy (*E. annuus*) is a **tall (60–150 cm)**, weedy annual of moist, disturbed sites, which is occasional in the southern part of our region. It has **numerous**, broadly lance-shaped, **toothed** leaves, stems with long spreading hairs below the inflorescence, **numerous narrow, white ray flowers up to 10 mm long**, disk flowers with a pappus of **white bristles plus short scales or whiskers** and several to many heads in an open, leafy cluster. **Rough-stemmed fleabane** or daisy (*E. strigosus*) is **30–70 cm tall** and has **few, usually entire** leaves, but otherwise it is similar to annual fleabane. Rough-stemmed fleabane is also an annual weed of the southern part of our region but it is usually found in drier disturbed sites than annual fleabane. • Horseweed, reported to be irritating to the nostrils of horses, is a Canadian native that has spread throughout the world. • The Latin *Conyza* was ascribed by Pliny to some form of 'fleabane' (see *Erigeron*, pp. 283–285) and derives from the Greek *konops*, 'a flea.'

Key to Daisies (*Erigeron*) and Asters (*Aster*)

It is sometimes difficult to distinguish daisies (*Erigeron*) from asters (*Aster*). Daisies usually flower earlier in the growing season than do asters, but there are exceptions and overlaps. Most species of daisies have involucral bracts nearly equal in length and arranged in a single series, but some have involucres like those of asters. The bracts of daisies are comparatively long and narrow, and they usually lack green tips. The ray flowers of daisies are usually more numerous and narrower than those of asters. Asters generally are taller and more leafy than daisies and have more flower heads per stem, but there are exceptions.

1a. Involucral bracts usually in 1–2 equal rows, green (but not leafy) or wax-papery throughout; ray flowers mostly very narrow; plants seldom with rhizomes (except *Erigeron peregrinus*); buds often nodding, becoming erect on opening; plants mostly blooming in spring and early summer .... *Erigeron*

    2a. Ray flowers numerous (25–40), thread-like, very short (1 mm long or less), whitish; disk flowers relatively few (less than 20); weedy annuals .... *Conyza canadensis*

    2b. Ray flowers few to numerous, well developed, conspicuous; disk flowers numerous; perennials or biennials 3

        3a. Ray flowers very numerous, thread-like, erect, short (to 4 mm long) .... *E. acris*

        3b. Ray flowers few to numerous, well developed and spreading, usually longer than 4 mm 4

            4a. Stem leaves well developed, gradually reduced in size up the stem, with clasping bases, lance-shaped or broader; plants tall and erect 5

                5a. Rays mostly 2–4 mm wide, numerous (25–80) .... *E. peregrinus*

                5b. Rays 1 mm wide or less, very numerous (over 150) .... *E. philadelphicus*

            4b. Stem leaves much reduced in size or absent, linear to lance-shaped; plants low and spreading; involucres woolly-hairy 6

                6a. Flowers yellow .... *E. aureus*

                6b. Flowers white to purplish .... *E. humilis*

1b. Involucral bracts usually in 3 or more rows and overlapping like shingles on a roof, the outer ones often progressively shorter, usually green at the tip and wax-papery at the base, sometimes green throughout and somewhat leafy; ray flowers comparatively broad; plants often with rhizomes; buds usually erect; plants blooming mostly in late summer or fall .... *Aster*

    2c. Involucral bracts and stalks of flower heads glandular .... *A. modestus*

    2d. Involucral bracts and stalks of flower heads not glandular 3

        3c. Heads solitary; plants dwarfed, of high elevations .... *A. alpigenus*

        3d. Heads several to many 4

            4c. Ray flowers few (13–21); plants without rhizomes; leaves cottony on lower surface .... *A. ledophyllus*

            4d. Ray flowers more numerous; plants often with rhizomes 5

                5c. Involucral bracts strongly graduated in size, green and mostly blunt at the tip .... *A. chilensis*

                5d. Involucral bracts not strongly graduated or, if so, then the bracts distinctly sharp pointed 6

                    6c. Outer involucral bracts with wax-papery (not green) margins near the base; leaves usually toothed .... *A. subspicatus*

                    6d. Outer involucral bracts without wax-papery margins (but sometimes whitish) near the base; outer bracts often enlarged and leafy; leaves usually not toothed .... *A. foliaceus*

PHILADELPHIA FLEABANE • *Erigeron philadelphicus*

GENERAL: Biennial or short-lived perennial, with an erect stem-base and a **taproot or fibrous roots**; stems 20–70 cm tall, with long-spreading hairs or hairless.

LEAVES: Basal leaves broadly lance-shaped, coarsely toothed, **hairy**, short stalked; stem leaves progressively reduced in size, lance-shaped, stalkless, clasping at base, often toothed.

FLOWERS: Ray flowers pink to pinkish-purple or white, **numerous (over 150), very narrow**; disk flowers yellow; involucres 4–6 mm high, the bracts lance-oblong, with broad, clear margins, hairy on midvein or hairless; heads **few to many**.

FRUITS: Sparsely hairy achenes; pappus hairs whitish, fragile.

ECOLOGY: Moist, open forests, thickets, streambanks, roadsides, clearings; scattered at low to middle elevations mostly from Vancouver Island south.

NOTES: Showy fleabane (*E. speciosus*) is another species with numerous, narrow ray flowers, but it has smaller, entire stem leaves and occurs mostly in western Washington and Oregon in our region. Bitter fleabane (*E. acris*) is a biennial to perennial with numerous, very narrow (to 0.4 mm wide), short (up to 4 mm long), erect, pink to purplish or white ray flowers and straw-coloured pappus hairs. It is more typically an eastern and northern species, and it is often weedy. It occurs sporadically along the eastern margin of our region on gravel bars, river terraces and streambanks and in meadows, wetlands, and clearings, from low to high elevations. • The common name 'fleabane' was first applied to European species of *Erigeron*. It was believed that bunches of the dried plants hung in a house would drive out fleas. *Erigeron* comes from the Greek *eri* meaning 'spring' and *geron* meaning 'an old man,' in reference to the white-hairy fruiting heads or possibly to some hairy spring-flowering species.

SUBALPINE DAISY • *Erigeron peregrinus*

GENERAL: Perennial herb, from a **rhizome or short stem-base**; stems single, unbranched, 10–70 cm tall, hairy or hairless.

LEAVES: Basal leaves narrowly or broadly lance- to spoon-shaped, tapering to the stalk, variable in size, 1–20 cm long, **essentially hairless, often hairy margined**; stem leaves similar to lower ones, sometimes clasping, ample or greatly reduced.

FLOWERS: Ray flowers pink, lavender or reddish-purple, sometimes whitish, **30–80**; disk flowers yellow; involucres 6–12 mm high, the bracts lance-oblong, **sticky-hairy or merely hairy**; heads **solitary or few**.

FRUITS: Hairy, **4–7 ribbed** achenes; pappus hairs white to tan.

ECOLOGY: Moist to wet meadows, streamsides and open forests from middle to high elevations; common in lowland bogs in southeast Alaska and other suitable habitats throughout our region.

NOTES: Subalpine daisy is one of the most typical species of subalpine meadows, and it is probably our most common daisy. • **Alice Eastwood's daisy** (*E. aliceae*) is similar but has distinctly hairy leaves, **2–4 ribbed** achenes and involucral bracts that are **hairy below and glandular above**. It occurs on rocky ridges or in meadows and sandy openings at fairly high elevations in the Cascades Mountains of Oregon (where it largely replaces subalpine daisy) and also in the Olympic Mountains. Subalpine daisy could also be confused with leafy aster (see notes, p. 288).

ARCTIC DAISY • *Erigeron humilis*

GENERAL: Perennial herb, with a short **taproot or short, brittle stem-base** and often some fibrous roots; stems single, **3–20 cm tall, hairy with greyish or dark hairs.**

LEAVES: Basal leaves **broadly lance- to spoon-shaped,** commonly hairless or nearly so by flowering time; stem leaves linear to lance-shaped, reduced, stalkless; leaves with **entire margins.**

FLOWERS: Ray flowers **white to purplish, numerous (about 50–150)**; disk flowers yellow; involucres 6–9 mm high, the bracts lance-oblong, purplish-black or greenish, with long, multicellular hairs with **purplish black** crosswalls; heads **solitary.**

FRUITS: Hairy achenes; pappus hairs white to tan.

ECOLOGY: Tundra, snowbeds, seepage sites, rocky ledges, and scree; in moist to wet alpine sites, also sometimes in bogs at lower elevations; common in northern southeast Alaska, usually at high elevations; rare on the Queen Charlotte Islands, scattered in the Coast Mountains to southwestern B.C.

NOTES: At least 20 species of *Erigeron* occur within our region; we have described a few of the most common. For more information, please consult Hultén (1968), Hitchcock and Cronquist (1973), and Douglas et al. (1989). • **Cut-leaved daisy** (*E. compositus* var. *glabratus*) is a small, tufted perennial with **3-lobed to divided basal leaves** and white to pink or blue ray flowers (sometimes rayless). It occurs at middle to high elevations on fairly dry, sandy or rocky sites, mostly along the eastern edge of our region, but it is locally common on some dry ridges in the southern B.C. Coast and the Cascade mountains. • The species name *humilis* means 'low-growing, lower than most of its kind.'

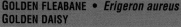

GOLDEN FLEABANE • *Erigeron aureus*
GOLDEN DAISY

GENERAL: **Dwarf perennial** herb from a **thick, branched stem-base,** finely hairy; stems with a few, small leaves, 2–15 cm tall.

LEAVES: **Mostly basal,** stalked, **elliptic to egg-shaped,** entire, rounded or blunt at tip.

FLOWERS: Ray flowers 25–70, **yellow,** 6–9 mm long; disk flowers yellow; involucral bracts 5–8 mm high, loose, **woolly-hairy,** the hairs sometimes with purple crosswalls; heads **solitary.**

FRUITS: Achenes; pappus of 10–20 bristles plus some outer bristles or narrow scales.

ECOLOGY: Rocky, relatively dry ridges, ledges and tundra; common at subalpine to alpine elevations.

NOTES: In similar, high-elevation habitats along the eastern margin of the southern half of our region and also in the Olympic Mountains, you could encounter **Lyall's goldenweed** (*Haplopappus lyallii*). It, too, is a dwarf species with solitary yellow heads, but its stems are **leafy** and the **lance-shaped to oblong** leaves are strongly **glandular-hairy.** • The species name *aureus* means, simply, 'golden.'

ALPINE ASTER • *Aster alpigenus*

GENERAL: Dwarf perennial herb from an erect stem-base and usually a **taproot, 3–30 cm tall**.

LEAVES: Mostly basal, entire, lance-shaped to linear, 2–15 cm long, often woolly-hairy when young; stem leaves few and much smaller.

FLOWERS: Ray flowers 10–40, violet to lavender, 7–15 mm long; disk flowers yellow; involucral bracts 5–13 mm high, overlapping, sometimes purplish tinged, often hairy on the margins; **heads solitary**.

FRUITS: Achenes, hairy on the upper portion; pappus of whitish bristles.

ECOLOGY: Subalpine meadows; common, sometimes locally abundant.

NOTES: Arctic aster (*A. sibiricus*) is a small, **rhizomatous** perennial with **leafy stems** and **1 to few heads**. It occurs sporadically north from Mt. Baker to Alaska, mostly along the eastern margin of our region, in high-elevation meadows and on rocky slopes at lower latitudes, descending to lower elevations further north. • The species name *alpigenus* means 'alpine.'

TEA-LEAVED ASTER • *Aster ledophyllus*

GENERAL: Perennial herb from a stout stem-base; **stems leafy, 30–60 cm tall**.

LEAVES: Numerous, stalkless, narrowly lance-shaped to elliptic, entire or with a few irregular teeth, **3–7 cm long**, more or less hairless above, **grey-cottony on lower surface**; lowermost leaves very small.

FLOWERS: Ray flowers 13–21, **lavender-purple**, 12–20 mm long; disk flowers yellow; involucral bracts 7–11 mm high, overlapping, narrow, sharp-tipped, tips commonly purplish; heads several.

FRUITS: Achenes, hairy mostly on upper portion; pappus of whitish bristles, a few of the outer bristles usually shorter than the rest.

ECOLOGY: Relatively dry meadows, glades, and open forests, mostly at subalpine elevations; common in the Cascade Mountains.

NOTES: Engelmann's aster (*A. engelmannii*) is a species of open forest and meadows at middle to high elevations in the eastern Cascade Mountains of Washington and adjacent B.C. Engelmann's aster is similar to tea-leaved aster, but it is a **larger** plant (**60–150 cm tall**) with **larger leaves (5–10 cm long)** and **(usually) white** ray flowers. **Olympic mountain aster** (*A. paucicapitatus*) also has **white** ray flowers but is **smaller (20–60 cm tall)** and has **smaller (2–4 cm long), glandular-hairy** leaves. It grows in meadows and on open rocky slopes from low to high elevations, and it occurs sporadically on central Vancouver Island and the Olympic Peninsula.

COMMON CALIFORNIA ASTER • *Aster chilensis*

GENERAL: Slender, somewhat sprawling perennial from a rhizome or branching stem-base; stems leafy, ascending to erect, hairy at least above, 50–100 cm tall.

LEAVES: Lower leaves lance-shaped, stalked, soon withering; **middle and upper leaves linear to narrowly oblong,** stalkless, 2–10 cm long, usually entire, hairless or sparsely hairy.

FLOWERS: Ray flowers 15–40, **blue or violet to white,** 5–15 mm long; disk flowers yellow; involucral bracts 5–7 mm high, **graduated,** green and mostly blunt at the tip; heads usually numerous on leafy-bracted branches.

FRUITS: Achenes, several veined, sparsely hairy; pappus of tawny bristles.

ECOLOGY: Meadows, open slopes, clearings, moist cliffs near the ocean; common primarily at lower elevations.

NOTES: *A. chilensis* includes *A. hallii* (*A. chilensis* var. *hallii*), the mostly white-rayed variety common in Washington and Oregon but apparently absent from B.C. • White-top aster (*A. curtus*) is a relatively uncommon species of dry, low-elevation, open habitats in the Strait of Georgia–Puget Sound area south to Oregon. It also has white-flowered heads, but the rays are few (1–3) and shorter than the pappus hairs (1–3 mm long). Oregon aster (*A. oregonensis*) is similar to white-top aster, but it is bigger, has 4–7 white rays that are 4–7 mm long, and occurs in open forest from southwest Washington south to California. Rough-leaved aster (*A. radulinus*) is another low-elevation species of dry, open forest and openings from southeastern Vancouver Island south to California. It has white to purple ray flowers 8–12 mm long, purple-edged involucral bracts, and sharply toothed, firm, rough-hairy leaves.

GREAT NORTHERN ASTER • *Aster modestus*

GENERAL: Perennial herb, with creeping rhizomes; stems single, simple or branched, 30–100 cm tall, sparsely to densely hairy and glandular up towards the flowers.

LEAVES: Basal leaves somewhat **smaller** than the others, usually withered by flowering time; stem leaves **lance-shaped,** stalkless, more or less clasping, hairless above, sparsely hairy beneath; margins smooth to few toothed.

FLOWERS: Ray flowers **violet or purple,** 20–45; disk flowers yellow; involucres 7–11 mm high, the bracts narrowly lance-shaped, **glandular,** greenish; heads few to many, **on glandular stalks.**

FRUITS: Sparsely hairy achenes; pappus hairs whitish or yellowish.

ECOLOGY: Moist to wet forests, openings, swamps, stream and river banks, and clearings; common at low to middle elevations in the northern half of our region, south to Oregon mostly in the B.C. Coast and the Cascade mountains.

NOTES: *A. modestus* is the only species of *Aster* in our region with **glandular involucral bracts.** • *Aster* is the Greek, Latin and English name for a star and describes the appearance of the flower heads. Asters are often confused with species of *Erigeron,* but the erigerons bloom earlier in the year. A good way to remember this is that *Aster* spp. are sometimes called 'Michaelmas' or 'Christmas' daisies because they can bloom as late as Christmas.

DOUGLAS' ASTER • *Aster subspicatus*

GENERAL: Perennial herb from a creeping rhizome or stem-base; stems leafy, hairy (at least on upper part), 20–80 cm tall.

LEAVES: Lower leaves lance-shaped, usually stalked; **middle leaves lance-shaped to oblong or narrowly elliptic**, stalkless, **usually toothed**, hairless above and beneath.

FLOWERS: Ray flowers **blue to purple**, 1–2 cm long; disk flowers yellow; involucral bracts firm, thick, overlapping, the outer ones typically with **wax-papery margins and a yellow-brown basal portion**; heads several to many, on hairy stalks in a leafy-bracted, open group.

FRUITS: Achenes, several ribbed, usually hairy; pappus hairs usually reddish or purplish-brown at maturity.

ECOLOGY: Beaches, meadows, streambanks, moist clearings; common at low to middle elevations throughout our region; the most common aster in coastal Alaska and north coastal B.C.

NOTES: This species is also known as *A. douglasii*. • Douglas' aster is sometimes difficult to distinguish from **leafy aster**, which has **mostly entire** leaves **often clasping** the stem, and **leafy** outer involucral bracts with **white margins at the base**. Douglas' aster is typically a coastal species, whereas leafy aster is more widespread. However, some taxonomists (e.g. Hultén 1968) think that both species should be included in *A. subspicatus*.

LEAFY ASTER • *Aster foliaceus*

GENERAL: Perennial herb from a creeping rhizome or stem-base; stems leafy, 20–60 cm tall.

LEAVES: Mostly entire; lower leaves broadly lance- to egg-shaped, usually stalked, often withering; middle leaves lance- to egg-shaped, stalkless **(sometimes clasping at base)**, 5–12 cm long, hairless to hairy.

FLOWERS: Ray flowers 15–60, **rose-purple to blue or violet**, 1–2 cm long; disk flowers yellow; involucral bracts overlapping, relatively large (some of the outer ones **enlarged and leafy**), **white margined at the base**; heads solitary to several, on hairy stalks in a **short**, leafy-bracted cluster.

FRUITS: Achenes, more or less hairy; pappus hairs white or straw-coloured, sometimes reddish.

ECOLOGY: Moist meadows, streambanks, glades and open forest at middle to high elevations, descending also to low elevations in the north; common throughout our region.

NOTES: *A. foliaceus* is included within *A. subspicatus* in Hultén (1968) and Welsh (1974), but our coastal-**lowland** *A. subspicatus* is readily distinguished from our coastal-**mountain** *A. foliaceus* (see notes above). Leafy aster is a highly variable species in terms of size, hairiness, number of heads and shape of involucral bracts. **Eaton's aster** (*A. bracteolatus*, also called *A. eatonii*) is similar but has a **long**, narrow, leafy-bracted inflorescence with numerous heads, and it usually has **pink or white** ray flowers. It occurs fairly frequently in moist sites from low to middle elevations in the southern part of our region. Leafy aster could also be confused with subalpine daisy (*Erigeron peregrinus*), especially when both species grow together in subalpine meadows, but **subalpine daisy** has **equal-sized, non-graduated** involucral bracts. • The species and common names are the same: *foliaceus* means 'leafy.'

CANADA GOLDENROD • *Solidago canadensis*

GENERAL: Perennial herb, with **long, creeping** rhizomes; stems leafy, 40–150 cm tall, hairy at least on upper part.

LEAVES: Basal leaves **lacking**, lower ones soon deciduous, stem leaves numerous, crowded, **only gradually reduced upwards**, lance-linear to narrowly elliptic, tapering to a stalkless base, saw-toothed to entire, essentially hairless to rough-hairy on both sides.

FLOWERS: Ray flowers yellow, 10–17, short (1–3 mm long); disk flowers yellow; involucres 3–5 mm high, 3–6 mm broad, the bracts long pointed, **somewhat overlapping and sometimes sticky-glandular**; heads numerous, in dense **pyramidal clusters**.

FRUITS: Short-hairy achenes; pappus hairs white.

ECOLOGY: Roadsides, meadows, thickets, bluffs, forest openings or edges, often in disturbed areas; scattered in appropriate habitats at low to middle elevations.

NOTES: Northern coastal examples of this plant are sometimes called *Solidago lepida* (see Hultén 1968). • Goldenrod was reputedly carried into battle during the Crusades and was commonly used as a substitute for highly taxed English tea during the American Revolution. • *Solidago* is another medicinal plant; the name comes from the Latin *solidus* (whole) and *ago* (to make)— i.e., to make whole, or cure. • Fans of Canadian folk music may remember Stan Rogers's version of 'Witch of the Westmorland.' In this epic tale, an injured knight's wounds are bound with goldenrod by a witch with 'one half the form of a maiden fair, with a jet-black mare's body.' He recovers, of course, though it is not clear if it was the goldenrod or because she 'kissed his pale lips once and twice and three times round again.'

NORTHERN GOLDENROD • *Solidago multiradiata*

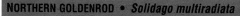

GENERAL: Perennial herb, with a **short** or rarely elongate **rhizome or branching stem-base**; stems usually solitary, hairy towards the flowers, 5–40 cm tall.

LEAVES: Basal and lower leaves **large**, broadly lance- to spoon-shaped, usually toothed, hairless except **conspicuously hairy-margined on the leaf stalks**; stem leaves similar to the basal but **becoming smaller above**.

FLOWERS: Ray flowers yellow, 12–18; disk flowers yellow, 15–21; involucres 5–8 mm high, 7–14 mm broad, the bracts **not obviously overlapping, not sticky**; heads several to many, in **dense, short-branched clusters**.

FRUITS: Short-hairy achenes; pappus hairs white.

ECOLOGY: Tundra, rocky ridges, grassy slopes, gravel bars, meadows, sometimes in dry open forest; widespread from middle to high elevations; also in lowlands in the far northern part of our region.

NOTES: Spikelike goldenrod (*S. spathulata*, also called *S. decumbens*) is taller (10–80 cm tall), **often strongly resinous and aromatic**; it has leaves that are hairless and **not hairy-margined on the stalks** and numerous heads in a **long, narrow cluster**. *S. spathulata* occurs on coastal sand dunes, river-banks, gravel bars, terraces, meadows and open dry forest and tundra, at low to high elevations, scattered in the southern half of our region. This species has a very wide altitudinal range: it is common on coastal sand dunes in Oregon and occurs in alpine tundra in the Cascade Mountains. • Northern goldenrod is one of the most common and widespread species of much of our alpine tundra, but it is rare or absent on the outer coast. • Goldenrods could be confused with yellow-flowered species of *Hieracium* or *Senecio*, but they are distinguished by their numerous small (usually less than 1 cm wide) heads. • All goldenrods contain small quantities of natural rubber in their latex.

NODDING BEGGARTICKS • *Bidens cernua*

GENERAL: Annual herb with fibrous roots; stems leafy, erect, simple or branched, hairless to sparsely hairy, 10–100 cm tall.

LEAVES: Opposite, stalkless, unlobed, hairless, lance-shaped; margins saw-toothed to almost smooth; 4–20 cm long.

FLOWERS: Ray flowers 6–8, yellow, or lacking; disk flowers yellow; involucral bracts in 2 series, the inner egg-shaped and dark streaked, the outer narrowly lance-shaped, green and somewhat leafy, **spreading or drooping**; heads **hemispheric**, solitary at ends of branches, nodding with age.

FRUITS: Achenes, narrowly wedge-shaped, 4 sided, flattened, ribbed, **convex and leathery** at the top, tan-coloured; pappus of **3–4 barbed bristles**.

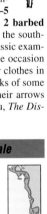

ECOLOGY: Moist disturbed soil, wet ditches, lakeshores; scattered at low elevations.

NOTES: Nodding beggarticks is a widespread, weedy species in much of the northern hemisphere. • **Vancouver Island beggarticks** (*B. amplissima*) is similar but has **deeply 3-lobed** leaves and **flat-topped** achenes. It is frequent in low-elevation wet, open habitats, but only on southeastern Vancouver Island and the adjacent B.C. mainland. **Common beggarticks** (*B. frondosa*) has **stalked, compound leaves with 3–5 leaflets, orange** disk flowers, **erect** outer involucral bracts and dark achenes with **2 barbed bristles.** It is a weed introduced from the eastern U.S., and it is scattered mostly in the southeastern part of our region. • The fruits (sometimes called seeds) of *Bidens* provide classic examples of adherent or stick-tight dispersal, hence 'beggarticks.' 'If in October you have occasion to pass through or along some half dried pool, these seeds will often adhere to your clothes in surprising numbers. It is as if you had unconsciously made your way through the ranks of some countless but invisible Lilliputian army, which in their anger had discharged all their arrows and darts at you, though none of them reached higher than your legs' (H.D. Thoreau, *The Dispersion of Seeds*).

MOUNTAIN SNEEZEWEED • *Helenium autumnale*

GENERAL: Perennial herb with **fibrous roots**; stems leafy, sparsely hairy to hairless, 40–120 cm tall.

LEAVES: Alternate, numerous, gland-spotted, lance-shaped, stalkless or with short, winged stalks that carry on down the stem, 4–15 cm long, lowest generally deciduous; margins shallowly toothed to nearly smooth.

FLOWERS: Ray flowers yellow, 10–20, wedge-shaped, **3 lobed at tip, pointing downwards**; disk **hemispheric**, flowers yellow; involucral bracts in 2–3 series, narrow, pointing downwards; heads several to numerous at the ends of branches.

FRUITS: Achenes, 4–5 angled and ribbed; pappus of several broad, sharp-pointed, translucent **scales**.

ECOLOGY: Occasional in streambanks, wet ditches, and other moist open places at low to middle elevations.

NOTES: Two **taprooted** species with big, yellow, sunflower-like heads occur on the south coast. **Deltoid balsamroot** (*Balsamorhiza deltoidea*) has big, **triangular, long-stalked, mostly basal** leaves and occurs sporadically in dry, open, grassy habitats in the Strait of Georgia–Puget Sound area and south to California, at low elevations. **Narrow-leaved mule's-ears** (*Wyethia angustifolia*) has large, **lance-shaped, basal** leaves and **several, smaller, alternate, stem** leaves. It grows in meadows and on open slopes at low to middle elevations in the Willamette valley and south to California.

HALL'S GOLDENWEED • *Haplopappus hallii*

GENERAL: A **much-branched shrub with a woody base** and erect annual stems to 50 cm tall.

LEAVES: Alternate, stiff, rough, deciduous, gradually reduced in size upward on the stem, more or less oblong, 2–5 cm long.

FLOWERS: Yellow, heads clustered towards the ends of the stems, resinous, with 5–8 rays; involucral bracts **hard and shiny** as if varnished.

FRUITS: Elongate achenes; pappus **bristles dingy white**, distinctly **unequal** in size.

ECOLOGY: A locally common dwarf shrub on rocky, open sites at middle to high elevations in the Cascade Mountains of Oregon.

NOTES: Although Hall's goldenweed is shrubby, we have treated it here (rather than in the 'Shrubs' section) because it is the only common sunflower-family shrub in our region. • This species represents a large genus of plants that form a prominent component of the flora in many dry mountains and deserts of western North America. They occur in dry southern parts of our region. • The generic name, spelled '*Aplopappus*' in some books, is from the Greek *haplous*, 'simple,' and *pappos*, 'seed-down,' and it refers to the unbranched pappus. This species is probably named after H.M. Hall, who did the respected monograph on this genus, or after Elihu Hall, an Oregon missionary who collected plants for Professor Asa Gray of Harvard University. It is also sometimes called 'hesperodoria,' which was a previous Latin name and means 'evening-flowering.'

ENTIRE-LEAVED GUMWEED • *Grindelia integrifolia*

GENERAL: Perennial **herb from a taproot** and often a stout branched stem-base; stems leafy, often somewhat hairy, 15–80 cm tall.

LEAVES: Toothed or entire, **resin-dotted**; basal leaves lance-shaped, up to 40 cm long; stem leaves alternate, stalkless and often clasping at their bases.

FLOWERS: Ray flowers yellow, 10–35; disk flowers yellow; involucral bracts **sticky glandular**, their long, slender, green tips loose or spreading; heads usually several to many, hemispheric.

FRUITS: Achenes, somewhat flattened; pappus of **2 to several firm but deciduous awns**.

ECOLOGY: Beaches, rocky shores, salt marshes, mostly maritime habitats; frequent from the Queen Charlotte Islands south; also in moist open non-maritime habitats in the Strait of Georgia–Puget Sound area through the Willamette Valley.

NOTES: Entire-leaved gumweed is an extremely variable species and so has been described under a number of different names, including *G. macrophylla*. • *G. integrifolia* is sometimes called 'Puget Sound gumweed' or 'resinweed.' It is named after David Grindel (1776–1836), a Russian botanist. The scientific and common names refer to the entire uppermost leaves of the plant (hence *integrifolia*). It is aptly named 'gumweed' because the flowers are surrounded by bracts covered with a white, extremely sticky latex or 'gum.'

CHILEAN TARWEED • *Madia sativa*

GENERAL: Coarse **annual, tar-scented** herb, conspicuously hairy and with **stalked glands** almost everywhere; stems leafy, 20–100 cm tall.

LEAVES: Alternate, linear to narrowly oblong, entire or slightly toothed; lower leaves somewhat crowded, **3–18 cm long**.

FLOWERS: Ray flowers yellow, **mostly about 13, 3–7 mm long**; disk flowers yellow, fertile; involucre broadly **urn-shaped, 6–12 mm high and about as wide**, the bracts covered in stalked glands; heads several, in open, leafy to dense clusters.

FRUITS: Achenes, flattened, curved and **lopsided**; ray achenes enfolded by the involucral bracts; **pappus lacking**.

ECOLOGY: Roadsides, clearings, other dry, open, disturbed sites; common at low elevations in the southern part of our region, from northwestern Washington south to California; also in adjacent southern B.C., where possibly introduced.

NOTES: Clustered tarweed (*M. glomerata*) is similar to Chilean tarweed but it has **narrower** leaves, **2–7 cm long**; very small heads in 1 to several small clusters; rays **1–3 or lacking, only 2 mm long**; and **spindle-shaped** involucres **only 3–5 mm wide**. It is scattered at low to middle elevations in the southern half of our region on roadsides and in other dry, open, disturbed sites. We have several other species of tarweeds, all in dry, open sites at low to middle elevations in the southern half of our region; use technical manuals for positive identification. **Little tarweed** (*M. exigua*) and **small-headed tarweed** (*M. minima*) both are **small annuals** with **tiny heads**. Elegant tarweed (*M. elegans*) is our showiest species, with **ray flowers 10–17 mm long**. • *Madia* comes from *madi*, the Chilean name for this crop plant once sown (*sativa* means 'sown') in fields for the seed from which the growers pressed a highly nutritious oil. Chilean tarweed grows widely in California, where the native people collected the seeds for winter use.

SILVERBACK LUINA • *Luina hypoleuca*

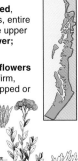

GENERAL: Perennial herb from a stout, branched, woody stem-base; **stems leafy**, erect, several to many, white-woolly, 15–40 cm tall.

LEAVES: Alternate, **elliptic to egg-shaped**, mostly similar in size and shape, stalkless, entire or nearly so, green and thinly hairy on the upper surface, **silvery white-woolly on the lower; basal leaves lacking**.

FLOWERS: Disk flowers dull yellow; **ray flowers lacking**; involucres 5–8 mm high, the bracts in a single series, lance-shaped, firm, hairy, of equal size; 10–17 heads on slender woolly stalks in a compact, flat-topped or mounded cluster.

FRUITS: Achenes, hairless or sparsely hairy, several-veined; pappus of numerous, fine, white bristles.

ECOLOGY: Common on open rocky slopes, cliff crevices, and talus slopes, at middle to subalpine elevations.

NOTES: Slender luina (*L. stricta*) has large, **lance-shaped basal** leaves, stem leaves **reduced in size upwards**, and a **long, narrow inflorescence**. It occurs sporadically in high-elevation meadows and on moist, open slopes in the Cascades from Mt. Rainier south. **Silvercrown** (*Cacaliopsis nardosmia*, also called *L. nardosmia;* **leaf drawing at right**) has **big** (up to 20 cm long and 25 cm wide), **circular to heart-shaped**, deeply **palmately divided** leaves that are **long stalked**, green above, and **thinly white-woolly below**. It is a species of well-drained meadows and open forest, occurring occasionally in the Cascades from Manning Park south and in the coastal ranges of western Oregon. Its leaves are similar to those of palmate coltsfoot (p. 294) which, however, have small, slender teeth in addition to deep lobes.

WOOLLY ERIOPHYLLUM • *Eriophyllum lanatum*
OREGON SUNSHINE

GENERAL: Perennial, **woolly** herb; stems usually several from the base, leafy, 25–60 cm tall.

LEAVES: Alternate or opposite, narrowly lobed to sometimes entire, 1–8 cm long.

FLOWERS: Ray flowers 8–13, yellow, **1–2 cm long**; disk flowers yellow; involucre 9–12 mm high, the bracts firm, erect, embracing the ray achenes; **heads single on long stalks.**

FRUITS: Achenes, slender, 4-angled, hairless to glandular or hairy; **pappus of 6–12 translucent scales, or a toothed crown.**

ECOLOGY: Dry, open habitats, bluffs, rocky slopes; common at low to middle elevations.

NOTES: Hairy goldfields (*Lasthenia maritima*, also called *Baeria maritima*) is a **somewhat succulent, weak annual** of rocky sea-cliffs and islands from southern Vancouver Island to California. It is 10–50 cm tall and has **opposite**, narrowly oblong leaves and small yellow heads with **short (1–3 mm)** rays and a conic receptacle. **Gold star** (*Crocidium multicaule*) is a **delicate**, several-stemmed **annual**, hairless except for **loose, cottony tufts** in the axils of smooth, slightly fleshy leaves. It is 5–30 cm tall, and it has basal and **alternate stem leaves** and bright-yellow heads with about 8 **rays 4–10 mm long** and a **conic** receptacle. This is an early-flowering species (*en masse* it can put on a dazzling display) of sandy flats, cliff ledges, rock outcrops and other dry, open sites at low elevations, scattered from the Strait of Georgia–Puget Sound area south in the valleys to California.

PATHFINDER • *Adenocaulon bicolor*

GENERAL: Perennial herb from fibrous roots, 30–100 cm tall; stems slender, erect, solitary, **white-woolly on lower part, with stalked glands on upper part.**

LEAVES: Mostly basal, large and thin, long-stalked, **broadly triangular to heart-shaped, green and essentially hairless above, white-woolly below**; margins smooth to coarsely toothed; stem leaves similar to basal leaves, few, alternate.

FLOWERS: Whitish, tubular disk flowers only, and only the outer 3–7 fertile; involucres 2–3.5 mm high, the bracts green, hairless, equal in size, pointing down when mature and eventually falling off; heads small, several to numerous, in a branched, **glandular** inflorescence.

FRUITS: Club-shaped achenes, becoming 5–8 mm long, with **stalked glands on upper portion; pappus lacking.**

ECOLOGY: Common in moist, shady forest and glades, at low to middle elevations.

NOTES: Unlike most members of the sunflower family, **pathfinder lacks both ray flowers and a pappus.** • If not in flower, pathfinder could be confused with the weedy **burdock** (p. 306), which has somewhat similar leaves but stout, **distinctly leafy, hairless stems**, and which usually grows in open, disturbed habitats. • The Squaxin used the crushed leaves for a poultice. • Wander through a patch of 'pathfinder' in the woods and you can always find your way back, since the silvery undersides of leaves turned over by your foot-steps will show you the way home. The species name *bicolor* refers to the fact that the upperside of the leaves are, in contrast, bright green. • Like several of our forest understorey herbs, pathfinder is a 'sunfleck' species, dependant on sunflecks (temporary patches of light on the forest floor) for a large frac-tion of its daily carbon gain.

PALMATE COLTSFOOT • *Petasites palmatus*

GENERAL: Perennial, with slender, creeping rhizomes; stems numerous, 10–50 cm tall, either with mostly female or mostly male flowers; **flowering stems precede leaves**.

LEAVES: Basal leaves **heart- or kidney-shaped**, deeply divided (to more than 2/3 towards base) into **5–7, toothed lobes, green and hairless above, white-woolly below**; stem leaves reduced to alternate bracts.

FLOWERS: Ray flowers **creamy white**; disk flowers **whitish to pinkish**; involucres 7–16 mm high, the bracts lance-shaped, with hairs at the base; heads several to many, on glandular and often white-woolly stalks.

FRUITS: Hairless achenes, 5–10 ribbed; pappus hairs numerous, white.

ECOLOGY: Moist to wet forest, thickets, swamps, openings, clearings; common and widespread at low to middle elevations.

NOTES: Palmate coltsfoot is also known as *P. frigidus* var. *palmatus*. • **Japanese butterbur** (*P. japonicus*) is an occasional species of low-elevation, wet ditches, fields and clearings in southwestern B.C. This introduction from Japan has **rounded to heart-shaped, unlobed, coarsely toothed** basal leaves. It has been cultivated by Japanese immigrants as an early spring vegetable. • The Quinault Indians in Washington State used the leaves of *P. palmatus* to cover berries in steam-cooking pits. • The coltsfeet are unusual in that the flowering stems come up before the leaves.

SWEET COLTSFOOT • *Petasites frigidus* var. *nivalis*

GENERAL: Perennial herb, with thick, creeping rhizomes; stems numerous, 10–50 cm tall, either with mostly female or mostly male flowers; **flowering stems precede leaves**.

LEAVES: Basal leaves **triangular to heart-shaped**, large, with **5–8 broad teeth or deeply lobed into 3–5 coarsely toothed** segments, **green and thinly hairy to hairless above, sparsely to densely white-woolly below**, stalked; stem leaves reduced to alternate, reddish bracts.

FLOWERS: Ray flowers **whitish or pink to purplish**; disk flowers **pink to purplish**; involucres 6–12 mm high, the bracts lance-shaped, with hairs at the base; heads several, in elongating flat-topped clusters, on glandular and often white-woolly stalks.

FRUITS: Hairless achenes, 5–10 ribbed; pappus hairs numerous, white.

ECOLOGY: Wet to moist meadows, seepage areas, streambanks, and lake shores; common from subalpine to alpine elevations.

NOTES: Sweet coltsfoot is also known as *P. nivalis* or *P. hyperboreus*. • Some Alaskan natives chewed coltsfoot root or soaked it in hot water and drank the tea for tuberculosis, chest problems, sore throat and stomach ulcers. • The name 'coltsfoot' was originally given to the closely related European species *Tussilago farfara* because the leaves resemble the foot of a colt. *Petasites* is from the Greek *petasos*, 'a broad-brimmed hat,' referring to the large basal leaves characteristic of this genus. Another common name for species of *Petasites* is 'butterbur.'

Key to Arnicas (*Arnica*) and Groundsels and Ragworts (*Senecio*)

1a. Leaves alternate, or all basal .... *Senecio*

2a. Leaves on entire length of stem approximately the same size,
or only slightly smaller upwards; basal leaves usually few at
flowering time, seldom clustered or tufted 3

    3a. Plants freely branched, often sprawling .... *S. fremontii* (see *S. integerrimus*)

    3b. Plants usually unbranched, upright 4

        4a. Leaves smooth-margined to toothed 5

            5a. Leaves triangular .... *S. triangularis*

            5b. Leaves lance-shaped to oval, not triangular 6

                6a. Leaves densely woolly on lower surface;
involucres 20–45 mm wide; ray flowers 3–7 mm wide;
maritime, north coastal plants .... *S. pseudoarnica*

                6b. Leaves essentially hairless below; involucres
8–16 mm wide; ray flowers 1–2 mm wide ...... *S. elmeri* (see *S. integerrimus*)

        4b. Leaves (at least some of them) prominently lobed or
deeply cleft to 2–3 times divided 7

            7a. Heads lacking ray flowers .... *S. vulgaris* (see *S. sylvaticus*)

            7b. Heads with ray flowers 8

                  8a. Involucral bracts not black-tipped;
upper part of stems with glandular hairs .... *S. viscosus* (see *S. sylvaticus*)

                8b. Involucral bracts black-tipped 9

                      9a. Leaves 2–3 times pinnately divided .... *S. jacobaea* (see *S. sylvaticus*)

                      9b. Leaves merely lobed and cleft .... *S. sylvaticus*

2b. Leaves on stem becoming noticeably smaller towards
upper part of stem; basal leaves often clustered or tufted 10

    10a. Plants hairless by flowering time, except for inconspicuous
woolly tufts at the base, in the leaf axils or in the inflorescence 11

        11a. Leaves smooth-margined to toothed, not lobed, wavy or pinnately divided . 12

            12a. Basal leaves usually smooth-margined,
sometimes irregularly toothed .... *S. integerrimus*

            12b. Basal leaves regularly toothed .... *S. lugens* (see *S. integerrimus*)

         11b. Leaves (or at least some of them) lobed, wavy or pinnately divided 13

            13a. Heads with ray flowers 14

                14a. Heads usually several 15

                  15a. Basal leaves smooth to wavy-margined,
or coarsely toothed .... *S. macounii*

                  15b. Basal leaves sharply toothed 16

                      16a. Basal leaves numerous (6 or more), thick and firm,
entire to toothed
above the middle .... *S. streptanthifolius* (see *S. pauperculus*)

                      16b. Basal leaves few (6 or fewer), thin and lax,
usually toothed almost to the base .... *S. pauperculus*

                14b. Heads solitary, rarely 2 15

                  15c. Base of involucres hairless .... *S. cymbalarioides* (see *S. newcombei*)

                  15d. Base of involucres hairy 16

                      16c. Basal leaves toothed,
never lobed .... *S. moresbiensis* (see *S. newcombei*)

                      16d. Basal leaves conspicuously 5–7 lobed .... *S. newcombei*

             13b. Heads without ray flowers 17

                17a. Disk flowers orange; involucral bracts purplish;
heads usually 1–6 .... *S. pauciflorus* (see *S. pauperculus*)

                17b. Disk flowers yellow; involucral bracts green;
heads 6–40 or more .... *S. indecorus* (see *S. pauperculus*)

    10b. Plants hairy at flowering time 18

        18a. Involucral bracts conspicuously black tipped ..... *S. lugens* (see *S. integerrimus*)

        18b. Involucral bracts not black tipped .... *S. elmeri* (see *S. integerrimus*)

(continued p. 296)

(continued from p. 295)

1b. Leaves opposite, except for some of the very small uppermost ones .... *Arnica*
   2c. Stems with more than 4 pairs of leaves 3
      3c. Involucral bracts with tuft of long,
      white hairs at tip ....*A. chamissonis* (see *A. amplexicaulis*)
      3d. Involucral bracts without tuft of white hairs at tip 4
         4c. Leaves toothed .... *A. amplexicaulis*
         4d. Leaves not toothed ....*A. longifolia* (see *A. amplexicaulis*)
   2d. Stems with 1–4 pairs of leaves 5
      5c. Pappus bristles have side-hairs, somewhat like the plume
      of a feather, tawny or straw-coloured 6
         6c. Heads broad, wider than high, somewhat hemispheric .... *A. mollis*
         6d. Heads narrow, higher than wide ....*A. diversifolia* (see *A. mollis*)
      5d. Pappus bristles with short, stiff side-hairs, usually white 7
         7c. Achenes hairless on the lower part, or all over; involucre
         with few or no long hairs; stem leaves seldom heart-shaped .... *A. latifolia*
         7d. Achenes short-hairy all over; involucre often densely
         white-hairy; stem leaves often heart-shaped .... *A. cordifolia* (see *A. latifolia*)

A. amplexicaulis

A. latifolia

A. mollis

S. triangularis

S. pseudo-arnica

S. macounii

S. sylvaticus

S. integerrimus

S. pauperculus

S. newcombei

STREAMBANK ARNICA • *Arnica amplexicaulis*

GENERAL: Perennial herb from creeping rhizomes; stems leafy, erect, unbranched except in the inflorescence, usually somewhat hairy and glandular at least in the upper portion, 15–80 cm tall.

LEAVES: Basal leaves small, often falling off by flowering time; stem leaves opposite, mostly stalkless, usually in **4–10 pairs**, lance- to egg-shaped, **toothed**, 2–12 cm long, nearly hairless to glandular-hairy.

FLOWERS: Ray flowers pale yellow, 8–14, 1–2 cm long, conspicuously toothed at tip; disk flowers yellow; involucres 7–15 mm high, the bracts lance-shaped, sharp pointed, hairy; heads 1–5 (sometimes up to 10), on stalks with yellowish hairs and often with stalked glands.

FRUITS: Achenes, cylindric, **sparsely hairy and sometimes glandular**; pappus **brownish**, feathery.

ECOLOGY: Moist forest, glades, streambanks, at low to middle elevations; common the length of our region, more so on the islands than on the inner mainland coast.

NOTES: Two more of our *Arnica* species have 5 or more pairs of stem leaves. **Seep-spring arnica** (*A. longifolia*) has 5–7 pairs of lance-shaped leaves with **smooth** margins. It grows in wet but well-drained sites around springs and seeps, at middle to high elevations in the Cascades of Washington south to California. **Meadow arnica** (*A. chamissonis*) has 5–10 pairs of entire to toothed leaves and a distinctive **tuft of hair** at the tip of each involucral bract. It is our **tallest** arnica (up to 1 m), and it occurs in moist meadows at middle to subalpine elevations the length of our region, but not on the outer coast.

MOUNTAIN ARNICA • *Arnica latifolia*

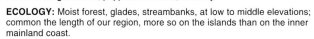

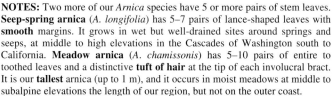

GENERAL: Perennial herb, from a horizontal rhizome, 10–60 cm tall; stems solitary or occasionally a few clustered together, sparsely hairy and often glandular.

LEAVES: Basal leaves rounded to lance-elliptic, rarely heart-shaped, usually withered by flowering time, often produced **on separate, short shoots**; stem leaves opposite, **2–4 (5) pairs**, egg-shaped to lance-elliptic, often becoming narrower and smaller above, thinly hairy and usually sparsely to densely glandular, stalked below, stalkless above, **usually coarsely toothed**.

FLOWERS: Ray flowers yellow, 8–12, conspicuously toothed at squared-off tips; disk flowers yellow; involucres 7–18 mm high, the bracts lance-shaped, sparsely (usually) to densely long-hairy and often glandular; heads usually 1–5, on hairy and sometimes glandular stalks.

FRUITS: Achenes, **hairless or sparsely hairy**; pappus hairs **white**, with **short stiff side-hairs**.

ECOLOGY: Moist, open forest, meadows, streambanks, and rocky slopes; common at middle to high elevations.

NOTES: Mountain arnica can be confused with heart-leaved arnica (*A. cordifolia*), especially when not in flower or fruit. The involucral bracts and achenes of **heart-leaved arnica** are generally much **hairier** than those of mountain arnica, which also has stem leaves that are seldom heart-shaped. *A. cordifolia* is a forest and meadow species of low to middle elevations, and it is uncommon west of the Coast-Cascade Mountains. These 2 species **hybridize**, resulting in a **narrower-leaved**, high-elevation plant called **slender arnica** (*A. gracilis*). • Taken internally, *Arnica* species cause a rise in body temperature; applied externally, they are antiseptic. Although *Arnica* species were widely used in Europe and parts of North America in herbal remedies, there are no written reports of their use by aboriginal peoples in our region.

297

HAIRY ARNICA • *Arnica mollis*

GENERAL: Perennial herb, from a freely rooted rhizome, 15–60 cm tall; stems solitary, sometimes branched above.

LEAVES: Basal leaves elliptic, often produced on **separate shoots**, often deciduous by flowering time; stem leaves 2–4 pairs, opposite, lance-shaped to elliptic, 2–20 cm long, reduced above, hairless to glandular and hairy, stalked below, stalkless above, **entire to coarsely toothed**.

FLOWERS: Ray flowers yellow, 14–20, toothed at the tips; disk flowers yellow; involucres 10–18 mm high, the bracts lance-shaped, hairy, and with stalked glands; heads 1–5, on hairy and glandular stalks.

FRUITS: Achenes, usually **moderately hairy and sometimes glandular**; pappus hairs **brownish, somewhat feathery** with side-hairs.

ECOLOGY: Frequent in moist meadows and open forests at middle to high elevations.

NOTES: Diverse arnica (*A. diversifolia*) appears to be a complex series of **hybrids** among hairy arnica or streambank arnica and mountain arnica and heart-leaved arnica. Diverse arnica has the **brownish pappus** of streambank arnica and hairy arnica and the **more-rounded, coarsely toothed** leaves of heart-leaved arnica and mountain arnica. Typically, diverse arnica has a **top-shaped** head that is narrower than those of other arnicas, and it grows in middle-elevation forests and openings sporadically in the southern half of our region.

ARROW-LEAVED GROUNDSEL • *Senecio triangularis*

GENERAL: Perennial herb, with a fibrous-rooted stem-base or rhizome; stems clustered, 30–150 cm tall.

LEAVES: Basal leaves thin, broadly to narrowly **triangular to triangular-heart-shaped, squared-off at the base**, strongly toothed, stalked, more or less hairless above, often short-hairy on the veins below; stem leaves similar, larger, gradually reduced upwards, becoming stalkless.

FLOWERS: Ray flowers yellow, usually about 8; disk flowers yellow; involucres 8–12 mm high, the bracts greenish, with black and tufted-hairy tips, otherwise hairless to sparsely hairy; heads few to numerous in a short, flat-topped cluster.

FRUITS: Hairless achenes.

ECOLOGY: Moist to wet, well-drained meadows, streambanks, slide tracks, thickets, open forest; typically a subalpine species, but also in seepage areas in middle-elevation forests; common and often abundant.

NOTES: The large, triangular, saw-toothed leaves make identification of arrow-leaved groundsel almost foolproof, but in the northern (Alaska panhandle and adjacent B.C.) and southern (southern Vancouver Island, Olympics and Washington Cascades) parts of our region watch out for **American sawwort** (*Saussurea americana*), which also grows in lush mountain meadows and has **similar leaves**, but **purplish flowers**. • With over 1,500 species throughout the world, *Senecio* is one of the largest genera of flowering plants. *Senecio* is also a very versatile group with species that grow in a wide range of habitats in our region, including beaches, tundra, bogs, meadows, forest understories and disturbed, weedy areas. • Other common names are 'triangle-leaved butterweed,' or 'arrowleaf butterweed,' presumably in reference to the yellow flowers. *Senecio* is from *senex*, meaning 'an old man,' because the receptacle lacks hairs or bristles (like a bald head).

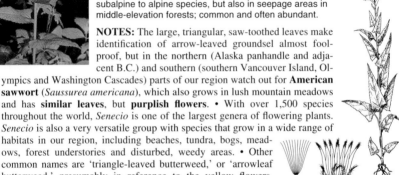

BEACH GROUNDSEL • *Senecio pseudoarnica*

GENERAL: Robust perennial herb from an erect to ascending rhizome; stems stout, more or less hairless below, **woolly-hairy above**, 10–70 cm tall.

LEAVES: Basal leaves usually smaller than stem leaves, which are alternate, **not much reduced in size upwards, thick,** spoon- or egg-shaped to oblong, 2–25 cm long, usually toothed, broadly stalked to stalkless, and **woolly-hairy** on the lower surface at least.

FLOWERS: Ray flowers yellow, long (10–25 mm); disk flowers yellow; involucres 10–20 mm high, the bracts green, sometimes purplish-tinged, woolly-hairy; heads large (up to 4.5 cm wide), solitary to several.

FRUITS: Hairless achenes.

ECOLOGY: Fairly common on sand dunes, sea beaches, and tidal flats; a **maritime** species.

NOTES: Beach groundsel is a widely distributed species found on the shores of the eastern and western Pacific and the western Atlantic. • The name 'groundsel' was originally applied to common groundsel (*S. vulgaris*). 'Groundsel' appears to have been derived from the Old English *grundeswylige* meaning 'ground-swallower'—an apt name for *Senecio*s, which are often rampant weeds. *S. vulgaris* was, however, also used by early herbalists as a treatment for inflammation or watering of the eyes. It may be that the name was mistakenly transcribed as *gundeswelge* at some time, from *gund* meaning 'matter discharged from eyes' and *swelge* meaning 'swallower.' The species name *pseudoarnica* suggests that beach groundsel looks like an arnica.

WOOD GROUNDSEL • *Senecio sylvaticus*

GENERAL: Annual herb from a **taproot**; stems leafy, erect, solitary, branched in the inflorescence, more or less hairy, 15–80 cm tall.

LEAVES: Basal leaves smaller than stem leaves, usually deciduous by flowering time; stem leaves lance-shaped, **deeply pinnately lobed and irregularly toothed**, sparsely to densely hairy, lower leaves stalked becoming stalkless upwards, 2–12 cm long.

FLOWERS: Ray flowers yellow, inconspicuous, **less than 2 mm long**; disk flowers yellow; involucres 5–7 mm high, the bracts lance-shaped, black tipped, clear edged, sparsely hairy; heads several to numerous, on hairy stalks.

FRUITS: Achenes, **stiffly hairy**; pappus hairs white, numerous.

ECOLOGY: Roadsides, clearings, logged-over areas; common in disturbed sites at low to middle elevations.

NOTES: We have 3 other similar weedy species of disturbed sites. **Common groundsel** (*S. vulgaris*) has **rayless** heads and numerous **black-tipped involucral bracteoles** as well as full-sized bracts, and it is common in the southern half of our region and sporadic north to the Queen Charlotte Islands and southeast Alaska. It is a common garden weed that can flower all year long in milder spots along the coast. **Tansy ragwort** (*S. jacobaea*) has deeply cut leaves, **ray flowers 4–10 mm long**, and black-tipped involucral bracts. It has become fairly abundant on southern Vancouver Island and in the lower Fraser Valley, Washington and Oregon. **Sticky ragwort** (*S. viscosus*) has numerous **sticky glands** on the stems and lobed leaves, **ray flowers 1–4 mm long**, glandular involucral bracts that **lack distinct black tips** and **hairless** achenes. It occurs sporadically on southern Vancouver Island and in the Kitimat and lower Skeena river valleys. • Tansy ragwort has been used as the source of a yellow dye, and it also contains an alkaloid **toxic** to horses and cattle.

WESTERN GROUNDSEL • *Senecio integerrimus*

GENERAL: Perennial herb from a short, erect, fibrous-rooted crown; stems leafy, stout, solitary, sparsely to densely hairy, **20–70 cm tall**.

LEAVES: Basal leaves **thick, somewhat succulent**, stalked, **lance-shaped to elliptic, entire to irregularly toothed**, hairy when young becoming hairless with age, 6–25 cm long (including the stalk); stem leaves alternate, becoming smaller and stalkless upwards.

FLOWERS: Ray flowers yellow, sometimes white or creamy, 6–16 cm long or sometimes lacking; disk flowers yellow; involucres 5–10 mm high, the bracts lance-shaped, **usually black-tipped**, hairless to hairy; heads several to numerous, often tightly clustered, the stalks hairy.

FRUITS: Achenes, several-ribbed, hairless or hairy; pappus hairs white.

ECOLOGY: Dry to moist meadows, grassy slopes, and open forest, from middle to high elevations; common in the Coast-Cascade mountain chain from about Bridge River country south.

NOTES: In the southern part of our region, western groundsel could be confused with **black-tipped groundsel** (*S. lugens*), which, however, has **regularly toothed, lance-shaped** basal leaves, and an interrupted range in our region (north of 56°N and mostly east of the coastal region, then occasionally south of 50°N in the Coast Mountains of B.C. and the Olympic Mountains). **Elmer's butterweed** (*S. elmeri*) occurs on moist, well-drained scree and talus slopes at high elevations, scattered in the Coast-Cascade mountain chain from the upper Lillooet River valley of southern B.C. south to central Washington. It is a **small (10–30 cm tall)**, erect perennial with **numerous, often tufted, coarsely toothed** basal leaves; several, often nodding, yellow heads; and hairy, **often purplish-black-tipped** involucral bracts. **Dwarf mountain butterweed** (*S. fremontii*) also grows on talus and scree slopes, ledges and rocky ridges at high elevations, and it is common in the southern part of our region from about Chilko Lake south in the Coast-Cascades to California. It is a **dwarf (10–20 cm tall), sprawling** perennial with **thick, somewhat fleshy, coarsely toothed**, lance- to spoon-shaped leaves, and several yellow heads with **dark-hairy**-tipped bracts. • The species name *integerrimus* is Latin for 'entire leaves.'

MACOUN'S GROUNDSEL • *Senecio macounii*

GENERAL: Perennial herb from short, thick, fibrous-rooted rhizomes; stems leafy, solitary, hairless to somewhat hairy, **10–80 cm tall**.

LEAVES: Basal leaves thick, lance-shaped to elliptic, **at least some regularly coarse toothed**, stalked, 2–20 cm long, thinly white-woolly at first becoming hairless by flowering time; stem leaves lance-shaped, progressively reduced and becoming stalkless upwards.

FLOWERS: Ray flowers yellow, 7–15 mm long; disk flowers yellow; involucres 5–10 mm high, the bracts lance-oblong, **not black-tipped**, hairless or sparsely woolly; heads 3–20 in compact to open, flat-topped groups.

FRUITS: Achenes, several-ribbed, hairless; pappus hairs white.

ECOLOGY: Dry, open forest, glades and forest edges; scattered at mostly low elevations.

NOTES: Macoun's groundsel is named for either James Macoun (1862–1920), curator of the National Herbarium of Canada, or more likely his father John Macoun (1831–1920), Government Naturalist of Canada—both early collectors on the West Coast.

CANADIAN BUTTERWEED • *Senecio pauperculus*

GENERAL: Perennial herb, with a fibrous-rooted, short, simple or slightly branched stem-base; stems leafy, solitary, more or less **hairless**, 20–70 cm tall.

LEAVES: Basal leaves thin, **broadly lance-shaped to elliptic or oblong, toothed throughout**, stalked, hairless; stem leaves lance-shaped, toothed or lobed, progressively reduced upwards, stalkless.

FLOWERS: Ray flowers yellow, **5–10 mm long**; disk flowers yellow; involucres 3–9 mm high, the bracts green or tinged with purple at the tip, hairless to somewhat woolly; heads **few to several** in an umbel-like cluster.

FRUITS: Achenes, several-ribbed, hairless or sometimes finely hairy; pappus hairs white.

ECOLOGY: Moist forest, meadows, stream-banks, lake-shores and marshes at low to middle elevations; scattered mostly along the eastern margin of our region, but also occasionally in northern southeast Alaska and on Vancouver Island.

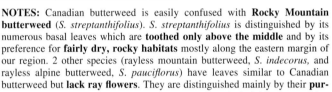

NOTES: Canadian butterweed is easily confused with **Rocky Mountain butterweed** (*S. streptanthifolius*). *S. streptanthifolius* is distinguished by its numerous basal leaves which are **toothed only above the middle** and by its preference for **fairly dry, rocky habitats** mostly along the eastern margin of our region. 2 other species (rayless mountain butterweed, *S. indecorus*, and rayless alpine butterweed, *S. pauciflorus*) have leaves similar to Canadian butterweed but **lack ray flowers**. They are distinguished mainly by their **purple** (*S. pauciflorus*) or **green** (*S. indecorus*) involucral bracts, and by the **bright-orange** rather than yellow flowers of *S. pauciflorus*.

NEWCOMBE'S BUTTERWEED • *Senecio newcombei*

GENERAL: Perennial herb from a short, fibrous-rooted rhizome; stems erect, leafy, hairless to hairy but usually conspicuously **white-woolly in the leaf axils**, 10–30 cm tall.

LEAVES: Basal leaves thin, **egg- to kidney-shaped, 5–7 lobed or coarsely round-toothed**, stalked, hairless to sparsely hairy; lower stem leaves similar to basal leaves, but upper leaves smaller and few-lobed to entire.

FLOWERS: Ray flowers yellow, 7–16 mm long; disk flowers yellow; involucres 5–12 mm high, the bracts lance-shaped, with a tuft of fine hairs at the tips and **somewhat hairy at the base**; heads **solitary**, on hairy stalks.

FRUITS: Achenes, several-ribbed, hairless; pappus hairs white.

ECOLOGY: Common on stream-banks, heaths, meadows, rocky bogs, scree and talus slopes, from low to high elevations but most abundant in the subalpine zone.

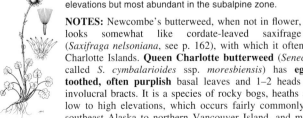

NOTES: Newcombe's butterweed, when not in flower, looks somewhat like cordate-leaved saxifrage (*Saxifraga nelsoniana*, see p. 162), with which it often grows on the Queen Charlotte Islands. **Queen Charlotte butterweed** (*Senecio moresbiensis*, also called *S. cymbalarioides* ssp. *moresbiensis*) has **egg-shaped, regularly toothed, often purplish** basal leaves and 1–2 heads with **often purplish** involucral bracts. It is a species of rocky bogs, heaths and open slopes from low to high elevations, which occurs fairly commonly on the islands from southeast Alaska to northern Vancouver Island, and most commonly on the Queen Charlotte Islands. **Alpine meadow butterweed** (*S. cymbalarioides*, not including *S. streptanthifolius*) resembles the above 2 species, but it has **involucral bracts that are hairless at the base**. It is fairly common in moist meadows and along stream-banks at middle to high elevations in the Cascade Mountains from southern B.C. south through Washington and Oregon. • Newcombe's butterweed is named after Charles Newcombe (1851–1924), an English physician and botanist.

FIELD PUSSYTOES • *Antennaria neglecta*

GENERAL: Perennial herb, mat forming with well-developed stolons; stems white-woolly, 5–30 cm tall.

LEAVES: Basal leaves spoon-shaped to broadly lance-shaped or elliptic, persistently **white-woolly below**, thinly so or hairless and **green above**; stem leaves linear to lance-shaped, stalkless, reduced upwards.

FLOWERS: Heads greenish-white, made up only of disk flowers; involucres 6–9 mm high, the bracts narrow, with long, pointed, **whitish tips**; several heads in a **compact, crowded cluster**.

FRUITS: Roughened achenes; pappus hairs numerous, fine, white.

ECOLOGY: Scattered in open, dry to moist, well-drained forest and openings at low to middle elevations.

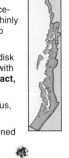

NOTES: Racemose pussytoes (*A. racemosa*) has a similar habit and leaves, but its upper stems are **glandular, not woolly-hairy**, its involucral bracts have **colourless-clear to pale-brownish tips,** and the heads are in a **long, open group**. *A. racemosa* grows in open forest and openings from low to high (mostly middle) elevations, sporadically in the southern part of the region, mostly in the Coast-Cascade mountain chain but also in the Olympics. • Many species of *Antennaria* have distinct male and female plants, and males may be rare or even absent from some areas. In these species, seed is often generated without fertilization, producing offspring genetically identical to their mother. • Flowers of pussytoes picked and dried soon after blooming will provide lovely bouquets throughout the winter; some people dye the blossoms. • *Antennaria* is from the Latin *antenna*, because tips of the pappus hairs of male flowers resemble insect antennae.

ALPINE PUSSYTOES • *Antennaria alpina*

GENERAL: Perennial, mat-forming herbs with leafy stolons; stems leafy, white-woolly, 5–10 cm tall.

LEAVES: Basal leaves lance- to spoon-shaped, up to 2.5 cm long, usually densely **white-woolly on both sides**; stem leaves linear-oblong, alternate.

FLOWERS: Heads greenish-black, with disk flowers only; involucres 4–7 mm high, the bracts slender, **sharp pointed, blackish-green at top, woolly at base**; several heads in a tight cluster.

FRUITS: Achenes, smooth or with tiny bumps; pappus hairs fine, white.

ECOLOGY: Well-drained, exposed ridges, gravelly slopes, tundra; common at subalpine to alpine elevations.

NOTES: Also known in part as *Antennaria media* or *A. friesiana*. • **Umber pussytoes** (*A. umbrinella*) is similar but has **blunt** involucral bracts that are **brownish at the tips**, and it occurs mostly at middle to subalpine (sometimes alpine) elevations the length of our region, but mostly along the eastern margin. • *Antennaria* species are called 'pussytoes' because the flowering heads, especially in fruit, resemble furry cats' paws.

ROSY PUSSYTOES • *Antennaria microphylla*

GENERAL: Perennial herb, **mat forming** with numerous leafy stolons; stems leafy, 5–40 cm tall.

LEAVES: Basal leaves spoon- or broadly lance-shaped, grey-woolly above and below.

FLOWERS: Heads **reddish-pink to white**, consisting only of disk flowers; involucres 4–7 mm high, the bracts woolly below, bright or pale **pink to white above**; 3–20 heads in a small, tight cluster.

FRUITS: Achenes, usually hairless; pappus hairs white.

ECOLOGY: Relatively dry, grassy slopes, meadows, river terraces, clearings, and open forests at **low to subalpine** elevations; fairly common, but mostly in the southern half of our region and not on the outer coast.

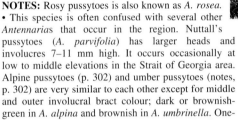

NOTES: Rosy pussytoes is also known as *A. rosea.* • This species is often confused with several other *Antennaria*s that occur in the region. Nuttall's pussytoes (*A. parvifolia*) has larger heads and involucres 7–11 mm high. It occurs occasionally at low to middle elevations in the Strait of Georgia area. Alpine pussytoes (p. 302) and umber pussytoes (notes, p. 302) are very similar to each other except for middle and outer involucral bract colour; dark or brownish-green in *A. alpina* and brownish in *A. umbrinella*. One-headed pussytoes (*A. monocephala*) has leaves that are green and lightly hairy above, and white-woolly below, and it has solitary heads. One-headed pussytoes occurs at subalpine to alpine elevations along the eastern edge of the northern part of our region.

WOOLLY PUSSYTOES • *Antennaria lanata*

GENERAL: Perennial herb from a branched stem-base, **tufted, not mat-forming**; stems leafy, densely white-woolly, 10–20 cm tall.

LEAVES: Basal leaves tufted, erect, lance-shaped, with 3 or more veins, densely white-woolly, 3–10 cm long; stem leaves narrower, alternate, progressively reduced upwards.

FLOWERS: Heads **greenish-black**; involucres 5–8 mm high, the bracts greenish and hairy at the base, **brown or greenish-black higher up, often white at the tip**; several heads in a compact cluster.

FRUITS: Achenes; pappus hairs white.

ECOLOGY: Common in meadows, heath, and snowbed sites at **subalpine and alpine** elevations.

NOTES: Woolly leaves are common on many alpine plants and may help retain heat and water in this often cold, windy environment. The white wool also reflects direct sunlight, which may prevent damage from ultraviolet radiation at high elevations where the air can be very clear and the sunlight can be intense—that is, when the clouds clear from the mountain tops.

PEARLY EVERLASTING • *Anaphalis margaritacea*

GENERAL: Perennial herb from **rhizomes**; stems usually unbranched, leafy, white-woolly, 20–100 cm tall.

LEAVES: Alternate, narrowly lance-shaped with a conspicuous midvein, **greenish above, white-woolly beneath**; margins often rolled under.

FLOWERS: Heads small, all of yellowish disk flowers; involucral bracts **dry, pearly white** with a dark triangular base; heads in dense, flat-topped clusters.

FRUITS: Very small, roughened, hairless to sparsely hairy achenes; pappus hairs white.

ECOLOGY: Rocky slopes, open forest, clearings, meadows, fields, pastures, roadsides; weedy native species common and widespread throughout our region, from low to subalpine elevations.

NOTES: Pearly everlasting is related to the pussytoes (*Antennaria* spp.) but has small, withering basal leaves and stem leaves that are **not much reduced in size upwards** on the stem. • Ditidaht healers rubbed this plant on the hands to soften them. The Kwakwaka'wakw dried the plants and mixed them with yellow-cedar pitch for a poultice. The Nlaka'pamux used pearly everlasting in an influenza medicine. • The common name derives from the pearly-white involucral bracts that retain their colour and shape when dried, making attractive dry bouquets. The plants usually do not bloom until midsummer, but the flowers can last until the first snows of winter.

SLENDER CUDWEED • *Gnaphalium microcephalum*

GENERAL: Perennial herb from a **taproot**; stems leafy, several, white-woolly, 20–70 cm tall.

LEAVES: Alternate, numerous, white-woolly, narrowly oblong, entire, 3–10 cm long; lower edges of leaves extending down the stem **like a narrow bracket**.

FLOWERS: Heads small, pale yellow, of disk flowers only; involucre **4–7 mm high**, the bracts dry, numerous, overlapping, **white to tan**, woolly only at the base; numerous in small clusters that are themselves aggregated in a broad group.

FRUITS: Achenes, small, smooth; pappus of **separate** white bristles.

ECOLOGY: Relatively dry open sites, often in sandy or rocky soil, or in recently burned forests; low to middle elevations.

NOTES: Several other species of *Gnaphalium* are common in the southern part of our region. **Cotton-batting cudweed** (*G. chilense*) is very similar to slender cudweed but it is an **annual or biennial** with leaves with **clasping flanges** at the bases and somewhat **yellowish involucres. Purple cudweed** (*G. purpureum*) is a native, **annual or biennial** weed that has a narrow **spike-like** inflorescence, **light-brown** involucral bracts often **tinged with purple,** and pappus bristles **united in a ring** at the base. **Lowland cudweed** (*G. palustre*) has **very small heads (involucre 2–4 mm tall)** in small leafy-bracted clusters. **Marsh cudweed** (*G. uliginosum*) is similar to lowland cudweed, but it has linear or **linear-lance-shaped (rather than oblong)** leaves and **darker** heads. It is fairly common on the south coast and ranges sporadically north to southeast Alaska. • The common name 'cudweed' was given to the softly felted-hairy European species because they were used to prevent or relieve chafings. The word 'cud' appears to have derived from the Anglo-Saxon and Dutch words for 'vulva.' Thus 'childing cudweed' (*G. germanicum*) was 'parturient cudweed' (Prior 1879). Other sources claim cudweed was given to cattle that had lost their cud. Also called 'chafeweed,' because it was used to prevent the backs of beasts of burden from becoming chafed by heavy loads.

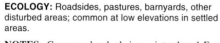

COMMON BURDOCK • *Arctium minus*

GENERAL: Coarse **biennial** herb; stems leafy, 0.5–1.5 m tall.

LEAVES: Alternate, large (up to 30 cm long and 25 cm wide), **egg- to heart-shaped**, stalked (the lower stalks hollow), nearly hairless above, **thinly white-woolly beneath**.

FLOWERS: Heads of **pink to purple**, disk flowers only, **1.5–2.5 cm** thick, nearly **stalkless or on short stalks**; involucre somewhat spherical, the bracts in several series, long, narrow, with spreading, **inwardly hooked tips**; in a fairly **long, scattered inflorescence**.

FRUITS: Achenes, oblong, 3-angled, several-ribbed, hairless; pappus of numerous short bristles.

ECOLOGY: Roadsides, pastures, barnyards, other disturbed areas; common at low elevations in settled areas.

NOTES: Common burdock is an introduced Eurasian weed, as is the related **great burdock** (*A. lappa*), which has mostly **long-stalked, 2.5–4 cm** thick heads in a **short, mounded cluster**. Great burdock is scattered in disturbed sites in the southern part of our region. • The hooked tips of the involucral bracts of burdock were the inspiration for Velcro. • This plant was named 'sea-urchin' by the Nuxalk when it was first introduced to the Bella Coola Valley. The Sahaptin boil the roots and drink the fluid for whooping cough. Burdock roots are also boiled and drunk for arthritis by contemporary Cowichan healers, and by herbalists as an ingredient in essiac tea. • *Arctium* means 'bear,' from the shaggy, hairy appearance of great burdock.

Thistles
(see p. 306)

Cirsium edule

Cirsium arvense

Cirsium brevistylum

Cirsium remotifolium

Cirsium vulgare

CANADA THISTLE • *Cirsium arvense*

GENERAL: Perennial from deep, wide-spreading roots and **creeping rhizomes**; stems leafy, rather thin, green, **without spiny wings**, 30 cm to 2 m tall, highly branched above.

LEAVES: Alternate, lance-shaped, irregularly lobed, spiny-toothed; hairless or green above, densely **white-hairy beneath**.

FLOWERS: Pink-purple, small heads of disk flowers only; involucre **1–2 cm high**, the bracts tipped with weak prickles; several to many heads in an open inflorescence; plants are **unisexual** (male or female, but not with flower parts of both); male heads showier.

FRUITS: Achenes, oblong, flattened, ribbed, 3–4 mm long; pappus of feathery, white bristles.

ECOLOGY: Fields, pastures, meadows, clearings, roadsides; common and often abundant at low to middle elevations, primarily in the settled or agricultural portions of our region.

NOTES: Canada thistle is the only thistle with male and female flowers on separate plants. It is distinguished from other thistles by the combination of green stems **without spiny wings**, small **almost spineless** heads and **creeping rhizomes**. • The **bull thistle** (*C. vulgare*) has **much larger heads** (involucres 2.5–4 cm high), **spiny-winged** stems and a deep, fleshy **taproot**. It is almost as common as Canada thistle. Both species originally came from Eurasia. These spiny plants are rarely eaten by grazing animals and can become abundant in pastures. • Peeled stems and roots of most thistles are edible and can provide nutritious food in an emergency. • The thistle (probably not this species) is the national flower of Scotland, adopted as far back as the 8th century AD. Legend has it that an invading Danish army was creeping, barefoot, towards a Scottish encampment when a soldier stepped on a thistle. He yelled so loud that the Scots awoke and defeated the Danes. The thistle was thereafter considered to be the guardian of Scotland and acquired the motto *nemo me impune lacessit* ('no one shall provoke me with impunity,' or in Scottish 'wha duar meddle wi me') as the emblem of that dour land.

EDIBLE THISTLE • *Cirsium edule*

GENERAL: Stout biennial or perennial herb from a **taproot**; stems leafy, thick and somewhat succulent but tapering and becoming slender above, fairly hairy, 50–200 cm tall.

LEAVES: Alternate, lance-shaped, irregularly lobed or coarsely toothed, teeth usually **more than half the width** of the leaf blade, spiny, green and sparsely hairy on both surfaces, or hairless except for the midrib on the lower surface.

FLOWERS: Heads pinkish-purple, of disk flowers only, nodding when young; styles exceed flowers by **at least 3 mm**; involucres **2–4 cm high**, cottony-hairy, the bracts slender, tapering, loose or spreading, outer bracts have **short spines**; single or in small clusters at the ends of branches.

FRUITS: Achenes, prismatic, several-nerved, hairless; pappus of feathery, white bristles.

ECOLOGY: Common in moist meadows, clearings, forest openings, usually at middle to high elevations but sometimes in the lowlands.

NOTES: Short-styled thistle (*C. brevistylum*) resembles edible thistle but has styles that are at most **only 1.5 mm longer** than the tubular flowers and leaves that are lobed **less than half the width** of the leaf blade. Short-styled thistle is common at low to middle elevations in the southern part of our region (sporadically north to the Queen Charlotte Islands), in moist meadows and open forests. **Spaced-out thistle** (*C. remotifolium*) is **weakly spiny** and has **creamy-white** heads. It occurs in low-elevation meadows and moist, open forest in western Washington and Oregon. • Bull thistle (and other thistles) were regarded by some aboriginal peoples, such as the Straits Salish, as having protective properties because of their prickly leaves. The leaves and roots were placed in bath water or held in the pocket as a talisman.

Other Families

If a plant family has several to many species in our area and is fairly easily recognized as a family, it is treated as a separate section in this book. If plants are truly unusual in appearance, they are featured in the 'Oddballs' section (pp. 350–355). If they live in the water, they are treated in the 'Aquatics' section (pp. 335–349). Other vascular plants that are not bizarre in appearance and belong to small families that live on land are described here.

In this section, species in the same family are described together. Families similar in leaf or flower characteristics are placed near each other, to facilitate comparison.

The plants considered here belong to the following families and genera:

Loranthaceae (Mistletoe Family): *Arceuthobium, Phoradendron*

Santalaceae (Sandalwood Family): *Comandra, Geocaulon*

Urticaceae (Nettle Family): *Urtica*

Chenopodiaceae (Goosefoot Family): *Atriplex, Salicornia, Suaeda, Chenopodium*

Nyctaginaceae (Four-o'clock Family): *Abronia*

Berberidaceae (Barberry Family): *Achlys, Vancouveria*; also *Mahonia* (p. 95)

Fumariaceae (Fumitory Family): *Corydalis, Dicentra*

Balsaminaceae (Balsam or Touch-me-not Family): *Impatiens*

Papaveraceae (Poppy Family): *Eschscholtzia, Meconella*

Oxalidaceae (Oxalis or Wood-sorrel Family): *Oxalis*

Geraniaceae (Geranium Family): *Erodium, Geranium*

Aristolochaceae (Birthwort Family): *Asarum*

Malvaceae (Mallow Family): *Sidalcea*

Lythraceae (Loosestrife Family): *Lythrum*

Hypericaceae (St. John's-wort Family): *Hypericum*

Cornaceae (Dogwood Family): *Cornus*; also *C. nuttallii* (p. 51), *C. stolonifera* (p. 90)

Apocynaceae (Dogbane Family): *Apocynum*

Primulaceae (Primrose Family): *Lysimachia, Glaux, Anagallis, Trientalis, Douglasia, Primula, Dodecatheon*

Solanaceae (Potato or Nightshade Family): *Solanum*

Menyanthaceae (Buckbean Family): *Fauria*; also *Menyanthes* (p. 339)

Convolvulaceae (Morning-glory Family): *Convolvulus, Cuscuta*

Cucurbitaceae (Cucumber or Gourd Family): *Marah*

Plumbaginaceae (Plumbago Family): *Armeria*

Plantaginaceae (Plantain Family): *Plantago*

Rubiaceae (Madder Family): *Galium, Sherardia*

Campanulaceae (Harebell Family): *Campanula*

Valerianaceae (Valerian Family): *Plectritis, Valeriana*

Araceae (Arum or Calla-lily Family): *Lysichiton*

Juncaginaceae (Arrow-grass family): *Triglochin*

WESTERN DWARF MISTLETOE • *Arceuthobium campylopodum*

GENERAL: Small, hairless, yellowish to greenish-brown, **leafless**, perennial plants **parasitic on the branches of conifers**; stems emerging from the host, **segmented, 2–20 cm long,** much branched, usually tufted; segments 1–3 mm thick, extra branches at the nodes fan-like.

LEAVES: Reduced to **tiny, opposite scales**.

FLOWERS: Yellowish-orange to green, small, inconspicuous; male flowers usually in pairs at nodes, stalkless on short lateral branches; female flowers 1 or 2 per node, stalkless or on stalks to 1 mm long.

FRUITS: Berries, **greenish or bluish**, sticky, egg-shaped; seeds single, sticky, explosively ejected from the berry.

ECOLOGY: Parasitic on a wide range of conifers (*Abies, Juniperus, Larix, Picea, Pinus, Tsuga*) in our region, **most commonly on western hemlock**; common but often overlooked, because it usually occurs high up in the host tree.

NOTES: Douglas' dwarf mistletoe (*A. douglasii*) is parasitic **on Douglas-fir** (*Pseudotsuga menziesii*), but it occurs mostly east of the Cascade Mountains. • Mistletoes cause 'witch's broom,' a disorganized growth of the tree. Mistletoe infections can cause significant reductions in the growth of conifer hosts. • The species name *campylopodum* means 'bent, curved' (*campylo*) 'foot, stalk' (*podum*), presumably in reference to the flower stalks.

OAK MISTLETOE • *Phoradendron flavescens*

GENERAL: Somewhat fleshy, finely short-hairy, yellowish-green, woody perennials, **parasitic on deciduous trees**; stems emerging from the host, branched, tufted, rather brittle, **segmented, 30–60 cm long**.

LEAVES: Opposite, thick, leathery, short-stalked, **egg-shaped to oval**, 1–4 cm long.

FLOWERS: Yellowish-green, small, inconspicuous; sexes on separate plants; male flowers stalkless in short (1–2 cm), 3-segmented spikes from upper leaf axils; female flowers stalkless in short, jointed axillary spikes, 3–12 per joint.

FRUITS: Berries, **pinkish-white**, slimy-sticky, egg- or pear-shaped; seeds single.

ECOLOGY: Parasitic in our region **mostly on Garry oak** in Oregon, especially in the Willamette Valley.

NOTES: Kozloff (1976) speculates that the fruits are dispersed by annoyed birds who rub their beaks against branches 'to get rid of the sticky stuff,' in so doing possibly pressing the seed into a place where it can germinate. • The common name 'mistletoe' appears to be derived from the Old English word *mistletan*. *Tan* means 'twig'; some sources say *mistl* means 'different,' hence 'different-twig.' Others say *mistl* comes from the Old German *mist* meaning 'dung,' because birds eat the berries and the seeds are deposited on trees in sticky bird droppings. • *Phoradendron* literally translated means 'tree-thief,' in reference to its parasitic habit. *Flavescens* describes the plant's yellowish colour.

CALIFORNIA COMANDRA • *Comandra umbellata* var. *californica*

GENERAL: Hairless perennial from rhizomes; stems usually clustered, erect, leafy, 5–35 cm tall; **parasitic on the roots of other plants**.

LEAVES: Alternate, nearly stalkless to short-stalked, lance-shaped to oblong or elliptic, 0.5–4.5 cm long, **rather thick and fleshy**, glaucous.

FLOWERS: Greenish-white to purplish, 3–7 mm long, usually 5-lobed, stalked; **several to many** in compact cluster atop stem.

FRUITS: Dry to somewhat fleshy, spherical, **blue to purplish-brown**, 4–10 mm long, 1-seeded.

ECOLOGY: Dry to moist, usually sandy or rocky, well-drained soil in open sites from low to subalpine elevations; scattered, locally common.

NOTES: California comandra is also known as *Geocaulon umbellatum*. • **Bastard toad-flax** (*Geocaulon lividum*, also called *Comandra livida*, **inset photo**) has **thin**, oval to oblong, short-stalked leaves, clusters of **1–4** flowers in the leaf axils and **fleshy, orange** fruits. It occurs in moist to fairly dry open forest or bog forest, occasionally in northern southeast Alaska and Prince William Sound, and in the Skeena-Nass drainages.

STINGING NETTLE • *Urtica dioica*

GENERAL: Perennial from strong spreading **rhizomes**, armed with stinging hairs, otherwise hairless to hairy; stems leafy, upright, **1–3 m tall**.

LEAVES: Opposite, narrowly lance-shaped to oval or heart-shaped, coarsely saw-toothed; stipules prominent, 5–15 mm long.

FLOWERS: Greenish, tiny; numerous in **dense, drooping clusters** or spikes in the leaf axils and at the stem tips; male and female flowers **in separate spikes** with female spikes usually uppermost.

FRUITS: Flattened, lens-shaped achenes.

ECOLOGY: Meadows, thickets, stream-banks, open forest; often growing *en masse* in disturbed habitats such as avalanche tracks, middens, slash piles, barnyards, roadsides, always in moist rich soil; common, locally abundant, from the lowlands to subalpine elevations.

NOTES: This species includes *U. lyallii* and *U. gracilis*. • **Dog nettle** (*U. urens*) is a **shorter (10–50 cm), taprooted annual**, with stipules less than 5 mm long, and male and female flowers **mixed** in the flower cluster. It is a weedy species, probably a native of Europe, and it is occasional in disturbed areas at low elevations in the southern half of our region (south of 51°N). • The stinging hairs are hollow, and each arises from a gland containing formic acid. As the brittle tips are broken, acid is secreted causing an irritating rash on contact with the skin. Nevertheless, the leaves can be cooked and eaten as greens when young. • Called 'Indian spinach,' the young leaves and stems were eaten by both coastal and interior tribes, but it is questionable whether this was a traditional use or whether it was introduced by Europeans. The plants were, however, an important source of fibre for making fish-nets, snares and tumplines. • Nettles can be used as a general spring tonic: 'If they would drink nettles in March / And eat mugwort in May / So many fine maidens / Would not go to clay.' (traditional).

ORACHE • *Atriplex patula*
SPEARSCALE

GENERAL: Somewhat fleshy annual, covered with a **whitish, mealy** substance (as if floured with cornmeal) when young, but becoming hairless and greenish with age; stems reclining to upright, usually branched, leafy, 10–100 cm tall.

LEAVES: Lower leaves opposite but upper alternate, stalked to stalkless, **lance-shaped to linear or oblong, rounded to arrowhead-shaped** at the base, with smooth or coarsely toothed margins, 2–12 cm long.

FLOWERS: Greenish, tiny, inconspicuous; numerous and crowded in **spikes at the ends of branches or in clusters in the leaf axils**; flowers male or female, mixed in the inflorescence or the male often above the female.

FRUITS: Membranous bladders enclosed by **2 lance-shaped to triangular, smooth to toothed bracts**.

ECOLOGY: Tidal marshes, beaches, saline soils; common but scattered along the coastline.

NOTES: Orache is an extremely variable species in many features, but perhaps most noticeably in leaf shape. Some taxonomists have segregated several species from the complex: *A. alaskensis* of the north coast, *A. subspicata* of the south coast, and *A. gmelinii* from Alaska to California. Others have delimited several varieties of *A. patula*. We will stick with the single complex species in this guide. • Orache is one of the best-known edible wild greens in some parts of the world, such as Europe. It is in the same family as spinach and can be used in much the same way, as a cooked potherb or in lasagna or other dishes. Like other greens containing oxalate salts, orache should not be used in large quantities. • The origin of 'orache' seems to be obscure, but possibly it came ultimately from a Greek word for 'a golden plant.' This was latinized to *aurago*, and from there became the French word *arrache*.

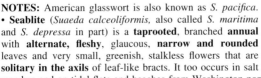

AMERICAN GLASSWORT • *Salicornia virginica*
PERENNIAL SALTWORT, PACIFIC SAMPHIRE

GENERAL: Fleshy, matted, hairless **perennial** from long, slender **rhizomes**; stems trailing (to 1 m long) and prostrate to ascending or erect, **jointed**; flowering stems numerous, upright, 5–30 cm tall, often brown-purple.

LEAVES: Essentially absent; reduced to tiny, opposite scales.

FLOWERS: Tiny; in groups of 3, **sunken in pits or hollows on the joints** of 1–4 cm long spikes at the branch tips; joints about 2.5 mm long and thick.

FRUITS: Membranous bladders with thin, papery walls enclosed by **spongy flower scales**; seeds 1 per bladder, hairy, falling separately from the fruit.

ECOLOGY: Common along the coast (in salt marshes and on tideflats and beaches); generally absent from beaches or shores with strong wave action and surf.

NOTES: American glasswort is also known as *S. pacifica.* • **Seablite** (*Suaeda calceoliformis*, also called *S. maritima* and *S. depressa* in part) is a **taprooted**, branched **annual** with **alternate, fleshy**, glaucous, **narrow and rounded** leaves and very small, greenish, stalkless flowers that are **solitary in the axils** of leaf-like bracts. It too occurs in salt marshes and on tidal flats and beaches from Washington north. • The tender, young stalks of *Salicornia* ssp., commonly known as 'sea asparagus,' are a well-known wild green vegetable, sometimes sold in seafood stores and chic or new-age restaurants. Aboriginal peoples apparently have eaten it only in recent times, but some people harvest it today as a source of income. • Although it has a somewhat glassy appearance, the common name comes from the fact that this plant was reduced to ashes to provide alkali (carbonate of soda) needed in glass-making.

LAMB'S-QUARTERS • *Chenopodium album*

GENERAL: Annual, 20–100 cm tall, usually branched, **greenish to greyish-mealy** (covered with flaky scales); stems leafy, often purple-striped with age.

LEAVES: Egg- or diamond-shaped, alternate, somewhat firm and succulent, coarsely but irregularly toothed or lobed; lower surface **greyish-green and covered with mealy particles.**

FLOWERS: Greenish, tiny; in **dense clusters or spikes in the leaf axils and at the stem tips**.

FRUITS: Thin, white, papery envelopes that enclose black, shiny, flattened seeds; 1 seed per envelope.

ECOLOGY: Disturbed sites, especially cultivated land, gardens, fields, roadsides; common at low to middle elevations (especially in settled areas) in the southern part of our region, scattered in the north, rare on the Queen Charlotte Islands.

NOTES: Red goosefoot (*C. rubrum*) occurs in salt marshes, moist saline meadows and disturbed soil, and it is scattered from southwestern B.C. to California. It is an annual with stems and leaves that **often turn reddish and are not covered with meal**. • Lamb's-quarters is a very characteristic and often abundant weed of agricultural areas, originally from Eurasia but now naturalized in much of North America. Relatives of this plant were used as staple grains across North America in prehistoric times. Through semi-domestication the size of the seeds was increased until they were much larger than today's *Chenopodium* seeds. Many aboriginal peoples have used the young leaves as a potherb in recent times. They contain oxalate salts, and should not be eaten in quantity or continuously over many days. • Lamb's-quarters should be *lammas quarter* because this plant blossomed around Lammas Day (August 1ˢᵗ), the first day of a harvest thanksgiving festival. The leaves are supposedly shaped like the foot of a goose, giving rise to both the Latin name *Chenopodium*, and the common name, 'goosefoot.'

YELLOW SAND-VERBENA • *Abronia latifolia*

GENERAL: Glandular-hairy perennial from **thick, heavy taproot**; stems **trailing along sand**, to 1 m long.

LEAVES: Thick and fleshy, opposite, circular or kidney-shaped to oblong-egg-shaped or deltoid, 1.5–6 cm long, long-stalked.

FLOWERS: Bright-yellow, on stout stalks, tubular at base, 8–10 mm long, flaring into 5 lobes; several to many in **rounded heads**.

FRUITS: Achenes, glandular-hairy, 8–12 mm long, with 4–5 thick, keel-like wings shaped like the dorsal fin of a perch.

ECOLOGY: Sandy sea beaches and dunes; scattered, locally common from the Queen Charlotte Islands (where rare) south.

NOTES: Pink sand-verbena (*A. umbellata*) is similar to yellow sand-verbena but has **pink** flowers. It is uncommon in similar beach habitats from western Washington to California and has been reported from Vancouver Island, but it has apparently been extirpated there. • Yellow sand-verbena usually occurs in association with other typical sand beach species such as large-headed sedge (p. 393), seashore bluegrass (p. 377), beach carrot (p. 216) and beach bindweed (p. 326). • The common name 'verbena' or 'vervain' rightly belongs to true verbena (*Verbena officinalis*). The sand-verbena resembles true verbena, but it has bright lemony-yellow flowers and grows in sand. *Abronia* is from *abros*, the Greek for 'graceful' or 'delicate.'

VANILLA-LEAF • *Achlys triphylla*
DEER FOOT

GENERAL: Perennial, spreading widely by slender rhizomes, hairless, without leafy aerial stems but sends up single leaves at intervals along the rhizomes, with a **vanilla-like fragrance** when dry.

LEAVES: All basal, on stalks 10–30 cm long, with **3 fan-shaped, asymmetrical, coarsely blunt-toothed leaflets** that are usually held nearly horizontally, but lateral leaflets sometimes in a near-vertical attitude; middle leaflet smaller, 3-lobed, resembles a goose foot (or a deer foot to some).

FLOWERS: White, small, **lacking** sepals and petals but with 8–20 **long, white stamens**; numerous in a long-stalked, **showy white spike** that is 2–5 cm long by 1 cm thick and sticks up above the leaves.

FRUITS: Achenes, dark grey-brown to reddish-purple, very finely hairy, leathery, **crescent-shaped**; inner side concave, with a somewhat **fleshy to leathery, thickened ridge**.

ECOLOGY: Moist, shady forests, glades, openings and forest edges, especially along streambanks, at low to middle elevations; common and locally abundant.

NOTES: In some spots, the leaves of vanilla-leaf form a nearly continuous, light-green carpet over the forest floor. The leaves are often fairly widely spaced along individual rhizomes, but the dense leaf layer results from numerous crossing rhizomes. After the leaves die and wither, the veins persist through much of the fall and winter as a lacy network. • Vanilla-leaf leaves were used by the Saanich of Vancouver Island, and probably by other groups in the plant's range, as an insect repellent. The Saanich dried the leaves and hung them in bunches in houses to keep flies and mosquitoes away. The 3-lobed leaves are often dried and hung in bundles to perfume the house with their sweet vanilla scent. • *Achlys* means 'mist' and is thought to describe the misty clouds of tiny white flowers.

INSIDE-OUT FLOWER • *Vancouveria hexandra*

GENERAL: Rhizomatous perennial, without leafy aerial stems.

LEAVES: All basal, 10–40 cm long, long-stalked, usually twice-divided into 3s; **9–15 leaflets heart- to egg-shaped**, 3 lobed, sparsely hairy; stalks brownish-hairy at least near the base.

FLOWERS: White, made up of 6–9 outer bracts that soon fall off, **6 sepals and 6 petals** that are a bit shorter than the sepals and have hooded, glandular tips; sepals and petals **bend backwards and flare**, so that the nodding flowers have the general aspect of a cyclamen or shootingstar; stamens finely purplish-glandular-hairy; flowers 10–30 on long, slender stalks in **open panicles**.

FRUITS: Follicles, about 1 cm long, purplish glandular-hairy, with several 3 mm long, **black** seeds nearly covered by a **fleshy outgrowth**.

ECOLOGY: Moist, shady forest, common from low to middle elevations.

NOTES: The delicate leaves of inside-out flower are suggestive of western meadowrue (p. 180). • The fleshy-appendaged seeds of inside-out flower are sometimes dispersed by wasps and ants. • The petals and sepals of this plant turn backwards so far that the flower looks like it is trying to turn itself inside-out to expose its 6 stamens (hence *hexandra*). This species was named after the explorer Capt. George Vancouver.

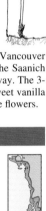

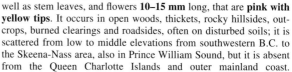

SCOULER'S CORYDALIS • *Corydalis scouleri*

GENERAL: Hairless and glaucous perennial from thick rhizomes; stems erect, hollow, simple or branched, **60–120 cm tall**.

LEAVES: Alternate, usually 3, **from near or above the middle** of the stem, large, much-divided in parsley fashion; ultimate segments **oblong-elliptic to lance-shaped**, rounded.

FLOWERS: Pink, showy, 20–30 mm long, **spurred; numerous** in long, usually branched, **spike-like** cluster atop stem.

FRUITS: Pod-like capsules, egg- to pear-shaped, bursting open elastically when ripe to eject the black, lustrous seeds.

ECOLOGY: Moist, usually shaded forest and stream-banks at low elevations; common in the Washington and Oregon portion of our region, rare on southern Vancouver Island.

NOTES: Pink corydalis (*Corydalis sempervirens*, also called rock harlequin) is a **taprooted**, smoky-green **annual or biennial** with **basal** as well as stem leaves, and flowers **10–15 mm** long, that are **pink with yellow tips**. It occurs in open woods, thickets, rocky hillsides, outcrops, burned clearings and roadsides, often on disturbed soils; it is scattered from low to middle elevations from southwestern B.C. to the Skeena-Nass area, also in Prince William Sound, but it is absent from the Queen Charlotte Islands and outer mainland coast.
• *Corydalis* is Greek for 'crested lark.' Presumably the rather ornate flowers were thought to resemble this bird. Scouler's corydalis is named after Dr. John Scouler, who accompanied David Douglas in his explorations of the Pacific Northwest.

PACIFIC BLEEDING HEART • *Dicentra formosa*

GENERAL: Hairless, soft, juicy perennial from slender, brittle rhizomes; flowering stems leafless, upright, **15–50 cm tall**.

LEAVES: All basal, numerous, long-stalked (only slightly shorter than flowering stems), fern-like, much divided into **narrowly oblong** ultimate segments.

FLOWERS: Pinkish-purple, heart-shaped at base, drooping; petals 4, outer 2 each with a short sac-like spur and spreading tip; **5–15** in clusters atop stem.

FRUITS: Pod-like capsules; seeds several, black, pebbled and shining, with small, white, oil-rich **appendage** attractive to ants, which disperse the seeds.

ECOLOGY: Moist forest, ravines, streambanks; low to middle elevations; common.

NOTES: Steer's head (*D. uniflora*) has a **single** 2-spurred flower atop the **short (4–10 cm tall)** stem. It occurs on gravelly, open, snowmelt-moist slopes at middle to subalpine elevations, occasionally in the Cascades from southern B.C. south to California, but mostly east of our region. • The heart shape of the pinkish-purple flowers gives rise to the common name. *Dicentra* means 'two-spurred,' in reference to the spurs on the two outer petals; *formosa* means 'beautiful, handsome, well-formed,' which it is indeed. • 'Steer's head,' the common name for *D. uniflora*, is an apt description of the flower.

COMMON TOUCH-ME-NOT • *Impatiens noli-tangere*
JEWELWEED

GENERAL: Hairless, **succulent, juicy annual**; stems leafy, upright to ascending, often branched, 20–80 cm tall.

LEAVES: Alternate, **elliptic-egg-shaped**, 3–12 cm long, stalked, **coarsely toothed**.

FLOWERS: Yellowish, often spotted with purple or reddish-brown, about 2.5 cm long; sepals 3, 1 of which is enlarged and has a strongly **down-curved spur** 6–10 mm long; petals 5, appearing as 3 because the lateral pairs are partially fused; **mostly in 2s** from upper leaf axils.

FRUITS: Capsules, 5 chambered, to 2.5 cm long, opening elastically and explosively; seeds numerous.

ECOLOGY: Moist forest, thickets, stream-banks, streamside areas; common at low to middle elevations.

NOTES: Policeman's helmet (*Impatiens glandulifera*) has **finely toothed** leaves **in part opposite or whorled**, and **red or pinkish** flowers each with a spur 4–5 mm long. It is an Asian ornamental species that has become established occasionally in moist bottomlands of the lower Fraser Valley and western Washington. **Spurless touch-me-not** (*I. ecalcarata*) is similar to *I. noli-tangere*, but the flowers **lack spurs**. It occurs sporadically in moist shady forests and thickets from southern B.C. to northwestern Oregon. • Originally the species name appears to have been *noli-me-tangere*, meaning 'touch-me-not.' The plant is so-called because the ripe fruits, when touched, suddenly burst open (hence *impatiens*, meaning 'impatient'). The phrase 'touch-me-not' is from the words of the risen Christ to Mary Magdalene, familiar from *noli-me-tangere* paintings. • The flowers of policeman's helmet resemble the shape of the helmets worn by the English 'bobby.'

CALIFORNIA POPPY • *Eschscholzia californica*

GENERAL: Hairless, usually **glaucous, taprooted perennial** with clear watery juice; flowering stems erect, 1 to several, 10–50 cm tall.

LEAVES: Mostly basal, numerous, **much-divided and parsley-like** with narrow ultimate segments, stalked.

FLOWERS: Yellow to orange, showy, **saucer-shaped**; petals usually 4, 1–5 cm long; stamens numerous; **solitary** atop long stalks.

FRUITS: Linear pod-like capsules, opening elastically from the base; seeds numerous.

ECOLOGY: Roadsides, clearings, dry rocky slopes at low elevations; native from the Columbia gorge south; widely cultivated as an ornamental elsewhere in the southern half of our region, and often escaping.

NOTES: Another species of the poppy family, **white meconella** (*Meconella oregana*), is a **small (2–10 cm tall) annual**, with **undivided**, spoon-shaped basal leaves, **opposite** stem leaves and small (5–9 mm wide) **white** flowers. It occurs sporadically in spring-moist meadows and grassy openings at low elevations, from southeastern Vancouver Island and the Gulf Islands south to California. • The genus is named for Johann Frederic Eschscholtz (1793–1831), a Russian scientist with Kotzebue's visit to California in 1816. 'Poppy' is from the Latin name for many poppies, *Papaver*. • *Meconella* is the diminutive of the Greek *mekon*, meaning 'poppy.'

REDWOOD SORREL • *Oxalis oregana*

GENERAL: Perennial with **sour, watery juice** and scaly rhizomes; flowering stems 5–15 cm tall, **brownish-hairy**.

LEAVES: Numerous, compound, **clover-like** with **3 heart-shaped and folded leaflets** with the narrow ends attached to the stalk, all basal on long (5–20 cm), stalks.

FLOWERS: White to pale-pinkish, sometimes with reddish veins, **12–20 mm long**; sepals and petals 5; stamens 10, of 2 unequal lengths; single atop long stalks.

FRUITS: Capsules, **football-shaped**, 5 chambered, **7–9 mm long**; seeds almond-shaped, corrugated.

ECOLOGY: Moist, forested sites at low to middle elevations; common in Washington and Oregon, rare in alluvial forest on western Vancouver Island and the southern Queen Charlotte Islands.

NOTES: Trillium-leaved sorrel (*O. trilliifolia*) has **2 to several, 10 mm long**, white or pinkish flowers per stalk and **very narrow capsules 2–3 cm long**. It grows in moist meadows and open forest from low to moderately high elevations, and it is scattered and locally common in Washington and Oregon. **Suksdorf's sorrel** (*O. suksdorfii*) is a **yellow-flowered** species of forest and clearings in southwestern Washington and Oregon. • The redwood sorrel normally holds its leaflets horizontally to maximize interception of light in the dim forest understory. But at times, such as in direct sunlight or at night, it creases the leaflets sharply downward, reportedly taking 6 minutes to fold up and 30 minutes to flatten out again. This may be an adaptation to conserve moisture, but the leaflets also fold in the rain, perhaps to reduce the impact of raindrops. • The Cowlitz, Quileute and Quinault of western Washington ate the leaves of redwood sorrel. The plants contain oxalic acid, which gives them a sour, tangy taste and is **potentially harmful**.

COMMON STORK'S-BILL • *Erodium cicutarium*
FILAREE

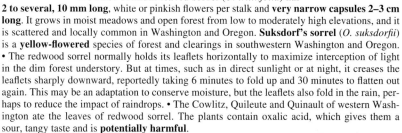

GENERAL: Taprooted, spreading, hairy **annual**; stems 3–40 cm tall, ascending, sparingly branching from the base, **usually somewhat reddish**.

LEAVES: Mostly basal (often hugging the ground), stalked, **much-divided and fern-like** with very narrow ultimate segments; stem leaves **opposite at swollen nodes**.

FLOWERS: Pink, small (8–15 mm wide); sepals 5, bristle-tipped; 5 petals; stamens 10, 5 short and sterile alternating with 5 longer and fertile; **few in umbel-like clusters** on long stalks from leaf axils.

FRUITS: Capsules, 3–5 cm long, **splitting open into 5 segments** each with 1 or 2 smooth seeds and tipped with a spirally twisting, persistent style.

ECOLOGY: Fields, clearings, waste places, at low elevations; common from southwestern B.C. south, also introduced in southeast Alaska.

NOTES: Common stork's-bill is a European weed introduced and now widespread in western North America and on several other continents. Thanks to the long-persistent styles, the fruits resemble stork's bills. As the fruits dry, they split lengthwise into 5 sharp-pointed segments, each attached to its portion of the separated style. The slender style becomes spirally twisted as it dries, but it straightens out again when wet. With alternate moisture and dryness, this uncoiling squirming action drives the attached seed into the ground. • A more correct common name should be 'heron's-bill,' since *Erodium* is from *erodios*, the Greek for 'a heron.' Very old names are 'pink-needle,' 'powke-needle' and 'pick-needle.'

HERB-ROBERT • *Geranium robertianum*
ROBERT GERANIUM

GENERAL: Taprooted annual with an unpleasant odour; stems branched, bent at the base to upright, spreading-hairy, 10–60 cm tall.

LEAVES: Egg-shaped to pentagonal in outline, **pinnately deeply divided** into **3–5 main segments that are themselves divided**, sparsely hairy on both sides, light green but sometimes reddish.

FLOWERS: Pink to reddish-purple, or pink with white stripes; sepals **glandular-hairy, bristle-tipped**; petals **7–15 mm long; usually 2** per fairly long stalk.

FRUITS: 5-parted capsules, the styles fused to form a central, pointed column 13–20 mm long.

ECOLOGY: Clearings, meadows, grassy openings, open forests, mostly at low elevations; an introduced Eurasian weed established and fairly frequent in southwestern B.C. south to California (but rare in western Oregon), rare northwards.

NOTES: The name 'herb-robert' is so ancient that no one is quite sure where it came from. The guesses cannot all be right: it was used to treat a disease in Germany called *Ruprechts-plage* after Robert, Duke of Normandy; it honours St. Robert, founder of the Cistercian order, who was born on April 29th, around the time the plant flowers; it is derived from *Ruprechtskraut* from the Latin *ruber*, because of its redness; it is associated with St. Rupert (or Rudbert) of Salzburg of the 8th century, who was invoked against bleeding wounds, ulcers, and erysipelas; it is associated with the house-goblin Knecht-Rupert; or it is named after Robin Goodfellow (Robin Hood).

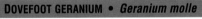

DOVEFOOT GERANIUM • *Geranium molle*

GENERAL: Taprooted annual, long-hairy and somewhat glandular; stems spreading, 10–40 cm tall.

LEAVES: Kidney-shaped in outline, about 2/3 divided into **5–7 broad, radiating, coarsely toothed lobes**; basal leaves long-stalked.

FLOWERS: Pink; sepals **soft-hairy, not bristle-tipped**; petals **3–5 mm long; usually 2** per stalk.

FRUITS: 5-parted capsules; styles fused to form a central, pointed column 6–8 mm long; point or **beak 1–2 mm long**, thread-like.

ECOLOGY: Fields, lawns, moist clearings and waste places; common at low elevations in the southern part of our region (southwestern B.C. south), rare on the Queen Charlotte Islands.

NOTES: Dovefoot geranium is a weedy species introduced from Eurasia, often found with common stork's-bill in sunny, exposed areas, where both start blooming early. **Bicknell's geranium** (*G. bicknellii*) is a native, **annual or biennial** species, spreading to erect and 20–80 cm tall, with **deeply 5-parted leaves, pale pink-purple** flowers, **bristle-tipped** sepals, petals 4–8 mm long, and capsules with **beaks 4–5 mm long**. It occurs in forest openings, along roadsides, in recently burned clearings, and on disturbed soil generally, where it behaves like a weed. It is common from southeast Vancouver Island and the Gulf Islands south in Washington, and in the middle Skeena and Nass drainages. **Cut-leaved geranium** (*G. dissectum*) is similar, but it has a capsule **beak 2–3 mm long** and short fruiting stalks. It is a weedy annual introduced from Europe, common at low elevations from southwestern B.C. to California and rare in the Queen Charlotte Islands. You may encounter 2 or 3 other small-flowered, weedy species of *Geranium*; consult technical manuals. • *G. molle* is called 'dovefoot' because of the shape of the leaves.

NORTHERN GERANIUM • *Geranium erianthum*
CRANE'S-BILL

GENERAL: Perennial from a thick, scaly **rhizome and woody stem-base**; stems leafy, hairy, 30–80 cm tall.

LEAVES: Palmately deeply divided into 3–5 irregularly lobed and toothed segments; blades broader than long; basal leaves long-stalked; stem leaves stalkless.

FLOWERS: Blue to pink-purple, short-stalked; petals twice as long as **very hairy** sepals; 3–5 in loose clusters, usually not much higher than surrounding leaves.

FRUITS: Capsules with styles fused to form a central, pointed column 25–33 mm long; when dry, the central column splits into 5, each part suddenly recoiling and ripping off a segment of the capsule, at the same time flinging out its single seed.

ECOLOGY: Moist, open forests, meadows, avalanche tracks, roadsides and clearings, from low elevations to above timberline; common and often abundant.

NOTES: Western geranium (*G. oreganum*) is also a fairly large showy perennial, but it has **reddish-purple** flowers and **lightly hairy** sepals, and it grows in moist meadows and forest at low to middle elevations from northwestern Washington to California (1 collection from Victoria). • *Geranium* is Greek for 'crane.' The species name *erianthum* comes from the Latin words meaning 'soft' and 'flower.'

WILD GINGER • *Asarum caudatum*

GENERAL: Evergreen perennial with extensive rhizomes; stems **trailing, rooting freely**, often forming large mats.

LEAVES: Heart- to kidney-shaped, shiny, long-stalked, **2 at each node**, 4–10 cm long, to 15 cm wide; leaf stalks and veins finely hairy.

FLOWERS: Purplish-brown to greenish-yellow, solitary, bell-shaped flowers with 3 flaring lobes that taper to long points; often concealed by leaves.

FRUITS: Fleshy capsules; seeds several, egg-shaped, with prominent fleshy appendage.

ECOLOGY: Rich bottomlands, moist, shaded forest, frequently in thick leaf mould that partly hides the flowers; common at low to middle elevations.

NOTES: The whole plant, when crushed, has a strong smell of lemon-ginger. The roots can be eaten fresh or dried and ground as a ginger substitute. • It has been reported that fungus gnats deposit eggs in the throats of the flowers, but when the larvae eat the flowers, they are poisoned and die (Meeuse and Morris 1984). • The Nuxalk made a tea from wild-ginger root which was drunk for stomach pains. It was applied as a poultice for headaches, intestinal pains and knee pains. It is known to have antibiotic properties. The Sechelt boiled the leaves, crushed them and put them in bath water or rubbed them directly on the painful limb for arthritis. The Squamish chewed the leaves and swallowed the juice for tuberculosis. They and the Stl'atl'imx and Saanich used wild ginger as a good-luck charm and a protective wash when bathing. The Skagit used the leaves in a medicinal preparation for tuberculosis. The Skokomish drank the leaf tea in quantity as an emetic and to settle the stomach. • The word 'ginger' dates back to the 13th century and means 'horn-root' or 'root with a horn shape,' and it has generally been applied to plants with this particular flavour or smell.

HENDERSON'S CHECKER-MALLOW • *Sidalcea hendersonii*

GENERAL: Taprooted perennial with short, thick rhizomes; stems leafy, hollow, **mostly hairless**, usually purplish tinged, 0.5–1.5 m tall.

LEAVES: Basal leaves long-stalked, round-toothed, heart-shaped at base; **stem leaves alternate**, progressively shorter stalked, **palmately 5 lobed** into oblong segments.

FLOWERS: Deep-pink, showy (like little hollyhocks); sepals 5, united at the base, the lobes fringed; petals 5, somewhat **heart-shaped**, broader and lobed at the tip; **stamens numerous**, about 50 or more; numerous in compound spikes atop stems.

FRUITS: Capsules, with 5–10 beaked, smooth chambers each with 1 kidney-shaped seed.

ECOLOGY: Wet meadows, tidal marshes and flats at low elevations; scattered from southwestern B.C. south to the mouth of the Umpqua River.

NOTES: Several other checker-mallows occur in the southern part of our region. **Rose checker-mallow** (*S. virgata*) has rose-pink flowers on stems 20–100 cm tall covered with **branched or star-like hairs**. **Meadow checker-mallow** (*S. campestris*) has **white to pale-pink** flowers on 0.5–2 m tall, hairy (usually with **unbranched hairs**) stems. Both species grow in meadows, fields, grassy slopes, and on roadsides in the Willamette Valley, though *S. virgata* usually is in moister habitats. • *Sidalcea* is also called 'marsh hollyhock.' The common name has nothing to do with holly, and it was probably originally 'holyhock' or 'holyoke' (from 'holy' and the Old English *hocc* or *hauc*, from the Latin *alcea*, a mallow-like plant). *Holli* may be a corruption of *cauli* or *coley* meaning 'cabbage,' because of the well-filled, double flowers. Another source says the name 'holyhock' was given to the close relative marsh mallow (*Althaea officinalis*) because it is a blessed or healing herb, although the true hollyhock appears to be *Alcea rosea*. • *Sidalcea* is a composite of two genus names: *Sida* (Greek for 'water-lily') and *Alcea* (mallow). The species was named for Dr. Louis Fourniquet Henderson (1853–1942), a professor of botany at the University of Oregon.

PURPLE LOOSESTRIFE • *Lythrum salicaria*

GENERAL: Perennial with strong rhizomes; stems erect, leafy, simple or branched above, angled, **0.5–2 m tall**.

LEAVES: Mostly opposite, some in 3s or alternate, **lance-shaped**, pointed, hairy, more or less heart-shaped at the base, 3–10 cm long.

FLOWERS: Reddish-purple, showy; sepals 5, fused basally into a tube; petals mostly 5, somewhat **crinkly**, 7–10 mm long; **stamens 8–10, of 3 distinct lengths**; numerous in long, crowded, interrupted spikes atop stems.

FRUITS: Capsules, long, 2-chambered; seeds numerous.

ECOLOGY: Marshes (brackish and freshwater), wet meadows, stream-banks, lake-shores, wet ditches and sloughs, at low elevations; scattered, locally abundant.

NOTES: Hyssop loosestrife (*L. hyssopifolia*) is a native, **pale-glaucous-green annual, 10–40 cm tall**, with mostly **alternate** leaves and flowers with **white to rose** petals 2–3.5 mm long; it also grows in marshy habitats mostly near the coast, from Washington to California. • Purple loosestrife is a Eurasian species that has become a nasty wetland weed in North America; it is also cultivated in flower gardens by misguided individuals. It is fast becoming known in North America as the 'beautiful killer' because it can completely take over wetlands and displace native species. • The name 'loosestrife' derives from *lysimachia* meaning 'to deliver from strife' (see *Lysimachia thyrsiflora*, p. 321), and was given by Turner (1548) to both genera. It appears to have some efficacy against gnats and flies, and was reputed to calm quarrelsome beasts of burden at the plough if placed upon the yoke.

WESTERN ST. JOHN'S-WORT • *Hypericum formosum*

GENERAL: Hairless perennial with slender stolons and rhizomes; stems **upright**, leafy, usually numerous, simple to branched, **10–80 cm tall**.

LEAVES: Opposite, lance-egg-shaped to oblong-elliptic, **1–3 cm long**, usually **purplish-black dotted**, stalkless and somewhat clasping at the base.

FLOWERS: Yellow (bronze-orange in bud), showy, **about 2 cm across**, stalked; sepals 5, triangular to egg-shaped, with dark dots; petals 5, about 10 mm long, with **dark dots or fine teeth along the margins**; stamens showy, **numerous (75–100)**, concentrated in several groups; few to several in clusters atop stem.

FRUITS: Capsules, 3-chambered, 6–9 mm long; seeds **yellowish**, 1 mm long or less, **net-veined but not pitted**.

ECOLOGY: Moist, open sites (meadows, streambanks, thickets) from low to subalpine elevations; scattered, locally common.

NOTES: Common St. John's-wort (*H. perforatum*) is quite similar but has **narrower, lance-shaped** leaves, narrowly lance-shaped sepals, and **brownish** seeds usually over 1 mm long and with **rows of pits**. It is a Eurasian perennial weed and a serious pest in fields, pastures and on roadsides and waste places, common from about Tacoma, Washington, south to California, and scattered north to central Vancouver Island and the lower Fraser Valley. • Common St. John's-wort was introduced to North America from Europe, where it has been used in medicine since ancient times. It spread to the northwest coast from California, where it was originally introduced and called 'Klamath weed.' In herbal medicine it has been widely employed to alleviate nervous disorders and it was applied to wounds where the nerves were exposed. However, it contains a phototoxin concentrated in the glandular dots on the leaves. Sensitive individuals become susceptible to skin burns and dermatitis, especially with exposure to sunlight. Recent studies indicate that 2 compounds isolated from this species strongly inhibit a variety of retroviruses, leading to speculation about its effect on HIV.

BOG ST. JOHN'S-WORT • *Hypericum anagalloides*

GENERAL: Low mat-forming perennial with numerous, branching, prostrate stems; upright stems leafy, hairless, **5–15 cm tall**.

LEAVES: Opposite, egg-shaped to elliptic, **rounded, 5–15 mm long**.

FLOWERS: Salmon-yellow, small (4–8 mm across); sepals 5, 2–3 mm long; petals 5, only slightly longer than sepals, **lacking black marginal spots**; stamens **15–25**; on **short, stout** stalks in few-flowered clusters.

FRUITS: Capsules, 3 chambered; seeds yellow, finely ridged.

ECOLOGY: Wet meadows, wetlands, wet ditches and clearings; at low to middle elevations.

NOTES: Scarlet pimpernel (*Anagallis arvensis*) resembles *H. anagalloides*, but it is an introduced annual from an unrelated family, the Primulaceae or primrose family. Scarlet pimpernel is also low, prostrate to ascending, hairless, and has opposite, egg-shaped but **pointed** leaves. Its flowers are **salmon-coloured**, borne on **long, thin**, curved stalks, and they are **10–17 mm wide**. It is a weedy species of fields, clearings, and waste areas, sporadic from southwestern B.C. south. • The Latin *hypericum* means 'above pictures,' from the early placement of plants over shrines to repel evil spirits. • St. John's-wort is named for John the Baptist. The spots seen when the leaf is held up to the light were believed to ooze blood on the day he was executed (August 27th or 29th). Folklore has it that if it was gathered on the eve of St. John's birthday (June 24th) and hung in the windows, it would protect the house against thunder and evil spirits.

BUNCHBERRY • *Cornus canadensis*
DWARF DOGWOOD

GENERAL: Low, trailing, rhizomatous perennial, **somewhat woody at the base**; stems erect, minutely hairy, 5–25 cm tall.

LEAVES: More or less evergreen, **short-stalked, 4–7 in a terminal whorl above 1 (or 2) pairs of leafy bracts** on the stem, oval-elliptic, 2–8 cm long, green above, whitish beneath; veins parallel.

FLOWERS: Small, **greenish-white or yellowish to purplish**; sepals, petals, and stamens 4; inflorescence consists of **4 white to purplish-tinged, petal-like bracts surrounding a central umbel-like cluster**.

FRUITS: Bright-red, fleshy, berry-like drupes, sweet though pulpy.

ECOLOGY: Moist coniferous and mixed forest and forest openings, meadows, bogs; often growing on tree trunks, logs, stumps in the most maritime forests; valley bottoms to subalpine elevations.

NOTES: Swedish dwarf cornel (*C. suecica*, also known as bog bunchberry) has **2 or more pairs of leaves** below the terminal, **stalkless** whorl, and dark-purplish sepals and petals. It grows from lowlands to alpine tundra, uncommonly in southeast Alaska, and more commonly in Prince William Sound. • Bunchberry has an explosive pollination mechanism. The petals of the mature, but unopened, flower buds suddenly reflex, triggered by a tiny 'antenna' projecting from one petal tip, and the anthers spring out simultaneously, catapulting their pollen loads into the air. • A Hesquiat myth tells of an unhappy wife who was driven to the top of a tree for punishment by her husband. As she climbed the tree she was bleeding from menstruation, and where the blood fell bunchberry grew. Her brother came to find her when he heard her singing. The wife died as a result of the ordeal and her brother disguised himself as his sister and sought for the husband in a nearby village. He was found out by mallard duck sisters because he did not harvest bracken fern like a woman.

SPREADING DOGBANE • *Apocynum androsaemifolium*

GENERAL: Perennial from rhizomes; stems **erect, branched**, leafy, hairless or hairy, often reddish, 20–70 cm tall; plants **with milky sap**.

LEAVES: Opposite, narrowly oval to elliptic or oblong, short-stalked, 3–8 cm long, **spreading and drooping**, hairless and green above, paler and usually hairy beneath.

FLOWERS: Pink or whitish with pink veins, sweet-scented, **bell-shaped with flaring lobes**, small **(6–8 mm long)**; showy in terminal and lateral clusters.

FRUITS: Very long (5–12 cm), paired, skinny, cylindric pods; **numerous seeds, each with long tuft of cottony hairs**.

ECOLOGY: Open hillsides and ridges, dry, warm, well-drained sites, fields, meadows, roadsides, also in dry forest; scattered, locally common, at low to subalpine elevations.

NOTES: In the southern part of our region you could encounter **hemp dogbane** (*A. cannabinum*), which has yellow-green leaves held **upright**, and **greenish-white** flowers only **2–5 mm long**. Hemp dogbane was used by a number of northwest aboriginal groups for fishnets, animal traps, sewing and so on. Fibre from hemp dogbane was traded to groups in the northern part of our range. • Spreading dogbane can be toxic to livestock, and sickness and death have been reported from its use for medicinal purposes by humans. • The stem fibres of spreading dogbane are strong, and similar to those of hemp dogbane, but much shorter, and considered of inferior quality. The fibre was sometimes used for cordage when hemp dogbane or stinging nettle were not available.

TUFTED LOOSESTRIFE • *Lysimachia thyrsiflora*

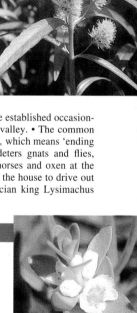

GENERAL: Hairless perennial from creeping rhizomes; stems leafy, erect, unbranched, 20–80 cm tall.

LEAVES: Opposite, scale-like on lower part of stem, large above, 3-16 cm long, **lance-shaped to narrowly elliptic**, stalkless, sometimes with sterile bulblet-bearing shoots in the axils, finely spotted with **red to purplish-black spots.**

FLOWERS: Yellow, spotted or streaked with purple, **saucer-shaped**, with usually 5 lobes; stamens 5, sticking out beyond the petals; numerous in dense **bottlebrush-like clusters on long stalks from the axils** of the 2 or 3 pairs of larger leaves near midstem.

FRUITS: Capsules, rounded, small (2.5 mm broad); seeds few, pitted.

ECOLOGY: Marshes, swamps, margins of streams and ponds, at low to middle elevations; scattered the length of our region, more common from southwestern B.C. south.

NOTES: Creeping jenny (*Lysimachia nummularia*) is a **prostrate, creeping** perennial with **round to oval** leaves and yellow flowers that are **single or in pairs** in the leaf axils. It is a garden escapee that has become established occasionally from southwestern B.C. south to the Willamette valley. • The common name comes from a translation of the Latin *lysimachia*, which means 'ending strife' or 'loosening strife.' This plant apparently deters gnats and flies, which may be why it was used to quiet 'quarrelsome beasts such as horses and oxen at the plough' (stopping their strife). Loosestrife also used to be burned inside the house to drive out serpents, flies and gnats. Pliny says that it was named after the Thracian king Lysimachus (ca. 360-281 BC), a companion of Alexander.

SEA MILK-WORT • *Glaux maritima*

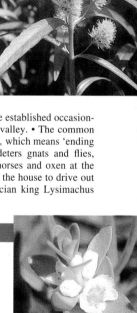

GENERAL: Hairless, **fleshy perennial** from rhizomes; stems leafy to the tip, 3–30 cm tall.

LEAVES: Numerous, **opposite low on the stem, alternate above, oval to oblong, rounded at tip**, stalkless and jointed at the base, 5–25 mm long.

FLOWERS: White or pinkish, small (4–5 mm long), **cup-shaped, single and stalkless in leaf axils** near the middle of the stem; flower parts in 5s.

FRUITS: Small capsules; seeds several, flattened.

ECOLOGY: Tideflats, salt marshes, sea beaches; common.

NOTES: This species also occurs in alkaline marshes and meadows inland of our region; our strictly coastal plants are

the subspecies *obtusifolia*. **Scarlet pimpernel** (*Anagallis arvensis*, also known as poor man's weatherglass) is in the same family (Primulaceae) as sea milk-wort, but it is a low **annual** with opposite, egg-shaped but **pointed** leaves, and **salmon-coloured** flowers on **long, thin, curved stalks**. It is a weedy species of fields, clearings, and waste places, sporadic from southwestern B.C. south. Scarlet pimpernel could also be confused with bog St. John's-wort (p. 319). • Haskin (1934) reports that some coastal tribes dug and ate the roots of sea milk-wort, and that the plant could contain 'a narcotic principal, for it is said that the Indians ate them only in the evening, since after eating they at once became very sleepy.' • *Glaux maritima* is called 'milk-wort' (along with the real milk-wort, *Polygala vulgaris*), because an infusion brewed from the plant was given to nursing mothers to increase their milk supply. *Glaux* is from the Greek *glaucos* ('bluish-green'), describing the colour of the plant, and *maritima* means 'of the sea.'

NORTHERN STARFLOWER • *Trientalis arctica*

GENERAL: Perennial from short, horizontal rhizomes that are slightly thickened at the tip, but **not noticeably tuberous**; stem erect, leafy, 5–25 cm tall.

LEAVES: Main leaves **oval-elliptic to broadly lance-shaped**, rounded at the tip, 1–7 cm long, in a **whorl** of 5–6 at the top of simple stems; **lower leaves few to several**, alternate, much smaller.

FLOWERS: White (pink-tinged), star-like; petals 5–7, sharp pointed, fused at the base; single on each of 1–3 thin stalks that arise from the centre of the leaf whorl.

FRUITS: Spherical 1-chambered capsules, splitting into 5 parts when dry.

ECOLOGY: Bogs, swamps, muskeg, boggy forest, seepage areas, wet thickets, meadows and heath, at low to (less commonly) high elevations; common except in the southernmost part of our region.

NOTES: Northern starflower is also known as *T. europaea* ssp. *arctica*. Northern star-flower differs from broad-leaved starflower in stem leaves (**several** vs. none) below the terminal leaf whorl, in flower colour (**white** vs. pink) and in habitat (**wetlands** vs. uplands) • The Latin name *Trientalis* means '1/3 of a foot in length' (approximately 10 cm), in reference to the size of the plant.

BROAD-LEAVED STARFLOWER • *Trientalis latifolia*
WESTERN STARFLOWER, INDIAN POTATO

GENERAL: Perennial from slender rhizomes with **enlarged, vertical tubers**; stem erect, 10–30 cm tall.

LEAVES: 4–8 in a terminal **whorl, egg-shaped to elliptic**, 3–10 cm long; other stem leaves **reduced to bracts**.

FLOWERS: Pink to rose, star-like; petals 5–9, usually 6 or 7, fused at the base; several on thin, curved stalks from the centre of the leaf whorl.

FRUITS: Spherical 1-chambered capsules, split into 5 parts when dry.

ECOLOGY: Open forest, thickets, meadows, at low to middle elevations; common from southwestern B.C. south, scattered northwards.

NOTES: Broad-leaved starflower is also known as *T. europaea* var. *latifolia* or *T. borealis* ssp. *latifolia*. • Broad-leaved starflower often grows in clumps around the bases of trees. • The plump firm tubers reportedly were gathered for food by some coastal aboriginal groups. • *Trientalis* species are called 'starflowers' because the flower stalks are very thin, leaving the flowers apparently hanging in the air like tiny woodland stars. The species name *latifolia* means 'broad-leaved.'

SMOOTH DOUGLASIA • *Douglasia laevigata*

GENERAL: **Mat-forming** perennial; stems prostrate to ascending, 4–8 cm tall, dichotomously branched, **ending in rosettes of leaves**.

LEAVES: Oblong to lance-shaped, 5–20 mm long, hairless or hairy; margins smooth or few-toothed.

FLOWERS: Crimson to deep-pink, fading to lavender, about 1 cm wide; sepals 5, fused at bottom half; petals 5, fused in a narrow funnel-shaped tube; stamens barely visible at the narrow throat where the round-tipped lobes spread at right angles from the tube; in **tight umbels** of 2–10 flowers atop a long, leafless stalk.

FRUITS: Capsules, opening from the top by 5 segments; seeds 1–3, brown, finely pitted.

ECOLOGY: Moist coastal bluffs, talus slopes, rocky ridges and ledges, at alpine to (occasionally) low elevations; scattered, locally common in the Olympic Mountains, the western Cascades from Snohomish County south, in the mountains of southwest Washington and northwest Oregon, and in the Columbia gorge, rare northwards on Vancouver Island and the Queen Charlotte Islands.

NOTES: Smooth douglasia resembles another, more common cushion plant: spreading phlox (*Phlox diffusa*). Note that *Douglasia*'s **deeper-pink or reddish** flowers are on **branched, leafless stalks**, and each has a single, undivided stigma. • The genus name honors David Douglas, intrepid early plant explorer of northwestern North America. The species name, *laevigata*, emphasizes the 'smooth leaves.'.

WEDGE-LEAF PRIMROSE • *Primula cuneifolia*
PIXIE-EYES   ssp. *saxifragifolia*

GENERAL: Fibrous-rooted perennial; **stems leafless**, 2–20 cm tall.

LEAVES: All in basal rosettes, lance-to egg-shaped, tapering to a stalked base, fairly thick, hairless, with **5–11 coarse teeth at the tip**.

FLOWERS: Deep-pink to rose or whitish, 1–2 cm wide; petals fused in a narrow, funnel-shaped tube that flares into 5 lobes (each with 2 blunt lobes); in umbels of 1–9 flowers atop long, leafless stalks.

FRUITS: Oval capsules; seeds angled.

ECOLOGY: Moist alpine heath and tundra, wet meadows; scattered in the northern part of our region, locally common in Prince William Sound and northern southeast Alaska, rare on northwestern Vancouver Island.

NOTES: Wedge-leaf primrose is very common on the Aleutian Islands and extends around the North Pacific to northern Japan • **Greenland primrose** (*P. egaliksensis*) has **oblong leaves** with **smooth to undulating margins**, and small (**5–9 mm broad**) **white or lilac** flowers. It grows in wet meadows, marshes, and along streams at middle to high elevations; it is locally common in northern southeast Alaska and rare on Vancouver Island. • The name 'primrose' is a classic example of a misinterpretation. It has nothing to do with roses; indeed, the flowers do not resemble roses at all. The original Latin name appears to have been *prima vera* or *fior di prima vera* meaning 'the first flower of spring,' and it gave rise to the French *primaverole*. This was then corrupted in English to *primerole* and then to *pryme rolles* from which 'primrose' came. The Latin, from *primus* ('first'), also recognises the early appearance of the flowers. • 'Pixie-eyes' is very apt, because the flowers with their yellow centres appear like eyes peeking out of the alpine tundra.

FEW-FLOWERED SHOOTINGSTAR • *Dodecatheon pulchellum*
PRETTY SHOOTINGSTAR

GENERAL: Hairless to glandular-hairy perennial; roots pale, **without bulblets**; flowering stems leafless, 5–50 cm tall.

LEAVES: Oblong-lance- to spoon-shaped, narrowed gradually to winged stalks, 3–20 cm long; margins smooth to weakly toothed.

FLOWERS: Magenta to lavender, 10–20 mm long; petals 5, **swept backwards**, united at the base in a yellowish collar with a wavy purplish ring; stamens 5, the stalks united into a **yellowish to orange** tube 1.5–3 mm long, surmounted by yellowish to reddish-purple anthers 4–7 mm long; 3–25 in an umbel atop the stem.

FRUITS: Capsules, cylindrical to egg-shaped, 1-chambered, **splitting up to tip**; seeds numerous.

ECOLOGY: Moist, often saline meadows, wet coastal rocks and bluffs, stream-banks; sea level to alpine, although mostly at low elevations in the northern part of our region; fairly common the length of our region.

NOTES: Few-flowered shootingstar is also known as *Dodecatheon pauciflorum*. • **Broad-leaved shootingstar** (*D. hendersonii*) has **egg-shaped to deltoid** leaf blades **contracted abruptly** to the stalk, **bulblets** present among the roots at flowering time and a **reddish-purple** stamen tube. It is a species of dry, grassy meadows or open woods, from southwestern B.C. (Strait of Georgia area) south to California. • The species name *pulchellum* refers to the plant's beauty. Note the similarity in flower shape to the closely related cultivated plant cyclamen.

TALL MOUNTAIN SHOOTINGSTAR • *Dodecatheon jeffreyi*
JEFFREY'S SHOOTINGSTAR

GENERAL: Hairless to glandular-hairy (especially in the inflorescence) perennial, forming large clumps connected by slender rhizomes, **without bulblets**; flowering stems leafless, 10–60 cm tall.

LEAVES: Lance-shaped, gradually narrowing to long stalks, 5–50 cm long; margins irregularly toothed to smooth.

FLOWERS: Purplish, magenta, lavender or sometimes white, 10–25 mm long; petals **4 or 5**, swept sharply backwards, united at the base in a short, yellowish tube with a reddish ring; stamens 4 or 5, the stalks free or narrowly fused, 1 mm long, **reddish to blackish-purple**, surmounted by yellow to reddish anthers 6–10 mm long; 3–20 in an umbel atop the stem.

FRUITS: Capsules, egg-shaped, 1-chambered, **opening at the top by a lid and splitting downwards**; seeds numerous.

ECOLOGY: Wet meadows, stream-banks, muskeg, pool margins, at sea level to high elevations; common.

NOTES: Shootingstars are among our most beautiful wildflowers, brightening up grassy slopes, meadows and muskeg. • Shootingstars provide a good example of 'buzz pollination.' The anthers shed pollen into the stamen tube, from which the pollen can be dislodged by sound waves set up by the buzzing of bumblebees. • 'Shootingstar' describes the flowers, whose stamens lead the way as the turned-back petals stream behind like the tail of a shooting star. *Dodecatheon* means 'twelve gods,' from the Greek *dodeka* ('twelve') and *theos* ('god'), which can be interpreted to mean a plant protected by the pantheon. • John Jeffrey was hired by a club of Scottish gentlemen to botanize in the Okanagan, Similkameen, Fraser, Willamette and Umpqua drainages in 1851–53.

EUROPEAN BITTERSWEET • *Solanum dulcamara*

GENERAL: Rhizomatous perennial, often **somewhat woody**; stems leafy, **vine-like**, 1–3 m tall or long, tending to climb or sprawl on other vegetation.

LEAVES: Alternate, stalked, 3–8 cm long, some unlobed and egg-shaped to somewhat heart-shaped, others with a pair of ear-like lobes or leaflets at the base, short-hairy to hairless.

FLOWERS: Blue-violet, resembling a shootingstar or a tomato flower; petals fused into a short tube at the base, with 5 pointed, reflexed lobes 5–9 mm long, like a star with the points arching backward; stamens 5, joined in a conspicuous **yellow cone**; 5–25 on branches from a short stalk off the stem.

FRUITS: Bright-red berries, shaped like fat footballs.

ECOLOGY: Waste places, thickets, roadsides, open forest, moist clearings, at low elevations; scattered in the southern half of our region, mostly in or near settled areas.

NOTES: European bittersweet is a Eurasian species, now established fairly widely in temperate North America, in our region mostly as a garden escapee. The leaves and fruits are moderately poisonous to humans and livestock. **Black nightshade** (*Solanum americanum* var. *nodiflorum*, also known as *S. nigrum* in part) is another weedy species, that is occasional mostly in the southern half of our region. It is an **annual taprooted** herb, and it has **white** flowers and **black** berries that are poisonous, at least when immature. • The term 'nightshade' was originally applied to this plant and to deadly nightshade (*Atropa belladonna*). An old herbal describes the narcotic *A. belladonna* as a *solatrum*, or soothing painkiller. In translation this was mistaken for the words *solem atrum*, meaning 'black sun' or 'eclipse.' • The common name 'bittersweet' and species name *dulcamara* ('sweet-bitter') describe the rind of the stem: 'When it is first tasted it is bitter, and afterwards sweet' (Turner 1548).

DEER-CABBAGE • *Fauria crista-galli*

GENERAL: Hairless perennial from shallow rhizomes that are thick, fleshy and covered with old leaf-bases; flowering stems leafless, 10–50 cm tall.

LEAVES: All basal, thick, broadly **kidney- to heart-shaped**, 5–14 cm wide, wider than long, **blunt-toothed**; stalks 10–30 cm long with sheathing stipules at base.

FLOWERS: White, top-shaped; petals fused at base into short (2–4 mm) tubes, spreading into 5 lobes 5–6 mm long with **wavy flanges** on the midveins and margins; 5–30 in loose flat-topped clusters atop stems.

FRUITS: Capsules, conic egg-shaped, 1 chambered; seeds smooth and shining.

ECOLOGY: Bogs, swamps, wet meadows, seepage areas in wet forest, at low to subalpine elevations; common, especially in the most maritime climates.

NOTES: Also known as *Nephrophyllidium crista-galli*, deer-cabbage and its aquatic cousin buckbean (p. 339) are related to the gentians, but they are often placed in their own family, the Menyanthaceae. • The attractively fringed white flowers have a foul odour, like bad cheese or mildewed laundry, which attracts pollinating flies. • When not in flower or fruit, deer-cabbage could be confused with broad-leaved marsh-marigold (p. 174), but the **lobes at the base of deer-cabbage's leaves do not touch**, whereas the lobes of broad-leaved marsh-marigold's leaves usually touch or overlap.

BEACH MORNING-GLORY • *Convolvulus soldanella*

GENERAL: Hairless fleshy perennial from deep rhizomes; stems leafy, **creeping but not twining**, 20–50 cm long.

LEAVES: Alternate, **thick and fleshy**; blades **kidney-shaped**, rounded at tip, heart-shaped at base, 1.5–4 cm wide, on stalks as long or longer.

FLOWERS: Pinkish-purple, showy, broadly funnel-shaped, **3–6 cm long**; petals wholly fused, pleated; single on stalks from leaf axils.

FRUITS: Capsules, more or less spherical, 2-chambered; seeds 2–4, large (6–8 mm long), smooth.

ECOLOGY: Coastal beaches and sand dunes; scattered from the Queen Charlotte Islands south to California.

NOTES: Beach morning-glory is also known as *Calystegia soldanella*. • Beach morning-glory is one of a distinctive assemblage of sand beach and dune species in our region, including yellow sand-verbena (p. 311), large-headed sedge (p. 393) and silver burweed (p. 278). • Another common name for *Convolvulus soldanella* is 'beach bindweed,' because it is a weed that twines (*convolvo* means 'to twine') around, or binds together, other plants. The species name, *soldanella*, means 'coin-shaped' and refers to the round leaves.

FIELD BINDWEED • *Convolvulus arvensis*
ORCHARD MORNING-GLORY

GENERAL: Hairless to hairy perennial from deep rhizomes; stems leafy, **trailing to somewhat twining**, 20–200 cm long, often forming carpets.

LEAVES: Alternate, the blades usually **arrowhead-shaped**, blunt or sharp pointed at the tip, 2–6 cm long, stalked.

FLOWERS: White to rose-purple, showy, **1.5–2.5 cm** long, shaped like a wide-mouthed funnel; petals wholly fused, twisted in bud, pleated in flower; 1 or 2 on erect stalks that exceed the leaves and have 2 linear bracts about midlength.

FRUITS: Capsules, shaped like a fat cone, 2 chambered, splitting lengthwise to release the smooth seeds.

ECOLOGY: Fields, thickets, roadsides, disturbed areas and waste places; low to middle elevations; common.

NOTES: Hedge bindweed (*C. sepium*, also called lady's-nightcap) is a rhizomatous perennial that **twines and clambers**, forming hedge-like growths over other vegetation and objects. It has large (**4–7 cm long**), showy, **white to pink** flowers, and it is also an **introduced weed**, common in moist to  wet habitats from southwestern B.C. south, and occasional on the Queen Charlotte Islands. **Nightblooming morning-glory** (*C. nyctagineus*) is a **native** perennial with **erect to trailing (not twining)** stems, and **creamy-white or pinkish-tinged** flowers. It grows on dry, rocky slopes or open forest, from Mt. Adams south in the Cascades and through the Willamette valley to California. • **Field bindweed** was **introduced** from Europe, and it now grows over much of temperate North America. It is a beautiful but pernicious **weed**, difficult to eradicate because of its deep rhizomes and low growth. • *C. arvensis* is sometimes called 'cornbind' and 'barebind' when it grows in fields of corn and barley (or 'bare'), respectively. 'Morning-glory' is more commonly used for the closely related genus *Ipomoea* .

MANROOT • *Marah oreganus*
BIGROOT

GENERAL: Climbing perennial from **swollen, woody roots**; stems leafy, **trailing or climbing**, with **branched, coiled tendrils**.

LEAVES: Alternate, large (15–20 cm across), irregularly **palmately lobed**, heart-shaped at base, stalked, rough-hairy above, sparsely hairy to hairless below.

FLOWERS: Whitish, bell-shaped, about 1 cm across; petals fused into a tube 3–6 mm long flaring to 5–8 pointed lobes 3–8 mm long; **male and female flowers separate on the same plant**; males several, in narrow-stalked clusters from leaf axils; females usually solitary, short-stalked, from the same axils.

FRUITS: Football-shaped bladders, inflated and **somewhat fleshy**, eventually dry and bursting irregularly at the tip, fibrous-netted and 2–4 chambered inside, weakly spiny or almost smooth outside, 3–8 cm long; seeds 1 or 2 per chamber, large (2 cm long), smooth.

ECOLOGY: Moist fields, clearings, thickets, bottomlands, open hillsides, at low elevations; common.

NOTES: Manroot's stems spread along the ground and climb onto other vegetation much like those of its cultivated relatives in the cucumber or gourd family. • Manroot, also known as 'wild cucumber,' was used by the Coast Salish to make a decoction for venereal disease and to treat kidney trouble and scrofula sores. The Squaxin mashed the upper stalk in water and bathed aching hands in the mixture. The Chehalis also applied a preparation to scrofula sores. • The large size of the roots is the source of both common names. *Marah* is one of the few Hebrew words used to name plants; it means 'bitter,' from the very bitter juice in the swollen roots. The same word forms the root of the name 'Mary'.

DODDERS • *Cuscuta* species

GENERAL: Parasitic, twining, leafless perennials (in our region) or annuals; stems **pinkish-yellow to orange or white, thread-like**, hairless, twining about herbs and shrubs and sticking to them by means of **suckers**.

LEAVES: Reduced to tiny scales.

FLOWERS: Whitish, creamy or yellow, small (2–4 mm long); sepals 4–5, fused and often fleshy at the base; petals fused into tubes or bells with 4–5 lobes; several to many, more or less stalkless, in clusters or globular masses.

FRUITS: Rounded capsules, falling without opening or opening along a ring near the base; seeds 1–4.

ECOLOGY: Parasitic on a variety of flowering plants, at low elevations; scattered, locally common.

NOTES: The characteristics used for distinguishing the various dodders are so technical that no useful purpose would be served here in describing the individual species in our region. However, **salt marsh dodder** (*C. salina*) is distinctive in that it **parasitizes salt-marsh plants** of the goosefoot (Chenopodiaceae) and sunflower (Asteraceae) families. • The dodders are unique in appearance and life cycle. 'Their small seeds germinate in the soil and produce slender stems without seed leaves. Unless the slowly rotating stem encounters a host plant within a short time, the dodder seedling withers and dies. If the stem comes in contact with the living stem of a susceptible plant, the dodder twines round it and at numerous points develops suckers, which penetrate the tissue of the host. Food is received through these suckers and the dodder loses all contact with the soil. After a period of growth, clusters of small flowers appear and large amounts of seed are produced' (Frankton and Mulligan 1987).

THRIFT • *Armeria maritima*
SEA-PINK

GENERAL: Perennial herb from taproot and branching stem-base; flowering stem leafless, 5–45 cm tall.

LEAVES: All basal, densely tufted, persistent, linear to narrowly lance-shaped, hairless to sparsely long-hairy, 5–10 cm long.

FLOWERS: Pink to lavender, small (4–7 mm long); sepals fused at the base, ribbed and soft-hairy; petals fused only at the base, with 5 long, delicate, **papery** lobes; short-stalked and numerous in **head-like clusters** with **papery bracts**; flowering stalks 1 to several.

FRUITS: Small, dry, **nut-like bladders,** often enclosed in the sepals, 1 chambered and 1 seeded.

ECOLOGY: Coastal beaches, bluffs, spits, sometimes somewhat inland along river-banks or in grassy meadows, at low elevations; scattered along the coastline.

NOTES: Thrift is not particularly common in our region, but it occurs around the globe on Arctic coasts and in Europe. • A 'pink' was an ornamental opening made in muslin to show the colour in Elizabethan dresses, which these flowers supposedly resembled. Alternatively, 'pink' may have derived from the Low German *pingsten* or Dutch *pinkster* for 'Whitsuntide' (the first 3 days of the week beginning with Pentecost Sunday) as pinks were also once called 'Whitsuntide gilliflowers' since they bloomed at that time of the year. 'Thrift' appears to be the passive participle of *threave* or *thrive* meaning 'to press close together,' because the plants grow in dense tufts. However, others claim that it is so called because it survives, or thrives, in poor, shallow soils. • *Armeria* is Latin for a species of carnation.

SEA PLANTAIN • *Plantago maritima* ssp. *juncoides*
SEASIDE PLANTAIN, GOOSE-TONGUE

GENERAL: Taprooted perennial, often slightly **woolly** at the short-branched crown; flowering stems 1 to several, sparsely hairy, 5–25 cm tall, usually slightly longer than the leaves.

LEAVES: All basal, **fleshy,** long (to 20 cm), **linear,** strongly ascending, mostly hairless.

FLOWERS: Greenish or membranous, very small, inconspicuous; 4 sepals; petals 4, fused below in a **hairy** tube spreading into lobes 1–1.5 mm long; numerous in **dense spikes** 2–10 cm long.

FRUITS: Capsules, egg-shaped to conic, **opening along an 'equator,' the top coming off like a lid;** seeds 2–4, brown or black.

ECOLOGY: Moist beaches (often in the crevices of large rocks), sandy or gravelly seashores, salt marshes; common the length of our coast.

NOTES: The leaves of seaside and Alaska plantains were eaten by the Dena'ina and other groups of Alaska. The succulent, salty-flavoured leaves were mixed with fish or marine mammal grease. Today they are jarred for winter use. Some say their use was learned from Russian traders and early European residents of our region. • Our sea plantain in the Americas belongs to ssp. *juncoides;* the species also occurs in Eurasia as ssp. *maritima.* • 'Plantain' is from the Latin *plantago* meaning 'foot-sole,' from the way some of the leaves lie flat on the ground.

ALASKA PLANTAIN • *Plantago macrocarpa*

GENERAL: Stout, mostly hairless perennial from a thick, heavy taproot; crown **not woolly**; flowering stems 1 to several, hollow, sometimes hairy in the upper part at least when young, 10–60 cm tall, usually longer than leaves.

LEAVES: All basal, **not fleshy**, several-veined, **lance-shaped**, long (7–45 cm), ascending, hairless, **narrowed at base to distinct stalks.**

FLOWERS: Greenish to brownish, very small, inconspicuous; 4 sepals; petals 4, fused below in a **hairless** tube spreading into lobes 1.5–2 mm long; numerous in spikes short and dense at flowering but elongating (to 3–10 cm in fruit) and looser at maturity.

FRUITS: Capsules, **large (5–7 mm long), conehead-shaped, falling without opening**; seeds usually 2, black, roughened.

ECOLOGY: Moist beaches and meadows, upper tidal marshes, bogs, shorelines, at low elevations; common along and near the coastline in the northern 2/3 of our region; south rarely to Washington and Oregon.

NOTES: Alaska plantain, with its large, unopening capsules, is distinct from other *Plantago* species at maturity, but it can be confused when young with sea plantain. However, **sea plantain has linear leaves without well-differentiated stalks**. • The species name *macrocarpa* means 'large-fruited.'

RIBWORT • *Plantago lanceolata*
ENGLISH PLANTAIN, BUCKHORN

GENERAL: Perennial from fibrous roots, hairless or tan-woolly at the base; flowering stems several, **groove-angled**, 15–60 cm tall, straggly-hairy, considerably longer than leaves.

LEAVES: All basal, strongly veined or ribbed lengthwise, **lance-shaped to narrowly elliptic or oblong**, 5–40 cm long, narrowed at base to stalk, hairless to hairy.

FLOWERS: Greenish, small; sepals 4, often long-hairy on midvein; petals 4, fused below in a short tube spreading into lobes 2–2.5 mm long; spikes dense, with numerous flowers, egg-shaped at first, becoming cylindric at maturity, 2–8 cm long, 1 cm thick, conspicuous by virtue of numerous long, yellow stamens that **stick well out**.

FRUITS: Capsules, oblong-egg-shaped, **splitting all the way around below the middle**; seeds 1–2, shining black.

ECOLOGY: Roadsides, fields, pastures, lawns, at low elevations; common weed from southwestern B.C. south, infrequent northwards.

NOTES: Ribwort is a Eurasian weed now widely established in much of temperate North America. • **Common plantain** (*P. major*) is another introduced weed that is even more widespread than ribwort. Common plantain is common throughout our region in disturbed areas. It has large, **broadly elliptic to egg-shaped** leaves with **strong parallel veins**. It is uncertain whether common plantain is a native or introduced species in North America. Eastern North American native people reportedly named it 'white man's foot' because they were not familiar with the plant prior to contact with white Europeans. • The lance-shaped leaves of *P. lanceolata* have several **prominent ribs**, giving rise to the name 'ribwort'. It was a highly prized herb in olden times, and the Saxons reputedly bound it to their heads with red wool to cure headaches. Old names like 'kemps' and 'cocks' derive from the Anglo-Saxon *cempa* or Danish *kaempe* for 'warrior,' because children used the plants to mock-fight with. (They twisted the flower stalk around itself and pushed it up tight against the inflorescence until the flowers shot off.)

CLEAVERS • *Galium aparine*

GENERAL: Weak, **taprooted annual**; stems **sprawling**, leafy, square with hooked bristles on the angles, 20–100 cm long or tall, tending to scramble over other vegetation.

LEAVES: Whorls of 6–8, linear to oblong, 1-veined, bristly along the margin (bristles pointed **backward**), round-tipped but with a sharp point, 1–7 cm long.

FLOWERS: Whitish or greenish, small (1–2 mm wide); petals fused at base into a very short tube that spreads into 4 lobes; **3–5 in small, stalked clusters** from the axils of leaf whorls.

FRUITS: Dry, 2-lobed little burs covered with hooked bristles.

ECOLOGY: Beaches, moist fields, clearings, ditches, open seashores; more widespread southwards; common at low to middle elevations, along seashores; more widespread southwards; common at low to middle elevations.

NOTES: Cleavers is a weedy but apparently native species. • **Field madder** (*Sherardia arvensis*) is a weedy, annual, Mediterranean introduction that is scattered but locally frequent in fields and waste places at low elevations from Vancouver Island and the adjacent mainland south, and rare on the Queen Charlotte Islands. It has **lance-shaped** leaves in **whorls of usually 6,** and **pink to lilac** flowers in small **heads within leaf-like bracts.** • The Cowichan rubbed cleavers on their hands to remove pitch. They also used the dried plants for starting fires. • The very young greens are eaten in some places as a potherb, and the fruits were formerly used by Belgian lace-makers as heads for their pins. In Scandinavia, masses of the stems and leaves were used as filters for milk. • Cleavers (or 'clivers') derives from the Anglo-Saxon *clife* and Dutch *kleefkruid* meaning 'cleaving (clinging) to clothes,' and from the Old English *clivers* meaning 'claws.' *Galium* is from *gala*, Greek for 'milk,' because the juice of Our Lady's bedstraw (*G.verum*) was used to curdle milk.

SWEET-SCENTED BEDSTRAW • *Galium triflorum*

GENERAL: Rhizomatous perennial; stems **sprawling,** leafy, square in cross-section and usually hooked-bristly on the angles, 20–100 cm long, sometimes ascending but usually scrambling over other vegetation.

LEAVES: In whorls of 5–6 (sometimes 4 on branchlets), **elliptic-lance-shaped, 1-veined,** bristly on the margins (bristles pointing **forward**) and hooked-bristly on underside of midrib, rounded but sharp-pointed at tip, 1–5 cm long, **vanilla-scented.**

FLOWERS: Greenish-white, small (2–3 mm wide); **usually 3 flowers per stalk** in loose, open clusters from axils of leaf whorls along the stem.

FRUITS: Dry, 2-lobed little burs covered with hooked bristles.

ECOLOGY: Moist forest, thickets, clearings, streambanks, usually in partial shade; common at low to middle elevations.

NOTES: Northern bedstraw (*G. boreale*) is an **upright** perennial with narrowly lance-shaped, pointed but blunt-tipped, **3-veined leaves in whorls of 4** and numerous **creamy-white** flowers in **showy terminal clusters.** It grows in moist to dry meadows, grassy openings, rocky slopes and forest edges and glades from low to high elevations, scattered the length of our region, but more common from Vancouver Island south and absent from much of the outer north coast. • A less robust species than cleavers, this native plant releases sweet-smelling coumarins when it is bruised or as it dries. It was used by some Ditidaht people to make a hair rinse, which was said to make the hair thick and lustrous. The dried flowers were used as a perfume.

NORTHERN WILD-LICORICE • *Galium kamtschaticum*

GENERAL: Rhizomatous perennial; stems single, **upright**, leafy, hairless or sparsely hairy, square in cross-section, 10–30 cm tall.

LEAVES: In **whorls of 4** (lower whorls smaller than upper), **oval to broadly egg-shaped or elliptic, 3-veined** (marginal hairs pointing **forward**), round-tipped but with a sharp point, 1–3 cm long.

FLOWERS: **Whitish to greenish**, small (about 3 mm wide); **1–3 (rarely to 6)** in small, open, **stalked clusters from the centre** of the uppermost leaf whorl.

FRUITS: Dry, 2-lobed little burs covered with **hooked bristles**.

ECOLOGY: Moist coniferous (especially alluvial) forest, thickets, stream-banks, grassy or mossy talus slopes; low to middle elevations; scattered from northern Washington north.

NOTES: Oregon bedstraw (*G. oreganum*, also known as *G. kamtschaticum* var. *oreganum*) is the **southern counterpart** of northern wild-licorice, occurring in moist forest and meadows from near sea level to subalpine elevations, common in Washington and Oregon. Oregon bedstraw has **more leaf whorls** than northern wild-licorice (**5–9** vs. 2–5) and **more flowers in a more-branched inflorescence**. • 'Bedstraw' derives from 'Our Lady's bedstraw,' the common name of *G. verum*. Legend has it that the Virgin lay on a bed that was a mixture of bracken and *G. verum*. The bracken did not acknowledge the child's birth and lost its flowers, but the bedstraw welcomed the child and blossomed.

SMALL BEDSTRAW • *Galium trifidum*

GENERAL: Perennial from slender rhizomes; stems numerous, sprawling, leafy, square in cross-section with bristles on the angles, 5–70 cm long or tall, often much branched, tending to scramble over other vegetation.

LEAVES: Whorls of 4 or 5–6, linear to narrowly elliptic, 1-veined, blunt-tipped, 0.5–2 cm long; margins with bristles pointing **backward**.

FLOWERS: Whitish, small (1–2 or 3 mm wide); in several to many **clusters of 1–3** on long, narrow stalks **from branch tips and axils of leaf whorls**.

FRUITS: Pairs of round, **smooth nutlets**.

ECOLOGY: Marshes, fens, bogs, swamps, banks of sluggish streams, muddy shores, sea beaches, wet ditches and clearings; common at low to fairly high elevations.

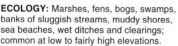

NOTES: *G. trifidum* includes *G. cymosum*, a plant of the south coast, with slightly longer leaves and larger flowers than typical *G. trifidum*. • Bedstraws are members of the coffee family, and they can be used to produce one of the most satisfying coffee substitutes to be found. The small, spherical burs should be collected when ripe but still greenish, spread out on a baking sheet and roasted in the oven until brown. They can then be ground and used in place of coffee.

COMMON HAREBELL • *Campanula rotundifolia*
BLUEBELLS-OF-SCOTLAND

GENERAL: Perennial from slender rhizomes or from a taproot and branched stem-base; stems 1 to several, leafy, ascending or erect, more or less hairless, 10–80 cm tall.

LEAVES: Basal leaves stalked, **oval to heart-shaped**, coarsely toothed, **usually withering** before flowers appear; stem leaves alternate, **linear to narrowly lance-shaped**, 1.5–8 cm long, the margins **smooth to indistinctly saw-toothed**.

FLOWERS: Purplish-blue, rarely white, large (1.5–3 cm long), bell-shaped, nodding; sepals hairy at fused base, the lobes awl-shaped; **single or 2–15** on thin wiry stalks in loose clusters atop stem.

FRUITS: Capsules, nodding, cylindrical to reverse-cone-shaped, opening by pores; seeds numerous, flattened.

ECOLOGY: Grassy slopes, gullies, canyons, rocky open ground and sites near waterfalls, from sea level to middle (sometimes subalpine) elevations; common.

NOTES: *C. rotundifolia* includes *C. latisepala*, which some taxonomists have recognized as a separate north-coast species distinguished by stalked, lance- to egg-shaped stem leaves, broadly triangular sepal lobes, and larger flowers that are usually produced 1 per stalk. • **Mountain harebell** (*C. lasiocarpa*) is a **dwarf alpine** species, usually less than 10 cm tall, with usually a **single** large, blue, bell-shaped flower per stalk; the sepal lobes are **toothed, hairy**, and very narrow. It is occasional in the mountains of the northernmost part of our region, from northern southeast Alaska to Prince William Sound, and rare on the Queen Charlotte Islands and in the northern Cascades. **Olympic harebell** (*C. piperi*) is also a **dwarf alpine** species, but it has **smaller (12–16 mm long)** flowers with **hairless** sepals, and it is restricted to rock crevices at high elevations in the **Olympic Mountains**. • Common harebell is known in Haida as 'blue rain flowers,' and children were warned not to pick them or it would rain.

SCOULER'S HAREBELL • *Campanula scouleri*

GENERAL: Perennial from slender rhizomes; stems leafy, lax, often curved at the base, hairless or short hairy, 10–40 cm tall.

LEAVES: Alternate, **sharply toothed**, the **lowermost egg-shaped**, stalked, 3–8 cm long, the others progressively narrower and less stalked upwards.

FLOWERS: **Pale-blue to whitish**, bell-shaped, 8–12 mm long, with 5 **recurved or spreading lobes** longer than the basal tube; style **sticks well out** from the flowers; usually several flowers on long slender stalks atop the stem.

FRUITS: Roundish capsules, opening by pores near the middle; seeds numerous, flattened.

ECOLOGY: Open or dense, relatively dry forest, thickets, open rocky slopes and outcrops, at low to middle elevations; common from southwestern B.C. south, rare northwards to southeast Alaska.

NOTES: Rough harebell (*Campanula scabrella*) grows in rocky areas at high elevations in the Cascades from central Washington through Oregon. It is a **taprooted**, spreading-hairy perennial with **smooth-margined, lance-shaped** leaves and **blue** flower bells 6–12 mm long. • Scouler's harebell is named for Dr. John Scouler, who accompanied David Douglas on his botanical explorations of the Pacific Northwest.

SEA BLUSH • *Plectritis congesta*

GENERAL: Annual; stem upright, leafy, **10–60 cm tall**.

LEAVES: Opposite, hairless, **oblong-elliptic**, stalkless; lowermost leaves spoon- or egg-shaped, short-stalked; margins **smooth or obscurely toothed**.

FLOWERS: Pinkish or whitish, small (2–8 mm long); petals 5, fused into **2 lips**, with a **thick spur**; several to many in **head-like or spike-like**, terminal clusters.

FRUITS: Dry, falling without opening, **sharply winged**, hairy or hairless, 1-seeded; convex side keeled, not grooved.

ECOLOGY: Vernally moist meadows, open rocky slopes and bluffs, at low elevations; common from the Strait of Georgia–Puget Sound area south to California, occasional on the Queen Charlotte Islands.

NOTES: Long-spurred plectritis (*Plectritis macrocera*) grows in similar habitats over a similar range (but not on the Queen Charlotte Islands), but it has mostly white to pinkish flowers about **equally 5-lobed,** and fruits with a **narrow groove** down the centre of the convex side. • 'Sea-blush' recognizes the colour of the flowers, which often grow in profusion on grassy bluffs near the ocean. *Plectritis* is from the Greek *plectros,* 'plaited', and *congesta* means 'congested' or 'crowded,' both referring to the inflorescence.

SITKA VALERIAN • *Valeriana sitchensis*

GENERAL: Fibrous-rooted **perennial** from a stout, branched rhizome or woody stem-base; stems leafy, square in cross-section, somewhat succulent, **30–120 cm tall**, smooth or sometimes short hairy.

LEAVES: Opposite, large (to 25 cm long), in 2–5 pairs on stem, stalked, **divided into 3–7 coarsely toothed leaflets**, the terminal leaflet largest and broadest.

FLOWERS: White to pale-pink, small (4–7 mm long), with a heavy, sweet scent; petals fused into 5-lobed, somewhat distended tube; **stamens protrude** giving head a fluffy appearance; numerous in **dense, terminal, hemispheric to flat-topped cluster.**

FRUITS: Numerous **ribbed** achenes, **oblong egg-shaped**, each topped by a **feathery plume** that aids in wind dispersal.

ECOLOGY: Moist meadows, thickets, stream-banks and open subalpine forest; widespread and often abundant at middle to (more commonly) high elevations.

NOTES: Scouler's valerian (*Valeriana scouleri*) is a **smaller (15–70 cm tall)**, less-leafy plant with **smooth-edged** leaflets and **lance-shaped** achenes. It grows at low to middle elevations in moist open forest, thickets and wet meadows, and on wet, rocky slopes and cliffs, from the Strait of Georgia–Puget Sound area south to California. • Sitka valerian is responsible for the strong sour odour detected in subalpine meadows after the first frost. The rhizomes also have a strong odour that some find unpleasant. • The Alaskan Tlingit name for this plant means 'medicine that stinks.' They applied crushed roots to a mother's nipples when weaning a child, rubbed them on sore muscles or blew them onto animal traps for luck. • Valerian was used in Europe as an aphrodisiac and love philtre. Cats and rats love it, and it has been suggested that the Pied Piper owed much of his success to valerian carried in his pockets. • One source says that the name 'valerian' is derived from Valeria, a part of Hungary where *V. officinalis* grew. Another proposes that the name comes from the Latin *valere* ('to be healthy'), and refers to its medicinal properties.

SKUNK CABBAGE • *Lysichiton americanum*
SWAMP LANTERN

GENERAL: Robust, hairless perennial 30–150 cm tall, from fleshy, upright underground stems; with a **skunky odour**, especially when flowering.

LEAVES: In **large basal rosette, lance-shaped to broadly elliptic, often huge** (to 1.5 m long by 0.5 m wide), thin, net-veined, tapering to short, stout, winged stalks.

FLOWERS: Greenish-yellow; numerous on a **spike on a thick, fleshy axis** which is **hooded by a bright-yellow, large bract**; appearing before or with the leaves in early spring, and later overtaken by their exuberant growth.

FRUITS: Berry-like and pulpy, green to reddish, **embedded** in the fleshy flower spike, 1- or 2-seeded.

ECOLOGY: Swamps, fens, muskeg, wet forest, mucky seepage areas, wet meadows; at low to middle elevations.

NOTES: 'In the ancient days, they say, there was no salmon. The Indians had nothing to eat save roots and leaves. Principal among these was the skunk-cabbage. Finally the spring salmon came for the first time. As they passed up the river, a person stood upon the shore and shouted: "Here come our relatives whose bodies are full of eggs! If it had not been for me all the people would have starved." "Who speaks to us?" asked the salmon. "Your uncle, Skunk Cabbage," was the reply. Then the salmon went ashore to see him, and as a reward for having fed the people he was given an elk-skin blanket and a war-club, and was set in the rich, soft soil near the river.' (Kathlamet story, related in Haskin 1934) • Wherever the leaves of this plant were available, they were used as 'Indian wax paper,' for lining berry baskets, berry-drying racks and steaming pits. Skunk cabbage was rarely used as food by the northwest coast peoples; it was mostly a famine food in early spring; and it was then eaten only after steaming or roasting.

SEA ARROW-GRASS • *Triglochin maritimum*

GENERAL: Hairless, **rather fleshy**, perennial from stout rhizome often covered with whitish fibrous remains of old leaf-bases, sometimes forming large clumps; flowering stems leafless, **20–120 cm tall.**

LEAVES: All basal, upright to spreading, **long and linear, half-round to somewhat flattened**, hairless, with sheathing bases.

FLOWERS: Small, **inconspicuous, greenish** but with feathery reddish stigmas, 6 flower scales, and 6 stamens; short-stalked and numerous in long, **narrow spike-like** clusters.

FRUITS: Dry, egg-shaped, splitting lengthwise into six 1-seeded segments that separate from the cylindrical flower axis.

ECOLOGY: Tidal marshes and mudflats, brackish meadows, sloughs; at low elevations, common the length of our region.

NOTES: Marsh arrow-grass (*T. palustre*) and slender arrow-grass (*T. concinnum*) are both uncommon inhabitants of saline or brackish marshes and meadows along our coast. Both are **usually smaller (less than 30 cm tall)** than sea arrow-grass and have narrower, more-rounded leaves; **slender arrow-grass** has **fruits similar** to those of sea arrow-grass, but **marsh arrow-grass** has **club-shaped** fruits that split into only **3 segments**. • The fleshy, succulent, whitish inner leaf-bases of sea arrow-grass were relished as a springtime vegetable by peoples of several coastal groups, including the Comox, Sechelt, Squamish and Straits Salish, as well as by the Kaigani Haida and Tlingit. The vegetative plants were preferred to the reproductive plants, which were believed to cause headaches. The leaf-bases were usually eaten raw, and at the right stage they have a mild, sweet, cucumber-like taste. The Kaigani Haida boiled them, usually in 3 changes of water. • **WARNING:** Arrow-grass contains cyanide-producing glycosides, and it is known to be poisonous, sometimes fatally, to livestock.

Aquatics

Vascular plants long ago conquered the land. They escaped from ancestral aquatic environments and no longer need the support and protection of water; the majority no longer need water as a medium for sex (fertilization). Some ferns and allies and flowering plants (most of them herbs), however, have ventured back into fresh water and, even further, into ocean shallows.

The plants covered in this section belong to a variety of flowering plant families, and they all grow in habitats that are submerged for at least part of the year. They are divided here into those that grow entirely underwater ('submerged' or 'floating') and those with feet in the water and heads in the air ('emergent'). As in the rest of this book, we are ignoring the algae, though they are often abundant in aquatic habitats. Good references to algae are Prescott (1964) for freshwater algae and Scagel (1972) for marine algae ('seaweeds'). Several of the mosses in the 'Bryophytes' section (e.g., *Fontinalis*, p. 463) can be considered aquatic as well.

Despite the fact that they are often not related to each other, aquatic plants share several features reflecting their common adaptations to life in an aquatic environment. Water supports them, so aquatic plants don't need to develop the strong, thickened stems seen in other plants; our aquatics are all herbs, and most of the submerged and floating species collapse when removed from their watery home. While rigid strength is not very important, flexibility is, because aquatic plants must be able to move with currents or waves. Leaves are often long and narrow, with a central cluster of non-thickened conducting tubes. These plants sometimes find oxygen hard to come by and carbon dioxide hard to get rid of, especially those with roots submerged in muddy bottoms. To address this problem, many aquatic plants have lots of spongy stem tissue through which gases can diffuse, and other processes by which they can actively 'pump' oxygen to their roots. Pollination and seed dispersal in land plants usually involve insects or wind, and most aquatic species still strive to raise their flowers above the surface of the water for pollination and eventual seed dispersal. In a few highly specialized aquatic plants, however, pollination and seed dispersal are effected in ways considerably different from—and often considerably more elaborate than—those common in the open air. Because of the uncertainty associated with sexual reproduction, asexual reproduction is very important for aquatic plants, and the result is often extensive 'clones' of genetically identical plants.

Most of our aquatic plants grow in fresh to brackish waters. Only 2 genera (*Phyllospadix* and *Zostera*) in our region are found in the ocean.

Aquatic plants are the food upon which all other aquatic organisms feed, directly or indirectly. Besides forming the anchor of the watery food chain, aquatic plants also provide habitat for a wide variety of organisms living in, or near, streams, lakes, ponds and ditches. Humans are one of the animal species that uses aquatic plants extensively; these plants provide materials for food and other uses (including clothes, mats and baskets).

Useful references to aquatic vascular plants in our region are Brayshaw (1985, 1989), Hotchkiss (1972) and Sculthorpe (1967).

Key to the Aquatics

1a. At least some part of the plants extending out of the water 2
  2a. Leaves grass-like; individual flowers inconspicuous 3
    3a. To 3 m tall; leaves basal; hundreds of brownish flowers clustered in dense terminal, cylindrical spikes; in marshes, ponds, lakeshores and wet ditches .... *Typha latifolia*
    3b. To 40 cm tall; leaves basal and on the stem; 3–12 greenish-white flowers in terminal clusters; in bogs and lake margins .... *Scheuchzeria palustris*
  2b. Leaves various but not grass-like; individual flowers conspicuous 4
    4a. Leaves alternate, compound (divided into leaflets) 5
      5a. Plants creeping to ascending, to 1 m long or tall; leaves pinnately divided into 5–7 leaflets; flowers reddish-purple, bowl-shaped .... *Potentilla palustris*
      5b. Plants upright, to 30 cm tall; leaves divided into 3 leaflets; flowers white, funnel-shaped .... *Menyanthes trifoliata*
    4b. Leaves all basal, not divided into leaflets 6
      6a. Blades of above-water leaves arrowhead-shaped, blades of submerged leaves lance-shaped or lacking; rhizomes with tubers .... *Sagittaria latifolia*
      6b. All leaf blades egg-shaped to lance-oblong; plants from fleshy corms .... *Alisma plantago-aquatica*

(1b continued on p. 340)

Alisma plantago-aquatica

Sagittaria latifolia

Scheuchzeria palustris

Typha latifolia

Potentilla palustris

Menyanthes trifoliata

WATER-PLANTAIN • *Alisma plantago-aquatica*

GENERAL: Marsh or semiaquatic perennial from a **fleshy, bulb-like** stem; flowering stem leafless, 80–120 cm tall.

LEAVES: All basal, long-stalked, sheathing at the base; blades **egg-shaped to lance-oblong,** pointy-tipped, rounded at the base, 10–30 cm long.

FLOWERS: White (occasionally light to deep-pink), **about 5 mm long**; sepals 3, greenish; petals 3, falling off early; ovaries 10–20, single-chambered; numerous in an open, branched, terminal cluster that sticks up well beyond the leaves.

FRUITS: Whorl of flattened, oblong-egg-shaped, **grooved** achenes.

ECOLOGY: Marshes, shorelines, wet ditches; usually emergent, sometimes largely submerged; low elevations.

NOTES: This species of water-plantain is distributed nearly worldwide. • Both the Latin name and the common name mean a plant with leaves like a plantain. *Alisma* is reputedly derived from the Celtic word *altis* meaning 'water.' The word 'plantain' is from the latin *planta* ('sole of the foot') and *ago*, (the general name in Chaucer's English for a cultivated plant), suggesting that a plantain has leaves resembling a footprint.

WAPATO • *Sagittaria latifolia*
ARROWHEAD

GENERAL: Marsh or semiaquatic perennial from **tuber-producing rhizomes**; flowering stem leafless, 20–90 cm tall.

LEAVES: All basal; stalks long, angled in cross-section, sheathing at the base; blades of above-water leaves **arrowhead-shaped,** to 25 cm long; submerged leaves lance-shaped or even bladeless and linear.

FLOWERS: White, 1–2 cm across; sexes often on separate flowers; sepals 3, greenish; petals 3, falling off early; ovaries and stamens numerous; in several whorls of 3 in a fairly long, narrow terminal cluster.

FRUITS: Sharp-beaked, flattened, **winged** achenes; numerous in a globular cluster.

ECOLOGY: Marshes, ponds, lakes, wet ditches; usually emergent but often partly submerged; low elevations.

NOTES: The thick, overwintering rhizomes and starchy tubers are eaten by ducks, muskrats and people. • The tubers of wapato were very important to the Chinook of the lower Columbia. Tubers were baked and provided an excellent source of starch. They were collected by canoe or by wading and dislodging the tubers, allowing them to float to the surface. The journals of Lewis and Clark relate that their diet while travelling in Oregon was elk meat and wapato bulbs purchased from the Indians. A Chinook myth describes wapato as the food 'before the salmon came to the Columbia.' • The common name 'wapato' or 'wapatoo' is the Chinook for 'tuberous plant.' The scientific name literally means 'broad-leaved arrowhead.'

SCHEUCHZERIA • *Scheuchzeria palustris*

GENERAL: Yellowish-green, **rush-like** perennial from yellowish-grey rhizomes; **stems leafy**, 10–40 cm tall, clothed at the base with dead leaves.

LEAVES: Linear, rounded, with pores at the tip, broadly sheathing at the base and with a prominent ligule where the leaf sheath joins the blade; basal leaves 5–25 cm or more long, erect; stem leaves reduced in size upwards, the blades somewhat channeled.

FLOWERS: Greenish-white, small, of 6 oblong segments about 3 mm long; 6 stamens; ovaries usually 3, distinct; on stalks in **cluster of 3–12 flowers** atop the stem.

FRUITS: Spreading follicles, greenish-brown, with 1 or 2 dark brown, fairly large (4–5 mm long) seeds.

ECOLOGY: Sphagnum bogs (creeping in the peat moss), lake margins; low to middle elevations.

NOTES: Scheuchzeria appears to be closely related to sea arrow-grass (*Triglochin maritimum*, p. 334), but they usually occupy different habitats: sea arrow-grass in tidal marshes, mudflats and other brackish to saline places, scheuchzeria in bogs and freshwater habitats. • The genus is named for Swiss botanist John Jakob Scheuchzer (1672–1733).

CATTAIL • *Typha latifolia*
REEDMACE

GENERAL: Marsh or semiaquatic perennial from coarse rhizomes; stems **pithy**, unbranched, cylindrical, 1–3 m tall.

LEAVES: Alternate, flat, long and narrow (somewhat grass-like), sheathing at the base, somewhat spongy, greyish-green, **1–2 cm wide**.

FLOWERS: Tiny; numerous, in a terminal **cylindrical spike**; lower portion of spike with female flowers, 15–20 cm long, 1–3 cm thick, dark brown; upper portion with male flowers, cone-shaped, disintegrating and leaving stem tip bare above the **persistent club-shaped female spike**.

FRUITS: Tiny ellipsoidal **nutlets**, about 1 mm long, designed to float in wind or water, with numerous **long, slender hairs** at the base.

ECOLOGY: Marshes, ponds, lakeshores, and wet ditches, in slow-flowing or quiet water; low to middle elevations.

NOTES: The **big bulrushes or tules** (*Scirpus* spp.) grow in similar habitats and often form large, almost exclusive colonies the way cattail does, but they have **few, very short basal leaves and open flower clusters**. • A number of coastal aboriginal peoples wove leaves of cattails and bulrushes into mats for bedding, sitting or kneeling on in canoes, as insulation for winter homes, or for capes, hats, blankets, or bags. Cattail seed fluff was used as stuffing for pillows and mattresses, as a wound dressing and for diapers. • Cattail provides important habitat and food for many marsh animals, including wrens, blackbirds, waterfowl and muskrats.

MARSH CINQUEFOIL • *Potentilla palustris*

GENERAL: Perennial from long, creeping, often floating, somewhat woody rhizomes; **stems prostrate to ascending**, frequently reddish below, to 1 m long.

LEAVES: Alternate, mainly on flowering stems; lower leaves **pinnately divided into 5–7 leaflets** that are **oblong, coarsely toothed**, pale-green above, glaucous to finely hairy below; upper leaves smaller.

FLOWERS: Strikingly **reddish-purple, bowl-shaped**, about 2 cm across; sepals and petals 5; stamens and ovaries numerous; few to several in loose terminal clusters.

FRUITS: Numerous **achenes**, plump, egg-shaped, brownish-purple, buoyant.

ECOLOGY: Marshes, fens, bogs, wet meadows, stream-banks, lake-shores, from low to middle (sometimes subalpine) elevations; usually partly submerged but with emergent flowering stems.

NOTES: Marsh cinquefoil is our **only aquatic cinquefoil** and the only one with **reddish**, not yellow, flowers. The flowers emit a fetid odour and also secrete nectar, thus attracting carrion flies as well as other kinds of flies and bees. • The similarity of marsh cinquefoil to strawberry was recognized by some aboriginal peoples. • The Haida used the stem in a medicinal preparation for tuberculosis. • The name 'cinque-foil' literally means '5 leaves,' and it refers to the fact that many species of *Potentilla* have leaves divided into 5 leaflets.

BUCKBEAN • *Menyanthes trifoliata*
BOGBEAN

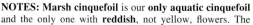

GENERAL: Aquatic to semiaquatic, hairless perennial from thick, submerged rhizomes covered with old leaf-bases; flowering stems ascending to erect, leafless, to 30 cm tall.

LEAVES: Alternate, crowded near base of flowering stem, on long (10–30 cm) stalks, each **divided into 3 elliptic, short-stalked leaflets**.

FLOWERS: White, usually tinged with purplish-pink, **funnel-shaped** with 5 petal lobes; inner surface of petals **frilly with long, white hairs**; few to several in fairly tight clusters atop stout leafless stems.

FRUITS: Oval, tardily splitting **capsules**; seeds several to many, smooth, shining, buoyant.

ECOLOGY: Bogs, fens, marshes, ponds, lake-shores; low to middle elevations.

NOTES: The showy flowers have a **very rank smell**. They are attractive to various flies and beetles as well as nectar- and pollen-feeding bees. • The Kwakwaka'wakw drank an extract made by boiling buckbean to treat stomach ailments. It was thought this medicine made a person gain weight. The stem and roots were ground, boiled and taken 3 times a day for spitting of blood. The rhizomes were used by some Alaskan tribes as emergency food. Rhizomes were dried, ground and washed in several changes of water to remove the bitterness, and then dried again. • The leaves have been used to make a bitter tonic that, taken in large doses, has a cathartic and emetic effect. Buckbean tea was also used to relieve fever and migraine headaches, for indigestion, to promote appetite and to eliminate intestinal worms. It was used externally to promote the healing of ulcerous wounds. • The original common name may have been 'goat's bean,' from the French *bouc* ('goat'). It was used to treat scurvy, and the common name may also have been derived from the German word for scurvy, *sharbock*.

Key to the Aquatics *(continued from p. 335)*

1b. Plants growing submerged or floating 7
7a. Plants growing in the ocean, intertidal or subtidal 8
   8a. Stems unbranched, to 50 cm long; rhizomes short, thick,
   irregularly knotted; leaves 2–4 mm wide, thick and opaque;
   intertidal or subtidal, usually where there is strong wave action .... *Phyllospadix scouleri*
   8b. Stems often branched, to 250 cm long; rhizomes long, uniformly slender;
   leaves 2–12 mm wide, thin and translucent; lowest intertidal or (usually) subtidal,
   usually on more sheltered shores where wave action is weak .... *Zostera marina*
7b. Plants growing in freshwater (or, for *Ruppia*, in brackish or
saline water in ponds, ditches, sloughs and tideflats) 9
   9a. Leaves whorled 10
      10a. Stems lax, to 1 m long; leaves 3–4 per whorl,
      finely divided, feather-like .... *Myriophyllum spicatum*
      10b. Stems upright, to 40 cm tall; leaves 6–12 per whorl, not divided .... *Hippuris vulgaris*
   9b. Leaves alternate or opposite 11
      11a. Leaves opposite; submerged leaves linear,
      floating and emergent leaves egg-shaped .... *Callitriche heterophylla*
      11b. Leaves alternate 12
         12a. Leaves bearing small (1–3 mm wide) bladders that trap tiny animals;
         flowers deep yellow, 1–2 cm long, like snapdragon flowers .... *Utricularia vulgaris*
         12b. Leaves without bladders 13
            13a. Leaves both submerged and floating, the two leaf types distinctly different 14
               14a. Submerged leaves finely divided; floating leaves
               palmately 3–5 lobed; flowers white, 1–2 cm wide .... *Ranunculus aquatilis*
               14b. Submerged leaves grass-like, not divided; floating leaves elliptic
               to oblong, not lobed; flowers inconspicuous, in stalked spikes 15
                  15a. Stems freely branched; submerged
                  leaves 3–10 mm wide; floating leaves
                  shiny green, 2–7 cm long, 13–19 veined .... *Potamogeton gramineus*
                  15b. Stems mostly unbranched; submerged
                  leaves 10–20 mm wide; floating leaves lustrous
                  coppery-green, 3–10 cm long, 20–30 veined .... *Potamogeton natans*
            13b. Leaves either submerged or floating, but not both 16
               16a. Leaves submerged, occasionally emergent, but not floating 17
                 17a. Leaves somewhat grass-like, hollow in cross-section,
                 in a basal rosette; stems leafless or essentially so 18
                   18a. Annual to 10 cm tall, emergent or
                   submerged; flowers white, to 1 mm long ....*Subularia aquatica*
                   18b. Perennial to 100 cm tall, submerged;
                   flowers pale blue or white, 1–2 cm long .... *Lobelia dortmanna*
               17b. Leaves not grass-like; stems leafy 19
                 19a. Leaves lance-egg-shaped,
                 4–10 cm long; in freshwater .... *Potamogeton richardsonii*
                 19b. Leaves thread-like, to 20 cm long;
                 usually in brackish or saline water .... *Ruppia maritima*
               16b. Leaves all floating 20
               20a. Leaves grass-like; flowers tiny, greenish;
               fruits like burs .... *Sparganium angustifolium*
               20b. Leaves not grass-like; flowers yellow, pink or purplish 21
                 21a. Leaves egg- or heart-shaped, large (10–45 cm long),
                 from massive rhizomes and thick, fleshy flowering stems;
                 flowers yellow, large (to 10 cm across) .... *Nuphar polysepalum*
               21b. Leaves elliptic to lance-shaped, to 15 cm long, from
                 slender rhizomes; flowers pink or purplish, to 3 cm across 22
                   22a. Plant covered with a gelatinous sheath;
                   flowers single, purplish, 2–3 cm across .... *Brasenia schreberi*
                 22b. Plant not covered with a gelatinous sheath;
                   flowers bright pink, 4–5 mm long,
                 numerous in a thumb-like spike .... *Polygonum amphibium*

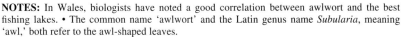

AWLWORT • *Subularia aquatica*

GENERAL: Hairless, aquatic annual with white, fibrous roots; flowering stem leafless or with a few leaves, erect, 2–10 cm tall, emergent or submerged.

LEAVES: Mostly basal, **awl-shaped**, somewhat grass-like, **rounded** in cross-section, 1–5 cm long.

FLOWERS: White, very small (to 1 mm long); sepals and petals 4; 6 stamens; submerged flowers do not open but do self-pollinate and set fruit; 2–8 on short ascending stalks in loose terminal clusters.

FRUITS: Slightly flattened, **ellipsoidal pod** (a silicle); seeds several, mucilaginous when wet.

ECOLOGY: Streams, shorelines, shallow ponds, seems to prefer fine gravelly substrates; usually submerged; scattered at low to middle elevations.

NOTES: In Wales, biologists have noted a good correlation between awlwort and the best fishing lakes. • The common name 'awlwort' and the Latin genus name *Subularia*, meaning 'awl,' both refer to the awl-shaped leaves.

WATER LOBELIA • *Lobelia dortmanna*

GENERAL: Hairless, fibrous-rooted, aquatic perennial; stems erect, hollow, unbranched, 20–100 cm tall.

LEAVES: Mostly in a submerged basal rosette, **linear, somewhat fleshy, hollow, curved**, 2–8 cm long; stem leaves few, alternate, bract-like.

FLOWERS: Pale-blue or white, 1–2 cm long; 5 sepals; petals 5, fused into a tube that is slit to below the middle on the upper side, 2-lipped, the lower lip larger and 3-lobed; 5 stamens; ovary 1, inferior; stalked, few, well spaced atop the stem and above the water.

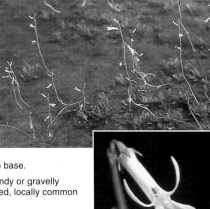

FRUITS: Capsules, 2 chambered; seeds roughened, squared off at the base.

ECOLOGY: Shallow water along sandy or gravelly margins of lakes and ponds; scattered, locally common at low elevations.

NOTES: Although it grows usually in shallow water, water lobelia has been observed producing flowers above the surface from a depth of about 2 meters. • *Lobelia* is the Latinized version of the name of Belgian botanist Matthias de L'Obel (1538–1616). This species is also known as 'water gladiole': the Latin *gladiolus* means 'a small sword,' in reference to the leaf shape.

WATER SMARTWEED • *Polygonum amphibium*

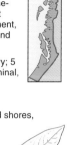

GENERAL: Aquatic to amphibious perennial with rhizomes or stolons; stems leafy, **prostrate or ascending, floating when aquatic,** with erect tips, 50–100 cm long.

LEAVES: Alternate, numerous, usually floating, **narrowly elliptic to oblong-lance-shaped,** stalked, to 15 cm long, margins smooth,somewhat pointed at the tip, pointed to somewhat heart-shaped at the base; stalks with prominent, cylindric, **sheathing stipules** 1–2 cm long and hairless to strongly hairy.

FLOWERS: Bright-pink, small (4–5 mm long) but showy; 5 petal-like segments; 8 stamens; numerous in 1 or 2 terminal, upright, **oblong or egg-shaped spikes** 1–3 cm long.

FRUITS: Achenes, lens-shaped, dark brown, smooth.

ECOLOGY: Ponds, sluggish streams, muddy banks and shores, in shallow water or on wet soil; common at low to middle elevations.

NOTES: Water smartweed is a cosmopolitan species that occurs on all continents, except perhaps Australia. • The explanation of 'smartweed' (from 'arsmart') was given under willow weed (*P. lapathifolium*, p. 127). It is not clear why species in this genus were used medicinally on the human hindquarters, but they were, for everything from poultices for external bleeding to treating piles and itchy skin diseases.

FLOATING-LEAVED PONDWEED • *Potamogeton natans*

GENERAL: Aquatic perennial from extensive, slender rhizomes that often produce overwintering tubers; stems submerged, leafy, rounded, greenish, mostly unbranched, to 2 mm thick and 1.5 m long.

LEAVES: Alternate, **of 2 types; submerged leaves linear** (1–2 mm wide), rounded, leathery, 5–20 cm long; floating leaves long-stalked, leathery, lustrous, coppery-green, **egg-shaped to narrowly elliptic,** rounded to somewhat heart-shaped at the base, 3–10 cm long, with 20–30 veins; stipules free of the rest of the leaf, long (to 10 cm), stiff, ultimately shredding into fibres.

FLOWERS: Tiny, inconspicuous; 4 flower segments; 4 ovaries; 4 stamens; stalkless and **whorled in 2–5 cm long, stalked spikes** that stick up out of the water.

FRUITS: Achenes, semi-fleshy at first then drying and hardening, green, shiny and wrinkled, short beaked, 1 seeded.

ECOLOGY: Lakes, ponds, sloughs; in shallow to moderately deep (1–3 m), usually standing water, fresh or brackish; common throughout our region at low to middle elevations.

NOTES: Floating-leaved pondweed is a cosmopolitan species and it is one of our most common aquatic flowering plants. It is distinguished from other pondweeds with broad floating leaves by its **long (usually over 10 cm), narrow (less than 2 mm wide)**, submerged leaves. If not in flower or fruit, it could be confused with **water smartweed,** which has **sheathing stipules without long, free tips, lacks submerged leaves**, and has darker-green leaves. • The Latin *Potamogeton* is from the Greek *potamos* ('a river') and *geiton* ('a neighbour'), alluding to the plant's habitat; *natans* means 'floating.' • Floating-leaved pondweed is sometimes called 'tench-weed,' possibly because it is found where tench (a European carp) swim, or because tench eat the slimy stems and leaves.

CLASPING-LEAVED PONDWEED • *Potamogeton richardsonii*
RICHARDSON'S PONDWEED

GENERAL: Aquatic perennial from slender rhizomes; stems submerged, leafy, round, green to brownish, sparingly branched, 1–2 mm thick and 30–100 cm long.

LEAVES: Alternate, **all submerged**, numerous and fairly close together, **lance-egg-shaped**, dark-green, stalkless, heart-shaped-clasping at the base, 4–10 cm long, 13–25 veined; **margins wavy**; stipules free of the rest of the leaf, soon **disintegrating into tufts of white threads**.

FLOWERS: Tiny, inconspicuous; 4 flower segments; 4 ovaries; 4 stamens; stalkless and whorled in stalked spikes that are 2–4 cm long, to 1 cm thick, and have 4–12 closely crowded whorls of flowers.

FRUITS: Achenes, semi-fleshy at first then drying and hardening, short beaked, 1 seeded.

ECOLOGY: Quiet lakes and sluggish streams, in shallow to fairly deep (0.5–3.5 m), clear water; common at low to middle elevations.

NOTES: Richardson's pondweed is also known as *Potamogeton perfoliatus* var. *richardsonii*. • Pondweeds overwinter by roots, rhizomes and tubers, as well as by seeds and special detachable winter buds. Seeds sprout only after being in cold water for several months; they do not survive drying.

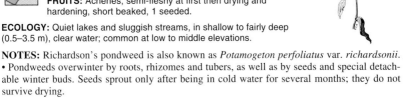

GRASS-LEAVED PONDWEED • *Potamogeton gramineus*

GENERAL: Aquatic perennial from slender rhizomes that produce elongated tubers in autumn; stems submerged, leafy, rounded, greenish, freely branched, 30–100 cm long.

LEAVES: Alternate, **of 2 types; submerged leaves** numerous, **linear to lance-shaped**, stalkless, 3–10 cm long, 3–10 mm wide; **floating leaves usually present**, stalked, **elliptic to oblong**, shiny, 2–7 cm long, 13–19 veined; stipules brownish, free of the rest of the leaf, to 3 cm long.

FLOWERS: Tiny, inconspicuous; flower parts in 4s; stalkless and whorled in stalked spikes that are 1–3.5 cm long and have 5–10 crowded whorls of flowers.

FRUITS: Achenes, semi-fleshy at first then drying and hardening, keeled, with very short beaks, 1 seeded.

ECOLOGY: Ponds, lakes, ditches, slowly flowing streams; common from low to subalpine elevations.

NOTES: Grass-leaved pondweed is widely distributed in the northern hemisphere. It is highly adaptable to local conditions, and is consequently an extremely variable species. It can grow in water to 2 m deep, or merely a few centimetres deep, and it can even be found stranded on muddy shores by receding water. The floating leaves are rounded at both ends, whereas the submerged leaves are pointed at both ends. • The species name *gramineus* means 'grass-like,' in reference to the leaves.

NARROW-LEAVED BUR-REED
• *Sparganium angustifolium*

GENERAL: Aquatic perennial from rhizomes; stems usually submerged or floating, 20–100 cm long.

LEAVES: Alternate, **floating, long and narrow** (2–8 mm wide); lower leaves sometimes as long as the stem; upper leaves usually with dilated sheathing bases.

FLOWERS: Tiny, greenish, numerous in **globular heads**; sepals/petals reduced to 3–6 linear scales; sexes separate on the same plant; **male heads 2–5**, stalkless, borne atop stem and above the 2–4 female heads, the lower 1 or 2 of which are stalked and **1–2 cm wide at maturity**.

FRUITS: Hardened, nutlet-like achenes, spindle-shaped, abruptly narrowed to 2 mm long beak; 1–2 seeds.

ECOLOGY: Ponds, lake-shores, sluggish streams; usually submerged or floating in shallow to fairly deep water, but sometimes partly emergent; low to middle elevations, extending sometimes to subalpine ponds.

NOTES: Narrow-leaved bur-reed is a widespread, highly variable complex that includes *S. emersum*, *S. multipedunculatum* and *S. simplex*, taxa that some treatments have recognized as separate species. • **Small bur-reed** (*S. minimum*) and **northern bur-reed** (*S. hyperboreum*) both have a **solitary male head**. **Small bur-reed** has **dark-green** leaves and **achene beaks about 1 mm long**; **northern bur-reed** has **yellow-green** leaves and **beakless achenes**. Small bur-reed is common in the southern half of our region, sporadic northwards; northern bur-reed is common from the Queen Charlotte Islands north. Where the ranges of the 2 species overlap, northern bur-reed usually occurs at higher elevations. • This species is called 'bur-reed' from the bur-like fruits and the narrow reed-like leaves.

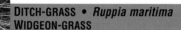

DITCH-GRASS • *Ruppia maritima*
WIDGEON-GRASS

GENERAL: Aquatic perennial from slender creeping rhizomes; stems **submerged**, round, **thread-like, branched**, to 80 cm long.

LEAVES: Mostly alternate, **submerged, delicate, thread-like**, to 20 cm long, stalkless, with membranous sheathing stipules.

FLOWERS: Tiny, inconspicuous, stalkless; sepals and petals lacking; 2 stamens; 4 ovaries; typically 2 on short spikes enclosed in the sheathing stipules.

FRUITS: Drupelets, 1 seeded, pear-shaped, pointed, 2–3 mm long, each borne on a slender **stalk** that **progressively elongates and often coils** as the fruits mature; stalk ultimately 3–30 cm long.

ECOLOGY: Quiet, shallow, brackish or saline water; ponds, ditches, sloughs, tideflats; common along the coastline.

NOTES: *R. maritima* includes *R. occidentalis* and *R. spiralis*. • When not in flower or fruit, **ditch-grass** is tough to distinguish from some of the narrow-leaved pondweeds, but the leaves are **usually in less-bushy clumps and the rhizomes are zig-zag**. Watch for ducks around ditch-grass; they yank up beakfuls of the plant, feeding on roots, fruits and foliage. Ditch-grass is water-pollinated. The pollen grains are released underwater (often adherent in strings), float upwards and tend to drift on the surface until some adhere to receptive stigmas. • Ditch-grass is also known as 'widgeon-grass' because ducks like to eat it. It is sometimes called 'tassel-grass,' because the bunches of delicate leaves look like tassels.

COMMON EEL-GRASS • *Zostera marina*

GENERAL: Submerged or partially floating marine perennials with long, slender rhizomes; stems leafy, flattened, **branching**, to 2.5 m long.

LEAVES: Alternate, 2-ranked, long and narrow (20–120 cm long by **2–12 mm wide**), tapemeasure-like, with closed basal sheaths and rounded tips.

FLOWERS: Tiny, lacking sepals and petals; male and female flowers alternating in 2 rows on the same spike; stalkless in 2 rows on one side of a flattened and somewhat fleshy axis (the spadix) enclosed in a tardily rupturing sheath (the spathe).

FRUITS: Bladdery, 1-seeded achenes, **flask-like**, ribbed, beaked.

ECOLOGY: Subtidal (to 6 m deep) or lowest intertidal, **typically sheltered shores**; forms large colonies on muddy substrates especially in estuaries, also occurs in spray pools along the exposed outer coast and on sandy substrates where there is weak wave action.

NOTES: Both eel-grass and surf-grass have a mixed mode of aquatic pollination. In surface pollination, pollen rafts, which superficially resemble snowflakes, form at low tide and are carried over the surface of the sea by winds and water currents. Some of these 'search vehicles' collide with the floating female stigmas, effecting pollination. In submarine pollination, small pollen bundles resembling whisk brooms travel underwater; ultimately some bump into underwater stigmas. • The crisp, sweet rhizomes and leaf-bases of eel-grass and surf-grass were eaten fresh or dried into cakes for winter food by the Straits Salish, Nuu-chah-nulth and Haida, and by the Kwakwaka'wakw, who ate eel-grass at special feasts. The Haida preferred eel-grass with herring spawn attached to the leaves, and a village on Moresby Island is named after eel-grass.

SCOULER'S SURF-GRASS • *Phyllospadix scouleri*

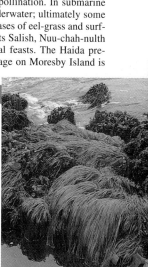

GENERAL: Submerged marine perennials with short, thick, fuzzy rhizomes; stems leafy, **mostly unbranched**, flattened, 5–50 cm long.

LEAVES: Alternate, 2-ranked, long and narrow (30–150 cm long by **2–4 mm wide**), with sheathing bases.

FLOWERS: Tiny, lacking sepals and petals; male and female spikes on separate plants; in caterpillar-like clusters, stalkless in 2 rows on one side of a flattened and somewhat fleshy axis (the spadix) enclosed in a tardily rupturing sheath (the spathe).

FRUITS: Bladdery, 1-seeded achenes, heart-shaped, stout beaked, flattened, with 2 flanges at the base, looking a bit like **extracted teeth**.

ECOLOGY: Intertidal and subtidal, exposed, **surf-beaten, rocky shores**; common usually where there is strong wave action.

NOTES: Scouler's surf-grass has recently been split into 2 species, *P. scouleri* with mostly 3-veined leaves, and *P. serrulatus* with 5–7 veined leaves, found in more-sheltered waters. • **Torrey's surf-grass** (*P. torreyi*) has **branched** stems and **narrower (about 1.5 mm)** leaves. It occurs in similar exposed marine habitats from about **51°N south**. • Surf-grass and eel-grass are difficult to distinguish when they lack flowers or fruits (as is often the case). **Surf-grass** is usually **bright or emerald green** and has **thick rhizomes** with lobed, **tuber-like, irregularly knotted** growths acting as **holdfasts** on rocks; eel-grass is **dull green** and has **slender rhizomes** with abundant roots at the nodes and usually is **not attached to rocky substrates**. The leaf sheaths of surf-grass have prominent, translucent margins; the leaf sheaths of eel-grass lack prominent translucent margins.

DIVERSE-LEAVED WATER-STARWORT
• *Callitriche heterophylla*

GENERAL: Small **aquatic or amphibious** perennial; stems leafy, **lax**, submerged or floating to emergent and prostrate on mud, 5–40 cm long, with small membranous ridges between the leaf-bases.

LEAVES: Opposite; submerged leaves linear, 1 veined, **notched** at the tip, 5–25 mm long; **floating and emergent leaves broadly egg-shaped**, 3 veined, to 1 cm wide.

FLOWERS: Tiny, inconspicuous, with a pair of tiny bracts but otherwise naked, consisting of a single 4-lobed ovary or a single stamen or both; stalkless, **1–3 in leaf axils**.

FRUITS: Four, achene-like, 1-seeded, brownish, squared-off egg-shaped, **wingless, irregularly** tiny-pitted.

ECOLOGY: Shallow ponds and lakes, sloughs, mudflats, shores of slow-moving streams; common but scattered at low elevations, less common on the north coast.

NOTES: Diverse-leaved water-starwort is also known as *C. bolanderi* (in part). • Several other water-starworts occur in our region; refer to technical manuals for reliable identification. **Spring water-starwort** (*C. verna*) is amphibious and has 2 types of leaves like diverse-leaved water-starwort, but it has **slightly wing-margined** fruits with **vertical lines** of tiny pit-like markings. It is scattered through most of our region at low to middle elevations. • *Callitriche* is the only genus of flowering plants in which aerial, floating and subsurface pollination systems have all been reported. *C. heterophylla* is one of several species that also has 'internal self-fertilization,' whereby pollen germinates in unopened anthers and grows down through the vegetative tissues of the plant until it reaches the ovary.

COMMON MARE'S-TAIL • *Hippuris vulgaris*

GENERAL: Aquatic or amphibious, hairless perennial from creeping rhizomes; stems leafy, **upright**, mostly unbranched, usually partly submerged, **10–40 cm tall**.

LEAVES: Whorled, stalkless, **linear** (10–35 mm long by 1–2 mm wide), **pointed, 6–12** per whorl; leaves stiff above water, limp underwater.

FLOWERS: Tiny, inconspicuous; petals lacking; stamen 1; ovary 1, single-celled; **single and stalkless in the axils** of leaves of the upper whorls.

FRUITS: Nutlets, 1 seeded, about 2 mm long.

ECOLOGY: Shallow ponds, lakeshores, streamsides, mudflats; usually in water; low to middle elevations.

NOTES: Common mare's-tail looks much like a horsetail (*Equisetum* spp.), but it is a flowering plant and does not have jointed, hollow stems. • **Four-leaved mare's-tail** (*H. tetraphylla*) is somewhat similar but has **elliptic to oblong-egg-shaped, blunt** leaves **4–6** per whorl. It occurs in tidal marshes, mudflats, and shallow ponds and is scattered from southwestern B.C. north and absent from the Queen Charlotte Islands. **Mountain mare's-tail** (*H. montana*) grows in **subalpine** wet meadows, boggy heath and shallow ponds, and along mossy streambanks; it is common (but often overlooked) from the Olympic Mountains and North Cascades north. It is a **small (to 10 cm tall)** plant with leaves **less than 10 mm long**, and is more terrestrial than aquatic. • The genus name derives from *hippos* (Greek for 'horse') and *oura* ('tail'). In old herbals it was called 'female horse-tail,' because it was thought to be the female part of the water horsetail (p. 430).

EURASIAN WATER-MILFOIL • *Myriophyllum spicatum*

GENERAL: Aquatic perennial from rhizomes; stems leafy, lax, 2–3 mm thick, 30–100 cm long.

LEAVES: Whorled, 3 or 4 per whorl, 1–3 cm long, **pinnately dissected into many thread-like segments, appearing feather-like**.

FLOWERS: Tiny, unisexual, with 4 quickly deciduous, 2.5 mm long petals; single and stalkless in axils of upper bract-like leaves, the inflorescence thus appearing **spike-like** and often sticking up out of the water.

FRUITS: 4 achenes, 1 seeded, rounded.

ECOLOGY: Lakes, ponds, sloughs, slow-moving streams; low to middle elevations; a serious aquatic weed in some water bodies.

NOTES: The formal taxonomy of **Eurasian water-milfoil** and closely related species is confusing. *M. spicatum* in the strict sense is a **Eurasian species introduced** to North America. **Verticillate water-milfoil** (*M. verticillatum*, also known as *M. spicatum* var. *spicatum*) is a more common **native** species with pinnately divided floral bracts. Siberian water-milfoil (*M. sibiricum*, also known as *M. spicatum* var. *exalbescens*, **inset photo**) is also a common native species, indistinguishable from Eurasian water-milfoil to all but the experts or those who really care (e.g., those whose reservoirs or favourite recreational lakes are choked with water-milfoil).

GREATER BLADDERWORT • *Utricularia vulgaris*

GENERAL: Aquatic perennial, free floating, **apparently without roots; stems floating or submerged**, leafy, to 1 m or more long, **about 1 mm thick**.

LEAVES: Alternate, numerous, 1–5 cm long, submerged or floating, **divided into numerous thread-like segments** round in cross-section, bearing small (1–3 mm wide), buoyant, valve-lidded **bladders** that trap small animals.

FLOWERS: Deep-yellow, 2-lipped (much like a snapdragon), 1–2 cm long; lower lip with a short, sac-like spur; 5–20 in a loose cluster atop a stout, above-water stalk.

FRUITS: Capsules, on down-curved stalks.

ECOLOGY: Ponds, lakes, sluggish streams; low to middle elevations.

NOTES: Flat-leaved bladderwort (*U. intermedia*) has **very narrow (about 0.4 mm wide)** stems and leaves with flat, blunt, bristly-edged ultimate segments, and **bladders on separate leafless branches**. **Lesser bladderwort** (*U. minor*) also has very narrow stems, and leaves with flattened, smooth-margined ultimate segments; **some leaves have bladders, some do not**. Both species are scattered the length of our region at low to middle elevations in lakes, ponds, muskeg pools and muck. • Bladderworts are **carnivorous** plants; their tiny bladders trap small crustaceans and other aquatic animals. Each bladder is closed at the narrow end by a water tight, valve-like door that has 4 stiff trigger-bristles on the outer surface. When set, the bladder has a partial vacuum; if a passing animal touches the trigger-bristles the door opens slightly, the walls of the bladder immediately expand, and the sudden inrush of water engulfs the prey. The door closes and the animal is imprisoned, decays, and is absorbed.

WHITE WATER-BUTTERCUP • *Ranunculus aquatilis*
WHITE WATER-CROWFOOT

GENERAL: Aquatic, mostly perennial; stems submerged, weak, sparingly branched, leafy, rooting at lower nodes, 1–2 mm thick, to 1 m long.

LEAVES: Alternate, **of 2 types: submerged leaves finely divided**, usually collapse when plant is taken from water; **floating leaves broad, flat, 3–5 palmately lobed**.

FLOWERS: White, 10–20 mm wide; 5 sepals and petals; **solitary and terminal on long stalks**.

FRUITS: Achenes, asymmetrically egg-shaped, hairy to hairless, short beaked, cross-ridged, 10–20 in a rounded cluster.

ECOLOGY: Ponds, sluggish streams, sloughs, water-filled ditches; common at low to middle elevations.

NOTES: White water-buttercup is also known as *R. trichophyllus*. • It often forms large clumps or floating mats. Contemporary author John Fowles used a very apt metaphor in a recent review of a dictionary: 'I can't open any dictionary without starting to drift through the countless reeds and pretty crowfoot rafts of other words.' • Studies have revealed that leaf form in white water-buttercup depends partly on photoperiod, partly on water level. • The common name 'crowfoot' is from the supposed resemblance of the leaves of some *Ranunculus* species to the foot of a crow.

WATERSHIELD • *Brasenia schreberi*

GENERAL: Aquatic perennial from slender, creeping rhizomes, **covered with a gelatinous sheath**, except for the upper surface of the leaves; stems submerged, long, slender, branching.

LEAVES: Alternate, arising from near the top of the stem, **elliptic, floating on the surface of the water**, 3–12 cm long, **centrally attached** to stalks 5–40 cm long.

FLOWERS: Purplish, 2–3 cm across; sepals and petals **3** (sometimes 4) each, narrowly oblong; stamens numerous, also purplish; 5–15 ovaries; **single on long stalks** arising from the leaf axils.

FRUITS: Leathery, indehiscent follicles, narrowly egg-shaped, ripening underwater and decaying to release the 1–2 seeds.

ECOLOGY: Ponds and sluggish streams, mostly at low elevations.

NOTES: The young leaves of watershield are, in Japan, said to be edible. To eat them, though, you would have to get past the thick layer of jelly-like mucilage secreted by unicellular glandular hairs. • Watershield has special overwintering buds. In autumn, the tips of the trailing stems become swollen with food reserves, and the youngest leaves at the tip remain dwarf. These apical buds are reddish-brown, translucent and sheathed in mucilage. They drop off and remain dormant on the bottom mud until spring. • The common name 'watershield' refers to the round shield- or target-shaped leaves. The species name commemorates Johann Christian Daniel von Schreber (1739–1810), a professor from Erlangen.

YELLOW POND-LILY • *Nuphar polysepalum*
SPATTERDOCK, COW-LILY

GENERAL: Aquatic perennial from **thick, massive** (sometimes monstrous: to 15 cm wide by 5 m long), **prehistoric-looking rhizomes**; flower stems thick, fleshy, long, arising directly from rhizomes.

LEAVES: Floating (sometimes submerged, sometimes emergent), **egg- or heart-shaped** with long (to 2 m) stalks that are round in cross-section and arise in alternate (appearing spiral) fashion from the rhizomes, leathery, 10–45 cm long.

FLOWERS: Yellow (tinged with green or red), large (to 10 cm across), waxy, cup-shaped, floating; sepals about 9, thick; petals 10–20, much smaller than the sepals and hidden by numerous reddish stamens; centre of flower dominated by a **large knob-like stigma; single, long-stalked**.

FRUITS: Ribbed, oval capsules, several-chambered, leathery, decaying and rupturing to liberate the numerous seeds in a jelly-like matrix.

ECOLOGY: Ponds, shallow lakes, sluggish streams; low to middle elevations.

NOTES: Yellow pond-lily is also known as *N. luteum* ssp. *polysepalum*, and as yellow waterlily. • **Fragrant waterlily** (*Nymphaea odorata*) has **large (6–12 cm across), white (tinged with pink), fragrant** flowers that open in the morning and close in the afternoon, and **round leaves to 25 cm across**. It is a native eastern North American species, introduced and scattered in the southern half of our region. **Pygmy waterlily** (*Nymphaea tetragona*) has **smaller (4–6 cm across), white, non-fragrant** flowers and **elliptic-oval leaves 5–12 cm long**. It is scattered at low to middle elevations in southern southeast Alaska and the central coast of B.C. • The Tsimshian drank an infusion from scrapings of the toasted rootstock or ate the boiled heart of the rootstock for bleeding of the lungs and as a contraceptive. The Haida still use water-lily-root medicine for numerous illnesses, including colds, tuberculosis, internal pains, ulcers, rheumatism, chest pains, heart conditions and cancer. The rhizomes were roasted and eaten for tuberculosis, in spite of being quite bitter. Another medicinal preparation for tuberculosis used the boiled rhizome along with red alder bark, 'little trees' (crowberry, p. 64) and sometimes pine bark or western hemlock branches. Other plants, such as bitter-cress (p. 146), were added occasionally to this mixture. The Nuxalk also used the rhizomes for a tuberculosis medicine and preparations for rheumatism, heart disease and gonorrhea. The rhizomes were also used for a blood tonic, in combination with strict ritual procedures. The Kwakwaka'wakw used the rhizomes as a medicine for bodily swelling or sickness in the bones. They drank an extract for asthma and chest pains. The heated leaves were applied to the chest for chest pains. The Quinault heated the roots and applied them to the seat of the pain, especially for rheumatism. • This plant is called 'west wind' in Hesquiat because during westerly storms it was said to bring calmer weather if a person took a leaf and slapped it against the water, yelling, 'West wind! West wind!' • The seeds of *Nuphar* spp. are edible and were an important food source to the Klamath and other coastal indigenous groups of California and Oregon; they are known as 'wok as.' The rhizomes of other *Nuphar* spp. were eaten by other indigenous cultures of North America, but the rhizomes of yellow pond-lily are not palatable and were considered poisonous by the Dena'ina.

Oddballs

Most plants make their own food through photosynthesis, but some plants get their food in other ways. Such plants often have little or no chlorophyll, and so do not look particularly green. The weird appearance of these botanical oddballs commonly arouses wonder and puzzlement ('What IS that thing?!'), and so we have grouped them in a special section on their own.

Insect-eating (insectivorous) plants have specialized structures (leaves in ours) for capturing insects. The insectivorous sundews and butterworts treated here (facing page) live in environments (usually bogs) where nitrogen, a key plant nutrient, is not readily available. The sundews and butterworts are photosynthetic, and therefore green or yellowish-green, but they supplement their diet with nutrients (especially nitrogen) from insects. They come from families of insectivorous plants: the sundew (*Drosera*), from the Droseraceae, which also includes the Venus' fly-trap (*Dionaea*); the butterwort (*Pinguicula*) from the Lentibulariaceae, which also includes the bladderworts (*Utricularia*) treated on p. 347.

Saprophytic plants live on dead and decaying vegetation. They can usually be found in soils rich in decomposing plant material. The saprophytes in this section are anomalies in the wintergreen family (Pyrolaceae), in the genera *Hemitomes*, *Allotropa*, *Pterospora* and *Hypopitys*. Close examination of these seeming apparitions reveals the familiar bell- or urn-shaped flowers of the wintergreen family.

Parasitic plants take their food from other living plants, and our species usually do not kill their host in the process. Parasitic plants are not green, and they are often very unusual in appearance. The terrestrial parasites connect with their host underground, and they are always found near their characteristic hosts. The root-parasites treated in this section are in the broomrape family (Orobanchaceae): broomrapes (*Orobanche*) and groundcones (*Boschniakia*). The paintbrushes (*Castilleja*, pp. 257–58), owl-clovers (*Orthocarpus*, p. 259) and toad-flaxes (*Comandra* and *Geocaulon*, p. 309) are partially parasitic, but not noticeably so since they are green. The mistletoes (*Arceuthobium* and *Phoradendron*, p. 348) are also parasites that are very unusual in appearance, but they are inconspicuous epiphytes (they grow on their tree hosts).

The roots of Indian-pipe (*Monotropa*), a member of the wintergreen family (Pyrolaceae), are connected to the roots of coniferous trees by a specialized combination of fungal filaments and plant roots called a mycorrhiza (meaning 'fungus-root'). Nutritionally it is a parasite, but a very special one, because it is not connected directly to its host.

Key to Oddballs

1a. Small (less than 25 cm tall) insect-eating plants; leaves either fleshy, greasy, and yellow-green, or fringed with sticky, glistening red 'tentacles'; usually in wetlands 2
    2a. Leaves fringed with sticky, glistening red 'tentacles'; flowers white .... *Drosera rotundifolia*
    2b. Leaves fleshy, greasy, and yellow-green; flowers dark lavender-purple .... *Pinguicula vulgaris*
1b. Various-sized plants; leaves not as above; not insect-eating;
in mature coniferous forests or shrubby sites 3
    3a. Plants fleshy, waxy-white or pinkish, blackening with age, pipe-shaped .... *Monotropa uniflora*
    3b. Plants of various colours and shapes, but not as above 4
        4a. Plants red-and-white striped like a candycane .... *Allotropa virgata*
        4b. Plants not red-and-white striped 5
            5a. Flowers urn- to bell-shaped; saprophytes (obtaining nutrition
from decaying vegetation) in rich humus in coniferous forests 6
                6a. Plant robust, reddish-brown, sticky-hairy ;
stems often persistent through the winter .... *Pterospora andromedea*
                6b. Plants smaller (to 30 cm tall); stems not persistent 7
                    7a. Plants to 15 cm tall, waxy-pink, drying brown, resembling a conifer's cone;
leaves scale-like, densely overlapping; flowers transparent .... *Hemitomes congestum*
                    7b. Plants to 30 cm tall, yellowish to pinkish, drying black,
not resembling a cone; flowers yellow to pink ....*Hypopitys monotropa*
            5b. Petals forming two unequal 'lips'; parasites growing with their 'hosts'
(e.g., salal, shrubby alder, stonecrop, sunflower family plants) 8
                8a. Plants yellowish, very short (to 5 cm tall); leaves basal;
flowers purple (occasionally yellowish); parasitic on (and so growing
with) stonecrops, sunflower family species, and other plants .... *Orobanche uniflora*
                8b. Plants yellow to red or brown, taller (to 40 cm tall), resembling
a conifer's cone; leaves scale-like, densely overlapping; flowers yellow,
purple, or brownish-red ; parasitic on (and so growing with) other species 9
                    9a. Plants yellow and red to purplish, to 12 cm high;
flowers yellow to purple; parasitic on salal;
Vancouver Island and adjacent mainland south .... *Boschniakia hookeri*
                    9b. Plants brownish, to 40 cm tall; flowers brownish-red;
usually parasitic on shrubby alders; southern Alaska north .... *Boschniakia rossica*

ROUND-LEAVED SUNDEW • *Drosera rotundifolia*

GENERAL: Small, **insect-eating** perennial, 5–25 cm tall.

LEAVES: Sticky, glandular, spreading, **in basal rosette**, 3–7 cm long; blades **round to broadly egg-shaped**, at least as broad as long, fringed with **long, reddish, glandular hairs (tentacles)** that exude drops of sticky fluid.

FLOWERS: White, small (petals 6–10 mm long), fully open only in strong sunlight; **few (3–10) in a coiled cluster**, all on one side of the stem.

FRUITS: Many-seeded, partitioned capsules.

ECOLOGY: Sphagnum bogs, fens, and wet meadows at low to middle elevations; throughout our region.

NOTES: Great sundew (*D. anglica*) is similar in most respects to round-leaved sundew, but it has **longer, narrower leaf blades** (usually at least 2 times as long as wide). Great sundew is found in the same habitats and over the same range as round-leaved sundew, but it is less common. • Coast Salish, Kwakwaka'wakw and other northwest coast groups used the leaves for removing corns, warts and bunyons. Known as 'many hearts' in Haida, it was used as a good luck charm for success in fishing. • Sundews are commonly pollinated by the same insects they ensnare in their sticky tentacles and use for food: mosquitoes, midges and gnats. • The sap is acrid and has the reputation for curdling milk. Fresh leaves were used in Europe in the preparation of cheeses and junkets, and for removing warts. The sap contains an antibiotic effective against several bacteria and was used to treat tuberculosis, asthma, bronchitis and coughs. • The common name is thought to come from a misspelling of the Saxon word *sin-dew*, which means 'always dewy,' which it is.

COMMON BUTTERWORT • *Pinguicula vulgaris*

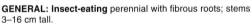

GENERAL: Insect-eating perennial with fibrous roots; stems 3–16 cm tall.

LEAVES: All basal, greenish-yellow, forming a rosette, fleshy, broadly lance-shaped to elliptic, smooth-edged with inrolled margins, greasy-slimy on upper surface.

FLOWERS: Dark lavender-purple, rarely white, 15 mm or more long; petals in funnel-like tube with **spur** and white hairs in throat; flowers borne **singly** on leafless, sticky stems.

FRUITS: Round capsules.

ECOLOGY: Fens, bogs, swamps and mossy seeps, rocky drip-faces and other moist sites, at low to subalpine elevations throughout our region.

NOTES: Hairy butterwort (*P. villosa*) is a less common, smaller species with **densely glandular** flowering stems and **smaller (up to 8 mm long), paler** flowers. It typically grows in wetlands at low to middle elevations, from north coastal B.C. and the Queen Charlotte Islands north to Alaska. • Butterworts (and sundews) usually grow on sites low in available nitrogen, and they supplement their diet by entrapping insects. Insects stick to the upper slimy surface of butterwort leaves. The leaf margins tend to roll inward to prevent insects from escaping. The plant then secretes juices that digest the soft tissues of the insect. • Butterwort supposedly encouraged or protected the productivity of milk cows, ensuring a supply of butter. Yorkshire farm women annointed the chapped udders of cows with butterwort juice. It was also thought to protect cows from elf arrows and humans from witches and fairies.

INDIAN-PIPE • *Monotropa uniflora*

GENERAL: Fleshy, waxy-white or pinkish perennial, **blackening with age**, appearing in **clusters** of flowering, unbranched stems 5–25 cm tall.

LEAVES: Linear or lance-shaped to oval, **scale-like**, up to 1 cm long.

FLOWERS: White, single, to 2 cm long, **narrowly bell-shaped, at first nodding or curved to 1 side**; petals sac-like and broadening at base.

FRUITS: Erect, oval to circular capsules, about 6 mm long, brown and splitting open when mature.

ECOLOGY: In humus in shaded, usually mature, coniferous forest; at low elevations, from the southern B.C. coast and Vancouver Island plus the Skeena and Nass river valleys area south to California; not on the mid-coast, not on the Queen Charlotte Islands.

NOTES: Roots of Indian-pipe are connected via fungi to the roots of nearby coniferous trees. In this manner Indian-pipe, which lacks chlorophyll and so cannot make its own food, obtains nutrition from the efforts of another plant (the conifer). • In the Straits Salish and Nlaka'pamux languages, the name for Indian-pipe means 'wolf's urine'; it is associated with wolves and is said to grow wherever a wolf urinates. Among the Nlaka'pamux it is an indicator for wood mushrooms in the coming season. It was used medicinally as a poultice for wounds that would not heal. • The common name 'Indian-pipe' refers to the pipe-like flowers. It is also called 'ghost flower,' 'corpse plant' and 'ice plant'—names inspired by the unusual colour and texture of the plant. • Note that while the flower hangs down, the fruit eventually points up. • Another **ghostly white plant** of low- to middle-elevation, moist coniferous forests is the **phantom orchid** (*Cephalanthera austinae*, also known as *Eburophyton austinae*). This **very rare** saprophyte grows to 50 cm tall, with 5–20 delicately scented, **white to cream, orchid** flowers with a **bright-yellow patch** within. Its range is from the lower Fraser Valley, the Gulf Islands and southeastern Vancouver Island south through the Olympic and Cascade Mountains.

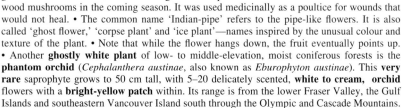

PINESAP • *Hypopitys monotropa*

GENERAL: Fleshy saprophyte to 30 cm tall, unbranched, **yellowish to pinkish, drying black**, usually hairy from a dense mass of fleshy roots.

LEAVES: Small, **scale-like**, lance-shaped to linear, thick, crowded near base of stem, lacking green colour.

FLOWERS: Yellowish to pinkish; petals 1–2 cm long, hairy on one or both surfaces, somewhat sac-like at base; **several to many** in terminal clusters, **at first nodding, more or less bent to 1 side**.

FRUITS: Erect, oval to round capsules, to 8 mm long, brown and splitting open when dry.

ECOLOGY: In humus in coniferous forests at middle elevations; from southeast Alaska and the Queen Charlotte Islands south to California

NOTES: The common name 'pinesap' refers either to the fact that this plant grows under pines (or other conifers) and 'saps' their juices, or to the resemblance of pinesap's flower colour and texture to congealed pine resin. • *Hypopitys* is from the Greek *hypos* (beneath) and *pitys* (tree). The species name *monotropa* means that the flowers all face one way. In the southern part of our region, along the west side of the Cascades north to the Olympics, watch for **fringed pinesap** (*Pleuricospora fimbriolata*). It is less common than *H. monotropa*, but it grows in similar habitats. The upright stems barely push the flowers up through the duff. The entire plant is **yellowish-white**, and its petals have **fringed margins**.

PINEDROPS • *Pterospora andromedea*

GENERAL: Robust **reddish-brown, sticky-hairy** saprophyte **to 1 m tall**, from a ball-like root mass.

LEAVES: Lance-shaped, like scales, sheathing the stem.

FLOWERS: White to yellow or pink, urn-shaped; petals fused, to 1 cm long; numerous in a slender inflorescence to 50 cm long.

FRUITS: Spherical capsules to 1.2 cm across, containing winged seeds.

ECOLOGY: Rich humus in coniferous forests.

NOTES: Pinedrops is the tallest saprophyte in our region, and its reddish-brown stems are often persistent through the winter. • No uses of pinedrops by coastal peoples are known. This plant was known as 'coyote's arrow' to some Okanagan people. • The flowers are thought to resemble drops of resin from pines (and other conifers) under which they grow. *Pterospora* comes from the Greek words *pteros* ('wing') and *sporos* ('seed'), because the tiny seeds have a lovely diaphanous wing on one side. The species name *andromedea* means that the flowers resemble those of the genus *Andromeda* (see p. 65).

CANDYSTICK • *Allotropa virgata*
SUGARSTICK

GENERAL: Red-and-white-striped saprophytic herb **to 50 cm tall**.

LEAVES: Scale-like, narrowly lance-shaped, to 3.5 cm long, more crowded near stem-base.

FLOWERS: White, red or brown sepals (petals absent) to 5 mm long; in a densely flowered spike to 15 cm long, each **urn-shaped** flower with a leaf under it.

FRUITS: Round capsules to 5 mm across.

ECOLOGY: Rich humus in coniferous forests at low to middle elevations; southern and southeastern Vancouver Island and the adjacent mainland south to California.

NOTES: Candystick (also called 'barber's pole' and 'devil's wand') is the only species in its genus. It is not found outside of western North America. • This plant, with its brilliant red-on-white stripes, looks just like the candy canes people place in children's Christmas stockings. *Allotropa* (from *allos*, 'other,' and *tropos*, 'turn') refers to the flowers, which turn upwards when young, but downwards as they get older; *virgata* means 'striped.'

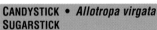

GNOME-PLANT • *Hemitomes congestum*

GENERAL: Waxy-pink saprophytic herb (brown when dry) to 15 cm high, from a fleshy rootstock; **leaves overlapping** in a dense spike somewhat **resembling a conifer's cone**.

LEAVES: Scale-like and overlapping; edges ragged and with irregular hairs.

FLOWERS: Thin and semi-transparent, **erect, pinkish, bell-shaped**; petals partly fused, to 1.5 cm long; in dense terminal spikes, each flower with a bract.

FRUITS: Hairy oval capsules.

ECOLOGY: Rich humus in damp coniferous forests at middle elevations; on Vancouver Island and the adjacent mainland south to California, with an outlier population in the Skeena River valley near Terrace.

NOTES: Gnome-plant is the only plant in its genus. It does not occur outside western North America. • When it first appears above ground, this gnome-like plant looks like a small blackened cauliflower head, a fungus or an inverted cone. Then it bursts open to reveal a crowded (*congestum*) head of pink-yellow flowers. The Latin name of the genus means 'half-sterile' or 'half-eunuch,' because often half of the anther cells are sterile.

VANCOUVER GROUNDCONE • *Boschniakia hookeri*
POQUE

GENERAL: Yellow to red or purple parasitic herb **to 12 cm tall**, from a thickened tuber-like underground stem.

LEAVES: Scale-like (like the scales on a conifer's cone), broad, **overlapping**.

FLOWERS: Yellow to purple; petals formed into 2 unequal lips, to 1.5 cm long; in a dense spike, each flower with a bract under it.

FRUITS: Capsules to 1.5 cm long; seeds tiny, numerous.

ECOLOGY: Usually growing with salal, at low elevations; southwestern B.C. (rare on the Queen Charlotte Islands) south to northern California.

NOTES: Species in this genus are **root-parasites**—that is, they are connected to the roots of nearby plants, and derive nutrition from them. Vancouver groundcone is parasitic on salal (p. 53) and probably other members of the heather family, such as kinnickinnick (p. 67). • The spherical root-bases of these fleshy plants were sometimes eaten raw by the Kwakwaka'wakw and Nuu-chah-nulth. The Kwakwaka'wakw name for this plant, *p'ukw'es*, apparently gave rise to the alternative English common name 'poque.' This plant was also used as a good luck charm by some of the central coastal groups of B.C. • A single groundcone plant can produce more than a third of a million seeds. • This species is named for 19th century British botanist Sir W.J. Hooker or his son Sir J.D. Hooker, or both.

NORTHERN GROUNDCONE • *Boschniakia rossica*

GENERAL: Brownish parasitic herb **to 40 cm tall**, from a thickened underground stem.

LEAVES: Scale-like (like the scales on a conifer's cone), broad, yellowish to purplish, **overlapping**.

FLOWERS: Brownish-red; petals formed into 2 unequal lips, to 1.5 cm long; in a **dense spike** to 25 cm long, each flower with a hairy-fringed bract under it.

FRUITS: Capsules to 1.5 cm long.

ECOLOGY: Moist sites at middle elevations, from extreme northern B.C. north to Alaska.

NOTES: Northern groundcone is parasitic on shrubby alders (usually), but also occasionally on birch, willow, huckleberry, spruce and leatherleaf (*Chamaedaphne calyculata*). It can be separated from Vancouver groundcone by its **larger size**, its **hairy-fringed flower bracts** and its geographic **distribution**. • Grizzly bears sometimes like to gorge on these thick, fleshy plants, which can be very abundant in floodplain cottonwood forests in the big northern valleys. • *Boschniakia* is called 'groundcone' from its resemblance to a large pine cone sitting on the ground. What might be taken for the cone scales are brownish, 2-lipped flowers. • The genus is named for Russian amateur botanist A. K. Boschniak.

NAKED BROOMRAPE • *Orobanche uniflora*

GENERAL: Short (to 5 cm tall), apparently annual, **parasitic** herb, **yellowish and glandular-hairy**.

LEAVES: Scale-like, lance-shaped, to 1 cm long.

FLOWERS: Yellowish-white to purple, to 3.5 cm long, irregular in shape; **single on long (to 10 cm long) stalks, 1–3 per plant**.

FRUITS: Capsules splitting lengthwise.

ECOLOGY: Moist, open sites or open woods, from low to middle elevations; southern Vancouver Island and the adjacent mainland south.

NOTES: Naked broomrape is parasitic on stonecrops, saxifrages, species in the sunflower family and other plants. • **Clustered broomrape** (*O. fasciculata*) is similar but **larger (to 15 cm tall)** and with **more numerous flowers (4–10 per plant**, vs. 1–3 per plant in naked broomrape). The flower stalks on *O. uniflora* are much longer than the stem; those of *O. fasciculata* are not. Clustered broomrape is parasitic on a variety of hosts (often *Artemisia* spp.) and can be found on open sites at low to middle elevations from Vancouver Island and the adjacent mainland south. • The genus name *Orobanche*, from *orobos* ('a clinging plant') and *ancho* ('to strangle'), alludes to the fact that species are parasitic on the roots of other plants. A British species is parasitic on Scotch broom (p. 83) and so is called 'broomrape'; perhaps we ought to introduce this to our region! The single flower (*uniflora*) is borne on a stem devoid of leaves ('naked'). • The family Orobanchaceae, to which both *Boschniakia* and *Orobanche* belong, is also called the 'cancer-root' family.

Poaceae (Grass Family)

Grasses tend to be overlooked in favour of other, more glamorous, flowering plants, but the grass family (Poaceae or Gramineae) is undoubtedly the most useful to humankind. Grasses now provide us with 3 times more food than do peas and beans, tubers, fruit, meat, milk and eggs put together. Grasses include sugar cane and cereals such as wheat, barley, oats, rye, corn and rice. They are used for forage and turf, and they are available as materials for woven, thatch, adobe, or bamboo structures. Barley can be brewed into beers and whiskeys, rice into sake, molasses (from sugar cane) into rum. Many species of wildlife, from large grazing mammals to waterfowl, depend on grass and grassland or wetland habitats for food, shelter and completion of their life cycles.

Grass flowers are small but complex, and they have acquired a peculiar but necessary terminology. The tiny flowers are borne in the axils of a small scale-like inner bract, the '**palea**,' and a larger outer bract, the '**lemma**'; the flower, lemma and palea together are called a '**floret**.' Below the florets are two more bracts, the '**glumes**'; florets and glumes together are called a '**spikelet**,' which is the basic unit of the inflorescence. Leaves of most grasses sheath the stem before diverging as a narrow blade, and where the sheathing part joins the blade are found 2 distinctive organs useful for identification: the '**ligule**' (typically a membranous flap or appendage), and the '**auricle**' (an ear-like lobe or flange). Grass stems are usually hollow in the internodes and round in cross-section. If your 'grass' specimen either has a solid stem or is triangular in cross-section, refer to the 'Sedges and Rushes' section, pp. 388–416.

The grass family is very large and complex. In our region there are over 200 grass species, most of which are indigenous. Introduced European grasses are an important component of the flora of the southern part of our region, especially in the summer-dry Douglas-fir area, which coincides with most of the human population and disturbed ground. Only the most common species encountered in our region are presented here.

Grasses in general were used widely by native peoples for lining steam-cooking pits, wiping fish, covering berries, stringing food for drying, spreading on floors and as bedding.

To assist in identification, the grasses are picture-keyed below first into tribes and then into genera. Detailed drawings of the flowering parts and leaf axils are provided to illustrate characteristics of individual species. Consult Hitchcock and Cronquist (1973) and Hultén (1968) for more information about our grasses.

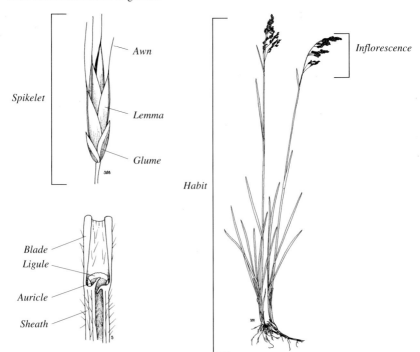

Spikelet · Awn · Lemma · Glume · Inflorescence · Habit · Blade · Ligule · Auricle · Sheath

Picture Key to Grass Tribes

1a. Inflorescence a spike (spikelets without stalks) .... Hordeae (Barley tribe)

1b. Inflorescence a panicle or raceme (spikelets with stalks) 2

2a. Each spikelet with 1 flower (floret); glumes small .... Agrostideae (Bentgrass tribe)

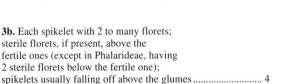

2b. Each spikelet with 2 to many flowers (florets) 3

3a. Each spikelet with 1 fertile floret above and 1 sterile floret below the fertile one; spikelets falling off with the glumes attached .... Paniceae (Panicum tribe)

3b. Each spikelet with 2 to many florets; sterile florets, if present, above the fertile ones (except in Phalarideae, having 2 sterile florets below the fertile one); spikelets usually falling off above the glumes 4

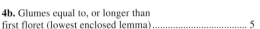

4a. Glumes shorter than first floret (lowest enclosed lemma); lemmas awnless, or awned from the tip .... Festuceae (Fescue tribe)

4b. Glumes equal to, or longer than first floret (lowest enclosed lemma) 5

5a. Glumes narrow; lemmas awned from the back, or awnless; sterile florets, if present, above the fertile ones .... Aveneae (Oat tribe)

5b. Glumes broad, boat-shaped; lemmas awned from a notched tip, or awnless; spikelets with 1 fertile floret above 2 sterile ones .... Phalarideae (Canary grass tribe)

Picture Key to Poaceae Genera

Hordeae (Barley tribe)

Inflorescence a spike

spikelets solitary at each node

spikelets 2 or 3 at each node

spikelets with flat side facing axis of spike

spikelets with narrow side facing axis of spike

spikelets 2 at each node, alike

spikelets 3 at each node, lateral pair reduced to awns

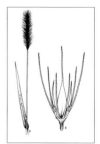

Agropyron
(quackgrass, wheatgrass)
p. 362

Lolium
(ryegrass)
p. 363

Elymus
(wildrye, dunegrass)
p. 363, 364

Hordeum
(barley)
p. 362

Paniceae (Panicum or Millet tribe)

Spikelets 2-flowered; 1 fertile floret above, 1 sterile floret below; fertile lemma and palea hardened

inflorescence not spiny or bristly

inflorescence spiny or bristly

spikelets in slender, finger-like, 1-sided racemes at tip of stems

spikelets on slender stalks in open panicles

inflorescence a stiff spiny panicle with 1-sided branches; ligules absent

inflorescence spike-like, cylindrical, bristly; ligules present

Digitaria
(crabgrass)
p. 386

Panicum
(panicum)
p. 386

Echinochloa
(barnyard-grass)
p. 387

Setaria
(bristlegrass, foxtail)
p. 387

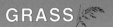
Agrostideae (Bentgrass tribe)

Spikelets 1 flowered

inflorescence spike-like — *inflorescence not spike-like*

spikes cylindrical; lemmas not bearded at base

Spikes thicken in the middle; lemmas with tuft of hairs at the base

glumes awned, with comb-like fringe of hairs on keel

glumes awnless; lemma awned from near middle

Ammophila
(European beachgrass)
p. 364

Phleum
(timothy)
p. 368

Alopecurus
(foxtail)
p. 368

panicle not drooping — *panicle drooping*

lemmas with tuft of stiff hairs at base

lemmas lacking tuft of hairs at base

Cinna
(wood reedgrass) p. 369

Calamagrostis
(reedgrass)
p. 365

Agrostis
(bentgrass)
p. 366-367

Phalarideae (Canary grass tribe)

Spikelets 3 flowered; glumes broad, boat-shaped

panicle open; lemmas awnless or awned

panicle spike-like; sterile lemmas awned

panicle compact; spikelets crowded, all turned in same direction; lemmas awnless

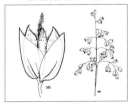

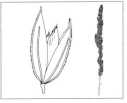

Hierochloe
(sweetgrass) p. 369

Anthoxanthum
(vernalgrass) p. 370

Phalaris
(canary grass) p. 370

Festuceae (Fescue tribe)

Spikelets 2 to many flowered; glumes shorter than 1st floret

lemmas with awns; inflorescence dense and spike-like or plume-like, or of dense 1-sided clusters

inflorescence of dense, 1-sided clusters; spikelets with short stiff hairs

inflorescence large and feathery; spikelets with long silky hairs

inflorescence spike-like, bristly like a bottlebrush

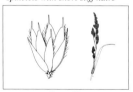

Dactylis
(orchard grass) p. 371

Phragmites
(common reed) p. 371

Cynosurus
(dogtail) p. 372

lemmas without awns

plants of saline habitats

plants not of saline habitats (though some are maritime)

strongly rhizomatous; stems solid; leaves in 2 ranks; male and female heads on separate plants; spikelets large

mostly tufted (some stolons); stems hollow; spikelets smaller, narrower

Distichlis
(saltgrass) p. 381

Puccinellia
(alkali grass) p. 381

glumes not papery; lemmas usually keeled on back; stems not bulbous at base

glumes papery; lemmas rounded on back; stems often bulbous at base

Melica
(oniongrass)
p. 372

lemmas with veins converging at tip, often cobwebby at base; spikelets usually small

lemmas with 7 prominent, parallel veins; spikelets often long and narrow, not cobwebby

lemmas with mostly 5 prominent, parallel veins, not cobwebby

Poa
(bluegrass)
pp. 377–379

Glyceria
(mannagrass)
pp. 379–380

Torreyochloa
(weak alkali grass)
p. 380

Festuceae (continued)

lemmas with awns; inflorescence usually open, if narrow the spikelets not densely crowded

spikelets widely spaced in loose, drooping, 1-sided racemes	*spikelets large, in panicles; lemmas awned from between 2 teeth at tip*	*annuals; spikelets small; lemmas awned from tip*	*perennials; spikelets small; lemmas awned from tip*

Pleuropogon (nodding semaphore grass) p. 373	**Bromus** (brome) pp. 373–374	**Vulpia** (annual fescues) p. 375	**Festuca** (perennial fescues) pp. 375–376

Aveneae (Oat tribe)

Spikelets 2- to many-flowered; glumes equal to or longer than 1st floret

lemmas included in (shorter than) glumes

small annuals with hair-like leaves; lemmas 2-toothed at tip, awned from below midlength	*perennials; lemmas with flattened, twisted awn arising from between 2 teeth at tip*	*perennials; lemmas 2 toothed at tip, with round, twisted awn arising from midlength*	*perennials; lower lemma awnless, upper lemma with short hook-like awn from just below the smooth tip*

Aira (early hairgrass) p. 383	**Danthonia** (oat-grass) page 383	**Vahlodea** (mountain hairgrass) p. 384	**Holcus** (velvet-grass) p. 385

lemmas reaching beyond (longer than) glumes

lemmas 3–4 toothed at tip, awned from below middle, rounded on back	*lemmas 2 toothed at tip, awned from above middle, keeled on back*	*lower lemma with twisted, bent awn from midlength; upper lemma with short straight awn from near tip*

Deschampsia (tufted hairgrass) p. 384	**Trisetum** (trisetum) p. 382	**Arrhenatherum** (tall oatgrass) p. 385

MEADOW BARLEY • *Hordeum brachyantherum*

GENERAL: Tufted perennial, sometimes hairy on leaf sheaths; stems erect but bent at base, 20–90 cm tall.

LEAVES: Flat, 3–8 mm wide, hairless to spreading hairy; no auricles; ligules short, about 0.5 mm long, minutely frilly at tip.

INFLORESCENCE: Spike, usually erect, 4–10 cm long, brittle and easily shattering when ripe; **spikelets 3 per node**; central spikelet stalkless, lateral spikelets usually sterile, on short curved stalks; glumes slender and awn-like, about 1 cm long; fertile lemma with **awn 1–1.5 cm long**.

ECOLOGY: Salt marshes, ocean beaches, moist meadows and clearings, grassy slopes, along streams; fairly common from sea level to middle or subalpine elevations, but most abundant in maritime habitats.

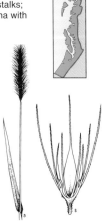

NOTES: Foxtail barley (*H. jubatum*, **inset photo**) is a showy, weedy species with a **thicker, nodding** spike and **2–6 cm long, purplish-red awns**; it is particularly common along roadsides. • The awned spikelets of both species can attach to clothing or the hair and skin of animals. The spikelets can cause injury by working into nose or mouth passages, or even through the intestines of animals eating them, but blacktail deer graze the leaves freely. • *Hordeum* is the Latin for barley, which got its English name because it was used to make *beere*, which became *beerlegh* or *berlegh*. • Some genera of the barley tribe (e.g., *Hordeum*, *Elymus*, *Agropyron*) are interfertile, and hybrids can readily occur.

QUACKGRASS • *Agropyron repens*
COUCHGRASS

GENERAL: Perennial from long, tough, wiry **rhizomes**; stems erect to curved at base, often hairy on leaf sheaths, up to 1 m tall.

LEAVES: Flat, firm, hairless to (more commonly) hairy, **5–10 mm wide; auricles well developed**; ligules very short, to 0.5 mm in length.

INFLORESCENCE: Spike, erect, stiff, 7–15 cm long; **spikelets 1 per node**, stalkless, **borne alternately and flatwise to the axis of the spike**, closely crowded, overlapping, about twice as long as the internodes; glumes awn-tipped; lemmas awnless, awn-tipped, or with straight awn up to 10 mm long.

ECOLOGY: Disturbed sites mostly at low elevations, scattered but widely distributed, in or near settled areas; especially common in fields, lawns, meadows, roadsides, waste areas.

NOTES: On the basis of what some might call obscure characters, *A. repens* has recently been segregated as *Elytrigia repens*, and *A. trachycaulum* has emerged as *Elymus trachycaulus*. • **Slender wheatgrass** (*A. trachycaulum*) is a native, **loosely tufted** bunchgrass. It has **short or no auricles, lacks rhizomes** and occurs in drier habitats (meadows, gravel bars, rocky slopes, open forest) and drier climates (e.g., Strait of Georgia–Puget Sound area, Willamette Valley). • Quackgrass is a European species that has become well established in the settled portions of our region as a vigorous, persistent weed. • 'Quack' and 'couch' apparently derive from the Anglo-Saxon *cwice* or *cwic* meaning 'vivacious'—presumably in reference to the growth of this persistent weed.

PERENNIAL RYEGRASS • *Lolium perenne*
ENGLISH RYEGRASS

GENERAL: Tufted, short-lived perennial, usually with rhizomes and numerous developing leaves at the base; stems hairless, curved at base, 30–80 cm tall.

LEAVES: Flat to folded, hairless, glossy, 3–4 mm wide; auricles usually well developed, up to 1.5 mm long; ligules about 1 mm long.

INFLORESCENCE: Spike, erect, 7–25 cm long; **spikelets 1 per node**, stalkless, crowded, **borne edgewise to axis of spike**; glumes 7 nerved, unawned; **lemmas sharp-pointed but unawned**.

ECOLOGY: Fields, pastures, lawns, roadsides, clearings, waste areas; scattered at low elevations, mostly in settled areas and more commonly in the southern half of our region.

NOTES: Italian ryegrass (*Lolium multiflorum*) is a **biennial or short-lived perennial** with short glumes and **awned lemmas**. Both ryegrasses are European species, widely distributed mostly in the southern part of our region as weeds or escapees from cultivation. Both are often grown for hay or pasture and are frequently planted as nurse-crops or for quick cover, as in grass-seeding mixtures. • *Lolium* and *Agropyron* both have 1 spikelet per node, but in ***Lolium*** the **spikelet** is attached **edgewise** to the axis of the spike vs. **flatwise** in *Agropyron* (except in the introduced forage species *A. cristatum*, crested wheatgrass). • *Lolium* is the Latin for a 'darnel' or a weed of grain fields. Th. Newton, in his Herbal to the Bible (1585), defined a darnel as 'all vicious, noisome and unprofitable graine encombring and hindering good corne.'

BLUE WILDRYE • *Elymus glaucus*

GENERAL: Tufted perennial usually forming small clumps, 0.5–1.5 m tall.

LEAVES: Flat or slightly inrolled, usually lax, hairless to roughened, **5–12 mm wide**; auricles usually well developed, claw-like and clasping; ligules short (about 1 mm long).

INFLORESCENCE: Spike, erect, stiff, 5–15 cm long; **spikelets usually 2 per node**, mostly 2-flowered and overlapping; **lemmas hairless to sparsely short-hairy**, virtually unawned to long-awned (awns up to 20 mm long).

ECOLOGY: Open forest (coniferous and deciduous), dry to moist openings, rocky slopes and clearings; common at low to middle elevations.

NOTES: **Hairy wildrye** (*Elymus hirsutus*) is similar but has **flexible, drooping spikes** and **lemmas fringed with long hairs**. It occurs the length of our region, mostly west of the Coast-Cascade Mountain crest, in dry to moist open forest, gravelly or rocky slopes, upper beaches, openings and clearings, and sometimes on avalanche tracks and in mountain gullies, at low to moderately high elevations. • It is simple to separate the genera *Elymus* and *Agropyron* on the basis of number of spikelets per node, but taxonomists have long disputed this separation. Some modern grass taxonomists maintain that there are good reasons to merge most of the 2 genera into *Elymus*. • This is one of our tallest grasses, and it provides forage for both domestic stock and wildlife. • *Elymus* is from the ancient Greek *elumos*, a name for some type of grain. The blue-grey colour (*glaucus*) and the resemblance to rye (*Secale cereale*) are the reasons for the species and common name.

DUNEGRASS • *Elymus mollis*
DUNE WILDRYE

GENERAL: Robust perennial, forming **large clumps with thick spreading rhizomes**; stems stout, erect, 0.5–1.5 m tall, usually finely hairy towards top.

LEAVES: Flat to folded, tough; sheaths hairless; blades hairless beneath, finely hairy above, with numerous prominent nerves, **6–15 mm wide**; auricles present on some leaves; **ligules short, barely 1 mm long**.

INFLORESCENCE: Spike, **stout, erect**, 10–30 cm long and **1–2 cm thick**; spikelets paired, 20–30 mm long; **glumes and lemmas usually very soft-hairy**, scarcely awned.

ECOLOGY: Coastal dunes, sand and gravel beaches, edges of shoreline forests; strictly maritime; often the dominant cover on offshore, treeless, sea-bird islands.

NOTES: Closely related to lymegrass (*E. arenarius*), a European species which occupies equivalent habitats. • Apparently *E. mollis* was the dominant grass on dunes immediately adjacent to the ocean until the introduction of European beachgrass, which now is the more abundant species on many dunes. • Dunegrass was used by the Vancouver Island Salish for weaving tumplines and packstraps and for tucking into the ravels of reef-nets for strength. The Nuu-chah-nulth sometimes used dunegrass for weaving basket handles. The Quinault wove tumplines from dunegrass, and they spread it out to dry salal berries on. The Haida split the stems in half, dyed them, and used them to twine and decorate baskets. The Tlingit used the stems as overlay for baskets, but they preferred other similar species. • Dunegrass is cultivated in Japan for making ropes, mats and paper.

EUROPEAN BEACHGRASS • *Ammophila arenaria*
MARRAM GRASS

GENERAL: Tough, coarse perennial in **tufts connected by deep**, **extensively creeping rhizomes**, 0.5–1.5 m tall.

LEAVES: Narrow (2–4 mm wide), inrolled, very long, stiff; no auricles; **ligules long (10–25 mm) and sharp-pointed**.

INFLORESCENCE: Panicle dense, **spike-like**, often thicker in the middle, 10–30 cm long and **1–2 cm thick**; spikelets crowded; glumes longer than lemmas; lemmas unawned but notched at tip, bearded at base with hairs 2–3 mm long.

ECOLOGY: Beaches and dunes along the immediate coast.

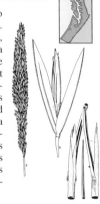

NOTES: *Ammophila* is closely related to *Calamagrostis*, differing in having **awnless** rather than awned lemmas. • European beachgrass is an excellent sand-binder native to Europe, which was introduced for this purpose along the Pacific coast. It is such a good sand-binder that it has increased sand deposition on the first dune ridge behind the beach and has changed the patterns of sand movement in some dune systems. The plants appear to do better where sand is accumulating, and they may decrease in vigour where the surface remains stable. • Studies in California have revealed that dune habitats dominated by European beachgrass (rather than by the native dunegrass) have a taller and more dense leaf canopy and fewer species of plants and burrowing insects. The borders of dense clumps of European beachgrass also have fewer searocket (p. 153) plants, apparently because the clumps shelter deer mice that eat the seeds of searocket. • In Europe, this species is used to make thatch, baskets, chair seats, brooms and mats. • The genus name *Ammophila* means 'sand lover'—and indeed it is.

BLUEJOINT • *Calamagrostis canadensis*

GENERAL: Tufted, coarse, hairless perennial up to 1 m tall, with creeping rhizomes; forms tussocks.

LEAVES: Usually flat, numerous, long, **rather lax, 3–8 mm wide**; collars usually lacking hairs; auricles absent; ligules 3–10 mm long.

INFLORESCENCE: Nodding panicle 10–25 cm long, from narrow and rather dense to loose and relatively open, usually purplish when mature; **lemma with usually straight awn, and numerous callus hairs about as long as lemma**.

ECOLOGY: Moist to wet thickets, meadows, stream-banks, shore-lines, wetlands, and clearings; common but only abundant locally, from low to high elevations.

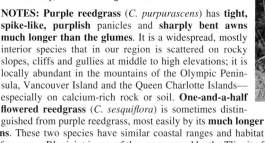

NOTES: Purple reedgrass (*C. purpurascens*) has **tight, spike-like, purplish** panicles and **sharply bent awns much longer than the glumes**. It is a widespread, mostly interior species that in our region is scattered on rocky slopes, cliffs and gullies at middle to high elevations; it is locally abundant in the mountains of the Olympic Peninsula, Vancouver Island and the Queen Charlotte Islands— especially on calcium-rich rock or soil. **One-and-a-half flowered reedgrass** (*C. sesquiflora*) is sometimes distinguished from purple reedgrass, most easily by its **much longer awns**. These two species have similar coastal ranges and habitat preferences. • Bluejoint is one of the grasses used by the Tlingit of Alaska for decorating fine spruce-root baskets. • Bluejoint is a very aggressive colonizer after disturbance. • *Calamagrostis* is from the Latin *calamos*, 'reed,' and *agrostis*, 'grass.' 'Reedgrass' is another common name for species in this genus.

NOOTKA REEDGRASS • *Calamagrostis nutkaensis*

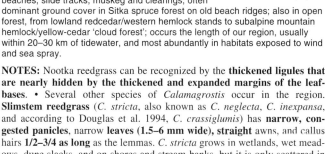

GENERAL: Tufted, robust perennial, hairless, 0.5–1.5 m tall, forming **large, tough clumps but also spreading by short rhizomes**.

LEAVES: Thick, **tough**, flat to folded, usually erect, **6–12 mm wide**; collars hairless; no auricles; **ligules thickened, 2–6 mm long**.

INFLORESCENCE: Panicle, **erect**, 12–30 cm long, narrow, **rather loosely flowered** but with stiff, erect branches, greenish-yellow to purplish; **lemmas with straight or bent awn from about midlength; callus hairs of unequal length, but not more than half as long as lemma**.

ECOLOGY: Exposed coastal headlands, cliffs, beaches, slide tracks, muskeg and clearings; often dominant ground cover in Sitka spruce forest on old beach ridges; also in open forest, from lowland redcedar/western hemlock stands to subalpine mountain hemlock/yellow-cedar 'cloud forest'; occurs the length of our region, usually within 20–30 km of tidewater, and most abundantly in habitats exposed to wind and sea spray.

NOTES: Nootka reedgrass can be recognized by the **thickened ligules that are nearly hidden by the thickened and expanded margins of the leaf-bases**. • Several other species of *Calamagrostis* occur in the region. **Slimstem reedgrass** (*C. stricta*, also known as *C. neglecta*, *C. inexpansa*, and according to Douglas et al. 1994, *C. crassiglumis*) has **narrow, congested panicles**, narrow **leaves (1.5–6 mm wide), straight** awns, and callus hairs **1/2–3/4 as long** as the lemmas. *C. stricta* grows in wetlands, wet meadows, dune slacks, and on shores and stream-banks, but it is only scattered in our region. • Nootka reedgrass was first described from Nootka Sound.

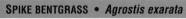

SPIKE BENTGRASS • *Agrostis exarata*

GENERAL: Tufted perennial, 30–120 cm tall; stems erect but sometimes bent at base and rooting from basal nodes.

LEAVES: Flat, rough, **2–10 mm wide**; auricles absent; **ligules 3–8 mm long**, usually somewhat torn at tip.

INFLORESCENCE: Panicle, narrow, tight and spike-like to interrupted and somewhat open, 5–18 cm long; numerous spikelets crowded to base of branches; glumes small, nearly equal, sharp-pointed to awn-tipped; single lemma shorter than glumes, **awnless or awned from above midlength; awns up to 5 mm long**; callus slightly bearded.

ECOLOGY: Common at upper levels of tidal marshes and rocky beaches, wet meadows, river bars, clearings, moist, open ground in general, from sea level to middle elevations.

NOTES: Small-leaved bentgrass (*A. microphylla*) is essentially an **annual** version of *A. exarata*, with a **bent awn 3–7 mm long**; it occurs on moist, open ground at low elevations from the Strait of Georgia area south. **Dune bentgrass** (*A. pallens*) is a species of coastal dunes and sea cliffs from southern Washington to California (rare on the Queen Charlotte Islands and the west coast of Vancouver island), which differs from *A. exarata* in its **narrow, wiry leaves**, its **short (1–3 mm), firm ligules** and **long, slender rhizomes. Northern bentgrass** (*A. mertensii*, also known as *A. borealis*) and **variable bentgrass** (*A. variabilis*) also have tight (but not spike-like) panicles, but they are **smaller (up to 25 cm tall), subalpine to alpine** species with **leaves less than 2 mm wide** and **panicles 2–6 cm long**. Both northern and variable bentgrass are sporadic in the coastal mountains, and they descend to lower elevations on the north coast. • Spike bentgrass is a common and very variable species, ranging from slender plants with narrow leaves and few-flowered panicles to robust plants up to 1 m or more tall. • The species name *exarata* means 'with embossed grooves, engraved,' in reference to the leaves. A 'bentgrass' was any grass that grew on a *bent* or common (i.e., neglected, unbroken ground).

HAIR BENTGRASS • *Agrostis scabra*

GENERAL: Densely tufted perennial with **roughened stems 20–70 m tall**; roots fibrous.

LEAVES: Numerous, fine, short, rough, mainly basal; auricles absent; ligules 2–3 mm long.

INFLORESCENCE: Panicle, large, diffuse, zig-zag, often purplish; **spikelets borne near the branch tips**; glumes equal, small; single lemma delicate, with or without a fine awn; **glumes and panicle branches also roughened**.

ECOLOGY: Dry to wet disturbed areas generally, especially clearings and roadsides; also on dry rocky slopes and gravelly river bars and on rocks near waterfalls; common at low to middle elevations.

NOTES: Idaho bentgrass (*A. idahoensis*) is similarly delicate and tufted, but **only 10–30 cm tall**, and with a **smaller, somewhat contracted panicle**; it occurs in moist openings at middle to subalpine elevations in the mountains, from southern B.C. southwards. **Oregon bentgrass** (*A. oregonensis*) is **30–80 cm tall** with an **open panicle** whose branches, unlike those of *A. scabra*, are **spikelet-bearing to below midlength**. Oregon bentgrass occurs in wet meadows, montane bogs and fens and along streams, at low to middle elevations from Vancouver Island south. Some taxonomists include *A. idahoensis* and *A. oregonensis* within *A. mertensii* (see notes under *A. exarata*, above). • Hair bentgrass is also called 'ticklegrass'; play with the panicle to find out why. The panicle breaks away with age, rolling along the ground like a tumbleweed in the wind. • The species name *scabra* means 'rough, scurfy,' in reference to the feel of the grass.

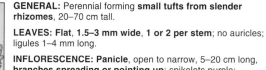

ALASKA BENTGRASS • *Agrostis aequivalvis*

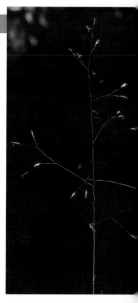

GENERAL: Perennial forming **small tufts from slender rhizomes**, 20–70 cm tall.

LEAVES: Flat, **1.5–3 mm wide, 1 or 2 per stem**; no auricles; ligules 1–4 mm long.

INFLORESCENCE: Panicle, open to narrow, 5–20 cm long, **branches spreading or pointing up**; spikelets purple; **glumes 3–4 mm long**; lemma about as long as glumes, **unawned**; palea nearly as long as lemma.

ECOLOGY: Bogs and open wet forest near the coast; common but not usually abundant at low to middle elevations.

NOTES: Alpine bentgrass (*A. humilis*) also has well-developed paleas (at least half as long as the lemmas). However, it is a **higher-elevation** species of subalpine to alpine meadows, streambanks and lake-shores, although it can descend to middle elevations on the outer coast. Alpine bentgrass is a tufted perennial **smaller (5–15 cm tall)** in stature than Alaska bentgrass; it has short, **mostly basal leaves, narrow, compressed panicles**, and **glumes about 2 mm long**.

COLONIAL BENTGRASS • *Agrostis capillaris*

GENERAL: Perennial, **tufted** but with a **few very short rhizomes**; slender stems 20–50 cm tall.

LEAVES: Flat to folded, 2–5 mm wide; auricles absent; **ligules mostly 1–2 mm long**.

INFLORESCENCE: Panicle, **open, diffuse**, 5–15 cm long; **branches delicate, not spikelet-bearing to the base**; spikelets not crowded, usually purple; glumes slightly unequal in size, pointed at tip; lemma shorter than glumes, awnless or short-awned; palea about half as long as lemma; anthers 1–1.3 mm long.

ECOLOGY: Lawns, fields, roadsides, clearings, moist open ground; widespread at low elevations; common lawn and turf grass, introduced from Europe for pastures and lawns; scattered throughout our region, most abundant in settled areas (e.g., lower Fraser Valley, southeast Vancouver Island, Puget Sound).

NOTES: Colonial bentgrass is also known as *A. tenuis*. • **Creeping bentgrass** (*A. stolonifera*, sometimes also known as *A. alba*) is another widespread turf grass introduced from Europe. It has **stolons but no rhizomes** and **longer (3–6 mm) ligules**, and it occupies moist to wet habitats like lawns, fields, ditches, pond edges, and meadows. **Redtop** (*A. gigantea*, also sometimes called *A. alba*) has **abundant rhizomes but not stolons, ligules 2–6 mm long,** and **densely spikeletted panicles**. It grows in relatively dry fields and waste places and on roadsides. • Colonial bentgrass is a common lawn grass, called 'colonial' because it grows in dense masses. The species name *capillaris* alludes to the thin leaves.

TIMOTHY • *Phleum pratense*

GENERAL: Short-lived perennial that forms large clumps; stems smooth, stiffly erect, up to 1 m tall; **base bulbous** with fibrous roots.

LEAVES: Wide (4–8 mm) and flat, tapering; auricles absent; ligules 2–3 mm long.

INFLORESCENCE: Panicle, very dense, spike-like, cylindrical, many times longer than broad, **up to 10 cm long, less than 1 cm thick;** spikelets crowded, flattened; **glumes with a comb-like fringe of hairs on the keels** and with short, stout, curved awns.

ECOLOGY: Roadsides, pastures, clearings; introduced from Eurasia and naturalized; common from low to middle elevations throughout our region in settled areas.

NOTES: Alpine timothy (*P. alpinum*), a common native grass of **middle- to high-elevation** meadows, heaths and streambanks, is similar but **smaller (to 60 cm tall)** and has a **shorter (less than 5 cm long), thicker panicle**. • Timothy is a palatable, leafy grass, one of the more-important domestic hay grasses in North America, and one of our more-common causes of hay fever. • Timothy is named for Timothy Hanson, the 19th-century U.S. agrologist who brought the grass from New York and championed its use in domestic pastures. It is known as 'real hay' in the Pemberton Valley of B.C. among some of the Stl'atl'imx elders. • *Phleum* is from *pleos*, the Greek name for a reedy grass.

SHORTAWN FOXTAIL • *Alopecurus aequalis*

GENERAL: Tufted perennial, erect or spreading; stems 15–60 cm tall, often with a curved base underwater.

LEAVES: Flat, 1–4 mm wide, lax when submerged; auricles absent; ligules 4–8 mm long, pointed.

INFLORESCENCE: Slender, spike-like panicle, 2–7 cm long, **about 4 mm thick,** pale green; **glumes about 2 mm long,** long-hairy; **lemma with short (1–2 mm) awn** attached near middle.

ECOLOGY: Stream-banks, roadside ditches, shallow ponds (where often submerged), wet clearings; common at low to middle elevations.

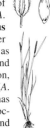

NOTES: Water foxtail (*A. geniculatus*) also has long-hairy glumes about 2 mm long, but its lemmas have **longer awns (4–5 mm long)** that are **bent** and **attached near the base,** and that **stick out** from the spike-like panicle. This species has been widely introduced from Eurasia along our coast, where it occupies habitats similar to those of *A. aequalis* but usually near settlements, and it is more common in the southern half of our region, ranging sporadically north to Juneau. **Meadow foxtail** (*A. pratensis*), another European introduction, is a stout, somewhat **stoloniferous perennial 30–90 cm tall**, with spike-like panicles much like those of water foxtail, but with **larger (about 5 mm long), long-hairy glumes,** as well as lemmas with **long, bent awns.** Meadow foxtail grows in wet meadows and fields, on roadsides and in swampy places; it is scattered but locally common, mostly in the southern half of our region. **Carolina meadow foxtail** (*A. carolinianus*) is an **annual,** smaller than the above 3 species, and it has spikelets like those of water foxtail, including the bent, protruding awn. It occurs sporadically in the region, mainly in the Strait of Georgia–Puget Sound area and south, and it grows in vernally moist, disturbed habitats, old fields, pastures and clearings. • **Rabbitfoot grass** (*Polypogon monspeliensis*) is a **tufted annual** with a dense, **bristly, spike-like panicle** that is tawny when mature and looks **like a bottlebrush.** Both glumes and lemma of rabbitfoot grass are awned, and its appearance and habitat preferences suggest *Alopecurus.* It is an introduction from Europe that now occurs scattered from northern southeast Alaska south (more common from Vancouver Island south) in waste places, ditches, clearings and vernal pools.

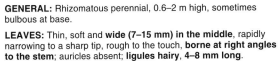

WOOD REEDGRASS • *Cinna latifolia*
NODDING WOOD-REED

GENERAL: Rhizomatous perennial, 0.6–2 m high, sometimes bulbous at base.

LEAVES: Thin, soft and **wide (7–15 mm) in the middle**, rapidly narrowing to a sharp tip, rough to the touch, **borne at right angles to the stem**; auricles absent; **ligules hairy, 4–8 mm long**.

INFLORESCENCE: Open, drooping panicle 15–30 cm long; 1-flowered spikelets detach whole at maturity leaving a bare axis; lemmas with a short, straight awn or awnless.

ECOLOGY: Moist woods, meadows, wet areas along streams and moist disturbed areas; widespread and often abundant at low to middle elevations.

NOTES: Wood reedgrass is a tall, sweet-smelling grass with short, wide leaves and prominent ligules; it increases tremendously on disturbed sites. • The Tlingit used this grass to decorate spruce root baskets. • *Cinna* (from the Greek *kinni*) is an ancient name for some grass.

COMMON SWEETGRASS • *Hierochloe odorata*

GENERAL: Erect perennial; **stems often solitary, usually purplish-based, 30–60 cm tall**; spreading from **long rhizomes; sweet-smelling**.

LEAVES: Stem leaves short and broad **(to 8 mm wide)**; non-flowering shoots often have long blades; auricles absent; ligules 3–5 mm long.

INFLORESCENCE: Panicle, open, pyramidal in shape; spikelets lustrous golden-yellow, tulip-shaped; glumes broad, longer than lemmas; lemmas hairy, **awnless**.

ECOLOGY: Moist meadows, lake-shores, stream-banks, streamside areas, forest openings, beaches, upper parts of tidal marshes; widely scattered from low to middle elevations in the northern part of our region and at middle to high elevations in the southern part.

NOTES: 2 other species of *Hierochloe* occur in the region. **Alpine sweetgrass** (*H. alpina*) is a **clump-forming alpine** species that has **distinctly awned lemmas**; it occasionally occurs in the coastal mountains of the northern part of our region. **Western sweetgrass** (*H. occidentalis*) has **stems 60–90 cm tall** and **leaves 7–12 mm wide**; it occurs in open forest from southwestern Washington to northern California. • The sweet, lingering fragrance of this grass is due to the presence of coumarin, which was formerly used as a flavouring agent. This grass was well-appreciated and highly respected among aboriginal North Americans. It was often obtained through trade from the Blackfoot and other plains groups by B.C. aboriginal peoples. Today, many people use it as a cleansing and purifying incense on ceremonial occasions. • In northern Europe, common sweetgrass was scattered in front of churches on saints' days. • *Hierochloe* is a combination of the Greek *hieros*, 'sacred,' and *chloe*, 'grass': 'holy grass' is another common name for the genus. Both common names and the species name result from the sweet smell of this species.

SWEET VERNALGRASS • *Anthoxanthum odoratum*

GENERAL: Tufted, sweet-scented perennial; stems hairless, 30–60 cm tall.

LEAVES: Flat, somewhat hairy at least towards the base, 3–7 mm wide; short (about 1 mm) hairy auricles present; ligules 2–3 mm long.

INFLORESCENCE: Panicle, narrow, spike-like, asymmetrical, tawny, 2–9 cm long; glumes sharp-pointed, longer than lemmas; **sterile lemmas 2, about 3 mm long, hairy, awned**; fertile lemma firm, hairless, about 2 mm long.

ECOLOGY: Lawns, pastures, meadows, roadsides; also in open forest, usually with Garry oak or Douglas-fir; scattered over much of the length of our region, rare in the northern half (where usually near settlements), more abundant in drier climates of the southern half, Strait of Georgia area to Willamette Valley.

NOTES: Annual vernalgrass (*A. puellii*, also known as *A. aristatum*) is a **smaller annual** species, also introduced, that grows in fields and waste places from the Strait of Georgia area south, typically in dry areas. • Sweet vernalgrass is a Eurasian species introduced to much of temperate North America. A grass of early spring, it usually withers by midsummer. Sweet vernalgrass was formerly used as a component of cured hay because of the sweet smell, which comes from a compound called 'coumarin.' If coumarin-containing hay rots, the coumarin is converted to a chemical that inhibits blood clotting. • *A. odoratum* is called 'sweet vernalgrass' because of its smell and early flowering. *Anthoxanthum* is from the Greek *anthos* ('flower') and *xanthos* ('yellow'), alluding to the tawny colour of the mature inflorescence.

REED CANARY GRASS • *Phalaris arundinacea*

GENERAL: Robust perennial, 0.7–2 m tall, with **long, scaly, pinkish rhizomes**; stems hollow.

LEAVES: Flat, 5–15 mm wide, roughened; sheaths open, margins overlapping; ligules 4–10 mm long, usually tattered and turned backward, slightly hairy; no auricles.

INFLORESCENCE: Panicle, compact (at least initially), to 25 cm long; **spikelets 3 flowered, crowded on side branches** of the inflorescence; glumes about the same size, 4–5 mm long, minutely hairy; **fertile lemma to 4 mm long, shiny, flax-like**; sterile lemmas to 2 mm long, brownish, hairy.

ECOLOGY: Wet places in disturbed sites, including clearings, ditches (especially along roads), marshy spots and depressions, stream-banks and along edges of wetlands; scattered and often locally abundant, more common in the southern half of our region; at low to middle elevations around areas of human habitation or agricultural activity.

NOTES: The Halq'emeylem and probably other Salish groups used the stems for decorating baskets. The stems were cut while still pliable and green in May and early June (when the wild roses bloom). They were cut into even lengths and soaked in boiling water, then dried for several days in the sun to bleach them white. They were split, soaked again and used like the stems of common reed (p. 371) to superimpose white patterns on the weave of split-root baskets. This process is described in Turner (1992).
• It is not clear whether reed canary grass is entirely introduced or whether it is indigenous in parts of the coast and has extended its range through human influence. • *Phalaris* may be called 'canary grass' either because *P. canariensis* is the source of canary seed, or because the genus was first described from the Canary Islands.

ORCHARD GRASS • *Dactylis glomerata*

GENERAL: Strongly tufted perennial, from short rhizomes; hollow stems to 1.5 m tall.

LEAVES: Sheaths split open partway; **blades flat**, hairless, roughened, **3–10 mm wide**, early growth light bluish-green; ligules 3–7 mm long, somewhat hairy; auricles absent.

INFLORESCENCE: 1-sided panicle 3–15 cm long, the branches ascending to erect; **3- to 5-flowered spikelets** flattened and borne at the end of short, stiff branches in **crowded asymmetric heads**; glumes 4–6 mm long, with a soft awn-tip, **outer glume stiffly hairy on the keel; lemmas 5–8 mm long, stiffly hairy on the keel**, with a soft awn-tip to 1 mm long.

ECOLOGY: Disturbed sites (especially roadsides) and pastures; widespread and often locally abundant at low to middle elevations; throughout our region but most common in the southern half, near areas of human habitation or disturbance.

NOTES: Orchard grass could be confused with reed canary grass. **Reed canary grass** usually has **wider leaves** and a **more narrow, pointed inflorescence**, and it usually grows in **wetter habitats** than does orchard grass. • Orchard grass was introduced from Eurasia. It is cultivated for hay and is used in grass-seeding mixtures on clearings and along road cuts. • The genus name is from the Greek *dactylos* ('finger'), perhaps in reference to the stiff branches of the panicle. It is called 'orchard grass' because it can be found growing in orchards under the drip from the trees.

COMMON REED • *Phragmites australis*

GENERAL: Stout, tall, **reed-like** perennial, spreading by rhizomes; stems hollow, erect, **2–3 m tall**.

LEAVES: Flat, 1–4 cm wide and 20–40 cm long, stiff, with **loose sheaths that twist in the wind, aligning the leaves on 1 side of the stem**; no auricles; **ligules 1.5–3 mm long, the top portion a fringe of hairs**.

INFLORESCENCE: Panicle, **large, feathery**, purple in flower, straw-coloured to greyish in fruit; spikelets 3–6 flowered; glumes unequal in size; **lemmas longer than the glumes, some awned and with numerous long, silky hairs** from near their bases at the axis of the spikelet.

ECOLOGY: Around pools, sloughs, springs, sluggish creeks and other permanent water bodies, sometimes at the edge of salt marshes, often forms dense fringing colonies; at low elevations.

NOTES: Common reed is also known as *P. communis*. • This is a widespread species, occurring throughout temperate and many tropical regions. It forms large, floating masses in some places, and it is sometimes harvested. Common reed is used in many parts of the world for thatch, mats, insulation, fuel, fertilizer and mulch. Its pulp is used to make paper, cellophane, cardboard and fibre board. *Phragmites* stems have been used to make pen points for calligraphy. The grains were consumed by North American aboriginal people, and the young shoots by the Japanese. • 600-year-old cigarettes found in the Red Bow Cliff Dwellings in Arizona were constructed of common reed stems stuffed with tobacco. The reed 'barrels' did not burn and were re-used.

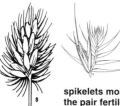

HEDGEHOG DOGTAIL • *Cynosurus echinatus*

GENERAL: Tufted annual, hairless; stems 20–50 cm tall, with inflated sheaths.

LEAVES: Flat, 2–5 mm wide; no auricles; **ligules prominent, 2–7 mm long**, rounded and ragged at tip.

INFLORESCENCE: Panicle, dense, more than 1 cm thick, **spike-like, bristly, sausage-shaped; spikelets mostly in pairs** on very short branches; **one spikelet of the pair fertile, the other flattened and fan-like**, consisting of glumes and sterile lemmas; glumes and lemmas of sterile spikelets have long-pointy tips; fertile spikelets have awn-tipped glumes 5–6 mm long and lemmas about the same length with **awns 3–10 mm long**.

ECOLOGY: Clearings, roadsides, meadows and dry forest edges (Garry oak, Douglas-fir and arbutus forest); scattered, locally abundant at low elevations in the drier, southern parts of our region.

NOTES: Hedgehog dogtail is a weedy, European species well established in parts of North America, including the Pacific Northwest. • **Crested dogtail** (*Cynosurus cristatus*) is a **perennial** species with a **thinner (less than 1 cm thick) inflorescence**. It is a Eurasian species that also occurs fairly frequently in fields and clearings in the drier southern parts of our region. • The common name derives from a translation of the Latin *echinos* (hedgehog), *kuon* (dog), and *oura* (tail), because the prickly spike is fringed mostly on 1 side like the tails of some dogs.

ALASKA ONIONGRASS • *Melica subulata*

GENERAL: Tufted perennial but also with short, thick rhizomes that bear **clusters of bulb-like stem bases**; stems 30–100 cm tall, spreading-hairy on the leaf sheaths.

LEAVES: Flat, thin, 3–7 mm wide, hairy on upper surfaces; no auricles; ligules 1–5 mm long, hairless, split or jagged at tips.

INFLORESCENCE: Panicle, narrow, 12–20 cm long, the relatively few branches single or in pairs, ascending to erect; **spikelets narrow, 12–20 mm long, loosely 2–5 flowered, tawny or purplish-bronze**, with the uppermost floret sterile; glumes narrow, of unequal length, faintly nerved, shorter than spikelet, the largest about 8 mm long; **lemmas sharp-pointed but unawned, 9–13 mm long, 7-nerved, hairy on the nerves and margins**.

ECOLOGY: Dry to moist meadows, open to shady slopes, stream-banks, floodplain forest; from near sea level to middle elevations; widespread but seldom abundant; can be one of the major grasses in park-like, floodplain, Sitka spruce forests with grassy ground cover, as on the Queen Charlotte Islands, some parts of Vancouver Island and the Olympic Peninsula.

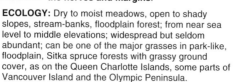

NOTES: Alaska oniongrass looks somewhat like a brome or fescue, but it has unawned lemmas, papery glumes rounded on the back and nearly closed leaf sheaths. • **Geyer's melic** (*M. geyeri*) is like Alaska oniongrass but has a **more-open panicle** and **smaller, mostly hairless lemmas;** it occurs in the coastal mountains from northwest Oregon to central California. • **Harford's melic** (*M. harfordii*) occurs in our region, but it has **awned lemmas** and it ranges from southern Vancouver Island and the Olympic Peninsula south to northern California. • Alaska oniongrass is not known to have been used by aboriginal peoples, but it has a bulb-like corm which is edible and pleasantly nutty tasting. • The name 'oniongrass' comes from the swollen stem-bases resembling onion bulbs. *Melica* is from an ancient Latin name for some grass.

NODDING SEMAPHORE GRASS • *Pleuropogon refractus*

GENERAL: Perennials in small clusters from rhizomes; stems 1–1.5 m tall; sheaths closed except for upper 2–7 cm.

LEAVES: Flat, soft, 3–7 mm wide, long but uppermost often reduced to about 1 cm in length; no auricles; ligules 1.5–3.5 mm long, minutely fringed.

INFLORESCENCE: Raceme (spikelets stalked but on a single axis), 10–25 cm long; **spikelets 5–12, widely spaced, becoming down-turned or drooping**, loosely 7–11 flowered, up to 3 cm long; **glumes papery**, unequal in size, shorter than spikelets, the larger ones somewhat lobed at tip; **lemmas 7–8 mm long, prominently parallel-nerved**, often 3 lobed at tip, **with 3–10 mm long awns**.

ECOLOGY: Stream-banks, edges of bogs and swamps, wet meadows, moist shady forest, from near sea level to nearly subalpine elevations; scattered, locally common.

NOTES: Nodding semaphore grass looks somewhat like a brome, but its inflorescence, with the spikelets angled downward and stalked but on a single axis, is distinctive. • Nodding semaphore grass is a plant of seasonally wet, partially shaded sites. Although considered uncommon, it is widely distributed in the southern half of our region within its rather narrow habitat requirements. Despite its wide range, it is not often found, and it usually occurs as small colonies of individuals, often associated with species of wider ecological amplitude such as red alder, salmonberry, lady fern, Sitka spruce and sword fern. • The nodding inflorescence suggests semaphore signals. *Pleuropogon* means 'side-beard,' from some species having awns at the base of the palea.

ALASKA BROME • *Bromus sitchensis*

GENERAL: Stout perennial, 0.5–1.8 m tall, **hairless**; rhizomes lacking.

LEAVES: Flat, thin, long, **7–15 mm wide, hairless to sparsely hairy above**; no auricles; ligules 2–8 mm long.

INFLORESCENCE: Panicle, large, 10–35 cm long, the long **branches erect to spreading or drooping and bearing spikelets toward ends**; spikelets large, 2–4 cm long, **strongly flattened**, 4–10 flowered; glumes shorter than lemmas, awnless; lemmas keeled (rather than rounded) on back, hairless to finely hairy, with 5–12 mm long awns.

ECOLOGY: Moist to dry meadows, stream-banks, sea beaches, bluffs, talus slopes and slide tracks, also open forest; common from the lowlands to subalpine elevations.

NOTES: Pacific brome (*B. pacificus*) is similar to *B. sitchensis*, but has **soft-hairy leaf sheaths and blades, hairy lemmas**, and **hairy ligules 3–5 mm long**. Pacific brome is less common; it grows in moist meadows, on beaches and in open forest, mostly at low elevations and along the immediate coast, but extending inland in the Puget Lowland. **California brome** (*Bromus carinatus*, also known as *B. marginatus*) is a variable species common in a variety of open habitats, mostly in the southern half of our region. It resembles California and Pacific brome, but it has **narrow panicles, narrower leaves (usually much less than 10 mm wide)** and panicle branches that are **spikelet-bearing to near the base. Smooth brome** (*B. inermis*) resembles California brome but it lacks strongly compressed spikelets (its **lemmas are rounded rather than keeled on the back**). Smooth brome occurs the length of our region, scattered but locally abundant in fields, meadows and other disturbed sites, often as a forage species in hayfields and pastures. There is some dispute about whether it is a native or introduced species, or both. • *Bromus* is an ancient name for an oat, indicating some food value. The grass is sometimes called 'oatgrass.' It is also called 'lobgrass,' as the flower heads (panicles) loll or *lob*, meaning 'hang about' to 1 side.

COLUMBIA BROME • *Bromus vulgaris*

GENERAL: Perennial, tall (60–120 cm), slender, loosely tufted; **stems often with hairy nodes**.

LEAVES: Lax, flat, 5–10 mm wide, and usually hairy on at least one surface; no auricles; **ligules 3–5 mm long**.

INFLORESCENCE: Open, drooping panicle with slender branches; few-flowered spikelets; **lemmas hairy only on margins; awn more than 5 mm long**.

ECOLOGY: Shaded to open forest, openings, thickets, moist to dry banks, also subalpine meadows and dry rocky slopes; common at low to subalpine elevations.

NOTES: Columbia brome is very similar to **fringed brome** (*B. ciliatus*), which has **shorter (2–4 mm) awns** and **shorter (about 1 mm) ligules**. Fringed brome grows in similar habitats at middle elevations in the B.C. Coast Mountains, usually along the eastern boundary of our region. **Orcutt's brome** (*B. orcuttianus*) is also very similar to Columbia brome, but it has **narrower** panicles with short, **stiffly spreading** branches and occurs occasionally on fairly dry, often wooded sites in the Oregon and southern Washington **Cascades**.

SOFT BROME • *Bromus hordeaceus*
SOFT CHESS

GENERAL: Annual, in **small tufts**, 20–80 cm tall, **usually soft-hairy throughout**.

LEAVES: Flat, 2–5 mm wide; no auricles; ligules about 1 mm long, usually hairy.

INFLORESCENCE: Panicle, erect, narrow, rather dense, 3–10 cm long; spikelets 5–9 flowered, usually **plump and fuzzy**; **lemmas rounded at tip**, 6–9 mm long, prominently nerved, with **awns 6–10 mm long**.

ECOLOGY: Fields, roadsides, clearings, rocky slopes, dry open forest, at low elevations; common in the southern half of our region, especially in areas of drier climate; scattered northwards on the Queen Charlotte Islands and in southeast Alaska, near settlements.

NOTES: Soft brome is also known as *B. mollis*. • This weedy European species is probably the most common and widespread of several introduced, annual brome grasses on the Northwest Coast. **Barren brome** (*B. sterilis*) is one of these weedy annuals, common in the Strait of Georgia–Puget Sound area in disturbed areas and rocky forest openings. Barren brome has an **open panicle** and lemmas with **sharp tips** and **long (2–3 cm) awns**. **Rip-gut brome** (*B. rigidus*) is similar in general appearance and habitat, but it has **bigger spikelets** and even **longer (3–6 cm) awns**. **Cheatgrass** (*B. tectorum*) resembles barren brome and rip-gut brome, but it has **smaller spikelets (less than 2.5 cm long)**. It is less frequent in our region than the other annual bromes, but it is locally common in the Willamette valley and the Strait of Georgia–Puget Sound area. • The name 'chess' is another word for a 'darnel,' a grass growing in a wheat field. The species name suggests a similarity to barley (*Hordeum*).

BARREN FESCUE • *Vulpia bromoides*

GENERAL: Slender **tufted annual, essentially hairless**, 10–50 cm tall; **stems grooved lengthwise.**

LEAVES: Folded to inrolled, narrow, about 1 mm wide; no auricles; ligules to 0.6 mm long.

INFLORESCENCE: Panicle, narrow, 3–10 cm long, **with short, erect branches**; spikelets 3–6 flowered; glumes unequal in size, the shorter 3–6 mm long; lemmas hairless, about 6 mm long, with **fairly long awns (6–13 mm long).**

ECOLOGY: Rock outcrops, grassy bluffs, rocky slopes, open forest, roadsides, and relatively dry, disturbed areas at low to sometimes middle elevations; common, locally abundant from the Strait of Georgia through the southern half of our region, scattered northwards.

NOTES: Barren fescue is also known as *Festuca bromoides* and *F. dertonensis.* • The 4 weedy, annual fescues that occur in our region are considered by many taxonomists (including Douglas et al. 1994) to belong to the genus *Vulpia*, and we have followed that treatment. All 4 species occupy similar habitats. **Small fescue** (*V. microstachys*) is much like barren fescue but its leaf sheaths are **often hairy**, and its lowest panicle branches are **spreading or bent downwards. Foxtail fescue** (*Vulpia myuros*, which includes *V. megalura*) has tight, narrow panicles **10–20 cm long**, with the shorter glumes averaging only **1.5 mm long**, and with **long-awned (about 13 mm)** lemmas. **Six-weeks fescue** (*V. octoflora*) also has long, narrow panicles, but its awns are fairly **short (1–7 mm long).** Barren fescue is introduced from Europe, but the other 3 weedy annual fescues are native. *V. myuros* is in the strict sense European, but *V. megalura* is native (apparently). • *Vulpia* is named after J.S. Vulpius (1760–1846), a German botanist. The common name suggests *V. bromoides* is like a sterile fescue (*Festuca*), and the species name that it is like a brome (*Bromus*).

WESTERN FESCUE • *Festuca occidentalis*

GENERAL: Tufted perennial, with a few slender stems 25–100 cm tall.

LEAVES: Inrolled, **hair-like, lax, soft**, mostly basal, **in large tufts**; no auricles; ligules to 0.5 mm long, fringed at tip.

INFLORESCENCE: Panicle, open, 7–20 cm long, usually **drooping at the top**; spikelets 3–5 flowered; **lemmas about 5 mm long**, tapering to a slender **awn 4–10 mm long**.

ECOLOGY: Meadows, open forest, forest openings and edges, rocky slopes, clearings; common at low to middle elevations.

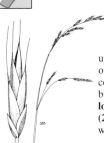

NOTES: Idaho fescue (*F. idahoensis*) is a densely tufted perennial with narrow leaves; it occurs in **similar but drier habitats** (and up to subalpine elevations) from the Strait of Georgia area south to California. It could be confused with western fescue, but it has fairly **tight, narrow panicles, longer (5–7.5 mm) lemmas and shorter (2–5 mm) awns.** • *Festuca* is an ancient word meaning 'a straw' or 'a mere nothing.'

RED FESCUE • *Festuca rubra*

GENERAL: Loosely tufted perennial, **usually with rhizomes**; stems 20–100 cm tall, often bent at the **reddish-purple base**; hairless to soft-hairy on leaf sheaths that disintegrate with age to brown, curled fibres.

LEAVES: Folded-inrolled, narrow (about 1.5 mm wide), hairless; no auricles; ligules short, less than 0.5 mm long.

INFLORESCENCE: Panicle, usually contracted and narrow, the branches erect to ascending, 3–20 cm long; spikelets often **reddish-purple or glaucous-green; lemmas hairless to hairy, 5–7 mm long,** with **short (1–3 mm) awns.**

ECOLOGY: Tidal marshes, beaches, stream-banks, mountain meadows, river flats, clearings, roadsides, fields; common from sea level to high elevations.

NOTES: Rocky Mountain fescue (*Festuca saxomontana*, sometimes called *F. ovina* in part) is a tufted, narrow-leaved perennial that somewhat resembles red fescue but **lacks rhizomes** and has **3–5 mm long**, short-awned lemmas. Rocky Mountain fescue occurs sporadically on relatively dry outcrops and rocky slopes and at forest edges in the Strait of Georgia–Puget Sound area and north in the Coast Mountains along the eastern edge of our region. In the alpine zone, it is largely replaced by **alpine fescue** (*F. brachyphylla*), a **dwarf, tufted species 5–25 cm tall.** • Red fescue is a widespread and very variable species. Apparently this species was (and still is in some spots) a major component of the natural vegetation in low elevation grasslands and mountain meadows, but now it is also common in many disturbed sites. • Many cultivars of red fescue have been developed for horticultural and agricultural purposes, and they are widely used in lawns, as forage and in grass-seeding mixtures for erosion control. • Red fescue is so-called because of the reddish bases of the stems and the often reddish spikelets.

BEARDED FESCUE • *Festuca subulata*

GENERAL: Tufted perennial, 50–100 cm tall; **stems leafy** to near the panicle.

LEAVES: Flat, lax, hairless, 3–10 mm wide; no auricles; ligules 0.3–0.7 mm long, fringed at tip with tiny hairs.

INFLORESCENCE: Panicle, open, loose, 10–35 cm long; **branches in 2s or 3s, drooping;** spikelets loosely 3–5 flowered; lemmas about 7 mm long, with tips narrowing to **5–20 mm long awns.**

ECOLOGY: Moist forest, forest glades and edges, riverbanks, meadows, clearings; common and locally abundant (e.g., in floodplain forests) from low to middle elevations, more common on Vancouver Island and the Queen Charlotte Islands than on the adjacent mainland.

NOTES: Crinkle-awn fescue (*F. subuliflora*) resembles bearded fescue, but it often has **hairy collars and hairy upper-leaf surfaces**; as well, its **ligules are distinctly fringed at the tip** with coarse hairs, and the **10–15 mm long awn is often kinked and twisted.** Crinkle-awn fescue grows in dense to open forest, glades and meadows, in shallowly rooted, loose tufts in rich, loamy soil. It occurs sporadically on Vancouver Island and the Gulf Islands and south at low to middle elevations to northern California. 2 introduced, large, perennial, European fescues with **flat, wide (mostly wider than 4 mm) leaves** occur in fields, meadows, roadsides and other disturbed areas in our region, especially from southwestern B.C. south: **tall fescue** (*F. arundinacea*) and **meadow fescue** (*F. pratensis*) both have **well-developed auricles**, but those of **tall fescue** are **fringed** with coarse hairs. • The species name suggests the lemmas are 'subulate' (awl-shaped).

ANNUAL BLUEGRASS • *Poa annua*

GENERAL: Annual, hairless, rooting at the nodes and **forming small mats; stems usually spreading or flattened,** 5–20 cm tall.

LEAVES: Usually folded, soft, 1–3 mm wide, hairless; no auricles; ligules about 1 mm long.

INFLORESCENCE: Panicle, usually pyramid-shaped, open, 3–8 cm long; branches smooth; spikelets 3–6 flowered, 4–6 mm long; lemmas about 3.5 mm long, distinctly 5-nerved, **hairy on the lower part of the nerves, but lacking cobwebby hairs at base.**

ECOLOGY: Lawns, fields, gardens, waste places; very common in disturbed, open habitats at low elevations.

NOTES: Howell's bluegrass (*Poa howellii*) is a **native annual** species, **erect and taller (40–80 cm)** than annual bluegrass, from which it also differs in its **rough panicle** branches and **lemmas that are finely hairy** over much of their surface and often have **cobwebby hairs at the base.** Howell's bluegrass is a species of meadows, dry rocky slopes and open woodland (often with Garry oak); it is scattered at low elevations in drier climate areas of the southern part of our region, from the Strait of Georgia–Puget Sound south. • *Poa* is a difficult genus taxonomically, and some of the more than 15 species that occur in our region are difficult to tell apart. • The bluegrasses rank high both as forage plants for wild and domestic animals, and for cultivated pasture and turf. • Annual bluegrass is a widely established Eurasian species that can be a troublesome weed in gardens and lawns. • The bluish-green colour of the stems of *Poa* species gives rise to the name 'bluegrass.'

SEASHORE BLUEGRASS • *Poa macrantha*
DUNE BLUEGRASS

GENERAL: Perennial, with **extensively creeping rhizomes and long runners creeping over the sand;** stems erect from curved base, usually hairless, **15–40 cm tall;** plants with separate sexes.

LEAVES: Inrolled, stiff, in dense basal tufts, up to 3 mm wide; no auricles; **ligules 1–1.5 mm long, thick, very hairy.**

INFLORESCENCE: Panicle, compact, at times dense and spike-like, 4–12 cm long; spikelets 5 flowered, about 12 mm long; **lemmas hairy on the keel and marginal nerves, 8–10 mm long.**

ECOLOGY: Coastal sand dunes; sporadic, but common in suitable habitat; on the outer coast as well as on beaches of the Strait of Georgia–Puget Sound.

NOTES: Seashore bluegrass is also known as *P. douglasii* ssp. *macrantha.* • **Little beach bluegrass** (*P. confinis*) is similar to seashore bluegrass in its strongly rhizomatous habit, habitat (coastal dunes and beaches) and distribution. It differs from seashore bluegrass in its **more-slender** stature, **shorter (1.5–4 cm long) panicle,** and much **smaller (2–4 mm long) lemmas. Eminent bluegrass** (*P. eminens*) is a **robust** species of salt marshes and gravelly beaches. It is **50–130 cm tall** and has **leaves 5–10 mm wide,** compact, elliptic **panicles 9–25 cm long,** and **spikelets 7–12 mm long.** It ranges from Kitimat/Douglas Channel, B.C., north through coastal Alaska. • Seashore bluegrass is one of the best native dune-stabilizing plants. • The species name *macrantha* emphasizes the large flowers.

KENTUCKY BLUEGRASS • *Poa pratensis*

GENERAL: Perennial, hairless, erect, 30–100 cm tall, with **long creeping rhizomes**, forming a dense sod.

LEAVES: Flat to folded, 2–4 mm wide, numerous, with distinct boat-shaped tips; no auricles; **ligules 1–3 mm long**.

INFLORESCENCE: Panicle open, **pyramid-shaped**, tending to be curved one-sided when mature, **usually with 3–5 branches at each joint**; spikelets relatively large, 3–5 flowered; **lemmas about 3.5 mm long, with basal cobwebby hairs**.

ECOLOGY: Introduced and widely established (although some phases of this species could be native) in meadows, pastures, clearings, roadsides, thickets and open forest from low to middle elevations; common at least near settlements.

NOTES: Lax-flowered bluegrass (*P. laxiflora*) is somewhat similar, but it has longer upper leaves and sparsely flowered panicles with **usually 2 branches per joint and drooping** lower panicle branches. Lax-flowered bluegrass is a native species of moist, shady forest glades, edges and rocky slopes, scattered at mostly low elevations from southeast Alaska to northern Oregon; it is fairly common and locally abundant on the Queen Charlotte Islands. **Bog bluegrass** (*P. leptocoma*), a native species of **high-elevation** stream-banks, bogs, meadows, rocky ridges and gullies, differs in that it is **tufted and lacks rhizomes**. • Kentucky bluegrass is an extensively used lawn and pasture grass, highly tolerant of close grazing and mowing. On the coast, Kentucky bluegrass seems to be represented by Eurasian subspecies introduced for lawns and pastures. • Kentucky bluegrass is the state flower of Kentucky, 'the bluegrass state.' Mandolin player Bill Monroe, a Kentucky native, named his band the 'Bluegrass Boys,' and the fast and furious country-tinged music they play has come to be called 'bluegrass music.'

FOWL BLUEGRASS • *Poa palustris*

GENERAL: Tall (40–120 cm), **loosely tufted** perennial, with fibrous roots; stems usually curved and purplish at base, sometimes spreading horizontally like stolons.

LEAVES: Flat or folded, soft, slender (1.5–3 mm wide) and boat-shaped at tips; auricles absent; **ligules 2–5 mm long**.

INFLORESCENCE: Panicle, **open, loose**, 10–30 cm long, with **fine-spreading branches; lower branches in whorls of 4 or 5**; lemmas usually bronze at tip, **cobwebby at base, about 2.5 mm long**.

ECOLOGY: Widespread in wetlands, meadows, streamside sloughs and levees, moist forest, wet ditches and clearings; at low to middle elevations.

NOTES: Fowl bluegrass is an introduced Eurasian species. • **Bulbous bluegrass** (*P. bulbosa*, **inset photo**) is another introduced, weedy perennial, but it has **florets modified** into long, usually **purplish bulb-like** structures. Bulbous bluegrass is common in disturbed, relatively dry habitats at low elevations in the southern half of our region, especially in the Strait of Georgia–Puget Sound area and south.

ARCTIC BLUEGRASS • *Poa arctica*

GENERAL: Loosely tufted, with **creeping rhizomes**; stems 10–60 cm tall, often purplish and curved at base.

LEAVES: Mostly basal, **flat or folded**, 2–4 mm wide, tips boat-shaped; auricles absent; ligules 1–3 mm long.

INFLORESCENCE: Open, pyramidal panicle, 5–10 cm long; spikelets large, often purplish, 3–5 flowered; lemmas usually with **tuft of cobwebby hairs at base.**

ECOLOGY: Common in high-elevation meadows and tundra, on rocky ridges and scree and along stream edges; occurs the length of our region but more inland, not so much along the outer coastal mountains, except from northern southeast Alaska west to the Aleutians.

NOTES: Arctic bluegrass is a variable species that has been divided into several varieties. It is called *P. grayana* by some taxonomists. It is very similar in appearance to some forms of Kentucky bluegrass but it differs in habitat and has **1 or 2 panicle branches per node and hairier lemmas**. • **Alpine bluegrass** (*P. alpina*) and narrow-flowered bluegrass (*P. stenantha*) are 2 other high-elevation bluegrasses that might be encountered. Both **lack rhizomes and cobwebby hairs** at the bases of the lemmas, but **alpine bluegrass** has **short, flat, mostly basal leaves 2–5 mm wide** and **fat, pear-shaped spikelets**, while **narrow-flowered bluegrass** has **narrow (1–2 mm wide), soft, lax leaves** and **narrow oblong-elliptic spikelets**. Both species occur the length of the B.C. coastal mountains and extend into the Cascade Mountains, but narrow-flowered bluegrass is the more coastal of the 2, and it descends to low elevations along the Alaska coast. **Bog bluegrass** (*P. leptocoma*) also occurs at high elevations; it is tufted but does have **cobwebby hairs** at the base of the lemmas and an **open, spreading panicle** (see notes under Kentucky bluegrass, p. 378).

NORTHERN MANNAGRASS • *Glyceria borealis*

GENERAL: Aquatic (usually) perennial, up to 1 m high, loosely tufted from creeping rhizomes.

LEAVES: Flat or folded, sometimes floating, **usually 2–5 mm wide**; no auricles; **ligules 5–10 mm long**.

INFLORESCENCE: Panicle, **long and narrow**, up to 40 cm long, **with ascending branches**; spikelets long (10–12 mm), **cylindrical**, many-flowered; **lemmas firm, 3–4 mm long, with 7 prominent veins**.

ECOLOGY: Wetlands (except bogs), stream-banks, lakeshores; often found in standing water; scattered, locally abundant in suitable habitats at low to middle elevations, but not on the outer coast.

NOTES: Slender-spiked mannagrass (*G. leptostachya*) and **western mannagrass** (*G. occidentalis*) are 2 other species in our region that have narrow panicles and long, cylindrical spikelets. **Slender-spiked mannagrass** has lemmas about the same length as those of northern mannagrass, but its spikelets are longer (12–18 mm) and its leaves are minutely roughened on the lower surface. **Western mannagrass** has **longer lemmas (5–6 mm long)**. Both slender-spiked mannagrass and western mannagrass are uncommon at low elevations along the coast from southeast Alaska and the Queen Charlotte Islands south to California, in swamps, marshes, wet meadows and along lake-shores and stream-banks. • Both the Latin *glyceria* (from the Greek *glyceros*, 'sweet') and the common name 'mannagrass' refer to the sweet taste of the grain.

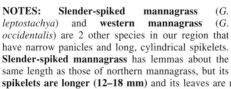
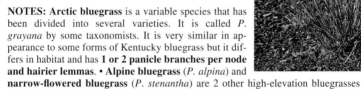

TALL MANNAGRASS • *Glyceria elata*

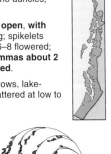

GENERAL: Loosely tufted, somewhat succulent perennial with creeping rhizomes, 1–1.5 m tall.

LEAVES: Flat, lax, **6–12 mm wide**; no auricles; ligules 3–6 mm long, **short-hairy**.

INFLORESCENCE: Panicle, **loose, open, with spreading branches** 15–30 cm long; spikelets **flattened, egg-shaped in outline**, 6–8 flowered; glumes small, 1 mm long or less; **lemmas about 2 mm long, firm, prominently 7 veined**.

ECOLOGY: Streamsides, wet meadows, lake-shores and shady, moist woods; scattered at low to middle elevations.

NOTES: Reed mannagrass (*G. grandis*) has stout stems that are **fat and soft** towards the base, **leaves 6–15 mm wide**, large, open panicles with numerous purplish spikelets, and **hairless ligules**, but it occurs only occasionally in our region. • Species of mannagrass have small grains that can be extracted by hand threshing and used as a cereal or meal, but they were not used by northwest coast peoples.

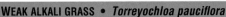

WEAK ALKALI GRASS • *Torreyochloa pauciflora*

GENERAL: Perennial, strongly rhizomatous; stems often bent at base, 30–150 cm tall, sometimes rooting at lower nodes.

LEAVES: Flat, **3–15 mm wide**, roughened on one or both surfaces; no auricles; **ligules 3–9 mm long, sharp-pointed and torn at tip**.

INFLORESCENCE: Panicle, open, rather loose, mostly 10–20 cm long, the branches ascending to spreading or drooping; **spikelets compressed, oblong to egg-shaped** in outline, 3–7 flowered; **lemmas 2–3 mm long, 5–7 veined, usually with a purplish band just below the wax-papery margin** of the tip.

ECOLOGY: Shallow water, marshes, swamps, wet meadows and wet forest openings; frequent from lowlands to subalpine zone.

NOTES: Weak alkali grass is also known as *Glyceria pauciflora* or *Puccinellia pauciflora*. This species has several features of *Glyceria*, but it also has the **open leaf sheaths** characteristic of *Puccinellia*, from which it is distinguished by its usually **much-longer ligules**, the **more-prominent veins of the lemma** and its broader leaves. • *Torreyochloa* is named for American botanist John Torrey (1796–1873).

ALASKA ALKALI GRASS • *Puccinellia nutkaensis*
PACIFIC ALKALI GRASS

GENERAL: Tufted perennial but sometimes with short stolons; stems erect, hairless, 20–70 cm tall (line drawing below; **photo is of *P. pumila***).

LEAVES: Flat to somewhat inrolled, 1–3 mm wide; no auricles; ligules 1–3.5 mm long.

INFLORESCENCE: Panicle, narrow, 5–20 cm long, the few slender **branches ascending to spreading**; spikelets 5–9 mm long, 4–6 flowered, green or purplish; lemmas 3–3.8 mm long, sparsely short-hairy at the base, with **somewhat frilly or lobed margins at tip.**

ECOLOGY: Sea beaches and tidal marshes; common at low elevations.

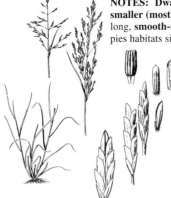

NOTES: Dwarf alkali grass (*P. pumila*, **shown in photo**) is **smaller (mostly 10–20 cm tall)**, and it has narrow panicles 5–10 cm long, **smooth-margined lemmas** and ligules 1–2 mm long. It occupies habitats similar to those of Alaska alkali grass all along the seacoast of our region. These two *Puccinellia*s are the common widespread alkali grasses of sea beaches and tidal marshes. A third, typically interior species, **Nuttall's alkali grass** (*P. nuttalliana*, which includes *P. borealis*) is only occasional along our coast, especially in the Strait of Georgia–Puget Sound area. It has panicles with **spreading to reflexed lower branches** when mature and **shorter (2–3 mm) lemmas**. • This genus was named for Benedetto Puccinelli (1808–1850), an Italian botanist.

SEASHORE SALTGRASS • *Distichlis spicata* var. *spicata*

GENERAL: A sod-forming perennial, 10–40 cm tall, with solid (not hollow) stems and vigorous, **scaly rhizomes.**

LEAVES: Yellowish-green, **short**, 2–4 mm wide, **stiff and erect**, **closely 2-ranked**; old leaves persistent; no auricles; ligules short, to 0.5 mm long, fringed with hairs.

INFLORESCENCE: Panicle, small and compact; spikelets large, compressed, overlapping; male and female flowers on separate plants; lemmas 3–6 mm long, **hardened, smooth, unawned.**

ECOLOGY: Tidal marshes, seashores; common at low elevations.

NOTES: The interior variety of this species (*D. spicata* var. *stricta* or alkali saltgrass) occurs in saline or alkaline meadows and on sandy lake-shores. • *Distichlis* is from the Greek *distichos* meaning '2-ranked,' and refers to the 2 rows of leaves.

NODDING TRISETUM • *Trisetum cernuum*

GENERAL: Tufted perennial; stems often bent at base, 40–120 cm tall.

LEAVES: Flat, **lax, 5–12 mm wide**, with thin, prominent tips; no auricles; **ligules 1.5–3 mm long**.

INFLORESCENCE: Panicle, open, loose, nodding, 10–30 cm long; **second glume longer and much wider than first, with a sharp tip**; lemmas 5–6 mm long, with **long (10 mm) bent awn** from just above middle, and **callus hairs about 1 mm long**.

ECOLOGY: Moist forest, stream-banks, upper beaches, thickets, and clearings; common at low to middle elevations.

NOTES: Nodding trisetum could be confused with **false melic** (*Schizachne purpurascens*), which is **uncommon** in our region, **lacks a sharp tip on the longer glume** and has **narrower leaves**, longer lemmas and longer callus hairs. If it lacks an inflorescence, nodding trisetum could also be confused with **nodding wood-reed** (p. 369), which, however, **has ligules 4–8 mm long. Tall trisetum** (*T. cernuum* var. *canescens*, also known as *T. canescens*) has **narrow, ascending panicles** and **leaves 4–7 mm wide**; it is frequent in open forest, meadows, and on streambanks in the southern part of our region. • *Trisetum* is from the Greek *treis* (three) and *seta* (bristles), in reference to the 3 awns on the lemmas of some species. The inflorescence is 'nodding'—hence *cernuum*.

SPIKE TRISETUM • *Trisetum spicatum*

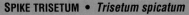

GENERAL: Erect, **densely tufted** perennial; stems 10–70 cm tall, hairless or (usually) hairy below the inflorescence.

LEAVES: Folded to flat, 1–5 mm wide, stiff; no auricles; ligules 0.5–2 mm long.

INFLORESCENCE: Panicle, dense, spike-like, 5–15 cm long, often turning dark purple or silvery; glumes slightly unequal in size; lemmas 4–5 mm long, with **long (5–6 mm) bent awn** from below divided tip.

ECOLOGY: Rocky slopes, outcrops, gravel bars, open forest, tundra, clearings, from low to high elevations; frequent the length of our region, tending to occur only at high elevations in the south, rare on the Queen Charlotte Islands.

NOTES: Spike trisetum is a widely distributed, highly variable species, more common in interior regions. It is one of the most widespread of our native species: it is not only widespread in cold areas of North America and Eurasia (a common distribution pattern for arctic-alpine species), but it also occurs in southern South America (a very unusual discontinuous distribution). • Species and common names allude to the upright spike.

TIMBER OAT-GRASS • *Danthonia intermedia*

GENERAL: Densely tufted perennial, 5–60 cm tall.

LEAVES: More or less inrolled, mainly basal, to 3 mm wide, long-hairy on the lower surface, with **long hairs where leaf blade joins the stem**; old leaves persistent; no auricles; ligules mostly a fringe of hairs, to 1 mm long; **sheaths usually hairless** but sometimes hairy.

INFLORESCENCE: Panicle, dense, tuft-like, 2–5 cm long, often purplish; **spikelets large, few** (3–11), usually 1 per short erect branch of panicle; glumes about 15 mm long; lemmas 7–10 mm long, **strongly hairy at the base and on the margins, toothed at tip, with bent, twisted awn up to 10 mm long**.

ECOLOGY: Rocky slopes, meadows, beaches, grassy openings, from low to high elevations; common from southwestern B.C. south, scattered northwards.

NOTES: Poverty oat-grass (*D. spicata*) has **lemmas less than 6 mm long** that are **hairy over the back as well as on the margins**. It grows in sandy or rocky habitats, usually in open forest or forest edges, sometimes also on rocky sites in muskeg or on lake-shores, sporadically along our coast. **California oat-grass** (*D. californica*) has **spreading panicle branches** and usually **hairy leaf sheaths**. It is fairly common in the southern half of our region, extending from the Queen Charlotte Islands south, on sandy and rocky ridges and lake-shores and in grassland and meadows, from low to middle elevations. • *Danthonia* is named for Etienne Danthione, a French botanist of the early 19th century.

EARLY HAIRGRASS • *Aira praecox*

GENERAL: Delicate, tufted annual, 5–25 cm tall.

LEAVES: Inrolled, **hair-like,** merely 0.5 mm wide, **very short, mostly basal**; auricles absent; ligules 1–3 mm long.

INFLORESCENCE: Panicle, compact, spike-like, 1–3 cm long, branches erect; glumes equal, longer than lemmas; lemmas 2, **about 3 mm long**, both with **twisted awns 2–3 mm long from below midlength**.

ECOLOGY: Dry (or moist only in the spring), gravelly or rocky sites near the ocean (bluffs, beaches, rock knolls, grassy meadows); common at low elevations in the southern half of our region, especially in the Strait of Georgia–Puget Sound area and along the Oregon and Washington coast, infrequent northwards.

NOTES: Silver hairgrass (*A. caryophyllea*, **inset photo**) is a similar small, slender annual, but it has an **open panicle 2–6 cm long** and **shorter (2–2.3 mm) lemmas**. It occupies similar habitats and a similar range to early hairgrass. • Both species are introduced from southern Europe and behave as weeds. They are part of a group of introduced, annual, spring-flowering grasses (like several *Vulpia* and *Bromus* species) that appear widely in the drier, Mediterranean-type climatic areas of our region, and that wither and turn brown as summer progresses and their habitats dry out. • The species name *praecox* means 'developing earlier than most.'

TUFTED HAIRGRASS • *Deschampsia cespitosa* ssp. *beringensis*

GENERAL: Densely tufted perennial with numerous stems 20–120 cm tall.

LEAVES: Flat to folded, **narrow**, to 3 mm wide, **rather stiff**; no auricles; **ligules prominent, pointed, 3–8 mm long**.

INFLORESCENCE: Panicle, **open, loose, 10–25 cm long, often nodding**; spikelets **bronze and glistening**, usually darkening at maturity, 2–3 flowered; lemmas thin, **about 4 mm long**, hairy at base, **awned from near base**.

ECOLOGY: Tidal marshes, beaches, meadows, gravelly river bars, rocky ridges, lake-shores, rocky areas in bogs; common from sea level to alpine.

NOTES: Slender hairgrass (*D. elongata*) is a native perennial with a **narrow panicle** with **ascending to erect branches** and **firm lemmas about 2.5 mm long**. It is frequent in our region from low to high elevations, in moist clearings, meadows and open forests, and along streams and lakes, often in disturbed sites near inhabited areas. **Annual hairgrass** (*D. danthonioides*) is an **annual** species of roadsides, dry slopes and vernal pools; it is scattered the length of our region but most abundant in the Strait of Georgia–Puget Sound area. • Tufted hairgrass is a variable species found in many habitats (coastal salt marshes to alpine tundra). Its range goes from the Arctic to high altitudes in the tropics. • *Deschampsia* is named for French botanist L.A. Deschamps (1774–1849).

MOUNTAIN HAIRGRASS • *Vahlodea atropurpurea*

GENERAL: Loosely tufted perennial, 20–80 cm tall.

LEAVES: Flat, soft, deep-green, 4–6 mm wide, with tips more or less prow-like; no auricles; **ligules 1.5–3.5 mm long**, hairy.

INFLORESCENCE: Panicle, open, loose, 5–10 cm long, **often nodding or with drooping branches; spikelets relatively large and often purplish in colour** at maturity; lemmas about 2.5 mm long, **hairy at base, awned from the middle**.

ECOLOGY: High-elevation meadows, alpine heath, snowbeds, stream-banks, and open subalpine forests, but most typically in high subalpine heath; common, locally abundant at high elevations.

NOTES: Mountain hairgrass is referred to in some texts as *Deschampsia atropurpurea*. • The species name means 'dark purple,' in reference to the colour of the spikelets.

TALL OATGRASS • *Arrhenatherum elatius*
FALSE OATGRASS

GENERAL: Stout **perennial** 80–150 cm tall; stems sometimes hairy at the nodes, **often swollen and bulb-like at the base** and sometimes rooting at the lower nodes, but without true rhizomes.

LEAVES: Flat, roughened, often hairy, **4–10 mm wide**; no auricles; ligules 1–3 mm long, finely hairy, fringed at tip.

INFLORESCENCE: Panicle, erect, narrow, silvery-green at flowering, later purplish, shiny, 10–30 cm long; **spikelets 2 flowered, large and oat-like**, the lower usually male only, the upper bisexual; glumes rather broad, papery; lemmas hairy at the base, 7-veined; **lower lemma with a stout, twisted, bent, awn 10–20 mm long** from about midlength; **upper lemma with a short, straight, awn up to 6 mm long** from near the tip.

ECOLOGY: Fields, pastures, meadows, roadsides, disturbed sites; common at low elevations in the southern half of our region, especially in settled areas; known also from southeast Alaska (Petersburg).

NOTES: Tall oatgrass is a European species widely introduced in North America and cultivated as a meadow and pasture grass. A grass of early summer (June and July), it later withers and disintegrates. • True oats (wild oat, *Avena fatua*; common oat, *A. sativa*) may also be encountered in disturbed habitats or as weedy escapees from cultivation. Both are **annuals** with rather **open, few-flowered panicles** of large spikelets. • The Latin *Arrhenatherum* is from the Greek *arrhen* ('masculine') and *ather* ('awn'), in reference to the awned male flowers.

COMMON VELVET-GRASS • *Holcus lanatus*
YORKSHIRE FOG

GENERAL: Tufted perennial, usually **softly grey-hairy (velvety)**; stems weak, rather succulent, 30–100 cm tall.

LEAVES: Flat, 3–10 mm wide; no auricles; ligules 1–2 mm long, hairy, fringed at tip.

INFLORESCENCE: Panicle, compact, pale grayish but usually purplish-tinged, 5–15 cm long; spikelets 2 flowered, the lower floret bisexual, the upper male only; glumes about equal in size, longer than lemmas, hairy; **lemmas smooth and shiny, somewhat leathery**, the lower lemma unawned, the **upper with a short hook-like awn** from just below the tip.

ECOLOGY: Fields, lawns, roadsides, railroad embankments, open waste ground; common to abundant at low elevations in the southern half of our region, especially in and around human settlements; sporadic, locally abundant northwards.

NOTES: Creeping velvet-grass (*H. mollis*) is similar, but it has **creeping rhizomes**, is **less hairy** on the stems, and is much less common than common velvet-grass. Both species have been introduced from Europe as meadow-grasses. • Common velvet-grass is one of several grass species that, in comparatively recent times, have developed populations tolerant to toxic concentrations of heavy metals (such as copper, zinc, lead and arsenic) in mine tailings—evolution in action on the slag heaps of civilization. • A 'fog' was an English North Country dialect word for a coarse winter grass, from the Old Norse *fogg* meaning 'long, lax, damp grass.' *Holcus* is Greek for 'millet' and *lanatus* means 'woolly'—hence velvet-grass.

HAIRY CRABGRASS • *Digitaria sanguinalis*

GENERAL: Branching annual, often **spreading to prostrate and tending to root from lower nodes**, can form patches over 1 m wide; **stems with hairy leaf sheaths**.

LEAVES: Flat, **4–8 mm wide**, hairy at least towards the base; no auricles; ligules about 2 mm long.

INFLORESCENCE: Racemes, **linear**, usually several (3–12), **finger-like in 2 or 3 whorls, 5–12 cm long; spikelets in pairs** (1 short stalked and the other stalkless) and in 2 rows on 1 side of the raceme, 2-flowered but the lower flower sterile; glumes unequal in size, fringed with hairs; **fertile lemma about 3 mm long, smooth and leathery; sterile lemma strongly veined, hairy**.

ECOLOGY: Lawns, gardens, roadsides, along railroad tracks; sporadic at low elevations in settled areas.

NOTES: Smooth crabgrass (*D. ischaemum*) is also a sprawling annual, but it has **hairless stems** and **fewer (1–5) racemes**. Both smooth and hairy crabgrass are introduced, European weeds that have become established in much of North America, though usually not abundantly in our region. • *Digitaria* is from the Latin *digitus* ('finger'), because of the finger-like arrangement of the inflorescence. The name 'crabgrass' might allude to the long, creeping stems that freely root at the nodes, which bear some resemblance to crabs.

WESTERN PANICUM • *Panicum occidentale*

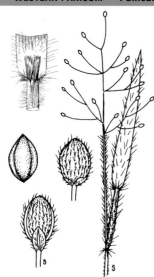

GENERAL: Tufted perennial; **stems yellowish-green**, leafy toward base, spreading, usually **velvety-hairy**, 15–40 cm tall.

LEAVES: Flat, **firm**, erect to ascending, **hairy (especially below)**, 5–10 mm wide; no auricles; **ligules 3–4 mm long, consisting of long hairs**.

INFLORESCENCE: Panicle, **open**, 3–9 cm long; spikelets up to 2 mm long, **short-hairy, 2 flowered**, the lower flower sterile; glumes unequal in size; **fertile lemma hardened**.

ECOLOGY: Moist, sandy ground (lake-shores, beaches, stream-banks), rocky and gravelly areas in bogs, meadows and open forest; common but scattered at low to middle elevations.

NOTES: Few-flowered panicum (*P. scribnerianum*) has a similar range but **drier** habitat preferences (gravelly knolls, rocky bluffs and open sandy flats). It has **shorter (about 1.5 mm) ligules, longer (about 3 mm) spikelets** and fewer panicle branches. • Another common name for *P. occidentale* is 'witch grass,' which may be a corruption of 'twitch grass' (see quackgrass, p. 362), or it may be something more interesting altogether. • *Panicum* is the largest genus of grasses, with about 600 species worldwide, mostly in warmer climates.

LARGE BARNYARD-GRASS • *Echinochloa crusgalli*

GENERAL: Tufted annual, **often branched and reddish-purple at base**; stems stout, erect but often curved at base, hairless, 0.5–1.5 m tall.

LEAVES: Flat, hairless, 5–15 mm wide; no auricles; no ligules.

INFLORESCENCE: Panicle, erect to nodding, purple-tinged, 10–20 cm long; panicle branches spreading to erect; **spikelets crowded, single or in clusters along 1 side** of the panicle branches, 3–4 mm long, **2 flowered**, the lower floret sterile; glumes unequal in size, **bristly, awnless; sterile lemma often awned; fertile lemma hardened, smooth, shiny,** unawned but abruptly pointed.

ECOLOGY: Moist clearings, wet ditches, cultivated fields, barnyards; common at low elevations, mostly in settled areas.

NOTES: Large barnyard-grass is a weedy species introduced from Eurasia. • Hitchcock et al. (1969) note that 'during the upland bird-hunting season the spikelets of *E. crusgalli* are shed at the slightest touch, often dropping into the eyes of hunting dogs, from which they are removed with some difficulty, since they tend to work into the eyelids.' This is a peculiar and somewhat anachronistic comment, but not without interest. What are those hunting dogs doing in the barnyards? Presumably, paint-ball players and local militia on maneuvers are similarly afflicted. • Earlier in this century, enterprising American seedsmen (hucksters) advertised a cultivated variety of barnyard-grass as 'billion dollar grass,' recommended for forage as green feed, silage or hay. However, it proved too succulent for hay and its use waned with the introduction of other productive crops of higher value. • *E. crusgalli* is also known as 'cocks-comb grass' or 'cockspur.' Both common names and the species name (*crusgalli*) refer to the shape of the inflorescence, which is like the comb of a rooster. The genus name is from *echinos*, Greek for 'hedgehog,' and *chloa*, meaning 'grass,' alluding to the prickly spikelets.

GREEN BRISTLEGRASS • *Setaria viridis*
GREEN FOXTAIL

GENERAL: Annual, erect but sometimes curved at base, branched at base, 30–100 cm tall.

LEAVES: Flat, up to 10 mm wide; no auricles; **ligules half membrane and half a terminal fringe of hairs,** about 2 mm long.

INFLORESCENCE: Panicle, narrow, cylindric, spike-like, up to 10 cm long and 15 mm wide; **spikelets with 2–3 upwardly barbed bristles at the base, 2 flowered,** the lower floret sterile; glumes of unequal length, veined; **fertile lemma leathery, cross-wrinkled** when mature, **nearly completely enclosed by the second glume and sterile lemma,** and not shed from them.

ECOLOGY: Cultivated fields, roadsides, waste places; common at low elevations in settled areas.

NOTES: We have 3 other species of *Setaria* in our region; all are weedy annuals. **Yellow bristlegrass** (*S. glauca*, also known as *S. lutescens*) has **5–6 bristles** per spikelet. **Bur bristlegrass** (*S. verticillata*) has **interrupted panicles. Foxtail millet** (*S. italica*) often has an **enlarged and lobed panicle,** and it is grown for food in parts of Eurasia. • Green bristlegrass is a weedy species introduced from temperate Eurasia. If squeezed through the hand, the inflorescence wriggles like a woolly bear caterpillar. • *Setaria* is from the Latin *seta* ('bristle') and refers to the bristle-like sterile branches of the inflorescence. The species name *viridis* means 'green,' hence the common name.

Sedges and Rushes

Sedges (family Cyperaceae) and rushes (family Juncaceae) resemble grasses in their long, narrow, parallel-veined leaves and inconspicuous flowers with several scale-like bracts. They are most easily distinguished through examination of their stems: those of sedges are generally triangular in cross-section and solid (not hollow), with the leaves in 3 rows (vs. 2 rows for grasses); those of rushes are round and solid ('pithy'). Remember: 'sedges have edges and rushes are round.' Both provide important forage and habitat for a variety of wildlife species.

The sedge family has several genera; the largest is *Carex*, which has its ovary and fruit (achene) enclosed in a membranous sac (the **perigynium**) in the axil of a single scale-like bract. The rush family has two genera, *Juncus* and *Luzula*, which have usually 2 series of 3 scale-like floral bracts that look like miniature brown lilies. Neither family has much economic importance. Pith from the culms of *Cyperus papyrus* was used by early Egyptians in papermaking. A few species of rushes and *Cyperus* may be grown as wetland ornamentals. Others are used locally in basketry and matting and making hats and chair seats. The pith has been used for candlewicks.

More information about sedges and rushes in our region is provided in Hultén (1968), Hitchcock and Cronquist (1973) and Taylor (1983).

> 'Oh, what can ail thee, Knight at arms
> Alone and palely loitering;
> The sedge is wither'd from the lake,
> And no birds sing.'—John Keats, 'La Belle Dame Sans Merci'

Key to Genera of the Sedge Family

1a. Flowers unisexual; achenes enclosed or wrapped in a sac (the perigynium) .... *Carex*
1b. Flowers bisexual; achenes not enclosed in perigynium 2
  2a. Scales of spikelets spirally arranged 3
  2b. Scales of spikelets in 2 vertical rows .... *Dulichium*
    3a. Spikelets with 1 (rarely 2) achenes .... *Rhynchospora*
    3b. Spikelets with several to many achenes 4
      4a. Styles thickened towards the base, forming a conspicuous
      tubercle on the achenes .... *Eleocharis*
      4b. Styles not thickened to form a tubercle 5
        5a. Flower bristles 10 or more .... *Eriophorum*
        5b. Flower bristles 8 or fewer 6
          6a. Spikelets atop leafy bracts .... *Scirpus*
          6b. Spikelets atop slightly modified, not leafy, scales .... *Trichophorum*

Key to Sedges (*Carex*)

1a. Spike solitary .... **Group I**

1b. Spikes more than 1, sometimes congested
in a head-like inflorescence 2

2a. Spikes all alike, usually with both male
and female flowers (or with sexes
on separate plants), stalkless .... **Group II**

2b. Spikes differentiated into a terminal
male spike and lateral female spikes;
lateral spikes usually stalked .... **Group III**

Group I: Sedges with a single terminal spike

1a. Mature perigynia reflexed (abruptly bent downward);
scales deciduous; stigmas 3 2
  2a. Perigynia broadly lance- to egg-shaped in outline, 3–4 mm long;
  plants forming tufts or hummocky mats .... *C. nigricans*
  2b. Perigynia narrowly lance-shaped in outline, 6–7 mm long;
  plants single or a few together .... *C. pauciflora*
1b. Mature perigynia not reflexed; scales persistent; stigmas 2 or 3 3
  3a. Plants with rhizomes; leaves flat; stigmas 2 .... *C. anthoxanthea*
  3b. Plants densely tufted; leaves quill-like, wiry; stigmas 2 or 3 .... *C. nardina*

Group II: Sedges with several spikes, each spike with both male and female flowers, or male and female spikes on different plants

1a. Perigynia large, 10–15 mm long, with 5 mm long beaks;
stigmas 3; plants of sandy beaches .... *C. macrocephala*
1b. Perigynia shorter than 7 mm, beakless or with beaks
shorter than 3 mm; stigmas 2 2
  2a. Male flowers at the upper part of each individual spike
  (in mature plants look for remains of stamen stalks);
  spikes aggregated in dense, oblong heads .... *C. stipata*
  2b. Male flowers at the base of each individual spike 3
    3a. Perigynia wing-margined, the lower part of the body
    not spongy thickened 4
      4a. Spikes aggregated into a dense head; perigynia with
      slender, round beaks, the upper 1–2 mm not finely toothed;
      scales shorter and noticeably narrower than the perigynia .... *C. macloviana*
      4b. Spikes in a loose, curved cluster; perigynia with a
      flattened beak, the margin finely toothed to the tip; scales
      about as long as the perigynia and nearly the same width .... *C. aenea*
    3b. Perigynia not wing-margined, at most thin-edged, the
    lower part of the body spongy thickened 5
      5a. Inflorescence interrupted-linear, the individual spikes
      well separated from each other, very small and few-flowered
      with 1–3 perigynia; plants solitary or loosely tufted .... *C. disperma*
      5b. Inflorescence more or less head-like, though sometimes
      long and narrow; all or most of the individual spikes
      closely aggregated and several-flowered 6
        6a. Perigynia whitish-dotted (frosted), with very short
        (less than 1 mm) beaks .... *C. canescens*
        6b. Perigynia not whitish-dotted, with long beaks 7
          7a. Perigynia appressed, broadest at or near the middle,
          indistinctly veined, the beak with saw-toothed margins .... *C. deweyana*
          7b. Perigynia spreading at maturity, broadest at or
          near the middle, distinctly veined on both surfaces,
          the beak with smooth margins .... *C. laeviculmis*

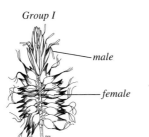

Group I

male

female

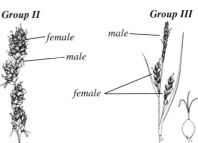

Group II

female

male

female

Group III

male

Group III: Sedges with terminal male and lateral female spikes

1a. Stigmas 2; achenes lens-shaped, flattened 2
    2a. Lowest bract with a long sheath; spikes few-flowered;
    perigynia golden-yellow at maturity .... *C. aurea*
    2b. Lowest bract usually sheathless; spikes many-flowered 3
        3a. Uppermost spike bisexual, female flowers on top;
        inflorescence nearly flat-topped, of 3–5 dark spikes .... *C. enanderi*
        3b. Uppermost spike male, or rarely with a few female
        flowers at the base; inflorescence otherwise 4
            4a. Perigynia with distinct veins .... *C. kelloggii*
            4b. Perigynia without veins 5
                5a. Perigynia papery .... *C. sitchensis*
                5b. Perigynia tough, leathery 6
                    6a. Female spikes erect on stiff stalks;
                    leaf sheaths fibrous-shreddy at base .... *C. obnupta*
                    6b. Female spikes drooping on slender stalks;
                    leaf sheaths not fibrous-shreddy .... *C. lyngbyei*
1b. Stigmas 3; achenes triangular in cross-section 7
    7a. Perigynia hairy .... *C. rossii*
    7b. Perigynia hairless 8
        8a. Scales of female spikes black or purplish-black or dark brown 9
        9a. Uppermost spike with female flowers above male flowers;
        perigynia strongly flattened, papery, light-green .... *C. mertensii*
        9b. Uppermost spike of male flowers only 10
            10a. Scales of female spikes not awn-tipped;
            roots not yellow-woolly .... *C. stylosa*
            10b. Scales of female spikes awn-tipped;
            roots usually yellow-woolly 11
                11a. Scales with short awn-tips (to 1 mm long);
                perigynia blackish when ripe .... *C. pluriflora*
                11b. Scales with long awn-tips (2–12 mm long);
                perigynia green or blue-green when ripe .... *C. macrochaeta*
        8b. Scales of female spikes greenish, not blackish 12
            12a. Perigynia beakless; plants bluish-green .... *C. livida*
            12b. Perigynia beaked; plants yellowish-green 13
                13a. Spikes close together, forming a head;
                perigynia 2–3 mm long .... *C. viridula*
                13b. Spikes remote, not forming a head;
                perigynia 3–8 mm long .... *C. rostrata*

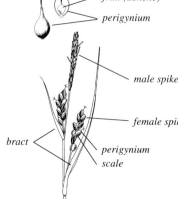

stigma

fruit (achene)

perigynium

male spike

female spike

bract

perigynium

scale

inflorescence

rhizome

SPIKENARD SEDGE • *Carex nardina*

GENERAL: Dwarf, **densely tufted; stems wiry, 2–15 cm tall**, about as long as leaves.

LEAVES: Very narrow, **hair-like**, **stiff**, roughened, erect or curving, 1 or 2 per stem; **old leaves and brownish leaf sheaths persistent and very conspicuous.**

INFLORESCENCE: Solitary, elliptic spike 5–15 mm long; male flowers at the top.

PERIGYNIA: Elliptic to narrowly egg-shaped, about 4 mm long, short-stalked, hairless, straw-coloured, tapering to a finely saw-toothed beak; scales brownish, wider and about as long as perigynia; 2 or 3 stigmas.

ECOLOGY: Dry, windswept ridges, talus slopes, ledges; common in the **alpine** zone virtually the length of our region (south to Mt. Hood, Oregon), mostly in and east of the B.C. Coast Mountains and the Cascades; rare on Vancouver Island and in the Olympic Mountains.

NOTES: *C. nardina* includes *C. hepburnii*. • **Brewer's sedge** (*C. breweri,* which includes *C. engelmannii*) has spikes similar to those of spikenard sedge and quill-like leaves, but instead of being densely tufted it has **1 to few stems from creeping rhizomes**. It, too, is a high-elevation species of the Cascades from southernmost B.C. to California. **Single-spike sedge** (*C. scirpoidea*) has stout scaly rhizomes, stems **10–40 cm tall, flat leaves**, solitary spikes (either all male or all female) and **very hairy perigynia**. It grows at middle to high elevations in meadows, heath and open rocky slopes, scattered the length of our region. • *Nardina* is from the Latin *nardus* meaning 'spikenard-like.' The word 'spikenard' means 'a spike, tuft, or ear of nard,' where 'nard' is a fragrant ointment that was extracted from the rhizomes of the original spikenard, *Nardostachys jatamansi*, an Indian plant in the valerian family. Spikenard sedge presumably acquired the name because of the resemblance of its inflorescence to spikenard.

BLACK ALPINE SEDGE • *Carex nigricans*

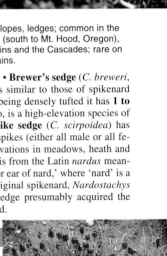

GENERAL: Tufted from stout creeping rhizomes, often forming **hummocky mats**; stems stiff, 5–35 cm tall, light-brown and clothed with old leaves at the base.

LEAVES: Numerous, **densely packed near base of stem,** usually shorter than stem, flat or somewhat channelled, **stiff, 1–3 mm wide.**

INFLORESCENCE: Spike **solitary** with male flowers at top; no bract at base.

PERIGYNIA: Brownish, lance- to narrowly egg-shaped, stalked at the base, tapering into a short beak at the tip, **spreading to reflexing at maturity and soon falling off**; scales dark brown, much shorter than perigynia; **3 stigmas.**

ECOLOGY: Snowbeds, wet meadows, and tundra, edges of rivulets and ponds; widespread at **high elevations,** often abundant.

NOTES: Black alpine sedge could be confused with **Pyrenean sedge** (*C. pyrenaica,* **inset photo**), which **lacks a rhizome,** has **narrower (about 1 mm wide)** channelled leaves and **less widely spreading perigynia** with 2 or 3 stigmas; it often grows in grassy tundra, on ledges and moist gravels, and in snowbeds on rocky ridges and boulder fields. Pyrenean sedge is also widespread in our region, but it is not nearly as common as black alpine sedge. • Black alpine sedge can survive with a very short growing season, and it is often the dominant plant in areas where the snow drifts and banks remain late into the summer. • The species name *nigricans* means 'black.'

FEW-FLOWERED SEDGE • *Carex pauciflora*

GENERAL: Stems 10–40 cm tall, **single or a few together** from a very slender rhizome, stiff, brownish, and curved at the base.

LEAVES: Narrow (0.5–1.5 mm wide), usually channelled, shorter than to as long as the stems.

INFLORESCENCE: Spike **solitary, very small**, without a bract; male flowers at the top of spike.

PERIGYNIA: Few (usually less than 7), **6–8 mm long, narrowly lance-shaped**, longer than the light-brown scales, greenish-brown, **bent back downwards at maturity**, 3-angled; **3 stigmas**; both scales and perigynia falling off at maturity.

ECOLOGY: Fairly frequent but scattered in *Sphagnum* **bogs and fens**, at low to middle elevations.

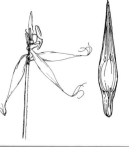

NOTES: The long, reflexed perigynia distinguish this species. • **Yellow bog sedge** (*C. gynocrates*, also known as *C. dioica* ssp. *gynocrates*) has male and female flowers on **different** plants, **2 stigmas**, and **plump, egg-shaped perigynia** that are mostly **spreading to ascending**. Yellow bog sedge grows in middle- to high-elevation bogs, fens, and wet meadows, mostly along the eastern edge of our region from Alaska to southern B.C. (Skagit Valley). • The common name 'few-flowered' is a translation of *pauciflora*.

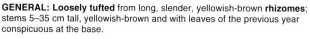

YELLOW-FLOWERED SEDGE • *Carex anthoxanthea*

GENERAL: Loosely tufted from long, slender, yellowish-brown **rhizomes**; stems 5–35 cm tall, yellowish-brown and with leaves of the previous year conspicuous at the base.

LEAVES: Flat, about 2 mm wide, erect or spreading, 2–4 per stem.

INFLORESCENCE: Solitary spike, narrowly cylindrical, 7–30 mm long; male flowers on top although spike sometimes either all female or all male.

PERIGYNIA: Narrowly elliptic, yellowish-green to straw-coloured, **4 mm long**, hairless, many-veined, short-beaked; scales chestnut-brown with green centres, about same length as perigynia; usually 3 stigmas.

ECOLOGY: Wet meadows, bogs, boggy forest, from sea level to above tree line; common from central Vancouver Island north, especially so from northern Vancouver Island to south-central Alaska.

NOTES: Coiled sedge (*C. circinata*) is similar to yellow-flowered sedge but it is **densely tufted** and has **stiff, hair-like, curved or curled leaves**. It occurs on moist cliffs, rocky knolls and talus slopes, and it is fairly common from the Olympic Mountains north (especially north of Vancouver Island). Coiled sedge and yellow-flowered sedge often grow in close proximity, but they have different ecological requirements. • The species name *anthoxanthea* means 'yellow-flowered.'

LARGE-HEADED SEDGE • *Carex macrocephala*

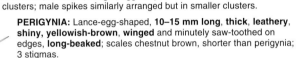

GENERAL: Stems single or few together from **long, horizontally spreading rhizomes buried in sand**, 10–40 cm tall, stiff, stout, dark-shreddy and clothed with old leaves at the base.

LEAVES: Clustered near the base, **4–8 mm wide, thick, yellowish-green, channelled**, sharp-pointed, often exceeding the stems.

INFLORESCENCE: Male and female spikes on **separate plants, in dense heads 4–6 cm long and 1–4 cm wide**, erect; female spikes numerous, stalkless, in tight, egg-shaped clusters; male spikes similarly arranged but in smaller clusters.

PERIGYNIA: Lance-egg-shaped, **10–15 mm long, thick, leathery, shiny, yellowish-brown, winged** and minutely saw-toothed on edges, **long-beaked**; scales chestnut brown, shorter than perigynia; 3 stigmas.

ECOLOGY: Sandy seashores, coastal dunes; common but scattered.

NOTES: Sand-dune sedge (*C. pansa*, also known as *C. arenicola*) also occurs on sandy beaches, dunes and rocky shores, but it has **much smaller (7–10 mm long) clusters of distinct, bisexual spikes**. It is an uncommon species ranging from the Queen Charlotte Islands to California. • Both of these beach sedges occur as tufts connected by long rhizomes that creep in a nearly straight line. • *Macro* means 'large' and *cephala* means 'head,' referring to the flower and fruiting spikes.

SAWBEAK SEDGE • *Carex stipata*

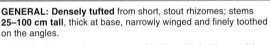

GENERAL: Densely tufted from short, stout rhizomes; stems **25–100 cm tall**, thick at base, narrowly winged and finely toothed on the angles.

LEAVES: About as long as stems, **flat, flaccid, 4–10 mm wide, yellowish-green**.

INFLORESCENCE: Several to many spikes, stalkless in **dense, thickly oblong clusters 3–10 cm long; male flowers at top** of each spike.

PERIGYNIA: Straw-coloured to brownish, narrowly lance- to egg-shaped, wingless, hairless, veined on both sides, sharp-edged to the **spongy, stub-stalked base**, tapering to **long, finely toothed beak**; scales brownish, shorter and narrower than perigynia; 2 stigmas.

ECOLOGY: Wet meadows, ditches and clearings, swamps, streamsides, lake-shores; common at mostly low elevations.

NOTES: Lesser panicled sedge (*C. diandra*), Cusick's sedge (*C. cusickii*) and Hood's sedge (*C. hoodii*) are all somewhat similar to sawbeak edge (though less robust). **Lesser panicled sedge** has **more than 10** spikes aggregated in a **tight head** and leaf sheaths that are **red-dotted but not copper-tinged at the top. Cusick's sedge** has **more than 10** spikes in an **interrupted head** and leaf sheaths that are **red-dotted and copper-tinged** at the top. **Hood's sedge** has **4–8 spikes** in a tight, **egg-shaped head** and leaf sheaths that are **not red-dotted** at the top. Lesser panicled sedge and Cusick's sedge are both wetland sedges of low to middle elevations, and they are common from Vancouver Island south to central Washington (*C.diandra*) or from Vancouver Island and the Queen Charlotte Islands and the adjacent mainland south to California (*C.cusickii*). Hood's sedge grows in moist to dry meadows and forest openings from low to high elevations, commonly from Vancouver Island and the adjacent mainland south to California. • Sawbeak sedge gets its common name from the finely toothed beak on the perigynia. The species name *stipata* means 'with a stipe or stalk' and probably refers to the stub-stalked base of the perigynia.

FALKLAND ISLAND SEDGE • *Carex macloviana*

GENERAL: **Densely tufted** from short, blackish rhizomes; numerous stems 30–85 cm tall, with lots of old, dry leaves at the base.

LEAVES: Flat, 2–4 mm wide, 3–5 per stem, shorter than stem.

INFLORESCENCE: Several stalkless spikes crowded into a **dense, roundish to oblong head up to 2.5 cm long**; male flowers hidden at the base of each spike.

PERIGYNIA: **Copper-coloured to dark olive-green** at maturity, **3.5–5 mm long**, egg-shaped, flattened, **wing-margined**, tapering to a slender beak; scales brownish, **about as wide and long as perigynia**; 2 stigmas.

ECOLOGY: Meadows, grassy slopes, gravelly shores, forest openings and edges, clearings; often relatively dry sites; common from low to subalpine elevations.

NOTES: Thick-headed sedge (*C. pachystachya*), **Hayden's sedge** (*C. haydeniana*) and **small-winged sedge** (*C. microptera*) closely resemble this species, but they differ in microscopic details of their perigynia. Some taxonomists maintain that there should be just 1 variable species: *C. macloviana*. **Dunhead sedge** (*C. phaeocephala*) has a similar head of stalkless spikes, but its **reddish-brown scales conceal** the perigynia. It grows mostly in the alpine zone the length of our region but primarily in its eastern parts. **Sheep sedge** (*C. illota*) is also similar to Falkland Island sedge, but it has a **small (6–15 mm long), black head** and s**maller (2.5–3.5 mm long) perigynia**. It occupies wet meadows, boggy shores and stream-banks from middle to high elevations from eastern Vancouver Island and the adjacent mainland south to California. • *C. macloviana* was described from the Falkland Islands.

BRONZE SEDGE • *Carex aenea*

GENERAL: **Densely tufted**; **slender**, wiry stems **30–100 cm tall**, bent over at the tip.

LEAVES: Shorter than stem, soft, flat, 2–4 mm wide.

INFLORESCENCE: Spikes 4–8, stalkless, in a **loose, curved cluster; lower spikes well separated**; male flowers at the base of each spike.

PERIGYNIA: Dull-green **becoming bronze, egg-shaped**, flattened, **wing-margined** and tapering to a long beak; scales brownish, as large as and **concealing** the perigynia; 2 stigmas.

ECOLOGY: Open, dry to moist forest, meadows, clearings; often grows in profusion in disturbed areas; scattered at low to middle elevations; mostly in the inland portions of our region.

NOTES: We have a bunch of species similar to bronze sedge and they are difficult to distinguish from it. **Meadow sedge** (*C. praticola*, **inset photo**) has shorter (to 70 cm tall) stems, **narrower perigynia**, and **silvery-green spikes**. It occurs most of the length of our region north to Lynn Canal (absent from the Queen Charlotte Islands) in meadows, open forest and on stream-banks from low to middle elevations. **Tracy's sedge** (*C. tracyi*, also known as *C. leporina*) has a **reddish-brown tip** on the perigynium beak in contrast to the whitish tip of meadow sedge. Tracy's sedge grows in wet meadows and swamps and along streams at low to middle elevations from the Queen Charlotte Islands to California, most commonly on Vancouver Island and southwards. **Bebb's sedge** (*C. bebbii*) grows in similar habitats on the mainland coast south from the Skeena River to Oregon. Bebb's sedge has perigynia with flat, **finely saw-toothed, reddish-brown beaks**.

DEWEY'S SEDGE • *Carex deweyana*

GENERAL: Loosely tufted; stems weak, spreading, 20–120 cm tall, roughened beneath the head, exceeding the leaves, clothed at the base with old leaves.

LEAVES: Flat, soft, thin, 2–5 mm wide.

INFLORESCENCE: Spikes 2–6, stalkless, forming a **loose head 2–6 cm long;** terminal spike with **female flowers at top;** lateral spikes usually all female and somewhat separated from each other.

PERIGYNIA: Pale-green, with **thin, papery** walls, about 5 mm long, lance-elliptic to egg-shaped, **rounded and spongy at the base, with sharp margins** minutely saw-toothed, tapering to a slender, flattened beak, **appressed;** scales thin, clear with green centres, slightly shorter than perigynia; 2 stigmas.

ECOLOGY: Open, often alluvial forest, stream-banks, clearings at low to middle elevations; abundant on Vancouver Island and the Queen Charlotte Islands, common in Washington and Oregon, but not in coastal Alaska except near towns on the Kenai Peninsula, where perhaps introduced.

NOTES: Dewey's sedge could be confused with smooth sedge (*C. laeviculmis*, below), which often occupies similar habitats and also has weak, spreading stems and leaves. However, **smooth sedge** is **densely tufted** and has **narrower leaves (1–2 mm wide),** as well as perigynia that are **spreading or ascending (not appressed)** at maturity. • The Rev. Chester Dewey was a professor and student of *Carex* at the University of Rochester.

SMOOTH SEDGE • *Carex laeviculmis*

GENERAL: Densely tufted, also with some short, slender rhizomes; **stems weak, very slender,** 15–90 cm tall.

LEAVES: Shorter than stems, **flat, weak, pale-green, 1–2 mm wide.**

INFLORESCENCE: Spikes all or mostly female, stalkless, erect-ascending, **fairly well separated** in a head **2–6 cm long;** terminal spike **female above.**

PERIGYNIA: Green to brownish-green, lance- to egg-shaped, few-veined on both surfaces, **wingless,** tapering to a somewhat flattened, **nearly smooth beak;** scales yellowish-brown with clear margins and green midvein; 2 stigmas.

ECOLOGY: Bogs, wet meadows, shorelines, stream-banks, wet forest, from low to middle elevations; common.

NOTES: Coastal stellate sedge (*C. phyllomanica*) is equally common over virtually the same range as smooth sedge, but it is restricted to bogs and fens. It has a **minutely saw-toothed** perigynium beak, and its spikes are **closer together** in a head **1.5–3.5 cm long. Star sedge** (*C. echinata*, also known as *C. angustior*, *C. cephalantha*, *C. muricata*, and *C. stellulata*) is very like coastal stellate sedge but it has **sharp-pointed scales** around the perigynia, whereas those of coastal stellate sedge are blunt. Star sedge is common in bogs and on the sandy shores of lakes and streams from Vancouver Island and the adjacent mainland south to California. • The common name derives from *laevi* and *culmis*, Latin for 'smooth' and 'stem or culm' respectively.

GREEN SEDGE • *Carex viridula*

GENERAL: Densely tufted in small clumps; stems stiff, 5–50 cm tall, pale brown and shreddy at the base with conspicuous remains of previous year's leaves.

LEAVES: Flat to channelled, **yellowish-green, 1–4 mm wide**.

INFLORESCENCE: Terminal spike **usually male**, linear; **lateral spikes female, 2–6, spherical-oblong**, ascending to spreading, nearly stalkless to short stalked, with **long narrow bracts sticking out** from the base.

PERIGYNIA: Yellowish-green, egg-shaped to elliptic, 2–3 mm long, **several-ribbed**, wingless, spreading, **abruptly contracted to straight beak**; scales much smaller than perigynia, yellowish-brown; stigmas 3.

ECOLOGY: Common in bogs, swamps, fens, wet meadows, dune slacks and lake-shores at low to middle elevations.

NOTES: Green sedge is also known as *C. oederi* var. *viridula*. • **Yellow sedge** (*C. flava*, **photo on right**) is very similar and grows in similar (but **more often calcium-rich or sandy**) habitats, but not south of Vancouver Island and more sporadically northwards; it is absent from the Queen Charlotte Islands. Yellow sedge has **spreading to reflexed perigynia 4–6 mm long** with **longer curved** beaks. • *C. viridula* is called 'green sedge' from the Latin *viridulus* meaning 'greenish,' in reference to the yellowish-green perigynia.

SOFT-LEAVED SEDGE • *Carex disperma*

GENERAL: Loosely tufted or solitary from long, slender rhizomes; stems **very slender, weak, usually nodding**, 10–40 cm tall, clothed with old leaves at the base.

LEAVES: Narrow (about 1–2 mm wide), **thin, soft**, mostly shorter than stem, light-green.

INFLORESCENCE: Very small, greenish spikes, **few-flowered, well separated from each other; male flowers at top** of spikes.

PERIGYNIA: Plump, elliptic to egg-shaped, greenish to brownish and **shining** at maturity, small (but longer and wider than the whitish-green scales), with faint lines, 2-angled, abruptly contracted into **tiny beak**; 2 stigmas.

ECOLOGY: Bogs, swamps, moist to wet forests, seepy openings, stream-banks; scattered at low to middle elevations; most commonly along the eastern edge of our region, but also on the Queen Charlotte Islands and Vancouver Island.

NOTES: **Bristle-stalked sedge** (*C. leptalea*) is **densely tufted** on slender rhizomes and also has thin, soft, lax, hair-like leaves, but it has a **solitary**, oblong spike with a few oval-elliptic, **many-veined, beakless** perigynia. It is a common species of bogs, swamps, fens, wet meadows, wet forest openings and shorelines from low to middle elevations, occurring the length of our region.

GREY SEDGE • *Carex canescens*

GENERAL: **Densely tufted**, from short, black rhizomes, often forming large clumps; stems erect to spreading, 20–80 cm high, brownish and clothed with old leaves at base.

LEAVES: Clustered near the base, long (but not longer than the stems), **soft, flat, 2–4 mm wide, bluish-green**.

INFLORESCENCE: **Loose cluster** of 4–7 small, silvery-brown spikes, **lower ones separated; male flowers at the base** of each spike.

PERIGYNIA: Small (2–3 mm long) but longer than the straw-coloured scales, oblong-egg-shaped, yellowish-green to whitish-brown, with a **very short beak**, 2-angled, 15–30 per spike; 2 stigmas.

ECOLOGY: Swamps, fens, bogs, stream-banks, lake-shores, wet meadows; common at low to subalpine elevations.

NOTES: Grey sedge is also known as *C. curta*, and includes *C. arctiformis*. • **Brownish sedge** (*C. brunnescens*) closely resembles grey sedge, but it has **smaller** spikes with fewer, **more strongly beaked** perigynia, and it is less common (especially south of B.C.) than grey sedge. It occurs in peatlands and wet forest openings at middle to subalpine elevations the length of our region. **Northern clustered sedge** (*C. arcta*) is similar to grey sedge but has a **tighter, oblong head** to 4 cm long and egg-shaped perigynia that are broadest near the base and **prominently beaked**. It grows in wet meadows, marshes, wet clearings and ditches at low to middle elevations from the Queen Charlotte Islands to California, most commonly from Vancouver Island and the adjacent mainland south. • The species name *canescens* is Latin for 'turning hoary-white,' referring to the silvery spikes.

ROSS' SEDGE • *Carex rossii*

GENERAL: Low, **dense tufts**; stems slender, 10–30 cm high.

LEAVES: **Narrow (1–2.5 mm wide)**, long, thin and somewhat lax, somewhat spreading, at least some longer than the stem, with **purplish sheaths at the base**.

INFLORESCENCE: Terminal spike male, 2 or 3 few-flowered female spikes clustered below; bracts well developed, leaf-like, usually longer than the inflorescence; **additional spikes on long stalks near the base of stem**, widely separated from the terminal spikes.

PERIGYNIA: Few per spike; **elliptic**, 3–4 mm long, greenish to straw-coloured, longer than the scales, 3-angled, **covered with short hairs**, with a stalk-like base; 3 stigmas.

ECOLOGY: Well-drained, relatively dry, open forests, gravelly or rocky slopes and flats, cutbanks, roadsides, clearings; at low to middle elevations, sometimes in subalpine zones.

NOTES: *C. rossii* includes *C. deflexa*; the plant is also known as *C. deflexa* var. *rossii*. • There are in this region at least 2 other species of similar appearance and habitat to *C. rossii*. **Short-stemmed sedge** (*C. brevicaulis*, also known as *C. deflexa* var. *brevicaulis*) occurs on dry, grassy slopes and coastal bluffs, and in open, rocky forest at low elevations; it is common from the Strait of Georgia–Puget Sound area south to California, with one locality on the Queen Charlotte Islands. Short-stemmed sedge has **plump, broad, orbicular** perigynia, relatively broad (to 3 mm), coarse, firm leaves and a **short bract** below the lowermost non-basal female spike. **Long-stoloned sedge** (*C. inops*, also known as *C. pensylvanica*) also has hairy perigynia and purplish leaf sheaths like those of Ross' sedge, but it **lacks the additional spikes on long stalks near the base of the stem** and has creeping **rhizomes or stolons**. It occurs in dry, open forest and grassy meadows and on rocky slopes at low to middle elevations, fairly commonly from the Strait of Georgia–Puget Sound area south to California.

GOLDEN SEDGE • *Carex aurea*

GENERAL: Loosely tufted from long, slender rhizomes with short runners; stems slender, from very short to greatly exceeding the leaves (5–40 cm tall), light brown at the base.

LEAVES: From near the base, 2–4 mm wide, more or less flat.

INFLORESCENCE: Male spike narrow, terminal; 3–5 oblong female spikes with 4–20 flowers each, the upper ones on short stalks, the lower ones on long stalks; long, leaf-like bracts.

PERIGYNIA: Rounded-egg-shaped, **beakless, coarsely ribbed, golden to orange** when mature, 2-angled; scales reddish-brown, shorter and narrower than perigynia, widely spreading at maturity; 2 stigmas.

ECOLOGY: Wet gravelly sites (gravel bars, lake-shores, stream-banks), bogs, fens, seepage meadows; from low to subalpine elevations; common mostly along our eastern boundary, absent from most of the outer coast.

NOTES: The round, golden perigynia make this sedge distinctive. The **spikes often lie on the ground when ripe.** • Some taxonomists recognize 2 other species in this group: **two-coloured scale sedge** (*C. bicolor*), in which the sheath of the lowest bract has **black, ear-like flanges** at its mouth and the **perigynia are bluish-white**; and **Garber's sedge** (*C. garberi* ssp. *bifaria*, also known as *C. hassei*), in which the terminal spike has **female flowers above** and male flowers below. Both of these species are sporadic mostly north of 58°N, and *C. garberi* also occurs occasionally from Vancouver Island south. • Golden (*aurea*) sedge is an apt name for this charming sedge whose perigynia turn a lovely golden to orange at maturity.

GOOSE-GRASS SEDGE • *Carex enanderi*
ENANDER'S SEDGE

GENERAL: Loosely tufted, from rhizomes or stolons; stems stiff, hairless, 12–40 cm tall, with brownish or purplish leaf sheaths at base.

LEAVES: Flat, 1–3 mm wide, shorter than stems.

INFLORESCENCE: Spikes 3–5, **oblong-cylindrical; terminal spike stalkless, with female flowers on top**; lateral spikes female, stalked, ascending to erect in a fairly tight cluster; **lowest bract leaf-like, longer than inflorescence**.

PERIGYNIA: Straw-coloured or greyish-green, sometimes purple-spotted, egg-shaped to elliptic, 2–3.5 mm long, **many-veined or many-ribbed** on both sides; **scales purplish-black, shorter and narrower** than perigynia; 2 stigmas.

ECOLOGY: Peaty/gravelly sites along streams and pools, wet meadows, **usually at high elevations;** fairly common but scattered.

NOTES: Goose-grass sedge is also called *C. eleusinoides.* • A Swedish clergyman, Sven Enander (1847–1928), despite being a student of willows, lends his name to this sedge. Why the plant has acquired the name 'goose-grass' is not known, though the same common name has been applied to other low, grass-like plants.

KELLOGG'S SEDGE • *Carex kelloggii*

GENERAL: Densely tufted, with short rhizomes; stems 10–80 cm tall, brownish and shreddy at the base, with conspicuous old leaves.

LEAVES: Flat above, channelled below, **1–3 mm wide**, usually exceeding the stems; **sheaths brown-spotted**.

INFLORESCENCE: Terminal spike usually male; lateral 3–5 spikes female, close together or slightly separated, **erect**, the upper stalkless, the lower short-stalked; **lowest bract leaf-like, much longer than inflorescence**.

PERIGYNIA: Light-green to straw-coloured, somewhat granular-bumpy on the surface, egg-shaped, 2–4 mm long, several-veined on both sides, abruptly short-beaked, short-stalked, falling off early; **scales purplish-brown to blackish, shorter than perigynia**; 2 stigmas.

ECOLOGY: Bogs, swamps, wet meadows, stream-banks, lake-shores, from low to subalpine elevations; common and widespread.

NOTES: *C. kelloggii* includes *Carex lenticularis*. • Albert Kellogg (1813–87) was a San Francisco physician and botanist who founded the Californian Academy of Sciences (and, as far as we know, was not responsible for creating corn flakes).

SITKA SEDGE • *Carex sitchensis*

GENERAL: Tufted from coarse, short, scaly, brown-purplish rhizomes; stems 40–150 cm tall, reddish brown at base, with conspicuous old leaves.

LEAVES: Flat with margins rolled under, **3–10 mm wide**, partitioned by **whitish, knot-like crosswalls** between the veins; **sheaths dark tinged at mouth**.

INFLORESCENCE: Long, cylindrical spikes; 1–4 erect, male, terminal spikes; lower 3–5 spikes female or with male flowers at top, **erect or drooping on slender stalks**; lowermost bract leaf-like, longer than inflorescence.

PERIGYNIA: Greenish or straw-coloured, oval to egg-shaped, 2–3.5 mm long, veinless, short-beaked; **scales purplish-brown with clear or whitish tip, longer than perigynia**; 2 stigmas.

ECOLOGY: Fens, swamps, marshes, wet meadows, lake-shores, from low to middle elevations; common and widespread.

NOTES: Water sedge (*C. aquatilis*, **inset photo**) is similar, but it has **long, cord-like** rhizomes, lower spikes that are **short-stalked or stalkless and erect**, and scales that are **shorter** than the perigynia and **lacking whitish tips**. Water sedge is scattered in bogs and fens, and on wet shores from low to high elevations the length of our region, but it occurs much more commonly to the east. Sitka sedge could be confused with **slough sedge** (p. 400), but slough sedge has **fibrous-shreddy sheaths** at the base of the stems and **plump, leathery** perigynia. • Sitka sedge often forms tall, dense stands that are an important part of prime waterfowl habitat in wet meadows and streamside areas. • *C. sitchensis* is named after Sitka in Alaska, from where it was first described.

LYNGBY'S SEDGE • *Carex lyngbyei*

GENERAL: Stems **single or in clumps** from well-developed creeping **rhizomes and stolons**, 20–100 cm tall, **purplish-brown at the base but not shreddy**, with conspicuous old leaves.

LEAVES: Flat with margins rolled under, 2–8 mm wide, shorter than stems, rough, abruptly pointed.

INFLORESCENCE: Spikes **all on slender, spreading or drooping stalks**; upper 2–3 spikes male, lower 2–4 spikes cylindrical, female or with male flowers at the top; lowermost bract leaf-like.

PERIGYNIA: Green to brown, egg-shaped, about 3 mm long, **plump, leathery and thick-walled**, obscurely veined on both sides, beakless or with a very short, whitish beak; scales reddish-brown to black, sharp tipped, much longer than perigynia; 2 stigmas.

ECOLOGY: Tidal marshes and flats, estuarine meadows, brackish marshes, gravel or cobble beaches; **very common along the coastline.**

NOTES: Lyngby's sedge is our most common shoreline sedge. It is often the dominant species in tidal marshes, growing in dense, nearly pure stands. • **Lesser saltmarsh sedge** (*C. glareosa*) and **Gmelin's sedge** (*C. gmelinii*) are both maritime species that also occur in tidal marshes in the northern half of our region. • Lyngby's sedge is a pioneer colonizer of tidal mudflats. It promotes rapid sedimentation as it grows, because eddies form around its stems. It is prime forage for geese during spring migration, and for trumpeter swans and grizzly bears, because it contains as much as 25% crude protein when young.

SLOUGH SEDGE • *Carex obnupta*

GENERAL: Densely tufted along long, **stout rhizomes**; stems coarse, stiff, 60–150 cm tall, **purplish and with shreddy sheaths (becoming web-like) at base**, with conspicuous old leaves.

LEAVES: Flat to channelled, with margins rolled under, 3–10 mm wide, coarse, firm, shorter than stems.

INFLORESCENCE: Upper 1–3 spikes male, often curving; lower 2–4 spikes cylindrical, female or with male flowers at top, stalkless or **on short erect stalks**, spreading or drooping; lowermost bract leaf-like, longer than spikes.

PERIGYNIA: Shiny yellowish-green or brown, elliptic, **plump, leathery and thick-walled**, 2-ribbed but nerveless on both sides, with very short beak; scales purplish-black, sharp-tipped, longer than perigynia; 2 stigmas.

ECOLOGY: Marshes, swamps, bogs, stream-banks, lake-shores, wet forest openings, meadows, clearings; common at low elevations.

NOTES: While similar in appearance to Lyngby's sedge, **slough sedge** has **shining** (not dull) perigynia, **fibrous-shreddy** lower leaf sheaths and lower spikes on **short, stiff, erect** (rather than long, spreading to drooping) stalks. The 2 species usually occur in different habitats from one another, although they can sometimes be found together in brackish sloughs and upper parts of tidal marshes. • Slough sedge is still a popular basket material for the Nuu-chah-nulth and the Makah. The inner leaves are split and flattened before being dried. Fine baskets are made from this sedge, often with cedar foundations and intricate designs from dyed strands of grass or coloured barks.

PALE SEDGE • *Carex livida*

GENERAL: Solitary or loosely tufted from long slender rhizomes; stems 10–50 cm tall, smooth.

LEAVES: Channelled (V-folded), firm, narrow **(1–3.5 mm wide),** very glaucous (appear light **bluish-green to blue-grey**), mostly basal, often longer than stems.

INFLORESCENCE: Terminal spike usually male; lateral 1–3 spikes female, nearly stalkless to short stalked, **erect to ascending,** with **few (5–15) perigynia;** lowermost bract leaf-like, nearly as long as inflorescence, **with long sheath at base.**

PERIGYNIA: Bluish-green to whitish or straw-coloured, elliptic to oblong-egg-shaped, **3–4.5 mm long, veinless, beakless or very short-beaked;** scales purplish-brown with green centre and clear margins, shorter than or equalling the perigynia; 3 stigmas.

ECOLOGY: Bogs, fens, shallow peatland pools, muddy stream-banks, wet forest openings; common at low to middle elevations.

NOTES: Woodrush sedge (*C. ablata,* also known as *C. luzulina*) is a somewhat similar species of middle- to high-elevation fens, bogs and wet meadows; it is scattered and locally common from southern Vancouver Island and the adjacent mainland south to California. It forms small **dense tufts;** it has **flat leaves 3–9 mm wide** and commonly **much shorter** than stems, and it has **yellowish-green, lance-shaped** perigynia with minutely saw-toothed margins and a short, **dark beak. Henderson's sedge** (*C. hendersonii*) grows in wet forest and in boggy or springy openings from low to middle elevations, sporadically over much the same range as woodrush sedge. Henderson's sedge is tufted and **50–100 cm tall;** it has **large, M-folded, green leaves 6–15 mm wide** and **as long as** stems; and it has narrowly elliptic, **greenish, many-veined,** short-beaked perigynia **4.5–6.5 mm long.** • The Latin name for the species means 'lead-coloured, bluish-grey, leaden,' and describes the colouration of the leaves and perigynia.

SEVERAL-FLOWERED SEDGE • *Carex pluriflora*

GENERAL: Loosely tufted with long, purplish-black rhizomes; roots covered with **yellowish felt;** stems arising singly or few together, 20–60 cm tall, clothed with old leaf bases.

LEAVES: About as long as the stems, flat with margins rolled under, 2–4 mm wide, glaucous.

INFLORESCENCE: Erect male terminal spike; 1–3 lateral female spikes, nodding on long, slender stalks; **lowest bract bristle-like and much shorter than inflorescence.**

PERIGYNIA: Pale-green to blackish-brown at maturity, egg-shaped, **plumply triangular** in cross-section, beakless, 3–4.5 mm long; scales black, slightly longer than perigynia; 3 stigmas.

ECOLOGY: Common in bogs, fens, marshes, stream-banks, wet meadows, from low to middle elevations.

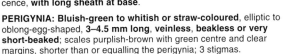

NOTES: Shore sedge (*C. limosa,* also called mud sedge) and **poor sedge** (*C. magellanica* ssp. *irrigua,* also called bog sedge and *C. paupercula*) are similar to several-flowered sedge in appearance and habitat, but they are **less common** in our region (both are absent from the Queen Charlotte Islands, and poor sedge probably does not occur south of B.C. to any great extent) and much more frequent inland. Both have the characteristic yellowish, felty roots of this group of sedges, but their perigynia are **bluish-green** and somewhat **flattened-triangular** in cross-section. The male spikes of **shore sedge** are **15–27 mm long,** whereas those of **poor sedge** are **4–12 mm long.** • 'Several-flowered' is the meaning of the Latin *pluriflora.*

LARGE-AWNED SEDGE • *Carex macrochaeta*

GENERAL: **Loosely tufted**, with short, densely matted rhizomes; roots covered with **yellowish felt**; stems 10–90 cm tall, **purplish-red and fibrous-shreddy at the base.**

LEAVES: Flat with margins rolled under, 2–5 mm wide, firm, shorter than stems.

INFLORESCENCE: Erect male terminal spike; 2–4 female lateral spikes, erect or more commonly spreading to nodding on slender stalks; **lowest bract leaf-like, about as long as inflorescence.**

PERIGYNIA: Straw-coloured or greenish, sometimes purplish-spotted, elliptic-lance-shaped, 3–5 mm long, **flattened-triangular** in cross-section, minutely beaked; scales **black**, longer than perigynia, with **awn 3–12 mm long**; 3 stigmas.

ECOLOGY: Common in wet meadows, sandy beaches, heaths, streambanks, rocky runnels and waterfall spray zones, from low to subalpine elevations; rare in Washington.

NOTES: Large-awned sedge is similar to **showy sedge** (*C. spectabilis*), which, however, **lacks the yellowish felt** on the roots and has **dark-reddish** scales with conspicuous, **pale midribs** that often stick out from the scales as **awn tips to 1 mm long**. Showy sedge grows in moist meadows and forest openings and on rocky slopes, from low to high elevations. It occurs commonly in most of our region, from Alaska south to the Olympic Mountains and through the Cascades to California; it is absent from the Queen Charlotte Islands. It is mostly subalpine in Washington and Oregon, and it dominates some subalpine meadows in the Olympic and Cascade mountains. • Large-awned sedge is an abundant and important summer forage species for mountain goats in B.C. and Alaska.

MERTENS' SEDGE • *Carex mertensii*

GENERAL: Densely tufted, often forming large clumps; stems **to 120 cm tall**, sharply triangular and **narrowly winged**, very rough on the angles.

LEAVES: Shorter than the stem, flat, 4–7 mm wide, from the lower half of the stem; basal leaves reduced to scales.

INFLORESCENCE: Terminal spike **male below, female above**; lateral 5–10 spikes female with a few male flowers at the base of most spikes, **large, cylindrical, crowded together, and drooping on slender stalks**.

PERIGYNIA: Whitish, oval, papery and flattened, about 5 mm long, with a very small, red-tipped beak; scales dark reddish-brown with lighter midrib, **much smaller than perigynia**; 3 stigmas.

ECOLOGY: Moist to wet forest openings, wet meadows, stream-banks, open rocky slopes, often in disturbed areas such as roadsides and clearings; common from low to moderately high (not alpine) elevations.

NOTES: This large sedge is distinctive with its broad, colourful spikes. • **Showy sedge** (*C. spectabilis*) is superficially similar, but it is somewhat smaller, with smaller spikes, a **male** terminal spike, **darker** perigynia, and **awn-tipped** scales. • Mertens' sedge was likely named for Carl Heinrich Mertens (1896–1830) who was from Bremen and was the first European botanical collector at Sitka, Alaska. He accompanied Lütke on the corvette *Senjavin*. It may have been named for F.C. Mertens, German botanist (1764–1831), but this is less likely.

LONG-STYLED SEDGE • *Carex stylosa*
VARIEGATED SEDGE

GENERAL: Densely tufted on short, stout, shreddy rhizomes; stems 10–50 cm tall, **purplish-red and fibrous-shreddy at base, which is clothed with conspicuous old leaves**.

LEAVES: Bunched near the base, flat with margins rolled under or channelled towards the base, 1–4 mm wide, firm, shorter than stems.

INFLORESCENCE: Terminal spike male; lateral 1–3 spikes female, stalked, erect to ascending, somewhat separate in a loose cluster; lowermost bract leaf-like but shorter than inflorescence.

PERIGYNIA: Straw-coloured to dark brown or purple, elliptic to egg-shaped, 2.5–3.5 mm long, hairless and smooth, minutely beaked; scales purplish-black, **about equalling or shorter than perigynia**; 3 stigmas; **thick style sticks out prominently.**

ECOLOGY: Bogs, fens, marshes, wet meadows, stream-banks, shorelines; sometimes forms dense, round tussocks on open, boggy slopes; low to high elevations, especially on the outer coast.

NOTES: This sedge is also called 'variegated sedge,' from the variable colours of the perigynia. • **Buxbaum's sedge or club sedge** (*C. buxbaumii*) has **single or loosely** tufted stems 30–100 cm tall from long rhizomes, **glaucous** leaves, **2–5 oblong-egg-shaped spikes** in a loose cluster **equalled or exceeded by the leaf-like lowermost bract**, and **blue-green** perigynia exceeded by narrow, purplish-brown scales with **awned or long, pointy tips**. It grows in marshes, fens, bogs, wet meadows and wet thickets and along shorelines. It is frequent but scattered at low to middle elevations in the southern half of our region and sporadic northwards.

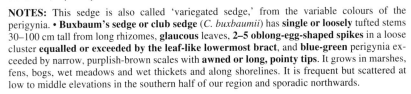

BEAKED SEDGE • *Carex rostrata*

GENERAL: Thick stems, **to 120 cm tall, in large clumps** from short, stout rhizomes and long, creeping stolons, sometimes forming a dense sod; base light brown, thick, spongy, conspicuously clothed with old leaves; **sheaths not shredding and becoming web-like.**

LEAVES: Upper leaves long, **exceeding stems, yellowish-green, rather thick**, more or less flat, up to 12 mm wide, conspicuously partitioned by **whitish, knot-like crosswalls** between the veins.

INFLORESCENCE: Long, with cylindrical spikes; 2–4 overlapping male spikes at the top; densely flowered, short-stalked or stalkless, erect female spikes below; lowest bract leaf-like, longer than spikes.

PERIGYNIA: Inflated, membranous but firm, **shining, yellowish-green to straw-coloured**, egg-shaped, 3–8 mm long, **several-ribbed**, abruptly tapering to a beak with **2 short points, spreading at maturity**; scales reddish-brown and narrower than the perigynia; 3 stigmas.

ECOLOGY: A very common, large water sedge that prefers perennially wet areas at low to middle elevations.

NOTES: **Inflated sedge** (*C. exsiccata*, also known as *C. vesicaria*) is similar and has similar habitat preferences, but it has **shreddy (becoming web-like)** sheaths, and **many-ribbed**, reddish-tinged perigynia gradually tapering to a long beak and **not spreading** at maturity. **Retrorse sedge** (*C. retrorsa*) has **many-ribbed, spreading or reflexed** perigynia contracted to a beak with **2 erect points** and leaf-like bracts **several times longer** than the inflorescence. Both species range from about 55°N south to California (*C. exsiccata*) or southwestern B.C. (*C. retrorsa*). Inflated sedge, which also occurs on the Queen Charlotte Islands, is by far the more common of the two. • **Slender sedge** (*C. lasiocarpa*) and **woolly sedge** (*C. lanuginosa*) are also big water sedges, but both have **densely hairy** perigynia. They both range from about 55°N south to California and are absent from the Queen Charlotte Islands.

TULE • *Scirpus lacustris*
HARD-STEMMED BULRUSH, SOFT-STEMMED BULRUSH

GENERAL: Stout perennial from thick, scaly, reddish-brown rhizomes, sometimes forming large colonies; stems **cylindrical, erect, in rows along rhizomes, 1–2 cm thick** towards the base, mostly **1–3 m tall.**

LEAVES: Few, mostly at or near the base of the stem, **reduced to prominent membranous sheaths** with poorly developed or no blades.

INFLORESCENCE: Spikelets brown, 8–15 mm long, **several to many in an open to compact, branched, terminal cluster**; main involucral bract 1–10 cm long, greenish, **appearing as an extension of the stem.**

FRUITS: Achenes, egg-shaped, nut-like, pointy-tipped, about 2 mm long, concealed by brownish to pale-grey, spirally arranged scales, each surrounded by several fragile, whitish bristles that are about as long as the achene.

ECOLOGY: Marshes, muddy shores, shallow water (fresh and brackish), at low elevations; occurs sporadically north of Vancouver Island, more frequently in the southern half of our region, where it is locally abundant.

NOTES: *S. lacustris* includes 2 subspecies: **hard-stemmed bulrush** (ssp. *validus* also known as *S. acutus*), with reddish-brown spikelets and **stems that are not easily crushed** between the fingers, and **soft-stemmed bulrush** (ssp. *glaucus* also known as *S. validus*), with greyish-brown spikelets and **stems that are soft and easily crushed** between the fingers. • The stems of this plant were important for making baskets and mats that were used as walls and roofs of temporary shelters, and as floor mats, door covers and seat covers, among other things. The stems were harvested in late summer or early fall, brought home in large bundles and then spread out to dry in the sun. The mats were made by laying the stems side by side, alternating top and bottom, and either sewing with a long needle or twining the stems together with a tough fibre such as stinging nettle or Indian hemp. The mats were light and insulating because of the pithy center of the stem. The Nuu-chah-nulth made baskets and basket lids from the stems. The Vancouver Island Salish traded tule mats to the Mainland Salish in exchange for mountain-goat wool. • The common name 'tule' is a Spanish word derived from the Nahuartl word *tollin* meaning 'a rush.' (Nahuartl is a North American Indian linguistic stock related to Shoshonean, comprising Aztec and other tribes from Central America and Mexico).

Gathering tules at Cowichan Lake E.S. Curtis (ca. 1915).

SMALL-FLOWERED BULRUSH • *Scirpus microcarpus*

GENERAL: Stems usually **clustered**, from a sturdy rhizome, stout, triangular, **leafy**, to 1.5 m tall.

LEAVES: Several, from both the base and the stem, **flat, 10–15 mm wide**; leaf sheaths often purplish-tinged and with **whitish, knot-like crosswalls**.

INFLORESCENCE: Numerous short spikelets in **small clusters at the ends of spreading stalks; involucral bracts several, leaf-like**.

FRUITS: Pale, lens-shaped, seed-like, pointy-tipped achenes, 1 mm long, each surrounded by 4–6 slightly longer bristles; scales greenish-black with prominent midrib.

ECOLOGY: Swamps, sloughs, stream-banks, wet ditches and clearings; common at low to middle elevations.

NOTES: *S. microcarpus* is also known as *S. sylvaticus* and *S. rubrotinctus*. • **Seacoast bulrush** (*S. maritimus*, also known as *S. paludosus*) has stems 20–150 cm tall arising from **tubers** along stout rhizomes. It has several to many spikelets aggregated in a **head-like** terminal cluster cradled by **1–4 long, leaf-like bracts**. Seacoast bulrush occurs in low-elevation marshes, shores, wet meadows and shallow water, in both fresh and brackish to saline conditions. It is common from about 53°N south, and has been reported from southeast Alaska. • Small-flowered bulrush was apparently used to weave light-duty baskets and as an ornamental trim in hide clothing. The leaves were sometimes laid over and under food in steaming pits. • The common name 'small-flowered' is a translation of *microcarpus*.

AMERICAN BULRUSH • *Scirpus americanus*

GENERAL: Perennial from long, stout rhizomes; **stems single or in small groups, sharply triangular**, erect, 15–100 cm tall.

LEAVES: Usually **channelled or folded and narrow (1–2 mm wide)**, sometimes flat and 2–4 mm wide, firm, several but all borne towards the base, shorter than stems.

INFLORESCENCE: Spikelets 1–7, **stalkless in a tight cluster**; main involucral bract prominent, leaf-like, 3–10 cm long, **appearing as a continuation of the stem**.

FRUITS: Dark-brown, lens-shaped, seed-like, pointy-tipped achenes, 2–3 mm long, each surrounded by 2–6 bristles equalling or shorter than achene; scales brown to blackish-purple, with firm **midrib extended as a short awn from the cleft tip**.

ECOLOGY: Fresh and brackish marshes, shores, wet meadows, ditches; common at low elevations.

NOTES: American bulrush is one of the most widespread flowering plants; it occurs on several continents, including Australia. • American and seacoast bulrush (mentioned above) often occur together in tidal marshes, but American bulrush seems to prefer coarser substrates, where freshwater influence is greater, while seacoast bulrush dominates on finer and more saline substrates. • American bulrush stems were used by the Nuu-chah-nulth as the foundation material for their beautiful wrapped-twine baskets of tall basket sedge. They were also used for weaving basket lids and handles. • 'Bulrush' has nothing to do with rushing bulls; is a corruption of *pole-rush* or 'pool-rush,' because the plant grows in pools of water.

TUFTED CLUBRUSH • *Trichophorum cespitosum*

GENERAL: Densely tufted perennial, often forming **tussocks**; stems slender, smooth, greyish-green, **circular in cross-section**, 10–40 cm tall, **clothed with leaf sheaths at the base**.

LEAVES: Several, light-brown, scale-like at base of stem; **single stem leaf about 5 mm long**.

INFLORESCENCE: Single, terminal spike, 2–4 flowered; midvein of lowest bract prolonged into a **blunt awn** (about as long as spike).

FRUITS: Brown, narrowly egg-shaped, 3-angled, minutely pointy-tipped, 1.5 mm long, seed-like achenes, each surrounded by 6 delicate, white bristles about twice as long as the achene; scales chestnut brown.

ECOLOGY: Bogs, fens, peaty/gravelly shores, wet tundra; common from lowland to alpine.

NOTES: Tufted clubrush is also called *Scirpus cespitosus*. • **Low clubrush** (*Scirpus cernuus*) is a tufted **annual** with numerous slender, hair-like stems 3–25 cm tall, 1 to few mostly reduced leaves, a solitary egg-shaped spikelet 2–5 mm long, a solitary involucral bract and tiny achenes **without surrounding bristles**. It is scattered and locally common in tidal marshes and on muddy flats, beaches and shores, from the Queen Charlotte Islands south through California. • Tufted clubrush sometimes turns bright yellow or orange in the fall. • The Latin *Trichophorum* means 'hair-carrier,' in reference to the long bristles surrounding the fruits.

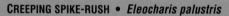

CREEPING SPIKE-RUSH • *Eleocharis palustris*

GENERAL: Perennial with rhizomes; stems oval in cross-section, arising **singly or in clusters from long, dark-brown rhizome**, with reddish sheaths at the base, 10–100 cm tall.

LEAVES: All basal and reduced to mere sheaths.

INFLORESCENCE: A **solitary terminal spikelet**, 5–25 mm long, brown, lance- to egg-shaped, with **2 or 3 empty scales** at the base; fertile scales several, spirally arranged; 2 stigmas.

FRUITS: Achenes, lens-shaped, yellow-brown, 1–1.5 mm long, surmounted by a **conical tubercle** (like a nose cone), surrounded by typically 4 bristles a bit longer than the achene.

ECOLOGY: Wet ditches, brackish tidal marshes, meadows, shorelines, shallow water, from low to middle elevations; common throughout our region and elsewhere over its broad, global range.

NOTES: Several other species of spike-rush occur in our region. **Kamchatka spike-rush** (*E. kamtschatica*) is a rhizomatous perennial similar to creeping spike-rush, but it has spikelets subtended by a **single, empty basal scale** and achenes with rounded, **bulbous tubercles**, and it occurs sporadically in low-elevation marshes, wet meadows and mudflats from northern Vancouver Island north through coastal Alaska. **Needle spike-rush** (*E. acicularis*) is a **mat-forming** perennial that has oblong-egg-shaped, **many-ribbed** achenes with **3 stigmas**. It grows in marshes and shallow water, and on mudflats and shorelines, scattered throughout our region. **Small spike-rush** (*E. parvula*) is a **very small (to 6 cm tall), mat-forming** perennial that has **3-angled** achenes with **3 stigmas**. It grows in salt marshes and on brackish tidal flats, scattered from southern Vancouver Island to California. **Ovoid spike-rush** (*E. ovata*) is a **tufted annual** 5–50 cm tall with **2 stigmas**. It occurs in marshes and wet, muddy places from the Queen Charlotte Islands south.

NARROW-LEAVED COTTON-GRASS • *Eriophorum angustifolium*

GENERAL: Stems arising **singly or a few together from widely spreading rhizomes**, rounded, to 80 cm tall, clothed at the base with dark-brown sheaths.

LEAVES: Both at the base and along the stem; stem leaves flat below the middle, triangular and channelled toward the tip, **2–6 mm wide**.

INFLORESCENCE: Spikelets drooping, 2–8 in a loose cluster; 2 or more **leafy involucral bracts**, longer than inflorescence.

FRUITS: Dark-brown to black, egg-shaped, 3-angled, 2–2.5 mm long, seed-like achenes, each surrounded by numerous, **long (2–3.5 cm) white bristles; scales brownish or greyish**, the slender midrib not reaching the tip.

ECOLOGY: Fens, bogs, wet meadows and stream-banks; widespread and common from low to high elevations throughout most of our region, south mostly at higher elevations to Mt. Jefferson, Oregon.

NOTES: Narrow-leaved cotton-grass is also known as *E. poly-stachion.* • When mature, the bristles of *E. angustifolium* form large, white clusters that resemble cotton balls, hence the name 'cotton-grass.' The bristles aid seed dispersal by wind. Some boggy areas turn white when the abundant cotton-grass is in fruit. • *Eriophorum* is Latin for 'wool-bearer'; *angustifolium* means 'narrow-leaved.'

CHAMISSO'S COTTON-GRASS • *Eriophorum chamissonis*

GENERAL: Extensive beds growing from spreading rhizomes or stolons; stems rounded, 20–70 cm tall, clothed at the base with dark-brown sheaths.

LEAVES: Mostly near the base, very narrow (0.5–2 mm wide), channelled throughout.

INFLORESCENCE: Solitary spikelet at tip of stem; no leafy involucral bracts.

FRUITS: Brown, oblong-egg-shaped, 3-angled, 2–3 mm long, seed-like achenes, each surrounded by numerous long, normally **cinnamon-coloured bristles; scales blackish**, the slender midrib not reaching the tip.

ECOLOGY: Fens, bogs, wet ditches; scattered at low to middle elevations.

NOTES: Chamisso's cotton-grass is also called *E. russeolum.* • This species is distinguished from other **single-headed** cotton-grasses (none of which is common in our region) by the **combination** of **rust-coloured bristles** and **spreading rhizomes**. • Chamisso's cotton-grass, with its distinctive, fluffy fruiting heads, is well known to many aboriginal peoples. In some languages, it is given the same name as is eagle down. • *E. chamissonis* is named for Albert Ludwig von Chamisso de Boncourt, a German poet-naturalist and the botanist on board the ship *Rurik*, which visited Alaska in 1816–1817.

407

WHITE BEAK-RUSH • *Rhynchospora alba*

GENERAL: Tufted perennial with short rhizomes; stems triangular, slender, leafy, 10–50 cm tall.

LEAVES: Very narrow (to 1 mm wide); lowest leaves reduced, often scale-like; upper leaves elongate, shorter than stems, channelled to flat, greyish-green.

INFLORESCENCE: Several to many small spikelets in 1–3 **compact, head-like clusters 5–15 mm wide**; terminal cluster largest and with a small involucral bract about as long as the inflorescence; lateral clusters (if any) on stalks; spikelets usually 2-flowered.

FRUITS: Achenes, brownish-green, lens-shaped, 1.5–2 mm long, tapering to **narrowly triangular tubercle**, each surrounded by **10–12 stiff bristles; scales whitish to pale brown.**

ECOLOGY: Bogs, fens, wet peaty or sandy soil; common from low to middle elevations.

NOTES: White beak-rush is our only local representative of the genus *Rhynchospora*, which is much more abundant (ca. 200 species) in warmer climates. • The common name derives from the Latin *rhynchospora* meaning 'beaked seed,' and *alba*, meaning 'white.'

DULICHIUM • *Dulichium arundinaceum*

GENERAL: Perennial herb; stems arising **singly or a few together** from rhizomes, **leafy, hollow,** rounded or obtusely triangular, 30–100 cm tall.

LEAVES: Relatively **short, flat, fairly wide (3–8 mm), numerous, in 3 ranks and rather evenly distributed** along the stem; lower leaves mere bladeless sheaths.

INFLORESCENCE: Spikes of 7–10 spikelets each, **in axils** of upper leaves; **spikelets linear, flattened,** several flowered, **in 2 rows and stalkless** on the axis of the spike.

FRUITS: Achenes, flattened, narrowly oblong, 2.5–3 mm long, **stalked and long beaked,** each surrounded by **6–9 downwardly barbed, brownish bristles**; scales longer than achenes.

ECOLOGY: Fens, wet meadows, margins of ponds and streams; fairly common at low to middle elevations.

NOTES: Dulichium is widespread in eastern North America, from Newfoundland to Florida. • The genus name *Dulichium* is of uncertain origin and meaning; the species name *arundinaceum* means 'reed-like.'

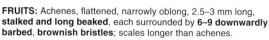

Key to the Rush Family

1a. Capsules 3 chambered; seeds numerous; leaves stiff, hairless .... *Juncus*
    2a. Involucral bract (lowest bract of the inflorescence) resembling an
    extension and continuation of the stem, inflorescence thus appearing lateral 3
        3a. Tufted alpine plants; flowers 1–4; involucral bract
        rarely more than 2 cm long; seeds conspicuously tailed .... *J. drummondii*
        3b. Tufted (*J. effusus* only) or with rhizomes; plants of
        low to subalpine elevations; flowers many; involucral
        bracts more than 5 cm long; seeds not tailed 4
            4a. Stems in dense clusters; stamens 3 .... *J. effusus*
            4b. Stems not in dense clusters, distributed along
            elongate rhizomes; stamens 6 .... *J. arcticus*
    2b. Involucral bract (lowest bract of the inflorescence)
    leafy or scale-like, not forming a continuation of the stem,
    inflorescence thus appearing terminal 5
        5a. Plants annual .... *J. bufonius*
        5b. Plants perennial 6
            6a. Inflorescence unbranched or sparsely branched,
            with 1–10 large, densely-flowered heads 7
                7a. Leaves rounded in cross-section; bracts of the
                inflorescence conspicuous, light brown .... *J. mertensianus*
                7b. Leaves flattened; bracts of the inflorescence
                inconspicuous or if evident greenish 8
                      8a. Rhizomes scaly; leaves without
                      crosswalls; stamens 6 .... *J. falcatus*
                      8b. Rhizomes not scaly; leaves laterally flattened
                      (iris-like), with partial crosswalls; stamens 3 or 6 .... *J. ensifolius*
            6b. Inflorescence freely branched, usually with
            more than 3 small, loosely-flowered heads 9
                9a. Leaves without crosswalls .... *J. tenuis*
                9b. Leaves with crosswalls 10
                      10a. Plants tufted, often producing plantlets;
                      flower scales much shorter than the capsules .... *J. supiniformis*
                      10b. Plants with rhizomes, never producing plantlets;
                      flower scales about as long as the capsules .... *J. acuminatus*
1b. Capsules 1 chambered; seeds 3; leaves flexible,
usually hairy on margins near base .... *Luzula*
    11a. Flowers 1–3 at the ends of branches of open inflorescences 12
        12a. Plants usually less than 30 cm tall; stem leaves
        1–3, to 5 mm wide; flower bracts strongly torn and frilly at tip .... *L. piperi*
        12b. Plants usually more than 30 cm tall; stem
        leaves usually 4 or more, 5–10 mm wide; flower
        bracts entire to slightly torn and frilly at the tip .... *L. parviflora*
    11b. Flowers 4 or more in spikes or heads 13
        13a. Inflorescence erect, not drooping; involucral
        bract leaf-like, well developed; flower bracts slightly frilly .... *L. multiflora*
        13b. Inflorescence tending to droop; involucral bract
        poorly developed; flower bracts strongly frilly .... *L. arcuata*

seed
stigmas
capsule
flower scales

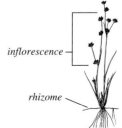

inflorescence

rhizome

COMMON RUSH • *Juncus effusus*

GENERAL: **Tufted** perennial from stout rhizomes; stems **leafless**, 25–130 cm tall, round, finely grooved, **1.5–3 mm thick**.

LEAVES: All basal, **reduced to brown sheaths**.

INFLORESCENCE: **Apparently lateral**, many-flowered, compact to open; lowermost bract 8–25 cm long, erect and **appearing as a continuation of the stem**; flower scales ('sepals' and 'petals') greenish or brownish, **2–3.5 mm long**; **stamens usually 3**, anthers about 1 mm long.

FRUITS: Capsules, egg-shaped, slightly shorter than or about as long as the scales, blunt or rounded at the tip; seeds ellipsoid, finely ridged, minutely pointed at tips.

ECOLOGY: Moist to wet fields, pastures, roadsides, ditches, clearings, tideflats, pond margins and bogs, at low to middle elevations; common, often abundant in disturbed habitats.

NOTES: Thread rush (*J. filiformis*) has even **longer** involucral bracts **(at least half as long as the stem)** and **slender stems (about 1 mm thick)**. It grows in moist meadows, marshes and bogs, and on sandy shores, from low to subalpine elevations; it is scattered through most of our region, south to northern Oregon. • Stems of common rush were used for weaving by the mainland Comox, and possibly by other groups, although some people said they were too brittle. The Quinault used them, mixed with cattail, to weave tumplines and string. • Rushes were once used as a charm to cure thrush in babies in Devon, England. 3 rushes taken from a stream were passed separately through the mouth of the patient. The rushes were then thrown in the stream and, as they were carried away, the child would be cured.

ARCTIC RUSH • *Juncus arcticus*

GENERAL: **Strongly rhizomatous** perennial; stems stout, arising comb-like from rhizome, **rounded**, 10–100 cm tall, 1.5–4 mm thick at base.

LEAVES: All basal, mostly **reduced** to bladeless, pointy-tipped, lustrous, **yellowish-brown sheaths**.

INFLORESCENCE: **Apparently lateral**, with several to many flowers clustered on 1 side of the stem, compact to 1 cm long or open to 15 cm long; involucral bract erect, rounded, sharply pointed, 4–25 cm long, **appearing like a continuation of the stem**; flower scales greenish to dark brown, **4–6 mm long; stamens 6**.

FRUITS: Capsules, about as long as the scales; seeds elliptic, finely net-veined, minutely pointed at tips.

ECOLOGY: Salt and brackish marshes, tideflats, wet meadows, sea beaches, sandy lake-shores and river bars; low to middle elevations.

NOTES: *J. arcticus* includes *J. balticus* (Baltic rush). • The closely related **Brewer's rush** (*J. breweri*, assonantly known as *J. lesueurii*) is very similar to arctic rush, but it has **longer (5–7 mm)** flower scales, a **spherical** inflorescence, and **flattened, twisted** stems. It occupies brackish or saline marshes and meadows, sandy beaches and dune slacks; it occurs sporadically from the Queen Charlotte Islands south to California. • Churches were once ceremonially strewn with rushes on some saints' days in Britain. In Grasmere, in England's Lakes District, rushes were carried around the village on August 5th (St. Oswald's day). Villagers carried shapes made out of rushes, such as the hand of St. Oswald, serpents on poles, harps and the child Moses in the bulrushes.

TOAD RUSH • *Juncus bufonius*

GENERAL: Fibrous-rooted **annual**, lacking rhizomes, light green, in age brown; stems solitary or tufted, simple or branched from the base, erect or sprawling, channelled, 5–30 cm tall.

LEAVES: Basal and along the stem, few to several, **very narrow** (mostly less than 1 mm wide), flat to rolled under, 0.5–10 cm long.

INFLORESCENCE: Terminal, commonly much-branched; flowers usually single at the nodes, in the axils of bracts; flower scales **greenish**, narrowly lance-shaped and sharp pointed, 3–8 mm long; stamens 6, the anthers mostly shorter than filaments.

FRUITS: Capsules, oblong-elliptic, rounded at the tip, chestnut-brown, shorter than scales; seeds cylindric-ellipsoid, very finely ridged, minutely pointed at tips.

ECOLOGY: Lake-shores, stream-banks, tideflats, roadsides, fields, gardens, clearings, trampled paths; from sea level to middle elevations; common and widespread in wet, open sites.

NOTES: A cosmopolitan, variable weed; in our region toad rush apparently consists of both native and introduced races. • **Three-flowered rush** (*J. triglumis*) is a dwarf (5–15 cm tall), densely tufted **perennial** with narrow, **rounded, basal** leaves. It has a **solitary, 1–3 flowered** terminal head about as long as the involucral bract, **pale-brown or white** flower scales, cylindrical, pointed capsules, and tailed seeds. It grows in wet, mossy sites, along stream-banks and next to snowbeds at **high elevations**, occasionally in the eastern or inland parts of the northern half of our region, and rarely on the Queen Charlotte Islands. • The species name *bufonius* translates from Latin as either 'of the toad' or 'living in damp places.'

DRUMMOND'S RUSH • *Juncus drummondii*

GENERAL: Small mats of tufted stems from short rhizomes; stems round in cross-section, 5–45 cm tall.

LEAVES: All basal, **reduced to mere sheaths or sheaths with short bristle-tips**.

INFLORESCENCE: Apparently lateral, with **1–3 flowers in a small cluster**; lowermost bract rounded, sharp pointed, **appearing as a continuation of the stem, comes to the top of inflorescence**; flower scales greenish-brown, about 6 mm long; 6 stamens.

FRUITS: Oblong-elliptic capsules with a **rounded, notched** tip and numerous small seeds with membranous tails at each end.

ECOLOGY: Moist, gravelly slopes, heaths, snowbeds, stream-banks, and meadows; common at high elevations throughout our region, especially on the mountains of the mainland.

NOTES: The **short (1–3 cm)** bract and the few flowers per stem help to distinguish this species from other low rushes. • **Parry's rush** (*J. parryi*) is similar to Drummond's rush. It grows in similar but **drier** high-elevation habitats, from southern B.C. frequently through the Cascades to California. Parry's rush has upper basal sheaths with **definite blades** 2–7 cm long, bracts **2–8 cm long** and capsules **pointed** at the tip. • An Irish tradition says that rushes go brown from the top downwards because St. Patrick cursed them. Rushes are supposed to bring luck and protection and are gathered on St. Bride's Eve (January 31st) and hung over doorways. It was considered lucky to find a green-topped rush. • Drummond's rush is named after either the famous botanical collector Thomas Drummond or his grandson, Scottish botanist J. R. Drummond (1851–1933).

MERTENS' RUSH • *Juncus mertensianus*

GENERAL: Tufted perennial with rhizomes; stems leafy, rounded to somewhat flattened, 5–30 cm tall, with brown to purplish basal sheaths.

LEAVES: Few to several basal leaves; stem leaves 1–4, **half rounded, with crosswalls**.

INFLORESCENCE: Terminal, several to many flowers in a **solitary, blackish-brown, hemispherical head**; involucral bract shorter to longer than the head; flower scales dark brown, 3–4 mm long, long pointed; 6 stamens.

FRUITS: Capsules, oblong egg-shaped, about as long as scales, abruptly rounded at tip; seeds cylindric-ellipsoid, finely net-veined, **minutely pointed at ends**.

ECOLOGY: Meadows, stream-banks, snowbeds, pond edges, heath, bogs and rocky runnels; common at middle to high elevations.

NOTES: Regel's rush (*J. regelii*) has **flattened**, grass-like leaves **without crosswalls**, **1–4 chestnut-brown heads** and tailed seeds. It grows in marshes and wet meadows and along stream-banks at middle to subalpine elevations, in the Cascades from southern B.C. to California. **Chestnut rush** (*J. castaneus*) has **flat but rolled under** and channelled leaves **without crosswalls, 1–3 brown heads, large, lustrous** capsules and tailed seeds. It occurs only in the northern part of our region (northern south-east Alaska and Prince William Sound) in marshes and bogs, and on lake-shores and river flats, from middle to subalpine elevations. • Mertens' rush is named after German botanist Karl Franz Mertens (1764–1831).

SICKLE-LEAVED RUSH • *Juncus falcatus*

GENERAL: Perennial with rhizomes; stems leafy, solitary or in clusters, rounded, 10–30 cm tall (line drawings below; **photo is *J. covillei*).**

LEAVES: Mostly basal, **flat (to 3 mm wide), stiff, grass-like**.

INFLORESCENCE: Terminal, usually single but sometimes with 2–3, several- to many-flowered, **compact, hemispherical** clusters; involucral bract 0.5–5 cm long, flat, extending slightly beyond head; flower scales chocolate brown, 4–6 mm long; 6 stamens.

FRUITS: Capsules, egg-shaped, firm, **leathery, slightly shorter than scales**, rounded and often dimpled at tip; **seeds angular-pear-shaped, loosely covered with a shiny, netted membrane**.

ECOLOGY: Coastal marshes, tideflats, dune slacks, rocky and sandy shores, stream-banks, bare soil in bogs, mostly at low elevations; common the length of our region, but usually not far from the sea.

NOTES: Coville's rush (*J. covillei*, **photo above**) also grows on wet lake-shores and sandy or gravelly banks at low elevations; it occurs sporadically from southern Vancouver Island south to California. It has the look of sickle-leaved rush, but it has **non-leathery** capsules that **slightly exceed** the flower scales and **cylindric-egg-shaped, non-shiny** seeds 0.3 mm long, about **half the length** of those of sickle-leaved rush. • The Latin species name parallels the common name: 'sickle-shaped.'

DAGGER-LEAVED RUSH • *Juncus ensifolius*

GENERAL: Perennial; **stems solitary or few (often in rows) from thick rhizomes, flattened, 2-edged**, leafy, 15–60 cm tall.

LEAVES: Laterally flattened like *Iris* leaves, 2–6 mm wide, 3–4 per stem.

INFLORESCENCE: Terminal, heads 1–10, each with several to many flowers; lowermost bract 1–10 cm long, shorter to longer than inflorescence; flower scales greenish-brown to brownish-purple, 3–4 mm long; 3 or 6 stamens.

FRUITS: Capsules, oblong, about as long as scales, rounded at the tip; seeds cylindric, minutely pointed at tips.

ECOLOGY: Usually on wet, sandy soil in bogs, marshes and wet meadows and on lake-shores and stream-banks, from low to subalpine elevations; common throughout most of our region.

NOTES: Bolander's rush (*J. bolanderi*) also has clusters of many-flowered, spherical heads, but its leaves are **rounded**, not flattened. It grows in wet meadows and marshes and on shores, mostly at low elevations from southwestern B.C. to California. • The species name *ensifolius* means 'sword-leaved.'

SLENDER RUSH • *Juncus tenuis*

GENERAL: Tufted perennnial; **stems more or less leafless**, round, 15–70 cm tall.

LEAVES: All basal or nearly so, 1–3 per stem, flattened, narrow (about 1 mm wide), as long as or shorter than stems.

INFLORESCENCE: Terminal, several to many flowers in a **compact to loose cluster**; involucral bract usually longer than inflorescence; flower scales greenish to tan, **sharp tipped**, 4–5 mm long; 6 stamens.

FRUITS: Capsules, cylindric-egg-shaped, rounded and dimpled at the tip, about as long as the scales; seeds ellipsoid, minutely pointed at tips.

ECOLOGY: Moist, usually disturbed sites (pastures, roadsides, ditches and clearings), at low to middle elevations; more common south of 55°N.

NOTES: Slender rush is a widespread, variable species that occurs across North America and in Eurasia, Australia and South America. • **Gerard's or mud rush** (*J. gerardii*) is similar to slender rush, but it has leafy stems and outer flower scales with rounded, hooded tips. It occurs occasionally in salt marshes and on tidal flats and stream-banks, mostly at low elevations, in the Strait of Georgia–Puget Sound area. • The species name *tenuis* is Latin for 'slender,' in reference to the leaves.

SPREADING RUSH • *Juncus supiniformis*

GENERAL: Tufted perennial from slender rhizomes, **sometimes with hair-like floating leaves and stems**; stems bent at the base, round, with basal sheaths and a few leaves, 10–30 cm tall.

LEAVES: 2–4 per stem, **half-round**, **with crosswalls, from firm and erect to flaccid.**

INFLORESCENCE: Terminal, branched, of 2–6, few to several-flowered heads; lowermost bract shorter than inflorescence; flower scales brown, narrowly lance-shaped, 3–4.5 mm long; stamens 3 or 6, the anthers shorter than the filaments.

FRUITS: Capsules, cylindrical, longer than scales, abruptly narrowed to a short beak; seeds cylindrical, finely ridged, minutely pointed at tips.

ECOLOGY: Common in marshes, bogs, mucky shores, ditches and shallow water, from low to middle elevations.

NOTES: Spreading rush is also known as *J. oreganus*. It is a variable species that **ranges from erect and non-proliferating to sprawling, very narrow, and producing plantlets in the upper nodes,** apparently depending on the degree and duration of submergence. • **Bog rush** (*J. stygius*) also grows in bogs and shallow mucky pools; it occurs sporadically in the northern part of our region, from about **54°N northwards** (but absent from the Queen Charlotte Islands). It has **1–3** small, pale, **few-flowered** heads, **hair-like** stems and **1–3 rounded**, very narrow stem leaves. • The species name *supiniformis* means 'spreading,' in reference to the plant's growth habit.

TAPERED RUSH • *Juncus acuminatus*

GENERAL: Tufted perennial, sometimes with very short rhizomes; stems leafy, rounded, 30–80 cm tall.

LEAVES: Half-round, hollow, prominently jointed by crosswalls.

INFLORESCENCE: Terminal, with erect to ascending branches, longer than involucral bract, **usually of 5 to many small, compact, 5-flowered to 20-flowered heads**; flower scales straw-coloured to greenish-brown, sharply pointed, 3–3.5 mm long; stamens 3 or sometimes 6.

FRUITS: Capsules, egg-shaped, 3 edged, uniformly tapered to pointed tip, about as long as scales; seeds oblong-ellipsoid, finely net-veined, minutely pointed at tips.

ECOLOGY: Wet lake-shores, ditches, meadows, marshes, bogs; common at low to middle elevations.

NOTES: Jointed rush (*J. articulatus*) is similar to tapered rush in leaves and capsules (**line drawing of capsule on right** is jointed rush), but the capsules are **slightly longer** than the scales, and the branches of the inflorescence are **spreading**. Jointed rush occurs on wet shores and mudflats and in tidal meadows at low to middle elevations from Vancouver Island to California and occasionally on the Queen Charlotte Islands and in southeast Alaska. **Pointed rush** (*J. oxymeris*) has tapered capsules similar to those of tapered rush, but its leaves are **laterally flattened** and **incompletely jointed**, and it has a **large, loose** inflorescence with **10–70** small heads. It grows at low elevations in wet meadows and on stream-banks and lake-shores, and it occurs fairly frequently from southwestern B.C. to California. • Again, the species and common names refer to the same thing—the 'acuminate' (meaning 'tapered to a pointed tip') fruits.

PIPER'S WOOD-RUSH • *Luzula piperi*

GENERAL: Strongly tufted perennial, with short rhizomes, 10–40 cm tall.

LEAVES: Basal leaves flat, relatively thick, 3–5 mm wide, with a few long, white hairs on margins (or hairless); **stem leaves 1–3,** reduced in size, 1–5 mm wide, with needle-like tips.

INFLORESCENCE: 1–3 flowers at ends of branches in an **open, drooping panicle;** flower scales purplish-brown, about 2 mm long; anthers 0.4–0.7 mm long.

FRUITS: Brown, egg-shaped capsules, surrounded by bracts that are **torn and frilly at the tip;** seeds yellow to brown, cylindric-ellipsoid, slightly appendaged at each end.

ECOLOGY: Moist meadows, heath, snowbeds, tundra, thickets, open forest, in the subalpine and alpine zones; frequent throughout our region as far south as the Olympic Mountains and Mt. Rainier, perhaps further.

NOTES: *Luzula piperi* is also known as *L. wahlenbergii* ssp. *piperi*. *L. wahlenbergii* is, in the strict sense, an arctic species that does not occur in our region. • The open-inflorescence wood-rushes (*L. piperi, L. parviflora, L. hitchcockii* and *L. divaricata*) are easily confused (see notes under *L. parviflora*, below). **L. piperi** can be distinguished by a tendency to **fewer, narrower leaves,** a **smaller** inflorescence and **more-shredded frilly** bracts.

SMALL-FLOWERED WOOD-RUSH • *Luzula parviflora*

GENERAL: Tufted perennial (or stems solitary or in small tufts from rhizomes), leafy, 20–80 cm high; basal sheaths chestnut or purplish-brown.

LEAVES: Both basal and along stem, **large (5–10 mm wide), flat,** with a few long, white hairs on margins; **stem leaves 3–5.**

INFLORESCENCE: Single or paired flowers in a **nodding, open to somewhat congested panicle;** flower scales greenish to brown, **about 2 mm long; anthers 0.3–0.6 mm long.**

FRUITS: Brown, egg-shaped capsules with numerous small seeds, surrounded by brownish bracts that are **smooth to slightly frilly at the tip;** seeds yellow to brown, cylindric-ellipsoid, **ridged on 1 side.**

ECOLOGY: Variety of moist sites in open forests, thickets, meadows, heath, stream-banks, roadsides, trails; widespread and common, from low to fairly high elevations.

NOTES: Small-flowered wood-rush can be distinguished from other open-flowered wood-rushes by its **height** (usually **more than 30 cm**) and the presence of usually **4 or more** broad stem leaves. • **Hitchcock's wood-rush** (*Luzula hitchcockii*, also known as *L. glabrata*; **inset photo**) is very similar but has **longer (1–1.5 mm)** anthers, **dark brown** scales that are **about 3 mm long,** and distinctly **beaked** capsules. It is frequent in heaths and meadows, on exposed ridges and in open forest, at subalpine and alpine elevations from southern B.C. (about 52°N) south through the Cascades to Crater Lake, Oregon. **Spreading wood-rush** (*L. divaricata*) is a related species that has **stiffly spreading** branches in an **erect, open** inflorescence; it grows primarily south of our region, in California. Most of what has been called *L. divaricata* in our region is probably a subspecies (ssp. *fastigiata*) of *L. parviflora*.

CURVED WOOD-RUSH • *Luzula arcuata*

GENERAL: Tufted, shortly rhizomatous perennial; **stems slender, somewhat arching,** 5–25 cm tall.

LEAVES: Basal leaves inrolled, channelled, or flat, 1–4 mm wide, usually purplish-tinged, hairless or sparingly hairy; **stem leaves 1–3,** the tips often brown or purplish.

INFLORESCENCE: Branched, 2–10 small head-like clusters on very slender, drooping or arching stalks; flower scales brown, 2–3.5 mm long; anthers 0.3–0.6 mm long.

FRUITS: Capsules, brown, egg-shaped, surrounded by **frilly bracts;** seeds brown, cylindric-egg-shaped, slightly pointed at both ends.

ECOLOGY: Dry to moist tundra, snowbeds, heath, at high elevations; common in the northern part of our region (north of 55°N), sporadic southward to Mt. Rainier.

NOTES: Spiked wood-rush (*L. spicata*) is also a small, high-elevation species that is fairly common the length of our region, mostly on dry rocky ridges and slopes, but not on the outer coast. It has a **solitary** (usually) **spike-like** inflorescence, nodding atop a slender, arching stem. • The common name and *arcuata* ('curved') refer to the arched flowering stalks.

L. arcuata   *L. spicata*

MANY-FLOWERED WOOD-RUSH • *Luzula multiflora*

GENERAL: Densely tufted perennial, 10–60 cm tall.

LEAVES: Basal and stem leaves, 2–6 mm wide, **with long, white hairs along the margin and where the leaves join the stem;** stem leaves 2–4, with blunt, thickened, brownish tips.

INFLORESCENCE: Clusters 1 to several, **dense, head-like, 8-15 flowered,** sometimes nearly stalkless and close to each other but usually on stiff, erect to ascending branches; flower scales greenish to chestnut brown to silvery, 2–4.5 mm long; anthers 0.5–2 mm long.

FRUITS: Brown, egg-shaped capsules, surrounded by somewhat frilly-edged bracts; seeds brown, spherical to egg-shaped, with a **prominent spongy appendage at the base.**

ECOLOGY: Common in dry to moist, open forests, grassy meadows, coastal bluffs, rocky slopes, beaches and shores from low to fairly high elevations.

NOTES: Many-flowered wood-rush (also known as *L. campestris*) is a very variable and widespread species, with several subspecies. • The species name *multiflora* is Latin for 'many-flowered.'

Ferns and Allies

This section contains descriptions of a heterogeneous group of plants referred to as the ferns and their 'allies.' These are vascular plants: that is, they have internal tubes for transporting fluids (in common with all other plants in this guide except bryophytes and lichens). However, they reproduce not by seeds but by spores (in common with the bryophytes and lichens). This places them in a position morphologically intermediate between the so-called 'lower plants' (such as the bryophytes) and the 'higher plants' (such as the flowering plants). It also imposes some limits on the biology of the ferns and their allies: because they reproduce by spores, rather than seeds, they must have abundant moisture available for reproduction. Most, but not all, of these plants are characteristically absent from drier sites.

The ferns and allies were used for a number of purposes by native groups on the coast, from food and medicine to scouring pads, decoration in baskets and diaper lining.

The northern Pacific coastal region is home to approximately 40 species of ferns, 7–8 species of grape ferns and rattlesnake ferns, 10 species of horsetails, 8 species of clubmosses, 6 species of spikemosses and 4–5 species of quillworts. This section begins with a key to the groups included: ferns (including grape and rattlesnake ferns), horsetails, clubmosses and spikemosses, and quillworts. We then provide keys for the species within each group. More information on ferns and allies is provided in Taylor (1970, 1973a), Vitt et al. (1988), Cody and Britton (1989) and Lellinger (1985), as well as in the general floras mentioned in the introduction to this guide.

Key to Ferns and Allies

1a. Leaves pinnatifid (divided or cut into numerous branches or lobes on 2 sides of a common axis) and feather-like or fan-shaped .... FERNS

1b. Leaves narrow, simple or branch-like 2

2a. Leaves whorled; stems jointed and ribbed .... HORSETAILS

2b. Leaves alternate or opposite; stem not ribbed 3

3a. Leaves short, flat .... CLUBMOSSES and SPIKEMOSSES

3b. Leaves quill-like, in basal rosettes; stem thick, corm-like .... QUILLWORTS

Ferns

The grape or rattlesnake ferns (*Botrychium* spp.) are relatively small, and they have fleshy roots and short, vertical, subterranean stems (rhizomes) that bear a single leaf divided into a sterile expanded blade and a fertile, spike-like or panicle-like portion. The spore sacs are free (not aggregated in clusters called 'sori') and they are short stalked, stalkless or sunken in the leaf tissue.

The 'true' ferns have creeping or erect rhizomes (often very scaly) and stalked, erect or spreading, often large **leaves** (**fronds**). The leaf blades are curled in bud ('fiddleheads'), and they are usually lobed, divided or variously compound. Fertile and sterile leaves are most often alike, but they are dissimilar in some genera. The **spore sacs** are grouped together in **sori**, which are sometimes enclosed or covered by a membrane called the '**indusium**.'

Recent taxonomic treatments (e.g., Douglas et al. 1991) of several of our ferns have resulted in new names and some new species that we acknowledge but do not necessarily accept, preferring to wait and see if the new taxonomy stands the test of time.

Key to Genera of Ferns

1a. Sporangia (**spore sacs**) in clusters on a leafless stalk that projects
from the upper side of the **leaf** (**frond**) (grape or rattlesnake ferns) .... *Botrychium*
1b. Sporangia borne on the underside of vegetative leaf or
on separate, modified, fertile leaf ('true' ferns) 2

  2a. Fronds of 2 distinct types; fertile leaves with contracted **leaflets** (**pinnae**) 3

    3a. Fertile leaves smaller and less divided than sterile leaves,
eventually dark brown .... *Matteucia* (see *Polystichum*)
    3b. Fertile leaves larger than sterile leaves, remaining green 4

      4a. Fronds once-pinnately divided .... *Blechnum*
      4b. Fronds 2–3 times pinnate; sterile leaves parsley-like .... *Cryptogramma*

  2b. Fronds all alike or nearly so 5

    5a. **Sori** (**clusters of spore sacs**) marginal, covered
(at least when young) by the rolled-under margins of the leaflets 6

      6a. Sori distinct; **indusium** (**protective membrane over sori**)
formed by rolled-under flaps of the **pinnules** (**ultimate segments of leaf**);
leaves deciduous .... *Adiantum*
      6b. Sori continuous; indusium formed by continuous
rolled-under margins of the leaflets 7

        7a. Rhizome and leaves with hairs only, lacking scales;
stipes (leaf stalks) tall (> 1 m), stout; leaves deciduous .... *Pteridium*
        7b. Rhizome scaly; stipes shorter, slender; leaves evergreen 8

          8a. Fertile leaves with linear, pod-like ultimate segments;
leaves hairless .... *Aspidotis* (see *Cryptogramma*)
          8b. Fertile leaves with wider, flattened ultimate segments;
leaves woolly beneath .... *Cheilanthes* (see *Cryptogramma*)

    5b. Sori not marginal, naked or covered by non-marginal indusia 9

      9a. Sori naked, without indusia 10

        10a. Spore sacs along the leaflet veins,
not aggregated into sori; lower surface of leaflets
covered with golden powder .... *Pityrogramma*
        10b. Sori discrete; lower surface of leaflets not golden-powdery 11

          11a. Fronds evergreen, merely pinnately lobed,
not divided all the way into leaflets .... *Polypodium*
          11b. Fronds deciduous, 2–4 times pinnate 12

            12a. Fronds in dense, vase-like tufts,
covered at base with conspicuous, persistent bases
of stipes of past years .... *Athyrium*
            12b. Fronds scattered or in small tufts,
not with conspicuous, persistent leaf stalk
bases of past years 13

              13a. Fronds 2–3 times pinnate, glabrous,
lacking fringe of marginal hairs .... *Gymnocarpium*
              13b. Fronds 1–2 times pinnate,
hairy along main axis and midribs,
with fringe of marginal hairs .... *Thelypteris*

      9b. Sori covered (at least when young) by indusia 14

        14a. Indusium elongate, flap-like,
attached along the edge 15

          15a. Fronds once pinnate, evergreen,
not taller than 35 cm .... *Asplenium*
          15b. Fronds twice pinnate, deciduous,
usually taller than 35 cm .... *Athyrium*
          15c. Fronds twice pinnate, evergreen, usually
taller than 35 cm; sori oblong, arranged in
chain-like rows .... *Woodwardia* (see *Athyrium*)

        14b. Indusium attached at a point 16

          16a. Indusium centrally attached, circular;
leaves evergreen, often sharp-toothed .... *Polystichum*

16b. Indusium laterally attached;
leaves deciduous or evergreen 17

    17a. Indusium hood-like, delicate,
soon shrivelling, its free tip thrown back
as sori mature .... *Cystopteris*

    17b. Indusium kidney- or horseshoe-shaped 18

        18a. Fronds twice pinnate,
hairy at least along main axis and
midveins; indusium (when present)
small and inconspicuous .... *Thelypteris*

        18b. Fronds 2–3 times pinnate, hairless
or merely scaly, not hairy; indusium
well developed and persistent .... *Dryopteris*

*Botrychium
lunaria*

*Botrychium
multifidum*

*Blechnum
spicant*

*Polystichum
munitum*

*Athyrium
filix-femina*

*Dryopteris
expansa*

*Pteridium
aquilinum*

*Gymnocarpium
dryopteris*

*Thelypteris
phegopteris*

*Pityrogramma
triangularis*

*Polypodium
glycyrrhiza*

*Asplenium
viride*

*Adiantum
pedatum*

*Cryptogramma
crispa*

*Cystopteris
fragilis*

419

BRACKEN FERN • *Pteridium aquilinum*

GENERAL: Fronds **large, solitary**, erect, deciduous, to 3 (sometimes 5) m tall; **rhizomes spreading**, much-branched below ground surface, clothed with numerous hairs.

LEAVES: Blades **triangular, 2–3 times pinnate, hairy**; stipes stout, straw-coloured to greenish, longer than the blades; leaflets 10 or more pairs, mostly opposite, the lowest pair narrowly to broadly triangular, upper ones progressively reduced and lance-shaped; ultimate segments round toothed, **margins rolled under**.

SORI: Marginal, continuous, covered by rolled leaf margin; indusium not evident.

ECOLOGY: Meadows, roadsides, clearings, sterile sandy soils, burns, avalanche tracks, dry to wet forests, acid sites such as lake-shores and bogs; often weedy; at low to subalpine elevations.

NOTES: This cosmopolitan species is the world's most widespread fern. In our region it occurs on a wide variety of habitats, but it is especially common on open and disturbed sites. The rhizomes are deep, so it can survive even intense fires and is often abundant on recently burned areas. • Bracken-fern leaves were used on the Northwest Coast as one of the protective plant layers in traditional pit ovens. The Nuu-chah-nulth often cooked then chewed the rhizomes and spat out the remnants to be used for tinder when dry. The rhizomes were harvested in summer or fall and eaten by nearly all coastal peoples, including the Nuxalk, Saanich, Kwakwaka'wakw, Nuu-chah-nulth and Haida. They dried and then cooked the rhizomes in a traditional pit oven or roasted them over a fire until the outer skin and the tough, central fibres could be removed. Because they are constipating, the rhizomes were generally eaten with fish eggs or oil. CAUTION: Despite the aboriginal use, you should not eat these plants; bracken has been implicated in livestock poisoning and stomach cancer.

DEER FERN • *Blechnum spicant*

GENERAL: Medium-sized, **evergreen, tufted** at the end of a short, stout rhizome.

LEAVES: Fronds of **2 kinds**: sterile leaves **often pressed to the ground**, 20–80 cm (to 1 m) tall or long, evergreen, leathery; stipes **purplish-brown**; leaflets 35–70 pairs, **widely spaced, oblong**, to 5 cm long and 3–7 mm wide, progressively reduced towards the top and bottom; fertile leaves similar but upright, arising from centre of clump, deciduous and with much **narrower** (to 2 mm wide) leaflets that are **sometimes rolled in near-tubes** around the sori.

SORI: Continuous, distributed **near the margin**; protected by a continuous translucent brown indusium attached close to the leaflet edge.

ECOLOGY: Moist to wet forests, wet slide areas under alder, stream-banks, occasionally in bogs; lowlands to middle or even subalpine elevations.

NOTES: Deer fern looks vaguely like sword fern, at least in growth habit, but the **leaflets are attached to the leaf axis all along their bases**, not on short stalks like those of sword fern. • The young leaves of deer fern were chewed by Hesquiat hunters and travellers as a hunger suppressant. The leaves were used as a medicine for skin sores, a use said by Hesquiat elders to have been learned by watching deer rub their antler stubs on this plant after their antlers had fallen off. • Often a major understorey plant in wet forest, deer fern is an important winter food for deer and elk in some areas.

SWORD FERN • *Polystichum munitum*

GENERAL: Large (to 1.5 m tall, but smaller in the north), **evergreen**, with **erect leaves forming a crown** from a stout, woody, scaly rhizome.

LEAVES: Stipe **dry-scaly**; blade lance-shaped, erect to arching, **once-pinnate**; leaflets alternate, pointed, **sharp toothed** with incurved spine-tips, each with a **small lobe pointing forward** at the bottom.

SORI: Large, circular, about halfway between the midvein and the margin; indusium **round** with fringed margins, **centrally attached**.

ECOLOGY: Moist forest at low to middle elevations; abundant and widespread from central Vancouver Island and adjacent mainland south, less common further north.

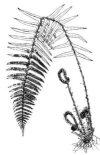

NOTES: The *Polystichum*s are all big, tufted, evergreen ferns with round sori which have indusia attached to their centres. At least 6 other *Polystichum*s may be encountered within our region; 2 of the most common are Braun's holly fern (*P. braunii*, also known in part as *P. andersonii* and *P. setigerum*) and mountain holly fern (*P. lonchitis*). **Braun's holly fern (lowermost photo)** is big (to 1 m tall) and scaly, and it has **twice-pinnate** leaves (divided 1 more time than are sword fern's) with **no basal lobes; mountain holly fern** is **simply pinnate** (like sword fern). Braun's holly fern is found in moist forest, shaded rocky slopes and streamside areas at low to subalpine elevations from southeast Alaska to Oregon. **Mountain holly fern** is like a smaller sword fern but it is **shinier and more leathery**, with wide-spreading, spiny-toothed leaves **10–60 cm long** (vs. 20–150 cm long in sword fern), stipes **less than 10 cm long** (vs. up to 50 cm long in sword fern). It can be found in dry coniferous forests or (more commonly) on cliffs and talus, from middle to subalpine elevations from Alaska to northern California. A third species, **narrow-leaved sword fern** (*P. imbricans*), is closely related and very similar to sword fern, but it is a **smaller (20–60 cm tall)** plant with **overlapping, somewhat infolded** leaflets and **scarcely scaly** stipes. Narrow-leaved sword fern grows in dry rocky openings and forest, typically in distinctly drier habitats than those of sword fern, at low elevations from southwestern B.C. to California. • Sword fern leaves were used by northwest coast peoples as a protective layer in traditional pit ovens, between food in storage boxes and baskets and on berry-drying racks. The leaves were also used as flooring and bedding. The large rhizomes were dug in the spring and eaten as a starvation food by the Quileute, Makah, Klallam, Squamish, Sechelt, Nuu-chah-nulth, Kwakwaka'wakw and Haida. The rhizomes were roasted over a fire or steamed in a traditional pit oven, then peeled and eaten. The Nuu-chah-nulth ate the cooked rhizomes especially to cure diarrhea. Sword fern is known in a number of Vancouver Island and Puget Sound languages as 'pala-pala plant,' because it was used in a traditional game known as 'pala-pala.' This game, played by children, involved seeing who could pull the most leaflets off a leaf in a single breath while saying 'pala' with each one. • Another large fern that is uncommon in our region but can be locally abundant and striking is the **ostrich fern** (*Matteucia struthiopteris*), an interior species found along the banks of major B.C. rivers (Skeena, Nass, Fraser), and also in Prince William Sound. Ostrich fern's leaves are similar to those of Braun's holly fern, but they are **deciduous** and the **sori are borne on specialized, brown pod-like leaflets on the separate fertile leaves**. Ostrich ferns provide the 'fiddleheads' available in springtime in our markets.

LADY FERN • *Athyrium filix-femina*

GENERAL: Fronds **clustered, erect and spreading, to 2 m tall**; rhizomes stout, ascending to erect, covered with scales and old leaf stalk bases.

LEAVES: Stipes short, fragile, scaly at the base, much shorter than the blades; blades narrowly to broadly **lance-shaped, tapering at both ends** (with a diamond-shaped profile), 2–3 times pinnate; leaflets 20–40 pairs, upper and lower ones progressively reduced; ultimate segments toothed or lobed.

SORI: Elongate and curved, oblong to horseshoe-shaped; indusium also elongate and curved, attached on 1 side, with hairs and teeth, **soon shrivelling**.

ECOLOGY: Moist to wet forests, swamps, thickets, openings, slidetracks, stream-banks, gullies, meadows and clearings; at all elevations.

NOTES: At first glance, lady fern could be confused with spiny wood fern. **Spiny wood fern**, however, is **broadly triangular (not diamond-shaped)** in outline, with the blade not tapering towards the base and the leaflet teeth with bristle-tips. • **Alpine lady fern** (*A. distentifolium*, also known as *A. alpestre*) is a **smaller (to 80 cm tall)**, less-common species typically found at **high elevations**, along streams, on wet cliff-faces and talus slopes or in meadows, throughout our region. Its leaves are much **narrower** in outline than those of lady fern, and appear to have been scorched by a flame and '**crinkled.**' • **Giant chain fern** (*Woodwardia fimbriata*) has **large (to 3 m)**, twice-divided, **evergreen** leaves with **elongated sori immediately adjacent to the midrib** on either side. It is a species of wet, shady woods and stream-banks at low to middle elevations from the Strait of Georgia–Puget Sound area to southern California, and it is very common in the redwood forests south of our region. • The leaves of lady fern were used by aboriginal people for laying out or covering food, especially berries for drying. The fiddleheads were eaten in the early spring when they were 7–15 cm tall. They were boiled, baked or eaten raw with grease.

SPINY WOOD FERN • *Dryopteris expansa*
SHIELD FERN

GENERAL: Fronds **clustered, erect and spreading, to 1 m tall**; rhizomes stout, ascending to erect, clothed with chaffy, brown scales.

LEAVES: Stipes scaly at the base, usually shorter than the blades; blades **broadly triangular to egg-shaped to broadly oblong**, 3 times pinnate; leaflets 5–20 pairs, the **lowest pair broadly triangular and asymmetrical**; ultimate segments toothed; the 2 basal ones much larger than the others (spur-like).

SORI: Rounded, partially covered by the rounded indusium.

ECOLOGY: Moist forests and openings, scree slopes; low to subalpine elevations.

NOTES: This species is also known as *D. assimilis*, *D. austriaca* and *D. dilatata*. • Two other *Dryopteris* species within our region, both somewhat similar to spiny wood fern, are male fern (*D. filix-mas*) and coastal wood fern (*D. arguta*). **Male fern** is large, with **deciduous, non-glandular** leaves that have the **broadly lance-shaped** outline of lady fern but are **1–2** rather than 2–3 times pinnate. This reportedly **poisonous** species occupies rocky wooded slopes, avalanche-track thickets and blocky lava fields, sporadically on the mainland coast from the Nass River south to the Washington Cascades. **Coastal wood fern** has **scale-like 'chaff'** on the leaf stalk and leaf axis (vs. hair-like in male fern), and it has **evergreen, glandular** leaves. Its habitat is similar to (but often sunnier than) that of male fern, and its range is from southeastern Vancouver Island to California at low elevations. • The pineapple-like rootstocks of some forms of spiny wood fern were an important starchy food.

OAK FERN • *Gymnocarpium dryopteris*

GENERAL: Fronds **usually solitary (but often in masses), erect**, deciduous, to 40 cm tall; rhizome long, slender, creeping, clothed with a few brown, fibrous scales.

LEAVES: Stipe shiny, straw-coloured, scaly at the base, equalling or longer than the blades; blades thin, **broadly triangular, 2–3 times pinnate, hairless**; leaflets to 20 pairs, the lowest pair triangular and asymmetrical; ultimate segments round toothed, the 2 basal ones larger than the others.

SORI: Small, **circular, lacking an indusium**.

ECOLOGY: Moist forests and openings, rocky slopes; at low to subalpine elevations.

NOTES: *G. dryopteris*—in its broad, circumboreal sense—includes *G. disjunctum*. The close relationship of *G. dryopteris* to *Dryopteris* is reflected by its inclusion in the latter genus by some taxonomists as *D. disjuncta*. • Oak fern's delicate, triangular blades (that look as though they are made up of 3 separate parts) held horizontal to the ground, and its lime-green colour, are distinctive. • This species can form an almost continuous carpet over the forest floor on some sites. It is a very attractive fern, and it forms a beautiful, luxuriant forest understorey. • *Gymnocarpium* means 'naked fruit,' because these plants have no indusia. The name 'oak fern' appears to have resulted from a translation of the species name: *Dryopteris* is Greek for 'oak' (*drys*) 'fern' (*pteris*). This fern does not grow near or on oaks, but 'oak fern' is a former name for *Polypodium vulgare*, from that species's habit of growing on oak branches.

NARROW BEECH FERN • *Thelypteris phegopteris*

GENERAL: Fronds **usually solitary, erect**, deciduous, to 40 cm tall; rhizomes slender, creeping, sparsely scaly.

LEAVES: Stipes slender, brown to straw-coloured, hairy and sparsely scaly, equal to or longer than the blades; blades **triangular to egg-shaped, twice pinnate, with hairs** on both surfaces and scales mainly on the midribs; leaflets 10–25 pairs, stalkless, the **lowest pair usually bent forward**, the others attached nearly at right angles to the leaf stalk.

SORI: Small, more or less **circular**, near the margin; **indusium lacking**.

ECOLOGY: Moist, rich forests, stream-banks, bogs, wet cliffs, and rocky seepage slopes at low to subalpine elevations.

NOTES: Narrow beech fern is also known as *Phegopteris connectilis*. • **Mountain fern** (*T. quelpaertensis*, also known as *T. limbosperma* or *T. oreopteris*) is another coastal species that differs in that it has a **leaf shaped much more like that of lady fern**, but with round, near-marginal sori with **indusia**. It occurs on wet cliffs, rocky slopes and talus slopes from sea level to the subalpine; it is sporadic from the Cascades of central Washington north. Mountain fern is **lemon-scented** when crushed. • This species is also called 'cowboy fern,' because the lowest pair of leaflets point downwards like spurs or spread out like bowed legs. The name 'beech fern' is the result of a confusing and deliberate mistranslation. Apparently this species was given the name *phegopteris* (from *phegos*, 'oak' and *pteris*, 'fern'). However, oak fern (see above) was also placed in this genus as *Thelypteris dryopteris*. Because there cannot be 2 'oak ferns' in the same genus, when the names were anglicized one was changed to beech fern, as if *phegos* were the same as *fagus* ('beech').

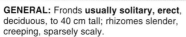

GOLDENBACK FERN • *Pityrogramma triangularis*

GENERAL: Small, **tufted, evergreen**, to 35 cm tall; leaves golden beneath, numerous from short, creeping, dark-scaly rhizomes.

LEAVES: Stipes long (twice as long as the blades), **wiry, shiny brown**; blades **broadly triangular** in outline, **2–3 times pinnate**, the 2 basal leaflets divided again and their lowest segments larger than upper ones; **covered with a white to golden, waxy powder below.**

SORI: In lines along the branching veins on the undersurface of the leaflets; **indusium absent.**

ECOLOGY: Dry, open to partly shaded, rocky slopes and crevices and shallow-soil meadows; from low to middle elevations.

NOTES: Goldenback fern is also known as *Pentagramma triangularis*. • This is one of our most beautiful ferns. In dry weather the leaves curl up, exposing the golden undersides. • *Pityrogramma* derives from the Greek *pityron* ('bran') and *gramma* ('letter' or 'line'), referring to the scaly, linear sori. The backs of the leaves are covered in golden powder, giving rise to the common name.

LICORICE FERN • *Polypodium glycyrrhiza*

GENERAL: Small to medium-sized, **evergreen**, to 70 cm tall (but often much smaller), from a creeping, reddish-**brown**, scaly, **licorice-flavoured rhizome**; often growing on deciduous tree trunks and branches.

LEAVES: Stipes straw-coloured, smooth, usually shorter than the blades; blades to 50 cm long, **once-pinnate**; leaflets **usually longer than 3 cm**, with **pointed tips** and finely scalloped or toothed margins.

SORI: Oval to round, 1 row on either side of the main vein, **without an indusium.**

ECOLOGY: On wet, mossy ground, logs and rocks (sometimes forms large sheets over rock slabs) or **(commonly) epiphytic** on tree trunks and branches, often bigleaf maple; at low elevations.

NOTES: Licorice fern is also known as *P. vulgare*. • Ferns in the genus *Polypodium* have evergreen, relatively little-divided (for a fern) leaves. 3 other species in this genus occur on rocks or sometimes on tree trunks in our region. **Leathery polypody** (*P. scouleri*, **inset photo on left**) is an outer coast species, **rarely found far from salt spray**, which has **extremely leathery** leaves, ultimate segments with **rounded tips** and a **white rhizome that is not licorice-flavoured**. It is found on rock cliffs and tree trunks from Cape St. James (Queen Charlotte Islands) south along the outer coast to California. **Pacific polypody** (*P. amorphum*, also known as *P. montense*) has **shorter (less than 3 cm long)** ultimate segments with **rounded tips, round sori**, and a rhizome with a **bitter** taste; it can be found in rock crevices at low to (usually) high elevations from the Nass River south. **Western polypody** (*P. hesperium*) may be a hybrid from *P. glycyrrhiza* and *P. amorphum*: its rhizome **tastes of licorice** and it has **oval sori**, but **mostly rounded** ultimate segments. This smaller species can be found in habitats similar to those of Pacific polypody south of about 55°N, but it does not reach the outer coast. • The sweet, licorice-flavored rhizomes were chewed for the flavour by the Squamish, Sechelt, Comox, Nuxalk, Haida and Kwakwaka'wakw. Occasionally the rhizomes were dried, steamed, scorched or eaten raw. The rhizomes were an important medicine for colds and sore throats. They were also mixed with bitter medicines as a sweetener.

GREEN SPLEENWORT • *Asplenium viride*

GENERAL: Densely tufted from short, scaly rhizomes, **soft not evergreen**, small; leaves to 14 cm tall; old stipes and leaf axes persist for years.

LEAVES: Bright-green (reddish-brown at base) stipes; blades long and narrow, **once-pinnate**; leaflets **oval to round**, round-toothed, **opposite at base, becoming alternate** upwards.

SORI: Several, **elongate, in sausage-like lines along veins** on the underside of the leaflets; indusium membranous, attached along 1 side of the sorus, delicate, tending to disappear as sorus ripens.

ECOLOGY: In moist, shaded, sheltered crevices on rocky limestone (or other basic rock) bluffs or talus slopes; middle to alpine elevations.

NOTES: If the spleenwort stipes are **purplish-brown** and the leaflets are **firm, evergreen**, and **opposite** (or nearly so), you are probably looking at the **maidenhair spleenwort** (*A. trichomanes*), which is found in similar habitats to those of green spleenwort (but generally at lower elevations) from southeast Alaska to Oregon. Both species prefer limestone or at least calcium-rich rocks as a substrate. • The Greek *asplenon* means 'without spleen,' deriving from the use of maidenhair spleenwort in Europe as a treatment for diseases of the spleen.

MAIDENHAIR FERN • *Adiantum pedatum*

GENERAL: Delicate, **palmately branched**; leaves **few or solitary** from stout (3–5 mm thick), scaly rhizomes, but form colonies in suitable habitats.

LEAVES: Lustrous, dark-brown to purplish-black, erect stipes 15–60 cm tall, the top of the leaf stalk **divided into 2 and these divisions divided again**; blade 10–40 cm across, set nearly at **right angles to the leaf stalk**, more or less parallel to the ground; each leaflet with **oblong or fan-shaped** ultimate segments smooth and flat on the lower margin and cleft into ragged, rectangular lobes on the upper margin.

SORI: Oblong, on the edges of the upper lobes of the leaflets; **flap-like indusium** formed by the **inrolled leaf margin**.

ECOLOGY: Shady, humus-rich sites in moist, often rocky forests, on stream-banks, cliffs and in the spray zone of waterfalls; low to middle (occasionally subalpine) elevations.

NOTES: Maidenhair fern is also known as *A. aleuticum*. • This delicate, black-stemmed fern was used in basketry by some Washington groups. The Hesquiat used the leaves in a medicine for strength and endurance, especially for dancers in winter. • Maidenhair fern reportedly has some medicinal properties. In olden times, maidenhair fern was exported to Europe as packaging and then used by herbalists to make cough medicine. It was also boiled with sugar to make the syrup called 'capillaire,' and it has some emetic properties. • This fern is called 'maidenhair fern' because of its fine, glossy, hair-like stalks, or because of the masses of dark root hairs. 'Maidenhair' was originally applied to European bog asphodel (*Narcithecium ossifragum*) because young girls used it to make their hair yellow. *Adiantum* means 'unwetted'; the foliage sheds rain.

PARSLEY FERN • *Cryptogramma crispa*
MOUNTAIN PARSLEY

GENERAL: Small, **evergreen, densely clustered** from short, ascending, branched rhizomes clothed with scales and old leaf stalk bases; sterile and fertile leaves **markedly different**.

LEAVES: Stipes **straw-coloured**; sterile leaves to 20 cm tall, blades egg-shaped, thick, crisply firm, usually **3 times branched**, leaflets mostly 3–10 pairs, largest at the base, ultimate segments finely toothed; fertile leaves to 30 cm tall, blades broadly lance-shaped, 2–3 times branched, leaflets mostly 3–10 pairs, **with inrolled margins** and **blunt tips**.

SORI: Continuous along the length of fertile leaflets, **covered by their rolled-under margins**.

ECOLOGY: Fairly dry, rocky, open sites (cliffs, ledges, crevices, talus slopes) at low to high elevations.

NOTES: Parsley fern is often called *C. acrostichoides*, and it includes *C. sitchensis*. • The evergreen sterile leaves, reminiscent of parsley, are distinctive in their rocky habitats. • 2 other small, evergreen ferns from dry cliff-faces and talus slopes are pod fern or Indian's-dream fern (*Aspidotis densa*, also known as *Cryptogramma densa* and *Cheilanthes siliquosa*) and lace fern (*Cheilanthes gracillima*), neither of which resemble parsley. **Pod fern** has 2 kinds of leaves like parsley fern and has wiry, **chestnut-brown** stipes, **3-times-branched** fertile leaves to 30 cm tall and ultimate segments that are **abruptly pointed**; its sterile leaves are smaller and often lacking. **Lace fern does not** have separate sterile and fertile leaves; its leaves are 25 cm tall, **twice branched** and **cinnamon-felted on the underside**. Both species occur in suitable habitats at low to middle elevations (*A. densa* favours limestone or serpentine, *C. gracillima* favours acid igneous rocks), from southern Vancouver Island and the adjacent mainland south to California.

FRAGILE FERN • *Cystopteris fragilis*

GENERAL: Delicate, small, to 30 cm tall; rhizomes short, creeping, densely scaly.

LEAVES: Stipes **straw-coloured, hairless**, short, equalling or shorter than the blades; blades lance-shaped, tapering at both ends, 2–3 times pinnate, **axis hairless** except for a few hairs towards the base of the leaflets; leaflets 8–18 pairs, lower ones reduced; ultimate segments irregularly toothed.

SORI: Small, **roundish**, partially covered with a **delicate, hood-like**, somewhat toothed or lobed **indusium, which soon withers and curls back**.

ECOLOGY: Cool, moist to dry, often calcium-rich, rocky forests and openings, rock cliffs, crevices, and ledges, talus slopes; at all elevations.

NOTES: Fragile fern could be confused with **young or stunted specimens of lady fern** (p. 422) which, however, have scaly stipes, at least near the base. • **Mountain bladder fern** (*C. montana*) is a sporadic but often overlooked species of shady, moist to wet forest, glades, rocky slopes with seepage and streambanks. It occurs at low to middle elevations in southeast Alaska, typically on nutrient-rich calcareous soils. *C. montana* looks more like a *Gymnocarpium* or *Dryopteris*, with **triangular-egg-shaped, twice-pinnate, narrowly dissected leaves**, but it has a hood-like indusium. • *Cystopteris* is from the Greek for 'bladder' (*kystos*) and 'fern' (*pteris*), referring to the hood-like indusium.

COMMON MOONWORT • *Botrychium lunaria*

GENERAL: Erect, deciduous, yellowish-green or bluish, 10–25 cm tall.

LEAVES: Stipes equalling or exceeding the length of the sterile blades; blades more or less **stalkless, oblong,** hairless, **somewhat leathery, once-pinnate**; 2–5 pairs of **roundish to fan-shaped leaflets.**

REPRODUCTIVE: Fertile stalk 0.5–8 cm long, equalling or exceeding the length of the fertile spike; fertile spike 1–7 cm long, 2–3 times pinnately compound, the numerous sporangia mostly stalkless and free.

ECOLOGY: Grassy slopes, fields, moist meadows, heath, turfy ledges, open forest; scattered at all elevations.

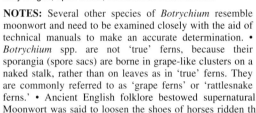

NOTES: Several other species of *Botrychium* resemble moonwort and need to be examined closely with the aid of technical manuals to make an accurate determination. • *Botrychium* spp. are not 'true' ferns, because their sporangia (spore sacs) are borne in grape-like clusters on a naked stalk, rather than on leaves as in 'true' ferns. They are commonly referred to as 'grape ferns' or 'rattlesnake ferns.' • Ancient English folklore bestowed supernatural powers on this plant. Moonwort was said to loosen the shoes of horses ridden through it, and it was believed that it could be inserted into locks to unlock doors. The spores of moonwort can reportedly make you invisible. • *Botrychium* is from the Greek word *botryos* ('a bunch of grapes') in reference to the sporangia; *lunaria* and 'moonwort' both refer to the half-moon-shaped leaflets.

LEATHERY GRAPE FERN • *Botrychium multifidum*

GENERAL: Erect, evergreen, 10–50 cm tall, from several thick, wrinkled roots.

LEAVES: Fleshy and leathery, with a **long leaf stalk attached near the base** of the plant, **2–4 times compound,** to 30 cm across; usually 1 new, green and 1 old, over-wintering leaf.

REPRODUCTIVE: Fertile leaf as tall or taller than the sterile leaf, with a much-branched, panicle-like, fertile spike.

ECOLOGY: Moist or wet meadows, fields, grassy slopes, lake-shores, stream-banks, swampy or alluvial (especially cottonwood) forests; from sea level to subalpine elevations.

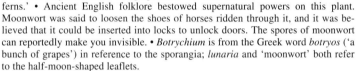

NOTES: 3 deciduous *Botrychium* species within our region are lance-leaved moonwort (*B. lanceolatum*), northwestern moonwort (*B. boreale*, also known as *B. pinnatum*), and rattlesnake fern (*B. virginianum*). The **lance-leaved moonwort** has a small, **stalkless, triangular blade** (with narrowly **lance-shaped segments**) **attached immediately below** the much-branched fertile spike; its home is open woods, sandy clearings, meadows and wet redcedar forests at middle to alpine elevations, from Alaska to northern Oregon (Mt. Hood), but not on the Queen Charlotte Islands or Vancouver Island. The somewhat similar **northwestern moonwort** has an **egg-shaped, stalkless blade** with broader, **oblong segments** and a fertile spike that is **longer** than the sterile leaf; it occurs on open, grassy meadows, stream-banks, heath and peaty ground at middle to subalpine elevations from Alaska to Washington. **Rattlesnake fern** is the **largest** of the 3, with large (to 20 cm wide), **broadly triangular, much-dissected blades** that are **thin**, not fleshy or leathery; it is a species of moist, usually deciduous forests, meadows, and wet clearings, from Skeena River to California, on Vancouver Island but absent from the Queen Charlotte Islands. Its common name refers to the fancied resemblance of the fertile leaf to the tail tip of a rattlesnake.

Horsetails

The horsetails are rhizomatous herbs with aerial, usually hollow, grooved, regularly jointed stems impregnated with silica, which makes them harsh to the touch. Slender, green branches (easily mistaken for leaves) and leaves are borne in whorls at the conspicuous nodes; the leaves are reduced to a series of teeth united by a sheath, and they usually lack chlorophyll (the stems and branches are green and photosynthetic). The spores are produced in cones atop the stems. The Equisetaceae has a single genus, *Equisetum*, with about 20 species worldwide.

Key to Species of Horsetails (*Equisetum*)

1a. Stems evergreen and perennial, usually unbranched;
cones sharp-pointed at tip (scouring-rushes) 2
    2a. Stems stout, 20–150 cm tall, 3–10 mm thick, 14–50 ridged;
    central cavity taking up 3/4 or more of the stem .... *E. hyemale*
    2b. Stems slender, 10–50 cm tall, 1–4 mm thick, 3–12 ridged;
    central cavity to 1/3 the diameter of stem .... *E. variegatum* (see *E. hyemale*)
1b. Stems annual, usually with regularly whorled
branches; cones blunt (Horsetails) 3
    3a. Fertile (cone-bearing) and sterile stems similar; cones produced in summer 4
        4a. Stems shallowly 10–30 ridged; central cavity
        1/2 to 4/5 the diameter of main stem .... *E. fluviatile*
        4b. Stems deeply 5–10 ridged; central cavity less
        than 1/3 the diameter of main stem .... *E. palustre* (see *E. fluviatile*)
    3b. Fertile (cone-bearing) and sterile stems dissimilar;
    cones produced in spring 5
        5a. Fertile stems usually not branched, fleshy, whitish pinkish or brown 6
            6a. Stems 5–20 mm in diameter; stem sheaths with 20–30 teeth;
            cones hollow, 4–10 cm long .... *E. telmatiea*
            6b. Stems 3–5 mm in diameter; stem sheaths with less
            than 20 teeth; cones solid, less than 4 cm long .... *E. arvense*
        5b. Fertile stems branched, green 7
            7a. Branches usually branched again; sterile stems with 2
            rows of spines on each of the ridges; stem
            sheaths brownish, the teeth cohering
            in several broad lobes .... *E. sylvaticum* (see *E. arvense*)
            7b. Branches usually not again branched; sterile stems with
            blunt bumps or cross-ridges; stem sheaths greenish, teeth free or nearly so 8
                8a. Fertile stems whitish or brownish, unbranched,
                soon withering; sterile stems with smooth or inconspicuous
                low bumps and first internodes of the primary
                branches much longer than the stem sheath .... *E. arvense*
                8b. Fertile stems becoming green, branched, persistent;
                sterile stems with conspicuous bumps and first
                internodes of the primary branches shorter than or
                equalling the length of the stem sheath .... *E. pratense* (see *E. arvense*)

E. hyemale	*E. fluviatile*	*E. telmatiea*	*E. arvense*

Clubmosses and Spikemosses

The clubmosses and spikemosses all have small, narrow, evergreen leaves that are alternate and more or less spirally arranged, or sometimes arranged in opposite pairs. They have sporangia (spore cases) in terminal cones or leaf axils.

Key to Species of Clubmosses (*Huperzia, Lycopodium*) and Spikemosses (*Selaginella*)

1a. Stems long-creeping with erect branches, or stems tufted and forking, or a single branch from a short rhizome; cones cylindrical, usually conspicuous .... (Clubmosses) 2

2a. Spore sacs in the axils of ordinary green leaves, not forming definite cones .... *Huperzia selago*

2b. Spore sacs in terminal cones 3

3a. Sterile branches horizontal; cones solitary; fertile (cone) leaves green, much like sterile leaves .... *L. inundatum*

3b. Sterile branches erect or ascending; cones with yellowish, scalelike leaves 4

4a. Cones sessile at the ends of leafy stems 5

5a. Aerial stems erect, freely forking, tree-like .... *L. dendroideum*

5b. Aerial stems tufted, bushy, or fan-like 6

6a. Aerial stems unbranched or few-forked, 13–25 cm tall; sterile leaves all alike, spirally arranged, not fused to stem .... *L. annotinum*

6b. Aerial stems fan-like, shorter than 13 cm; sterile leaves in 4–5 rows, scale-like, partially fused to stem 7

7a. Sterile branchlets rounded; leaves all alike, in 5 rows .... *L. sitchense* (see *L. alpinum*)

7b. Sterile branchlets flattened; leaves in 4 rows, those of upper and lower side unlike the marginal .... *L. alpinum*

4b. Cones stalked 8

8a. Leaves awl-shaped with long hair-tips .... *L. clavatum*

8b. Leaves scale-like; plants bushy, with flattened branchlets ... *L. complanatum*

1b. Stems usually short-creeping, often mat-forming; branches prostrate (sometimes pendent), not forking; cones 4 angled, inconspicuous .... (Spikemosses) 9

9a. Sterile leaves clearly in 4 ranks and of 2 sizes, rounded at tip .... *Selaginella douglasii* (see *S. oregana*)

9b. Sterile leaves spirally arranged, of one size, usually bristle- or hair-tipped 10

10a. Stems slender, creeping, not mat-forming or pendent; leaves soft; cones not 4-angled, thicker than stem .... *S. selaginoides*

10b. Stems terrestrial and mat-forming or epiphytic and pendent; leaves thick, firm; cones 4-angled, not appreciably thicker than stem 11

11a. Plants usually forming loose mats; stem leaves merely sessile, not with bases fused to stem .... *S. wallacei*

11b. Leaves fused at the base to the stem 12

12a. Plants usually epiphytic on trees; stems pendent, festooning; branches strongly curled when dry .... *S. oregana*

12b. Plants terrestrial, densely tufted; branches not or slightly curled when dry .... *S. densa* (see *S. wallacei*)

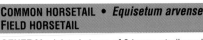

COMMON HORSETAIL • *Equisetum arvense*
FIELD HORSETAIL

GENERAL: Jointed **stems of 2 types**, sterile and fertile; sterile stems to 70 cm tall, green, **branched**, hollow (the central cavity taking up about half of the stem), **10–12 ridged**, sheaths green, appressed to stem, with 10–12 brownish or blackish teeth, **first internode of main branches longer** than the stem sheath; fertile stems to 30 cm tall, **brownish to whitish, unbranched**, usually thick and succulent, **soon withering**; rhizomes creeping, branched, dark-felted, tuber-bearing.

CONES: Long-stalked, 2–3.5 cm long, blunt-tipped, **persistent**.

ECOLOGY: On a wide variety of soils, in moist to wet forests, meadows, swamps, fens and alpine seepage areas, often weedy (as on roadsides and cutbanks); from lowlands to alpine areas.

NOTES: Meadow horsetail (*E. pratense*) is uncommon but widely scattered in the northern half of our region (Skeena River north, not on the Queen Charlotte Islands), in moist forests, meadows and clearings and along stream-banks. It differs from common horsetail in having **green, persistent, branched** fertile stems, and in that the first internode of the primary branches on sterile stems is **shorter than, or equal to**, the stem sheath, which has white-tipped teeth. • **Wood horsetail** (*E. sylvaticum*) is similar to both common and meadow horsetails, but it has **branches that branch again**. It grows in shady coniferous forests, swamps, bog edges and clearings; it is scattered in the northern part of our region, over much the same range as meadow horsetail. • Ancient Romans ate young, fertile common-horsetail shoots as if they were asparagus. They also used them to make tea and as a thickening powder. • Common horsetail is one of the most widespread plants in the world, and often turns up as a bad garden weed (sometimes called 'devil guts'). It was the first vascular plant to send green shoots up through the debris of the 1980 eruption of Mt. St. Helens.

SWAMP HORSETAIL • *Equisetum fluviatile*
WATER HORSETAIL

GENERAL: Stems **unbranched or with branches sporadic or more numerous in whorls**, especially near the top; **fertile and sterile stems alike**, annual, hollow (the central cavity taking up **70% or more** of the stem), to 100 cm tall, **10–30 ridged**; sheaths green, the teeth dark brown to blackish; rhizomes creeping, shiny, often reddish.

CONES: Short-stalked, blunt-tipped, **deciduous**, to 2.5 cm long.

ECOLOGY: Lake edges, marshes, fens, bogs, ditches and other wet sites; low to moderate elevations; often forms large, conspicuous colonies **in shallow water**.

NOTES: Swamp horsetail can be distinguished from other species of *Equisetum* in our region by the **soft annual stems** that collapse easily when squeezed, because of the **thin walls and large central cavity**. • In similar habitats at low to middle elevations in the southern half of our region (and rarely along the north coast to Lynn Canal), look for **marsh horsetail** (*E. palustre*), a similar species with a **smaller central stem cavity (less than 1/3** the diameter of the stem) and **fewer (5–10)** stem ridges. • *Equisetum* species have an affinity for gold in solution, and they concentrate it more than most plants, so they have been used in bioassays for the metal. • *Equisetum* is from the Latin *equus* ('horse') and *setum* ('bristle'); *fluviatile* means 'growing in a stream.'

SCOURING-RUSH • *Equisetum hyemale*

GENERAL: Stems **all alike, unbranched, stout, evergreen**, hollow (the central cavity taking up **3/4 or more** of the stem), **bluish-green, to 1.5 m tall, 3–10 mm thick, 14–50 ridged**; sheaths green to ashy-grey, usually also with **black bands** at the tip and in the middle or at the base, the teeth dark brown to blackish; rhizomes creeping, slender, blackish, deep in the soil.

CONES: Short-stalked, to 2.5 cm long, **hard-pointed, persistent**.

ECOLOGY: Common on moist to wet sites, often along major streams and rivers with connections east of coastal mountains, on open sandbars as well as in shaded alluvial forests, also in disturbed habitats such as roadsides, railway embankments and old fields; at low to middle elevations; uncommon north of 51°N.

NOTES: If your scouring-rush is **smaller (to 50 cm tall)** and **thinner (less than 4 mm thick)** than *E. hyemale*, with **fewer (3–12)** ridges and a small central cavity, it is likely **northern scouring-rush** (*E. variegatum*). Northern scouring-rush is frequent at sea level to alpine elevations from Prince William Sound to southern Washington, on sandy shores and stream-banks and in thickets and wet meadows. • The cell walls of *Equisetum* species are impregnated with silicon dioxide. They were used by aboriginal peoples on the coast primarily as abrasives for polishing wooden objects such as canoes, dishes, arrow shafts and gambling sticks. The Tlingit and Coast Salish used horsetail rhizomes to decorate baskets. • The name 'scouring-rush' was given to this species because it was used in Europe to scour utensils made of wood or pewter. It was also used for honing the reeds of woodwind instruments.

GIANT HORSETAIL • *Equisetum telmatiea*

GENERAL: Stems **of 2 types**, sterile and fertile; sterile stems **branched**, hollow (central cavity 2/3 to 3/4 the diameter of the stem), to 3 m tall, 2 cm thick, 14–30 ridged, the sheaths to 2.5 cm long, pale below, dark above; fertile stems **unbranched, fleshy**, to 60 cm tall; rhizomes black, covered with felt, bearing pear-shaped tubers at the joints.

CONES: Stout, short-stalked, long (to 10 cm long), **blunt-tipped**.

ECOLOGY: Moist to wet places, stream-banks, swamps, seepage areas, gullies, roadside ditches, usually near standing or flowing water, often forming dense colonies; at low to middle elevations.

NOTES: Giant horsetail often forms dense patches in wet areas; these patches have an attractive, delicate texture as a result of the numerous, thin branches. Small specimens of this usually large species can be distinguished from common horsetail by the **larger, looser sheath** and **more-numerous (20–30)**, 2-ribbed teeth. • Giant horsetail was the preferred horsetail for native groups on the coast. The young spore-bearing and vegetative shoots of the giant horsetail were an important springtime vegetable of some Coast Salish and Nuu-chah-nulth peoples. They were picked when young and eaten raw, sometimes with oil, after the papery sheaths had been removed. CAUTION: the green parts of this and other species are poisonous to livestock and probably to humans, at least if eaten in large quantities. • Horsetails are a very ancient group of plants that grew to the size of trees when dinosaurs roamed the earth. Lying on the wet ground and with a little imagination, one can view horsetail patches as ancient forests in miniature. Look up through their dense foliage for a glimpse of pterodactyls! • *E. telmatiea* is called 'giant horsetail' because of its size. The species name means 'of muddy water or marshes.'

STIFF CLUBMOSS • *Lycopodium annotinum*

GENERAL: Horizontal stems creeping on or near surface of ground, sometimes arching, to 1 m long, rooting at intervals, leafy; erect stems shiny, **simple or once to twice forked**, to 25 cm tall.

LEAVES: In 8 ranks, **whorl-like, usually spreading, firm, sharp-pointed.**

CONES: Stalkless, solitary at the branch tips; cone leaves straw-coloured, egg-shaped, tapering to a slender point, marginally toothed.

ECOLOGY: Moist forest, thickets, bog edges, and subalpine heath, also on rocky areas with thin soils; widespread at low to subalpine elevations.

NOTES: Stiff clubmoss is easily recognized by its **erect, leafy, fertile branches, each with a single, stalkless cone**. It varies in appearance depending on altitude; it has shorter, stiffer stems and firmer leaves at higher elevations. It is the most common forest clubmoss in coastal Alaska and north coastal B.C. • While there are no reports of the spores of *Lycopodium* species being used by B.C. native groups, the spore powder (known as 'vegetable sulphur') was supposedly used by other North American natives as a drying agent for wounds and a treatment for nose bleeds and diaper rash. The spores may also be used today as a dusting powder for condoms and a body powder for babies and bedridden patients.

RUNNING CLUBMOSS • *Lycopodium clavatum*

GENERAL: Horizontal stems **extensively creeping** on surface of ground, sometimes arching, to 1 m or more long, rooting at intervals, leafy; erect stems **irregularly branched**, to 25 cm tall.

LEAVES: Bright-green, **crowded, ascending to spreading**, in about 10 ranks, lance-shaped, **tipped with soft, white bristles**.

CONES: Several (2–4) on a long, forked, scaly stalk; cone leaves yellowish, rounded, tapering to a white, hair-like point, irregularly toothed.

ECOLOGY: Moist to dry open forests or edges of swamps and bogs; openings, clearings and roadcuts (often on acid sandy soil); occasionally in high-elevation heath and tundra; at all elevations.

NOTES: Bog clubmoss (*Lycopodiella inundata*, also known as *Lycopodium inundatum*) is a **short-creeping** species that is never upright (except for the **unbranched, leafy, cone-bearing stems**); it is found at low elevations on wet shoreline areas and bogs from south of Petersburg to northwest California. • Running clubmoss was used in modern times by the Nuu-chah-nulth and the Nuxalk as a Christmas decoration inside the house. In Ditidaht, it is called 'causing one to be confused in the woods'; it was believed that anyone who handled it would become lost. In several coastal languages including Hesquiat, Haida and Tlingit, this plant is known as 'deer's belt.' • *L. clavatum* is also known as 'staghorn clubmoss' because of the appearance of the cone-bearing stems.

GROUND-PINE • *Lycopodium dendroideum*

GENERAL: Horizontal stems in the form of creeping rhizomes well below the surface of the ground, rooting throughout; stems erect, to 30 cm tall, irregularly branched, **bushy-forked, appearing tree-like.**

LEAVES: Numerous, in 6 to 9 ranks, long-pointed, prickly to the touch.

CONES: Stalkless, solitary at the branch tips, cone leaves yellowish-brown, heart-shaped, abruptly sharp pointed.

ECOLOGY: Moist to fairly dry, deciduous and coniferous forests, thickets, openings and bog edges; scattered at low to middle elevations.

NOTES: Ground-pine is also known as *L. obscurum.* • Another branched, tree-like clubmoss is **ground-cedar** (*L. complanatum,*

p. 434), which has **stalked cones** and **scale-like leaves reminiscent of western redcedar**, hence the common name. It can be found in moist to dry forests, rocky slopes and sandy openings, at low to middle elevations from Alaska (Lynn Canal only) to northern Oregon (but not on Vancouver Island). • The genus name *Lycopodium* is from the Greek *lycos* ('wolf') and *podus* ('foot'), after a fancied resemblance of the leafy stems of clubmoss to a wolf's paw. • *L. dendroideum* is called 'ground-pine' (or 'princess-pine') because the plant resembles a miniature coniferous tree. • This and some other species of *Lycopodium* have been observed to form 'fairy rings' when growing in openings, old fields or alpine heath.

FIR CLUBMOSS • *Lycopodium selago*

GENERAL: Horizontal rooting stems short, withering but persistent; **erect stems simple or several times dichotomously branched,** usually clustered, **often forming tight, more or less flat-topped tufts,** to 20 cm tall.

LEAVES: In 8 ranks, **usually ascending, crowded,** lance-shaped, firm, pointed.

CONES: Not obvious; **spore cases borne in the axils of ordinary green leaves near the branch tips**, in bands alternating with bands of sterile leaves (fertile leaves produced early in the season, followed later by sterile leaves).

ECOLOGY: Moist, open, low-elevation to subalpine forest and parkland, heath, bogs; shaded, acid cliffs and boulders; high-elevation heath and tundra.

NOTES: This species is also known as *Huperzia selago, H. miyoshiana, H. haleakalae* (in part), and *H. occidentalis* (in part), and it is sometimes called mountain clubmoss. • This plant was used as a purgative by the Ditidaht and was known as a 'strong medicine.' Fir clubmoss is reported to contain a chemical that may be effective against Alzheimer's disease. • The spore powder ('vegetable sulphur') of all clubmosses is very flammable and was used in fireworks, stage lighting and early flash photography. • The species name *selago* is an old name for *Lycopodium.*

ALPINE CLUBMOSS • *Lycopodium alpinum*

GENERAL: Horizontal stems creeping on surface of ground, to 50 cm long, rooting at intervals, sparsely leafy; erect stems **to 10 cm tall**, whitish, **tufted, forked several times, branches somewhat flattened.**

LEAVES: Bluish-green, in 4 ranks, partially fused to stem, **of 3 forms**: the dorsal (outer) ones lance-shaped, the ventral (inner) ones shorter and trowel-shaped, the lateral leaves concave, with deltoid, free tips and **flange-like bases fused to the branch.**

CONES: Stalkless, solitary at the branch tips; cone leaves yellow, broadly triangular.

ECOLOGY: Dry to moist sites in open, higher-elevation forests, rocky slopes and high-elevation heath and tundra.

NOTES: Alaska or Sitka clubmoss (*L. sitchense*), a species with **light-green, 5-ranked, essentially similar leaves** and **rounded (not flattened)** vegetative branches, is sometimes difficult to distinguish from alpine clubmoss. It occupies habitats similar to those of alpine clubmoss, but it can be found in open forest more frequently than can *L. alpinum*. Its range stretches from Alaska to the central Oregon Cascades, and it is most commonly found in subalpine heath. • The Gitksan may have used alpine or Alaska clubmoss in medicinal preparations. • The species name *alpinum* and common name 'alpine clubmoss' emphasize the high-elevation habitats of this species.

GROUND-CEDAR • *Lycopodium complanatum*

GENERAL: Horizontal stems creeping on or slightly below the ground surface, to 1 m or more long; upright aerial stems arising at intervals, **to 35 cm tall**, much branched, with crowded to loosely forking branchlets; **branchlets flattened, constricted** between yearly growths.

LEAVES: In 4 ranks; lateral leaves fused to stem for **more than half their length**, the free tips narrowly lance-shaped, pointy-tipped, often somewhat glaucous; inner leaves much smaller.

CONES: Cylindric, **1–3 on stalks**; cone leaves yellowish, round to deltoid.

ECOLOGY: Moist to dry, usually coniferous forests, rocky slopes, sandy openings and clearings; low to middle elevations.

NOTES: Ground-cedar is somewhat similar and apparently related to alpine clubmoss and Alaska or Sitka clubmoss, from which it can be distinguished by its **larger size (to 35 cm tall** vs. to 10 or 15 cm tall), **loose, elongated branches**, much reduced inner leaves, **stalked cones** and, to some extent, by its habitat. • The irregular growth pattern often gives ground-cedar a straggly look. • *L. complanatum* is called 'ground-cedar' because the scale-like leaves are reminiscent of the leaves of *Thuja* species.

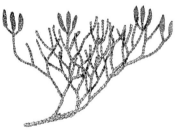

OREGON SELAGINELLA • *Selaginella oregana*

GENERAL: Usually **festooning deciduous trees** (most commonly bigleaf maple), occasionally sprawling over wet ground; stems **long (to 30 cm), loose and freely branched**.

LEAVES: Bright-green, **oval to triangular**, loosely overlapping, **spirally arranged**, grooved on the back, with short (usually less than 2 mm) **bristles on the tip**.

CONES: 1 or more at the ends of branches, fairly inconspicuous; the cone leaves in 4 tight rows so the cones appear square in cross-section.

ECOLOGY: Usually hanging from the branches of bigleaf maple (rarely other deciduous trees), occasionally sprawling over moist, shaded rocks and banks; at low elevations.

NOTES: Douglas' selaginella (*S. douglasii*) is a **creeping terrestrial** species with **oval leaves of 2 sizes in 4 distinct rows**. It grows at low elevations on moist shady cliffs, rocks, banks and tree bases, **primarily along the Columbia River**. • The big, hanging curtains of 'mosses' on maples along the coast and in the rainforests in Olympic National Park are usually made up of Oregon selaginella interspersed with moss. During dry weather the branches curl up, forming ringlets. • The 1 record in the Queen Charlotte Islands may be a remnant population established from Oregon selaginella transported from Vancouver Island by Haida warriors using it as kneepads in their canoes. • *Selaginella* is the diminutive of *selago*, an old name for *Lycopodium*.

MOUNTAIN-MOSS • *Selaginella selaginoides*
MOUNTAIN SPIKEMOSS

GENERAL: Small, creeping, branching stems, **2–5 cm long**, forming **small mats**; fertile stems erect, 3–15 cm tall.

LEAVES: Small (2–4 mm long), **narrowly egg-shaped, spirally arranged**, with bristles on the edges, not grooved on the back; tip sharp-pointed but **not extended into a bristle**.

CONES: Unbranched, upright, terminal and fairly inconspicuous; **cone leaves slightly larger** than the lower, sterile leaves.

ECOLOGY: Bogs, stream-banks, marshy shores, wet forests and wet rocky ledges; low (in Alaska) to middle elevations; widespread but never abundant.

NOTES: Mountain spikemoss does not look much like a *Selaginella*; it **looks like a moss with a distinctive yellowish-green colour**. • In the spikemosses (*Selaginella* spp.), spores are borne in sporangia (little sacs) in the axils of modified, fertile leaves. The fertile cone leaves are usually only slightly different from the sterile leaves, so the cones in *Selaginella* are usually fairly inconspicuous—unlike those of most clubmosses (*Lycopodium* spp.).

WALLACE'S SELAGINELLA • *Selaginella wallacei*

GENERAL: Horizontal stems **to 20 cm long**, forming **loose, tangled mats**; upright stems numerous, **cord-like**, branched or simple, often intertwined, to 4 cm high.

LEAVES: Narrowly oblong, about 3 mm long, **arranged spirally**, not clearly in rows, closely overlapping, grooved on the back; tips **extended into stiff bristles.**

CONES: Numerous, terminal, usually unbranched, slightly curved, 1–2 cm long; **cone leaves very similar to sterile leaves** but clearly in 4 rows, so the whole cone appears square in cross-section.

ECOLOGY: Rocky cliff-faces and ledges, mossy bluffs, rocky slopes, both in the open and in moderate shade; from low to middle elevations.

NOTES: Compact selaginella (*S. densa*) is similar to Wallace's selaginella, but it can be distinguished by its **flattened branches** and its general habit. Compact selaginella is **'denser' (more compactly branched)** and forms **small cushions** on the ground. It can be found from southern Vancouver Island and the adjacent mainland south to northwestern California, generally at subalpine or alpine elevations in the Cascades and Olympics. **From Lynn Canal north**, it is replaced by the closely related **northern selaginella** (*S. sibirica*). • The 'resurrection plant' available in many nurseries is a spikemoss (*S. lepidophylla*) from the southern United States and Mexico.

BRISTLE-LIKE QUILLWORT • *Isoetes echinospora*

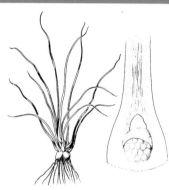

GENERAL: Aquatic herb with tufted, grass-like leaves, from a **2-lobed, bulb-like corm**, which has been interpreted to be a very short stem.

LEAVES: Several to many (10–30 or more), **erect**, soft, green to yellowish-green, to 20 cm long, **grass-like**, cylindric, tapering to a long, very slender tip.

SPORANGIA: Oblong to oval, to 10 mm long by 3 mm wide, **at the base of the leaf on the inner side.**

ECOLOGY: In shallow (to about 1 m deep), standing or slowly flowing water, often growing on sand or gravel; low to middle elevations.

NOTES: Bristle-like quillwort is also known as *I. muricata, I. braunii, I. setosa* and *I. maritima* (in part). • **Nuttall's quillwort** (*I. nuttallii*) is the only quillwort in our region that grows in **non-submerged** conditions; it ranges from southeast Vancouver Island south, in wet sites (especially vernal pools and seepage areas) at low elevations. There are several other quillworts in our region, but they cannot be distinguished without microscopic examination of their spores. If you have a microscope and a burning desire to identify your quillwort, a good reference is Cody and Britton (1989). • Quillworts, like spikemosses and clubmosses, produce spores borne in chambers (sporangia) in their leaf axils. • The common name 'quillwort' describes this plant's appearance: a bunch of quills. The species name *echinospora* means 'prickly spores'; the spores of this species appear spiny when viewed under a microscope. The Latin *isoetes* means 'equal-to-a-year,' perhaps in reference to the evergreen nature of the leaves.

Bryophytes (Mosses and Liverworts)

Flowering plants, conifers, ferns, clubmosses, spikemosses and horsetails are all vascular plants—that is, they have well-developed water- and food-conducting systems. Bryophytes (mosses, liverworts [hepatics], and hornworts) are non-vascular plants—that is, they have less developed conductive tubes. The other group treated in this book, the lichens, are actually composite organisms composed of simple non-vascular plants (algae) living with fungi.

Having vascular tissues allows plants to grow tall and thrive in places where water is not always available. Since bryophytes have poorly developed conducting tubes, they remain small and usually grow in wet places. Because the climate over much of our region is so wet, bryophytes are usually abundant. Those moss species that live in dry places have the ability (unusual in plants) to dry up and, upon re-wetting, to begin to photosynthesize almost immediately.

Life cycles of mosses and liverworts are similar. A single-celled green **spore**, blown through the air, lands on the ground, or on a branch, stump or tree trunk. If the landing spot is moist, the spore will germinate and grow into the **gametophyte** (the conspicuous moss or liverwort plant, the one you usually see). On the branches of the gametophyte, male and female sex organs produce sperm and eggs. The sperm swim to the eggs and fertilize them; the fertilized egg is the start of the **sporophyte** generation. The sporophyte consists of a capsule on a stalk (**seta**), growing out of the gametophyte. The capsules of mosses often have teeth (**peristome teeth**) around the pores their tips. Spores are released from the capsule, and the life cycle begins again.

Moss and liverwort leaves are usually only 1 cell thick, except along the midvein (**costa**). The leaves of mosses are attached to the stems by the **alar cells**, which are sometimes different in appearance from the other cells on the leaf. All bryophytes lack true roots; instead they are attached to substrates by **rhizoids**.

So, is it a moss, or is it a liverwort? In most mosses, the capsule stalk elongates, then the capsule enlarges and matures; in liverworts, the capsule enlarges and matures before the stalk elongates. As a result, you do not often see the stalks and capsules on liverworts. Liverworts usually have different (often reduced or absent) leaves underneath (**ventral**). Because the ventral leaves are usually pressed flat to the stem, and the 2 rows of lateral leaves come out nearly opposite each other, all leaves are flattened (in a distinctive fashion) in the same plane. This leaf arrangement is rare in mosses. Moss capsules usually open at the tip, and the pore often is surrounded by peristome teeth; liverwort capsules split lengthwise into 4 sections (valves). Although most liverworts are leafy, like mosses, a few (e.g., lung liverwort and snake liverwort, p. 446) are flattened and not differentiated into stem and leaves (**thalloid**).

Most bryophytes are mosses (some 8,000–9,000 species worldwide). The liverworts, or hepatics, are also a large group (about 6,000 species worldwide), but they are much more common in the southern hemisphere and much less important in our region. Hornworts (*Anthoceros* spp.) are a small group both worldwide and in our region, and they are not described in this book. A good reference to the bryophytes of northwestern North America is Vitt et al. (1988).

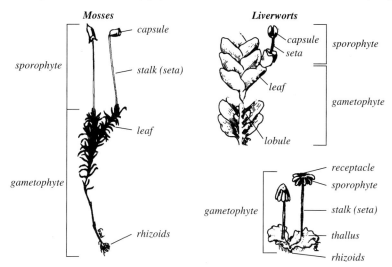

Mosses — capsule, stalk (seta), leaf, sporophyte, gametophyte, rhizoids

Liverworts — capsule, seta, leaf, lobule, sporophyte, gametophyte, receptacle, stalk (seta), thallus, rhizoids

Hepatics (Liverworts)

Hepatics produce spores. These germinate to produce leafy or ribbon-like plants called **gametophytes**. In this form, the hepatic produces a **sporophyte** consisting of a **foot**, a clear, short **stalk** and a **capsule**. Usually, the capsule develops in a sheath of fused leaves (the 'perianth'), but when the spores are mature, the stalk elongates and the **capsule splits into segments**, releasing its spores and beginning the cycle again.

In some hepatics lacking definite leaves and stems (complex thalloid hepatics), capsule stalks do not elongate. Instead, the entire spore-producing structure (the sporophyte) grows on top of a stalk produced by the plant thallus (the gametophyte).

Leafy hepatics have stems with leaves in 2 or 3 ranks. These leaves never have a midrib, and often they are rounded, have 2–4 points, and are folded ('complicate-2-lobed'). The leaves are attached either transversely, oriented as shingles on a roof ('**succubous**') or opposite to shingle orientation ('**incubous**') when viewed from the upper surface. (NB: 'Succubous' and 'incubous' both pertain to leaf arrangement, **not** to demonic nocturnal sex.) Often, the leaves on the lower surface of the stem (**underleaves**) are reduced or lacking. Most leafy hepatics are placed in the Jungermanniales.

There are 2 types of thalloid hepatics:

1) **Simple thalloids** are composed of 1 type of tissue and produce spore capsules on elongating stalks (as in leafy hepatics). These belong to the Metzgeriales.

2) **Complex thalloids** have fascinating internal structure, much like a greenhouse, and produce smaller sporophytes; they belong in the Marchantiales.

There are more than 220 species of hepatics in our region; they are most abundant on moist substrates, but some also occur as epiphytes in periodically dry forests.

COMMON SCISSOR-LEAF LIVERWORT • *Herbertus aduncus*

GENERAL: Plants **rusty-red to brownish**, forming **loose, sometimes straggly mats** 2–10 cm or longer on tree trunks and branches; stems radially symmetric, almost thread-like or at least very slender, unbranched, or occasionally branched.

LEAVES: About 1 mm long, lance-shaped, **divided into 2 sharp lobes** to halfway or more, these difficult to observe as they are usually **upright**, pressed to the stem and curved to 1 side; cells very irregularly thick-walled and knobby throughout the leaf; leaves on the lower surface of the stem similar to upper leaves.

SPOROPHYTES: Rarely produced.

ECOLOGY: On trees or growing in open tundra; the wiry stems form spreading, descending or hanging mats on the bases, trunks and branches of coniferous trees in lowland rainforest habitats from Oregon northward; the rare occurrence of this species in acidic tundra is of phytogeographic interest.

NOTES: Common scissor-leaf liverwort is also known as *Herberta adunca*. • The **reddish colour, wiry stems and upright leaves** of *H. aduncus* superficially resemble a moss, for which it can easily be mistaken. However, careful examination will reveal **2-lobed leaves**, a feature mosses never have.

MAPLE LIVERWORT • *Barbilophozia lycopodioides*

GENERAL: Plants large, **rich-green**, 3–5 or up to 8 cm long, with creeping to ascending, little-branching stems; **gemmae rarely** growing at the tips of the stems.

LEAVES: 1.5–2.5 mm long, wavy, **overlapping like shingles**; upper leaves obliquely attached, oblong-rounded, with **4 equal, slenderly tapered lobes**; leaves on the lower side of the stem tiny, but present, lance-shaped, 2 lobed with many hair-like outgrowths along the edges; cells rounded-square.

SPOROPHYTES: Rarely produced; emerging from tube of fused, pleated leaves fringed with hair-like outgrowths.

ECOLOGY: Common on **forest floor humus and moist soil at middle and higher elevations**; especially characteristic of humid, subalpine forests, occasionally on soil associated with rock ledges; not common in low-elevation rain forests.

NOTES: This large, rich-green hepatic is characterized by **4-lobed leaves that overlap like shingles**. The lobes and upper portions of the leaves are wavy and end in slenderly tapered points. Gemmae are rare. • *B. hatcheri* often grows with *B. lycopodioides*; it is distinguished by its **sharply pointed leaf lobes** and its shoots usually have **reddish masses of gemmae** at their tips. *B. barbata* is common on cliff-faces; it has straight leaves attached at the sides and is darker in colour and non-wavy. Other hepatics with large leaves that overlap like shingles have 3-lobed leaves. • Species here considered in the genus *Barbilophozia* are also found in the literature placed in the genera *Lophozia* and *Orthocaulis*.

SNOW-MAT LIVERWORT • *Orthocaulis floerkei*

GENERAL: Plants **reddish-green to brownish**; stems dense, ascending, 2–5 cm long, forming **extensive mats**.

LEAVES: 1.0–1.5 mm long, stiffly spreading, **overlapping like shingles**; upper leaves concave, closely overlapping, **3 lobed, sharp pointed**; leaves on the lower side of the stem **relatively large**, 2 lobed, lance-shaped, with one to several hair-like outgrowths along the lower edges; **no gemmae**; cells round.

SPOROPHYTES: Occasional, short-lived; emerging from a deeply pleated, toothed, oval-cylindric tube of fused leaves.

ECOLOGY: Common in **subalpine forests on humus and acidic soils**; often found with *B. lycopodioides* and *B. hatcheri*, but probably more restricted in its preference to subalpine habitats.

NOTES: Snow-mat liverwort is also known as *Barbilophozia floerkei*. • The **3-lobed leaves that overlap like shingles** distinguish *O. floerkei* from species of *Bazzania*, which have leaves that **overlap like reversed shingles**, from *Barbilophozia lycopodioides* and *B. hatcheri* which have **4-lobed leaves** and from species of *Lophozia* which have **2-lobed leaves**. Several other hepatics with 3-lobed leaves occur in our region, including species of *Tritomaria*, but these commonly have either gemmae or unequally lobed leaves. Other species of *Orthocaulis* with 3-lobed leaves do not have well-developed leaves on the lower side of the stem as does *O. floerkei*.

HARD SCALE LIVERWORT • *Mylia taylorii*

GENERAL: Plants beautiful, **reddish-green to carmine-red**, sometimes pale-green in smaller populations, robust, forming dense, spreading, creeping to ascending **mats** 3–6 or sometimes 12 cm long, sometimes in **thick turfs**; stems mostly simple, with many root-like filaments on the lower side.

LEAVES: 1.5–2.5 mm long, upright, pressed to the stem, with spreading outer portions, **overlapping like shingles, lacking lobes**, round to oval, concave; edges curved **downward, smooth**; leaves on the lower side of the stem slenderly lance-shaped, tiny, not obvious.

SPOROPHYTES: Not common; emerging from a cylindric tube of fused leaves, flattened sideways and fringed with hair-like outgrowths.

ECOLOGY: Most often **on logs** in lowland forests and in forested peatlands; occasionally on tree bases or humus.

NOTES: **Concave, unlobed leaves, overlapping like shingles and with their edges bent backwards**, distinguish this species. The reddish colour is distinctive in well-developed plants. Hard scale liverwort is one of our prettiest hepatics. It forms large, thick mats. • *M. anomala* is common on *Sphagnum fuscum* **hummocks in bogs**. It is **smaller** and has **narrower leaves** than *M. taylorii*, and it has **yellow gemmae** on the upper leaves.

CEDAR-SHAKE LIVERWORT • *Plagiochila porelloides*

GENERAL: Plants relatively large, **dark-green to olive-green**, shiny, 1–10 cm long, forming creeping to ascending **mats**.

LEAVES: About 1–2 mm long, **overlapping like shingles**; upper leaves oval, **not lobed; edges nearly smooth to strongly toothed**, with the upper and lower edges bent backwards; no leaves on the lower side of the stem.

SPOROPHYTES: Short-lived; emerging from an elongate, flattened, toothed, abruptly squared-off tube of fused leaves.

ECOLOGY: On **rocks, cliff-faces, logs, tree bases and stream-banks** in shaded low-elevation to subalpine forests; occasional in the alpine in humid habitats.

NOTES: **Oval, unlobed leaves, overlapping like shingles and with their edges strongly bent backward**, identify the genus *Plagiochila*. *Mylia* has smooth leaf edges that are less strongly bent downwards, while other hepatics have smaller, rounded leaves that overlap like shingles and have edges that are not bent backward. • *Plagiochila* is the largest genus of liverworts in the world. Cedar-shake liverwort (*P. porelloides*, often called *P. asplenioides* ssp. *porelloides*, **inset photo**), like many Pacific coast bryophytes, occurs in similar habitats at north-temperate latitudes around the world. • The toothed leaves of cedar-shake liverwort are unusual for a liverwort.

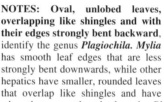

THREE-TOOTHED WHIP LIVERWORT • *Bazzania tricrenata*

GENERAL: Plants slender, **reddish-brown to deep-green**, 3–5 cm long, forming **spreading mats**.

LEAVES: 1–1.5 mm long, **overlapping like reversed shingles**, upper leaves closely overlapping, convex, egg-shaped, with **2–3 irregular, small lobes** at the tips; lower leaves smaller, oval, with 3–4 irregular lobes at the tips; cells square.

SPOROPHYTES: Occasional, short-lived, emerging from oval-spindle-shaped, slender, puckered, red tubes of fused leaves.

ECOLOGY: On **lower portions of tree trunks**, on humus surrounding the **bases of trees** and occasionally on rock surfaces in lower and middle-elevation forests and peatlands.

NOTES: 3-lobed leaves that **overlap like reversed shingles** are characteristic of the genus *Bazzania*; there are several species in our region. **Three-toothed whip liverwort** has leaves tipped with **2 or 3 notches** that are irregular in shape and size. *B. trilobata* is **larger** and has **3 equal-sized lobes**. Species of *Calypogeia* are **smaller**; their leaves overlap like reversed shingles and have **2 small notches** each. Both of these genera have well-developed leaves on the lower side of the stem. *Lepidozia* and *Kurzia* species are **much smaller** and have **3-lobed, club-shaped** leaves.

LITTLE HANDS LIVERWORT • *Lepidozia reptans*

GENERAL: Plants tiny, **light to olive-green**, 1.5–3 cm long, with widely spaced, **pinnate**, spreading branches, forming **loose mats** over other bryophytes, usually creeping or trailing.

LEAVES: Less than 1 mm long, **overlapping like reversed shingles**, widely-spaced, **3–4 lobed about half way** to the base; upper leaves curved downward, **resembling club-shaped mitts**; leaves on the lower side of the stem somewhat smaller, upright, otherwise similar; cells rounded.

SPOROPHYTES: Not uncommon; arising from a long, prominent, slenderly spindle-shaped tube of fused leaves that is finely toothed at the opening.

ECOLOGY: On **decaying wood**, especially rotten stumps and logs in montane and boreal forests; occurring with *Tetraphis pellucida* and *Calypogeia* species.

NOTES: Leaves with 3–4 lobes that overlap like reversed shingles are also found in species of *Bazzania*, which have **larger plants** and **much shallower lobes** (restricted to mere notches at the tips) than does *L. reptans*, and by species of *Kurzia* (formerly *Microlepidozia*) and *Blepharostoma trichophyllum,* which have **leaves divided to the base into 3 thread-like lobes**. • The stage of decay of the rotting wood is important to *Lepidozia*. 'Kickable' stumps—those with a pleasant soft sound when kicked— almost always have *Lepidozia* and *Tetraphis*; stumps in early stages of decay have harder substrates and often have species of *Lophozia*, *Brachythecium* and *Pohlia nutans* species on them, and you have a sore toe. This quick feedback helps you learn the habitat preferences of *Lepidozia reptans*.

COMMON FOLD-LEAF LIVERWORT • *Diplophyllum albicans*

GENERAL: Plants **reddish, often dark-brown**, 1–5 cm long, forming mats on moist, shaded or protected substrates; some populations occur as **creeping plants** while others are more dense with ascending plants forming **mats.**

LEAVES: 1.0–1.6 mm long, flattened, **overlapping like reversed shingles, 2 lobed and folded lengthwise** with upper lobes smaller than lower lobes; lower lobes **oblong**, toothed, blunt to sharply pointed, with a central group of elongated cells forming a pale band for about half of the leaf; no leaves on the lower side of the stem.

SPOROPHYTES: Present for only a short time, emerging from a deeply pleated, cone-shaped tube of fused leaves.

ECOLOGY: On **seepy rock surfaces** at all elevations, but especially common at lower elevations.

NOTES: Upper leaves that are **much longer than wide** are characteristic of this small genus of 5 or so species. *D. albicans* is the only one with a **pale band** of elongate cells in the lower portion of the lower lobe. *Scapania* species are somewhat similar, but they have **rounded upper leaves**.

YELLOW-LADLE LIVERWORT • *Scapania bolanderi*

GENERAL: Plants **pale-green to yellow-green**, 1–5 cm long, forming spreading, descending or creeping **mats or cushions**, little branched or unbranched.

LEAVES: 1.5–2.5 mm long, flattened, **overlapping like reversed shingles;** upper leaves **2 lobed and folded lengthwise**, oval, the lobes attached along their lower edges, with small upper-lobes and large under-lobes; **edges strongly toothed** all around; no leaves on the lower side of the stem; cells rounded, thin-walled.

SPOROPHYTES: Present for only a short time; emerging from a keeled, flattened, abruptly squared-off tube of fused leaves.

ECOLOGY: Abundant in lowland forests **on tree bark, stumps, logs, trunks** and, more rarely, soil; especially noticeable in mature, shaded forests on trunks of large cedar, hemlock and Douglas-fir along with species of *Dicranum.*

NOTES: Although there are quite a few species of *Scapania* in our region, this is by far the most common. Other large species of the genus usually occur **on rock** (*S. americana*) and **seepage areas** (*S. undulata*), **in fens** (*S. paludicola*), and **near water** (*S. irrigua*). *Diplophyllum* species also have leaves on which the upper lobes are smaller than the lower ones, but the **toothed leaf edges** distinguish *S. bolanderi* from these hepatics. **Common fold-leaf liverwort** (*D. albicans*) is a common species on moist rock surfaces, but it has leaves that are **much longer than wide.**

PURPLE-WORM LIVERWORT • *Pleurozia purpurea*

GENERAL: Plants large, **purplish to dark reddish-green**, superficially resembling **worms**, unbranched to occasionally branched, forming **creeping mats**.

LEAVES: Complex arrangement consisting of large, **concave, egg-shaped** lower leaves with **ragged** upper edges forming upward, **cupped** leaves surrounding inner and smaller upper leaves in the shape of large lobules; these inner lobules are helmet-shaped, water-holding organs.

SPOROPHYTES: Not known from our region.

ECOLOGY: A species of northern **bogs and soligenous fens**, occurring along the edges of pools and lawns, sometimes in spreading mats encroaching on the water surface.

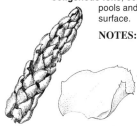

NOTES: These **large, purplish-red** plants, forming **stringy masses** along the edges of bog pools, remind one of *Scorpidium scorpioides*, which occurs in exactly the same habitat in continental rich fens. • *Pleurozia* has unique leaves with the upper lobes developed into **sac-shaped water-holding structures**, while the lower lobes are **upwardly concave**; no other hepatic has this leaf structure.

FLAT-LEAVED LIVERWORT • *Radula complanata*

GENERAL: Plants **yellow-green**, dull, 1–2 cm long, with regular, evenly spaced, once or twice pinnate branches; stems **creeping**.

LEAVES: 0.6–1.0 mm long, **overlapping like reversed shingles**, upper leaves 2 lobed and folded lengthwise; upper lobes large, oval, smooth-edged; lower lobes smaller, almost square, attached to upper lobes along the lower edge; no leaves on the lower side of the stem; **gemmae usually abundant**, giving the upper lobe edges a ragged appearance.

SPOROPHYTES: Common, short-lived; emerging from an oblong, flattened, **spade-shaped tube of fused leaves**.

ECOLOGY: Common on **cliff-faces and rock surfaces** and as an epiphyte **on tree trucks and branches**, where it occurs as closely attached stems.

NOTES: The **yellowish** plants, about **twice as large** as those of *Frullania* and about **half the size** of *Porella,* nicely help to distinguish flat-leaved liverwort. The total **absence of leaves on the lower side** of the stem (seen with a hand lens) also distinguishes *Radula* from these other common epiphytes. The **spade-shaped tubes** of fused leaves are helpful in identification. Flat-leaved liverwort is the only species in this genus common in our region.

TREE-RUFFLE LIVERWORT • *Porella navicularis*

GENERAL: Plants **large, dark-green**, shiny, coarse, up to 10–15 cm long, forming descending, spreading or creeping **mats**; stems often regularly once **pinnately branched**.

LEAVES: Flattened; upper leaves closely **overlapping like reversed shingles**, divided into large, round, upper lobes and smaller, **tongue-shaped under-lobes**; edges of underlobes rolled under; leaves on the lower side of the stem tongue-shaped, their edges rolled under; cells rounded, with strongly thickened corners.

SPOROPHYTES: Present only for a short time, emerging from a fat, 3-cornered, pleated tube of fused leaves; plants unisexual, male plants with conspicuous, short side branches containing sex organs.

ECOLOGY: Common on **tree trunks and branches** in lowland forests; occasionally found on rock faces; the most conspicuous hepatic of the lowland rain forest.

NOTES: Tree-ruffle liverwort can be easily distinguished from hanging millipede liverwort by its **large size**, the **rounded leaves** on the lower side of the stem and its **lack of helmeted under-lobes**. Several other species of *Porella* occur in our region, including *P. cordeana*, which has **ruffled lower edges** on the underleaves and a **brighter green** colour; it occurs on rocks and trees. *Scapania* has **upper lobes that are smaller** than the lower ones.

HANGING MILLIPEDE LIVERWORT • *Frullania nisquallensis*

GENERAL: Plants **small, reddish-brown to red-black**, 3–8 cm long, growing **closely pressed** to the substrate or **sometimes forming hanging mats** from branches, regularly to irregularly **pinnately branched**.

LEAVES: About 1 mm long, flattened; **overlapping like reversed shingles**; upper leaves 2 lobed and folded lengthwise, with large upper lobes and **small under-lobes forming small helmets** attached to the base by a narrow, constricted point; leaves on the lower side of the stem are slightly larger than the under-lobes, heart-shaped; edges bent backward, the notch cutting about 1/4 the way to the base; cells rounded, with irregularly thickened walls, several strongly coloured cells forming an oblique line through the upper lobe.

SPOROPHYTES: Present for only a short time, emerging from a pleated, puckered, cone-shaped tube of fused leaves; plants unisexual; male plants recognized by many short, side branches with sex organs.

ECOLOGY: Common on **trunks and branches of trees**, especially maple and alder in lowland forests, sometimes on conifers; also on cliff-faces.

NOTES: Hanging millipede liverwort is the most common small hepatic in our region. The **closely attached, reddish** plants on trunks of alder and maple can be easily identified. *Porella* and *Scapania* are **much larger**. *Radula* is usually **yellowish**; it has **flattened, spade-like tubes** of fused leaves and has **no helmeted under-lobes**. • The helmets of *Frullania* are water-storage containers for this plant, which lives in a stressful habitat. It has been reported that some *Frullania*s produce helmets that are mini-ecosystems housing rotifers and water-bears.

COMB LIVERWORT • *Riccardia multifida*

GENERAL: Plants shiny, **pale-green**, flattened, ribbon-like, 1.0–1.5 cm long with **many fan-shaped branches**, 2–3 times pinnate; plants small, narrow (0.8–1.0 mm wide), 6–7 cells thick near the middle, 1 cell thick at edges, **lacking a midrib**; usually **branching** at angles of 45° to 65°.

SPOROPHYTES: Arising from a fleshy, club-shaped sheath.

ECOLOGY: On **wet soil** along streams and near rock outcrops and other mesic areas; found from sea level to the alpine, but most common at lower elevations in lowland rain forests.

NOTES: Several other species of *Riccardia* occur in our region. These are distinguished by the number and angle of the branches and by the number of cell layers in the plant body. *Riccardia* is **much smaller** than the other thalloid hepatics. Only *Metzgeria* and *Apometzgeria* can be as narrow as *Riccardia*, but plants of these two genera are **longer and have a distinct midrib**. *Aneura* is the only other genus without a midrib; *Aneura pinguis* is **larger and unbranched** or nearly so, and it grows in calcareous fens.

RING PELLIA • *Pellia neesiana*

GENERAL: Plants **dark to rich-green**, shiny, flattened, ribbon-like, 4–8 mm wide, unbranched or branching in pairs; **midrib well developed**, but thallus gradually thinning toward the somewhat **wavy edges**; unisexual; male plants with sex organs in small blisters along the midrib; female plants with sex organs growing under a flap of tissue at the tip of the branch (the involucre).

SPOROPHYTES: Capsules dark, spherical, growing on long, colourless, transparent, short-lived stalks; open by splitting lengthwise into 4 segments.

ECOLOGY: On **moist, inorganic soil** along stream-banks, on lake-shores, and in swampy areas; although this species can be found from sea level to the alpine, it is more common at low elevations.

NOTES: Whereas ring pellia is common along the coast, *P. endiviifolia* is frequent farther **inland**; the involucre of the latter species forms a **complete ring**. The presence of a **midrib** and the **lack of complex markings and pores** on the upper surface distinguish *Pellia* from *Aneura*, *Riccardia*, *Marchantia* and other complex thalloid hepatics. Other genera resembling *Pellia* and also found in our region include *Moerkia*, which is distinguished by a **strong midrib** and a thallus **1–2 cells** thick. *Moerkia* is much less common than *Pellia*. • This liverwort was called 'resembling fish scales' in Hesquiat. It was used in a medicine for treating children's sore mouths.

445

LUNG LIVERWORT • *Marchantia polymorpha*

GENERAL: Plants large, flattened, ribbon-like, 7–13 mm wide; branches in pairs, coarse, dull, with **indistinct pores** and **black mottles** across the upper surface; usually with flaring, circular **cups containing several disc-shaped gemmae**; midrib well developed, present as a depressed, darkened area on the upper surface; lower surface black-purple, covered with triangular scales; unisexual; male plants with sex organs contained in sacs on a flattened, **lobed disc** at the top of a long (1–3 cm) stalk; female plants with sex organs positioned beneath **finger-like lobes** radiating outwards from the tops of long stalks; male and female plants usually in separate colonies.

SPOROPHYTES: Develop from sex organs on female plants; stalks very short, not elongating, normally not visible; capsules elliptic, opening by a fragmented tip; the stalks do not elongate.

ECOLOGY: On soil, often in disturbed areas; especially common on wet, organic soil after forest fires.

NOTES: This large, complex thalloid hepatic is only confused with other members of the Marchantiales. *Conocephalum* has distinct **hexagonal markings**, while other common genera such as *Preissia* and *Asterella* are smaller, have **stalkless** male sex organs and **never have gemmae cups**. *Lunularia cruciata*, introduced from Australia, is a common **greenhouse weed**, but it is smaller and has **gemmae contained in semi-circles**. • Lung liverwort occurs frequently as a garden weed and a pest in tree nurseries, where it can kill seedlings. For those with hepaticidal tendencies, it may be killed by application of a chemical called 'Panacide,' marketed under a variety of trade names and available from garden shops. • The **umbrella-like** male and female structures are distinctive for this charming little plant. You may remember lung liverwort from high school biology class, where it is often used as an example of a liverwort.

SNAKE LIVERWORT • *Conocephalum conicum*

GENERAL: Plants flattened, ribbon-like, with coarse, **hexagonal markings** on the upper surface, each hexagon with a **dot or pore** in its centre; plants from 1.0 to 2.2 cm wide, occasionally with paired branches, **strongly aromatic**; gemmae cups **lacking**, lower surface with abundant root-like filaments.

SPOROPHYTES: Capsules occasional, growing on the lower side of cone-shaped heads at the tips of long, upright stalks; male sex organs produced on stalkless pads.

ECOLOGY: On moist, inorganic soil in mesic localities such as behind waterfalls and on sandy banks and moist rock faces.

NOTES: Snake liverwort is the largest of the thalloid hepatics. The pronounced **hexagonal markings** distinguish it from *Marchantia*. Snake liverwort releases a **pleasant odour** when crushed. • These complex thalloids (*Conocephalum* and *Marchantia*) have complex internal structures, seen in *Conocephalum* as hexagons (the 'greenhouse walls') and pores (the 'vents' to the greenhouses). Inside, tiers of green cells (looking for all the world like cacti) photosynthesize to produce food for the plant. • This plant was called 'seal's tongue' in some languages, such as Haida, and it was used as an eye medicine by the Ditidaht.

PEAT MOSSES

The genus *Sphagnum* (the peat mosses), with about 40 species in our region, is a common component of forests, cliff-faces, bogs and fens. It has a number of special features that make its morphology distinct and identification of species difficult.

The branches occur in **'fascicles' or clusters**, each with some of the branches spreading at about 90° and the remainder hanging down along the stem. The stems are upright and, in addition to the clusters of branches, have **stem leaves**. These are critical to the identification of most species. The branches are covered by concave leaves without midribs. The **branch leaves** are 1 cell thick and consist of a net-like pattern of **small, green, living cells** without pores or strengthening ribs ('fibrils') alternating with **large, clear, dead cells** with **pores** and **fibrils**. For each large dead cell there are 2 small, green, living cells. The green cells have a variety of shapes when viewed in cross-section, and these are characteristic of groups of species. For example, one group has triangular green cells exposed on the concave leaf surface while another group has triangular cells exposed on the convex surface.

Sphagnum stems produce pairs of branches and elongate after development of the clusters of branches. The top portion, containing the young clusters of branches, is visible as a compact head or **'capitulum'** at the tip of the plant. The sporophytes of *Sphagnum* species are all nearly identical and of little taxonomic significance. All species have black, shiny capsules positioned on short-lived, clear stalks ('**pseudopodia**'). Capsules have a lid (an '**operculum**') and **open by an implosive mechanism** that blows the spores upwards on dry, sunny days. If one listens carefully while standing in an extensive patch of fruiting *Sphagnum*, one can hear the capsules imploding. The capsules implode as specialized cells called 'pseudostomates' (long thought to be non-functional stomates) in the middle of the capsule contract inward due to water loss.

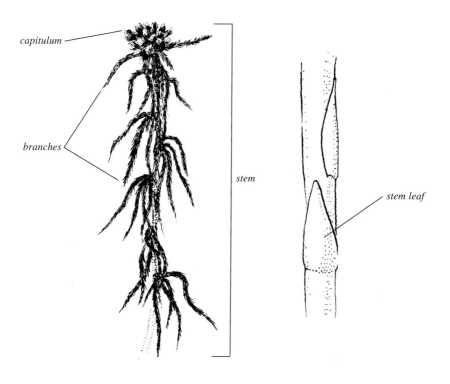

Small Red Peat Moss
S. capillifolium

FAT BOG MOSS • *Sphagnum papillosum*

GENERAL: Plants **yellowish-brown, fat, swollen, soft;** stems brown, with **1–3 (sometimes 5) pores and fibrils** in the outer cells; spreading branches **all short and stubby.**

LEAVES: Stem leaves large, tongue-shaped, once divided, fringed across the broad, rounded tip; branch leaves very concave, hood-shaped, rough at the tip on the convex surface; green cells oval to trapezoidal, exposed equally or more so on the inner surface, with minute papillae on the surface in contact with the colourless, transparent cells.

ECOLOGY: Forming **lawns and low hummocks** in **acidic poor fens,** sometimes on **floating mats** around small 'bog' lakes, also in mats surrounding pools in soligenous fens, **only rarely in bogs;** from sea level to the subalpine; often with *S. magellanicum* and *S. rubellum.*

NOTES: The **large, fat plants** and their **brown** colour distinguish this species from most other sphagnums. • *S. austinii* (also known as *S. imbricatum*) is also brown, but it has **small, narrowly tapered, spreading branches scattered** among the normal, fat, short ones, and it forms **hard, crusty hummocks.** *S. magellanicum* **is red.** Under the compound microscope, the presence of papillae between colourless, transparent cells and green cells is distinctive; *S. austinii* has elongate 'comb fibrils' while *S. magellanicum* and other large, fat species, such as *S. palustre* and *S. centrale*, are smooth.

SPREAD-LEAVED PEAT MOSS • *Sphagnum squarrosum*
SHAGGY SPHAGNUM

GENERAL: Plants large, **whitish- to yellowish-green, bristly;** capitulum with a large, **pinkish bud** at the tip; stems **without fibrils or pores.**

LEAVES: Stem leaves oval, slightly fringed at the broad tip; branch leaves 2.0–3.5 mm long, concave, spreading at right angles and bent backwards, the tips toothed and egg-shaped (not hood-shaped), abruptly narrowed from a broad, basal portion; green cells exposed on outer surface.

ECOLOGY: Primarily a **fen and swamp** species; found along streams, on peaty soils **in forests,** on wet cliff shelves and in woodlands and open, sedge-dominated fens where it forms loose mats; **never in bogs and rarely in poor fens.**

NOTES: Easily distinguished by its **large plants** with **leaves spreading at right angles and bent backwards.** No other species has this combination; however, the closely related, but **smaller,** *S. teres* can sometimes resemble this species in size and leaf orientation. • The soft, absorbent qualities of sphagnum moss made it ideal for use in personal hygiene and baby care. Northwest coast aboriginal peoples preferred it over other types of mosses for bedding, menstrual pads, wound dressings and baby diapers. Sphagnum mosses were also used to wipe fish in preparation for smoking. • Some species of *Sphagnum*, along with certain species of *Dicranum, Mnium, Atrichum* and *Polytrichum,* have antibiotic properties. • *Squarrosum* means 'rough,' *S. squarrosum* is so-called because the overlapping leaves have protruding tips that spread in all directions.

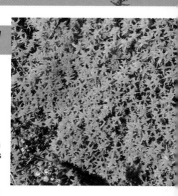

YELLOW-GREEN PEAT MOSS • *Sphagnum angustifolium*
POOR-FEN SPHAGNUM

GENERAL: Plants small, **yellow-green**, slender; capitulum **bushy, rounded**, not star-shaped; stems without fibrils or pores; 2 young hanging branches.

LEAVES: Stem leaves 0.5–0.8 mm long, **small, triangular, blunt**, without pores or fibrils, widely spaced; branch leaves slender, toothed at tip, not hood-shaped; most colourless, transparent cells with 1 large pore at the tip plus only 1–2 additional pores in the corners of the cell on the outer surface; green cells triangular, exposed on outer surface only.

ECOLOGY: A species of **poor fen lawns**; less common in bogs and rarely emergent in carpets; often associated with *S. magellanicum* and *S. pacificum*.

NOTES: The lack of red or brown colouration, the presence of **2 side-by-side hanging branches** in the lower capitulum and the small, **triangular, blunt stem leaves** distinguish yellow-green peat moss. *S. pacificum* has **pointed stem leaves**, *S. lindbergii* has **brown stems**, and *S. mendocinum* and other emergent-aquatic species have distinctive branch-leaf **pore patterns**. The **rather small, yellow-green** plants with **'pom-pom' shaped heads** also help distinguish yellow-green peat moss from green forms of other species.

BROWN-STEMMED BOG MOSS • *Sphagnum lindbergii*

GENERAL: Plants medium-sized, **brown**, robust; capitulum with a **large bud** at the tip; stems brown, without pores or fibrils; pitted retort cells restricted to leaf-bases, other cells without pores; 1 or 2 young hanging branches.

LEAVES: Stem leaves **large, fan-shaped, deeply torn** across the upper portion and broad-meshed in a large, middle, triangular area from the tip nearly to the base; branch leaves slender, toothed at the tip; most colourless, transparent cells with 2–5 small pores at corners on outer surface; green cells triangular, exposed on outer surface only.

ECOLOGY: A species of **bog and poor fen pools**; forms emergent to semi-aquatic carpets in hollows and pool edges; also found in acid seeps at high elevations, often in association with *S. compactum*.

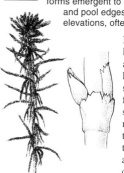

NOTES: Brown-stemmed bog moss is easily recognized by its **brown** stems, **brown** plants, and **deeply torn stem leaves**. The arctic *S. lenense* has a somewhat similar stem leaf, but it is small, has a coppery colour and occurs on hummocks. • Brown-stemmed peat moss is a characteristic species of bogs and poor fen pools. It is, perhaps, the **most aquatic** of all the west coast species. • Look closely at the leaves of the peat mosses (you will need a microscope) to see why they are so absorptive. Much of the leaf is composed of large, clear, dead cells, and this distinctive characteristic allows leaves of *Sphagnum* to absorb large amounts of fluid. This makes them useful in gardening, as surgical dressings or for personal hygiene.

SMALL RED PEAT MOSS • *Sphagnum capillifolium*

GENERAL: Plants small, **reddish**, with a **rounded, convex** capitulum; stems **without pores** or fibrils; 1 young, hanging branch.

LEAVES: Stem leaves twice as long as wide, **broadly egg-shaped**, narrower above than below, blunt, with at least a few fibrils and pores (or poorly formed gaps) in the upper part; branch leaves slender, toothed at tip; colourless, transparent cells with many large pores on both surfaces; green cells triangular, exposed on inner surface only.

ECOLOGY: Forming hummocks in **wooded edges around bogs and poor fens**, more rarely in open peatlands, where it is mostly replaced by *S. rubellum*.

NOTES: Small red peat moss is also known as *S. nemoreum*. • Both *S. capillifolium* and **S. rubellum** are reddish, but the latter is distinguished by **tongue-shaped, non-pitted** stem leaves and **flat-topped** capitula. Neither has any outer stem cells with pores as do *S. russowii* and *S. girgensohnii*. • Small red peat moss was used especially by northern interior natives (e.g., Tahltan and Gitksan) because it is so abundant in their territories. It was dried and used for bedding, menstrual pads and baby diapers. Wet *Sphagnum* species are reported to have healing properties and were placed on wounds. The Carrier believed that red forms caused bad sores. • *Capillifolium* means 'with hair-like leaves.'

WHITE-TOOTHED PEAT MOSS • *Sphagnum girgensohnii*
COMMON GREEN SPHAGNUM

GENERAL: Plants medium-sized, **green**, robust, forming loose mats; capitulum **star-shaped, flat-topped**; stems with **many pitted cells** in the outer, colourless, transparent layer; 1 young hanging branch.

LEAVES: Stem leaves broadly tongue-shaped, **torn along the edge across a flat top**; branch leaves similar to those of small red peat moss.

ECOLOGY: A species of **woodlands**, more common at higher elevations, especially in subalpine and upper montane forests, but also along bog and fen edges at low elevations.

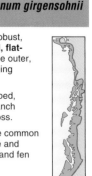

NOTES: The large, yet slender plants, **green** colour, and **flat-topped, torn stem leaves** (that look like they were cut with pinking shears) distinguish **white-toothed peat moss**. *S. fimbriatum* has stem leaves that are **torn all round**, while *S. capillifolium*, *S. warnstorfii*, *S. rubellum*, and *S. russowii* are all **red**. Of these, only *S. russowii* and *S. fimbriatum* have outer stem cells with pores as does *S. girgensohnii*. • *Sphagnum* spp. are commonly called 'peat mosses' and are widely used in gardening. When dry, peat moss species can absorb large amounts of fluid.

TRUE MOSSES

The gametophyte generation of the true mosses begins when spores germinate to produce clusters of green, branched filaments: the protonema. These produce **gametophytes**: structures with stems, leaves, sex organs, and a membranous hood (the **calyptra**) protecting the developing sporophyte. The **sporophyte** generation is relatively long-lived and it is always attached to the gametophyte. It is composed of a **foot**, a **stalk** and a **capsule** with an urn, a lid (the **operculum**) and a circle of teeth inside the mouth (the **peristome**).

Moss stems sometimes have green, filamentous, branched structures (**paraphyllia**) or scale-like structures that cover branch buds (**pseudoparaphyllia**). Some species have stems covered with many-celled, root-like filaments that are never green. Any of these stem structures may be sufficiently abundant to form a woolly covering of hair. Leaves of mosses may or may not have a midrib, and the leaf blades are mostly 1 cell thick, except for members of the Polytrichales. Leaf cells may be almost any shape, but the cells that attach the leaf to the stem (the **alar cells**) are often different. Moss leaves often have a strikingly different appearance when dry than when moist. Some species have very shiny leaves, but in others the leaves are quite dull.

Sporophytes grow from female sex organs, located either at the tips (**acrocarpous**) or along the sides (**pleurocarpous**) of branches. Species with sporophytes along their branches usually are branched and creeping, while those with sporophytes at their tips are less frequently branched. Sporophytes may be well developed with long stalks and inclined capsules with a double or single peristome, or they may be reduced with short stalks, completely covered, upright capsules and no peristome.

There are about 700 species of mosses in this area; they are abundant at all elevations, but generally they are more showy and noticeable at lower elevations in coastal rain forests.

BLACK ROCK MOSS • *Andreaea rupestris*
GRANITE MOSS

GENERAL: Plants **tiny, black to dark-reddish**, forming **compact cushions or tufts** 5–30 mm high on rock, **tightly attached** to substrate and difficult to remove; stems upright to ascending, unbranched to obscurely branched.

LEAVES: Usually less than 1 mm long, broadly lance-shaped, sharply to bluntly pointed, **widely spreading when moist**, upright and pressed to the stem when dry; no midrib; upper leaf cells papillose on back of leaf, rounded to star-shaped, thick-walled.

SPOROPHYTES: Common, raised on short stalks (pseudopodia) produced by the gametophyte; capsules black, football- to spindle-shaped, splitting by 4 longitudinal slits, the capsule segments remain attached at their tips.

ECOLOGY: Mostly restricted to **periodically dry, acid rock surfaces** at all elevations; although found at lower elevations in open areas, in general a species of cooler climates that has nearly cosmopolitan distribution.

NOTES: There are quite a few small, blackish mosses on rocks, but the **acidic** substrate, **widely spreading leaves** when moist and **tight adherence** to the substrate are key characteristics for species of ***Andreaea***. Black rock moss occurs in drier sites than do other species. In all there are 10 species of this genus in our region. The leaves of some have a midrib; those of others, like *A. rupestris*, do not. The species can be distinguished only under the compound microscope.

JUNIPER HAIRCAP MOSS • *Polytrichum juniperinum*
JUNIPER MOSS

GENERAL: Plants **bluish-green, shiny**, short to long, slender to stout, upright, unbranched, occur in **mats** or more rarely as **closely associated individuals**; stems about 1 cm to more than 10 cm high.

LEAVES: 4–8 mm long, upright-spreading when dry, becoming wide-spreading when moist, thick, with a **short, toothed, reddish bristle-point**; leaves structured as those of awned haircap moss (below).

SPOROPHYTES: Common; stalks upright, wiry, long, reddish; capsules upright, **4 angled**, becoming horizontal with age, puckered at base; peristome with 64 short, blunt teeth; calyptrae long, covering entire capsule with **long hairs**.

ECOLOGY: Common, almost weedy, **on disturbed mineral soils**.

NOTES:. Complex leaves, with lamellae covered by the leaf blade (thus **shiny and bluish-green**) and short, **reddish bristle-points** distinguish **juniper haircap moss**. *P. strictum* has slender, elongate stems covered by a whitish, felty covering of hairs and it is somewhat smaller. Many species of *Polytrichum* have the lamellae exposed. • Although it sometimes occurs with awned haircap moss, juniper moss is generally more common in mesic sites from sea level to the alpine. It is common after

fire, often with *Marchantia polymorpha*, but it is replaced by *P. strictum* on organic soils. • Species of *Polytrichum* can be recognized by the characteristic 'lamellae' on their leaves: dark-green ridges running lengthwise along the leaf midrib. Juniper haircap moss occurs throughout the world, except in some tropical regions.

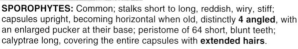

AWNED HAIRCAP MOSS • *Polytrichum piliferum*

GENERAL: Plants somewhat shiny, short, stout, upright, unbranched, occuring in **mats** or sometimes as **closely associated individuals**; stems generally short, about 1–4 cm high.

LEAVES: 4–7 mm long, becoming spreading when moist, upright-spreading when dry, thick, with a conspicuous, **long, clear, toothed bristle-point**; midrib strong with many green lamellae on the inner surface, wrapped and covered by the leaf blade causing one to see a single line running the length of the inner surface of the leaf representing the overlap of the inrolled leaf blade; leaf-bases expanded, clear and sheathing the stem.

SPOROPHYTES: Common; stalks short to long, reddish, wiry, stiff; capsules upright, becoming horizontal when old, distinctly **4 angled**, with an enlarged pucker at their base; peristome of 64 short, blunt teeth; calyptrae long, covering the entire capsules with **extended hairs**.

ECOLOGY: A species of **dry, usually acidic, sites**, often on **sandy or gravelly substrates** in open, disturbed areas; common along roadsides, on exposed **rock outcrops**, and in severe alpine areas.

NOTES: The **long, clear bristle-points** distinguish this species from all other Polytrichaceae; *P. juniperinum* and *P. strictum* both have **reddish** bristle-points. All other mosses with clear bristle-points have delicate leaves only 1 cell thick. • Awned haircap moss is often associated with other Polytrichaceae, especially *P. juniperinum* and *Pogonatum urnigerum*. Species of *Oligotrichum* occur in moister sites. • Awned haircap moss and juniper haircap moss, both dry site species, have infolded leaf edges covering the green lamellae that help prevent drying out.

COMMON HAIRCAP MOSS • *Polytrichum commune*
HAIRY-CAP MOSS

GENERAL: Plants **dark green**, robust, unbranched, 4–45 cm or more long, unisexual; males have enlarged heads at the tip, females produce sporophytes; lower portion covered by **grey, root-like filaments**.

LEAVES: 6–10 mm long, spreading at right angles and bent backward from a sheathing base when moist, upright-pressed to the stem and rolled when dry, **lance-shaped** from a membranous, sheathing base, **sharply pointed** but not awned; midrib covered on the inner surface with 20–55 vertical tiers of cells 4–9 cells high, each tier tipped by a U-shaped cell; edges coarsely toothed.

SPOROPHYTES: Regularly present, at the tip of the plant; stalks wiry, very long, slender; capsules **horizontal, 4 angled**; peristome of 64 short, rounded teeth and an expanded central membrane; calyptrae naked, with a tuft of **hairs at the tip, covering the entire capsule**.

ECOLOGY: Terrestrial in moist forests from sea level to the subalpine; also sometimes in moist areas associated with cliff-faces at elevations up to the alpine; widespread in our region.

NOTES: The **4-angled capsules** identify all species in the genus *Polytrichum*. Only **common haircap moss** has **U-shaped cells** at the tip of the leaf lamellae. *Pogonatum alpinum* can be of similar size to *Polytrichum commune*, but it has capsules that are **round in cross-section** with **papillose cells** at the tips of the leaf lamellae. *Polytrichum juniperinum* and *P. strictum* both have leaf blades that overlap the lamellae, making the leaves **shiny with a blue-green colour**.

GREY HAIRCAP MOSS • *Pogonatum urnigerum*

GENERAL: Plants with a **whitish-green cast**, generally short, stout, 2–6 cm high, occurring as **closely set individuals** or sometimes forming **extensive mats**; stems unbranched or forked, upright.

LEAVES: 3–7 mm long, widely spreading when moist, upright when dry, **broadly lance-shaped**, broader than most other members of the family, **strongly toothed in upper portion**; inner surface completely covered by 30–50 short lamellae 4–7 cells high; basal area expanded, clear, sheathing the stem.

SPOROPHYTES: Not common; stalks 10–40 mm long, short, wiry, upright; capsules **upright, cylindric**, without any hint of angles, not puckered at base; peristome of 32 short, white teeth.

ECOLOGY: Common at all elevations **on exposed, acidic, inorganic soils**, especially on roadside banks and other exposed mesic habitats having appropriate soils.

NOTES: *Pogonatum* species are easily distinguished using features of the cells at the tips of the leaf lamellae; unfortunately these are not visible in the field. Some helpful field hints include: *P. alpinum* is **dark-green** and has **narrow leaves** with **small teeth** along the edges, *P. urnigerum* has **broad leaves** with **coarse teeth** and *P. dentatum* is **whitish-green**, with even **broader** leaves and shorter plants. Also similar, but generally larger, are *Polytrichum lyallii* and *P. commune*.

453

SMALL HAIR MOSS • *Oligotrichum aligerum*

GENERAL: Plants medium-sized, **olive green to dark green**, occurring as **loosely organized mats**; stems **1–2 cm** high, stiff, upright, unbranched, developing as individuals.

LEAVES: 2–5 mm long, widely-spreading and stiff when moist, pressed to the stem and upright when dry, lance-shaped from a slightly wider, **sheathing base**, with sharp points; midrib single, strong, ending at the tip of the leaf; inner surface of leaves covered in their middle portion with 6–12 rows of short lamellae (1–8 cells high), these loosely arranged and wavy; **short stubby lamellae** present on the **outer leaf surface** give the leaf a **rough appearance**.

SPOROPHYTES: Common, at the tip of the plant; stalks long, wiry; capsules cylindric, round, upright to almost upright; peristome of 32 short teeth; calyptrae naked or with a few hairs.

ECOLOGY: On inorganic, acidic soil, often in small disturbed soil patches in open areas; common along roadsides at lower and middle elevations.

NOTES: This is one of several smaller polytrichaceous mosses found on acidic soil banks. Species of *Polytrichum* have **4-angled capsules** and lamellae nearly completely covering the upper leaf surface. *Pogonatum* species either have **many lamellae**, like the *Polytrichums*, or they have **broader leaves**. *O. parallelum* is **larger** than *O. aligerum* and has **lamellae confined** to the midrib, and *O. hercynicum* is an **alpine** species **without well-developed lamellae** on the outer leaf surfaces.

LARGE HAIR MOSS • *Oligotrichum parallelum*

GENERAL: Plants **rich green**, unbranched, upright, robust, forming **loose mats**; stems **2–5 cm** high.

LEAVES: 3–6 mm long, widely spreading when moist, wavy and contorted when dry, broadly lance-shaped to oblong, sharply pointed; leaf blade mostly 1-cell thick; outer leaf blade with a few low lamellae in the upper part; no border along the edges; strong midrib, with 4–6 upright, straight lamellae on its inner surface, **without a distinctive sheathing base**.

SPOROPHYTES: Often present; stalks wiry, upright, long; capsules cylindric, smooth, upright; peristome of 32 small teeth.

ECOLOGY: On acidic soil at higher elevations, especially on humid cliff shelves, banks and stream edges; occasionally at lower elevations in moist habitats.

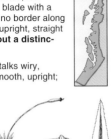

NOTES: Species of *Atrichum* also have lamellae restricted to the upper midrib surface, but they have a **leaf border** of elongate cells while *Oligotrichum* species do not. All 3 species of *Oligotrichum* in our region have at least a few low lamellae present on the outer leaf surface. *O. parallelum* has broad leaves **without sheathing bases**, and the lamellae of its inner leaf surface are **straight**; both *O. aligerum* and *O. hercynicum* have **wavy lamellae**.

CRANE'S-BILL MOSS • *Atrichum selwynii*

GENERAL: Plants **rich-green**, unbranched, forming **loose mats on soil**; stems 1–4 cm high.

LEAVES: 3–8 mm long, loosely wide-spreading when moist, **upright and twisted when dry**, lance- to tongue-shaped, broadly but sharply pointed, **bordered** by elongate cells; blade 1 cell thick; midrib strong, with 2–6 low, straight lamellae 2–12 cells high and restricted to the inner surface of the midrib; basal area not much expanded.

SPOROPHYTES: Often present; stalks long, dark, wiry; capsules upright to somewhat inclined, cylindric, smooth; peristome of 32 rather long, conspicuous, whitish teeth; calyptrae without hairs.

ECOLOGY: Occurring **on shaded, moist, inorganic soil banks, stream edges and soil-covered rock ledges**; especially common on soil exposed by **up-turned tree bases**; restricted to acidic soils; found at all elevations, but more frequent at lower elevations where appropriate habitats are more common.

NOTES: 3 species of *Atrichum* occur along the west coast and can be distinguished by leaf characteristics. *A. selwynii* has **broader** leaves with **blunter** tips; *A. tenellum* and *A. undulatum* have **narrower** leaves and **sharper** leaf tips. *A. undulatum* is common as a **garden and roadside weed** near the coast, while *A. selwynii* is the **most common** species of natural habitats. All of these differ from other members of the Polytrichaceae by having **lamellae only on the inner surface** of the midrib and **leaves bordered** by elongate cells. False-polytrichum (p. 462) is a look-alike, but it lacks lamellae.

CORD MOSS • *Funaria hygrometrica*

GENERAL: Plants small, **light-green, almost bulb-shaped**, produce characteristic sporophytes, almost always annuals; stems unbranched, short, less than 1 cm high.

LEAVES: 2–5 mm long, oval to egg-shaped, sharply pointed, **upright**, concave, shiny, **contorted when dry**; midrib single, ending just before the tip; edges more or less smooth; leaf cells rectangular, large, thin-walled, smooth, similar throughout the leaf.

SPOROPHYTES: Nearly always present, at the tip of the plant; stalks elongate, **contorted, yellow**, very readily absorb moisture; capsules asymmetric, **pear-shaped, hanging**, 16 ribbed and **bright yellow** when mature, green otherwise; peristome double, but superficially appears single; calyptrae large.

ECOLOGY: A **weed**; found commonly **on disturbed, compacted soil** (high in nitrogen from 'you-know-what'), also in greenhouses; occurs naturally after fire in moist depressions, or where campfires have been; common at low and middle elevations.

NOTES: Weedy mosses with upright stems and sporophytes at the tip of the plant include *Funaria* with **broad** leaves, **contorted** stalks and **fat** capsules, *Leptobryum pyriforme* with **linear** leaves and **pear-shaped** capsules, *Bryum argenteum* with **bulb-shaped silvery** plants and *Ceratodon purpureus* with **lance-shaped** leaves, leaf edges **rolled under** and **purple** stalks and capsules. **Other** *Bryum* species have **widely spreading** leaves when moist and **hanging, cylindric** capsules.

RED BRYUM • *Bryum miniatum*

GENERAL: Plants **wine-red to golden-brown**, in **spongy cushions** emerging from seeps on exposed rocks; stems 2–5 cm high, little branched, upright, lighter above.

LEAVES: 2–3 mm long, narrowly egg-shaped to oblong, **blunt, concave**; midrib narrow, ending near the tip; leaf cells thin-walled, hexagonal, smooth, similar throughout, but narrower and longer near the edges.

SPOROPHYTES: Rare; stalks long, upright, pale; capsules hanging, smooth; peristome of 2 well-developed series.

ECOLOGY: Typical of **seepy rock surfaces** along the coast and at **low elevations**; associated with exposed rock shelves along stream-banks and along the coast.

NOTES: No other moss forms such **brilliant red cushions** with **blunt, concave, closely overlapping leaves.** *B. pseudotriquetrum* has red stems and sometimes blunt leaves, but it is never the colour of *B. miniatum.* **Other red *Bryum*** species that occur in our area have **sharply pointed leaves.** *Pohlia wahlenbergii* occurs in **calcium-rich seeps** and is **reddish**, but it has **sharply pointed**, distinct leaves and a peculiar **dull, whitish** stem.

TALL CLUSTERED THREAD MOSS • *Bryum pseudotriquetrum*

GENERAL: Plants **greenish to reddish**, occurring in **cushions or mats or as individuals among other mosses**; variable in form; stems unbranched or rarely branched, red, without any covering of hairs, about 2–8 cm high.

LEAVES: Up to 4 mm long, egg-shaped but variable, tips blunt to sharp; midrib ending near or extending just beyond the tip; edges **bordered** by longer cells, smooth, **extend downwards** along the stem at base; cells hexagonal, thin-walled, smooth.

SPOROPHYTES: Not common; stalks reddish to pale-green, upright, long; capsules hanging, smooth, cylindric; peristome well developed and double.

ECOLOGY: Extremely variable; occurring in **seeps, rich fens, swampy areas or streamside banks**, seemingly always in areas with **calcium-rich** water or soil; often associated with swamp moss (p. 460); common at all elevations.

NOTES: While there are more than 25 species of *Bryum* in our region, only a few can be identified in the field. **Tall clustered thread moss** is probably the **most common** species, especially in **wet, seepy or fen areas**. It can be recognized by the leaves **extending down the reddish stems** and the lack of any other distinguishing features. Most other *Bryum*s are species of drier habitats. *Pohlia* species have **toothed** leaf edges and **longer** leaf cells.

MAGNIFICENT MOSS • *Plagiomnium venustum*

GENERAL: Plants medium to large, **olive green to light green**, in **loose to dense mats**, 2–4 cm high; stems upright, without obvious spreading shoots.

LEAVES: 3–5 mm long, spreading when moist, strongly contorted when dry, egg-shaped, widest in upper portion, not extending down along the stem; edges with obvious, **single teeth nearly to base**, bordered by long cells; midrib single, ending near or just beyond the tip.

SPOROPHYTES: Common, at the tip of the plant; stalks 1–4 per plant, long, slender, green; capsules broadly cylindric, smooth, hanging; peristome double.

ECOLOGY: On humus, **rotting logs and lower portions of tree trunks**; most common in coastal rain forests.

NOTES: Magnificent moss has leaves with **single teeth, more than 1** stalked capsule per plant, leaf-bases that **do not extend** down the stem, and **bisexual** plants. This species is not as large as badge moss (below), which is more restricted to moist soil habitats.

BADGE MOSS • *Plagiomnium insigne*
COASTAL LEAFY MOSS

GENERAL: Plants large, showy, from 3–8 cm high; wide-spreading, glistening leaves when moist, becoming shrivelled and dull when dry; fertile plants unisexual, the male plants distinguished by conspicuous flattened heads; sterile stems arched, like those of strawberries.

LEAVES: Mostly 5–7 mm long, oval to egg-shaped, sharp-pointed, with **sharp teeth to the base**, bordered by long cells, extending down the stem; cells hexagonal, large, smooth, thin-walled.

SPOROPHYTES: Common, at the tip of the plant; stalks long, green, slender, 3–6 per plant; capsules broadly cylindric, smooth, hanging; peristome greenish-yellow, double, well developed.

ECOLOGY: On humus in moist, shaded, lowland forests, also on soil along trails and other shaded, open areas; **sometimes forms lush, extensive mats**.

NOTES: Badge moss, a handsome species, is the **largest '*mnium*.'** The genus *Plagiomnium* has borders of single teeth. Badge moss can be distinguished from magnificent moss, the only other large *Plagiomnium* in our region, by its **unisexual** plants, leaf edges that **extend down** the stems for a noticeable length and **3–6** stalked capsules per plant. Magnificent moss has smaller, bisexual plants, and leaves that do not extend down the stem; it generally has 1–4 stalks per stem.

FAN MOSS • *Rhizomnium glabrescens*
LARGE LEAFY MOSS

GENERAL: Plants upright, unbranched, unisexual; stems naked, up to 3 cm high, shiny, with large leaves; male plants have large, **rose-like clusters** of leaves at the tip; female plants have capsules.

LEAVES: 3–6 mm long, widely-spreading when moist, shrivelled and pressed to the stem when dry, **oval**, blunt or broadly and sharply pointed; midrib strong, ending near the tip; **edges smooth**, bordered by 3–4 rows of elongate cells in several layers, appearing very thick; leaf cells uniform throughout, hexagonal, smooth, thin-walled.

SPOROPHYTES: Common, at the tip of the plant; stalks elongate, straight; capsules cylindric, smooth, hanging; peristome double.

ECOLOGY: Very common on **rotting logs, humus and soil over rocks** in low- and middle-elevation forests; the most common species of leafy moss in low-elevation forests.

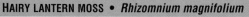

NOTES: Both **magnificent moss** and **badge moss** have leaves edged with **single teeth**, while *Mnium spinulosum* leaves have **double teeth**. Hairy lantern moss (below) has stems covered with **root-like filaments**, and *R. pseudopunctatum* is a species of **wetlands** with a less-developed leaf border. • The unisexual plants of fan moss found on logs in coastal forests are easily recognized and should be hard to confuse with other species. Only *R. nudum*, which also has naked stems, could cause problems, but it is a middle-elevation to **subalpine** species with leaves that are **nearly circular**, not oval as in fan moss. • *R. punctatum* was used by the Makah as a poultice for swellings.

HAIRY LANTERN MOSS • *Rhizomnium magnifolium*

GENERAL: Plants large, shiny, about 2–8 cm high, often forming extensive **mats**; stems unisexual, covered with densely branched, **root-like filaments**.

LEAVES: 5–11 mm long, widely-spreading when moist, shrivelled when dry, **broadly oval**, blunt; midrib single, ending mostly just below the tip; **edges smooth**, bordered by 1–2 rows of linear cells in 1–2 layers forming a delicate border; leaf cells hexagonal, thin-walled, smooth, similar throughout.

SPOROPHYTES: Common, at the tip of the plant; stalks elongate, straight; capsules cylindric, smooth, hanging; peristome double.

ECOLOGY: A species of **wet, shaded depressions** and slow-moving forested streams; often on **sandy soil on streambanks**, where the large plants often reach over 1 cm in width; occurs sporadically in low- and middle-elevation rainforests.

NOTES: The **large size**, stems covered with **root-like filaments, smooth** leaf edges and **unisexual** plants distinguish **hairy lantern moss** from all others. *R. nudum* is a middle-elevation to subalpine species with **circular leaves** and **no root-like filaments** on the stems; *R. pseudopunctatum* is smaller and **bisexual** and it has no root-like filaments on its stem; and **badge moss** is as large as hairy lantern moss, but its leaves are edged with teeth. • All species of *Mnium*, *Plagiomnium* and *Rhizomnium* in our area are commonly referred to as 'leafy mosses.'

MENZIES' RED-MOUTHED MNIUM • *Mnium spinulosum*

GENERAL: Plants **lush-green, in mats**; stems about 1–2 cm high, upright, unbranched, usually with abundant sporophytes.

LEAVES: 3–5 mm long, upright-spreading to spreading when moist, shrivelled and pressed to the stem when dry; lance-oval, gradually and sharply pointed, bordered by several rows of linear cells; edges with **large, double teeth** in upper half of leaf; leaf cells hexagonal, smooth, thin-walled throughout.

SPOROPHYTES: Common, at the tip of the plant; stalks long, slender, 1–4 per plant; capsules cylindric, hanging, smooth; **peristome deep red**, double, well developed.

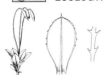

ECOLOGY: On soil and needles under coniferous trees in moist, shaded, low- to middle-elevation forests; prefers **heavily shaded habitats** beneath Douglas-fir, hemlock and other coniferous trees.

NOTES: Often forms large, **dark-green, glistening mats** on coniferous needles. • Within *Mnium*, *M. lycopodioides* and *M. thomsonii* are smaller species growing in association with **cliff-faces;** *M. edgeatum* could be confused with *M. spinulosum*, but its capsules have **yellowish** peristome teeth and its leaves have smaller teeth. *M. spinulosum* can always be identified microscopically by the many-layered leaf borders that are at least 3 cells thick; other related species have borders 1–2 cells thick. The **deep-red peristome** is also a critical character of *M. spinulosum*. *Plagiomnium venustum* and *P. insigne* are superficially similar, but they have **single teeth** on the leaf edges. The number of sporophyte stalks is variable: some plants have only 1 per stem, while others may have up to 4 per stem. • The genus *Mnium* has leaves with double teeth while species in *Plagiomnium* have single teeth, and species in *Rhizomnium* have no teeth. All of these 'leafy mosses' were previously placed in *Mnium*.

MENZIES' TREE MOSS • *Leucolepis acanthoneuron*

GENERAL: Plants **light green**, glossy, **tree-shaped**, about 4–8 cm high; stems upright, with a **circle of branches** at their tips.

LEAVES: Branch leaves 1.5–2.0 mm long, broadly lance-shaped, sharply pointed, with a midrib, **bordered** by elongate cells, **strongly toothed**; leaf cells hexagonal, smooth, delicate, similar throughout; male and female plants well separated when sex organs are present.

SPOROPHYTES: Common, growing at the tip of the plant; stalks elongate, slender; capsules **hanging**, smooth, dark, egg-shaped to cylindric.

ECOLOGY: Frequent in moist lowland rainforests, where it can form large populations **on logs, boulders, wet organic soil and humus**; occasionally extends upwards onto the lower portions of tree trunks.

NOTES: Menzies' tree moss is also known as *Leucolepis menziesii*. • Menzies' tree moss is a member of the Mniaceae, with whom it shares leaf and leaf-cell characteristics. The **umbrella-like** plants distinguish it from all other mosses in our region except **tree moss** (p. 474); tree moss, however, is **much more tree-like** in appearance. *Pleuroziopsis ruthenica* is a common northern species with **fern-like** stems. The **hanging capsules** that are often present in **Menzies' tree moss** also distinguish it from tree moss, which has upright capsules. • The Saanich peoples used this moss to make a yellow dye for baskets.

SWAMP MOSS • *Philonotis fontana*

GENERAL: Plants **yellow-green to glaucous-green**, upright, unbranched, in **cushions or mats**, dull, but often glistening due to superficial water droplets, varies from 1–10 cm high; **stems red**; fertile plants sometimes with several umbrella-like branches at the tip.

LEAVES: 1.5–2.0 mm long, loosely spreading when moist, upright-pressed to the stem when dry, lance-shaped to egg-shaped, sharply pointed; leaf edges curved downward; midrib strong, single; leaf cells oblong, thick-walled throughout the leaf, each with a papilla at either the lower or upper end.

SPOROPHYTES: Uncommon, at the tip of the plant, but sometimes seemingly on the sides of branches because of continued stem growth; stalks long, straight; capsules round, upright, smooth when young, becoming 16 ribbed, asymmetric and horizontal when old; peristome double, with 16 teeth, upright.

ECOLOGY: In **seeps** and on **moist soil, banks and rock faces**; always associated with **calcium-rich water**; common along forestry roads, often in small ditches with seepy water; often associated with *Pohlia wahlenbergii*.

NOTES: The **glaucous-green** colour and **calcium-rich, seepy habitat** are good identifying features of **swamp moss**. *Pohlia wahlenbergii* has a similar colour and habitat, but it has **broader leaves**, non-papillose, thin-walled cells and **hanging capsules**. The papillae of *Philonotis* are projections from the cell ends—very different from those of most other mosses. Swamp moss is the most common of several species of *Philonotis*.

APPLE MOSS • *Bartramia pomiformis*

GENERAL: Plants **glaucous-green to yellow-green**, unbranched to only occasionally branched, about 2–10 cm high; stems often have an abundant, **reddish covering of hairs**.

LEAVES: 4–9 mm long, contorted when moist, more so when dry, narrowly **lance-shaped** from a slightly widened base; edges bent backwards; midrib strong, single, ending at or slightly beyond the tip; leaf cells square to rectangular, papillose from cell ends.

SPOROPHYTE: Often present, at the tip of the plant; stalks short; capsules spherical, each with a small mouth, 16 ribbed, upright when young, becoming horizontal and somewhat asymmetric when old; peristome double but reduced and fragile.

ECOLOGY: On **moist, acidic to neutral cliff-faces** at all elevations; common on roadsides, cliffs and shaded cliffs in forested and tundra habitats.

NOTES: Several species can be confused with apple moss: *Bartramia ithyphylla* has **stiff, upright** leaves and it is common at **higher elevations**; *Plagiopus oederiana* occurs on **calcium-rich rock** and has leaves obscurely arranged in 3 rows with many bumps on the leaf cells; and the genus *Amphidium*, with 3 species, has **linear leaves**, partially exposed to completely covered oval capsules on short stalks, and many bumps on the leaf cells. • The young capsules look like apples, hence the common name.

LOVER'S MOSS • *Aulacomnium androgynum*

GENERAL: Plants small, **pale green to yellowish-green**, about 0.5–4 cm high, forming **cushions and tufts**; stems unbranched, upright, without abundant covering of hairs, often tipped by a short, naked stalk with a **ball of reddish gemmae** at the top.

LEAVES: 1.5–3.5 mm long, loosely upright-spreading and straight when moist, contorted, upright and pressed to the stem when dry, **lance-shaped** and sharply but broadly pointed; midrib single, ending just below the tip; leaf cells uniform throughout, about as wide as long, with a single central papilla.

SPOROPHYTE: Occasional, at the tip of the plant; stalks long; capsules curved, slightly asymmetric, ribbed, horizontal when mature; peristome double.

ECOLOGY: A characteristic species of **burnt tree stumps**; common in cut-over areas and in second-growth forests.

NOTES: This species of *Aulacomnium* is the smallest of the 4 species of this genus in our region. It is the only one that is commonly found on tree stumps. It is also the only species in our region that has a **cluster of gemmae at the tip of a short stalk**. Ribbed bog moss, which is common on **organic soil**, also has gemmae, but in this species the **gemmae occur all along the stem**, while in lover's moss they are restricted to a ball at the tip. • This species is present relatively early in succession and is replaced by *Tetraphis* species and several hepatics later on when the wood becomes softened by decay. It occurs with *Dicranum tauricum* or other *Dicranum* species and sometimes with scattered isolated stems of *Pleurozium* or *Rhytidiadelphus* species.

RIBBED BOG MOSS • *Aulacomnium palustre*
GLOW MOSS

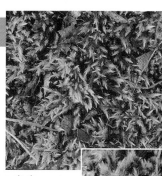

GENERAL: Plants medium-sized, unbranched to occasionally branched; stems upright, 3–9 cm high, with abundant, **reddish covering of hairs**, often tipped by a short, leafless stalk that has small, **lance-shaped gemmae along its entire length** (although there may be more towards the tip).

LEAVES: 2–5 mm long, **yellow-green** when young, becoming **brownish or reddish-green** when older, spreading when moist, contorted when dry, **lance-shaped and broadly sharp-pointed**; edges bent backward; midrib strong, single and ending just below the tip; cells uniform, as wide as long, each surface with a single, cone-shaped papilla.

SPOROPHYTES: Occasional, at the tip of the plant; stalks long; capsules cylindric, asymmetric, ribbed, horizontal when mature; peristome double.

ECOLOGY: On **organic soils and occasionally on rotten logs**; most common on **disturbed, peaty banks** in peatlands, where it occurs on acid peat in bogs and on acidic microhabitats in rich fens; also on organic soils in tundra and subalpine habitats.

NOTES: Mats of ribbed bog moss can cover large areas on wet sites. • The **reddish fuzz** covering the stems, which contrasts with the **yellowish younger leaves**, is characteristic of **ribbed bog moss**. When present, the stalks at the tip of the plant that bear small gemmae along their entire lengths are definitive. While ribbed bog moss occurs on disturbed peaty banks, lover's moss occurs on tree bases and stumps. *A. turgidum* is an **arctic-alpine** species with **stiff, blunt, oval** leaves and gametophytes resembling **upright, scaly cocktail sausages**. • Ribbed bog moss sometimes grows up the bases of bushy plants (e.g., *Spiraea*). Asexual reproduction is common in this plant—look for clusters of green, leafy-looking 'brood bodies' on the ends of short, green stalks.

FALSE-POLYTRICHUM • *Timmia austriaca*

GENERAL: Plants large, **olive-green**, upright, unbranched, forming **loose mats**; stems about 3–8 cm high, **dark red, without** a covering of hairs.

LEAVES: 5–6 mm long, wide-spreading when moist, upright-pressed to the stem and somewhat inwardly curving when dry, **lance-shaped**, broadly and sharply pointed, the **lower portion orange and expanded to a sheathing base**; upper leaf cells small, square, bulging on the inner surface, flat on the outer surface; lower cells elongate and smooth.

SPOROPHYTES: At the tip of the plant; stalks long, single; capsules upright to inclined, smooth, long-cylindric; peristome of 2 series, the inner of 64 filaments, the outer of 16 teeth; calyptrae hood-shaped, usually remaining attached to the upper stalk until quite late in the year.

ECOLOGY: On calcium-rich and neutral **soil ledges** and **moist stream-banks and in rock crevices**; sometimes forms mats on forest litter in open, montane forests; occasional from sea level to the alpine, but nowhere common in our area.

NOTES: The **unbranched, upright, rather large** plants, their leaves with **orange sheathing bases** and the lack of any lamellae on the leaf surfaces distinguish false-polytrichum. The upper leaf blades are 1 cell thick and appear very translucent due to a bulging inner surface and flat outer surface. Several other species of the genus occur in North America; each has a different pattern of upper-leaf-cell structure. • This moss looks like a *Polytrichum*, but *Timmia* has **orange leaf-bases** and *Polytrichum* has lamellae (green ridges running length-wise along the leaf midrib). *Polytrichum* leaves appear opaque, whereas *Timmia* leaves are **translucent**. • *Timmia* is named for Joachim Timm, a German botanist; *austriaca* means 'from Austria.' Mt. Timmia on Ellesmere Island was named for this genus, thus making a mountain out of a moss-hill.

GOBLIN'S GOLD • *Schistostega pennata*

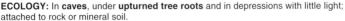

GENERAL: Plants **very small**, 4–7 mm high, **flat**, unbranched, each with 10 or so **pinnate** leaves; clusters of green, branched filaments (protonemata) persistent, luminescent, with lens-shaped cells, forming **golden, gleaming mats of thread-like plants**.

LEAVES: 0.7–1.2 mm long, narrowly elliptic, sharp-pointed, their **bases merging** together along the stem; leaf cells large, hexagonal throughout.

SPOROPHYTES: Occasional, at the tip of the plant; stalks slender, straight; capsule tiny, hemispheric, upright; peristome absent.

ECOLOGY: In **caves**, under **upturned tree roots** and in depressions with little light; attached to rock or mineral soil.

NOTES: This interesting, infrequent moss produces persistent protonemata that concentrate light through lens-shaped cells, enabling the moss to grow in extreme low-light conditions. Sometimes the protonemata occur alone, but occasionally plants with sporophytes are present. • The **flat** plants with leaves growing **in 2 rows** and their large leaf cells and **tiny capsules** distinguish **goblin's gold**. • Look for goblin's gold under upturned tree roots in moist, lowland forests by first spotting a golden sheen, usually at the junction of tree and soil or sometimes just behind the shallow pool of water that occurs in the depression.

COMMON WATER MOSS • *Fontinalis antipyretica*

GENERAL: Plants **large, dark green to brownish, branched**, up to 40 cm long, occurring **submerged** in flowing water; stems conspicuously **3-angled**.

LEAVES: 4–9 mm long, large, broadly lance-shaped to almost egg-shaped, sharply pointed, **abruptly keeled** and, when removed from the stem, lie folded; midrib lacking; leaf cells elongate, thin-walled, cells at the base of the leaf larger and clear.

SPOROPHYTES: Rare; stalks short; capsules completely covered by the leaves, nearly spherical; peristome highly modified into a trellis-like inner layer and 16 outer teeth.

ECOLOGY: In flowing water attached to rocks or logs; not uncommon in lowland rain forest, becoming rare at high elevations.

NOTES: Strongly **keeled leaves in 3 rows** along the entire length of the stems distinguish this species. 3 other species of the genus occur in our region; none of these are as distinctly 3-rowed as is common water moss. These are distinguished from one another with difficulty and at best identified only with some frustration. • *Fontinalis* is the only truly aquatic genus of true mosses in our area. Although fens and bogs sometimes have emergent species of *Sphagnum* and such species as *Calliergon*, these never occur in streams as does *Fontinalis*. Common water moss prefers acidic waters.

CLEAR MOSS • *Hookeria lucens*

GENERAL: Plants dark, **flattened**, rather robust, up to 8 cm long, with a distinctly **limp appearance**; stems creeping, forming small **open patches** or sometimes occurring as **isolated individuals**.

LEAVES: 2–5 mm long, flattened, **translucent, shiny, egg-shaped, with blunt tips**; midrib absent; leaf cells quite large, thin-walled, hexagonal.

SPOROPHYTES: Uncommon, growing from the side of the stem; stalks dark and straight; capsules inclined, smooth, with a long beak; peristome double.

ECOLOGY: On moist humus in lowland rainforests.

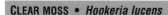

NOTES: Leaves of both *Isopterygium* and *Plagiothecium* have flattened arrangements, but they are more slender than leaves of **clear moss** (with the exception of *P. undulatum* (p. 475), which is similar or larger in size to *H. lucens* and has **wavy leaves** and a rather **dull, whitish-green** appearance). Another species of *Hookeria*, **H. acutifolia**, is common in our region and can be distinguished from clear moss by its **sharp leaf tips**. Some hepatics are superficially similar, but they have leaves attached in 2 or 3 distinct rows.

MENZIES' NECKERA • *Metaneckera menziesii*

GENERAL: Plants large, **glossy, olive-green, descending**, forming extensive **mats on tree trunks**; stems up to 20 cm long, **pinnately branched**, with many **branched, green filaments** (paraphyllia) and often many, **small, narrowly tapered branchlets**.

LEAVES: 1.2–3.2 mm long, oblong, **strongly transversely wavy**, abruptly squared off at tip usually with a small abrupt point, asymmetric; **midrib single**, ending about 3/4 of the way up the leaf; arranged in a **flattened** (complanate) orientation along the stem; leaf cells diamond-shaped, smooth.

SPOROPHYTES: Common, from the side of the stem; stalks very short; capsules oblong, **completely covered** in the extended protective leaves of the female plant (perichaetum), protruding downward beneath the stems; peristome double.

ECOLOGY: Abundant and frequent **on coniferous trees** and **calcium-rich cliff-faces** at low elevations along the coast; abundant on cliff-faces farther inland.

NOTES: This frequent and abundant epiphyte has **strongly wavy leaves**, flattened together in **1 plane**. It can only be confused easily with **Douglas' neckera** (below) and *Neckera pennata*; these differ in that their leaves **lack a midrib** and their plants **do not have small, green filaments** along the stem. The *Metaneckeras* also often have abundant narrowly tapered, **whip-like branchlets**, a feature that neither of the *Neckeras* has.

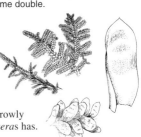

DOUGLAS' NECKERA • *Neckera douglasii*

GENERAL: Plants large, **olive-green to light green, rather glossy**, irregularly branched, generally descending, about 5–10 (but up to 40) cm long.

LEAVES: 2.4–3.0 mm long, **flattened and strongly transversely wavy**, broadly lance-shaped and sharp-pointed; **no midrib**; leaf cells oblong to elongate, firm-walled; alar cells not distinctive.

SPOROPHYTES: Often present; growing from the side of the stem; stalks short; capsules upright, oblong, smooth, projecting just above separated leaves; peristome double.

ECOLOGY: Common in lowland and montane **forests**, where it forms **large, hanging mats on trunks and branches of trees**.

NOTES: Douglas' neckera can be easily distinguished by the flattened leaf arrangement and wavy, shiny leaves. **Menzies' neckera**, which is common in similar habitats, can be distinguished from Douglas' neckera by its **leaves with a midrib**, the **small, green filaments** (paraphyllia) along the stem and its **completely covered capsules**. Both species share a flattened leaf arrangement and wavy leaves. The *Metaneckeras* often have slender, fragile branches that are easily broken off. Menzies' neckera occurs eastward into the Rockies, while Douglas' neckera is restricted to the rainforests west of the Coast Mountains and the Cascades. • Douglas' neckera was named for the Scottish botanist David Douglas, who in 1826 was the first to climb Mt. Hooker in the Canadian Rockies.

PLUME MOSS • *Dendroalsia abietina*

GENERAL: Plants **olive-green to grey-green**, dull; main stems creeping, giving rise to densely and regularly **once-pinnate** secondary stems usually less than 20 cm long; when moist these are straight, elongate, descending, **fern-like** plants; **when dry they curl inwards**, forming down-curled plants.

LEAVES: 1.6–2.2 mm long, broadly lance-shaped, sharp-pointed, upright and straight wet or dry, saw-toothed towards the tip; stem leaves longer than branch leaves; edges bent backward in the upper portion; midrib single, ending just below the tip; leaf cells oval, with 1 strong papilla on the outer surface.

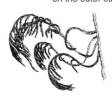

SPOROPHYTES: Growing on the underside of female plants, from the side of the stem; stalks very short; capsules oblong, partially exposed in the leaves, visible only from beneath the stems.

ECOLOGY: Epiphytic or occasionally on calcium-rich cliff-faces in forests dominated by **Garry oak and bigleaf maple**; confined to the **drier, Mediterranean-type climatic zones** in the southern portion of our region, northwards to southern British Columbia.

NOTES: The stems of plume moss that **bend downwards when dry** but that open into elongate plumes when wet cannot be mistaken for any other moss. The stems are regularly pinnately branched, and individual plants are unisexual. Other epiphytes, such as *Homalothecium*, *Neckera*, *Metaneckera* and *Orthotrichum*, all have stems that **turn upwards when dry**.

HANGING MOSS • *Antitrichia curtipendula*

GENERAL: Plants **rusty-green to orange-green**, forming **large, loose cushions and mats**; stems **once pinnately branched**, up to 15 cm long.

LEAVES: 2–4 mm long, loosely and widely spreading when moist and dry, broadly egg-shaped and quickly narrowing to a sharply pointed tip; stem and branch leaves similar, not at all pleated; edges rolled under; **1 long and 2 shorter, obscure midribs**; cells oblong, irregularly thick-walled, smooth, those at the base orange and set off from the upper ones.

SPOROPHYTES: Not common, from the side of the stem; stalks long; capsules straight or slightly curved, smooth; peristome double.

ECOLOGY: Forming large mats and 'balloons' that **festoon tree trunks and branches** in low elevation forests, especially in more-open gaps with lots of light.

NOTES: The **large, orangish cushions** that often form **balls and balloons on tree branches** are characteristic of hanging moss. The stems are loosely branched, and the branches are spreading and usually **angled downwards** from the stems. In some ways, this species resembles **goose-necked moss** (p. 472), a species of the **forest floor and tree bases** that is **light green** in colour, often grows **upright** and has leaves with only a **single midrib**. • That characteristic 'rainforest look' shown in photos of the lowland coastal forests is due to a combination of *Antitrichia* balls and cat-tail moss and coiled-leaf moss curtains.

465

TANGLE MOSS • *Heterocladium procurrens*

GENERAL: Plants **yellow-green to olive-green**, coarse, dull; stems with **many widely-spaced branches; small, green filaments** (paraphyllia) common along the stems.

LEAVES: Branch leaves 0.4–0.8 mm long, egg-shaped with short to slenderly tapered points, **flattened together in 1 plane to spreading** when moist, loosely upright when dry; **midrib single**, often forked near the tip, ending about mid-leaf; upper cells diamond-shaped, papillose; stem leaves 1–2 mm long, oval, abruptly narrowed to a thread-like tip; cells smooth.

SPOROPHYTES: From the side of the stem; stalks upright, long, smooth; capsules oblong, dark brown to nearly black, smooth, horizontal, curved; peristome well developed, double.

ECOLOGY: On tree bases, soil and cliff shelves at subalpine and middle-elevation zones; occasionally at lower elevations.

NOTES: The **widely spreading**, rather short branch leaves are **flattened** together **in 1 plane they** have a **single midrib** and **lack a hair-point. They** are useful features for distinguishing **tangle moss.** Tangle moss could be confused with ***Claopodium***, which has **contorted leaves (when dry)** and with ***Eurhynchium***, which has **smooth leaf cells.** 2 additional species of *Heterocladium* are present in our region; both have papillose stem leaves.

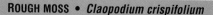

ROUGH MOSS • *Claopodium crispifolium*

GENERAL: Plants dull, **lime-green to olive-green, regularly once-pinnate**, with the stem and branch tips yellow-green; stems with some **small, green filaments** (paraphyllia) along the stem, 4–8 mm long.

LEAVES: 1–2 mm long, heart-shaped, sharply pointed, straight and spreading when moist, contorted and loosely upright when dry; **midrib strong**, ending just beyond the tip as a **yellow to clear point, shiny and contrasting** with the dull leaf surfaces; cells diamond-shaped to short-oblong, each with a single, strong papilla.

SPOROPHYTES: Occasionally present, from the side of the stem; stalks long, rough, black; capsules oblong, horizontal, smooth; peristome double.

ECOLOGY: On logs and tree bases in low- to middle-elevation forests, often along streams and in other light-gap situations; less common on moist, calcium-rich boulders and cliff-faces.

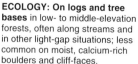

NOTES: The **shiny midrib** that ends beyond the leaf tip in a **yellowish point** characterizes both *C. crispifolium* and *C. bolanderi*. **C. bolanderi,** however, is **less regularly branched,** has leaf cells with 2–3 papillae per cell and is **more common on rock surfaces.** Similar species such as *Heterocladium*, *C. whippleanum* and *Thuidium* all lack the clear to yellowish, extended midrib.

YELLOW MOSS • *Homalothecium fulgescens*

GENERAL: Plants **golden-green, shiny**, coarse, forming **extensive mats**; stems 5–22 cm long, **irregularly branched**, the branches **spreading when moist** and **conspicuously upturned when dry**.

LEAVES: 2.5–4.0 mm long, lance-shaped, sharply pointed, with small teeth along the edges and deep longitudinal pleats; midrib slender, ending just below the tip; leaf cells elongate, smooth.

SPOROPHYTES: Occasional, from the side of the stem; stalks long, rough; capsules cylindrical, smooth, upright to curved when old; peristome double.

ECOLOGY: Common **on trunks of maple, cottonwood, alder and oak** in coastal areas; also found on logs, cliffs and boulders.

NOTES: Shiny, golden-green plants that form **extensive spreading mats on deciduous trees** are characteristic of **yellow moss**. When wet, its branches are spreading, but they become **upturned when dry**. There are 6 species of the genus in our region and they are difficult to tell apart; *H. fulgescens* **is more irregularly branched and coarser** than the others, and it is the **most common species at low elevations**.

GOLDEN SHORT-CAPSULED MOSS • *Brachythecium frigidum*

GENERAL: Plants **yellow-green, soft, shiny**, forming **large mats**; stems **creeping, often arching** towards the tips with **many spreading branches**.

LEAVES: 2–3 mm long, egg-shaped, sharply pointed (slenderly tapered), rather broad, somewhat pleated, toothed at upper edges; midrib slender, ending about 3/4 of the way up the leaf, **wide-spreading and slightly sickle-shaped when moist, little altered when dry**; branch and stem leaves not very different.

SPOROPHYTES: Common; stalks upright, blackish, with many small papillae, especially in upper portion; capsules short-cylindrical, slightly curved, horizontal; peristome well developed, double.

ECOLOGY: Widespread throughout our region, but especially common in lowland rainforest; occurs **on logs, moist forest-floor litter, soil and tree bases**, occasionally on low-hanging branches.

NOTES: In our region this species is probably the most common member of a **large and difficult genus** of about 20 species. All species are more or less yellow-green and have **lance-shaped, sharply pointed, pleated leaves** and stems that tend to **sprawl or creep and branch frequently but irregularly**. Other common species of this genus are *B. rivulare* (found **on stones and soil banks near running water**), *B. salebrosum* (found **on logs** in the boreal and montane forest areas), *B. groenlandicum* (found in the **subalpine**), *B. turgidum* and *B. mildeanum* (found in **rich fens**) and *B. starkei* (found on **moist forest humus**). *Homalothecium* species are also similar in appearance, but they have **strongly upturned branches when dry** and most often grow on rocks or are epiphytic. • The name *Brachythecium* means 'short capsule,' in reference to the relatively short, thick capsule on the sporophyte.

BLUNT-LEAVED MOSS • *Scleropodium obtusifolium*

GENERAL: Plants **yellow-green to dark-green, shiny, in extensive, flat mats**; stems sometimes arching, **irregularly branched**, but never regularly pinnately branched.

LEAVES: About 1.5 mm long, **closely set and overlapping** one another, **very concave, egg-shaped** and sharp-pointed, sometimes ending in an short, abrupt point; midrib single, ending about 3/4 of the way up the leaves; cells elongate, smooth; alar cells swollen.

SPOROPHYTES: Rarely present, from the side of the stem; stalks dark, rough; capsules inclined, smooth, curved; peristome well developed, double.

ECOLOGY: On **irrigated boulders, rock-faces and cliffs near swiftly running streams**; occasionally on exposed roots overhanging water; often associated with black-tufted rock moss and streamside moss; common in lowland forests if appropriate streams are present, extending to the subalpine.

NOTES: The habitat of blunt-leaved moss is distinctive, and its **concave, egg-shaped** leaves that are **pressed to the stem** and that **densely overlap** one another are good field characters. *Brachythecium* and *Homalothecium* both have lance-shaped leaves, while other mosses in general have more-branched stems than does blunt-leaved moss or leaves that curve strongly to 1 side. 2 other species of *Scleropodium* occur in our region; both have less-concave, narrower leaves.

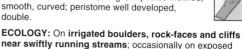

CAT-TAIL MOSS • *Isothecium myosuroides*

GENERAL: Plants **glossy and dingy green, varying from whitish-green to pale brownish-green**; stems form **long, narrowly tapered strands hanging from branches** or form **creeping, irregularly branched mats**; when the plant occurs atop a branch or log, branching is variable.

LEAVES: Up to 2.0 mm long, upright, elliptic and variably sharp-pointed; edges sharply toothed; **midrib well developed** and ending about 2/3 of the way up the leaf; cells long, rather thick-walled; alar cells well developed.

SPOROPHYTES: Common; stalks brownish, slender; capsules rather short-cylindrical, symmetric, almost upright to inclined; peristome well developed, double.

ECOLOGY: By far the most common and most variable species of the coastal rainforests where it is '**dirt common**' from sea level to middle elevations.

NOTES: At some localities, every tree branch is covered by cat-tail moss. It can also cover boulders and logs, but it is **noticeably absent** from ground-surface and cliff-face habitats. **Coiled-leaf moss** (p. 469) has a similar colour and occurs in the same habitats—it can be abundant in the rainforest, sometimes forming hanging drapes. When examined closely, coiled-leaf moss has **leaves that curve strongly to one side**. • In addition to the confusion caused to students and amateurs by the extreme variability of cat-tail moss, bryologists who have studied this genus disagree about the correct names. Various sources list it as *I. stoloniferum*, *I. myosuroides* and *I. spiculiferum*. *I. cristatum* is a second species in this genus which occurs in our region.

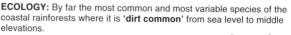

COILED-LEAF MOSS • *Hypnum circinale*

GENERAL: Plants **glossy, light green to sometimes whitish-green, creeping, irregularly and finely branched**, forming **slender, descending to hanging mats on tree trunks and rock surfaces**.

LEAVES: Up to 2.2 mm long, **strongly curved to 1 side**, gradually narrowed from a broad base; **no midrib**; leaf points long, curved, with many small teeth, remaining sickle-shaped when removed from the stems; leaf cells elongate, thin-walled throughout; alar cells square.

SPOROPHYTES: Grow from the side of the stem; stalks long; capsules relatively short, inclined, smooth.

ECOLOGY: One of the most common species of lowland rainforests that forms **large, hanging, dense mats that have a braided appearance**.

NOTES: Other species that can be confused with coiled-leaf moss are: *Isothecium myosuroides* which can be distinguished by its **straight leaves with midribs**, *Drepanocladus uncinatus* which can be distinguished by its **pleated, midribbed** leaves, and other *Hypnum* species, of which *H. subimponens* is most frequent. *H. subimponens* is **larger** than *H. circinale*, **lush green** in colour and **regularly pinnately branched**, and it has long-cylindric capsules.

CURLY HYPNUM • *Hypnum subimponens*

GENERAL: Plants **rich, yellow-green**, forming **mats** that often have a **dark brown cast** to the older areas; stems **creeping, regularly pinnately branched**, the outer layer consisting of enlarged, clear cells.

LEAVES: 1.5–3.0 mm long, **strongly curved to 1 side**, smooth, egg-shaped, long and slenderly sharp pointed; upper cells elongate; alar cells small, square.

SPOROPHYTES: Common; stalks long, reddish; capsules long-cylindric, curved, smooth, upright or nearly so; peristome well developed, double.

ECOLOGY: Common in lowland rainforests **on logs, cliff-faces, boulders, tree bases and tree trunks**.

NOTES: Regularly pinnately branching stems, smooth leaves **strongly curved to 1 side** and the **glossy, yellow-green** colour are features of this species. Several similar species can be readily distinguished from curly hypnum: *Drepanocladus uncinatus* and *Ptilium crista-castrensis* both have **strongly pleated** leaves; *Hypnum circinale* is **smaller** and **whitish-green**, and has short capsules; and both *H. dieckei* and *H. lindbergii* have swollen alar cells and occur **on rocks or are terrestrial**.

OREGON BEAKED MOSS • *Kindbergia oregana*

GENERAL: Plants large, **yellow-green to orange-green**; stems 6–30 cm long, **creeping to arched**, once-pinnate, with branches evenly and closely spaced.

LEAVES: 1.2–2.0 mm long, stem and branch leaves **of 2 shapes**; stem leaves widely spreading, broadly elliptic, quickly narrowed to a sharp tip; branch leaves much smaller, narrower, less spreading; midrib strong, single; cells elongate, with clearly defined alar cells.

SPOROPHYTES: Frequent, growing from the side of the stem; stalks black with small papillae; capsules inclined, smooth, curved, each with a **long beak**.

ECOLOGY: Common in lowland rainforests along the coast; forms **mats on logs, humus and tree bases**.

NOTES: Species of *Kindbergia* are sometimes placed in the genera *Stokesiella* and *Eurhynchium* (e.g., *Stokesiella oregana*, *Eurhynchium oreganum*). • The **regularly once-pinnately branched** stem with **widely spreading** and **well-separated stem and branch leaves** is diagnostic of this large, showy, coastal species. Another coastal rainforest species that is regularly pinnate is ***Ptilium crista-castrensis***, but its leaves are **strongly curved to 1 side**. Another species of *Kindbergia*, **K. praelonga** is **smaller**, and **much less** regularly branched.

SLENDER BEAKED MOSS • *Kindbergia praelonga*

GENERAL: Plants **dirty green to olive-green**, irregularly once to twice pinnately branched, mostly with **arching, creeping** stems to about 10 cm long.

LEAVES: Up to 1.5 mm long; stem and branch leaves well separated from one another; stem leaves widely diverging, larger, broadly elliptic, gradually narrowed to a sharp point; branch leaves smaller, narrower, with shorter points; leaf cells elongate, similar throughout (except for alar cell region).

SPOROPHYTES: Occasional; growing from the side of the stem; stalks black, with small papillae; capsules inclined, smooth, curved, similar to those of Oregon beaked moss.

ECOLOGY: Forms **irregular mats on logs, humus and tree bases** in rich lowland forests and montane forests; often found with Oregon beaked moss, but occurs in a wider diversity of forested habitats.

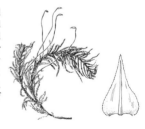

NOTES: *Kindbergia* differs from *Brachythecium* and *Homalothecium* in its separated stem and branch leaves and the long-beaked lid on its capsules. Whereas Oregon beaked moss is a beautiful, richly and evenly branched moss, **slender beaked moss** is **scruffy, unevenly and irregularly branched,** and overall a **much-smaller, more-untidy** plant. The branching of slender beaked moss is **often twice pinnate**, in contrast to the consistently once-pinnate branching of Oregon beaked moss.

BIG RED STEM • *Pleurozium schreberi*
RED-STEMMED FEATHERMOSS

GENERAL:. Plants large, **olive-green, robust**, almost upright to ascending, forming **extensive, loosely interwoven colonies**, about 7–16 cm high; stems conspicuously **red, smooth**, with branches swollen, **widely spaced, irregularly once pinnate**.

LEAVES: 2–3 mm long, oblong-elliptic, quickly narrowing to a broad, abruptly short-pointed tip; edges smooth; no midrib; upper cells elongate; alar cells clearly defined.

SPOROPHYTES: Sporadic, common in some populations, growing from the side of the stem; stalks long, slender, reddish; capsules short-cylindric, inclined to horizontal, curved, dark; peristome well developed, double.

ECOLOGY: Prefers **acidic, poor soils and drier conditions**; along the coast in lowland rainforests, *Pleurozium* is largely replaced by shaggy moss and species of *Kindbergia*, but it sometimes ocurs in bogs and scrub forest.

NOTES: The **smooth, red** stems, robust and semi-upright plants, **blunt, short, upright** leaves and **once pinnate** branches serve to easily distinguish **big red stem**. *Rhytidiadelphus* species, in contrast, have **long, slender, pleated** leaves and **step moss** is **twice pinnately branched**. • Along with step moss, *Pleurozium* species are the most common terrestrial mosses in the boreal and intermontane forests. They are not as abundant along the coast, but they are still frequently found. • Capsules are rare in *P. schreberi,* and there is no known mechanism of asexual reproduction. This is unusual in a moss distributed fairly widely around the globe. Crum (1976) suggests that a lack of male plants may underlie the sexual difficulties in *Pleurozium*. • The word *Pleurozium* comes from the Latin *pleuro*, meaning 'ribs,' and it presumably refers to the arrangement of the branches on either side of the stem, which resembles a rib cage.

SPEAR MOSS • *Calliergonella cuspidata*

GENERAL: Plants **large, yellow-green, shiny, irregularly branched, upright**, up to 10 cm high; the lack of branches near the tip and the flattened arrangement of the leaves of the stems give the plants a **spear-like shape**; outermost layers of stem cells swollen and clear, giving stems a clear-green appearance.

LEAVES: About 2 mm long, egg-shaped to elliptic, blunt; **no midrib**; cells elongate throughout, except for the clear, swollen alar cells.

SPOROPHYTES: Rare, growing from the side of the stem; stalks long, slender, reddish; capsules inclined, curved, smooth.

ECOLOGY: Frequent **in yards** and on **grassy roadsides** in urban areas; less common in natural habitats where it occurs in **fens** and other moist, **swampy** habitats.

NOTES: These fairly large, **yellow-green, shiny, upright, irregularly branched** mosses can be confused with **big red stem** (distinguished by its **red stems**), *Calliergon* species (whose leaves have a **strong midrib**) or *Scleropodium* species (which also have **leaf midribs**). Although the stems are somewhat flattened near the tips, they should not be confused with the **really flattened** leaves of species of *Hookeria* and *Plagiothecium*; neither of these genera has plants that are upright and irregularly branched, like those of *Calliergonella* species. • Although this species can be common in human-altered habitats, it is not abundant in natural situations in our region.

BENT-LEAF MOSS • *Rhytidiadelphus squarrosus*

GENERAL: Plants large, **light green to reddish-green**, forming **extensive mats** up to 15 cm high; stems variable, **upright, unbranched to arching and irregularly branched, without** small green filaments (paraphyllia) along the stem.

LEAVES: 2.5–3.2 mm long, spreading at right angles with upper portions bent backwards when moist or dry, heart-shaped, sharply pointed, **not pleated**; midrib short and double; cells elongate, similar throughout.

SPOROPHYTES: Not common, from the side of the stem; stalks long, upright; capsules short, oblong, smooth, asymmetric, horizontal; peristome double.

ECOLOGY: *R. squarrosus* occurs in yards, on roadsides and in other disturbed habitats; common as a **yard weed** in Vancouver and Seattle.

NOTES: Leaves spreading at right angles give **bent-leaf moss** a **bristly star-shaped** appearance when viewed from above; this is usually sufficient to identify this species. ***R. loreus*** has **pleated** leaves, in contrast to the unpleated leaves of *R. squarrosus*, and ***R. triquetrus*** has a truly **unkempt look** about it when compared to the neat, trim *R. squarrosus*. ***R. subpinnatus*** is an **ascending, arched** plant with **many side branches**, while *R. squarrosus* is unbranched to irregularly branched; it also differs from *R. squarrosus* in that it occurs along streams in lowland and middle-elevation forests and is occasionally found in subalpine and alpine seeps. ***Campylium*** species, especially *C. stellatum*, also have leaves that spread at right angles but they are not common in our region and are **restricted to rich fens**.

GOOSE-NECKED MOSS • *Rhytidiadelphus triquetrus*
ELECTRIFIED CAT'S-TAIL MOSS

GENERAL: Plants large, **upright to ascending**, coarse, up to 20 cm long, with **irregular, widely spaced, once-pinnate branching**; stems and branches without small, green filaments (paraphyllia); uppermost portion **often curved to 1 side**.

LEAVES: 3.5–5.0 mm long, egg-shaped with long, slender tips, spreading **(messy), somewhat pleated** leaves; midribs strong, double; cells elongate and irregularly thickened throughout.

SPOROPHYTES: Infrequent, growing from the side of the stem; stalks long; capsules inclined, curved, smooth.

ECOLOGY: Terrestrial on **humus-rich substrates** in montane forests; less common in lowland rainforests, where it is replaced by *R. loreus*; sometimes extending onto logs and tree bases where it occurs intermixed with *Hylocomium splendens*, *R. loreus* and *Kindbergia* species; also on sandy-gravelly soils in beach and streamside forests.

NOTES: The **coarse, irregular** appearance of this species is due to the irregularly spreading, rather large leaves and the irregular branching. The **curved stem tips** give the plants a characteristic 'goose-necked' look. Other species that are as large as and could be confused with goose-necked moss are ***R. loreus*** (which has **curved leaves**), ***R. squarrosus*** (which has **no pleats** on its neatly **right-angle-spreading** leaves), ***Rhytidium rugosum*** (which has transversely **wrinkled** leaves), and ***Rhytidiopsis robusta*** (which has **pleated leaves** that are **strongly curved to 1 side** growing on robust stems that are not much branched).

LANKY MOSS • *Rhytidiadelphus loreus*

GENERAL: Plants large, **yellow-green to dark green**, ascending to creeping, **widely spaced pinnately branched**, in **loose mats** up to 15 cm high, with branches tapering to fine points; stems and branches **lack** small green filaments (paraphyllia); stems very stiff, giving an overall tidy appearance.

LEAVES: 3.5–4.0 mm long, regularly spreading and **somewhat curved, noticeably pleated**, broad, egg-shaped, gradually narrowed to a rather long, slender point; **midrib double**, indistinct.

SPOROPHYTES: Occasional, growing from the side of the stem; capsules inclined, smooth, cylindrical, asymmetric.

ECOLOGY: Often the **dominant ground cover** in lowland and middle-elevation rainforests, replacing both goose-necked moss and stair step moss in coastal rainforests.

NOTES: When compared to other terrestrial feathermosses that form extensive, loosely interwoven colonies, **lanky moss** is the only one with **slightly curved, pleated leaves**. *R. loreus* is much larger than species of *Kindbergia*, less bristly than *R. triquetrus* and only once-pinnately branched, while *Hylocomium splendens* is twice pinnately branched.

PIPECLEANER MOSS • *Rhytidiopsis robusta*

GENERAL: Plants large, **yellow-green to pale green**, creeping, up to 15 cm long, with **few branches**; stems **with abundant small green filaments** (paraphyllia) and closely set leaves.

LEAVES: 1.5–2.0 mm long, **strongly curved** to 1 side wet or dry, lance-shaped, sharp-pointed, with distinct **longitudinal pleats; midrib double**, ending near mid-leaf; cells elongate, smooth.

SPOROPHYTES: Rare, growing from the side of the stem; stalks long; capsules smooth, asymmetric, cylindrical, curved and horizontal; peristome double.

ECOLOGY: A moss characteristic of **subalpine forests** where it can form **large, pure mats on the forest floor**; sporadic and becoming rare at lower elevations, where it sometimes occurs on logs.

NOTES: The **large, little-branched** plants with leaves that are **uniformly strongly curved to 1 side** distinguish this handsome species, as does its habitat. *Rhytidium rugosum*, in comparison, has **transversely wrinkled** leaves (like crumpled paper) and a **single midrib**. Only *Rhytidiadelphus loreus* and *Drepanocladus uncinatus* have pleated, sickle-shaped leaves, but the first is **richly branched** and the second is **much smaller** than *Rhytidiopsis robusta*, with more-slender leaves. • *Rhytidiopsis* means 'looking like *Rhytidium*.'

473

STEP MOSS • *Hylocomium splendens*
STAIR STEP MOSS

GENERAL: Plants large, robust, somewhat shiny, up to 20 cm long; stems **twice pinnately branched**, with **abundant small, green filaments** (paraphyllia) visible with a hand lens; annual growth increments visible as **individual, arched segments**, each arising just behind tip of the previous year's.

LEAVES: 2–4 mm long; branch leaves narrowly egg-shaped, sharply pointed; stem leaves elliptic below, gradually tapering to a longer, wavy, slender point; midribs 2, inconspicuous; cells elongate.

SPOROPHYTES: Not uncommon, growing from the side of the stem; capsules inclined, smooth, curved and cylindrical.

ECOLOGY: Common in lowland and middle elevation forests, often forming the dominant ground cover; most common in forests dominated by western redcedar and hemlock on humus rich soils; prefers slightly calcium-rich soils and is replaced by *Sphagnum* species on acidic, organic soils and by big red stem on drier, more-acidic soils.

NOTES: This species' 3–5 cm long **step-like annual increments** are distinctive. 2 other species of the genus occur in our region, but neither of these has the distinctive **stair-steps**. Step moss is often associated with species of *Rhytidiadelphus*, especially **lanky moss** (with leaves **strongly curved to 1 side**), and **goose-necked moss** (with **bristly, backward-bending** leaves). Farther inland, step moss is associated with **big red stem**, which has **once-pinnate, red stems** and **no paraphyllia**. Coastal plants of step moss (subspecies *giganteum* of some authors) with distinctive stem leaves are 3–5 times larger than the inland plants. • The age of step moss may be estimated by counting its annual 'steps.'

TREE MOSS • *Climacium dendroides*

GENERAL: Plants large, robust, **tree-shaped**, about 2–10 cm high, growing from underground, horizontal stems; stems branched, upright, with **small green filaments** (paraphyllia).

LEAVES: 2.5–3.0 mm long; midrib strong, single, elongate; cells thin-walled throughout; branch leaves loosely arranged, egg-shaped or narrower, sharp-pointed, pleated, toothed; stem leaves upright, closely pressed to the stem, broader, abruptly short-pointed, not pleated.

SPOROPHYTES: Rare; arising from top of upright stems; stalks long; capsules upright, smooth, dark, shortly cylindrical; peristome double; calyptrae split.

ECOLOGY: Widespread throughout our region, from sea level to alpine tundra, but most common at low elevations in **moist, humus-rich woods, peaty swamps, fens**, calcium-rich **tundra** (often at the edges of peatlands), **lake edges and in floodplain forests**; can become a weed in yards in areas of high rainfall.

NOTES: The upright stems of tree moss are branched only near the tips, so they look like **small trees**. The stems are coarse and stand **stiffly upright**, and they are **interconnected by underground horizontal stems**. The only other mosses in our region that have a tree-like appearance are *Leucolepis acanthoneuron*, which can be distinguished from *Climacium dendroides* by its **bordered leaves** and much **more-umbrella-like appearance**, and *Pleuroziopsis ruthenica*, which has **more-fern-like** stems and **longer, narrower** leaves and colourless, transparent lamellae on the upright stems. *P. ruthenica* is found only in the northern portion of our region.

SMALL FLAT MOSS • *Pseudotaxiphyllum elegans*

GENERAL: Plants **small, pale green to yellow-green, delicate, glossy,** forming **mats;** stems to 3.5 cm long, creeping, **strongly flattened,** not much branched; branches small, brittle, deciduous, growing towards the tips of stems.

LEAVES: 0.5–2.0 mm long, flattened with the tips pointed downwards when dry, **lance-shaped,** sharp-pointed, somewhat asymmetric; edges with small teeth; midrib very short and double; upper cells elongate; alar cells not clearly defined.

SPOROPHYTES: Uncommon, from the side of the stem; stalks upright, long; capsules egg-shaped, smooth, nodding; peristome well developed, double.

ECOLOGY: On soil banks, tree bases, forest humus and rotten logs from sea level to the subalpine; especially common on **compacted, bare soil patches** along disturbed trails at low elevations.

NOTES: The rather **small, shiny, flattened** plants are characteristic of **small flat moss.** Its **lack** of leaves that are obviously strongly curved to 1 side distinguishes it from *Hypnum* and *Drepanocladus* species, and its **slender leaves** and **small size** distinguish it from *Plagiothecium* species. A few other small, flattened species in different genera are present along the coast; these can be distinguished by using Ireland (1969).

WAVY-LEAVED COTTON MOSS • *Plagiothecium undulatum*

GENERAL: Plants **large, whitish-green to pale green, glossy,** with a **conspicuously flattened** appearance, forming **mats** in shaded areas; stems little branched, **spear-shaped,** from 3 to more than 15 cm long.

LEAVES: 1.5–4.0 mm long, narrowly egg-shaped to lance-shaped, sharply pointed, **transversely wavy,** somewhat asymmetric, flattened on all parts of the stem; upper cells elongate, similar below.

SPOROPHYTES: Common, from the side of the stem; stalks black, long; capsules inclined, smooth, curved,

ECOLOGY: A species of **shaded** habitats in lowland to montane forests, occurring on **logs, humus, tree stumps and moist soil,** more rarely on rock surfaces; common along streams, in secondary and primary forests dominated by cedar, hemlock, or Douglas-fir.

NOTES: Large, flattened plants that form **whitish-green mats** are characteristic of **wavy-leaved cotton moss.** Other flattened mosses in our region include smaller species of *Plagiothecium* and species of *Isopterygium* (none of which has **wavy** leaves), as well as the 2 species of *Hookeria* (which have **extra-large hexagonal cells,** see p. 463).

TWISTED ULOTA • *Ulota obtusiuscula*

GENERAL: Plants small, **olive-green to reddish-green**, forming **dense cushions and tufts on tree trunks and branches**; stems 1–3 cm high, irregularly branched.

LEAVES: 1.5–4 cm long, **contorted** when dry, contorted to upright when moist, lance-shaped from an **expanded base**, gradually narrowed to a slender, sharp point; upper leaf cells rounded, with small papillae; inner basal leaf cells clear, thick walled, becoming thin walled and rectangular near edges.

SPOROPHYTES: Nearly always present, at the tip of the plant, with additional branches growing from beneath; stalks short; capsules upright, 8 ribbed, football-shaped, mouth not especially small; peristome double; calyptrae cone-shaped, hairy.

ECOLOGY: Epiphytic, **usually on alder, maple or other broad-leaved trees**, but sometimes on conifers in lowland rainforests.

NOTES: Dense cushions of plants with contorted leaves (when dry) are characteristic of species in the genus *Ulota*. **U. phyllantha has brood-bodies** at the stem tips and occurs in areas subjected to **salt spray** while *U. megalospora* has **creeping main stems**. *Orthotrichum* species have **less-contorted** leaves.

LYELL'S BRISTLE MOSS • *Orthotrichum lyellii*

GENERAL: Plants **olive-green to brownish**, dull, irregularly branched, forming **loose tufts and mats on trees**; stems vary in length from 1 to more than 10 cm, **descending along trunks**.

LEAVES: 2–6 sometimes 8 mm long, wide-spreading when moist, loosely upright when dry, lance-shaped, sharp-pointed; edges smooth, flat; midrib strong, ending at leaf tip; upper cells rounded, papillose; lower cells longer, smooth; alar cells not clearly defined.

SPOROPHYTES: Common, at the tip of the plant; stalks short; capsules **partially exposed** beyond the leaves, cylindrical, **8 ribbed**, upright; peristome well developed, double, the outer teeth bent backwards and twisted.

ECOLOGY: On tree trunks and branches of deciduous trees in lowland rainforests; less common on coniferous trees, rare on rock.

NOTES: Several species of *Orthotrichum* are common epiphytes of lowland and montane forests while several others are common on mesic to dry rock outcrops. Associated with *O. lyellii* (which has **partially** exposed capsules and capsules **ribbed** along their **entire length**) and *O. speciosum* (which has **projecting** capsules **ribbed only in the upper half**) and *O. striatum* (which has **smooth, completely covered** capsules). Another species, *O. consimile*, forms **tiny cushions** with **projecting** capsules; it is especially common **on elderberry twigs**.

BOTTLE MOSS • *Amphidium lapponicum*

GENERAL: Plants **olive-green to light green**, dense, growing in **cushions**, about 1–3 cm high, **bisexual**; stems with scattered, **reddish, root-like filaments.**

LEAVES: 1.5–3.0 mm long, spreading and somewhat curved backward when moist, **contorted** when dry, linear to narrowly lance-shaped, sharp-pointed, often ending in a single, clear cell; **edges smooth**; upper cells square, becoming longer and clear below, covered by dense, elliptic, cuticular papillae over both cell cavities and crosswalls.

SPOROPHYTES: Common, at the tip of the plant; stalks short; capsules partially exposed beyond the leaves, short-oblong, sometimes constricted in the middle, distinctly 8 ribbed for their entire length; peristome absent.

ECOLOGY: On moist rock cliffs, especially on siliceous rock, but also on basalt and other slightly basic rock.

NOTES: The **tightly twisted, narrow, lance-shaped** leaves and **dense cushions** of **bottle moss** found **in rock crevices** are characteristic of the species. 2 other species of this genus are found in the area: *A. californicum* (which has **notched** upper leaf edges) and *A. mougeotii* (which has **narrower, linear** leaves, **finer, cuticular papillae, and **unisexual** plants). • Bottle moss occurs in crevices (often vertical ones) that receive periodic runoff from rainfall and become dry in between rains. The cushions absorb and hold water for these dry periods.

HAIRY SCREW MOSS • *Tortula ruralis*
SIDEWALK MOSS

GENERAL: Plants dull, **dark green to reddish-brown**, forming **cushions or mats, unisexual**; stems 1–5 sometimes 8 cm high, upright, unbranched or rarely branched beneath capsules.

LEAVES: 3–4.5 mm long, **strikingly spreading at right angles and curving backwards** when moist, upright-twisted when dry, broadly oblong, quickly narrowed to a long, **clear, toothed bristle-point**; edges strongly rolled under; midrib strong, extending beyond the leaf blade in the bristle-point; upper cells densely papillose, square; lower cells oblong, clear, smooth.

SPOROPHYTES: Not common, at the tip of the plant; stalks long, straight; capsules narrowly cylindrical, smooth, upright; peristome with a long, white tube of fused teeth, single.

ECOLOGY: On soil, in crevices and on rock surfaces in **periodically dry** habitats from sea level to the alpine.

NOTES: The broadly oblong leaves with long, clear bristle-points distinguish hairy screw moss from *Grimmia* (which has **lance-shaped** leaves), *Racomitrium* (which is **much more branched**) and *Polytrichum piliferum* (which has complex leaves with **lamellae**). • Hairy screw moss is replaced at **high elevations** by *T. norvegica* (which has **red bristle-points**) and near the coast by *T. princeps* (which has **bisexual** plants). More than 15 species of *Tortula* occur in our region. • *Tortula* means 'twisted,' in reference to the leaves and the capsule teeth; *ruralis* means 'of the countryside.'

RED ROOF MOSS • *Ceratodon purpureus*
FIRE MOSS

GENERAL: Plants small, **reddish-green**, forming **mats or tufts**, 1–2.5 cm high; stems unbranched, upright.

LEAVES: 0.7–3.0 mm long, spreading when moist, **contorted when dry**, lance-shaped, sharply pointed; edges bent backwards, smooth except for a few notches near the tip; upper cells square, smooth; lower cells somewhat longer; alar cells not clearly defined.

SPOROPHYTES: Common, at the tip of the plant; stalks **reddish when young, purple when old**, upright, slender; capsules almost upright, smooth and greenish when young, becoming horizontal, 8 ribbed, and **reddish-brown to purplish** when mature; peristome single, of 16 upright teeth.

ECOLOGY: The most-common moss in the world, known from the sidewalks of New York to the Antarctic; in our region on **sandy soils** along roadsides and **compacted soil** in disturbed areas, abundant on roofs; in undisturbed sites on **soil exposed** by upturned trees and on rotting logs.

NOTES: When mature, **red roof moss** is easily identified by the **dark reddish to purplish, ribbed** capsule, which is **abruptly bent** at its junction with the stalk. Young capsules look completely different, but still have a reddish tinge. When sterile, red roof moss is distinguished by its weedy habitat, **smooth** upper leaf cells, and leaf edges that are **rolled under** and **notched** near the tip. • On burned-over sites, red roof moss often occurs with *Pohlia nutans* and other pioneers such as *Bryum caespiticiam Funaria hygrometrica* and *Marchantia polymorpha*. The **deeply furrowed capsules** and **stalk colour** are good features for identifying red roof moss. • *Ceratodon* is from the Latin *cerato* meaning 'horn-shaped,' in reference to the forked capsule teeth; *purpureus* describes the reddish-purple colour of this species.

CURLY THATCH MOSS • *Dicranoweisia cirrata*

GENERAL: Plants small, **olive-green to yellow-green**, forming **cushions or more extensive mats** 1–2 cm high; stems upright, unbranched, slender.

LEAVES: 2–3 mm long, upright-spreading when moist, **twisted to contorted when dry**, narrowly lance-shaped, sharp pointed; edges narrowly curved backwards below; midrib slender, ending at the tip; upper cells rounded, smooth; lower cells somewhat longer.

SPOROPHYTES: Common, at the tip of the plant; stalks slender, long, upright; capsules narrowly cylindrical, smooth, upright; peristome single, of 16 reddish, short teeth.

ECOLOGY: Very common **on logs, fence-posts, roofs, tree trunks, and other woody substrates**; rare on rock, abundant at low elevations along the coast, and sometimes common on trees along the city streets of Vancouver and Seattle.

NOTES: Curly thatch moss is best identified by its **habitat** and its **lack** of impressive size, colour or morphology. The upright, **smooth** capsules, **twisted** leaves and **smooth** leaf cells are also helpful. Another species, *D. crispula*, occurs almost exclusively on **acidic rocks at high elevations**.

WET ROCK MOSS • *Dichodontium pellucidum*

GENERAL: Plants **dark green to olive-green**, forming **cushions and small turfs** 1.5–5 cm high; stems unbranched, upright.

LEAVES: 1–4 mm long, wide-spreading, curved backwards when moist, contorted when dry, **oblong-lance-shaped**, broadly pointed; edges flat, with a few irregular teeth at the tip; midrib slender, ending near the tip; upper cells rounded, **strongly bulging and papillose**; lower cells long, smooth.

SPOROPHYTES: Not common, at the tip of the plant; stalks dark, upright, long; capsules brown, upright, smooth, shortly cylindrical; peristome single, of 16 teeth.

ECOLOGY: In wet or moist habitats, especially **wet stream-banks** (where the species grows **on rock surfaces),** **gravelly soils and moist crevices**; common from sea level to the alpine, prefers slightly basic substrates.

NOTES: When compared to other small, acrocarpous mosses, **wet rock moss** has **broader** leaves and **bulging**, papillose cells that **protrude** noticeably at the upper edges of the leaves. *Barbula* species can be generally similar to wet rock moss, but they have either **densely papillose** upper leaf cells or leaf edges that **roll under**. *Oncophorus* species occur in habitats similar to those of wet rock moss, but they have **smooth** upper leaf cells and **narrower**, lance-shaped leaves.

SILKY TUFTED MOSS • *Blindia acuta*

GENERAL: Plants small, **blackish**, forming **cushions or expanding into extensive mats**, about 1–5 (sometimes 10) cm high; stems upright, unbranched.

LEAVES: 2–3 mm long, stiffly upright when moist or dry, lance-shaped and gradually narrowed to a sharp, slender point; edges smooth; midrib strong, filling the extended tip; cells short; alar cells well developed and reddish.

SPOROPHYTES: Common, at the tip of the plant; stalks short, curved, slender; capsules shortly oblong to nearly spherical, smooth, **hanging on curved stalks**; peristome single, reddish, of 16 upright teeth.

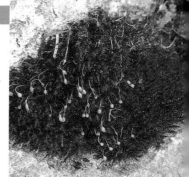

ECOLOGY: Restricted to wet, acidic rock surfaces, including **boulders at the edges of streams, cliff-faces**, even sometimes **submerged in waterfalls and fast running water**; from the coast into the alpine.

NOTES: Silky tufted moss is a **small, blackish** moss found **on acidic rocks**. It has **conspicuously curved** stalks when wet or dry and **short, fat** capsules. It is closely related to the smallest of all mosses in our region: species of the genus *Seligeria*. These species are **no more than 1 mm high** with stalks 2–3 mm long, and they occur **exclusively on calcium-rich rock**.

DUSKY FORK MOSS • *Dicranum fuscescens*
CURLY HERON'S-BILL MOSS

GENERAL: Plants medium-sized, **olive-green**, forming **large, loose cushions or mats**, 1–6 cm high; stems upright, unbranched or occasionally branched, **covered by whitish hairs**.

LEAVES: 4–10 mm long, **loosely upright and sickle-shaped to strongly curved to 1 side and twisted when dry**, straighter and more-spreading when moist, narrowly lance-shaped, sharp-pointed, the upper portion V-shaped in cross-section; edges toothed towards the tip; midrib extending to the tip; upper cells indistinctly papillose, square; lower cells smooth, long; alar cells well developed, reddish.

SPOROPHYTES: Common, at the tip of the plant; stalks single, green, upright, long; capsules inclined, somewhat asymmetric, smooth when young, becoming lightly 8 ribbed when old; peristome well developed, of 16 reddish inwardly curving teeth.

ECOLOGY: On rotting logs in rainforest extending to the subalpine; rarely on terrestrial or on rock surfaces; not common in peatlands.

NOTES: *Dicranum* species are conspicuous among forest mosses. They occur sporadically on forest litter, boulders, tree bases and trunks, logs and terrestrial sites. About 20 species of *Dicranum* are found in our region. **Dusky fork moss** is one of the smaller species; it has leaves that are **strongly curved to 1 side**, short upper leaf cells and **single stalks**. *D. polysetum* is larger with **transversely wrinkled** leaves. *D. scoparium* is also larger than *D. fuscescens* with long, **strongly pitted** upper leaf cells and **ridges on the back** of the midribs. • *D. fuscescens* and *D. scoparium* are the 2 most common coastal species of the genus.

BROOM MOSS • *Dicranum scoparium*

GENERAL: Plants upright, little branched, with a **densely matted covering of hairs** on lower stems, forming **large cushions** or **mats**, 2–8 cm high.

LEAVES: 5–12 mm long, **contorted and upright to strongly curved to 1 side** moist or dry; lance-shaped and sharply pointed; midrib single, ending in the tip; **upper leaf cells longer than wide**, with irregularly thickened walls, becoming longer below; alar cells well developed, large, yellowish or brownish, forming a well-marked group.

SPOROPHYTES: Often present, growing at the tip of the plant; stalks single, straight, long; capsules curved, inclined, cylindrical, smooth; peristome single.

ECOLOGY: Common throughout our region **on tree bases, humus and logs** in lowland to montane forests; abundant in subalpine forests where it forms mats on logs and humus.

NOTES: Broom moss used to be known as *D. howellii*. • Medium to large, upright plants with leaves strongly curved to 1 side characterize the genus. *D. scoparium* has upper leaf cells that are **longer than wide** and 4 low, **longitudinal ridges** on the backs of the leaf midribs. Other common species of this genus have upper cells that are about as wide as long, except for *D. polysetum*, which has **wavy leaves**, and *D. majus*, which is larger, has **many sporophytes** and has **no ridges** on the backs of the leaf midribs. • Male plants of our common *Dicranum* species are just tiny buds on the leaves of female plants. This may combine the advantage of having the sexes on separate plants (outbreeding) with the advantage of having both sexes on the same plant (reproduction is more sure); it may explain why species of *Dicranum* are very commonly seen with sporophytes.

BLACK FISH HOOK MOSS • *Campylopus atrovirens*

GENERAL: Plants slender, **blackish-green to golden-brown**, forming **cushions and mounds** 1–5 cm high; stems upright, unbranched or occasionally branched, with scattered, **reddish, root-like filaments** along the stems.

LEAVES: 4–9 mm long, **upright moist or dry**, slender, lance-shaped, gradually narrowed to a fine point, **concave**, the tip usually clear; **midrib very broad**, extending nearly the entire width of the leaf; leaf blade restricted to basal area, cells short; alar cells well developed.

SPOROPHYTES: Not found in this area.

ECOLOGY: Restricted to **peaty mounds** in peatlands from the Fraser valley northwards.

NOTES: Although several other species of *Campylopus* occur along the west coast, all of which are characterized by **concave leaves** and extremely broad midribs, black fish hook moss is the **most common**. It occurs frequently in coastal **bogs and soligenous fens**, where the emergent, **turfy mounds** it forms are a good identifying feature.

COMMON BEARD MOSS • *Schistidium apocarpum*

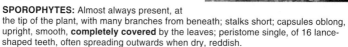

GENERAL: Plants small, **reddish-green**, forming **cushions or mats** on dry rocks; stems variable in length, from 0.2–8 cm.

LEAVES: Up to 2 mm long, spreading when moist, upright and pressed to the stem when dry, broadly lance-shaped, ending in a sharp point, usually with a **short, clear bristle-point**; edges rolled under, smooth; upper cells rounded, thick-walled, smooth; lower cells longer, otherwise similar.

SPOROPHYTES: Almost always present, at the tip of the plant, with many branches from beneath; stalks short; capsules oblong, upright, smooth, **completely covered** by the leaves; peristome single, of 16 lance-shaped teeth, often spreading outwards when dry, reddish.

ECOLOGY: On dry rock surfaces, cliff-faces, roadcuts, boulders, and walls that are often calcium-rich; at all elevations.

NOTES: Common beard moss is the **most common** member of the *Grimmia* complex of genera. Some books place it in the genus *Grimmia*. • These small, reddish to blackish-green plants forming cushions on dry rocks have, as characteristic features, rather broad **leaves** ending in **short, clear bristle-points** and **completely covered**, smooth capsules with **well-developed peristomes**. Species of *Grimmia* have **clear leaf bristle-points**, but they either have **projecting capsules** or, if the capsules are completely covered, they have **no peristome**. *Racomitrium* species are **much larger** than *Grimmia* species, while **rock-growing** *Orthotrichum* species **never** have clear leaf bristle-points. Another species of this genus, *S. rivulare*, can be very similar, but it occurs on **periodically wet rocks** and has leaves that **do not** have clear bristle-points.

STREAMSIDE MOSS • *Scouleria aquatica*

GENERAL: Plants **black to greenish-black, coarse, robust, highly branched**, forming **mats at water level**; stems up to 15 cm long.

LEAVES: 3–5 mm long, **spreading at right angles** when moist, upright and pressed to the stem when dry, broadly elliptic to oblong, **bluntly pointed; edges rolled under** towards the base of the leaf and **strongly toothed towards the tip**; midrib strong, single, ending just below the tip; leaf cells small, rounded and indistinct.

SPOROPHYTES: Occasionally present, at the tip of the plant, with many branches growing below; stalks very short; capsules completely covered by the leaves, spherical, black, with an expanded fist-like central axis (columella); **no peristome**.

ECOLOGY: A characteristic moss of the **splash zone of fast-flowing** lowland and montane **streams**; most abundant along the coast, but also common in the interior.

NOTES: The **large blackish plants** and **splash-zone habitat** are characteristics that easily distinguish **streamside moss**. As the water level goes down, this species shows up. • *Schistidium rivulare* can be confused with streamside moss, but it is **smaller** and has leaves with edges that are **rolled under** and **smooth** to near the tip and a capsule **with a peristome**. *Racomitrium aciculare* is also somewhat similar, but it has leaves with wavy cells and **broad, toothed tips** that are less strongly spreading when moist. • **Streamside moss** forms extensive, **black mats just above high water** where it is constantly washed by wave action.

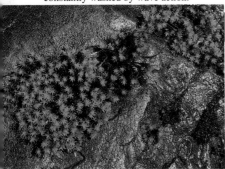

BLACK-TUFTED ROCK MOSS • *Racomitrium aciculare*

GENERAL: Plants **blackish below, dark green to light green above**, forming **cushions and tufts**; stems upright to ascending, unbranched or nearly so, 2–5 cm long.

LEAVES: 1.5–3.5 mm long, strongly **spreading** and curved backwards when moist, upright and pressed to the stem when dry, oblong, **blunt, with widely spaced, blunt teeth across the tip; edges flat**; midrib strong, ending just below the tip; upper cells small, thick walled, rounded.

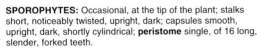

SPOROPHYTES: Occasional, at the tip of the plant; stalks short, noticeably twisted, upright, dark; capsules smooth, upright, dark, shortly cylindrical; **peristome** single, of 16 long, slender, forked teeth.

ECOLOGY: On wet rocks, especially where periodically wet; common at low and middle elevations along the coast.

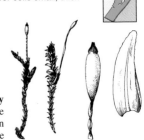

NOTES: All **other species of *Racomitrium*** have **narrowly pointed or bristle-tipped** leaves. *Scouleria* species are **larger** and have leaves that **spread at right angles** when moist. • Black-tufted rock moss often occurs with streamside moss and *Schistidium rivulare*. These mosses are all restricted to sites that are wet by splashing water and completely dry at times when water levels are low.

ROADSIDE ROCK MOSS • *Racomitrium canescens*

GENERAL: **Woolly mats** that are **yellow-green when moist** but become **whitish-green upon drying**, with **many side branches**; stems 2–8 cm long.

LEAVES: 1.8–3.0 mm long, wide-spreading when moist, irregularly upright-twisted when dry, broadly **lance-shaped and ending in a short, clear bristle-tip**; edges rolled under; upper cells shortly oblong, strongly papillose; lower cells similar but longer.

SPOROPHYTES: Often present, at the tip of the plant, associated with additional branching; stalks long, twisted, reddish; capsules cylindrical, upright, smooth, dark; peristome single, of 16 teeth divided into 32 filaments.

ECOLOGY: One of the most common terrestrial mosses in our region; forms **extensive mats along roadsides, on roofs and in open, exposed areas**, especially on acid substrates at lower elevations; generally not found in shaded areas but can occur at the edges of forests, on boulders, and on non-shaded cliff-faces along streams; also terrestrial at higher elevations into the tundra zone.

NOTES: **Yellow-green carpets** seen from the car while travelling are most often **roadside rock moss**. The many branches with **uniformly papillose** leaf cells distinguish it from such species as **hoary rock moss**, which has **smooth cells beneath a papillose, clear bristle-point**.

HOARY ROCK MOSS • *Racomitrium lanuginosum*

GENERAL: Plants **whitish-hoary or greyish-green** in appearance, rough, **irregularly branched**, upright to ascending; stems 4–12 cm long.

LEAVES: 3–4.5 mm long, widely spreading when moist, loosely pressed to the stem when dry, **narrowly lance-shaped and slenderly pointed**; midrib strong, single; cells near the tip of the leaf **clear, coarsely papillose**; upper leaf cells green, smooth, with wavy walls, oblong to elongate, similar but longer below.

SPOROPHYTES: Occasionally present, at the tip of the plant, with many branches arising below, thus seemingly from the side of the stem; stalks relatively short, contorted; capsules upright, smooth, projecting well above the leaves; peristome single, of 16 long filaments.

ECOLOGY: Forming **large, whitish-green cushions on acidic rocks**; occasionally in peatlands and even epiphytic at higher elevations; common in dry alpine tundra inland, but **at all elevations** near the coast.

NOTES: The distinctive features of **hoary rock moss** include the **whitish or greyish cast** and leaves with papillose, col-ourless, **transparent bristle-tips** strongly contrasting to smooth, green lower cells. The colourless, transparent bristle-points are sometimes re-duced in plants from higher-elevation peatlands. Other similar species include **roadside rock moss** (which has a **yellow-green** cast and **all leaf cells papillose**) and *Hedwigia ciliata* (which has leaves **lacking a midrib**). Species of *Grimmia* often have leaves with colourless, transparent points, but these species are **smaller** and form **tighter** cushions on dry rocks. • *Lanuginosum* means softly hairy, woolly or cottony and refers to the long, white leaf tips that give the plant a distinctive cottony appearance.

Introduction

More than a thousand different kinds of lichens make their home in Washington, Oregon, B.C. and Alaska. Only a few hundred of these, however, are widespread and conspicuous. In coastal regions, the richest habitats for lichens include rocky headlands, ventilated forests and the alpine. Old-growth forests also appear to be important to many species.

Lichens are the banners of the fungal kingdom. Think of them as fungi that have discovered agriculture. Instead of invading or scavenging for a living like other fungi—moulds, mildews, mushrooms—lichen fungi cultivate algae within themselves. Algae are photosynthesizers, and so can supply the fungus with carbohydrates, vitamins and proteins. In return the fungus appears to provide the alga with protection from the elements. A lichen is the physical manifestation of this relationship, much as a gall is the manifestation of, for example, a larval insect feeding on a leaf.

While most lichen fungi cultivate green algae, in some cases the photosynthesizer (photobiont) is actually a cyanobacterium (blue-green 'alga'). In a few lichen species, both types of photobionts are present: the paler green algae scattered throughout and the darker, blue-green cyanobacteria localized in small colonies called '**cephalodia**.'

Lichens reproduce in several ways. Sometimes the fungal partner produces saucer-like fruiting bodies (**apothecia**). Sometimes the inner 'stuffing' (**medulla**) of the lichen may become exposed here and there at the surface as clusters of tiny, powdery balls (**soredia**). In other cases the upper surface may bear tiny, wart-like outgrowths (**isidia**). When soredia or isidia are carried to new localities, by birds for example, they may grow into new lichens.

Lichen Life Forms

Lichens come in many different shapes, but they never form leafy stems as mosses do. The following account includes 7 growth forms: dust, crust, scale, leaf, club, shrub and hair.

Dust: Intimately attached; composed entirely of tiny, powdery granules.

Crust: Intimately attached; lower surface absent; hard upper surface present.

Scale: Tiny, shell-like lobes with a cottony lower surface; forming overlapping colonies.

Leaf: Small to large leaf-like or strap-like lobes, usually with holdfasts and a hard (non-cottony) lower surface.

Club: Unbranched or sparsely branched cylindrical stems, usually upright.

Shrub: Much-branched, cylindrical stems, usually tufted.

Hair: Intricately branched filaments, tufted to hanging.

DUST LICHENS • *Lepraria* species

GENERAL: Continuous dust lichens, consisting of **whitish, greenish, bluish or greyish** powdery granules; fruiting bodies absent (**photograph shows *Lepraria incana***).

HABITAT: On shaded, sheltered bark, wood or vertical rock outcrops in humid sites; common.

NOTES: Though dust lichens are easy to recognize as a group, telling them apart can be difficult and may involve

the use of thin-layer chromatography. The genus *Lepraria* has not been critically studied in North America, and it appears to contain several species as yet undescribed and unnamed. Most

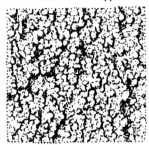

dust lichens do not produce fruiting bodies; reproduction occurs entirely through the dissemination of the powdery granules. They tend to grow in habitats sheltered from the rain, deriving moisture directly from the air. • *Lepraria* is from the Latin meaning 'dry scurf,' and it is related etymologically to the word leprosy.

SEA TAR • *Verrucaria maura*

GENERAL: A thin, **continuous** (or sometimes finely discontinuous) **crust** lichen; upper surface **black**, often finely cracked when dry (when viewed through a hand lens), and usually bearing scattered tiny, **black, pimple-like fruiting bodies** (perithecia); no white medulla.

HABITAT: Forming a black stain near **high tide line on seashore rocks**; common.

NOTES: Sea tar is easily recognized, at least to genus, by its **habitat, colour** and **minute 'pimples.'** The pimples are ac-

tually tiny fruiting bodies: immersed, sac-like perithecia, each of which opens by a pore. Together with other similar *Verrucaria* species, sea tar forms the lowest of 3 or 4 conspicuous life zones on seaside rocks. Perched below the *Verrucaria*

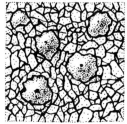

zone is the barnacle zone, and above it is either an orange *Caloplaca* zone or a whitish *Physcia* zone. • *Verrucaria* is from the Latin meaning 'wart,' and it refers to the pimple-like perithecia; *maura* is Greek and means 'dark' or 'obscure.'

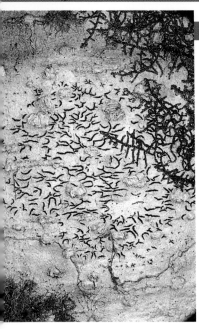

PENCIL SCRIPT • *Graphis scripta*

GENERAL: A **continuous crust** lichen; upper surface **pale whitish-grey**, smooth, bearing numerous **black hieroglyphic squiggles**.

HABITAT: On the smooth bark of deciduous trees and shrubs, especially alder, at lower elevations; common.

NOTES: The squiggles are diagnostic and represent an unusual form of fruiting body called a 'lirella.' If you examine the lirellae of lichens growing adjacent to a colony of pencil script, you will probably notice that some of them are **shorter, thicker and blunter** than the rest. These belong to various members of the genus *Opegrapha*. • This species has been identified from prehistoric amber, dating from 70 to 25 million years ago. • *Graphis scripta* means 'written drawing.' We think you get the picture.

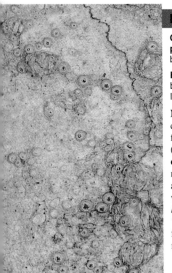

BARK BARNACLE • *Thelotrema lepadinum*

GENERAL: A **continuous crust** lichen; upper surface **pale whitish-grey**, thin, smooth to minutely warty, bearing numerous **barnacle-like fruiting bodies**.

HABITAT: On smooth-barked trees, especially alder, but also conifers, in open to shady, humid forests at lower elevations; common.

NOTES: If coastal rocks have barnacles, why not coastal trees? The bark barnacle is unlikely to be confused with any other lichen: each of its fruiting bodies (apothecia) is contained in a **2-layered blister that opens by a pore**. • In Europe, lichens growing on human skulls were once valued at their weight in gold as a remedy for epilepsy. • *Thelotrema* is from the Greek words meaning 'perforated nipple'; *lepadinum* is also Greek and means 'pertaining to limpets,' although the fruiting bodies of this species bear a much closer resemblance to barnacles.

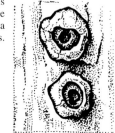

BULL'S-EYE • *Placopsis gelida*

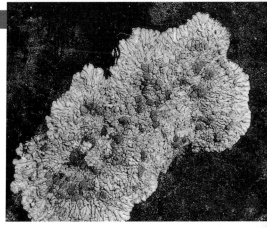

GENERAL: A small, disc-shaped, **lobed crust** lichen, 20–50 mm broad; upper surface **whitish-grey** or greenish-grey, often somewhat roughened, bearing **tiny, powdery balls (soredia)**, also bearing **fleshy pink 'warts' (cephalodia) and saucer-like fruiting bodies (apothecia)**.

HABITAT: On sloping rock surfaces in open sites at lower elevations; best developed over freshly exposed rock in humid localities; common.

NOTES: The bull's-eye can hardly be confused with any other lichen. It might perhaps be mistaken at first for a leaf lichen, because of its marginal lobes, but bull's-eye **grows tightly** against the substrate; it has **no lower surface**. • *Placopsis* is Greek for 'resembling a flat round plate'—which this lichen most certainly does. *Gelida* is Latin and means 'frosty,' perhaps referring to this lichen's pale upper surface.

CLADONIA SCALES • *Cladonia* species

GENERAL: Small to medium-sized scale lichens; lobes **tiny**, about 0.5–5 mm wide, usually tightly massed and **overlapping**; upper surface **greenish or greyish**, occasionally giving rise to upright hollow stalks (podetia).

HABITAT: On soil, moss, decaying logs and the bases of trees at all elevations; common.

NOTES: In coastal regions, cladonia scales are by far the most conspicuous of scale lichens. They are easily recognized by their **white lower surface** which, because the scales are curved upward around the edges, is usually **plainly visible** from above; this is true of no other scale lichens. • Though easy to recognize as a group, the cladonia scales are notoriously difficult to identify to species. Still, it can be 'fun' trying (consult a technical manual such as Thomson 1967). Characteristics to watch for are colour, size, lobation and the presence of tiny, powdery balls (soredia) on the surface.

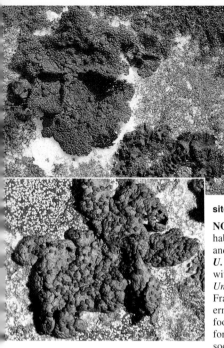

PUNCTURED ROCKTRIPE • *Umbilicaria torrefacta*

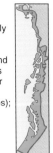

GENERAL: A medium-sized, **circular, few-lobed leaf** lichen, 15–40 mm across, attached centrally by a **single holdfast** (umbilicus); upper surface **dark brown,** apparently chinky-cracked, abundantly and **minutely perforate** toward margins (best viewed against the sky); lower surface brown or blackish, often in part platy, lacking holdfasts (rhizines); fruiting bodies (apothecia) often present, much-fissured.

HABITAT: On acid outcrops and boulder-beds in exposed, open sites at lower and middle elevations; frequent.

NOTES: *U. hyperborea* (inset photo) is similar in habit and ecology, but it has a **pimply upper surface** and **lacks** the **tiny perforations** of *U. torrefacta*. *U. deusta* has **minute wart-like outgrowths** (visible with a hand lens) **over its upper surface**. • The *Umbilicaria*s or 'rocktripes' were used by Sir John Franklin and other early northern explorers as an emergency food. They are best prepared for this purpose by soaking in soda water to remove acids

which can cause severe intestinal discomfort. Parboiling with an old pair of hiking boots might improve the flavour. • Rocktripes are a source of scarlet dyes. Known in Scotland as *corkir*, these dyes were once used for dyeing tartan cloth.

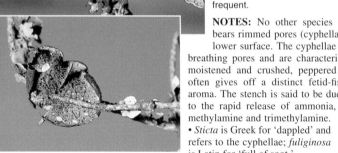

PEPPERED MOON • *Sticta fuliginosa*

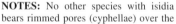

GENERAL: A small, **loosely attached, roundish leaf** lichen, 30–70 mm across, broadly attached; upper surface **brownish to blackish,** bearing numerous **tiny wart-like outgrowths (isidia),** otherwise smooth to weakly wrinkled; **lower surface pale brownish,** weakly wrinkled, pitted with scattered **rimmed pores** (cyphellae).

HABITAT: On conifers and mossy acid rock in humid forests at lower elevations; frequent.

NOTES: No other species with isidia bears rimmed pores (cyphellae) over the lower surface. The cyphellae apparently function as breathing pores and are characteristic of *Sticta*. • When moistened and crushed, peppered moon often gives off a distinct fetid-fish aroma. The stench is said to be due to the rapid release of ammonia, methylamine and trimethylamine. • *Sticta* is Greek for 'dappled' and refers to the cyphellae; *fuliginosa* is Latin for 'full of soot.'

LETTUCE LUNG • *Lobaria oregana*

GENERAL: A large, **loosely attached leaf** lichen; lobes **broad**, 20–35 mm wide; upper surface **yellowish-green**, strongly ridged, **deeply indented between the ridges, no soredia or isidia**; lobe margins frilly; lower surface pale brownish and finely hairy, except with scattered **pale, yellowish, naked** patches.

HABITAT: On trees in cool, humid forests, especially at middle elevations; restricted primarily to old-growth forests; still common, but going fast in many parts of its range.

NOTES: Lettuce lung might be confused with *L. pulmonaria*; that species, however, bears **soredia** and is **not at all yellowish**. *L. oregana* is a lichen of cool places; its strong association with coastal old-growth forests throughout much of its range is thought to reflect a sensitivity to temperatures higher than about 15°C, especially when moist. • Recent research suggests that this nitrogen-fixing lichen is important in the nutrition of some forest ecosystems. • Lettuce lung was used in a medicinal preparation by the Hesquiat to treat the coughing up of blood. • *Lobaria* is Latin meaning 'lobed.'

LUNGWORT • *Lobaria pulmonaria*

GENERAL: A large, **loosely attached leaf** lichen; lobes broad, 20–30 mm wide; upper surface **pale bluish-green (bright green when moist)**, strongly ridged, **deeply indented between the ridges**, bearing **tiny, powdery balls (soredia) or tiny, wart-like outgrowths (isidia)** along the ridges and lobe margins; lower surface brownish and finely hairy, with scattered **whitish, naked** patches.

HABITAT: On trees in humid forests, both coniferous and deciduous, at lower elevations; common.

NOTES: *L. linita* is similar to *L. pulmonaria*, but it **lacks soredia and isidia** and occurs **primarily over mossy rocks at upper elevations**; in very humid climates it may also colonize

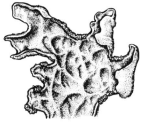

the trunks of trees down to sea level. • Lungwort was used by early European physicians in the treatment of pneumonia and other lung diseases, on the basis of its resemblance to that part of the body. It was also used in a similar way, for different reasons, by the Sechelt people. • As a rhyming scientific name in our region, *Lobaria pulmonaria* is second only to *Chrysanthemum leucanthemum*.

FRECKLE PELT • *Peltigera britannica*

GENERAL: A large, **loosely appressed leaf** lichen; lobes **broad**, 20–50 mm wide; upper surface **pale greyish-green** (dry) **to bright green** (moist), bearing scattered **'warts'** (cephalodia), and often bearing erect, flattened brown fruiting bodies (apothecia); lower surface without veins or with only broad, **inconspicuous veins**, cottony, blackening abruptly inward of lobe margins; holdfasts (rhizines) scarce.

HABITAT: On moss, humus, rocks and decaying logs in open forests at lower and middle elevations; rarely on trees; common.

NOTES: Freckle pelt is often mistaken for *P. aphthosa*, but that species is rare in coastal localities. *P. aphthosa* has **tightly appressed** cephalodia, whereas in *P. britannica* the cephalodia are **loosely appressed** and can be **readily dislodged** with the flick of a fingernail. *P. leucophlebia* is also similar

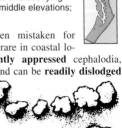

to freckle pelt, but it has well-developed veins that **darken gradually inward**. • In humid habitats, the green lobes of this species are occasionally found growing intermixed with blue-grey lobes. These are outgrowths of the cephalodia, which in turn are colonies of cyanobacteria. The cephalodia supply the lichen fungus and its green-algal partner with nitrogen.

FROG PELT • *Peltigera neopolydactyla*

GENERAL: A large, **loosely appressed leaf** lichen; lobes **broad**, 10–25 mm wide; upper surface **hairless**, olive-green to pale or dark **bluish-grey**, lacking cephalodia, often bearing **brownish, tooth-like fruiting bodies** (apothecia) on raised lobes along the lobe margins; lower surface whitish, **cottony**, bearing low, broad, brownish or blackish veins and **long, slender holdfasts** (rhizines).

HABITAT: On rock, moss, soil and logs in open to shady forests at all forested elevations; common.

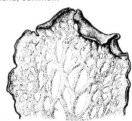

NOTES: The frog pelt's **broad** lobes, **naked** upper surface, **veins** and **long, slender rhizines** are distinctive; this species is unlikely to be confused with any other lichen except, perhaps, *P. pacifica* and *P. polydactylon*—both of which have **frilly** lobe margins. • Frog pelt comes in 3 colours: olive-green, milky blue and dark slate-blue. No explanation for this colour variation has yet been proposed, but it is possible that different races may be involved. • The Gitksan word for this and other similar lichens translates into English as 'frog's blanket.' • The *Peltigeras* are among the most conspicuous ground-dwelling lichens; nowhere are they more varied than in our region, home to at least 27 species.

SEASIDE KIDNEY • *Nephroma laevigatum*

GENERAL: A medium-sized, **loosely appressed leaf** lichen; lobes **broad**, 4–8 mm wide; upper surface **olive-brown to blackish-brown**, smooth, hairless, somewhat shiny; **inner portions (medulla) yellow or orange**; lower surface smooth or weakly wrinkled, hairless, pale brownish-orange; **fruiting bodies** common, brown, **positioned on the lower surface**.

HABITAT: On acid rock, especially in open, seaside sites; frequent.

NOTES: Only in *Nephroma* are the fruiting bodies (apothecia) located over the lower surface. And only in **seaside kidney**, among the *Nephroma* species occurring in our region, is the **medulla yellowish or orange**. • This species has a blue-green photobiont, and it is therefore probably an important contributor of nitrogen to its immediate environment. • *Nephroma* is from the Greek meaning 'sick kidney'; *laevigatum* is from the Latin meaning 'smooth.'

PIMPLED KIDNEY • *Nephroma resupinatum*

GENERAL: A medium-sized, **loosely appressed leaf** lichen; lobes **broad**, 5–10 mm wide; upper surface **brownish-grey**, smooth, minutely hairy toward the margins; inner portions (medulla) white; **lower surface minutely hairy**, pale creamy to brownish, bearing **sparse, naked protuberances** (papillae); **fruiting bodies** (apothecia) common, brown, **located on the lower surface**.

HABITAT: On trees and mossy rocks in open to somewhat shady forests; frequent.

NOTES: Just what physiological function, if any, pimpled kidney's protuberances perform is uncertain, but they do help to identify the species. *N. helveticum* is somewhat similar, but it has **frilly** lobe margins and **lacks protuberances** (papillae) over the lower surface. • *Resupinatum* is from the Latin meaning 'bent back,' and it may refer to the apothecia. Though located on the lower surface, they are often somewhat curved upward, making them visible from above.

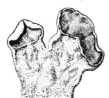

491

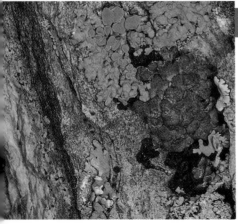

PINCUSHION ORANGE
CUSHION ORANGE • *Xanthoria polycarpa*

GENERAL: A small, **loosely appressed leaf** lichen, forming small, **loose, disc-shaped 'pincushions'**; lobes very narrow, about 0.2–0.3 mm wide; upper surface pale orange or **bright orange**, bearing **numerous orange fruiting bodies** (apothecia).

HABITAT: On **deciduous trees and shrubs** in open sites, also occasionally on conifers; at lower elevations; common.

NOTES: The lichen we find in our region is not typical of *X. polycarpa* in all regards, and it may represent a separate species. Another tiny orange lichen, *X. candelaria*, will often be found growing with *X. polycarpa*; its **lobes are upright** and they **terminate** in tiny, powdery balls (**soredia**) or tiny, wart-like outgrowths (**isidia**). • These and other *Xanthoria* species require large quantities of calcium or nitrogen, and they therefore often grow on or near bird droppings. • *Xanthoria* is a mix of Greek and Latin and means 'pertaining to the colour yellow.'

QUESTIONABLE ROCK-FROG • *Xanthoparmelia cumberlandia*

GENERAL: A medium-sized or large, disc-shaped, **loosely appressed leaf** lichen; lobes proportionately rather broad, 1–4 mm wide; upper surface **pale yellowish-green**, shiny, **lacking soredia and isidia**, often bearing fruiting bodies (apothecia); lower surface pale brown, bearing numerous holdfasts (rhizines).

HABITAT: On rock in open outcrops and boulder-beds, mostly at lower elevations; common.

NOTES: Questionable rock-frog is unique among coastal rock-dwelling lichens in being **appressed** and **yellowish** and in **lacking soredia**. • *Xanthoparmelia* is an enormous genus consisting of more than 400 species worldwide. It is best represented in arid regions, especially the American southwest; only 2 or 3 species are known to occur along the Pacific coast. Although *Xanthoparmelia* is still sometimes included in *Parmelia*, it is apparently not closely related to that genus.

The Rag Lichens (*Platismatia*)

The north Pacific is unusually rich in rag lichens. Of the 5 species occurring here, 3 (*P. herrei*, *P. lacunosa* and *P. stenophylla*) are found nowhere else. These sizeable leaf lichens are sure to catch the eye.

Key to *Platismatia*

1a. Lobes narrow, averaging 1–3 (sometimes 5) mm wide, elongate; upper surface smooth to weakly wrinkled 2

    2a. Isidia present along lobe margins; fruiting bodies (apothecia) usually absent .... *P. herrei*

    2b. Isidia absent; fruiting bodies usually present .... *P. stenophylla (see P. herrei)*

1b. Lobes broader, averaging 6–15 mm wide, short; upper surface smooth to strikingly ridged.. 3

    3a. Lobe margins more or less frilly (lacerate); upper surface smooth to occasionally broadly wrinkled; isidia, if present, irregularly scattered (i.e. not necessarily confined to ridges or lobe margins) .... *P. glauca*

    3b. Lobe margins more or less even; upper surface generally becoming deeply wrinkled or ridged; isidia, if present, restricted to ridges or lobe margins 4

        4a. Upper surface strikingly net-ridged, the spaces between the ridges deep and often bowl-like; isidia absent (or rarely present) along the margins; restricted to very humid climates .... *P. lacunosa* (see *P. norvegica*)

        4b. Upper surface weakly to rather strongly net-ridged, the spaces between the ridges remaining shallow and saucer-like; isidia often abundant and located both over the ridges of the upper surface and along the lobe margins; widespread .... *P. norvegica*

TATTERED RAG • *Platismatia herrei*

GENERAL: A medium-sized, **loosely attached leaf** lichen; lobes **narrow, 1–2 (sometimes 4) mm wide**, **pale bluish-green** to **whitish-grey** above, the margins often frilly and always in part lined with **tiny, wart-like outgrowths (isidia)**; lower surface white to black, **shiny**, typically **lacking holdfasts** (rhizines).

HABITAT: On trees, especially Douglas-fir, in open, humid forests at lower elevations; common.

NOTES: *P. stenophylla* is similar in general appearance to *P. herrei*, but it has **smooth, 'clean' lobe margins** and **lacks isidia.** It is less common and less widespread than *P. herrei*, occurring north only to Vancouver Island. *Cetraria chlorophylla*, though **brownish**, is also similar to *P. herrei*, but it bears tiny, powdery balls (**soredia**), not isidia, along the lobe margins. • *Platismatia* is Greek and means 'plate-like,' while *herrei* commemorates the astonishing Californian ichthyologist and lichenologist, Albert William Christian Theodore Herre (1868–1962).

RAGBAG • *Platismatia glauca*

GENERAL: A large, **loosely attached leaf** lichen; lobes **broad, 10–20 mm wide**, pale bluish-green to whitish-grey above, the margins often frilly and bearing tiny, powdery balls (soredia) or tiny, wart-like outgrowths (isidia); lower surface white to black, **shiny**, typically **lacking holdfasts** (rhizines).

HABITAT: On trees in open and shady forests alike, occurring at all forested elevations; common.

NOTES: Ragbag is a bewilderingly variable species. It also has a broad distribution, occurring on every continent except Antarctica. Both these facts suggest that the ragbag may be of great evolutionary age. • As the common name implies, some forms have a very tattered appearance. *Glauca* is Greek and means 'silvery,' 'gleaming,' or 'bluish-green'—all appropriate descriptors for this species.

LAUNDERED RAG • *Platismatia norvegica*

GENERAL: A large, **loosely attached leaf** lichen; lobes broad, **10–20 mm wide**, pale bluish-green to whitish-grey above; upper surface more or less net-ridged, the ridges bearing minute white flecks (pseudocyphellae) and tiny, wart-like outgrowths (isidia); **lobe margins not frilly, lacking isidia**; lower surface white to black, shiny, typically **lacking holdfasts** (rhizines).

HABITAT: On trees in open and shady forests alike, restricted to humid regions at lower elevations; common.

NOTES: Laundered rag is similar to ragbag, but it has a **much more-wrinkled upper surface**. Also similar to laundered rag is *P. lacunosa*, an elegant lichen restricted to highly oceanic climates that can be distinguished by the **much-deeper, bowl-like indentations** that pock its upper surface. • The species name *norvegica* means 'Norwegian,' and it says something about this species' global distribution.

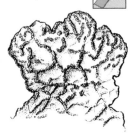

FORKING BONE • *Hypogymnia inactiva*

GENERAL: A medium-sized, **semi-upright (or occasionally hanging) leaf** lichen; lobes narrow, **1–2 mm wide**, regularly forking, **hollow**, the interior of the lobes **dark** (check upper portions), **soredia absent**; upper surface pale greyish to pale greenish; lower surface black, lacking holdfasts (rhizines).

HABITAT: On conifers in open forests at lower elevations throughout our region; common.

NOTES: Forking bone can be easily mistaken for forking tube lichen (*H. imshaugii*); in *H. imshaugii,* however, the interiors of the lobes are **white** (check upper portions). Forking bone and forking tube lichen are both restricted to western North America. • *Hypogymnia* is from the Greek meaning 'naked bottom,' in reference to the absence of

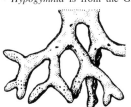

holdfasts (rhizines) in this genus. The epithet *inactiva* was applied to this species not because it is less industrious than other *Hypogymnia*s, but because it lacks the reactive chemical profile of closely related species.

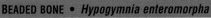

BEADED BONE • *Hypogymnia enteromorpha*

GENERAL: A medium-sized, **hanging leaf** lichen; lobes narrow, **2–5 mm wide**, the longest ones **weakly constricted at intervals**, irregularly or regularly branching, **hollow**, the interior of the lobes **dark** (check upper portions), **soredia absent**; upper surface pale greyish to pale greenish; lower surface black, lacking holdfasts (rhizines).

HABITAT: On conifers in open and shady forests at all forested elevations; common.

NOTES: The **lobe constrictions** are diagnostic, but they are often restricted to well-developed lobes. Until a few years ago, the name *H. enteromorpha* was routinely applied to as many as 9 different *Hypogymnia*s, including *H. inactiva*. • Checking the lobe tips of beaded treepipe with a hand lens will reveal tiny openings into the central cavity; these are probably breathing pores. • *Enteromorpha* is Greek and means 'intestine-shaped'; it refers to both the elongate, hollow lobes and the constrictions.

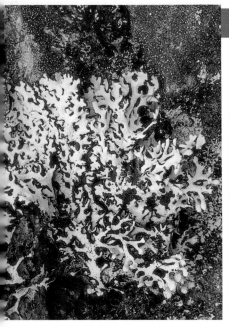

HOODED BONE • *Hypogymnia physodes*
HOODED TUBE LICHEN

GENERAL: A medium-sized, **appressed leaf** lichen; lobes narrow, 1–2 mm wide, **hollow, the interior of the lobes pale (check upper portions), bearing tiny, powdery balls (soredia) on the insides of burst lobe tips**; upper surface pale greyish to pale greenish; lower surface black, without holdfasts (rhizines).

HABITAT: On trees, moss and boulders in open to somewhat shaded sites at all forested elevations; common.

NOTES: *H. vittata* is similar to *H. physodes*, but it is usually somewhat **brownish**, and has a **dark**, rather than pale, central cavity (check upper portions). Also somewhat similar to these species is *H. tubulosa*, in which, however, the **soredia are located externally over the tips of the lobes**. Both species are much less common than hooded bone. • Among the most pollution-tolerant of the macrolichens, hooded bone is a familiar species of city parks and boulevards. • *Physodes* is from Greek and means 'inflated-looking' or 'puffed out.'

TICKERTAPE BONE • *Hypogymnia duplicata*

GENERAL: A medium-sized, **hanging leaf** lichen; lobes narrow, 1–2 mm wide, **hollow, the interior of the lobes pale (check upper portions), the lobe tips somewhat upturned**; upper surface whitish; lower surface black, without holdfasts (rhizines); soredia absent.

HABITAT: On trees and shrubs, especially conifers, in open, usually coastal localities at lower elevations; common.

NOTES: *H. duplicata*'s long, narrow, pendent, upturned lobes are distinctive. Some forms of *H. heterophylla* may be similar, but in that species the interiors of the lobes are **dark**, not pale, and the lobes themselves bear **numerous side-branches**. Tickertape bone is more common north of the Canadian border, while *H. heterophylla* occurs primarily in Washington, Oregon and California, seldom extending inland more than a few hundred metres from the coast. • *Duplicata* is Latin and means 'doubled.'

WAXPAPER LICHEN • *Parmelia sulcata*

GENERAL: A medium-sized, **loosely appressed leaf** lichen; lobes narrow, 1–3 mm wide; upper surface **pale greyish**, bearing **tiny, powdery balls (soredia) in long narrow cracks;** lower surface black and with numerous black holdfasts (rhizines).

HABITAT: On trees and (occasionally) rock in open or somewhat shaded sites at all forested elevations; common.

NOTES: *P. saxatilis* is similar to waxpaper lichen, but it produces tiny, **wart-like outgrowths (isidia)**, not soredia, and it is **more common on rock**. • Waxpaper lichen has long been used by north Europeans and Canadian Inuit as a natural dye, yielding a variety of hues, from yellowish-brown to dark or even rusty brown. Brown dyes from *Parmelia* species were called *crottle* by the Scots. • This species is commonly used by rufous hummingbirds to decorate and thereby camouflage their nests.

HOODED ROSETTE • *Physcia adscendens*

GENERAL: A small, **loosely appressed leaf** lichen; lobes narrow, to 0.5–1 mm wide, terminating in **hood-shaped swellings** bearing **tiny, powdery balls (soredia)** (visible with a hand lens); upper surface **pale greyish**, dull, with small white spots; lobe margins clothed with **long, slender 'eyelashes' (cilia);** lower surface white.

HABITAT: On deciduous trees and shrubs in open or somewhat shady sites at low elevations; common.

NOTES: Only *P. adscendens*, *Hypogymnia physodes* and *H. vittata* have **hood-shaped lobe tips**. In the 2 *Hypogymnia* species, however, the lobes are **hollow**, the lower surface is **black** and there are **no cilia**. The closely related *P. tenella* is also similar to hooded rosette, but it **lacks the hood**. • Recent studies have shown that the algal partners in the soredia of various *Physcia* species are sometimes commandeered by the germinating spores of other lichens, especially *Xanthoria*. • *Physcia* is from the Greek meaning 'sausage,' blister' or 'the large intestine.' Why? Your guess is as good as ours.

ANTLERED PERFUME • *Evernia prunastri*

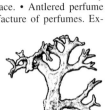

GENERAL: A medium-sized, **semi-erect or somewhat hanging leaf** lichen; lobes **elongate**, 1–4 mm wide, **divergently branching**; upper surface **pale greenish**, dull, **soft**, often weakly striate; lobe margins bearing **tiny, powdery balls (soredia); inner portions (medulla) loose and cottony**; lower surface whitish-green, lacking holdfasts (rhizines).

HABITAT: On deciduous and coniferous trees and shrubs in open sites at lowland elevations; common.

NOTES: The **inset photo** shows the closely related **spruce moss** (*E. mesomorpha*). • Antlered perfume is apt to be confused with ***Ramalina farinacea***. That species, however, is **much more compact** and has a distinctly **tough, not soft**, upper surface. • Antlered perfume has been used since the 16th century in the manufacture of perfumes. Extracts of this lichen act as a fixative to keep the desired fragrance lingering in the desired spot for hours. • *Evernia* comes from the Greek word meaning 'sprouting well.' With a recorded growth rate in this species of only 2 mm/year, this name seems a trifle inappropriate. Stone and McCune (1990) give a method for determining age in *E. prunastri* based on branching patterns.

FISHNET • *Ramalina menziesii*

GENERAL: A large, **hanging leaf** lichen; lobes **elongate**, 0.2–15 mm wide, in part **net-like**; upper surface **pale greenish**, weakly shiny, **hard**; soredia absent; lower surface pale greenish, lacking holdfasts (rhizines).

HABITAT: On the branches of trees and shrubs in open sites at low elevations; though restricted to coastal localities in Canada and Alaska, this species is not uncommon in humid inland sites farther south.

NOTES: The **perforated, net-like lobes** of fishnet are **unique** among North American lichens. In suitable sites, it festoons the branches of trees from top to bottom. This is among the fastest-growing lichens; growth rates of up to 90 mm/year have been recorded, though the average is probably closer to 35 mm. • Fishnet is one of a small number of lichens restricted to western North America. More than half of the lichens of our region occur in appropriate habitats throughout the northern world. • *Ramalina* is Latin, meaning 'twiggy.'

SULPHUR STUBBLE • *Chaenotheca furfuracea*

GENERAL: A minute club lichen, **stubble-like**, arising from a **pale yellowish-green basal dust**; clubs (stalks) **1–2 mm** tall, **pale yellowish**, mostly unbranched, terminating in **tiny, powdery yellow or brown balls** (mazaedia).

HABITAT: On sheltered wood and rock faces, most common among the roots of fallen trees in shady sites; apparently restricted to lower elevations; frequent, but easily overlooked.

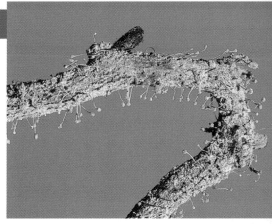

NOTES: Sulphur stubble is unlikely to be mistaken for any other species. It belongs to a distinctive group of lollipop-like lichens, the Caliciales. Though sulphur stubble itself is most common over freshly exposed roots, other Caliciales are typical of sheltered tree trunks, especially in old-growth forests, where they form delicate 'five-o'clock shadows.' • *Chaenotheca* is Greek and means 'chain box,' probably in reference to the fact that the spores in this genus are produced in loose, upwelling chains. (Gently rubbing the mazaedia with a forefinger results in a sooty smudge of spores). *Furfuracea* is from the Latin meaning 'covered in bran,' which makes this species a bran-name lichen.

DEVIL'S MATCHSTICK • *Pilophorus acicularis*

GENERAL: A medium-sized, **upright club** lichen, 10–30 mm tall, often arising from a thin, whitish crust; clubs (pseudopodetia) **clustered, whitish** to pale greenish, minutely roughened, mostly unbranched, terminating in **shiny black balls** (apothecia).

HABITAT: Over rock in cool, moist forests, often near waterfalls, at all forested elevations; common.

NOTES: Devil's matchstick is unmistakable. The related ***P. clavatus*** is somewhat similar, but it has **elongate, rather than ball-shaped, fruiting bodies. Both species are shown in the photo**. • Most lichens, when dry, are extraordinarily resistant to

cold. Even prolonged exposure (in the labratory) to temperatures as low as –196° C has proven harmless to some. On the other hand, many species are very sensitive to heat. • *Pilophorus* is Greek and means 'ball-bearing'; *acicularis* is Latin, meaning 'a small pin.'

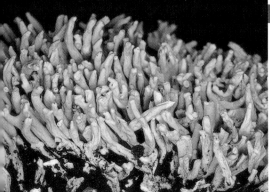

WATERWORM • *Siphula ceratites*

GENERAL: A medium-sized, **upright club** lichen, 10–30 mm tall, growing unattached; clubs (pseudopodetia) **clustered, white**, longitudinally furrowed, **solid, blunt-tipped, lacking fruiting bodies.**

HABITAT: Usually in standing water (or temporary pools) in **peatlands**, restricted to very humid climates at low to middle elevations.

NOTES: This extraordinary lichen can be confused only with ***Thamnolia vermicularis*** which, however, is **hollow**, not solid, and which is restricted to rather exposed sites, usually above treeline. Unlike most other lichens, which require wetting and drying at more or less frequent intervals, the waterworm withstands soaking for months at a time. • *Siphula* is probably derived from Latin and means 'a small tube'—a peculiar name for a solid lichen. *Ceratites* is Greek and means 'horn-like.'

LIPSTICK CLADONIA • *Cladonia macilenta*

GENERAL: A medium-sized, **upright club** lichen, 10–20 mm tall, arising from clusters of tiny grey basal scales (squamules); clubs (podetia) unbranched, **pale greyish**, hollow, **covered in tiny, powdery balls (soredia)**, often terminating in blunt or **pointed tips**, these often bearing **bright-red fruiting bodies** (apothecia).

HABITAT: On conifer bark and decaying wood, best developed close to the ground; restricted to lower elevations; common.

NOTES: Lipstick cladonia is one of several similar club-like *Cladonias*. The key points distinguishing *C. macilenta* are the **greyish colour**, the **powdery soredia** and the **red apothecia**. • Like most other members of its genus, lipstick cladonia originates as a cluster of tiny scales; only later are the fertile clubs (podetia) formed. • *Cladonia* is Greek and means 'club-like.' *Macilenta* is Latin and means 'thin' or 'lean,' which indeed this species is.

FALSE PIXIE CUP • *Cladonia chlorophaea*

GENERAL: A medium-sized, **upright club** lichen, 10–15 mm tall, arising from clusters of tiny, grey basal scales (squamules); clubs (podetia) unbranched, **pale greenish**, hollow, **covered in powdery or somewhat granular soredia**, terminating in **flaring cups**, these occasionally ringed with brown fruiting bodies (apothecia).

HABITAT: On acid mineral soil, moss and humus, especially in open sites, at all elevations; sometimes on tree bases; common.

NOTES: *C. chlorophaea* has many variants and chemical strains, some of which can be recognized as distinct species. The most common of these in coastal localities is *C. asahinae*. Other similar lichens include *C. fimbriata* (a **taller, trombone-shaped** species with **very fine soredia**), and *C. pyxidata* (**lower inset photo**) (like *C. chlorophaea*, but **lacking soredia**). • All of these species are often called 'pixie cup lichens,' because of their resemblance to tiny goblets. Pixies aside, the cups apparently assist in the dispersal of the soredia through rain splash or, more likely, through increased exposure to air currents.

DRAGON CLADONIA • *Cladonia squamosa*

GENERAL: A medium-sized, **upright club** lichen, 15–45 mm tall, arising from clusters of tiny, greenish basal scales (squamules); clubs (podetia) often **somewhat branched**, pale greenish, hollow, **covered in tiny scales (squamules)**, occasionally terminating in **narrow, open cups**, these sometimes ringed with brown fruiting bodies (apothecia).

HABITAT: On mossy ground, decaying wood in open or somewhat shady sites, mostly at lower and middle elevations; common.

NOTES: Like a dragon, *C. squamosa* is squamose, that is, it is covered in scales. *C. bellidiflora* is also scaly, but it **lacks cups** and has **red**, not brown, fruiting bodies (apothecia). • The dragon cladonia comes in 2 strains that can be distinguished chemically: one contains squamatic acid and other contains thamnolic acid. • Roughly 70 species of *Cladonia* occur in our region, making this one of the most diverse of lichen genera. • Lichens concentrate radioactive fallout to much higher concentrations than flowering plants do. The radioactivity may then be concentrated further as it passes up the food chain, in some cases ending with humans (as happened for example, with reindeer lichens, reindeer and their herders following the Chernobyl accident).

COASTAL REINDEER • *Cladina portentosa*

GENERAL: A medium-sized to large, **upright shrub** lichen, 4–7 (to sometimes 10) cm tall, **pale yellowish-green**, intricately branching from a distinct main stem; branches hollow, mostly **in 3s**, in part with a **shiny surface** (visible with a hand lens).

HABITAT: Forming extensive carpets over the ground in open sites, especially at lower elevations near the ocean; common.

NOTES: Roughly half a dozen *Cladina* species occur along the Pacific coast. Of those that are **pale yellowish-green, *C. arbuscula*** usually **lacks a distinct main stem** whereas *C. mitis* tends to **branch in 4s**, and to have a **more-uniformly cottony** surface. *C. arbuscula* is said to taste bitter, whereas *C. mitis* and *C. portentosa* taste mild. We are certain this is true. • *Cladina* is from the Latin meaning 'small branches,' which is a fair description. *Portentosa* is also Latin, and it means 'monstrous' or 'hideous,' which is not at all fair.

COMMON CHRISTMAS-TREE • *Sphaerophorus globosus*

GENERAL: A medium-sized, **tufted shrub** lichen, to 2–5 cm tall, **whitish** or greenish-brown, shiny, solid, much branched; branches stiff, occasionally bearing **terminal ball-shaped, black**, powdery, **fruiting bodies** (mazaedia); soredia absent.

HABITAT: On trunks and branches of conifers in open or somewhat shady forests at low to middle elevations; frequent.

NOTES: The sometimes thick, sometimes slender, stiff, ball-tipped branches of *S. globosus* are distinctive. The only species likely to be mistaken for it is *S. melanocarpus*, a lichen of very humid localities along the outer coast that is characterized by **flattened branches**. • The name *Sphaerophorus globosus* derives from Greek and Latin and means 'spherical ball-bearer,' referring to the fruiting bodies.

BLOOD-SPATTERED BEARD • *Usnea wirthii*

GENERAL: A medium-sized, **tufted** to somewhat hanging **shrub** lichen, 2–4 cm long, **pale yellowish-green**, often **red-spotted**, much branched; branches stiff, bearing tiny, powdery balls (soredia) near the tips, reinforced by a **pale-yellow central cord**.

HABITAT: On conifers in open lowland forests; frequent.

NOTES: *U. wirthii's* **tufted** growth habit, **pale-yellow** central cord and (sparse) **red spotting** distinguish it from all other species. • Though most *Usnea* species are not so easy to identify, the genus itself is readily recognized by the characteristic tough, thread-like central cord. Check for this by slowly pulling the lichen lengthwise like a party cracker. The central cord is unique to this genus, and provides anatomical strength, elasticity and, possibly, a storage area for energy-rich polysaccharides. • *Usnea* appears to derive from Arabic and to mean, inaccurately, 'moss.'

METHUSELAH'S BEARD • *Usnea longissima*

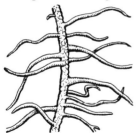

GENERAL: A large, **hanging hair** lichen, **15–35 cm or more** long, **pale yellowish-green**, consisting of a single, **unbranched** (or sparsely branched) central strand and numerous short lateral branchlets; white central cord becoming in part exposed (decorticate); soredia absent; central cord white.

HABITAT: Over various trees and shrubs in open, well-ventilated forests; infrequent, but locally abundant.

NOTES: Methuselah's beard is unlikely to be confused with any other *Usnea* because of its **whitish central cord**. Some forms might, however, be mistaken for *Alectoria*, but that genus **lacks a central cord**. • As the name suggests, *U. longissima* is the longest of lichens: specimens from coastal B.C. have measured 6 m in length (after tedious unraveling). This species disperses mostly, if not entirely, from small pieces carried to new localities. It is best developed in old-growth forests and will probably not persist in short-rotation second-growth forests. It has already disappeared from many localities throughout much of its range. In Europe, for example, it is all but gone. • The fibres of this lichen were used by the Haida to strain impurities from hot pitch before the pitch was used as medicine.

COMMON WITCH'S HAIR • *Alectoria sarmentosa*

GENERAL: A large, **hanging hair** lichen, 15–30 cm long, **pale green**, intricately branched; the branches **lacking a central cord**; soredia absent.

HABITAT: On conifers in open forests, especially at middle and upper forested elevations; common.

NOTES: Common witch's hair is superficially similar to various *Usnea* species, but it **lacks a central cord**. It is very similar to the endemic species *A. vancouverensis* which, however, differs in chemistry, is **more greyish-green**, and occurs **only at lower elevations**. • *Alectoria* means 'unmarried,' and it presumably refers to the relative absence of fruiting bodies in these lichens. *A. sarmentosa* itself, however, is often fertile: look for tiny, brown 'saucers' (apothecia) scattered among the branches. • The fibres of *Alectoria* species were used by the Nuxalk as false whiskers and hair for decorating dance masks. Some interior peoples wove ponchos and footwear from this lichen, but this type of clothing was considered inferior to hides. Deer are known to browse on this species, especially in winter.

SPECKLED HORSEHAIR • *Bryoria fuscescens*

GENERAL: A medium-sized to large, **hanging hair** lichen, 5–15 cm long, **dark medium-brown** or blackish, intricately branched, the branches even, rather pliant, **bearing tiny, powdery balls (soredia).**

HABITAT: On conifers in open forests at all forested elevations; frequent.

NOTES: Speckled horsehair is easily confused with other horsehair lichens with soredia, including ***B. glabra*** (which has rather **stiff and wiry** basal branches) and ***B. lanestris*** (which has **slender, distinctly brittle** branches). • These lichens disperse more or less entirely by asexual means, whether by fragmentation or by the soredia being borne away by birds and other animals. • The Coast Salish are said to have used *Bryoria* as a source of yellow dye. • *Bryoria* is derived from *Bryopogon* (an earlier, but invalid, name for these lichens) and *Alectoria* (the name of a related genus). *Fuscescens* is from the Latin, meaning 'becoming dark.' Quite so.

Glossary

(Page numbers indicate where the terms are illustrated.)

achene: a small, dry, 1-seeded, nut-like fruit (pp. 270; 390; 506)

acrocarpous: (bryophytes) bearing the sporophyte at the tip of the main stem or branch

adnate: attached

alar cells: cells at the basal angles of the leaf that attach the leaf to the stem

alluvium: deposits laid down by a river

alternate: arranged singly, not opposite (p. 508)

annual: living for only one year

anther: the pollen-bearing portion of a stamen (pp. 270, 506, 509)

antheridium: male sex organ; in bryophytes, a globose to shortly cylindric sac one cell layer thick

apex: the tip (p. 508)

apical: at the apex or tip

apothecium: (lichens) a disc-shaped or elongate fruiting body in which spores are produced

appressed: lying close or flat against a surface

archegonium: a female sex organ; in bryophytes

areole: (lichens) a small, discrete, greenish patch on the lichen surface

aril: a fleshy outgrowth of the seed coat

auricle: a projecting, ear-shaped lobe or appendage (pp. 356, 508)

awn: a bristle-shaped appendage (p. 356)

axil: the angle between the leaf and the stem (p. 508)

axillary: arising from an axil

banner: an upper, usually enlarged petal of a flower, as found in the pea family (p. 506)

basally: towards the base

beard: a clump of hairs

biennial: living for 2 years, usually flowering and producing fruit in the second year

bilobed: divided into 2 lobes (p. 506)

biodiversity: the full range of life in all its forms—including genes, species and ecosystems—and the ecological processes that link them

biomass: total weight of living organisms in an area

bipinnate: twice pinnate, leaflets again pinnate (p. 505)

blade: the broad part of a leaf or petal (pp. 356, 506, 508)

bract: a reduced or specialized leaf associated with a flower or inflorescence (pp. 270, 390, 507, 509)

branchlet: a small branch

bulb: a short, vertical, thickened underground stem with thickened leaves or leaf-bases

bulbil: a small, bulb-like, reproductive structure often located in a leaf axil, or replacing a flower

buttressed: propped up

calcareous: calcium-rich; soil rich in lime

callus: the firm, thickened base of a lemma

calyptra [calyptrae]: thin covering or hood fitted over the upper part of a moss spore capsule

cambium: vascular cambium is the tissue that produces the conducting tubes (xylem and phloem) in plants

capitulum: a tight, head-shaped cluster of flowers (as in asters) or branches (as in sphagnums) (p. 447)

capsule: a dry, dehiscent fruit composed of more than 1 carpel (p. 409); in bryophytes, the spore-containing sac (p. 437)

carpel: a fertile leaf bearing undeveloped seed(s) (p. 506)

Leaf Shapes

Linear   *Lanceolate*   *Oblong*   *Elliptic*   *Oval*   *Ovate*   *Obovate*   *Spatulate*

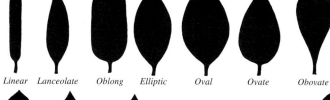

Cuneate   *Deltoid*   *Cordate*   *Reniform*   *Orbicular*   *Lyrate*

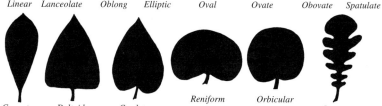
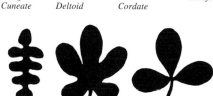
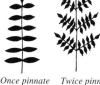

Pinnatifid   *Palmate*   *Trifoliate*   *Once pinnate (pinnate)*   *Twice pinnate (bipinnate)*   *3 times pinnate (tripinnate)*

cephalodium [cephalodia]: warty outgrowths containing cyanobacteria, in or on a lichen thallus

ciliate: fringed with hairs or hair-like outgrowths

circumboreal: occurring in the boreal zone around the world

circumscissile: opening so that the top comes off as a lid

clambering: trailing over the ground

clasping: holding or surrounding tightly (p. 508)

claw: stalk-like base of a petal or sepal (p. 506)

cleft: cut about halfway to the midrib or base, or a little deeper; deeply lobed (p. 508)

climax: a relatively stable community of plants and animals, dominant in a given locality so long as conditions remain stable

complanate: flattened together, compressed in 1 plane

complicate-bilobed: folded lengthwise and 2 lobed

compound: divided into smaller parts: leaves, divided into leaflets; inflorescences into smaller clusters (p. 507)

cordate: heart-shaped, with the notch at the base (p. 505)

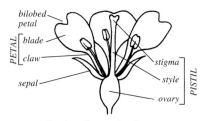

Section of a regular flower with an inferior ovary.

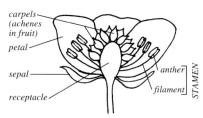

Section of a regular flower with numerous carpels.

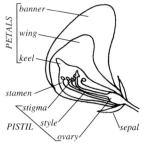

Section of an irregular flower with a superior ovary.

corm: a short, vertical, thickened underground stem without thickened leaves

cortex: the outer layer of a thallus or stem

costa: the midrib or nerve of a moss leaf

crenate: scalloped or with rounded teeth

crisped: with irregularly-curled, wavy edges

cultivar: a cultivated variety

cuneate: wedge-shaped or triangular, with the narrow end at the point of attachment (p. 505)

cuticular: of or belonging to the cuticle (the non-cellular outer covering)

cyanobacteria: a group of organisms related to true bacteria (sometimes called 'blue-green algae')

cyphella [cyphellae]: a recessed pore, such as on the undersurface of *Sticta*

deciduous: falling after completion of its normal function, often at the approach of a dormant season

decorticate: lacking a cortex

decumbent: reclining or lying flat on the ground, but with ascending tips

dehiscence: the act or method of opening, as in fruit, anthers or spore capsules

dehiscent: opening by a definite pore(s) or along a regular line(s) to discharge seeds or spores

deltoid: shaped like an equilateral triangle with one side at the base (p. 505)

dichotomous: branching into 2 equal parts, like a 'Y'

dimorphic: occurring in 2 forms, as in ferns with sterile and fertile leaves

disc flower: (aster family, Asteraceae) a flower with a tubular corolla (p. 270)

disjunct: disconnected; in biogeography, referring to populations of the same species that are separated by unusually great distances

dorsal: on the upper (outer) side, the side away from the stem; opposite to ventral (p. 508)

drupe: a fleshy or pulpy, 1-seeded fruit in which the seed has a stony covering

elliptic: shaped like an ellipse, oval or oblong with the ends rounded and widest in the middle (p. 505)

emergent: coming out from

endemic: growing only in a particular region

entire: without indentation or division (p. 508)

epiphyte: a plant growing on another plant

even-aged: all of similar age, referring to a population of plants (usually trees)

fascicle: a small bundle or cluster

fen: a wetland of slow-moving, often alkaline water with sedge (not *Sphagnum*) peat underfoot

fibril: a thickening of a clear cell of a *Sphagnum* that projects into the cells and forms oblique to transverse bars across the cell

filament: the stalk of a stamen (pp. 506, 509)

flexuous: bent in a zig-zag manner

floodplain: a plain built up by stream deposits through repeated flooding

floret: a tiny flower, usually part of a cluster; used also to describe the specialized flower of a grass

follicle: a dry fruit composed of a single carpel, splitting open along the seed-bearing suture

gametophyte: the gamete-producing part or phase of a plant; in bryophytes, the conspicuous green, leafy or thallose plant (p. 437)

gemma [gemmae]: a small body of a few cells serving in vegetative reproduction

glandular-hairy: with glands and hairs

glandular: with glands

gemma [gemmae]**:** a small body of a few cells serving in vegetative reproduction

glandular-hairy: with glands and hairs

glandular: with glands

glaucous: covered with a white, waxy powder which can be rubbed off

globose: shaped like a sphere

glume: (grasses) 1 of 2 empty bracts at the base of a spikelet (p. 356)

gynobasic: with an enlarged stem end, to which the flower parts are attached

hairpoint: a thin, hair-like extension (p. 508)

herb: a plant without woody above-ground parts, the stems dying back to the ground each year

herbaceous: herb-like

hybridization: the process of creating a hybrid by cross-breeding different species

hypanthium: a ring or cup around the ovary

hypha [hyphae]**:** tiny, multicellular fungal threads making up the main body of a fungus or lichen

incubous: with leaves overlapping like shingles if the base of the plant is at the ridge of the roof and the tip is at the eaves; opposite of succubous

incurved: curved upwards and inwards

indusium: an outgrowth covering and protecting a spore cluster in ferns (p. 510)

inflexed: incurved

inflorescence: a flower cluster (pp. 356, 390, 409, 507)

internode: portion of a stem between 2 nodes

intertidal: occurring in the shore area between normal high and low tides

involucre: a set of bracts beneath an inflorescence (in Asteraceae and Apiaceae)(pp. 270, 507); a protective covering around the hood of a capsule (as in hepatics)

irregular flower: a flower with petals (or less often sepals) dissimilar in form or orientation (p. 506)

isidium: a tiny, wart-like outgrowth of a lichen, with a cortex and containing algae; functions as a vegetative propagule

keel: a sharp or conspicuous longitudinal ridge, like the keel of a boat; the 2 partly united lower petals of many species of the Fabaceae (p. 506)

lacerate: torn or with an irregularly jagged margin

lamella [lamellae]**:** a green ridge or plate on the midrib or blade of some moss leaves or on the undersurfaces of lichens (as in *Umbilicaria*)

lanceolate: lance-shaped, much longer than wide, widest below the middle and tapering to both ends (p. 505)

lateral: on the side of

layering: a form of vegetative reproduction in which branches droop to the ground and root

leader: the terminal shoot of a tree

lemma: the lower of the 2 bracts immediately enclosing the individual grass flower (p. 356)

lenticel: a slightly raised area on root or stem bark

ligule: (grasses) the flat, usually membranous projection from the summit of the sheath (p. 356); (composites) the strap-shaped part of the marginal (ray) flower

linear: line-shaped; very long and narrow with essentially parallel sides (p. 505)

lip: a projection or expansion of something, such as the lower petal of an orchid or violet flower (p. 117)

lirella [lirellae]**:** a lichen fruiting body with an elongate disc (see pencil script, p. 486)

lobe: a rounded or strap-shaped division of the thallus of lichens; or a divison of the leaf in liverworts and vascular plants (p. 508)

lobule: small lobe (p. 437)

lyrate: pinnatifid with the terminal lobe largest and rounded (p. 505)

margin: an edge (p. 508)

mazaedium: [mazaedia] a lichen fruiting body in which a mass of spores and sterile hairs is formed by the disintegration of the club-shaped fruiting bodies (asci) of the fungus

medulla: inner part of a lichen thallus, usually consisting of loosely packed fungal hyphae

mesic: of habitats that are neither very wet nor very dry

midrib: the central rib of a leaf

midvein: the central vein of a leaf (p. 508)

minerotrophic: nourished by mineral-rich waters, describing wetlands

montane: on or of the mountains

mucilaginous: sticky, producing gummy or gelatinous substances

nectary: a gland that secretes nectar (p. 509)

net-veined: with a network of veins (p. 508)

node: the place where a leaf or branch is attached

oblanceolate: lanceolate with the broadest part above the middle (p. 505)

Types of Inflorescences

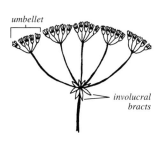

umbellet

involucral bracts

Spike   *Raceme*   *Panicle*   *Compound Umbel*

oblique: an angle of leaf attachment between 0° and 90° to the stem

oblong: shaped more or less like a rectangle (other than a square) (p. 505)

obovate: shaped like a long section through a hen's egg, with the larger end toward the tip (p. 505)

oolichan: a small, oily fish (*Thaleichthys pacificus*)

operculum: lid of a moss capsule

opposite: situated across from each other, not alternate or whorled; or, situated directly in front of organs of another kind (p. 508)

orbicular: essentially circular in outline (p. 505)

outwash: the stratified drift deposited by streams of meltwater flowing away from a glacier

oval: broadly elliptic (p. 505)

ovary: the structure which encloses the young, undeveloped seeds (ovules) (pp. 117, 506)

ovate: shaped like a long section through a hen's egg, with the larger end toward the base (p. 505)

palea: the upper of the 2 bracts immediately enclosing the individual grass flower

palmate: divided into lobes diverging like fingers (p. 505)

panicle: a branched inflorescence blooming from the bottom up (p. 507)

papilla [papillae]: minute, wart-like protuberance

papillose: (cells) with one to many papillae

pappus: (Asteraceae) the modified hairs or bristles on top of the achene (p. 270)

parallel-veined: with veins running parallel to one another, not branching to form a network (p. 508)

paraphyllium [paraphyllia]: minute leaf-like or thread-like structure borne on the stems and among the leaves of some mosses

parasite: an organism that gets its food/water chiefly from a live organism to which it is attached

pencilled: marked with thin lines

perennial: growing for 3 or more years, usually flowering and producing fruit each year

perianth: (flowers) the sepals and petals of a flower, collectively; (hepatics) a tube, apparently of 2–3 fused leaves, surrounding a developing sporophyte

perichaetium [perichaetia]: (bryophytes) a special leaf surrounding the female organ (archegonium) at the base of a sporophyte stalk (seta)

periglacial: close to, or recently exposed by, retreating glaciers

perigynium: [perigynia] the inflated sac enclosing an achene in sedges (p. 390)

peristome: the fringe of teeth surrounding the mouth of a moss capsule

perithecium: a flask-shaped fruiting body of a lichen, immersed in the thallus and with a dark and often protuding opening

petal: a member of the inside ring of modified flower leaves, usually white or brightly coloured (pp. 117, 270, 506)

petiole: a leaf-stalk (p. 508)

photobiont: the photosynthetically active component organism in a lichen, the alga or cyanobacterium

photosynthesis: the process by which green plants produce their food (carbohydrates) from water, carbon dioxide and minerals, using the sun's energy

phytogeography: study of the geographical distribution and relationships of plants

pinna: [pinnae] the primary division of a pinnate leaf (p. 510)

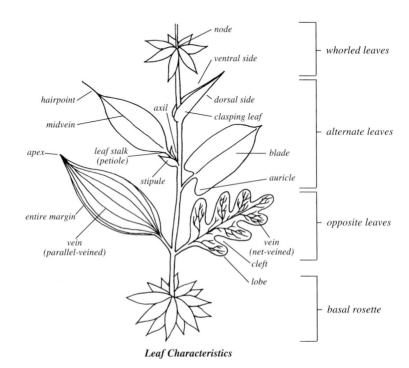

Leaf Characteristics

pinnate: feather-formed; of a compound leaf in which the leaflets are placed on each side of the common axis (p. 510)

pinnatifid: pinnately cleft halfway to the middle

pinnule: the secondary or ultimate leaflet or division of a pinnately compound leaf (p. 510)

pistil: the female organ of a flower, usually differentiated into an ovary, style and stigma (p. 506)

pleurocarpous: (bryophytes) producing sporophytes laterally from a bud or short branch

plicate: folded like a fan

podetium [podetia]: a stalk-like elevation of a lichen thallus supporting 1 or more apothecia

pollinium: [pollinia] a mass of waxy pollen, as in orchids

pome: a fruit with a core, such as an apple

potherb: an herb cooked as a vegetable

protonema [protonemata]: branched thread-like or plate-like growths arising from spores and on which the leafy parts of mosses develop

pseudocyphellum [pseudocyphellae]: a white patch, dot, or line on the surface of some lichens, caused by a break in the cortex and the extension of the inner medulla to the surface

pseudopodium [pseudopodia]: a stalk produced by the gametophyte that functions as a sporophyte stalk in the moss genera *Andreaea* and *Sphagnum*

quadrangular: 4-sided in cross-section

raceme: an unbranched inflorescence with stalked flowers blooming from the bottom up (p. 507)

rachis: the main axis (as in a compound leaf) (p. 510)

radially symmetrical: developing uniformly on all sides, like spokes on a wheel

rank: row, as a vertical row of leaves on a stem

ray flower: (aster family, Asteraceae) a flower with a strap-like (ligulate) corolla (p. 270)

receptacle: the end of the stem to which flower parts (or, in Asteraceae, the flowers) are attached (p. 270)

recurved: curved under (usually referring to leaf margins)

reflexed: abruptly bent or turned back or down

refugium [refugia]: a localized area, such as an ice-free mountaintop, where plants survived a period of glaciation, isolated from adjacent populations by ice

regular flower: a flower in which the members of each circle of parts (or at least the sepals and petals) are similar in size, shape, and orientation (p. 506)

reniform: kidney-shaped (p. 505)

retort cells: (*Sphagnum*) cells with a short projecting neck at the upper end, terminating in a pore, found in the cortex of branches

rhizine: in lichens, thread-like branched, unbranched, tufted, or brush-like organ of attachment, composed of fungal hyphae

rhizoid: a thread-like growth, simple or unbranched, which absorbs nutrients and anchors mosses and hepatics, never with chlorophyll (p. 437)

rhizomatous: with rhizomes

rhizome: underground, often elongate stem; distinguished from a root by the presence of nodes, buds, or scale-like leaves (p. 390)

riparian: of or pertaining to a river

rosette: a cluster of organs (usually leaves) arranged in a circle, often in a basal position (p. 508)

runner: a slender stolon

samara: a dry, usually winged fruit (e.g., a maple fruit)

saprophyte: an organism living on dead organic matter, neither parasitic nor making its own food

scale: any small, thin or flat structure (pp. 390, 409)

schizocarp: a fruit that splits into several parts

scree: rocky debris at the foot of a rock wall; talus

sepal: a member of the outside ring of modified flower leaves, usually green (pp. 117, 506)

serrate: saw-toothed, having sharp, forward-pointing teeth

sessile: without a stalk

seta: [setae] a stalk supporting a bryophyte capsule (p. 437)

sheath: an organ which partly or completely surrounds another organ, as the sheath of a grass leaf surrounds the stem (p. 356)

sheathing: partly or wholly surrounding an organ

silicle: a pod-like fruit much like a silique, but shorter, not much longer than wide

silique: a pod-like fruit of certain members of the mustard family, much longer than wide

site: a plot of ground or place of location

snag: the roughly pointed piece left when a tree trunk, branch, tooth, etc. is unevenly broken off

soligenous fen: a peatland affected by water originating, at least in part, from areas of mineral soil, percolating through it and/or carrying minerals in from the surrounding area

soredia: (lichens) microscopic clumps of several algal cells surrounded by fungal hyphae and erupting at the thallus surface as a powder

soredium [soredia]: a small, powdery propagule of a lichen, containing algal cells and fungal hyphae, breaking through the outer layer (cortex) to be released

sorus: [sori] a cluster of small spore cases (sporangia) on the underside of a fern leaf (p. 510)

spatulate: shaped like a spatula, rounded above and narrowed to the base (p. 505)

spike: a more or less elongate inflorescence with non-stalked flowers (p. 507)

spikelet: a small or secondary spike; the floral unit, or ultimate cluster, of a grass inflorescence (p. 356)

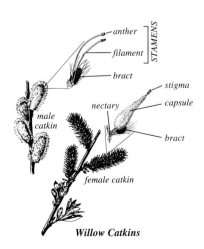

Willow Catkins

spinulose: covered by tiny spines

sporangium: [sporangia] a spore case

spore: a 1- to several-celled reproductive body produced in an ascus (lichens), capsule (mosses and hepatics) or sporangium (ferns and allies); capable of giving rise to a new plant

sporophyll: a spore-bearing leaf

sporophyte: the spore-bearing part or phase of a plant; in bryophytes composed of a foot, stalk and capsule; in vascular plants, the leafy plant (p. 437)

spur: a hollow appendage on a petal or sepal (p. 117)

spurred: with a spur

squamule: a small, scale-like lobe

stamen: the pollen-bearing organ of a flower (p. 506)

stand: a standing growth, especially of trees, such as a stand of white spruce

stigma: the tip of the female organ in plants, where the pollen lands (pp. 270, 390, 409, 506, 509)

stipe: a stalk-like support (p. 510)

stipule: an appendage at the base of a leaf-stalk (p. 508)

stolon: a horizontally-spreading stem or runner on the ground, usually rooting at nodes or tips

stoloniferous: with stolons

stoma, stomate [stomata]: a tiny opening in the epidermis of plants, bounded by a pair of guard cells which can close off the opening by changing shape

striate: marked with fine, parallel ridges

style: the stalk, or middle part, of the female organ in plants (connecting the stigma and ovary) (p. 506)

styptic: causing contraction of tissues such as blood vessels, stopping bleeding

sub-: almost

substrate: the surface on which something grows

subtend: to be directly below and close to

subtidal: occurring below normal low tide

succession: the process of change in plant community composition and structure over time

succubous: with leaves overlapping like shingles on a roof if the base of the plant is the 'eaves' and the tip is the 'ridge'; the opposite of incubous

suture: a seam or line of fusion; usually applied to the vertical lines along which a fruit splits open

talus: rocky debris at the foot of a rock wall; scree

taproot: a primary descending root

tepal: a sepal or a petal, when these structures cannot be distinguished

terminal: at the end, or top, of

terraces: a relatively level surface cut into the face of a steep, natural slope along the side of a valley

terrestrial: living on or growing in the earth

thallus: a main plant body, not differentiated into a stem and leaves, in lichens and in some hepatics (p. 437)

till: non-sorted glacial drift, deposits of clay, sand, pebbles and boulders

trailing: flat on the ground, but not rooting

trifoliate: 3-leaved (p. 505)

tripinnate: 3 times pinnate, leaflets twice divided again (p. 505)

tubercle: a small swelling or projection on an organ

tussocks: compact tufts of grasses or sedges

umbel: an often flat-topped inflorescence in which the flower stalks arise from a common point, much like the stays of an umbrella (p. 507)

umbellet: 1 of the umbel clusters in a branched (compound) umbel (p. 507)

umbelliferous: bearing umbels

umbilicus: the depression or 'belly-button' on the upper surface of a thallus, coinciding with the point of attachment on the lower surface of umbilicate lichens (as in *Umbilicaria*)

unarmed: without spines, prickles or thorns

unawned: not awned

utricles: small, thin-walled, 1-seeded, inflated fruits

valve: one of the pieces into which a pod or capsule splits

vein: a strand of conducting tubes (a vascular bundle), especially if visible externally (p. 508)

ventral: on the lower (inner) side, closest to the stem; opposite to dorsal (p. 508)

vermifuge: a remedy that destroys intestinal worms

whorled: arranged in rings of 3 or more (p. 508)

wing: a thin, flat extension or projection from the side or tip, one of the 2 side petals in a flower of the pea family (Fabaceae) (p. 506)

withe: a slender, flexible branch or twig

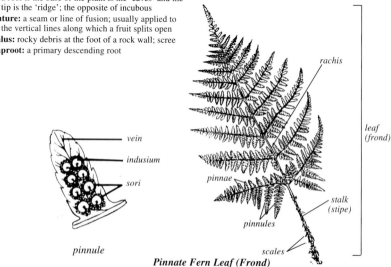

Pinnate Fern Leaf (Frond)

References Cited

Anderson, L.E., H.A. Crum, and W.R. Buck. 1990. List of the mosses of North America north of Mexico. *The Bryologist* 93: 448–499.

Boyd, R. 1986. Strategies of Indian burning in the Willamette Valley. *Canadian Journal of Anthropology* 5: 65–77.

Brayshaw, T.C. 1976. *Catkin Bearing Plants of British Columbia*. Occasional Paper No. 18, Royal British Columbia Museum, Victoria, British Columbia.

Brayshaw, T.C. 1985. *Pondweeds and Bur-reeds and Their Relatives, of British Columbia*. Occasional Paper No. 26, Royal British Columbia Museum, Victoria, British Columbia.

Brayshaw, T.C. 1989. *Buttercups, Waterlilies and their Relatives in British Columbia*. Memoir No. 1, Royal British Columbia Museum, Victoria, British Columbia.

Calder, J.A., and R.L. Taylor. 1968. *Flora of the Queen Charlotte Islands. Part 1. Systematics of the Vascular Plants*. Monograph No. 4. Canada Dept. of Agriculture, Ottawa, Ontario.

Clark, L. J., 1973. *Wildflowers of British Columbia*. Gray's Publishing Ltd., Sidney, British Columbia.

Cody, W.J., and D.M. Britton. 1989. *Ferns and Fern Allies of Canada*. Publ. 1829/E, Research Branch, Agriculture Canada, Ottawa, Ontario.

Craighead, J.J., F.C. Craighead, and R.J. Davis. 1963. *A Field Guide to Rocky Mountain Wildflowers*. Houghton Mifflin Company, Boston, Massachusetts.

Crum, H.A. 1976 (revised edition). *Mosses of the Great Lakes Forest*. Contributions from the University of Michigan Herbarium, Volume 10, Ann Arbor, Michigan.

Douglas, G.W., 1982. *The Sunflower Family (Asteraceae) of British Columbia. Volume I—Senecioneae*. Occasional Paper No. 23, Royal British Columbia Museum, Victoria, British Columbia.

Douglas, G.W., G.B. Straley, and D. Meidinger. 1989. *The Vascular Plants of British Columbia. Part 1—Gymnosperms and Dicotyledons (Aceraceae through Cucurbitaceae)*. Special Report Series 1, British Columbia Ministry of Forests, Research Branch, Victoria, British Columbia.

Douglas, G.W., G.B. Straley, and D. Meidinger. 1990. *The Vascular Plants of British Columbia. Part 2—Dictotyledons (Diapensiaceae through Portulacaceae)*. Special Report Series 2, British Columbia Ministry of Forests, Research Branch, Victoria, British Columbia.

Douglas, G.W., G.B. Straley, and D. Meidinger. 1991. *The Vascular Plants of British Columbia. Part 3—Dicotyledons (Primulaceae through Zygophyllaceae) and Pteridophytes*. Special Report Series 3, British Columbia Ministry of Forests, Research Branch, Victoria, British Columbia.

Douglas, G.W., G.B. Straley, and D. Meidinger. 1994. *The Vascular Plants of British Columbia. Part 4—Monocotyledons*. Special Report Series 4, British Columbia Ministry of Forests, Research Branch, Victoria, British Columbia (in press).

Dunn, D.B., and J.M. Gillett. 1966. *The Lupines of Canada and Alaska*. Monograph 2, Research Branch, Canada Department of Agriculture, Ottawa, Ontario.

Egan, R.S. 1987. A fifth checklist of the lichen-forming, lichenicolous and allied fungi of the continental United States and Canada. *The Bryologist* 90: 77–173.

Frankton, C., and G.A. Mulligan. 1987. *Weeds of Canada*. N.C. Press Limited and Agriculture Canada, Ottawa, Ontario.

Gilkey, H.M., and L.J. Dennis. 1967. *Handbook of Northwestern Plants*. Oregon State University Bookstores, Corvallis, Oregon.

Grigson, G. 1974. *A Dictionary of English Plant Names*. Allen Lane, A Division of Penguin Books, London, United Kingdom.

Gunther, E. 1973. *Ethnobotany of Western Washington*. University of Washington Press, Seattle, Washington.

Hebda, R.J., and R.W. Mathewes. 1984. Holocene history of cedar and native Indian cultures of the North American Pacific Coast. *Science* 225: 711–713.

Hitchcock, C.L., A. Cronquist, M. Ownbey, and J.W. Thompson. 1955, 1959, 1961, 1964, 1969. *Vascular Plants of the Pacific Northwest. Parts 1–5*. University of Washington Press, Seattle, Washington.

Hitchcock, C.L., and A. Cronquist. 1973. *Flora of the Pacific Northwest*. University of Washington Press, Seattle, Washington.

Hosie, R.C. 1969. *Native Trees of Canada*, Queens Printer, Ottawa, Ontario.

Hotchkiss, N. 1972. *Common Marsh, Underwater and Floating-leaved Plants of the United States and Canada*. Dover, New York, New York.

Hultén, E. 1968. *Flora of Alaska and Neighbouring Territories*. Stanford University Press, Stanford, California.

Ireland, R.R. 1969. *A taxonomic revision of the genus Plagiothecium for North America, north of Mexico*. Publications in Botany 8, National Museums of Canada, Ottawa, Ontario.

Kuhnlein, H.V., and N.J. Turner. 1991. Traditional Plant Foods of Canadian Indigenous Peoples. Nutrition, Botany and Use. Volume 8. In: *Food and Nutrition in History and Anthropology*, edited by S. Katz. Gordon and Breach Science Publishers, Philadelphia, Pennsylvania.

Lellinger, D.B. 1985. *A Field Manual of the Ferns and Fern Allies of the United States and Canada*. Smithsonian Institution Press, Washington, D.C.

Lyons, C.P. 1974. (1st ed. 1952). *Trees, Shrubs and Flowers to Know in British Columbia*. J.M. Dent and Sons, Toronto, Ontario.

Mathews, D. 1988. *Cascade-Olympic Natural History*. Raven Editors and Portland Audubon Society, Portland, Oregon.

McCutcheon, A.R., S.M. Ellis, R.E.W. Hancock, and G.H.N. Towers. 1992. Antibiotic screening of medicinal plants of British Columbian native peoples. *Journal of Ethnopharmacology* 37: 213–223.

Meeuse, B., and S. Morris. 1984. *The Sex Life of Flowers*. Facts on File, New York, New York.

Minore, D., and M.E. Dubrasich. 1978. *Big huckleberry abundance as related to environment and associated vegetation near Mount Adams, Washington*. Research Note PNW–322, USDA Forest Service, Pacific Northwest Forest and Range Experiment Station, Portland, Oregon.

Norton, H. 1979. The association between anthropogenic prairies and important food plants in western Washington. *Northwest Anthropological Research Notes* 13: 175–200.

Peck, M.E. 1961. *A Manual of the Higher Plants of Oregon*. Binford & Mort, Portland, Oregon.

Prescott, G.W. 1964. *How to Know the Freshwater Algae*. W.C. Brown Co., Dubuque, Iowa.

Prior, R.C.A. 1879. *On Popular Names of British Plants: Being an Explanation of the Origin and Meaning of the Names of Our Indigenous and Most Commonly Cultivated Species*. Frederic Norgate, London, United Kingdom.

Scagel, R.F. 1972. *Guide to Common Seaweeds of British Columbia*. Handbook No. 27, Royal British Columbia Museum, Victoria, British Columbia.

Scoggan, H.J. 1978–79. *The Flora of Canada*. National Museum of Natural Sciences Publications in Botany No. 7 (1–4), National Museums of Canada, Ottawa, Ontario.

Sculthorpe, C.D. 1967. *The Biology of Aquatic Vascular Plants*. Edward Arnold, London, United Kingdom.

Stewart, H. 1984. *Cedar: Tree of Life*. Douglas & McIntyre, Vancouver, British Columbia.

Stone, D.F., and B. McCune. 1990. Annual branching in the lichen *Evernia prunastri* in Oregon. *The Bryologist* 93: 32–36.

Stotler, R. and B. Crandall–Stotler. 1977. A checklist of the liverworts and hornworts of North America. *The Bryologist* 80: 405–428

Suttles, W. (editor). 1990. *Northwest Coast, Vol. 7, Handbook of North American Indians*. (W.C. Sturtevant, general editor). Smithsonian Institution, Washington, D.C.

Szczawinski, A.F. 1959. *The Orchids (Orchidaceae) of British Columbia*. Handbook No. 16, Royal British Columbia Museum, Victoria, British Columbia.

Szczawinski, A.F. 1962. *The Heather Family (Ericaceae) of British Columbia*. Handbook No. 19, Royal British Columbia Museum, Victoria, British Columbia.

Taylor, T.M.C. 1966. *The Lily Family (Liliaceae) of British Columbia*. Handbook No. 25, Royal British Columbia Museum, Victoria, British Columbia.

Taylor, T.M.C. 1970. *Pacific Northwest Ferns and Their Allies*. University of Toronto Press, Toronto, Ontario.

Taylor, T.M.C. 1973a. *The Ferns and Fern Allies of British Columbia*, Handbook No. 12, Royal British Columbia Museum, Victoria, British Columbia.

Taylor, T.M.C. 1973b. *The Rose Family (Rosaceae) of British Columbia*. Handbook No. 30, Royal British Columbia Museum, Victoria, British Columbia.

Taylor, T.M.C. 1974a. *The Figwort Family (Scrophulariaceae) of British Columbia*. Handbook No. 33, Royal British Columbia Museum, Victoria, British Columbia.

Taylor, T.M.C. 1974b. *The Pea Family (Leguminosae) of British Columbia*. Handbook No. 32, Royal British Columbia Museum, Victoria, British Columbia.

Taylor, T.M.C. 1983. *The Sedge Family (Cyperaceae) of British Columbia*. Handbook No. 43, Royal British Columbia Museum, Victoria, British Columbia.

Thompson, L.C., and M.D. Kinkade. 1990. Languages. In W. Suttles (editor). *Northwest Coast. Vol. 7, Handbook of North American Indians*. Smithsonian Institution, Washington, DC. pp. 30–51.

Thomson, J.W. 1967. *The Lichen Genus Cladonia in North America*. University of Toronto Press, Toronto, Ontario.

Turner, N.J. 1975. *Food Plants of British Columbia Indians Part 1: Coastal Peoples*. Handbook No. 34, Royal British Columbia Museum, Victoria, British Columbia.

Turner, N.J. 1982. Traditional use of devil's-club (*Oplopanax horridus*: Araliaceae) by native peoples in western North America. *Journal of Ethnobiology* 2 (1): 1–11.

Turner, N.J. 1991. Burning mountain sides for better crops: Aboriginal landscape burning in British Columbia. In K.P. Cannon (editor), *Archaeology in Montana, Special Issue* 32: 57–74.

Turner, N.J. 1992. 'Just when the wild roses bloom': The legacy of a Lillooet basket weaver. *TEK TALK: A Newsletter of Traditional Ecological Knowledge* 1: 2–5, UNESCO, World Congress for Education and Communication on Environment and Development.

Turner, N.J., and A.F. Szczawinski. 1978. *Wild Coffee and Tea Substitutes of Canada*. Edible Wild Plants of Canada Series No. 2, National Museum of Canada, Ottawa, Ontario.

Turner, N.J., and R.J. Hebda. 1990. Contemporary use of bark for medicine by two Salishan native elders of southeast Vancouver Island. *Journal of Ethnopharmacology* 229: 59–72.

Turner, N.J., L.C. Thompson, M.T. Thompson, and A.Z. York. 1990. *Thompson Ethnobotany. Knowledge and Usage of Plants by the Thompson Indians of British Columbia*. Royal British Columbia Museum, Memoir No. 3, Victoria, British Columbia.

Turner, N.J., L.M.J. Gottesfeld, H.V. Kuhnlein, and A. Ceska 1992. Edible wood fern rootstocks of western North America: solving an ethnobotanical puzzle. *Journal of Ethnobiology* 12: 1–34.

Vitt, D.H., J.E. Marsh, and R.B. Bovey. 1988. *Mosses, Lichens and Ferns of Northwest North America*. Lone Pine Publishing, Edmonton, Alberta.

Welsh, S.L. 1974. *Anderson's Flora of Alaska and adjacent parts of Canada*. Brigham Young University Press, Provo, Utah.

Index to Common and Scientific Names

Primary entries are in bold-face type; species mentioned in the 'Notes' sections only are not.

INDEX

Paul Alaback
University of Montana
Missoula, Montana

Joe Antos
University of Victoria
Victoria, B.C.

Trevor Goward
Naturalist, Lichenologist
Clearwater, B.C.

Ken Lertzman
Simon Fraser University
Burnaby, B.C.

Andy MacKinnon
B.C. Forest Service,
Research
Victoria, B.C.

Jim Pojar
B.C. Forest Service,
Research
Smithers, B.C.

Rosamund Pojar
Biologist, Naturalist
Smithers, B.C.

Andrew Reed
University of Victoria
Victoria, B.C.

Nancy Turner
University of Victoria
Victoria, B.C.

Dale Vitt
University of Alberta
Edmonton, Alberta

More Great Books About The Outdoors!

Plants of Northern British Columbia
Edited by MacKinnon, Pojar & Coupé

This extensive field guide describes everything you need to know to identify over 500 species of trees, shrubs, grasses, sedges, mosses, lichens and flowering plants in northern British Columbia. Complete with almost 600 colour photographs, this informative volume will delight both professionals and amateurs.

352 pages • 570 colour photographs • 600 B & W illustrations
softcover • $19.95 CDN • $15.95 US • ISBN 1-55105-015-3
Over 15,000 copies sold!

Mosses, Lichens and Ferns of Northwest North America
By Dale Vitt, Janet Marsh and Robin Bovey

This photographic field guide covers the area from southern Oregon to Alaska and from the Pacific Coast to Montana and Saskatchewan. Over 370 species are featured in the text, each illustrated with full-colour photographs and distribution maps. Many more similar species are mentioned along with habitat descriptions and keys to identification. This is a perfect book with which to explore the small and beautiful world in your own backyard.

300 pages • over 400 colour photographs • softcover • $24.95 • ISBN 0-919433-41-3

Ocean to Alpine
By Joy and Cam Finlay

Organized by region, this nature guide to more than 350 places throughout BC satisfies the year-round needs of those who travel in search of wildlife. It sets out the birds, plants, mammals and marine life common to each area and presents striking photographs of the region. Essential directions and information on hiking and accommodation, as well as a mileage guide of what you'll see along the road, round out this useful book.

256 pages • 54 colour photographs • 6 maps
softcover • $14.95 CDN • $11.95 US • ISBN 1-55105-013-7

Mushrooms of Western Canada	**Mushrooms of Northwest North America**
By Helene Schalkwijk-Barendsen	*By Helene Schalkwijk-Barendsen*
ISBN 0-919433-47-2 • $19.95 CDN	ISBN 1-55105-046-3 • $19.95 US

This comprehensive field guide covers the area from Alaska south to California, from the Pacific Coast to the Dakotas and Manitoba. A total of 560 species are meticulously illustrated in full colour. Includes information on identification and edibility, habitat, distribution, and an illustrated glossary. Written in everyday language, this guide is a beautiful and easy-to-use reference for the amateur or professional naturalist.

416 pages • 560 colour illustrations • softcover

New Books To Look For!

Trees, Shrubs and Flowers to Know in British Columbia and Washington
By C.P. Lyons

Ches Lyons' well-known and loved field guides to the plants of BC and Washington—best sellers since 1952—have been fully updated, revised and combined in a single rich volume.
ISBN 1-55105-044-7

Hiking the Ancient Forests of Washington and British Columbia
By Randy Stoltmann

The best walks and hikes in the old-growth forests spring to life in this guide to temperate rainforest trails. Detailed maps and directions are included for all of the 31 featured trails.
ISBN 1-55105-045-5

Look for these fine books at your local book shop or contact Lone Pine Publishing:

CANADA
206, 10426 81 Avenue
Edmonton, AB T6E 1X5
Ph (403) 433-9333
Fax (403) 433-9646

202A, 1110 Seymour Street
Vancouver, BC V6B 3N3
Ph (604) 687-5555
Fax (604) 687-5575

USA
#180 16149 Redmond Way
Redmond, WA 98052
Ph (206) 343-8397

1-800-661-9017